Lecture Notes in Computer Science 3954

Commenced Publication in 1973
Founding and Former Series Editors:
Gerhard Goos, Juris Hartmanis, and Jan van Leeuwen

T0180417

Aleš Leonardis   Horst Bischof
Axel Pinz (Eds.)

Computer Vision –
ECCV 2006

9th European Conference on Computer Vision
Graz, Austria, May 7-13, 2006
Proceedings, Part IV

 Springer

Volume Editors

Aleš Leonardis
University of Ljubljana
Faculty of Computer and Information Science
Visual Cognitive Systems Laboratory
Trzaska 25, 1001 Ljubljana, Slovenia
E-mail: alesl@fri.uni-lj.si

Horst Bischof
Graz University of Technology
Institute for Computer Graphics and Vision
Inffeldgasse 16, 8010 Graz, Austria
E-mail: bischof@icg.tu-graz.ac.at

Axel Pinz
Graz University of Technology
Institute of Electrical Measurement and Measurement Signal Processing
Schießstattgasse 14b, 8010 Graz, Austria
E-mail: Axel.Pinz@tugraz.at

Library of Congress Control Number: 2006924180

CR Subject Classification (1998): I.4, I.3.5, I.5, I.2.9-10

LNCS Sublibrary: SL 6 – Image Processing, Computer Vision, Pattern Recognition, and Graphics

ISSN   0302-9743
ISBN-10   3-540-33838-1 Springer Berlin Heidelberg New York
ISBN-13   978-3-540-33838-3 Springer Berlin Heidelberg New York

Springer is a part of Springer Science+Business Media

springer.com

© Springer-Verlag Berlin Heidelberg 2006
Printed in Germany

Typesetting: Camera-ready by author, data conversion by Scientific Publishing Services, Chennai, India
Printed on acid-free paper   SPIN: 11744085   06/3142   5 4 3 2 1 0

Preface

These are the proceedings of the 9th European Conference on Computer Vision (ECCV 2006), the premium European conference on computer vision, held in Graz, Austria, in May 2006.

In response to our conference call, we received 811 papers, the largest number of submissions so far. Finally, 41 papers were selected for podium presentation and 151 for presentation in poster sessions (a 23.67% acceptance rate).

The double-blind reviewing process started by assigning each paper to one of the 22 area chairs, who then selected 3 reviewers for each paper. After the reviews were received, the authors were offered the possibility to provide feedback on the reviews. On the basis of the reviews and the rebuttal of the authors, the area chairs wrote the initial consolidation report for each paper. Finally, all the area chairs attended a two-day meeting in Graz, where all decisions on acceptance/rejection were made. At that meeting, the area chairs responsible for similar sub-fields thoroughly evaluated the assigned papers and discussed them in great depth. Again, all decisions were reached without the knowledge of the authors' identity. We are fully aware of the fact that reviewing is always also subjective, and that some good papers might have been overlooked; however, we tried our best to apply a fair selection process.

The conference preparation went smoothly thanks to several people. We first wish to thank the ECCV Steering Committee for entrusting us with the organization of the conference. We are grateful to the area chairs, who did a tremendous job in selecting the papers, and to more than 340 Program Committee members and 220 additional reviewers for all their professional efforts. To the organizers of the previous ECCV 2004 in Prague, Vaclav Hlaváč, Jirí Matas and Tomáš Pajdla for providing many insights, additional information, and the superb conference software. Finally, we would also like to thank the authors for contributing a large number of excellent papers to support the high standards of the ECCV conference.

Many people showed dedication and enthusiasm in the preparation of the conference. We would like to express our deepest gratitude to all the members of the involved institutes, that is, the Institute of Electrical Measurement and Measurement Signal Processing and the Institute for Computer Graphics and Vision, both at Graz University of Technology, and the Visual Cognitive Systems Laboratory at the University of Ljubljana. In particular, we would like to express our warmest thanks to Friedrich Fraundorfer for all his help (and patience) with the conference software and many other issues concerning the event, as well as Johanna Pfeifer for her great help with the organizational matters.

February 2006

Aleš Leonardis,
Horst Bischof,
Axel Pinz

Organization

Conference Chair

Axel Pinz   Graz University of Technology, Austria

Program Chairs

Horst Bischof   Graz University of Technology, Austria
Aleš Leonardis   University of Ljubljana, Slovenia

Organization Committee

Markus Brandner	Local Arrangements	Graz Univ. of Technology, Austria
Friedrich Fraundorfer	Local Arrangements	Graz Univ. of Technology, Austria
Matjaž Jogan	Tutorials Chair	Univ. of Ljubljana, Slovenia
Andreas Opelt	Local Arrangements	Graz Univ. of Technology, Austria
Johanna Pfeifer	Conference Secretariat	Graz Univ. of Technology, Austria
Matthias Rüther	Local Arrangements	Graz Univ. of Technology, Austria
Danijel Skočaj	Workshops Chair	Univ. of Ljubljana, Slovenia

Conference Board

Hans Burkhardt   University of Freiburg, Germany
Bernard Buxton   University College London, UK
Roberto Cipolla   University of Cambridge, UK
Jan-Olof Eklundh   Royal Institute of Technology, Sweden
Olivier Faugeras   INRIA, Sophia Antipolis, France
Anders Heyden   Lund University, Sweden
Bernd Neumann   University of Hamburg, Germany
Mads Nielsen   IT University of Copenhagen, Denmark
Tomáš Pajdla   CTU Prague, Czech Republic
Giulio Sandini   University of Genoa, Italy
David Vernon   Trinity College, Ireland

Area Chairs

Michael Black   Brown University, USA
Joachim M. Buhmann   ETH Zürich, Switzerland

Rachid Deriche   INRIA Sophia Antipolis, France
Pascal Fua   EPFL Lausanne, Switzerland
Luc Van Gool   KU Leuven, Belgium & ETH Zürich, Switzerland
Edwin Hancock   University of York, UK
Richard Hartley   Australian National University, Australia
Sing Bing Kang   Microsoft Research, USA
Stan Li   Chinese Academy of Sciences, Beijing, China
David Lowe   University of British Columbia, Canada
Jiří Matas   CTU Prague, Czech Republic
Nikos Paragios   Ecole Centrale de Paris, France
Marc Pollefeys   University of North Carolina at Chapel Hill, USA
Long Quan   HKUST, Hong Kong, China
Bernt Schiele   Darmstadt University of Technology, Germany
Amnon Shashua   Hebrew University of Jerusalem, Israel
Peter Sturm   INRIA Rhône-Alpes, France
Chris Taylor   University of Manchester, UK
Bill Triggs   INRIA Rhône-Alpes, France
Joachim Weickert   Saarland University, Germany
Daphna Weinshall   Hebrew University of Jerusalem, Israel
Andrew Zisserman   University of Oxford, UK

Program Committee

Motilal Agrawal	Stan Birchfield	Octavia Camps
Jörgen Ahlberg	Laure Blanc-Feraud	David Capel
Miguel Alemán-Flores	Nicolas P. de la Blanca	Barbara Caputo
Yiannis Aloimonos	Volker Blanz	Stefan Carlsson
Amir Amini	Rein van den Boomgaard	Vicent Caselles
Arnon Amir	Patrick Bouthemy	Tat-Jen Cham
Elli Angelopoulou	Richard Bowden	Mike Chantler
Adnan Ansar	Edmond Boyer	Francois Chaumette
Helder Araujo	Yuri Boykov	Rama Chellappa
Tal Arbel	Francois Bremond	Tsuhan Chen
Antonis Argyros	Thomas Breuel	Dmitry Chetverikov
Karl Astrom	Lisa Brown	Ondrej Chum
Shai Avidan	Michael Brown	James Clark
Vemuri Baba	Thomas Brox	Bob Collins
Subhashis Banerjee	Alfred Bruckstein	Dorin Comaniciu
Aharon Bar-Hillel	Andres Bruhn	Tim Cootes
Kobus Barnard	Roberto Brunelli	Joao Costeira
Joao Pedro Barreto	Antoni Buades	Daniel Cremers
Chiraz Ben Abdelkader	Michael Burl	Antonio Criminisi
Marie-Odile Berger	Brian Burns	James Crowley
Marcelo Bertalmio	Darius Burschka	Kristin Dana
Ross Beveridge	Aurelio Campilho	Kostas Daniilidis

Trevor Darrell

James W. Davis

Fernando DelaTorre

Herve Delingette

Frank Dellaert

Frederic Devernay

Michel Dhome

Sven Dickinson

Zachary Dodds

Ondrej Drbohlav

Mark S. Drew

Zoran Duric

Pinar Duygulu

Charles Dyer

Alexei Efros

Jan-Olof Eklundh

James Elder

Ahmed Elgammal

Mark Everingham

Aly Farag

Paolo Favaro

Ronald Fedkiw

Michael Felsberg

Rob Fergus

Cornelia Fermüller

Vittorio Ferrari

Frank P. Ferrie

James Ferryman

Mario Figueiredo

Graham Finlayson

Bob Fisher

Patrick Flynn

Wolfgang Förstner

Hassan Foroosh

David Forsyth

Friedrich Fraundorfer

Daniel Freedman

Andrea Fusiello

Xiang Gao

Nikolas Gebert

Yakup Genc

Guido Gerig

Jan-Mark Geusebroek

Christopher Geyer

Georgy Gimel'farb

Joshua Gluckman

Jacob Goldberger

Dmitry Goldgof

Venu Govindaraju

Etienne Grossmann

Frederic Guichard

Yanlin Guo

Allan Hanbury

Horst Haussecker

Eric Hayman

Tamir Hazan

Martial Hebert

Bernd Heisele

Anders Heyden

R. Andrew Hicks

Adrian Hilton

Jeffrey Ho

Tin Kam Ho

David Hogg

Ki-Sang Hong

Anthony Hoogs

Joachim Hornegger

Kun Huang

Slobodan Ilic

Atsushi Imiya

Sergey Ioffe

Michael Isard

Yuri Ivanov

Allan D. Jepson

Hailin Jin

Peter Johansen

Nebojsa Jojic

Mike Jones

Fredrik Kahl

J.K. Kamarainen

Chandra Kambhamettu

Yoshinari Kameda

Kenichi Kanatani

Qifa Ke

Daniel Keren

Renaud Keriven

Benjamin Kimia

Ron Kimmel

Nahum Kiryati

Josef Kittler

Georges Koepfler

Vladimir Kolmogorov

Pierre Kornprobst

Jana Kosecka

Danica Kragic

Kiriakos Kutulakos

InSo Kweon

Shang-Hong Lai

Ivan Laptev

Erik Learned-Miller

Sang Wook Lee

Bastian Leibe

Christophe Lenglet

Vincent Lepetit

Thomas Leung

Stephen Lin

Michael Lindenbaum

Jim Little

Yanxi Liu

Alex Loui

Brian Lovell

Claus Madsen

Marcus Magnor

Shyjan Mahamud

Atsuto Maki

Tom Malzbender

R. Manmatha

Petros Maragos

Sebastien Marcel

Eric Marchand

Jorge Marques

Jose Luis Marroquin

David Martin

Aleix M. Martinez

Bogdan Matei

Yasuyuki Matsushita

Iain Matthews

Stephen Maybank

Helmut Mayer

Leonard McMillan

Gerard Medioni

Etienne Memin

Rudolf Mester

Dimitris Metaxas

Krystian Mikolajczyk

Majid Mirmehdi

Anurag Mittal

J.M.M. Montiel

Theo Moons

Philippos Mordohai

Greg Mori

Pavel Mrázek

Jane Mulligan

Joe Mundy

Vittorio Murino

Hans-Hellmut Nagel

Vic Nalwa

Srinivasa Narasimhan

P.J. Narayanan

Oscar Nestares

Heiko Neumann

Jan Neumann

Ram Nevatia

Ko Nishino

David Nister

Thomas O'Donnell

Masatoshi Okutomi

Ole Fogh Olsen

Tomáš Pajdla

Chris Pal

Theodore Papadopoulo

Nikos Paragios

Ioannis Pavlidis

Vladimir Pavlovic

Shmuel Peleg

Marcello Pelillo

Francisco Perales

Sylvain Petitjean

Matti Pietikainen

Filiberto Pla

Robert Pless

Jean Ponce

Rich Radke

Ravi Ramamoorthi

Deva Ramanan

Visvanathan Ramesh

Ramesh Raskar

Christopher Rasmussen

Carlo Regazzoni

James Rehg

Paolo Remagnino

Xiaofeng Ren

Tammy Riklin-Raviv

Ehud Rivlin

Antonio Robles-Kelly

Karl Rohr

Sami Romdhani

Bodo Rosenhahn

Arun Ross

Carsten Rother

Nicolas Rougon

Mikael Rousson

Sebastien Roy

Javier Sanchez

Jose Santos-Victor

Guillermo Sapiro

Radim Sara

Jun Sato

Yoichi Sato

Eric Saund

Hanno Scharr

Daniel Scharstein

Yoav Y. Schechner

Otmar Scherzer

Christoph Schnörr

Stan Sclaroff

Yongduek Seo

Mubarak Shah

Gregory Shakhnarovich

Ying Shan

Eitan Sharon

Jianbo Shi

Ilan Shimshoni

Ali Shokoufandeh

Kaleem Siddiqi

Greg Slabaugh

Cristian Sminchisescu

Stefano Soatto

Nir Sochen

Jon Sporring

Anuj Srivastava

Chris Stauffer

Drew Steedly

Charles Stewart

Tomáš Suk

Rahul Sukthankar

Josephine Sullivan

Changming Sun

David Suter

Tomáš Svoboda

Richard Szeliski

Tamas Sziranyi

Hugues Talbot

Tieniu Tan

Chi-keung Tang

Xiaoou Tang

Hai Tao

Sibel Tari

Gabriel Taubin

Camillo Jose Taylor

Demetri Terzopoulos

Ying-li Tian

Carlo Tomasi

Antonio Torralba

Andrea Torsello

Panos Trahanias

Mohan Trivedi

Emanuele Trucco

David Tschumperle

Yanghai Tsin

Matthew Turk

Tinne Tuytelaars

Nuno Vasconcelos

Olga Veksler

Svetha Venkatesh

David Vernon

Alessandro Verri

Luminita Aura Vese

Rene Vidal

Markus Vincze

Jordi Vitria

Julia Vogel

Toshikazu Wada

Tomáš Werner

Carl-Fredrik Westin

Yonatan Wexler

Ross Whitaker

Richard Wildes

Chris Williams

James Williams

Lance Williams
Richard Wilson
Lior Wolf
Kwan-Yee K. Wong
Ming Xie
Yasushi Yagi
Hulya Yalcin

Jie Yang
Ming-Hsuan Yang
Ruigang Yang
Jingyi Yu
Ramin Zabih
Changshui Zhang
Zhengyou Zhang

Cha Zhang
Song-Chun Zhu
Todd Zickler
Michael Zillich
Larry Zitnick
Lilla Zöllei
Steven Zucker

Additional Reviewers

Vitaly Ablavsky
Jeff Abrahamson
Daniel Abretske
Amit Adam
Gaurav Aggarwal
Amit Agrawal
Timo Ahonen
Amir Akbarzadeh
H. Can Aras
Tamar Avraham
Harlyn Baker
Patrick Baker
Hynek Bakstein
Olof Barr
Adrien Bartoli
Paul Beardsley
Isabelle Bégin
Ohad Ben-Shahar
Møarten Björkman
Mark Borg
Jake Bouvrie
Bernhard Burgeth
Frédéric Cao
Gustavo Carneiro
Nicholas Carter
Umberto Castellani
Bruno Cernuschi-Frias
Ming-Ching Chang
Roland Chapuis
Thierry Chateau
Hong Chen
Xilin Chen
Sen-ching Cheung
Tat-Jun Chin
Mario Christhoudias

Chi-Wei Chu
Andrea Colombari
Jason Corso
Bruce Culbertson
Goksel Dedeoglu
David Demirdjian
Konstantinos Derpanis
Zvi Devir
Stephan Didas
Miodrag Dimitrijevic
Ryan Eckbo
Christopher Engels
Aykut Erdem
Erkut Erdem
Anders Ericsson
Kenny Erleben
Steven Eschrich
Francisco Estrada
Ricardo Fabbri
Xiaodong Fan
Craig Fancourt
Michela Farenzena
Han Feng
Doug Fidaleo
Robert Fischer
Andrew Fitzhugh
Francois Fleuret
Per-Erik Forssén
Ben Fransen
Clement Fredembach
Mario Fritz
Gareth Funka-Lea
Darren Gawely
Atiyeh Ghoreyshi
Alvina Goh

Leo Grady
Kristen Grauman
Ralph Gross
Nicolas Guilbert
Abdenour Hadid
Onur Hamsici
Scott Helmer
Yacov Hel-Or
Derek Hoiem
Byung-Woo Hong
Steve Hordley
Changbo Hu
Rui Huang
Xinyu Huang
Camille Izard
Vidit Jain
Vishal Jain
Christopher Jaynes
Kideog Jeong
Björn Johansson
Marie-Pierre Jolly
Erik Jonsson
Klas Josephson
Michael Kaess
Rahul Khare
Dae-Woong Kim
Jong-Sung Kim
Kristian Kirk
Dan Kushnir
Ville Kyrki
Pascal Lagger
Prasun Lala
Michael Langer
Catherine Laporte
Jean-Marc Lavest

Albert Law
Jean-Pierre Lecadre
Maxime Lhuillier
Gang Li
Qi Li
Zhiguo Li
Hwasup Lim
Sernam Lim
Zicheng Liu
Wei-Lwun Lu
Roberto Lublinerman
Simon Lucey
Gian Luca Mariottini
Scott McCloskey
Changki Min
Thomas Moeslund
Kooksang Moon
Louis Morency
Davide Moschini
Matthias Mühlich
Artiom Myaskouvskey
Kai Ni
Michael Nielsen
Carol Novak
Fredrik Nyberg
Sang-Min Oh
Takahiro Okabe
Kenki Okuma
Carl Olsson
Margarita Osadchy
Magnus Oskarsson
Niels Overgaard
Ozge Ozcanli
Mustafa Ozuysal
Vasu Parameswaran
Prakash Patel
Massimiliano Pavan
Patrick Perez
Michael Phelps

Julien Pilet
David Pisinger
Jean-Philippe Pons
Yuan Quan
Ariadna Quattoni
Kevin Quennesson
Ali Rahimi
Ashish Raj
Ananath Ranganathan
Avinash Ravichandran
Randall Rojas
Mikael Rousson
Adit Sahasrabudhe
Roman Sandler
Imari Sato
Peter Savadjiev
Grant Schindler
Konrad Schindler
Robert Schwanke
Edgar Seemann
Husrev Taha Sencar
Ali Shahrokni
Hong Shen
Fan Shufei
Johan Skoglund
Natalia Slesareva
Jan Sochman
Jan Erik Solem
Jonathan Starck
Jesse Stewart
Henrik Stewenius
Moritz Stoerring
Svetlana Stolpner
Mingxuan Sun
Ying Sun
Amir Tamrakar
Robby Tan
Tele Tan
Donald Tanguay

Leonid Taycher
Ashwin Thangali
David Thirde
Mani Thomas
Tai-Peng Tian
David Tolliver
Nhon Trinh
Ambrish Tyagi
Raquel Urtasun
Joost Van-de-Weijer
Andrea Vedaldi
Dejun Wang
Hanzi Wang
Jingbin Wang
Liang Wang
Martin Welk
Adam Williams
Bob Woodham
Stefan Wörz
Christopher Wren
Junwen Wu
Wen Wu
Rong Yan
Changjiang Yang
Qing-Xiong Yang
Alper Yilmaz
Jerry Yokono
David Young
Quan Yuan
Alan Yuille
Micheal Yurick
Dimitrios Zarpalas
Guoying Zhao
Tao Zhao
Song-Feng Zheng
Jie Zhu
Loe Zhu
Manli Zhu

Sponsoring Institutions

Advanced Computer Vision, Austria
Graz University of Technology, Austria
University of Ljubljana, Slovenia

Table of Contents – Part IV

Face/Gesture/Action Detection and Recognition

Segmentation and Grouping

Object Recognition, Retrieval and Indexing

Low-Level Vision, Segmentation and Grouping

Robust Multi-view Face Detection Using Error Correcting Output Codes

Hongming Zhang[1,2], Wen Gao[1,2], Xilin Chen[2], Shiguang Shan[2], and Debin Zhao[1]

[1] Department of Computer Science and Engineering, Harbin Institute of Technology,
Harbin, 150001, China
[2] Institute of Computing Technology, Chinese Academy of Sciences,
Beijing, 100080, China
{hmzhang, wgao, xlchen, sgshan, dbzhao}@jdl.ac.cn

Abstract. This paper presents a novel method to solve multi-view face detection problem by Error Correcting Output Codes (ECOC). The motivation is that face patterns can be divided into separated classes across views, and ECOC multi-class method can improve the robustness of multi-view face detection compared with the view-based methods because of its inherent error-tolerant ability. One key issue with ECOC-based multi-class classifier is how to construct effective binary classifiers. Besides applying ECOC to multi-view face detection, this paper emphasizes on designing efficient binary classifiers by learning informative features through minimizing the error rate of the ensemble ECOC multi-class classifier. Aiming at designing efficient binary classifiers, we employ spatial histograms as the representation, which provide an overcomplete set of optional features that can be efficiently computed from the original images. In addition, the binary classifier is constructed as a coarse to fine procedure using fast histogram matching followed by accurate Support Vector Machine (SVM). The experimental results show that the proposed method is robust to multi-view faces, and achieves performance comparable to that of state-of-the-art approaches to multi-view face detection.

1 Introduction

Automatic detection of human faces is significant in applications, such as human-computer interaction, face recognition, expression recognition and content-based image retrieval. Face detection is a challenge due to variability in orientations, partial occlusions, and lighting conditions. A comprehensive survey on face detection can be found in [1].

Many approaches have been proposed for face detection, these approaches can be classified as two categories: global appearance-based technique and component-based technique. The first one assumes that a face can be represented as a whole unit. Several statistical learning mechanisms are explored to characterize face patterns, such as neural network [2,3], probabilistic distribution [4], support vector machines [5,6], naive Bayes classifier [7], and boosting algorithms [8,9]. The second method treats a face as a collection of components. Important facial features (eyes, nose and mouth) are first extracted, and by using their locations and relationships, the faces are detected [10].

A. Leonardis, H. Bischof, and A. Pinz (Eds.): ECCV 2006, Part IV, LNCS 3954, pp. 1–12, 2006.
© Springer-Verlag Berlin Heidelberg 2006

So far there are three ways for multi-view face detection. The first scheme is a view-based approach. In the training stage, separate face detectors are built for different views. In the testing stage, all these detectors are applied to the image and their results are merged into final detection results [4,7,9]. [11] uses a pose estimator to select a detector to find faces of the chosen view. The second scheme is described in [12] for rotated-face detection, which calculates the in-plane rotation angle of input image, and rotates the input image for a frontal face detector. The third way is to approximate smooth functions of face patterns across various views [13] or face manifold parameterized by facial pose [14].

Motivated by the idea that face patterns can be naturally divided into distinct classes according to separated facial poses, this paper proposes a novel method that detects multi-view faces using a multiclass classifier based on error correcting output codes (ECOC). With its inherent error-tolerant property, ECOC can improve the robustness to pose variation for face detection.

Dietterich and Bakiri [15,16] presented the idea of reducing multiclass problems to multiple binary problems based on ECOC. ECOC classifier design concept has been used in many applications, such as text classification [17] and face verification [18]. In ECOC related applications, one key issue is the problem how to construct optimal binary classifiers for an effective ECOC multi-class classifier. In [19], an approach is presented to learn good discriminator in linear feature space for object recognition.

In the proposed method, we emphasize on designing efficient binary classifiers by learning informative features through minimizing the error rate of the ensemble ECOC multi-class classifier. Aiming at designing efficient binary classifiers, we propose to use spatial histogram features as representation and use hierarchical classifiers that combine histogram matching and support vector machine (SVM) as binary classifiers.

Section 2 briefly describes the background of ECOC-based multi-class classification method. The overview of the proposed ECOC-based multi-view face detection approach is given in Section 3. Face representation used in the proposed method is described in Section 4. In Section 5, the method of learning an ECOC-based multi-view face detector through minimizing error rate is presented. Experimental results are provided in Section 6. Conclusions are given in Section 7.

2   Background of ECOC-Based Multi-class Classification

Let $S = \{(x_1, y_1), ..., (x_m, y_m)\}$ be a set of m training samples where each instance x_i belongs to a domain X, and each label y_i takes values from a discrete set of classes $Y = \{1, ..., k\}$. The task of learning a multiclass classifier is to find a function $H : X \rightarrow Y$ that maps an instance x into a class label y, $y \in Y$.

To understand the method for solving multiclass learning problems via ECOC, consider a $\{0,1\}$-valued matrix Z of size $k \times n$ where k is the number of classes and n is the length of the unique binary string assigned to each class as its *code word*. The k rows are well separated with large Hamming distance between any pair. For each column, the instances are relabeled as two *super classes* according to the binary vales (1s and 0s).

The multiclass learning method consists of two stages. (1) In the training stage, a set of n binary classifiers is constructed, where each classifier is to distinguish between the two super classes for each column. These binary classifiers are called *base classifiers*. (2) In the testing stage, each instance is tested by the base classifiers, and is represented by an output vector of length n. The distance between the output vector and the code word of each class is used to determine the class label of the instance.

3 Overview of the Proposed ECOC-Based Face Detection Method

We divide face patterns into three categories: frontal faces, left profile faces, right profile faces, according to facial pose variation out of plane. Adding non-face patterns together, we have four classes to be recognized in total. Therefore, we format multi-view face detection as a multi-class problem with four classes, and explore the problem of learning ECOC-based classifier for multi-view face detection.

Since $k = 4$, we construct a complete code of length $n = 7$, as shown in Table 1. No columns or no rows are identical or complementary in the code. For each column, one base classifier is needed to identify the super classes (refer to Section 2). In total, seven base classifiers $\{b_0, b_1, ..., b_6\}$ are to be constructed to form an ensemble classifier. According to information theory, this code has error correcting ability for any base classifier.

Table 1. ECOC codes for face detection

	b_0	b_1	b_2	b_3	b_4	b_5	b_6
Non face pattern (C_0)	0	0	0	0	0	0	0
Front face pattern (C_1)	1	1	1	1	0	0	0
Left profile face pattern (C_2)	1	1	0	0	1	1	0
Right profile face pattern (C_3)	1	0	1	0	1	0	1

We utilize an exhaustive search strategy to detect multiple faces of different sizes at different locations in an input image. The process of object detection in images is summarized in Fig. 1. It contains three steps: image sub sampling, object classification and detection results fusion.

In the Step 1, the original image is repeatedly reduced in size by a factor 1.2, resulting in a pyramid of images. A small window (image window) with a certain size 32x32 is used to scan the pyramid of images. After a sub image window is extracted from a particular location and scale of the input image pyramid, it is fed to the following procedures in the Step 2. Firstly, spatial histogram features are generated from this image window. Secondly, an ECOC-based multi-view face pattern classifier is used to identify whether the sub window contains a multi-view face. The Step 3 is a stage for detection results fusion. Overlapped face instances of different scales are merged into final detection results.

In the step 2, the input to the multi-view face detector is a vector x, which is constituted by spatial histogram features (refer to Section 4 for details) obtained on the

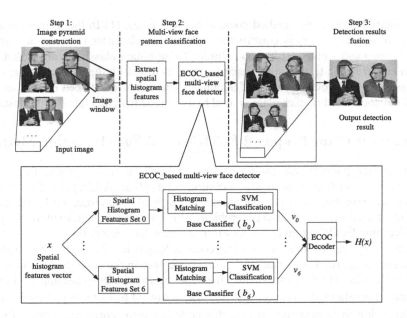

Fig. 1. The process of multi-view face detection in images

image window. For each base classifier, specific spatial histogram features are used as input. Histogram matching and SVM classification are performed hierarchically to identify which super class the vector belongs to (refer to Section 5 for details). The binary outputs by the base classifiers is transformed into an {0,1}-output vector of length $n = 7$, given as

$$V = [v_0, v_1, ..., v_6],\tag{1}$$

where v_j is the output of j th classifier, $j = 0,1,...,6$. The distance between the output vector and the code word of each class is determined by Hamming distance:

$$L_{c_i} = \sum_{j=0}^{6} |Z_{ij} - v_j|, (i = 0,...,3).\tag{2}$$

The test instance is assigned to the class label whose code word has minimum distance, by the ECOC decode rule given by

$$H(x) = \arg\min_{c_i} \{L_{c_i} \mid i = 0,1,...,3\}.\tag{3}$$

4   Spatial Histogram Features for Face Representation

For each column, we refer the super class labeled by 1s as *object*, and labeled by 0s as *non-object*. Similar to our previous work [21], spatial histogram features in are used for object representation, as illustrated in Fig. 2. Spatial templates are used to encode spatial distribution of patterns. Each template is a binary rectangle mask and is denoted as $rt(x, y, w, h)$, where (x, y) is the location and (w, h) is the size of the mask respectively. We model the sub image within the masked window by histogram. This kind of histograms is called as *spatial histograms*. For a sample P, its spatial histogram associated with template $rt(x, y, w, h)$ is denoted as $SH^{rt(x,y,w,h)}(P)$.

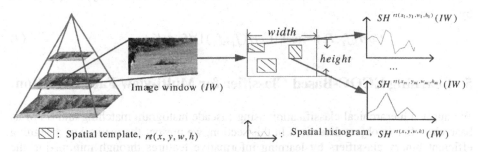

Fig. 2. Object spatial distribution is encoded by spatial histograms

Suppose a database with n object samples and a spatial template, we represent object histogram model over the spatial template by the average spatial histogram of the object training samples, defined as:

$$SH^{rt(x,y,w,h)} = \frac{1}{n}\sum_{j=1}^{n} SH^{rt(x,y,w,h)}(P_j), \qquad (4)$$

where P_j is an object training sample, and $rt(x, y, w, h)$ is the spatial template. For any sample P, we define its *spatial histogram feature* as its distance to the average object histogram, given by

$$f^{rt(x,y,w,h)}(P) = D(SH^{rt(x,y,w,h)}(P), SH^{rt(x,y,w,h)}), \qquad (5)$$

where $D(H_1, H_2)$ is the similarity of two histograms measured by intersection [20]. An object pattern is encoded by m spatial templates. Therefore, an object sample is represented by a spatial histogram feature vector in the feature space:

$$F = [f^{rt(1)}, ..., f^{rt(m)}]. \qquad (6)$$

Feature discriminating ability: For any spatial histogram feature $f_j (1 \le j \le m)$, its discriminative ability is measured by Fisher criterion

$$J(f_j) = \frac{S_b}{S_w}, \qquad (7)$$

where S_b is the between-class scatter, and S_w is the total within-class scatter.

Features correlation measurement: Given two spatial histogram features f_1 and f_2, we calculate the correlation between two features f_1 and f_2 as

$$Corr(f_1, f_2) = \frac{I(f_1 \mid f_2)}{H(f_1)}, \tag{8}$$

where $H(f_1)$ is entropy of f_1, $I(f_1 \mid f_2)$ is the mutual information of f_1 and f_2. Let F_s be a feature set, the correlation between F_s and a feature $f_t \notin F_s$ is given by

$$Corr(f_t, F_s) = \max\{Corr(f_t, f_k) \mid \forall f_k \in F_s\}. \tag{9}$$

5   Learning ECOC-Based Classifier for Multi-view Face Detection

We apply a hierarchical classification using cascade histogram matching and SVM as base classifier to object detection. In this section, we present the method of designing efficient binary classifiers by learning informative features through minimizing the error rate of the ensemble ECOC multi-class classifier.

5.1   Cascade Histogram Matching

Histogram matching is a direct method for object recognition. Suppose P is a sample and its spatial histogram feature with one template $rt(x, y, w, h)$ is $f^{rt(x,y,w,h)}(P)$, P is classified as object pattern if $f^{rt(x,y,w,h)}(P) \geq \theta$, otherwise P is classified as non-object pattern. θ is the threshold for classification. We select most informative spatial histogram features and combine them in a cascade form to perform histogram matching. We call this classification method as *cascade histogram matching*. If n spatial histogram features $f_1, ..., f_n$ with associated classification thresholds $\theta_1, ..., \theta_n$ are selected, the decision rule of cascade histogram matching is as follows:

$$CH(P) = \begin{cases} 1 & \text{object} & \text{if } f_1(P) \geq \theta_1 \wedge ... \wedge f_n(P) \geq \theta_n \\ 0 & \text{non - object} & \text{otherwise} \end{cases} \tag{10}$$

For each column, suppose that we have (1) spatial histogram features space $F = \{f_1, ..., f_m\}$, (2) positive and negative training sets: SP and SN, (3) a positive validation set $VP = \{(x_1, y_1), ..., (x_n, y_n)\}$, and a negative validation set $VN = \{(x_1', y_1'), ..., (x_k', y_k')\}$, where x_i and x_i' are samples with m dimensional spatial histogram feature vectors, $y_i = 1$ and $y_i' = 0$, (4) acceptable detection rate: D. The method for training cascade histogram matching is given in the following procedure:

1. Initialization: $F_{select} = \varnothing$, $ThreSet = \varnothing$, $t = 0$, $Acc(pre) = 0$, $Acc(cur) = 0$;
2. Compute Fisher criterion $J(f)$ using SP and SN, for each feature $f \in F$;
3. Find the spatial histogram feature f_t which has the maximal Fisher criterion value, $f_t = \arg\max_{f_j}\{J(f_j) \mid f_j \in F\}$;

4. Perform histogram matching with f_t on the validation set $V = VP \cup VN$, find a threshold θ_t such that the detection rate d on the positive validation set VP is greater than D, i.e., $d \geq D$;

5. Compute the classification accuracy on the negative validation set VN,

$$Acc(cur) = 1 - \frac{1}{k}\sum_{i=1}^{k}|CH(x_i') - y_i'|. \; CH(x) \text{ is the output by histogram matching}$$

with f_t and θ_t, $CH(x) \in \{0,1\}$;

6. If the classification accuracy satisfies condition: $Acc(cur) - Acc(pre) \leq \varepsilon$ (ε is a small positive constant), the procedure exits and returns F_{select} and $ThreSet$, otherwise process following steps:

   (a) $Acc(pre) = Acc(cur)$, $SN = \varnothing$, $F_{select} = F_{select} \cup \{f_t\}$, $F = F \setminus \{f_t\}$, $ThreSet = ThreSet \cup \{\theta_t\}$, $t = t+1$,

   (b) Perform cascade histogram matching with F_{select} and $ThreSet$ on an image set containing no target objects, put false detections into SN,

   (c) Go to step 2 and continue next iteration step.

5.2 Construction of the ECOC-Based Multi-view Face Detector

Cascade histogram matching is the coarse object detection stage. To improve detection performance, we employ SVM classification [22] as fine detection stage. By minimizing error rate, we construct an ECOC-based multi-view face detector.

Suppose that we have (1) a spatial histogram features space $F = \{f_1,...,f_m\}$, (2) a training set $s = \{(x_1, y_1),...,(x_n, y_n)\}$ and a testing set $v = \{(x_1', y_1'),...,(x_k', y_k')\}$, where x_i and x_i' are samples with m dimensional spatial histogram feature vectors, $y_i \in \{0,1,2,3\}$ and $y_i' \in \{0,1,2,3\}$, (3) ECOC code matrix Z of size $k \times n$, ($k = 4$, $n = 7$) as listed in Table 1. The construction of the ECOC-based multi-view face detector is performed as the following procedure:

1. Using the method for training cascade histogram matching (see section 5.1), construct a cascade histogram matching classifier as base classifier for each column. These base classifiers $\{b_0,...,b_6\}$ constitute the ECOC multi-class classifier;

2. Set classification accuracy $Acc(pre) = 0$; for each column, find f_m^i with maximum Fisher criterion, $F_{select}^i = \{f_m^i\}$ and $F_{ori}^i = F \setminus \{f_m^i\}$, $i = 0,1,...,6$;

3. Compute each base classifier's error rate; find the base classifier b_t ($0 \leq t \leq 6$), which has maximum error rate, and update the base classifier as follows:

   (a) Compute Fisher criterion $J(f)$ and feature correlation $Corr(f, F_{select}^t)$ on the training sample set, for each feature $f \in F_{ori}^t$;

(b) Compute *Thre* as follows:

$$\begin{cases} MinCorr = \min\{Corr(f, F^t_{select}) \mid f \in F^t_{ori}\} \\ MaxCorr = \max\{Corr(f, F^t_{select}) \mid f \in F^t_{ori}\}, \\ Thre = MinCorr * (1 - \alpha) + MaxCorr * \alpha \end{cases}$$

here α is a balance weight ($0 < \alpha < 1$), we choose $\alpha = 0.2$ in experiments;

(c) Find $f' \in F^t_{ori}$ with large Fisher criterion as below:

$$f' = \arg\max_{f_j}(J(f_j) \mid Corr(f_j, F^t_{select}) \le Thre);$$

(d) Train a SVM classifier C on the training set s, using f' and F^t_{select}; update b_t with cascade histogram matching and the SVM classifier C; update the ECOC multi-class classifier with b_t;

4. Evaluate the ECOC multi-class classifier on the testing samples set v, and compute the classification accuracy:

$$Acc(cur) = 1 - \frac{1}{k}\sum_{i=1}^{k}S(C(x_i'), y_i'), S(x, y) = \begin{cases} 1 & x \ne y \\ 0 & x = y \end{cases}.$$

Here, $C(x)$ is the classification output by the classifier C, $C(x) \in \{0,1,2,3\}$;

5. If the classification accuracy satisfies condition: $Acc(cur) - Acc(pre) \ge \varepsilon$ (ε is a small positive constant), process following steps:

(a) $Acc(pre) = Acc(cur)$, $F^t_{select} = F^t_{select} \cup \{f'\}$, $F^t_{ori} = F^t_{ori} \setminus \{f'\}$,

(b) Go to step 3 and continue next iteration step.

6. The procedure exits and returns the ECOC multi-class classifier, which is constituted by b_i and F^i_{select} ($i = 0,1,...,6$).

6 Experimental Results

We implement the proposed approach and conduct experiments to evaluate its effectiveness. Our training sample set consists of 11,400 frontal face images, 4,260 left profile face images, 4,080 right profile face images, and 17,285 non-face images, each of standard size 32x32.

The exhaustive spatial template set within 32x32 image window is 832,351, a very large amount. After reducing redundancy, 180 spatial templates are evaluated to extract spatial histogram features. For each base classifier, about 9~15 spatial templates are learned for cascade histogram matching and 20~25 are learned for SVM classification with RBF kernel function in our experiment. The multi-view face detector is composed of these base classifiers.

Experiment 1: Error-Tolerant Performance Evaluation
In order to evaluate the error-tolerant performance of the ECOC-based multi-view face detector, we collect another sample set for testing. This set contains 5,400 frontal face images, 3,011 left profile face images, 3,546 right profile face images, and 6,527 non-face images, each of standard size 32x32.

In Table 2, classification error rates of binary classifiers in the ECOC-based multi-view face detector are presented. Table 3 shows classification error rates of the ECOC-based multi-view face pattern classifier. The error rates are decreased after using ECOC to combine all the base classifiers. These results demonstrate that the system has error-tolerant ability and it is be able to recover from the errors of single base classifier.

Table 2. Classification error rates of the base classifiers

	b_0	b_1	b_2	b_3	b_4	b_5	b_6
Error rate	18.4%	18.4%	18.3%	17.9%	4.7%	25.0%	22.9%

Table 3. Classification error rates of the ECOC-based multi-view face pattern classifier

Class	Number of testing samples	Error rate
Non face pattern (C_0)	6257	4.8%
Front face pattern (C_1)	5400	1.6%
Left profile face pattern (C_2)	3011	5.5%
Right profile face pattern (C_3)	3546	4.7%
Total	18214	4.0%

Experiment 2: Testing Results on Standard Data Sets
We test our system on two standard data sets. One is MIT+CMU set [2,4], which contains 130 images with 507 frontal faces. The other is CMU-PROFILE [7], which consists of 208 images with 441 faces from full frontal view to side view. About 347 faces are in profile pose.

The ROC curves are shown in Fig. 3. In Fig. 4, some face detection examples are given. The examples demonstrate that our approach can handle multiple faces with complex backgrounds. Comparison results are shown in Table 4 and Table 5. Our system exhibits superior performance than [2,9,11,14] with higher detection rate, and achieves comparable performance compared with the system of [7,8].

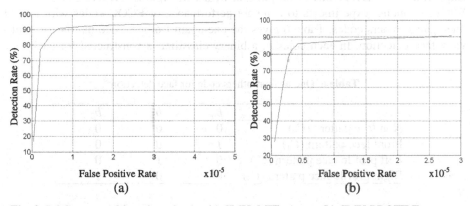

Fig. 3. ROC curves of face detection on (a) CMU+MIT test set, (b) CMU-PROFILE test set

Fig. 4. Some examples of multi-view face detection

Table 4. Face detection rates on MIT+CMU set

False alarms	31	65	167
Jones and Viola [8](frontal)	85.2%	92.0%	93.9%
Rowley et.al [2]	85.0%	N/A	90.1%
Schneiderman and Kanade [7]	N/A	94.4%	N/A
Li and Zhang [9]	89.2%	N/A	N/A
Our approach	90.7%	92.3%	94.2%

Table 5. Face detection rates on CMU-PROFILE set

False alarms	91	700
Jones and Viola [11](profile)	70%	83%
Schneiderman and Kanade [7]	86%	93%
Osadchy, Miller, LeCun [14]	67%	83%
Our approach	82%	90%

Experiment 3: Performance Comparison with One-Against-Others Codes

We also conduct experiments to compare performance of ECOC codes with that of one-against-others codes. Table 6 gives the one-against-others code matrix for multi-view face detection. In each column, a binary classifier is constructed for each face

Table 6. One-against-others code for face detection

	b_0	b_1	b_2
Non face pattern (C_0)	0	0	0
Front face pattern (C_1)	1	0	0
Left profile face pattern (C_2)	0	1	0
Right profile face pattern (C_3)	0	0	1

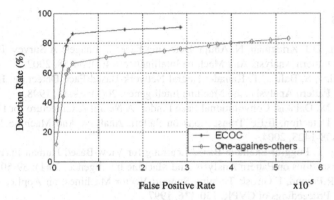

Fig. 5. Face detection performance comparison between ECOC with one-against-other: ROC on CMU-PROFILE test set

class against other face classes and non-face class. This code has no error correcting ability for base classifiers.

Fig. 5 shows the ROC comparison between the system using ECOC codes and the system using one-against-others codes. The comparison result shows that ECOC-based system achieves superior performance with higher detection rates.

7 Conclusions

In this paper, we solve multi-view face detection problem by using ECOC. The key issue is how to train effective binary classifiers for an efficient ECOC-based multi-view face detector. Our method constructs binary classifiers by learning informative features through minimizing the error rate. For purpose to obtain efficient binary classifiers, our method employs spatial histogram features as representation and hierarchical classifiers as binary classifiers. Extensive experiments show that ECOC improves the robustness to pose variation for face detection, and the proposed approach is efficient in detecting multi-view faces simultaneously. Tests on standard data sets show that the proposed method achieves performance comparable to that of state-of-the-art approaches to multi-view face detection.

The proposed approach of constructing ECOC-based multi-classifier by learning base classifiers can be viewed as a general framework of multi-classes problem based on a given code matrix. In the future work, we plan to apply this approach in multi-class objects detection with more kinds of objects.

Acknowledgements

This research is supported by National Nature Science Foundation of China (60332010), 100 Talents Program of CAS, China, the Program for New Century Excellent Talents in University (NCET-04-0320), ISVISION Technologies Co. Ltd.

References

1. M.H. Yang, D.J. Kriegman, N. Abuja: Detecting Faces in Images: A Survey. IEEE Transactions on Pattern Analysis And Machine Intelligence, 24(1): 34-58, 2002.
2. H.A. Rowley, S. Baluja, T. Kanade: Neural Network-Based Face Detection. IEEE Transactions on Pattern Analysis And Machine Intelligence, 20(1): 29-38, 1998.
3. C. Garcia, M. Delakis: Convolutional Face Finder: A Neural Architecture for Fast and Robust Face Detection, IEEE Transactions on Pattern Analysis And Machine Intelligence, 26(11): 1408-1423, 2004.
4. K.K. Sung, T. Poggio: Example-Based Learning for View-Based Human Face Detection. IEEE Transactions on Pattern Analysis And Machine Intelligence, 20(1): 39-50,1998.
5. E.Osuna, R.Freund, F.Girosi: Training Support Vector Machines: an Application to Face Detection. Proceedings of CVPR, 130-136, 1997.
6. S.Romdhani, P.Torr, B.Scholkopf, A.Blake: Computationally efficient face detection. Proceedings of the 8th International Conference on Computer Vision, Volume 2: 695-700, 2001.
7. H. Schneiderman, T. Kanade: A Statistical Method for 3D Object Detection Applied to Faces and Cars. IEEE Conference on Computer Vision and Pattern Recognition, 2000.
8. P. Viola, M. Jones: Robust Real Time Object Detection. IEEE ICCV Workshop on Statistical and Computational Theories of Vision, 2001.
9. S.Z. Li, Z.Q. Zhang: FloatBoost Learning and Statistical Face Detection. IEEE Transactions on Pattern Analysis and Machine Intelligence, 2004 (26): 9, 1112-1123.
10. K.C. Yow, R. Cipolla: Feature-Based Human Face Detection. CUED/F-INFENG/TR 249, 1996.
11. M. Jones, P. Viola: Fast Multi-view face detection. Technical Report TR2003-96, Mitsubishi Electric Research Laboratories, 2003.
12. H.A. Rowley, S. Baluja, T. Kanade: Rotation Invariant Neural Network-Based Face Detection. Computer Vision and Pattern Recognition, 38-44, 1998.
13. Y.M. Li, S.G. Gong, H. Liddell: Support vector regression and classification based multi-view face detection and recognition. Proceeding of Fourth IEEE International Conference on Face and Gesture Recognition, 300-305, 2000.
14. M. Osadchy, M.L. Miller, Y. LeCun: Synergistic Face Detection and Pose Estimation with Energy-Based Models. In Neural Information Processing Systems Conference, 2004.
15. T.G. Dietterich, G. Bakiri: Error-correcting output codes: A general method for improving multi-class inductive learning programs. In Proceedings of the Ninth National Conference on Artificial Intelligence (AAAI-91), AAAI Press, 1991, 572-577.
16. T.G. Dieteerich, G. Bakiri: Solving multi-class learning problems via error correcting output codes. Journal of Artificial Intelligence Research, 2,263-286, 1995.
17. R. Ghani: Using error-correcting codes for text classification. Proceedings of ICML-00, 17th International Conference on Machine Learning, 2000, pp 303-310.
18. J. Kittler, R. Ghaderi, T. Windeatt, J. Matas: Face verification via error correcting output codes. Image and Vision Computing. 21(13-14): 1163-1169, 2003).
19. S. Mahamud, M. Hebert, and J. Shi: Object recognition using boosted discriminants. In IEEE Conference on Computer Vision and Pattern Recognition (CVPR'01), 2001.
20. M. Swain, D. Ballard: Color indexing. International Journal of Computer Vision, 7(1): 11-32, 1991.
21. H.M. Zhang, W. Gao, X.L Chen, D.B. Zhao: Learning Informative Features for Spatial Histogram-Based Object Detection. Proceedings of International Joint Conference on Neural Networks 2005, 1806-1811, 2005.
22. V. Vapnik: Statistical Learning Theory. Wiley, New York, 1998.

Inter-modality Face Recognition

Dahua Lin[1] and Xiaoou Tang[1,2]

[1] Dept. of Information Engineering, The Chinese University of Hong Kong,
Hong Kong, China
dhlin4@ie.cuhk.edu.hk
[2] Microsoft Research Asia, Beijing, China
xitang@microsoft.com

Abstract. Recently, the wide deployment of practical face recognition systems gives rise to the emergence of the inter-modality face recognition problem. In this problem, the face images in the database and the query images captured on spot are acquired under quite different conditions or even using different equipments. Conventional approaches either treat the samples in a uniform model or introduce an intermediate conversion stage, both of which would lead to severe performance degradation due to the great discrepancies between different modalities. In this paper, we propose a novel algorithm called Common Discriminant Feature Extraction specially tailored to the inter-modality problem. In the algorithm, two transforms are simultaneously learned to transform the samples in both modalities respectively to the common feature space. We formulate the learning objective by incorporating both the empirical discriminative power and the local smoothness of the feature transformation. By explicitly controlling the model complexity through the smoothness constraint, we can effectively reduce the risk of overfitting and enhance the generalization capability. Furthermore, to cope with the nongaussian distribution and diverse variations in the sample space, we develop two nonlinear extensions of the algorithm: one is based on kernelization, while the other is a multi-mode framework. These extensions substantially improve the recognition performance in complex situation. Extensive experiments are conducted to test our algorithms in two application scenarios: optical image-infrared image recognition and photo-sketch recognition. Our algorithms show excellent performance in the experiments.

1 Introduction

The past decade has witnessed a rapid progress of face recognition techniques and development of automatic face recognition (AFR) systems. In many of the face recognition systems, we are in confront of a new situation: due to the limitations of practical conditions, the query face images captured on spot and the reference images stored in the database are acquired through quite different processes under different conditions. Here we give two cases arising from practical demands. The first case is a surveillance system operating from morning to night in an adverse outdoor environment. To combat the weak illumination in the nights or cloudy days, the system employ infrared cameras for imaging and

A. Leonardis, H. Bischof, and A. Pinz (Eds.): ECCV 2006, Part IV, LNCS 3954, pp. 13–26, 2006.

compare the infrared images with the optical images registered in the database, as shown in fig.1. In another case, the police call for a photo-sketch recognition system to recognize the identity of a suspect from a sketch when his photos are unavailable, as shown in fig.2. The images acquired by different processes, which we say are in different *modalities*, often present great discrepancies, thus it is infeasible to use a single model to carry out the comparison between these images. These new applications bring forward a great challenge to the face recognition systems and require new techniques specially designed for the *Inter-Modality Face Recognition*.

Before introducing our approach to the problem, we give a brief review on the statistical pattern recognition methods. An important difficulty for face recognition lies in the high dimension of the sample space. To alleviate the curse of the dimensionality, it is crucial to reduce the dimension while preserving the important information for classification. LDA (Fisherface)[1] is the most popular dimension reduction method for face recognition, which pursues a feature subspace to maximize the trace-ratio of the between-class scattering matrix and the within-class scattering matrix. To solve the singularity of within-class scatter matrix incurred by small sample size problem, a variety of improved LDA-based algorithms are proposed[2][3][4][5][6][7]. However, these algorithms fail to address the overfitting fundamentally. We argue that the poor generalization of LDA in the small sample size case originates from the formulation of the objective, which merely emphasize the separability of the training samples without considering the factors affecting the generalization risk.

In this paper, we propose a general algorithm for various inter-modality face recognition problems, where two issues arise: **1)** How to enable the comparison between samples in different modalities without the intermediate conversion? **2)** How to enhance the generalization capability of the model? To tackle the former issue, we propose a novel algorithm called *Common Discriminant Feature Extraction* as illustrated in fig.3, where two different transforms are simultaneously learned to transform the samples in both the query modality and the reference modality to a common feature space, where the discriminant features for the two modalities are well aligned so that the comparison between them is feasible. Motivated by the statistical learning theory[10] which states that the

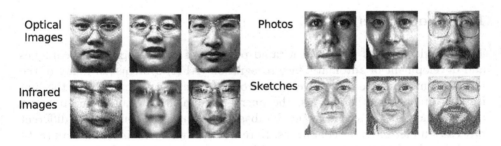

Fig. 1. The optical images vs. the infrared images

Fig. 2. The photos vs. the sketches

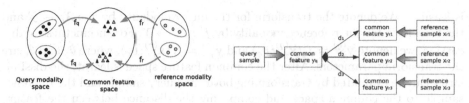

Fig. 3. Illustration of common feature space

Fig. 4. The query procedure

model complexity has important impact on the generalization risk, we formulate the learning objective by incorporating both the empirical discriminative power and the local consistency. The empirical discriminative power comprises the intra-class compactness and inter-class dispersion, which together reflect the separability of the training samples; while the local consistency[11] is inspired by the local preservation principle emerging from the machine learning literatures[12][13], which measures the local smoothness of the feature transformation. It is believed that by explicitly imposing the smoothness constraint and thus preserving the local structure of the embedded manifold, we can effectively reduce the risk of overfitting. Based on the formulation, we derive a new algorithm which can efficiently solve the global optima of the objective function by eigen-decomposition.

Considering that linear transforms lack of capability to separate the samples well in the complicated situations where the sample distribution is nongaussian, we further derive two nonlinear extensions of the algorithm to exploit the nonlinearity of the sample space. The first extension is by kernelization, which offers an elegant and efficient way to extract nonlinear features. The second extension is a multi-mode framework. The framework learns multiple models adapting to the query samples captured in distinct conditions and makes the final decision by a belief-based weighted fusion scheme. Comprehensive experiments are conducted to validate the effectiveness of our algorithms.

2   Common Discriminant Feature Extraction

2.1   Formulation of the Learning Problem

In the problem, there are two types of samples: the query samples captured on spot and the reference samples stored in the database, which are in different modalities. The vector space of the query samples and the reference samples are denoted by $\mathcal{X}_q$ and $\mathcal{X}_r$ respectively, whose dimensions are denoted by d_q and d_r. Suppose we have a training set of N_q samples in the query space and N_r samples in the reference space from C classes, denoted by $\{(\mathbf{x}_i^{(q)}, c_i^{(q)})\}_{i=1}^{N_q}$ and $\{(\mathbf{x}_j^{(r)}, c_j^{(r)})\}_{j=1}^{N_r}$. Here $c_i^{(q)}$ and $c_j^{(r)}$ respectively indicates the class label of the corresponding sample. To enable the comparison of the query samples and the reference samples, we transform them to a d_c-dimensional *Common Discriminant Feature Space*, denoted by $\mathcal{Y}$, which preserves the important discriminant information and aligns the samples in two different modality so that the comparison is feasible. We denote the transform for the query modality by $f_q : \mathcal{X}_q \to \mathcal{Y}$ and the transform for the reference modality by $f_r : \mathcal{X}_r \to \mathcal{Y}$. For succinctness of discussion, we denote $\mathbf{y}_i^{(q)} = f_q(\mathbf{x}_i^{(q)}; \theta_q)$ and $\mathbf{y}_j^{(r)} = f_r(\mathbf{x}_j^{(r)}; \theta_r)$, where θ_q and θ_r are the transform parameters. After the common feature space is learnt, the dissimilarity can be evaluated by transforming both the query sample and the reference sample to the common space and computing the distance between the feature vectors, as in fig.4.

To obtain the feature transforms with good generalization capability, we formulate the learning objective integrating both the empirical separability and the local consistency of the transform operators.

The empirical separability. The *empirical separability* describes the separability of the training samples. It involves two related goals: the intra-class compactness and the inter-class dispersion, which are measured by *average intra-class scattering* and *average inter-class scattering* respectively as follows:

$$J_1(\theta_q, \theta_r) = \frac{1}{N_1} \sum_{i=1}^{N_q} \sum_{j:c_j^{(r)}=c_i^{(q)}} \|\mathbf{y}_i^{(q)} - \mathbf{y}_j^{(r)}\|^2, \tag{1}$$

$$J_2(\theta_q, \theta_r) = \frac{1}{N_2} \sum_{i=1}^{N_q} \sum_{j:c_j^{(r)} \neq c_i^{(q)}} \|\mathbf{y}_i^{(q)} - \mathbf{y}_j^{(r)}\|^2, \tag{2}$$

where N_1 is the number of pairs of samples from the same class, N_2 is the number of pairs of samples from different classes. To better distinguish the samples from different classes, we should drive the query samples towards the reference samples from the same class and far from those of distinct classes. Based on the rationale, we derive the formulation of empirical separability by unifying the intra-class compactness and the inter-class dispersion:

$$J_e(\theta_q, \theta_r) = J_1(f_q, f_r) - \alpha J_2(f_q, f_r) = \sum_{i=1}^{N_q} \sum_{j=1}^{N_r} u_{ij} \|\mathbf{y}_i^{(q)} - \mathbf{y}_j^{(r)}\|^2, \tag{3}$$

where $u_{ij} = \begin{cases} \frac{1}{N_1} & (c_i^{(q)} = c_j^{(r)}) \\ -\frac{\alpha}{N_2} & (c_i^{(q)} \neq c_j^{(r)}) \end{cases}$, and the α reflects the trade-off between the two goals. Minimization of $J_e(\theta_q, \theta_r)$ will lead to the feature space best separating the training samples.

The local consistency. To reduce the risk of overfitting, we introduce the notion *local consistency* into the formulation to regularize the empirical objective, which is a notion emerging from spectral learning[11] and manifold learning [14][12]. The local consistency for f_q and f_r are respectively defined by

$$J_l^{(q)}(\theta_q) = \frac{1}{N_q} \sum_{i=1}^{N_q} \sum_{j=1}^{N_q} w_{ij}^{(q)} ||\mathbf{y}_i^{(q)} - \mathbf{y}_j^{(q)}||^2; \tag{4}$$

$$J_l^{(r)}(\theta_r) = \frac{1}{N_r} \sum_{i=1}^{N_r} \sum_{j=1}^{N_r} w_{ij}^{(r)} ||\mathbf{y}_i^{(r)} - \mathbf{y}_j^{(r)}||^2, \tag{5}$$

where $\mathcal{N}(i)$ is the set of indices of the neighboring samples of i, $w_{ij}^{(q)} = \exp(-\frac{||\mathbf{x}_i^{(q)} - \mathbf{x}_j^{(q)}||}{\sigma_q^2})$ and $w_{ij}^{(r)} = \exp(-\frac{||\mathbf{x}_i^{(r)} - \mathbf{x}_j^{(r)}||}{\sigma_r^2})$ reflect the affinity of two samples. It has been shown that[14] such a definition corresponds to the approximation of $\int_{\mathcal{M}} ||\nabla f(\mathbf{x})||^2$ over the manifold $\mathcal{M}$ on which the samples reside. This clearly indicates that minimization of J_l will encourage consistent output for the neighboring samples in the input space, and thus result in the transform with high local smoothness and best locality preservation. Hence, a smooth transform that is expected to be less vulnerable to overfitting can be learnt by imposing the local consistency constraint.

Integrating the empirical objective and the local consistency objective, we formulate the learning objective to minimize the following objective function:

$$J(\theta_q, \theta_r) = J_e(\theta_q, \theta_r) + \beta \left(J_l^{(q)}(\theta_q) + J_l^{(r)}(\theta_r) \right) = \sum_{i=1}^{N_q} \sum_{j=1}^{N_r} u_{ij} ||\mathbf{y}_i^{(q)} - \mathbf{y}_j^{(r)}||^2$$

$$+ \sum_{i=1}^{N_q} \sum_{j=1}^{N_q} v_{ij}^{(q)} ||\mathbf{y}_i^{(q)} - \mathbf{y}_j^{(q)}||^2 + \sum_{i=1}^{N_r} \sum_{j=1}^{N_r} v_{ij}^{(r)} ||\mathbf{y}_i^{(r)} - \mathbf{y}_j^{(r)}||^2, \tag{6}$$

where we introduce $v_{ij}^{(q)} = \frac{\beta w_{ij}^{(q)}}{N_q}$ and $v_{ij}^{(r)} = \frac{\beta w_{ij}^{(r)}}{N_r}$. For convenience. β is a regularization coefficient controlling the trade-off between the two objectives.

2.2   Matrix-Form of the Objective

To simplify the further analysis, we introduce the following matrix notations:

$d_c \times N_q$ matrix $\mathbf{Y}_q = \left[\mathbf{y}_1^{(q)}, \mathbf{y}_2^{(q)}, \dots, \mathbf{y}_{N_q}^{(q)} \right]$, $d_c \times N_r$ matrix $\mathbf{Y}_r = \left[\mathbf{y}_1^{(r)}, \mathbf{y}_2^{(r)}, \dots, \mathbf{y}_{N_r}^{(r)} \right]$

$N_q \times N_r$ matrix $\mathbf{U} : \mathbf{U}(i,j) = u_{ij}$,

$N_q \times N_q$ diagonal matrix $\mathbf{S}_q : \mathbf{S}_q(i,i) = \sum_{j=1}^{N_r} u_{ij}$, $N_r \times N_r$ diagonal matrix $\mathbf{S}_r : \mathbf{S}_r(j,j) = \sum_{i=1}^{N_q} u_{ij}$,

$N_q \times N_q$ matrix $\mathbf{V}_q : \mathbf{V}_q(i,j) = v_{ij}^{(q)}$, $N_r \times N_r$ matrix $\mathbf{V}_r : \mathbf{V}_r(i,j) = v_{ij}^{(r)}$,

$N_q \times N_q$ diagonal matrix $\mathbf{D}_q : \mathbf{D}_q(i,i) = \sum_{j=1}^{N_q} v_{ij}^{(q)}$, $N_r \times N_r$ diagonal matrix $\mathbf{D}_r : \mathbf{D}_r(i,i) = \sum_{j=1}^{N_r} v_{ij}^{(r)}$.

Then we can rewrite the objectives in matrix form as:

$$J_e(\theta_q, \theta_r) = \sum_{i=1}^{N_q} \sum_{j=1}^{N_r} u_{ij} ||\mathbf{y}_i^{(q)} - \mathbf{y}_j^{(r)}||^2 = \text{tr} \left(\mathbf{Y}_q \mathbf{S}_q \mathbf{Y}_q^T + \mathbf{Y}_r \mathbf{S}_r \mathbf{Y}_r^T - 2\mathbf{Y}_q \mathbf{U} \mathbf{Y}_r^T \right). \tag{7}$$

$$J_l^{(q)}(\theta_q) = 2\text{tr} \left(\mathbf{Y}_q (\mathbf{D}_q - \mathbf{V}_q) \mathbf{Y}_q^T \right); \tag{8}$$

$$J_l^{(q)}(\theta_r) = 2\text{tr} \left(\mathbf{Y}_r (\mathbf{D}_r - \mathbf{V}_r) \mathbf{Y}_r^T \right). \tag{9}$$

Combine the three formulas above, we can derive that

$$J(\theta_q, \theta_r) = \text{tr}\left(\mathbf{Y}_q \mathbf{R}_q \mathbf{Y}_q^T + \mathbf{Y}_r \mathbf{R}_r \mathbf{Y}_r^T - 2\mathbf{Y}_q \mathbf{U} \mathbf{Y}_r^T\right). \qquad (10)$$

where $\mathbf{R}_q = \mathbf{S}_q + 2(\mathbf{D}_q - \mathbf{V}_q)$ and $\mathbf{R}_r = \mathbf{S}_r + 2(\mathbf{D}_r - \mathbf{V}_r)$.

It is conspicuous that the transform $f(\mathbf{x})$ and its double-scaled version $2f(\mathbf{x})$ are essentially the same with respect to classification, however the latter transform will result in the objective value four times the former one. Hence, we should impose constraint on the scale of features in order to prevent trivial solutions. Since Euclidean distance will be used in the target feature space where all dimensions are uniformly treated, it is reasonable to require the feature vectors satisfy isotropic distribution. It can be expressed in terms of unit covariance as follows

$$\frac{1}{N_q} \mathbf{Y}_q \mathbf{Y}_q^T + \frac{1}{N_r} \mathbf{Y}_r \mathbf{Y}_r^T = \mathbf{I}. \qquad (11)$$

2.3   Solving the Linear Transforms

Linear features are widely used in the literatures due to its simplicity and good generalization. Accordingly we first investigate the case where f_q and f_r are linear transforms, parameterized by the transform matrix $\mathbf{A}_q$ and $\mathbf{A}_r$. Denote the sample matrices[1] by $\mathbf{X}_q = \left[\mathbf{x}_1^{(q)}, \mathbf{x}_2^{(q)}, \ldots, \mathbf{x}_{N_q}^{(q)}\right]$ and $\mathbf{X}_r = \left[\mathbf{x}_1^{(r)}, \mathbf{x}_2^{(r)}, \ldots, \mathbf{x}_{N_r}^{(r)}\right]$, then we have

$$\mathbf{Y}_q = \mathbf{A}_q^T \mathbf{X}_q \qquad \mathbf{Y}_r = \mathbf{A}_r^T \mathbf{X}_r \qquad (12)$$

Combining Eq.(10), Eq.(11) and Eq.(12), the optimization problem of the transform matrices $\mathbf{A}_q$ and $\mathbf{A}_r$ is given by

$$\text{minimize} \quad J(\mathbf{A}_q, \mathbf{A}_r) = \text{tr}\left(\mathbf{A}_q^T \mathbf{M}_{qq} \mathbf{A}_q + \mathbf{A}_r^T \mathbf{M}_{qr} \mathbf{A}_r - 2\mathbf{A}_q^T \mathbf{M}_{qr} \mathbf{A}_r\right), \quad (13)$$

$$\text{s.t} \quad \mathbf{A}_q^T \mathbf{C}_q \mathbf{A}_q + \mathbf{A}_r^T \mathbf{C}_r \mathbf{A}_r = \mathbf{I}. \qquad (14)$$

For Eq.(13) $\mathbf{M}_{qq} = \mathbf{X}_q \mathbf{R}_q \mathbf{X}_q^T$, $\mathbf{M}_{rr} = \mathbf{X}_r \mathbf{R}_r \mathbf{X}_r^T$, and $\mathbf{M}_{qr} = \mathbf{X}_q \mathbf{R}_q \mathbf{X}_r^T$. While for Eq.(14), $\mathbf{C}_q = \frac{1}{N_q} \mathbf{X}_q \mathbf{X}_q^T$ and $\mathbf{C}_r = \frac{1}{N_r} \mathbf{X}_r \mathbf{X}_r^T$ are the covariance matrices.

To solve the optimization problem, we introduce the matrices

$$\mathbf{M} = \begin{pmatrix} \mathbf{X}_q \mathbf{R}_q \mathbf{X}_q^T & -\mathbf{X}_q \mathbf{U} \mathbf{X}_r^T \\ -\mathbf{X}_r \mathbf{U}^T \mathbf{X}_q^T & \mathbf{X}_r \mathbf{R}_r \mathbf{X}_r^T \end{pmatrix} \qquad \mathbf{A} = \begin{pmatrix} \mathbf{A}_q \\ \mathbf{A}_r \end{pmatrix} \qquad \mathbf{C} = \begin{pmatrix} \mathbf{C}_q & 0 \\ 0 & \mathbf{C}_r \end{pmatrix} \quad (15)$$

According to Eq.(13), Eq.(14), and Eq.(15), the optimization problem can be written as

$$\mathbf{A} = \underset{\mathbf{A}^T \mathbf{C} \mathbf{A} = \mathbf{I}}{\text{argmin}} \mathbf{A}^T \mathbf{M} \mathbf{A}, \qquad (16)$$

where both $\mathbf{M}$ and $\mathbf{C}$ are $(d_q + d_r) \times (d_q + d_r)$ symmetric matrices.

---

[1] Here we assume that the samples $\mathbf{X}_q$ and $\mathbf{X}_r$ have zero mean vectors, otherwise, we can first shift them by subtracting the mean vectors.

To solve the constraint optimization problem, we have the following lemma

Lemma 1. *The matrix* $\mathbf{A}$ *satisfies* $\mathbf{ACA}^T = \mathbf{I}$ *where* $\mathbf{C}$ *is symmetric, if and only if* $\mathbf{A}$ *can be written as* $\mathbf{A} = \mathbf{V}\mathbf{\Lambda}^{-\frac{1}{2}}\mathbf{U}$ *where columns of* $\mathbf{V}$ *are eigenvectors and* $\mathbf{\Lambda}$ *are diagonal matrix of eigenvalues satisfying* $\mathbf{CV} = \mathbf{V}\mathbf{\Lambda}$, *and* $\mathbf{U}$ *are orthogonal matrix satisfying* $\mathbf{U}^T\mathbf{U} = \mathbf{I}$.

The lemma suggests a two-stage diagonalization scheme to obtain the optimal solution. In the first stage, we solve the $\mathbf{V}$ and $\mathbf{\Lambda}$ by eigenvalue decomposition on $\mathbf{C}$ and compute the whitening transform $\mathbf{W} = \mathbf{V}\mathbf{\Lambda}^{-\frac{1}{2}}$. It can be easily shown that $\mathbf{T}^T\mathbf{CT} = \mathbf{I}$. Considering that $\mathbf{C}$ is a block-diagonal matrix, it be accomplished by eigen-decomposition on $\mathbf{C}_q$ and $\mathbf{C}_r$ respectively as $\mathbf{C}_q = \mathbf{V}_q\mathbf{\Lambda}_q\mathbf{V}_q^T$ and $\mathbf{C}_r = \mathbf{V}_r\mathbf{\Lambda}_r\mathbf{V}_r^T$. When the dimensions of $\mathcal{X}_q$ and $\mathcal{X}_r$ are high, the covariance matrices may become nearly singular and incur instability. To stabilize the solution, we approximate the covariance by discarding the eigenvalues near zero and the corresponding eigenvectors as follows:

$$\widetilde{\mathbf{C}}_q = \widetilde{\mathbf{V}}_q\widetilde{\mathbf{\Lambda}}_q\widetilde{\mathbf{V}}_q^T \qquad \widetilde{\mathbf{C}}_r = \widetilde{\mathbf{V}}_r\widetilde{\mathbf{\Lambda}}_r\widetilde{\mathbf{V}}_r^T \tag{17}$$

Subsequently, $\mathbf{T}$ can be obtained by $\mathbf{T} = \begin{pmatrix} \widetilde{\mathbf{V}}_q\widetilde{\mathbf{\Lambda}}_q^{-\frac{1}{2}} & 0 \\ 0 & \widetilde{\mathbf{V}}_r\widetilde{\mathbf{\Lambda}}_r^{-\frac{1}{2}} \end{pmatrix}$.

Then the learning objective is transformed to be

$$\mathbf{U} = \underset{\mathbf{U}}{\arg\min}\, \mathbf{U}^T\left(\mathbf{T}^T\mathbf{MT}\right)\mathbf{U}, \qquad \text{s.t } \mathbf{U}^T\mathbf{U} = \mathbf{I}, \tag{18}$$

In the second stage we solve $\mathbf{U}$ by eigen-decomposition on the matrix $\mathbf{M}_W = \mathbf{T}^T\mathbf{MT}$ and taking the eigenvectors associated with the smallest eigenvalues of $\mathbf{M}_W$, then $\mathbf{A} = \mathbf{TU}$. Exploiting the fact that $\mathbf{T}$ is block-diagonal, we further simplify the computation by partitioned matrix multiplication. The whole procedure is summarized in Table 1.

Table 1. The Procedure of Solving the Linear Transform

---

1. Compute $\mathbf{R}_q$, $\mathbf{R}_r$ and $\mathbf{U}$ as in section 2.2.
2. Compute $\mathbf{M}_{qq} = \mathbf{X}_q\mathbf{R}_q\mathbf{X}_q^T$, $\mathbf{M}_{qr} = \mathbf{X}_q\mathbf{U}\mathbf{X}_r^T$ and $\mathbf{M}_{rr} = \mathbf{X}_r\mathbf{R}_r\mathbf{X}_r^T$.
3. Compute $\mathbf{C}_q = \frac{1}{N_q}\mathbf{X}_q\mathbf{X}_q^T$ and $\mathbf{C}_r = \frac{1}{N_r}\mathbf{X}_r\mathbf{X}_r^T$.
4. Solve $\widetilde{\mathbf{V}}_q$, $\widetilde{\mathbf{\Lambda}}_q$, $\widetilde{\mathbf{V}}_r$ and $\widetilde{\mathbf{\Lambda}}_r$ by performing eigenvalue-eigenvector analysis on $\mathbf{C}_q$ and $\mathbf{C}_r$ and removing the trailing eigenvalues and corresponding eigenvectors.
5. Compute $\mathbf{T}_q = \widetilde{\mathbf{V}}_q\widetilde{\mathbf{\Lambda}}^{-\frac{1}{2}}$ and $\mathbf{T}_r = \widetilde{\mathbf{V}}_r\widetilde{\mathbf{\Lambda}}^{-\frac{1}{2}}$. Denote their numbers of columns by $\widetilde{d}_q$ and $\widetilde{d}_r$.
6. Compute $\mathbf{M}_W = \begin{pmatrix} \mathbf{T}_q^T\mathbf{M}_{qq}\mathbf{T}_q & -\mathbf{T}_q^T\mathbf{M}_{qr}\mathbf{T}_r \\ -\mathbf{T}_r^T\mathbf{M}_{qr}^T\mathbf{T}_q & \mathbf{T}_r^T\mathbf{M}_{rr}\mathbf{T}_r \end{pmatrix}$.
7. Solve $\mathbf{U}$ by taking the eigenvectors corresponding to the d least eigenvalues of $\mathbf{M}_W$.
8. Denote the first $\widetilde{d}_q$ rows of $\mathbf{U}$ by $\mathbf{U}_q$ and the rest $\widetilde{d}_r$ rows by $\mathbf{U}_r$. Then we have $\mathbf{A}_q = \mathbf{T}_q\mathbf{U}_q$ and $\mathbf{A}_r = \mathbf{T}_r\mathbf{U}_r$.

---

3   Kernelized Common Discriminant Feature Extraction

Kernel-based learning is often used to exploit the nonlinearity of the sample space. The core principle is to map the samples to a Hilbert space with much higher dimension or even infinite dimension so that the inner product structure of that space reflects the desirable similarity. Suppose the original sample space is denoted by $\mathcal{X}$ and a positive definite kernel is defined on it by $k : \mathcal{X} \times \mathcal{X} \to R$. For a set of observed samples: $\{\mathbf{x}_i\}_{i=1}^n$, the $n \times n$ *Gram matrix* is given by $\mathbf{K}$ with $\mathbf{K}(i,j) = k(\mathbf{x}_i, \mathbf{x}_j)$.

According to the kernel theory, each positive definite kernel k induces a Hilbert space $\mathcal{H}$ and a feature map $\phi : \mathcal{X} \to \mathcal{H}$ satisfying that for every $\mathbf{x}_1, \mathbf{x}_2 \in \mathcal{X}$, $\langle \phi(\mathbf{x}_1), \phi(\mathbf{x}_2) \rangle = k(\mathbf{x}_1, \mathbf{x}_2)$. With this kernel trick, we can compute the inner product in the original space without explicitly evaluating the feature map.

Given the Hilbert space, we can extract the features by projecting the high-dimensional mapping to a lower-dimensional feature space. Assume the basis of the projection is a linear combinations of the Hilbert mappings of the training samples. Denote $\mathbf{\Phi} = [\phi(\mathbf{x}_1), \ldots, \phi(\mathbf{x}_n)]$, then we have $\mathbf{P} = \mathbf{\Phi A}$, where $\mathbf{A}$ is an $n \times d$ matrix storing the expansion coefficients and d is the dimension of the final feature space. Then for any sample $\mathbf{x} \in \mathcal{X}$, it is transformed to

$$\mathbf{y} = \mathbf{P}^T \phi(\mathbf{x}) = \mathbf{A}^T \mathbf{\Phi}^T \phi(\mathbf{x}) = \mathbf{A}^T \mathbf{k}(\mathbf{x}), \tag{19}$$

where $\mathbf{k}(\mathbf{x}) = [\phi(\mathbf{x}_1, \mathbf{x}), \phi(\mathbf{x}_1, \ldots, \phi(\mathbf{x}_n, \mathbf{x})]^T$. Specially, for the training set $\mathbf{X} = [\mathbf{x}_1, \ldots, \mathbf{x}_n]$, the matrix of the transformed vectors can be expressed as

$$\mathbf{Y} = [\mathbf{y}_1, \mathbf{y}_2, \ldots, \mathbf{y}_n] = [\mathbf{P}\phi(\mathbf{x}_1), \mathbf{P}\phi(\mathbf{y}_2), \ldots, \mathbf{P}\phi(\mathbf{y}_n)] = \mathbf{A}^T \mathbf{K}. \tag{20}$$

Actually, the learning of Common Discriminant Feature Extraction relies on inner products, thus it can be extended to the nonlinear case by kernel theory. Denote the Gram matrices for the query samples and the reference samples by $\mathbf{K}_q$ and $\mathbf{K}_r$, and the coefficient expansion matrices for transform operators by $\mathbf{A}_q$ and $\mathbf{A}_r$. According to Eq.(20), we have the feature vectors for the training set expressed as follows:

$$\mathbf{Y}_q = \mathbf{A}_q^T \mathbf{K}_q \qquad \mathbf{Y}_r = \mathbf{A}_r^T \mathbf{K}_r. \tag{21}$$

Then from Eq.(10), the joint objective function can be written by

$$J(\mathbf{A}_q, \mathbf{A}_r) = \mathrm{tr}(\mathbf{A}_q^T \mathbf{K}_q \mathbf{R}_q \mathbf{K}_q^T \mathbf{A}_q + \mathbf{A}_r^T \mathbf{K}_r \mathbf{R}_r \mathbf{K}_r^T \mathbf{A}_r - 2\mathbf{A}_q^T \mathbf{K}_q \mathbf{U} \mathbf{K}_r^T \mathbf{A}_r) \tag{22}$$

$$\text{s.t} \quad \mathbf{A}_q \left(\frac{1}{N_q} \mathbf{K}_q \mathbf{K}_q^T\right) \mathbf{A}_q^T + \mathbf{A}_r^T \left(\frac{1}{N_r} \mathbf{K}_r, \mathbf{K}_r^T\right) \mathbf{A}_r = \mathbf{I}. \tag{23}$$

Comparing Eq.(13) and Eq.(23), we see that the mathematical form of the optimization problem is essentially the same, except that the matrices $\mathbf{X}_q$ and $\mathbf{X}_r$ are replaced by the Kernel Gram matrices $\mathbf{K}_q$ and $\mathbf{K}_r$. Thus the optimization procedure derived above is also applicable here.

4 Multi-mode Framework

In practical systems, the reference images are often captured in a controlled condition, while the query images on spot are subject to significant variation of illumination and pose. To address this problem, we develop a Multi-Mode Framework. For each query mode, we learn a common feature space for comparing the query samples in that mode and the reference samples. Here, we denote the transform matrices for the k-th mode by $\mathbf{A}_{qk}$ and $\mathbf{A}_{rk}$.

Considering that uncertainty may arise when we judge which mode a query sample belongs to, we adopt a soft fusion scheme. In the scheme, the *fused distance* is introduced to measure the dissimilarity between the query samples and the reference samples, which is a belief-based weighted combination of the distance values evaluated in the common spaces for different modes. We denote the belief that the i-th query sample belongs to the k-th mode by b_{ik}, and denote the features of the i-th query sample and the j-th reference sample in the common space for the k-th mode by $\mathbf{y}_{ik}^{(q)} = \mathbf{A}_{qk}^T \mathbf{x}_i^{(q)}$ and $\mathbf{y}_{jk}^{(r)} = \mathbf{A}_{rk}^T \mathbf{x}_i^{(r)}$ respectively, then the fused distance is given by

$$d(\mathbf{x}_i^{(q)}, \mathbf{x}_j^{(r)}) = \sum_{k=1}^M b_{ik} ||\mathbf{y}_{ik}^{(q)} - \mathbf{y}_{jk}^{(r)}||^2 \qquad \text{s.t} \sum_{k=1}^M b_{ik} = 1. \qquad (24)$$

When the belief values for training samples are known, for a new query sample $\mathbf{x}$, its belief values w.r.t to the modes can be computed by smooth interpolation from the training samples adjacent to it. We re-formulate the learning objective with the following extensions:

1) Evaluate the empirical separability based on fused distance: $J_e = \sum_{i=1}^{N_q} \sum_{j=1}^{N_r} u_{ij} d(\mathbf{x}_i^{(q)}, \mathbf{x}_j^{(r)})$;
2) The local consistency comprises the local consistency of transforms for all modes;
3) Each query samples in the training set corresponds to M belief values. To ensure each mode covers a continuous and smooth region in the sample space so that the computation of beliefs for new samples is stable, we further enforce the local consistency on the belief values: $J_l^{(b)} = \sum_{i=1}^{N_q} \sum_{j=1}^{N_q} v_{ij}^{(q)} \sum_{k=1}^M (b_{ik} - b_{jk})^2$. Consequently, the multimode formulation of the learning objective is derived as follows:

$$J = J_e + \beta \sum_{i=1}^M (J_l^{(q)} + J_l^{(r)}) + \gamma J_l^{(b)}, \qquad (25)$$

where γ controls the contribution of the local consistency of beliefs. Eq.(25) can be expanded as follows:

$$J = \sum_{i=1}^{N_q} \sum_{j=1}^{N_r} u_{ij} \sum_{k=1}^M b_{ik} ||\mathbf{y}_{ik}^{(q)} - \mathbf{y}_{jk}^{(r)}||^2 + \sum_{k=1}^M \sum_{i=1}^{N_q} \sum_{j=1}^{N_q} v_{ij}^{(q)} ||\mathbf{y}_{ik}^{(q)} - \mathbf{y}_{jk}^{(q)}||^2$$

$$+ \sum_{k=1}^M \sum_{i=1}^{N_r} \sum_{j=1}^{N_r} v_{ij}^{(r)} ||\mathbf{y}_{ik}^{(r)} - \mathbf{y}_{jk}^{(r)}||^2 + \sum_{i=1}^{N_q} \sum_{j=1}^{N_q} v_{ij}^{(q)} \sum_{i=1}^M (b_{ik} - b_{jk})^2. \qquad (26)$$

Based on the generalized formulation, we derive the optimization scheme by alternate optimizing the transform matrices and the belief values.

1) Optimizing Transform Matrices. Denote $J_A = J_e + \beta \sum_{i=1}^{M}(J_l^{(q)} + J_l^{(r)})$, since $J_l^{(b)}$ does not relate to the features, with the belief values given, we can obtain the optimal transform matrices by minimizing J_A. Rearranging the order of sums, we can write it by

$$J_A = \sum_{k=1}^{M}\left\{\sum_{i=1}^{N_q}\sum_{j=1}^{N_r}b_{ik}u_{ij}\|\mathbf{y}_{ik}^{(q)} - \mathbf{y}_{jk}^{(r)}\|^2 + \sum_{i=1}^{N_q}\sum_{j=1}^{N_q}v_{ij}^{(q)}\|\mathbf{y}_{ik}^{(q)} - \mathbf{y}_{jk}^{(q)}\|^2 + \sum_{i=1}^{N_r}\sum_{j=1}^{N_r}v_{ij}^{(r)}\|\mathbf{y}_{ik}^{(r)} - \mathbf{y}_{jk}^{(r)}\|^2\right\}. \tag{27}$$

Thus J_A can be decomposed into

$$J_A = \sum_{k=1}^{M} J_k(\mathbf{A}_k^{(q)}, \mathbf{A}_k^{(r)}) \tag{28}$$

$$J_k(\mathbf{A}_k^{(q)}, \mathbf{A}_k^{(r)}) = \sum_{i=1}^{N_q}\sum_{j=1}^{N_r}b_{ik}u_{ij}\|\mathbf{y}_{ik}^{(q)} - \mathbf{y}_{jk}^{(r)}\|^2 + \sum_{i=1}^{N_q}\sum_{j=1}^{N_q}v_{ij}^{(q)}\|\mathbf{y}_{ik}^{(q)} - \mathbf{y}_{jk}^{(q)}\|^2 + \sum_{i=1}^{N_r}\sum_{j=1}^{N_r}v_{ij}^{(r)}\|\mathbf{y}_{ik}^{(r)} - \mathbf{y}_{jk}^{(r)}\|^2. \tag{29}$$

Compare Eq.(6) and Eq.(29), we see that they share the same mathematical form except that u_{ij} is replaced by $b_{ik}u_{ij}$. Because J_k is solely determined by the features of the k-th mode, we can optimize $\mathbf{A}_k^{(q)}$ and $\mathbf{A}_k^{(r)}$ for each mode individually by the aforementioned procedure with the belief values fixed.

2) Optimizing Belief Values. Denote $J_B = J_e + \gamma J_l^{(b)}$, which is the part of objective depending on the belief values. With the transform matrices given, we can optimize the beliefs by minimizing J_B:

$$J_B = \sum_{i=1}^{N_q}\sum_{j=1}^{N_r}\sum_{k=1}^{M}u_{ij}\sum_{k=1}^{M}b_{ik}\|\mathbf{y}_{ik}^{(q)} - \mathbf{y}_{jk}^{(r)}\|^2 + \sum_{i=1}^{N_q}\sum_{j=1}^{N_q}\sum_{k=1}^{M}v_{ij}^{(q)}\sum_{i=1}^{M}(b_{ik} - b_{jk})^2. \tag{30}$$

For succinctness, we denote $e_{ik} = \sum_{j=1}^{N_r}u_{ij}\|\mathbf{y}_{ik}^{(q)} - \mathbf{y}_{jk}^{(r)}\|^2$, then it can be simplified to

$$J_B = \sum_{i=1}^{N_q}\sum_{k=1}^{M}e_{ik}b_{ik} + \sum_{i=1}^{N_q}\sum_{j=1}^{N_q}\sum_{k=1}^{M}v_{ij}^{(q)}\sum_{i=1}^{M}(b_{ik} - b_{jk})^2. \tag{31}$$

We introduce the following notations: $\mathbf{E}$ is an $M \times N_q$ matrix with $\mathbf{E}(i, k) = e_{ik}$, $\mathbf{B}$ is an $M \times N_q$ matrix with $\mathbf{B}(i, k) = b_{ik}$, then the optimization problem can be written in a matrix form as

$$\mathbf{B} = \underset{\mathbf{B}}{\arg\min}\, J_B = \underset{\mathbf{B}}{\arg\min}\, \mathrm{tr}(\mathbf{E}^T\mathbf{B} + 2\mathbf{B}(\mathbf{D}_q - \mathbf{V}_q)\mathbf{B}^T), \quad \text{s.t } \mathbf{B}^T\mathbf{1}_M = \mathbf{1}_{N_q}. \tag{32}$$

Here $\mathbf{D}_q - \mathbf{V}_q$ is positive-semidefinite. This is a convex quadratic optimization program with linear constraint and can be efficiently solved by quadratic programming.

3) The whole procedure of optimization. We adopt the alternate optimization strategy in our framework. First we cluster all the query samples in the training set by Gaussian Mixture Model and set the initial belief values to be the posteriori evaluated by GMM. After that, we optimize the transform matrices for each mode based on Eq.(29) and the belief values based on Eq.(32) alternately until convergence.

5 Experiments

Experiment Settings

We conduct experiments in two inter-modality recognition applications.

1) Infrared-optical recognition. The reference images are captured by optical cameras with controlled illumination condition, while the query images are acquired in an uncontrolled environment. To cope with the adverse illumination condition, we use infrared cameras to capture the query images. In our experiment, two configurations are constructed to test our algorithms. Both configurations share the same set of reference samples. The reference set consists of 64 samples from 16 persons with each person having 4 samples. In the first configuration, we select 800 images with mild expression variation to form the query set. The second configuration is a much more challenging one, which consists of 1600 images subject to significant pose and illumination variation. Some examples of the images are displayed in fig.1. It can be seen that the infrared images are seriously blurred and distorted due to the limitation of infrared imaging.

2) Sketch-photo recognition. The reference set is composed of 350 images from FERET face database[16]. The 350 images represent 350 different persons. The query set comprises 700 sketches composed by artists. Each person has 2 samples in the query set. Fig.2 shows some examples of the photos and the corresponding sketches. We can see that the sketches present greatly different characteristics from the photos. In addition, some texture information is lost in the sketches.

All the photos are normalized to reduce the influence of interference factors. For each image, we first perform affine transformation on it to fix the eye centers and mouth center of the face to standard positions. Then we crop it to the size of 64×72. After that we apply histogram equalization and mask the background region using a face-shape mask. After preprocessing, we obtain the original vector representation for each image by scanning the 4114 remaining pixels to a vector. To accelerate the process of training and testing and suppress the noise, we employ PCA to reduce the space dimension and preserve 0.98% of the energy in the principal space.

Experiment Results

1) We first investigate how the selection of parameters α and β affects the generalization performance. In the experiments, we find that the performance is not sensitive to the α when α ranges from 0.2 to 2. However, the parameter β significantly influence the results. Fig.5, fig.7 and fig.9 show the change of performance w.r.t the number of features when β takes different values. We can see that when

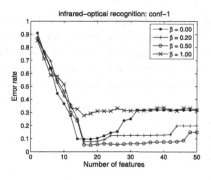

Fig. 5. Performance of CDFE in conf-1 of infrared-optical recognition

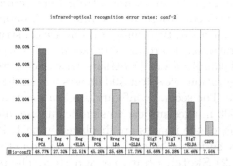

Fig. 6. Comparison of algorithms in conf-1 of infrared-optical recognition

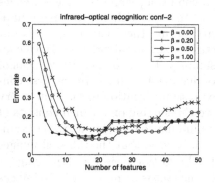

Fig. 7. Performance of CDFE in conf-2 of infrared-optical recognition

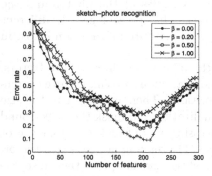

Fig. 8. Comparison of algorithms in conf-2 of infrared-optical recognition

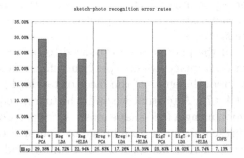

Fig. 9. Performance of CDFE in sketch-photo recognition

Fig. 10. Comparison of algorithms in sketch-photo recognition

$\beta = 0$, that is, the local consistency does not contribute to the formulation, the performance degrades drastically as the number of features increases. When β becomes larger, the change of performance becomes stable. However, if β is too large, the performance may degenerate. This is mainly due to over-smoothing. From the results, we can see that for infrared-optical recognition, the algorithm

	Reg. + KPCA	Reg. + KLDA	RReg. + KPCA	RReg. + KLDA	EigT. + KPCA	EigT. + KLDA	CDFE
infrared-optical. conf-1	24.3%	15.6%	20.4%	8.34%	22.7%	9.56%	1.98%
infrared-optical. conf-2	50.6%	21.8%	47.9%	15.0%	45.7%	15.3%	4.42%
sketch-optical.	32.2%	20.8%	24.3%	11.7%	25.8%	12.8%	5.43%

Fig. 11. Comparison of the algorithms with kernelized features

achieves best performance when $\beta = 0.5$, while for sketch-photo recognition, the algorithm achieves best performance when $\beta = 1.0$. The analysis above indicates the important role of local consistency for the generalization ability.

2) We compare the common discriminant feature extraction (CDFE) with other approaches for inter-modality recognition. In previous works, it is typical to first convert the query images to the reference modality and then apply conventional algorithms to classify the converted sample. In the experiments, we test the combination of three conversion methods (linear regression (Reg), ridge regression (RReg), and Eigentransformation (EigT)[9]) and three feature extraction methods (PCA[17], LDA[1], and Enhanced LDA[4]). The results are illustrated in fig.6, fig.8, and fig.10 for the infrared-optical recognition and the sketch-photo recognition respectively. It can be seen from the results that the CDFE consistently outperforms the other methods by a large margin. In all the configurations, CDFE at least reduces the error rate by half compared with the most competitive methods in conventional approaches.

3) We test the kernelized extension of the CDFE and compare it with the conversion-classification paradigm. For fair comparison, in the traditional approach, we also use kernelized method to extract features. Here, we test Kernel PCA and Kernel LDA. Gaussian kernel is used in the testing. The results are listed in fig.11. All the results given in the table are the best performances obtained through cross-validation. We can see our algorithm outperforms the conventional ones by a surprisingly large margin. In our view, such a remarkable improvement is owing to incorporation of local consistency, which on one hand fully exploits the potency of kernel method, on the other hand effectively controls the complexity of the operator.

4) We finally test the multi-mode framework in the conf-2 of infrared-optical recognition. In this configuration, due to diverse poses and illumination conditions, there are multiple modes in the sample distribution. In our experiments, the error rate decreases when we increase the number of modes. The lowest error rate 3.25% is attained when $M = 5$. Compared to the single mode case, in which error rate is 7.56%, it is an encouraging improvement.

6   Conclusion

In this paper, we studied the inter-modality face recognition problem. We proposed a new notion of common discriminant feature space and formulated the learning objective with local consistency. In the extensive experiments, our algorithms have achieved significant improvement over conventional methods.

Acknowledgement

The work described in this paper was fully supported by grants from the Research Grants Council of the Hong Kong Special Administrative Region and a joint grant (N_CUHK409-03) from HKSAR RGC and China NSF. The work was done in The Chinese University of Hong Kong.

References

1. P. N. Belhumeur, J. P. Hespanha, D. J. Kriegman: Eigenfaces vs. Fisherfaces: Recognition Using Class Specific Linear Projection. IEEE Trans. on PAMI **19**(7) (1997) 711–720
2. W. Zhao, R. Chellappa, A. Krishnaswamy: Discriminant Analysis of Principal Components for Face Recognition. Proc. of FGR'98 (1998)
3. J. Yang, F. Frangi, J. Yang, D. Zhang, Z. Jin: KPCA Plus LDA: A Complete Kernel Fisher Discriminant Framework for Feature Extraction and Recognition. IEEE Trans. on PAMI **27**(2) (2005) 230–244
4. C. Liu, H. Wechsler: Enhanced Fisher Linear Discriminant Models for Face Recognition. Proc. of CVPR'98 (1998)
5. X. Wang, X. Tang: A Unified Framework for Subspace Face Recognition. IEEE Trans. on PAMI **26**(9) (2004) 1222–1228
6. X. Wang, X. Tang: Unified Subspace Analysis for Face Recognition. In: Proc. of ICCV'03. (2003)
7. X. Wang, X. Tang: Dual-Space Linear Discriminant Analysis for Face Recognition. In: Proc. of CVPR'04. (2004)
8. X. Tang, X. Wang: Face Sketch Synthesis and Recognition. In: Proc. of ICCV'03. (2003)
9. X. Tang, X. Wang: Face Sketch Recognition. IEEE Trans. CSVT **14**(1) (2004) 50–57
10. V.N. Vapnik: Statistical Learning Theory. John Wiley and Sons, Inc. (1998)
11. D. Zhou, O. Bousquet, T.N. Lal, J. Weston, B. Scholkopf: Learning with Local and Global Consistency. In: Proc. of NIPS'04. (2004)
12. X. He, S. Yan, Y. Hu, H. Zhang: Learning a Locality Preserving Subspace for Visual Recognition. In: Proc. of ICCV'03. (2003)
13. X. He, Y. Hu, P. Niyogi, H. Zhang: Face Recognition Using Laplacianfaces. IEEE Trans. PAMI **27**(3) (2005) 328–340
14. M. Belkin, P. Niyogi: Laplacian Eigenmaps and Spectral Techniques for Embedding and Clustering. In: Proc. of NIPS'01. (2001)
15. T. Kim, J. Kittler: Locally Linear Discriminant Analysis for Multimodally Distributed Classes for Face Recognition with a Single Model Image. IEEE Trans. on PAMI **27**(3) (2005) 318–327
16. P.J. Phillips, H. Moon, S.A. Rizvi, P.J. Rauss: The FERET Evaluation Methodology for Face Recognition Algorithms. IEEE Trans. PAMI (2000) 1090–1104
17. M. Turk, A. Pentland: Eigenfaces for Recognition. J. Cogn. Neuro. **3**(1) (1991) 71–86

Face Recognition from Video Using the Generic Shape-Illumination Manifold

Ognjen Arandjelović and Roberto Cipolla

Department of Engineering, University of Cambridge, CB2 1PZ, UK

Abstract. In spite of over two decades of intense research, illumination and pose invariance remain prohibitively challenging aspects of face recognition for most practical applications. The objective of this work is to recognize faces using video sequences both for training and recognition input, in a realistic, unconstrained setup in which lighting, pose and user motion pattern have a wide variability and face images are of low resolution. In particular there are three areas of novelty: (i) we show how a photometric model of image formation can be combined with a statistical model of generic face appearance variation, learnt offline, to generalize in the presence of extreme illumination changes; (ii) we use the smoothness of geodesically local appearance manifold structure and a robust same-identity likelihood to achieve invariance to unseen head poses; and (iii) we introduce an accurate video sequence "reillumination" algorithm to achieve robustness to face motion patterns in video. We describe a fully automatic recognition system based on the proposed method and an extensive evaluation on 171 individuals and over 1300 video sequences with extreme illumination, pose and head motion variation. On this challenging data set our system consistently demonstrated a nearly perfect recognition rate (over 99.7%), significantly outperforming state-of-the-art commercial software and methods from the literature.

1 Introduction

Automatic face recognition (AFR) has long been established as one of the most active research areas in computer vision. In spite of the large number of developed algorithms, real-world performance of AFR has been, to say the least, disappointing. Even in very controlled imaging conditions, such as those used for passport photographs, the error rate has been reported to be as high as 10% [6], while in less controlled environments the performance degrades even further. We believe that the main reason for the apparent discrepancy between results reported in the literature and observed in the real world is that the assumptions that most AFR methods rest upon are hard to satisfy in practice.

In this paper, we are interested in recognition using *video sequences*. This problem is of enormous interest as video is readily available in many applications, while the abundance of information contained within it can help resolve some of the inherent ambiguities of single-shot based recognition. In practice, video data can be extracted from surveillance videos by tracking a face or by instructing a cooperative to move the head in front of a mounted camera.

A. Leonardis, H. Bischof, and A. Pinz (Eds.): ECCV 2006, Part IV, LNCS 3954, pp. 27–40, 2006.

We assume that both the training and novel data available to an AFR system is organized in a database where a sequence of images for each individual contains some variability in pose, but is not obtained in scripted conditions or in controlled illumination. The recognition problem can then be formulated as taking a sequence of face images from an unknown individual and finding the best matching sequence in the database of sequences labelled by the identity.

Our approach consists of using a weak photometric model of image formation with offline machine learning for modelling *manifolds* of faces. Specifically, we show that the combined effects of face shape and illumination can be effectively learnt using Probabilistic PCA (PPCA) [40] from a small, unlabelled set of video sequences of faces in randomly varying lighting conditions, while a novel manifold-based "reillumination" algorithm is used to provide robustness to pose and motion pattern. Given a novel sequence, the learnt model is used to decompose the face appearance manifold into albedo and shape-illumination manifolds, producing the classification decision by robust likelihood estimation.

2   Previous Work

Good general reviews of recent AFR literature can be found in [5, 46]. In this section, we focus on AFR literature that deals specifically with recognition from image sequences, and with invariance to pose and illumination.

Compared to single-shot recognition, face recognition from image sequences is a relatively new area of research. Some of the existing algorithms that deal with multi-image input use temporal coherence within the sequence to enforce prior knowledge on likely head movements [26, 27, 47]. In contrast to these, a number of methods that do not use temporal information have been proposed. Recent ones include statistical [3, 35] and principal angle-based methods with underlying simple linear [16], kernel-based [45] or Gaussian mixture-based [24] models. By their very nature, these are inherently invariant to changes in head motion pattern. Other algorithms implement the "still-to-video" scenario [28, 31], not taking full advantage of sequences available for training.

Illumination invariance, while perhaps the most significant challenge for AFR [1] remains a virtually unexplored problem for recognition using video. Most methods focus on other difficulties of video-based recognition, employing simple preprocessing techniques to deal with changing lighting [4, 13]. Others rely on availability of ample training data but achieve limited generalization [3, 37].

Two influential generative model-based approaches for illumination-invariant single-shot recognition are the illumination cones [7, 18] and the 3D morphable model [10]. Both of these have significant shortcomings in practice. The former is not readily extended to deal with video, assuming accurately registered face images, illuminated from several well-posed directions for each pose which is difficult to achieve in practice (see §5 for data quality). Similar limitations apply to the related method of Riklin-Raviv and Shashua [34]. On the other hand, the 3D morphable model is easily extended to video-based recognition, but it requires a (in our case prohibitively) high resolution [13], struggles with non-Lambertian effects (such as specularities) and multiple light sources, and has convergence problems in the presence of background clutter and partial occlusion (glasses, facial hair).

Broadly speaking, there are three classes of algorithms aimed at achieving pose invariance. The first, a model-based approach, uses an explicit 2D or 3D model of the face, and attempts to estimate the parameters of the model from the input [10, 23]. This is a view-independent representation. A second class of algorithms consists of global, parametric models, such as the eigenspace method [30] that estimates a single parametric (typically linear) subspace from all the views for all the objects (also see [29]). In AFR tests, such methods are usually outperformed by methods from the third class: view-based techniques e.g. the view-based eigenspaces [32] (also [26, 27]), in which a separate subspace is constructed for each pose. These algorithms usually require an intermediate step in which the pose of the face is determined, and then recognition is carried out using the estimated view-dependent model. A common limitation of these methods is that they require a fairly restrictive and labour-intensive training data acquisition protocol, in which a number of fixed views are collected for each subject and appropriately labelled. This is not the case with the proposed method.

3   Face Motion (and Other) Manifolds

Concepts in this paper heavily rely on the notion of face *manifolds*. Briefly, under the standard rasterized representation of an image, images of a given size can be viewed as points in a Euclidean *image space*, its dimensionality being equal to the number of pixels D. However, the surface and texture of a face is mostly smooth making its appearance quite constrained and confining it to an embedded *face manifold* of dimension $d \ll D$ [3, 9]. Formally, the distribution of observed face images of the subject i can be written as the integral:

$$p^{(i)}(\mathbf{X}) = \int p_F^{(i)}(\mathbf{x}) p_n(f_i(\mathbf{x}) - \mathbf{X}) d\mathbf{x}. \tag{1}$$

where p_n is the noise distribution, $f^{(i)} : \mathbb{R}^d \rightarrow \mathbb{R}^D$ the embedding function and $\mathbf{x}$ an intrinsic face descriptor. Fig. 1 (a) illustrates the validity of the notion on an example of a face motion image sequence. For the proposed method, the crucial properties are their (i) continuity and (ii) smoothness.

3.1   Synthetic Reillumination of Face Motion Manifolds

One of the key ideas of this paper is the *reillumination* of video sequences. Our goal is to take two input sequences of faces and produce a third, synthetic one, that contains the same poses as the first in the illumination of the second.

The proposed method consists of two stages. First, each face from the first sequence is matched with the face from the second that corresponds to it best in terms of pose. Then, a number of faces close to the matched one are used to finely reconstruct the reilluminated version of the original face. Our algorithm is therefore global, unlike most of the previous methods which use a sparse set

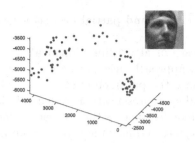 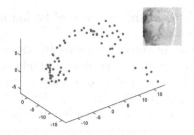

(a) Face Motion Manifold (FMM)   (b) Shape-Illumination Manifold

Fig. 1. Manifolds of (a) face appearance and (b) albedo-free appearance i.e. the effects of illumination and pose changes, in a single motion sequence. Shown are projections to the first 3 linear principal components, with a typical manifold sample on the top-right.

of detected salient points for registration, e.g. [4, 8, 16]. We found that facial feature localization using trained Support Vector Machines (similar to [4, 8]), as well as algorithms employed in commercial systems FacePass® [15, 41] and FaceIt® [22] failed on data sets used for evaluation in this paper (see §5) due to the severity of illumination conditions. We next describe the two stages of the proposed algorithm in detail.

Stage 1: Pose Matching. Let $\{\mathbf{X}_i\}^{(1)}$ and $\{\mathbf{X}_i\}^{(2)}$ be two motion sequences of a person's face in two different illuminations. Then, for each $\mathbf{X}_i^{(1)}$ we are interested in finding $\mathbf{X}_{c(i)}^{(2)}$ that corresponds to it best in pose. Finding the unknown mapping c on a frame-by-frame basis is difficult. Instead, we formulate the problem as a minimization task with the fitness function taking the form:

$$f(c) = \sum_j d_E \left(\mathbf{X}_j^{(1)}, \mathbf{X}_{c(j)}^{(2)} \right)^2 + \omega \sum_j \sum_k \frac{d_G^{(2)} \left(\mathbf{X}_{c(j)}^{(2)}, \mathbf{X}_{c(n(j,k))}^{(2)}; \{\mathbf{X}_j\}^{(2)} \right)}{d_G^{(1)} \left(\mathbf{X}_j^{(1)}, \mathbf{X}_{n(j,k)}^{(1)}; \{\mathbf{X}_j\}^{(1)} \right)} \quad (2)$$

where $n(i, j)$ is the j-th of K nearest neighbours of face i, d_E a pose dissimilarity function and $d_G^{(k)}$ a geodesic distance estimate along the FMM of sequence k. The first term is easily understood as a penalty for dissimilarity of matched pose-signatures. The latter enforces a globally good matching by favouring mappings that map geodesically close points from the domain manifold to geodesically close points on the codomain manifold.

Pose-matching function: The performance of function d_E in (2) at estimating the goodness of a frame match is crucial for making the overall optimization scheme work well. Our approach consists of filtering the original face image to produce a quasi illumination-invariant *pose-signature*, which is then compared with other pose-signatures using the Euclidean distance. Note that these signatures are *only* used for frame matching and thus need not retain any power of discrimination between individuals – all that is needed is sufficient pose information. We use a distance-transformed edge map of the face image as a pose-signature,

(a) Original   (b) Reilluminated

Fig. 2. (a) Original images from a novel video sequence and (b) the result of reillumination using the proposed genetic algorithm with nearest neighbour-based reconstruction

motivated by the success of this representation in object–configuration matching across other computer vision applications, e.g. [17, 38].

Minimizing the fitness function: Exact minimization of the fitness function (2) over all functions c is an NP-complete problem. However, since the final synthesis of novel faces (Stage 2) involves an entire geodesic neighbouring of the paired faces, it is inherently robust to some non-optimality of this matching. Therefore, in practice, it is sufficient to find a good match, not necessarily the optimal one.

We propose to use a genetic algorithm (GA) [12] as a particularly suitable approach to minimization for our problem. GAs rely on the property of many optimization problems that sub-solutions of good solutions are good themselves. Specifically, this means that if we have a globally good manifold match, then local matching can be expected to be good too. Hence, combining two good matches is a reasonable attempt at improving the solution. This motivates the chromosome structure we use, depicted in Fig. 3 (a), with the i-th gene in a chromosome being the value of $c(i)$. GA parameters were determined experimentally from a small training set and are summarized in Fig. 3 (b,c).

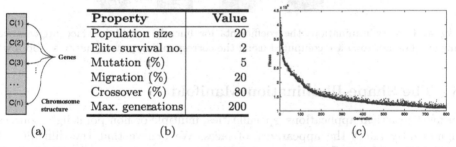

Property	Value
Population size	20
Elite survival no.	2
Mutation (%)	5
Migration (%)	20
Crossover (%)	80
Max. generations	200

(a)   (b)   (c)

Fig. 3. (a) The chromosome structure used in the proposed GA optimization, (b) its parameters and (c) population fitness (see (2)) in a typical evolution. Maximal generation count of 200 was chosen as a trade-off between accuracy and matching speed.

Estimating geodesic distances: The definition of the fitness function in (2) involves estimates of geodesic distances along manifolds. Due to the nonlinearity of FMMs [3, 27] it is not well approximated by the Euclidean distance. We estimate the geodesic distance between every two faces from a manifold using the Floyd's algorithm on a constructed undirected graph whose nodes correspond to face images (also see [39]). Then, if $\mathbf{X}_i$ is one of the K nearest neighbours of $\mathbf{X}_j$:

$$d_G(\mathbf{X}_i, \mathbf{X}_j) = \|\mathbf{X}_i - \mathbf{X}_j\|_2. \tag{3}$$

Otherwise:

$$d_G(\mathbf{X}_i, \mathbf{X}_j) = \min_k \left[d_G(\mathbf{X}_i, \mathbf{X}_k) + d_G(\mathbf{X}_k, \mathbf{X}_j) \right]. \tag{4}$$

Stage 2: Fine Reillumination. Having computed a pose-matching function c^*, we exploit the smoothness of FMMs by computing $\mathbf{Y}_i^{(1)}$, the reilluminated frame $\mathbf{X}_i^{(1)}$, as a linear combination of K nearest-neighbour frames of $\mathbf{X}_{c^*(i)}^{(2)}$. Linear combining coefficients $\alpha_1, \ldots \alpha_K$ are found from the corresponding pose-signatures by solving the following constrained minimization problem:

$$\{\alpha_j\} = \arg\min_{\{\alpha_j\}} \left\| \mathbf{x}_i^{(1)} - \sum_{k=1}^{K} \alpha_k \mathbf{x}_{n(c^*(i),k)}^{(2)} \right\|_2 \tag{5}$$

subject to $\sum_{k=1}^{K} \alpha_k = 1.0$, where $\mathbf{x}_i^{(j)}$ is the pose-signature corresponding to $\mathbf{X}_i^{(j)}$. In other words, the pose-signature of a novel face is first reconstructed using the pose-signatures of K training faces (in target illumination), which are then combined in the same fashion to synthesize a reilluminated face, see Fig. 2 and 4. Optimization of (5) is readily performed by differentiation.

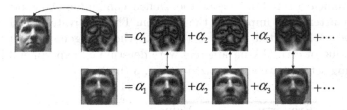

Fig. 4. Face reillumination: the coefficients for linearly combining face appearance images (bottom row) are computed using the corresponding pose-signatures (top row)

4   The Shape-Illumination Manifold

In most practical applications, specularities, multiple or non-point light sources significantly affect the appearance of faces. We believe that the difficulty of dealing with these effects is one of the main reasons for poor performance of most AFR systems when put to use in a realistic environment. In this work we make a very weak assumption on the process of image formation: the only assumption made is that the intensity of each pixel is a linear function of the albedo $a(j)$ of the corresponding 3D point:

$$X(j) = a(j) \cdot s(j) \tag{6}$$

where $\mathbf{s}$ is a function of illumination, shape and other parameters not modelled explicitly. This is similar to the reflectance-lighting model used in Retinex-based algorithms [25], the main difference being that we make no further assumptions on the functional form of $\mathbf{s}$. Note that the commonly-used (e.g. see [10, 18, 34]) Lambertian reflectance model is a special case of (6) [7]:

$$s(j) = \max(\mathbf{n}_j \cdot \mathbf{L}, 0) \tag{7}$$

where $\mathbf{n}_i$ is the surface normal and $\mathbf{L}$ the intensity-scaled illumination direction.

The image formation model introduced in (6) leaves the image pixel intensity as an unspecified function of face shape or illumination parameters. Instead of formulating a complex model of the geometry and photometry behind this function (and then needing to recover a large number of model parameters), we propose to learn it implicitly. Consider two images, $\mathbf{X}_1$ and $\mathbf{X}_2$ of the same person, in the same pose, but different illuminations. Then from (6):

$$\Delta \log X(j) = \log s_2(j) - \log s_1(j) \equiv d_s(j) \tag{8}$$

In other words, the difference between these logarithm-transformed images is not a function of face albedo. As before, due to the smoothness of faces, as the pose of the subject varies the difference-of-logs vector $\mathbf{d}_s$ describes a manifold in the corresponding embedding vector space. These is the Shape-Illumination manifold (SIM) corresponding to a particular pair of video sequences, see Fig. 1 (b).

The Generic SIM: A crucial assumption of our work is that the Shape-Illumination Manifold of all possible illuminations and head poses is *generic for human faces* (gSIM). This is motivated by a number of independent results reported in the literature that have shown face shape to be less discriminating than albedo across different models [11, 20] or have reported good results in synthetic reillumination of faces using the constant-shape assumption [34]. In the context of face manifolds this means that the effects of *illumination and shape* can be learnt offline from a training corpus containing typical modes of pose and illumination variation.

It is worth emphasizing the key difference in the proposed offline learning from previous approaches in the literature which try to learn the *albedo* of human faces. Since offline training is performed on persons not in the online gallery, in the case when albedo is learnt it is necessary to have means of generalization i.e. learning what *possible* albedos human faces can have from a small subset. In [34], for example, the authors demonstrate generalization to albedos in the rational span of those in the offline training set. This approach is not only unintuitive, but also without a meaningful theoretical justification. On the other hand, previous research indicates that illumination effects can be learnt *directly* without the need for generalization [3].

Training data organization: The proposed AFR method consists of two training stages – a one-time offline learning performed using *offline training data* and a stage when *gallery data* of known individuals with associated identities is collected. The former (explained next) is used for learning the generic face shape contribution to face appearance under varying illumination, while the latter is used for subject-specific learning.

4.1 Offline Stage: Learning the Generic SIM (gSIM)

Let $\mathbf{X}_i^{(j,k)}$ be the i-th face of the j-th person in the k-th illumination, same indexes corresponding in pose, as ensured by the proposed reillumination algorithm

Fig. 5. Learning complex illumination effects: Shown is the variation along the 1st mode of a single PPCA space in our SIM mixture model. Cast shadows (e.g. from the nose) and the locations of specularities (on the nose and above the eyes) are learnt as the illumination source moves from directly overhead to side-overhead.

in §3.1. Then from (8), samples from the generic Shape-Illumination manifold can be computed by logarithm-transforming all images and subtracting those corresponding in identity and pose:

$$\mathbf{d} = \log \mathbf{X}_i^{(j,p)} - \log \mathbf{X}_i^{(j,q)} \tag{9}$$

Provided that training data contains typical variations in pose and illumination (i.e. that the p.d.f. confined to the generic SIM is well sampled), this becomes a standard statistical problem of high-dimensional density estimation. We employ the Gaussian Mixture Model (GMM). In the proposed framework, this representation is motivated by: (i) the assumed low-dimensional manifold model (1), (ii) its compactness and (iii) the existence of incremental model parameter estimation algorithms (e.g. [21]).

Briefly, we estimate multivariate Gaussian components using the Expectation Maximization (EM) algorithm [12], initialized by k-means clustering. Automatic model order selection is performed using the well-known Minimum Description Length criterion [12] while the principal subspace dimensionality of PPCA components was estimated from eigenspectra of covariance matrices of a diagonal GMM fit, performed first. Fitting was then repeated using a PPCA mixture. We obtained 12 components, each with a 6D principal subspace. Fig. 5 shows an example of subtle illumination effects learnt with this model.

4.2   Robust Likelihood for Novel Sequence Classification

Let gallery data consist of sequences $\{\mathbf{X}_i\}^1, \ldots, \{\mathbf{X}_i\}^N$, corresponding to N individuals, $\{\mathbf{X}_i\}^0$ be a novel sequence of one of these individuals and $\mathcal{G}(\mathbf{x}; \boldsymbol{\Theta})$ a Mixture of Probabilistic PCA corresponding to the generic SIM. Using the reillumination algorithm of §3.1, the novel sequence can be reilluminated with each from the gallery, producing samples $\{\mathbf{d}_i\}$, assumed identically and independently distributed, from a *postulated* subject-specific SIM. We compute the probability of these observations under $\mathcal{G}(\mathbf{x}; \boldsymbol{\Theta})$:

$$p_i = \mathcal{G}(\mathbf{d}_i; \boldsymbol{\Theta}) \tag{10}$$

Instead of classifying $\{\mathbf{X}_i\}^0$ using the likelihood given the *entire* set of observations $\{\mathbf{d}_i\}$, we propose a more robust measure. To appreciate the need for robustness, consider the histograms in Fig. 6 (a). It can be observed that the probability of the most similar faces in an inter-personal comparison, in terms of (10), approaches that of the most *dissimilar* faces in an *intra-personal* comparison (sometimes even exceeding it). This occurs when the correct gallery

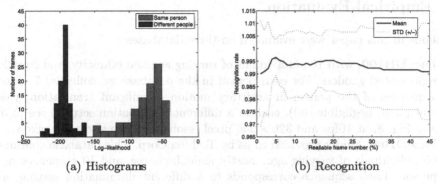

(a) Histograms

(b) Recognition

Fig. 6. (a) Histograms of intra-personal likelihoods across frames of a sequence when two sequences compared correspond to the same (red) and different (blue) people. (b) Recognition rate as a function of the number of frames deemed 'reliable'.

Algorithm 1: Offline training	**Algorithm 2:** Recognition (online)
Input: database of sequences $\{X_i\}^j$ **Output:** model of gSIM $\mathcal{G}(d; \Theta)$	**Input:** sequences $\{X_i\}^G, \{X_i\}^N$ **Output:** same-identity likelihood ρ

1: gSIM iteration
     for all j, k
	1: **Reilluminate using** $\{X_i\}^G$
	     $\{Y_i\}^N = \text{reilluminate}(\{X_i\}^N)$

2:     Reilluminate using $\{X_i\}^k$
       $\{Y_i\}^j = \text{reilluminate}(\{X_i\}^j)$
	2: **Postulated SIM samples**
	     $d_i = \log X_i^N - \log Y_i^N$

3:     Add gSIM samples
       $\mathbb{D} = \mathbb{D} \bigcup (\{Y_i\}^j - \{X_i\}^j)$
	3: **Compute likelihoods of** $\{d_i\}$
	     $p_i = \mathcal{G}(d_i; \Theta)$

4: Computed gSIM samples
     end for
	4: **Order** $\{d_i\}$ **by likelihood**
	     $p_{s(1)} \geq \cdots \geq p_{s(N)} \geq \cdots$

5: GMM $\mathcal{G}$ from gSIM samples
     $\mathcal{G}(d; \Theta) = \text{EM\_GMM}(\mathbb{D})$
	5: **Inter-manifold similarity** ρ
	     $\rho = \sum_{i=1}^{N} \log p_{s(i)}/N$

Fig. 7. A summary of the proposed offline learning and recognition algorithms

sequence contains poses that are very dissimilar to even the most similar ones in the novel sequence, or vice versa (note that small dissimilarities are extrapolated well from local manifold structure in (5)). In our method, the robustness to these, unseen modes of pose variation is achieved by considering the mean log-likelihood given only the most probable faces. In our experiments we used the top 15% of faces, but we found the algorithm to exhibit little sensitivity to the exact choice of this number, see Fig. 6 (b). A summary of proposed algorithms is shown in Fig. 7.

5   Empirical Evaluation

Methods in this paper were evaluated on three databases:

- **FaceDB100**, with 100 individuals of varying age and ethnicity, and equally represented genders. For each person in the database we collected 7 video sequences of the person in arbitrary motion (significant translation, yaw and pitch, negligible roll), each in a different illumination setting, see [2, 3] and Fig. 8, at 10fps and 320 × 240 pixel resolution (face size ≈ 60 pixels).
- **FaceDB60**, kindly provided to us by Toshiba Corp. This database contains 60 individuals of varying age, mostly male Japanese, and 10 sequences per person. Each sequence corresponds to a different illumination setting, at 10fps and 320 × 240 pixel resolution (face size ≈ 60 pixels), see [2].
- **FaceVideoDB**, freely available and described in [19]. Briefly, it contains 11 individuals and 2 sequences per person, little variation in illumination, but extreme and uncontrolled variations in pose and motion, acquired at 25fps and 160 × 120 pixel resolution (face size ≈ 45 pixels).

Data acquisition: The discussion so far focused on recognition using fixed-scale face images. Our system uses a cascaded detector [42] for localization of faces in cluttered images, which are then rescaled to the unform resolution of 50 × 50 pixels (approximately the average size of detected faces).

Methods and representations: We compared the performance of our recognition algorithm with and without the robust likelihood of §4.2 (i.e. using only the most reliable vs. all detected faces) to that of:

- State-of-the-art commercial system FaceIt® by Identix [22] (the best performing software in the most recent Face Recognition Vendor Test [33]),
- Constrained MSM (CMSM) [16] used in a state-of-the-art commercial system FacePass® [41],
- Mutual Subspace Method (MSM) [16], and
- KL divergence-based algorithm of Shakhnarovich *et al.* (KLD) [35].

In all tests, both training data for each person in the gallery, as well as test data, consisted of only a single sequence. Offline training of the proposed algorithm was performed using 20 individuals in 5 illuminations from the FaceDB100 – we

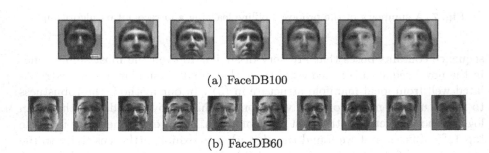

(a) FaceDB100

(b) FaceDB60

Fig. 8. Different illumination conditions in databases FaceDB100 and FaceDB60

emphasize that these were not used as test input for the evaluations reported in this section. The methods were evaluated using 3 face representations:

- raw appearance images $\mathbf{X}$,
- Gaussian high-pass filtered images – already used for AFR in [4, 14]:

$$\mathbf{X}_H = \mathbf{X} - (\mathbf{X} * \mathbf{G}_{\sigma=1.5}), \qquad (11)$$

- local intensity-normalized high-pass filtered images – similar to the Self Quotient Image [43]:

$$\mathbf{X}_Q = \mathbf{X}_H/(\mathbf{X} - \mathbf{X}_H), \qquad (12)$$

the division being element-wise.

5.1 Results

A summary of experimental results is shown in Table 1. The proposed algorithm greatly outperformed other methods, achieving a nearly perfect recognition (99.7+%) on all 3 databases. This is an extremely high recognition rate for such unconstrained conditions, small amount of training data per gallery individual and the degree of illumination, pose and motion pattern variation between different sequences. This is witnessed by the performance of Simple KLD method which can be considered a proxy for gauging the difficulty of the task, seeing that it is expected to perform well if imaging conditions are not greatly different between training and test [35]. Additionally, it is important to note the excellent performance of our algorithm on the Japanese database, even though offline training was performed using Caucasian individuals only.

As expected, when plain likelihood was used instead of the robust version proposed in §4.2, the recognition rate was lower, but still significantly higher than that of other methods. The high performance of non-robust gSIM is important as an estimate of the expected recognition rate in the "still-to-video" scenario of the proposed method. We conclude that the proposed algorithm's performance seems very promising in this setup as well. Finally, note that the standard deviation of our algorithm's performance across different training and test illuminations is much lower than that of other methods, showing less dependency on the exact imaging conditions used for data acquisition.

Table 1. Average recognition rates (%) and their standard deviations (if applicable)

		gSIM, rob.	gSIM	FaceIt	CMSM	MSM	KLD
Face DB100	$\mathbf{X}$	**99.7/0.8**	97.7/2.3	64.1/9.2	73.6/22.5	58.3/24.3	17.0/8.8
	$\mathbf{X}_H$	–	–	–	85.0/12.0	82.8/14.3	35.4/14.2
	$\mathbf{X}_Q$	–	–	–	87.0/11.4	83.4/8.4	42.8/16.8
Face DB60	$\mathbf{X}$	**99.9/0.5**	96.7/5.5	81.8/9.6	79.3/18.6	46.6/28.3	23.0/15.7
	$\mathbf{X}_H$	–	–	–	83.2/17.1	56.5/20.2	30.5/13.3
	$\mathbf{X}_Q$	–	–	–	91.1/8.3	83.3/10.8	39.7/15.7
Face VideoDB	$\mathbf{X}$	**100.0**	91.9	91.9	91.9	81.8	59.1
	$\mathbf{X}_H$	–	–	–	100.0	81.8	63.6
	$\mathbf{X}_Q$	–	–	–	91.9	81.8	63.6

Representations: Both the high-pass and even further Self Quotient Image representations produced an improvement for all methods over raw grayscale. This is consistent with previous findings in the literature [1, 4, 14, 43].

Unlike in previous reports of performance evaluation of these filters, we also ask the question of *when* they help and how much in *each case*. To quantify this, consider "performance vectors" s_R and s_F, corresponding to respectively raw and filtered input, whose each component is equal to the recognition rate of a method on a particular training/test data combination. Then the vector $\Delta s_R \equiv s_R - \bar{s}_R$ contains relative recognition rates to its average on raw input, and $\Delta s \equiv s_F - s_R$ the improvement with the filtered representation. We then considered the *angle* ϕ between vectors Δs_R and Δs, using both the high-pass and Self Quotient Image representations. In both cases, we found the angle to be $\phi \approx 136°$. This is an interesting result: it means that while on average both representations increase the recognition rate, they actually *worsen* it in "easy" recognition conditions. The observed phenomenon is well understood in the context of energy of intrinsic and extrinsic image differences and noise (see [44] for a thorough discussion). Higher than average recognition rates for raw input correspond to small changes in imaging conditions between training and test, and hence lower energy of extrinsic variation. In this case, the two filters decrease the SNR, worsening the performance. On the other hand, when the imaging conditions between training and test are very different, normalization of extrinsic variation is the dominant factor and performance is improved.

This is an important observation: it suggests that the performance of a method that uses either of the representations can be increased further in a straightforward manner by detecting the difficulty of recognition conditions, see [2].

Imaging conditions: Finally, we were interested if the evaluation results on our database support the observation in the literature that some illumination conditions are intrinsically more difficult for recognition than others [36]. An inspection of the performance of the evaluated methods has shown a remarkable correlation in relative performance across illuminations, despite the very different models used for recognition. We found that relative recognition rates across illuminations correlate on average with $\rho = 0.96$.

6   Summary and Conclusions

The proposed method for AFR from video has been demonstrated to achieve a nearly perfect recognition on 3 databases containing extreme illumination, pose and motion pattern variation, significantly outperforming state-of-the-art commercial software and methods in the literature.

The main direction for future work is to make a further use of offline training data, by taking into account probabilities of both intra- and inter-personal differences confined to the gSIM. This is the focus of our current work. Additionally, we would like to improve the computational efficiency of the method by representing each FMM by a strategically chosen set of sparse samples.

References

1. Y Adini, Y. Moses, and S. Ullman. Face recognition: The problem of compensating for changes in illumination direction. *PAMI*, 19(7):721–732, 1997.
2. O. Arandjelović and R. Cipolla. A new look at filtering techniques for illumination invariance in automatic face recogition. *FG*, 2006.
3. O. Arandjelović, G. Shakhnarovich, J. Fisher, R. Cipolla, and T. Darrell. Face recognition with image sets using manifold density divergence. *CVPR*, 2005.
4. O. Arandjelović and A. Zisserman. Automatic face recognition for film character retrieval in feature-length films. *CVPR*, 1:860–867, 2005.
5. W. A. Barrett. A survey of face recognition algorithms and testing results. *Systems and Computers*, 1:301–305, 1998.
6. BBC. Doubts over passport face scans. *BBC Online, UK Edition*, October 2004.
7. P. N. Belhumeur and D. J. Kriegman. What is the set of images of an object under all possible illumination conditions? *IJCV*, 28(3):245–260, 1998.
8. T. L. Berg, A. C. Berg, J. Edwards, M. Maire, R. White, Y. W. Teh, E. Learned-Miller, and D.A Forsyth. Names and faces in the news. *CVPR*, 2:848–854, 2004.
9. M. Bichsel and A. P. Pentland. Human face recognition and the face image set's topology. *Computer Vision, Graphics and Image Processing*, 59(2):254–261, 1994.
10. V. Blanz and T. Vetter. Face recognition based on fitting a 3D morphable model. *PAMI*, 25(9):1063–1074, 2003.
11. I. Craw, N. P. Costen, T. Kato, and S. Akamatsu. How should we represent faces for automatic recognition? *PAMI*, 21:725–736, 1999.
12. R. O. Duda, P. E. Hart, and D. G. Stork. *Pattern Classification*. John Wily & Sons, Inc., New York, 2nd edition, 2000.
13. M. Everingham and A. Zisserman. Automated person identification in video. *CIVR*, pages 289–298, 2004.
14. A. Fitzgibbon and A. Zisserman. On affine invariant clustering and automatic cast listing in movies. *ECCV*, pages 304–320, 2002.
15. K. Fukui and O. Yamaguchi. Facial feature point extraction method based on combination of shape extraction and pattern matching. *Systems and Computers in Japan*, 29(6):2170–2177, 1998.
16. K. Fukui and O. Yamaguchi. Face recognition using multi-viewpoint patterns for robot vision. *Int'l Symp. of Robotics Research*, 2003.
17. D. M. Gavrila. Pedestrian detection from a moving vehicle. *ECCV*, 2:37–49, 2000.
18. A. S. Georghiades, D. J. Kriegman, and P. N Belhumeur. Illumination cones for recognition under variable lighting: Faces. *CVPR*, pages 52–59, 1998.
19. D. O. Gorodnichy. Associative neural networks as means for low-resolution video-based recognition. *International Joint Conference on Neural Networks*, 2005.
20. R. Gross, I. Matthews, and S. Baker. Generic vs. person specific active appearance models. *BMVC*, 2004.
21. P. Hall, D. Marshall, and R. Martin. Merging and splitting eigenspace models. *PAMI*, 22(9):1042–1049, 2000.
22. Identix. Faceit. *http://www.FaceIt.com/*.
23. B. Kepenekci. *Face Recognition Using Gabor Wavelet Transform*. PhD thesis, The Middle East Technical University, 2001.
24. T. Kim, O. Arandjelović, and R. Cipolla. Learning over sets using boosted manifold principal angles (BoMPA). *BMVC*, 2005. (to appear).
25. R. Kimmel, R. Elad, D. Shaked, R. Keshet, and I. Sobel. A variational framework for retinex. *IJCV*, 52(1):7–23, 2003.

26. K. Lee and D. Kriegman. Online learning of probabilistic appearance manifolds for video-based recognition and tracking. *CVPR*, 1:852–859, 2005.

27. K. Lee, M. Yang, and D. Kriegman. Video-based face recognition using probabilistic appearance manifolds. *CVPR*, 1:313–320, 2003.

28. Y. Li, S. Gong, and H. Liddell. Modelling faces dynamically across views and over time. *ICCV*, 1:554–559, 2001.

29. X. Liu and T. Chen. Video-based face recognition using adaptive hidden Markov models. *CVPR*, 1:340–345, 2003.

30. H. Murase and S. Nayar. Visual learning and recognition of 3-D objects from appearance. *IJCV*, 14:5–24, 1995.

31. S. Palanivel, B. S. Venkatesh, and B Yegnanarayana. Real time face recognition system using autoassociative neural network models. *ASSP*, 2:833–836, 2003.

32. A. Pentland, B. Moghaddam, and T. Starner. View-based and modular eigenspaces for face recognition. *CVPR*, 84–91, 1994.

33. P. J. Phillips, P. Grother, R. J. Micheals, D. M. Blackburn, E. Tabassi, and J. M. Bone. FRVT 2002: Overview and summary. *Technical report, National Institute of Justice*, March 2003.

34. T. Riklin-Raviv and A. Shashua. The quotient image: Class based re-rendering and recognition with varying illuminations. *PAMI*, 23(2):219–139, 2001.

35. G. Shakhnarovich, J. W. Fisher, and T. Darrel. Face recognition from long-term observations. *ECCV*, 3:851–868, 2002.

36. T. Sim and S. Zhang. Exploring face space. *Face Processing in Video*, 2004.

37. J. Sivic, M. Everingham, and A. Zisserman. Person spotting: video shot retrieval for face sets. *CIVR*, 2005.

38. B. Stenger, A. Thayananthan, P. Torr, and R. Cipolla. Filtering using a tree-based estimator. *ICCV*, 2:1063–1070, 2003.

39. J. B. Tenenbaum, V. de Silva, and J. C. Langford. A global geometric framework for nonlinear dimensionality reduction. *Science*, 290(5500):2319–2323, 2000.

40. M. E. Tipping and C. M. Bishop. Mixtures of probabilistic principal component analyzers. *Neural Computation*, 11(2):443–482, 1999.

41. Toshiba. Facepass. *http://www.toshiba.co.jp/mmlab/tech/w31e.htm*.

42. P. Viola and M. Jones. Robust real-time face detection. *IJCV*, 57(2), 2004.

43. H. Wang, S. Z. Li, and Y. Wang. Face recognition under varying lighting conditions using self quotient image. *FG*, pages 819–824, 2004.

44. X. Wang and X. Tang. Unified subspace analysis for face recognition. *ICCV*, 2003.

45. L. Wolf and A. Shashua. Learning over sets using kernel principal angles. *JMLR*, 4(10):913–931, 2003.

46. W. Zhao, R. Chellappa, P. J. Phillips, and A. Rosenfeld. Face recognition: A literature survey. *ACM Computing Surveys*, 35(4):399–458, 2004.

47. S. Zhou, V. Krueger, and R. Chellappa. Probabilistic recognition of human faces from video. *Computer Vision and Image Understanding*, 91(1):214–245, 2003.

A Theory of Spherical Harmonic Identities for BRDF/Lighting Transfer and Image Consistency

Dhruv Mahajan[1], Ravi Ramamoorthi[1], and Brian Curless[2]

[1] Columbia University
{dhruv, ravir}@cs.columbia.edu
[2] University of Washington
curless@cs.washington.edu

Abstract. We develop new mathematical results based on the spherical harmonic convolution framework for reflection from a curved surface. We derive novel identities, which are the angular frequency domain analogs to common spatial domain invariants such as reflectance ratios. They apply in a number of canonical cases, including single and multiple images of objects under the same and different lighting conditions. One important case we consider is two different glossy objects in two different lighting environments. Denote the spherical harmonic coefficients by $B_{lm}^{light,material}$, where the subscripts refer to the spherical harmonic indices, and the superscripts to the lighting (1 or 2) and object or material (again 1 or 2). We derive a basic identity, $B_{lm}^{1,1}B_{lm}^{2,2} = B_{lm}^{1,2}B_{lm}^{2,1}$, *independent* of the specific lighting configurations or BRDFs. While this paper is primarily theoretical, it has the potential to lay the mathematical foundations for two important practical applications. First, we can develop more general algorithms for inverse rendering problems, which can directly relight and change material properties by transferring the BRDF or lighting from another object or illumination. Second, we can check the consistency of an image, to detect tampering or image splicing.

1 Introduction

Recent work by Basri and Jacobs [2], and Ramamoorthi and Hanrahan [15] has shown that the appearance of a curved surface can be described as a spherical convolution of the (distant) illumination and BRDF. This result often enables computer vision algorithms, previously restricted to point sources without attached shadows, to work in general complex lighting. Many recent articles have explored theoretical and practical applications for Lambertian surfaces (e.g., [1, 16]). However, there has been relatively little work in vision on using the convolution formulae for general glossy objects.

The main goal of this paper is to derive new formulae and identities for direct frequency domain spherical (de)convolution. As with most previous work in the area, we assume curved homogeneous objects (single BRDF) of known shape lit by complex distant illumination, and neglect cast shadows and interreflections. As explained in section 2, we also assume the BRDF is radially symmetric, which is a good approximation for most specular reflectance. A first example of our framework (section 3.1) is illumination estimation from a single image of a glossy material with known BRDF. By the convolution theorem, a glossy material will reflect a blurred version of the lighting.

A. Leonardis, H. Bischof, and A. Pinz (Eds.): ECCV 2006, Part IV, LNCS 3954, pp. 41–55, 2006.
© Springer-Verlag Berlin Heidelberg 2006

Fig. 1. One application of our framework. We are given real photographs of two objects of known geometry (shown in inset; note that both objects can be arbitrary, and one of them is a sphere here only for convenience). The two objects have different (and unknown) diffuse and specular material properties. Both objects are present in the first image under complex lighting, but the cat is not available in the second image, under new lighting. *Unlike previous methods, none of the lighting conditions or BRDFs are known* (lightings on left shown only for reference). Our method enables us to render or relight the cat, to obtain its image in lighting 2 (compare to actual shown on the right). This could be used for example to synthetically insert the cat in the second image.

It is appealing to sharpen or deconvolve this by dividing in the frequency domain by the spherical harmonic coefficients of the BRDF. The basic formula is known [15], but cannot be robustly applied, since BRDF coefficients become small at high frequencies. Our first contribution is the adaptation of Wiener filtering [4, 11] from image processing to develop robust deconvolution filters (figures 2 and 5).

Deconvolution can be considered a particular case, involving a single image of an object with known reflectance in unknown lighting. In this paper, we study single (section 3) and multiple (section 4) images under single and multiple lighting conditions. *Our main contribution is the derivation of a number of novel frequency domain identities.* For example, one important case we consider (section 4.3) is that of two different glossy[1] materials in two different lighting environments. Denote the spherical harmonic coefficients by $B_{lm}^{light,material}$, where the subscripts refer to the harmonic indices, and the superscripts to the lighting (1 or 2) and object or material (again 1 or 2). We derive an identity for the specular component, $B_{lm}^{1,1} B_{lm}^{2,2} = B_{lm}^{1,2} B_{lm}^{2,1}$, directly from the properties of convolution, *independent* of the specific lightings or BRDFs.

We show (section 4.4) that this and a related class of identities can be considered the frequency domain analog of fundamental spatial domain invariants, such as reflectance ratios (Nayar and Bolle [13]) or photometric invariants (Narasimhan et al. [12]).

---

[1] Parts of the theory (in sections 3.2 and 4) address only purely specular (or purely Lambertian) objects. However, as discussed in the paper and shown in our results, the theory and algorithms can be adapted in practice to glossy objects having both diffuse and specular components. Hence, we use the term "glossy" somewhat loosely throughout the paper.

This paper is motivated by two important practical applications. The first is inverse rendering [10, 15]. Besides estimation of lighting and BRDFs, we also develop more general algorithms, which directly relight and change material properties by transferring the BRDF or lighting from another object or illumination. For example, our identity above enables us to render the fourth light/BRDF image (say $B_{lm}^{2,2}$), given the other three, *without explicitly estimating any lighting conditions or BRDFs*. A common example (figure 1) is when we observe two objects in one lighting, and want to insert the second object in an image of the first object alone under new lighting.

The second, newer application, is to verify image consistency and detect tampering (Johnson and Farid [7], Lin et al. [8]). The widespread availability of image processing tools enables creation of "forgeries" such as splicing images together (one example is shown in figure 6). Most previous work has focused on checking consistency at a signal or pixel level, such as the camera response [8], or wavelet coefficients (Ng et al. [14]). However, (in)consistencies of lighting and shading also provide valuable clues. This paper takes an important first step in laying theoretical foundations for this new area.

2   Background

We now briefly introduce the spherical convolution and signal-processing framework [2, 15] needed for our later derivations. We start with the Lambertian case,

$$B(\mathbf{n}) = \int_{S^2} L(\omega) \max(\mathbf{n} \cdot \omega, 0)\, d\omega, \tag{1}$$

where $B(\mathbf{n})$ denotes the reflected light as a function of the surface normal. B is proportional to the irradiance (we omit the albedo for simplicity), and $L(\omega)$ is the incident illumination. The integral is over the sphere S^2, and the second term in the integrand is the *half-cosine* function. The equations in this paper do not explicitly consider color; the (R,G,B) channels are simply computed independently.

A similar mathematical form holds for other radially symmetric BRDFs, such as the Phong model for specular materials. In this case, we reparameterize by the reflected direction $\mathbf{R}$ (the reflection of the viewing ray about the surface normal), which takes the place of the surface normal:

$$B(\mathbf{R}) = \frac{s+1}{2\pi} \int_{S^2} L(\omega) \max(\mathbf{R} \cdot \omega, 0)^s\, d\omega, \tag{2}$$

where s is the Phong exponent, and the BRDF is normalized (by $(s+1)/2\pi$).

If we expand in spherical harmonics $Y_{lm}(\theta, \phi)$, using spherical coordinates $\omega = (\theta, \phi)$, $\mathbf{n}$ or $\mathbf{R} = (\alpha, \beta)$, and $\rho(\theta)$ for the (radially symmetric) BRDF kernel, we obtain

$$L(\theta, \phi) = \sum_{l=0}^{\infty} \sum_{m=-l}^{l} L_{lm} Y_{lm}(\theta, \phi) \quad B(\alpha, \beta) = \sum_{l=0}^{\infty} \sum_{m=-l}^{l} B_{lm} Y_{lm}(\alpha, \beta) \quad \rho(\theta) = \sum_{l=0}^{\infty} \rho_l Y_{l0}(\theta).$$

$$\tag{3}$$

It is also possible to derive analytic forms for common BRDF filters ρ. For the Lambertian case, almost all of the energy is captured by $l \leq 2$. For Phong and

Torrance-Sparrow, good approximations [15] are Gaussians: $\exp[-l^2/2s]$ for Phong, and $\exp[-(\sigma l)^2]$ for Torrance-Sparrow, where σ is the surface roughness parameter.

In the frequency domain, the reflected light B is given by a simple product formula or spherical convolution (see [2, 15] for the derivation and an analysis of convolution),

$$\boxed{B_{lm} = \Lambda_l \rho_l L_{lm} = A_l L_{lm}}$$ (4)

where for convenience, we define A_l and the normalization constant Λ_l as

$$\Lambda_l = \sqrt{\frac{4\pi}{2l+1}} \qquad A_l = \Lambda_l \rho_l.$$ (5)

The remainder of this paper derives new identities and formulae from equation 4, $B_{lm} = A_l L_{lm}$. Practical spherical harmonic computations are possible from only a *single image*, since a single view of a sufficiently curved object (assuming a distant viewer) sees all reflected directions. Most glossy BRDFs (such as Torrance-Sparrow) are approximately radially symmetric, especially for non-grazing angles of reflection [15]. Most of the theory in this paper also carries over to general isotropic materials, if we consider the entire light field, corresponding to multiple views [9].

3   Theoretical Analysis: Single Image of One Object

We develop the theory for the simplest case of a single image of one object in this section, with multiple objects and lighting conditions discussed later in section 4.

3.1   Known BRDF: Deconvolution to Estimate Lighting

We start by considering a known BRDF, where we want to determine the lighting. Given a single image of a curved surface, we can map local viewing directions to the reflected direction, determining $B(\mathbf{R})$, and then B_{lm} by taking a spherical harmonic transform. If the material includes a diffuse component, we use the dual lighting estimation algorithm [15], which finds the specular B_{lm} consistent with the diffuse component. As per equation 4, B_{lm} will be a blurred version of the lighting, filtered by the glossy BRDF.

From equation 4 in the spherical harmonic domain, we derive

$$L_{lm} = \frac{B_{lm}}{A_l} = A_l^{-1} B_{lm},$$ (6)

where the last identity makes explicit that we are convolving with a new radially symmetric kernel A_l^{-1}, which can be called the inverse, sharpening or deconvolution filter.

Unfortunately, it is difficult to apply equation 6 directly, since A_l in the denominator will become small for high frequencies, or alternatively the inverse filter A_l^{-1} will become very large. This will lead to substantial amplification of noise at high frequencies.

These types of problems have been well studied in image processing, where a number of methods for deconvolution have been proposed. We adapt Wiener filtering [4, 11] for this purpose. Specifically, we define a new inverse filter,

$$A_l^* = \frac{1}{A_l}\left(\frac{|A_l|^2}{|A_l|^2+K}\right) = \frac{A_l}{|A_l|^2+K} \qquad L_{lm} = A_l^* B_{lm},$$ (7)

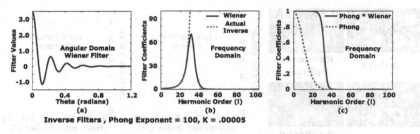

Inverse Filters , Phong Exponent = 100, K = .00005

Fig. 2. Deconvolution filter in the angular (a), and frequency (b) domains. The combined effect (multiplication in the frequency domain) of Phong and deconvolution filters is in (c).

where K is a small user-controlled constant. When $|A_l|^2 \gg K$, the expression in parentheses on the left is close to 1, and $A_l^* \approx A_l^{-1}$. When $|A_l|^2 \ll K$, $A_l^* \approx A_l / K$.

Figure 2 shows a deconvolution filter A_l^* in the angular (a) and frequency (b) domains. The convolution of this filter with the original Phong filter (blue graph in c) lets through most frequencies without attenuation, while filtering out the very high frequencies. Figure 5 shows an application of deconvolution with real images and objects.

3.2   Known Lighting: Identity Obtained by Eliminating the BRDF

We now consider the converse case, where the lighting is known, but the BRDF is not. We will *eliminate* the BRDF to derive an identity that must hold and can be checked *independent of the BRDF*. This is the first of a number of frequency domain identities we will derive in a similar fashion. First, from equation 4, we can write

$$A_l = \frac{B_{lm}}{L_{lm}}. \tag{8}$$

This expression could be used to solve for BRDF coefficients.[2] However, we will use it in a different way. Our key insight is that the above expression is independent of m, and must hold for all m. Hence, we can eliminate the (unknown) BRDF A_l, writing

$$\frac{B_{li}}{L_{li}} = \frac{B_{lj}}{L_{lj}} \tag{9}$$

for all i and j. Moving terms, we obtain our first identity,

$$B_{li}L_{lj} - B_{lj}L_{li} = 0. \tag{10}$$

In effect, we have found a redundancy in the structure of the image, that can be used to detect image tampering or splicing. The lighting L and image B are functions on a 2D (spherical) domain. However, they are related by a 1D radially symmetric BRDF, leading to a 1D redundancy, that can be used for consistency checking in equation 10.

To normalize identities in a $[0...1]$ range, we always use an error of the form

$$\text{Error} = \frac{|\,B_{li}L_{lj} - B_{lj}L_{li}\,|}{|\,B_{li}L_{lj}\,| + |\,B_{lj}L_{li}\,|}.$$

---

[2] Since natural lighting usually includes higher frequencies than the BRDF, we can apply equation 8 directly without regularization, and do not need to explicitly discuss deconvolution.

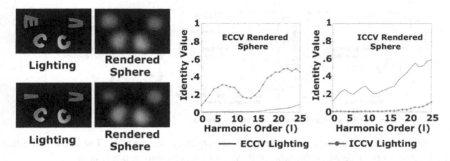

Fig. 3. Left: The synthetic images used. These correspond to closeups of specular spheres rendered with "ECCV" and "ICCV" lighting. To the naked eye, the two images look very similar. **Middle and Right:** The graphs show that our identity can clearly distinguish consistent image/lighting pairs (lower line) from those where lighting and image are inconsistent (upper line).

There are many ways one could turn this error metric into a binary consistency checker or tamper detector. Instead of arbitrarily defining one particular approach, we will show graphs of the average normalized error for each spherical harmonic order.

Figure 3 applies our theory to synthetic data of an ideal Phong BRDF, with noise added. We show closeups of (a rectangular region in) spheres generated with "ECCV" and "ICCV" lighting. To the naked eye, these look very similar, and it is not easy to determine if a given image is consistent with the lighting. However, our identity in equation 10 clearly distinguishes between consistent (i.e., the image is consistent with the lighting [ECCV or ICCV] it is supposed to be rendered with) and inconsistent illumination/image pairs. As compared to Johnson and Farid [7], we handle general complex illumination. Moreover, many of the identities in later sections work directly with image attributes, not even requiring explicit estimation or knowledge of the illumination (though we still require known geometry, and assume homogeneous materials.)

Our framework could be used to blindly (without watermarking) detect tampering of images, making sure a given photograph (containing a homogeneous object of known shape) is consistent with the illumination it is captured in.[3] To the best of our knowledge, ours is the first theoretical framework to enable these kinds of consistency checks. Example applications of tamper detection on real objects are shown in figures 4 and 6.

3.3 Combining Diffuse and Specular

We now consider the more general case of an unknown glossy BRDF with both specular *and* Lambertian (diffuse) reflectance. To our knowledge, this is the first such combined diffuse plus specular theory of the single image case.

---

[3] Our identities are "necessary" conditions for image consistency, under our assumptions and in the absence of noise. They are not theoretically "sufficient." For example, if an unusual material were to zero out a certain frequency, tampering at that frequency may go undetected. Also note that noise tends to add high frequencies, while materials tend to filter out high frequencies, causing the consistency errors to rise (become less reliable) with harmonic order.

Common Parameterization: While both diffuse and specular components are radially symmetric, they are so in different parameterizations (normal vs reflected direction). Hence, we first express the diffuse irradiance in the reflected parameterization,

$$B_{lm} = K_d D_{lm} + A_l^{\text{spec}} L_{lm}, \tag{11}$$

where D_{lm} are the spherical harmonic coefficients of the irradiance written in the reflected parameterization[4]. They depend only on the lighting, which is assumed known, and are small [9] for $|m| > 2$. The parameters of reflectance are the diffuse coefficient K_d and the specular BRDF filter coefficients A_l (we drop the superscript from now on).

Determining A_l and Image Consistency: For example, we can now eliminate K_d,

$$\frac{B_{li} - A_l L_{li}}{D_{li}} = \frac{B_{lj} - A_l L_{lj}}{D_{lj}} \implies A_l = \frac{B_{li} D_{lj} - B_{lj} D_{li}}{L_{li} D_{lj} - L_{lj} D_{li}}. \tag{12}$$

This can be used to directly estimate the specular BRDF coefficients, irrespective of the diffuse coefficient K_d. As a sanity check, consider the case when $K_d = 0$. In this case, $B_{li} = A_l L_{li}$, so the expression above clearly reduces to A_l. Hence, equation 12 can be considered a new robust form of reflectance estimation that works for both purely specular and general glossy materials. Further note that we estimate an accurate *non-parametric* BRDF representation specified by general filter coefficients A_l.

Since the formula above is true for all i, j, we get an identity for image consistency. An application to detect splicing for a real object is shown in the left graph of figure 6.

$$\frac{B_{li} D_{lj} - B_{lj} D_{li}}{L_{li} D_{lj} - L_{lj} D_{li}} = \frac{B_{lm} D_{ln} - B_{ln} D_{lm}}{L_{lm} D_{ln} - L_{ln} D_{lm}}. \tag{13}$$

4   Theoretical Analysis: Two Materials and/or Lighting Conditions

Section 3 analyzed the single object, single image case. In this section[5], we first consider two different objects (with different materials) in the same lighting. Next, we consider one object imaged in two different lighting conditions. Then, we consider the two lighting/two BRDF case corresponding to two images (in different lighting conditions), each of two objects with distinct BRDFs. Finally, we discuss some broader implications.

4.1   Two Objects/BRDFs: Same Lighting

We consider a single image (hence in the same lighting environment) of two objects, with different BRDFs. Let us denote by superscripts 1 or 2 the two objects,

---

[4] D_{lm} depend linearly on lighting coefficients L_{lm} as $D_{lm} \approx \sum_{n=0}^{2} A_n^{\text{Lamb}} L_{nm} T_{lmn}$, with $T_{lmn} = \int_{S^2} Y_{nm}(\frac{\alpha}{2}, \beta) Y_{lm}^*(\alpha, \beta) \, d\Omega$. The $\alpha/2$ in the first term converts from normal to reflected parameterization. The coefficients T_{lmn} can be determined analytically or numerically [9].

[5] This section will primarily discuss the purely specular case. For consistency checking, we have seen that in the reflective reparameterization, the diffuse component mainly affects frequencies D_{lm} with $|m| \leq 2$. Therefore, it is simple to check the identities for $|m| > 2$. Diffuse relighting is actually done in the spatial domain, as discussed in section 4.4. Section 5 provides experimental validation with objects containing both diffuse and specular components.

$$B^1_{lm} = A^1_l L_{lm} \qquad B^2_{lm} = A^2_l L_{lm}. \tag{14}$$

From these, it is possible to eliminate the lighting by dividing,

$$\frac{B^2_{lm}}{B^1_{lm}} = \frac{A^2_l}{A^1_l} = \gamma_l. \tag{15}$$

We refer to γ_l as the *BRDF transfer function*. Given the appearance of one object in complex lighting, multiplication of spherical harmonic coefficients by this function gives the appearance of an object with a different material. γ_l is *independent* of the lighting, and can be used in any (unknown) natural illumination. Also note that γ_l is *independent of* m, so we can average over all m, which makes it robust to noise—in our experiments, we have not needed explicit regularization for the frequencies of interest. Moreover, we do not need to know or estimate the individual BRDFs.

It is also possible to use these results to derive a frequency space identity that depends only on the final images, and does not require explicit knowledge of either the lighting condition or the BRDFs. We know that equation 15 should hold for all m, so

$$\frac{B^2_{li}}{B^1_{li}} = \frac{B^2_{lj}}{B^1_{lj}} \quad \Longrightarrow \quad B^2_{li}B^1_{lj} - B^1_{li}B^2_{lj} = 0. \tag{16}$$

This identity can be used for consistency checking, making sure that two objects in an image are shaded in consistent lighting. This enables detection of inconsistencies, where one object is spliced into an image from another image with inconsistent lighting. As with equation 10, the images B are 2D functions, but related by a 1D radially symmetric BRDF, leading to redundancies in the spherical harmonic coefficients.

Finally, note that the single image identity (equation 10) is a special case of equation 16, where one of the objects is simply a mirror sphere (so, for instance, $B^1 = L$).

4.2   Two Lighting Environments: Same Object/BRDF

We now consider imaging the same object in two different lighting environments. Let us again denote by superscripts 1 or 2 the two images, so that,

$$B^1_{lm} = A_l L^1_{lm} \qquad B^2_{lm} = A_l L^2_{lm}. \tag{17}$$

Again, it is possible to eliminate the BRDF by dividing,

$$\frac{B^2_{lm}}{B^1_{lm}} = \frac{L^2_{lm}}{L^1_{lm}} = L'_{lm}. \tag{18}$$

We refer to L'_{lm} as the *lighting transfer function*. Given the appearance of an object in lighting condition 1, multiplication of spherical harmonic coefficients by this function gives the appearance in lighting condition 2. L'_{lm} is *independent* of the reflectance or BRDF of the object. Hence, the lighting transfer function obtained from one object can be applied to a different object. Moreover, we never need to explicitly compute the material properties of any of the objects, nor recover the individual lighting conditions.

The relighting application does not require explicit knowledge of either lighting condition. However, if we assume the lighting conditions are known (unlike the previous subsection, we need the lighting known here since we cannot exploit radial symmetry to eliminate it), equation 18 can be expanded in the form of an identity,

$$B^2_{lm} L^1_{lm} - B^1_{lm} L^2_{lm} = 0. \tag{19}$$

This identity can be used for consistency checking, making sure that two photographs of an object in different lighting conditions are consistent, and neither has been tampered.

4.3   Two Materials *And* Two Lighting Conditions

Finally, we consider the most conceptually complex case, where both the lighting and materials vary. This effectively corresponds to two images (in different lighting conditions), each containing two objects of different materials. We will now use two superscripts, the first for the lighting and the second for the material.

	Lighting 1	Lighting 2
BRDF 1	$B^{1,1}_{lm} = A^1_l L^1_{lm}$	$B^{2,1}_{lm} = A^1_l L^2_{lm}$
BRDF 2	$B^{1,2}_{lm} = A^2_l L^1_{lm}$	$B^{2,2}_{lm} = A^2_l L^2_{lm}$

Simply by multiplying out and substituting the relations above, we can verify the basic identity discussed in the introduction to this paper,

$$B^{1,1}_{lm} B^{2,2}_{lm} = B^{1,2}_{lm} B^{2,1}_{lm} = A^1_l A^2_l L^1_{lm} L^2_{lm}, \tag{20}$$

or for the purposes of consistency checking,

$$\boxed{B^{1,1}_{lm} B^{2,2}_{lm} - B^{1,2}_{lm} B^{2,1}_{lm} = 0.} \tag{21}$$

An interesting feature of this identity is that we have completely eliminated all lighting and BRDF information. Consistency can be checked based simply on the final images, without estimating any illuminations or reflectances. Note that if the second object is a mirror sphere, this case reduces to the two lightings, same BRDF case in equation 19.

Equation 20 also leads to a simple framework for estimation. The conceptual setup is that we can estimate the appearance of the fourth lighting/BRDF image (without loss of generality, say this is $B^{2,2}_{lm}$), given the other three, *without explicitly computing any illumination or reflectances*. Clearly, this is useful to insert the second object into a photograph where it wasn't present originally, assuming we've seen both objects together under another lighting condition. From equation 20, we have

$$B^{2,2}_{lm} = \frac{B^{1,2}_{lm} B^{2,1}_{lm}}{B^{1,1}_{lm}} \tag{22}$$

$$= B^{1,2}_{lm} \left(\frac{B^{2,1}_{lm}}{B^{1,1}_{lm}} \right) = B^{1,2}_{lm} L'_{lm} \tag{23}$$

$$= B^{2,1}_{lm} \left(\frac{B^{1,2}_{lm}}{B^{1,1}_{lm}} \right) = B^{2,1}_{lm} \gamma_l. \tag{24}$$

This makes it clear that we can visualize the process of creating $B_{lm}^{2,2}$ in two different ways. One approach is to start with the *same* object in another lighting condition $B_{lm}^{1,2}$ and apply the lighting transfer function L'_{lm} obtained from *another* object. Alternatively, we start with *another* object in the *same* lighting condition, i.e. $B_{lm}^{2,1}$ and apply the BRDF transfer function γ_l. The BRDF transfer function is found from the image of both objects in lighting condition 1. In practice, we prefer using the BRDF transfer function (equation 24), since γ_l is more robust to noise. However, the equations above make clear that both interpretations are equivalent, following naturally from equation 20. Since *none* of the lightings or BRDFs are known, it would be very difficult to render $B_{lm}^{2,2}$ with alternative physics-based inverse rendering methods.

4.4 Implications and Discussion

We now briefly discuss some of the broader implications of our theory, and previous spatial domain identities and invariants analogous to our frequency domain results.

Multiple lighting conditions and BRDFs: Let us consider r lighting conditions and s BRDFs, instead of assuming $r = s = 2$, with superscripts $i \le r$ and $j \le s$, so that

$$B_{lm}^{i,j} = A_l^j L_{lm}^i \implies \mathbf{B}_{lm} = \mathbf{L}_{lm}\mathbf{A}_l^T, \tag{25}$$

where in the last part, for a given spherical harmonic index (l, m), we regard $\mathbf{B}_{lm}$ as an $r \times s$ matrix obtained by multiplying column vectors $\mathbf{L}_{lm}$ ($r \times 1$), corresponding to the lighting conditions, and the transpose of $\mathbf{A}_l$ ($s \times 1$), corresponding to the BRDFs.

Equation 25 makes it clear that there is a *rank 1 constraint* on the $r \times s$ matrix $\mathbf{B}_{lm}$. Section 4.3 has considered the special case $r = s = 2$, corresponding to a 2×2 matrix, where the rank 1 constraint leads to a single basic identity (equation 21). In fact, equation 21 simply states that the determinant of the singular 2×2 matrix $\mathbf{B}_{lm}$ is zero.

Spatial Domain Analog: Equation 25 expresses the image of a homogeneous glossy material in the *frequency domain* as a *product* of lighting and BRDF. Analogously, a difficult to analyze frequency domain convolution corresponds to a simple spatial domain product. For example, the image of a textured Lambertian surface in the *spatial domain* is a *product* of albedo ρ_k and irradiance E_k, where k denotes the pixel.

$$B_k^{i,j} = \rho_k^j E_k^i \implies \mathbf{B}_k = \mathbf{E}_k\boldsymbol{\rho}_k^T. \tag{26}$$

These identities enable spatial domain techniques for re-rendering the diffuse component (which in our case has constant albedo since the material is homogeneous), while still using the frequency domain for the specular component.[6] We use the *spatial domain analogs* of equations 20 and 24 to compute the diffuse component of $B^{2,2}$.

---

[6] We first separate diffuse and specular components by observing that in a parameterization by surface normals, B_{lm} will have essentially all of its diffuse energy for $l \le 2$, while the specul~ energy falls away much more slowly, and therefore mostly resides in $l > 2$. Since only the front facing normals in a single image, we use fitting to remove the terms with $l \le 2$, and thereby separate diffuse and specular. As expected for the extremes when the specular intensity is very small relative to the limit, a purely Lambertian surface) or vice versa (a purely

In this case, the spatial analog of the BRDF transfer function γ in equation 24 simply corresponds to the ratio of the (in our case uniform) diffuse albedos of the two objects.

Analogies with Previous Spatial Domain Results: While the exact form of, and rank 1 constraint on, equation 26 is not common in previous work, many earlier spatial domain invariants and algorithms can be seen as using special cases and extensions.

Reflectance ratios [13] are widely used for recognition. The main observation is that at adjacent pixels, the irradiance is essentially the same, so that the ratio of image intensities corresponds to the ratio of albedos. Using superscripts for the different pixels as usual (we do not need multiple super- or any subscripts in this case), we have $B^2/B^1 = \rho^2/\rho^1$. The analogous frequency domain result is equation 15, corresponding to the two BRDFs, same lighting case. In both cases, by dividing the image intensities (spherical harmonic coefficients), we obtain a result *independent of the illumination*.

Similarly, a simple version of the recent BRDF-invariant stereo work of Davis et al. [3] can be seen as the two lighting, same BRDF case. For fixed view and point source lighting, a variant of equation 26 still holds, where we interpret ρ_k^j as the (spatially varying) BRDF for pixel k and fixed view, and E_k^i as the (spatially varying) light intensity at pixel k. If the light intensity changes (for the same pixel/BRDF), we have $B^2/B^1 = E^2/E^1$. The frequency domain analog is equation 18. In both cases, we have *eliminated the BRDF* by dividing image intensities or spherical harmonic coefficients.

Narasimhan et al. [12] also assume point source lighting to derive spatial domain photometric invariants. By contrast, our frequency domain framework handles general complex lighting (but is limited to homogeneous objects with known shape, and a global spherical harmonic analysis as opposed to local pixel operations.) Narasimhan et al. [12] consider a variant of equation 26 with a summation of multiple terms (such as diffuse plus specular). For each term, ρ encodes a material property such as the diffuse albedo, while E encodes illumination and geometric attributes. Their work can be seen as effectively deriving a rank constraint on **B**, corresponding to the number of terms. For diffuse objects, this is a rank 1 constraint, analogous to that in the frequency domain for equation 25. For diffuse plus specular, this is a rank 2 constraint. They then effectively use the rank constraint to form determinants that eliminate either material or geometry/lighting attributes, as in our frequency domain work. Jin et al. [6] use a similar rank 2 constraint for multi-view stereo with both Lambertian and specular reflectance.

Finally, we note that some of our frequency domain results have no simple spatial domain analog. For example, the concept of angular radial symmetry does not transfer to the spatial domain, and there is no known spatial analog of equations 10, 13, and 16.

5   Experimental Validation and Results

We now present some experiments to validate the theory, and show potential applications. We start with diffuse plus specular spheres in figure 4, since they correspond most closely with our theory. We then describe results with a complex cat geometry (figures 1, 5 and 6). All of these results show that the theory can be applied in practice with real data, where objects are not perfectly homogeneous, there is noise in measurement and calibration, and specular reflectance is not perfectly radially symmetric.

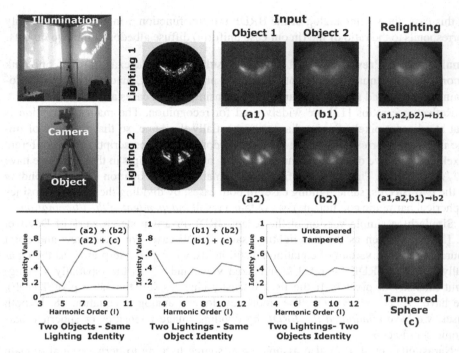

Fig. 4. Top Left: Experimental setup. **Top Middle:** Two lightings (shown only for reference) and images of two glossy (diffuse plus specular) spheres in that lighting. **Top Right:** We can accurately render (b1), given (a1,a2,b2), and render (b2), given (a1,a2,b1). **Bottom:** We tamper (b2) to generate (c) by squashing the specular highlights slightly in photoshop. While plausible to the naked eye, all three identities in section 4 clearly indicate the tampering (red graphs).

Experimental Setup: We ordered spheres from http://www.mcmaster.com. The cat model was obtained at a local craft sale. All objects were painted to have various specular finishes and diffuse undercoats. While homogeneous overall, small geometric and photometric imperfections on the objects were visible at pixel scale and contributed "reflection noise" to the input images. To control lighting, we projected patterns onto two walls in the corner of a room. We placed a Canon EOS 10D camera in the corner and photographed the objects at a distance of 2-3m from the corner (see top left of figure 4). This setup has the advantage of more detailed frontal reflections, which are less compressed than those at grazing angles. However, frontal lighting also gives us little information at grazing angles, where the BRDF might violate the assumption of radial symmetry due to Fresnel effects; we hope to address this limitation in future experiments. To measure the lighting, we photographed a mirror sphere. To measure BRDFs (only for deconvolution), we imaged a sphere under a point source close to the camera, determining A_l by simply reading off the profile of the highlight, and K_d by fitting to the diffuse intensity. For all experiments, we assembled high-dynamic range images.

Glossy Spheres: Figure 4 shows the two lighting, two materials case. The top right shows a relighting application. We assume (b1) is unknown, and we want to synthesize it from the other 3 lighting/BRDF images (a1,a2,b2). We also do the same for rendering

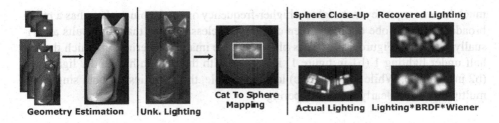

Fig. 5. Deconvolution on a real cat image. **Left:** Geometry estimation, using example-based photometric stereo (we take a number of images with the cat and example sphere; the sphere is also used to find the BRDF). **Middle:** Input image under unknown lighting, and mapping to a sphere using the surface normals. **Right:** Closeups, showing the original sphere map, and our deconvolved lighting estimate on top. This considerably sharpens the original, while removing noise, and resembles the BRDF*Wiener filter applied to the actual lighting (bottom row).

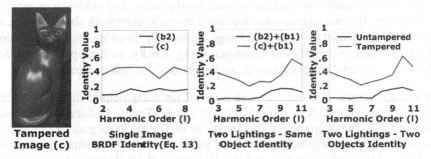

Fig. 6. Image consistency checking for cat (labels are consistent with figure 1). The tampered image (c) is obtained by splicing the top half (b1) under lighting 1 and the bottom half (b2) under lighting 2. Image (c) looks quite plausible, but the splicing is clearly detected by our identities.

(b2) assuming we know (a1,a2,b1). The results are visually quite accurate, and in fact reduce much of the noise in the input. Quantitatively, the L_1 norm of the errors for (b1) and (b2) are 9.5% and 6.5% respectively. In the bottom row, we tamper (b2) by using image processing to squash the highlight slightly. With the naked eye, it is difficult to detect that image (c) is not consistent with lighting 2 or the other spheres. However, all three identities discussed in the previous section correctly detect the tampering.

Complex Geometry: For complex (mostly convex) known geometry, we can map object points to points on the sphere with the same surface normal, and then operate on the resulting spherical image. Deconvolution is shown in figure 5. We used a sphere painted with the same material as the cat to aquire both the cat geometry, using example-based photometric stereo [5] for the normals, and the BRDF (needed only for deconvolution). Errors (unrelated to our algorithm) in the estimated geometry lead to some noise in the mapping to the sphere. Our deconvolution method for lighting estimation substantially sharpens the reflections, while removing much of the input noise.

The cat can also be used directly as an object for relighting/rendering and consistency checking. An example of rendering is shown in figure 1. Note that this is a very challenging example, since we are using the BRDF transfer function from a much lower-frequency material to a higher-frequency one—the blue sphere has a much broader specular lobe than the green cat. Nevertheless, we see that the results are visually plausible. Figure 6 illustrates photomontage image tampering, in which the top half under lighting 1 (b1 in figure 1) is spliced with the bottom half under lighting 2 (b2 in figure 1). While the image (c) looks plausible, the identities for both single and multiple images clearly detect tampering.

6   Conclusions and Future Work

In this paper, we have derived a set of novel frequency space identities. These identities often eliminate the lighting and/or BRDF, enabling a new class of inverse rendering algorithms that can relight or change materials by using BRDF/lighting transfer functions. In the future, similar ideas may be applied to other problems, such as BRDF-invariant stereo or lighting-insensitive recognition. We would also like to extend our identities and algorithms to work with textured objects, local patches, and unknown or approximate geometry. Beyond inverse rendering, our theoretical framework also makes a contribution to the relatively new area of image consistency checking, describing a suite of frequency domain identities to detect tampering. Finally, we have presented a new unified view of spatial and frequency domain identities and rank constraints.

Acknowledgements. We thank Sameer Agarwal for many helpful discussions. This work was supported by NSF grant #0430258 ("CyberTrust - Restore the Trustworthiness of Digital Photographs: Blind Detection of Digital Photograph Tampering"), as well as NSF grants #0098005, #0305322 and #0446916, the Washington Research Foundation, Microsoft Research, and the University of Washington Animation Research Labs.

References

1. R. Basri and D. Jacobs. Photometric stereo with general, unknown lighting. In *CVPR 01*, pages II–374–II–381, 2001.
2. R. Basri and D. Jacobs. Lambertian reflectance and linear subspaces. *PAMI*, 25(2):218–233, 2003.
3. J. Davis, R. Yang, and L. Wang. BRDF invariant stereo using light transport constancy. In *ICCV 05*, 2005.
4. R. Gonzalez and R. Woods. *Digital Image Processing*. Pearson Education, 2003.
5. A. Hertzmann and S. Seitz. Example-based photometric stereo: Shape reconstruction with general, varying BRDFs. *PAMI*, 27(8):1254–1264, 2005.
6. H. Jin, S. Soatto, and A. Yezzi. Multi-view stereo beyond lambert. In *CVPR 03*, pages 171–178, 2003.
7. M. Johnson and H. Farid. Exposing digital forgeries by detecting inconsistencies in lighting. In *ACM Multimedia and Security Workshop*, 2005.
8. Z. Lin, R. Wang, X. Tang, and H. Shum. Detecting doctored images using camera response normality and consistency. In *CVPR 05*, 2005.
9. D. Mahajan. A theory of spherical harmonic identities for inverse rendering, BRDF/lighting transfer and image consistency checking. Master's thesis, Columbia, 2006.
10. S. Marschner. *Inverse Rendering for Computer Graphics*. PhD thesis, Cornell, 1998.

11. Wiener N. Extrapolation, interpolation and smoothing of stationary time series. In *the MIT Press*, 1942.
12. S. Narasimhan, V. Ramesh, and S. Nayar. A class of photometric invariants: Separating material from shape and illumination. In *ICCV 03*, pages 1387–1394, 2003.
13. S. Nayar and R. Bolle. Reflectance based object recognition. *IJCV*, 17(3):219–240, 1996.
14. T. Ng, S. Chang, and Q. Sun. Blind detection of photomontage using higher order statistics. In *IEEE International Symposium on Circuits and Systems*, 2004.
15. R. Ramamoorthi and P. Hanrahan. A signal-processing framework for inverse rendering. In *SIGGRAPH 01*, pages 117–128, 2001.
16. D. Simakov, D. Frolova, and R. Basri. Dense shape reconstruction of a moving object under arbitrary, unknown lighting. In *ICCV 03*, pages 1202–1209, 2003.

Covariant Derivatives and Vision

Todor Georgiev

Adobe Systems, 345 Park Ave, W10-124, San Jose, CA 95110, USA

Abstract. We describe a new theoretical approach to Image Processing and Vision. Expressed in mathemetical terminology, in our formalism
image space is a fibre bundle, and the image itself is the graph of a section on it. This mathematical model has advantages to the conventional
view of the image as a function on the plane: Based on the new method
we are able to do image processing of the image as viewed by the human
visual system, which includes adaptation and perceptual correctness of
the results. Our formalism is invariant to relighting and handles seamlessly illumination change. It also explains simultaneous contrast visual
illusions, which are intrinsically related to the new covariant approach.

Examples include Poisson image editing, Inpainting, gradient domain
HDR compression, and others.

1 Introduction

It is a known fact that the human visual system does change the physical contents (the pixels) of the perceived image. We do not see luminance or color as
they are, measured by pixel values. Higher pixel values do not always appear
brighter, but perceived brightness depends on surrounding pixels. A popular
example is the simultaneous contrast illusion [14, 15], where two identical gray
patches appear different because of different surroundings. As a result of adaptation, difference in *lightness* (perceived brightness) does not equal difference in
pixel value. Some of those effects were already well understood in the general
framework of Land's Retinex theory [8]. Researchers like Horn [6], Koenderink
[7], and others, have later contributed to the theory. Petitot [18] has proposed
rigorous "neurogeometry" description of visual contours in images based on Riemannian connections.

Following the above authors, we introduce the geometric idea of Image Space
as fibred manifold and provide an understanding on how image processing in
Image Space differs from image processing in the conventional approach, where
images are simply functions on the plane. Compared to [18], we model lightness
perception instead of contours, and we are using general linear connections that
are not Riemannian.

Viewing Image Space as Fibred Manifold allows us to do image processing
on "the image as we see it", and not on the physical image as function of x, y.
Based on this construction, image processing is invariant with respect to certain
specific changes in pixel values, for example due to change of lighting. A shadow
on the image should not change the result of image processing operations, even

A. Leonardis, H. Bischof, and A. Pinz (Eds.): ECCV 2006, Part IV, LNCS 3954, pp. 56–69, 2006.

if it changes pixel values. A good edge detection (or face detection) system is not influenced by change of lighting.

We discuss in detail one example of how this new approach works: Writing the Laplace equation in terms of connections automatically improves the results of Poisson image editing [10]. Other examples include Inpainting [2], Gradient domain high dynamic range compression [5], and the Bilateral filter [13], [4].

2 Image Space as Fibred Manifold

2.1 Motivation

Intuitively, our approach can be described as follows. A grayscale image is not a collection of pixels, but a collection of "fibres". Instead of each pixel having brightness, we have "a mark" on each fibre. The bundle of fibres is "dynamic" in the sense that we can freely "slide" fibres relative to one-another. This happens as part of the Retinex-type adaptation of our visual system. Even though the mark on the fibre (pixel value) remains the same, its relation to the other fibres is different. This creates the preception of lightness as different from luminance.

On a more rigorous level, we propose to use the mathematical concept of Fibre Bundle [12], [9]. It assumes no a priori relation among fibres, other than topological. The relation (comparison between fibres) is added later, when we introduce a *connection*. It gives meaning to pixels by making comparison of lightness possible.

The relation among pixels is to some extent 'added' by the observer and is due to both pixel value and adaptation of the visual system. If captured in appropriate mathematical formalism, this will influence image processing.

The ultimate goal is to be able to do image processing on the internal image that we see, while actually touching only the physical pixels.

2.2 Image Space

In the traditional approach grayscale images are represented as surfaces in R^3: Pixels are defined by their coordinates x, y in the image plane, and their corresponding values z in R^+. Thus, the conventional model of image space is Cartesian product of the image plane and the positive real line of pixel values, $R^2 \times R^+$. This structure contains two natural projections: For any point in image space we can immediately say which pixel it is, and what the pixel value is – according to the two components of the Cartesian product. In this model the image is a function $z = f(x, y)$, and there is a natural comparison between any two pixel values: simply $z_2 - z_1$. It is customary to assume that brightness of different pixels can be compared in this way.

However, as noticed in section 2.1, there are examples of same pixel values appearing different or difference in lightness not equal to difference in pixel value. Retinex and other adaptation theories are fundamentally based on considering this difference between pixel values and lightness.

The fact that the human visual system does not compare pixels by their luminance alone, suggests that we need a model of image space in which pixel values, even if well defined, are not comparable a priori. It should be possible to add comparison or "difference in observed lightness" later, after a given adaptation.

We propose a model that replaces the Cartesian product structure of Image Space with a Fibred Space structure (see also [7]). The new structure is "weaker" because it "forgets" (in the mathematical sense) one of the projections (on z). In this paper we will show on several examples how this fibred space structure can be useful. Intuitively, the new structure is essentially a Cartesian product with one of the projections relaxed. By having the freedom of introducing this projection later (based on the concept of *connection*) we gain control on effects of adaptation.

This situation is similar to the model of space-time in classical mechanics [9]. There is a natural projection on time, in the sense that all observers have one absolute time. For example, they can synchronize their watches.

However, there is no natural projection onto space. One observer thinks that a given object does not move: It is always "here", in the sense that projection onto space is giving the same location at any time. However, another observer who passes by in a car would see that this same object moving. It projects onto different locations in space throughout time. Projection onto space is different for different observers!

In this way, space-time in classical mechanics is not simply a Cartesian product of space and time. Space in mechanics is relative, it depends on how we define the second projection. Time is absolute. Space acts like our "fibres" in images - it depends on the frame of reference or, which is the same, on the observer. Current pixel values are simply one possible set of coordinates for the image, like the coordinates of objects relative to one particular observer (in a given moving car). Other pixel values may describe the same mental image.

To continue the analogy, velocity in mechanics is like perceived gradients in images. It is different from the point of view of different observers, just like perceived image gradient depends on the state of adaptation of the observer.

2.3   Fibred Space

By definition [12], a Fibred Space (E, π, B) consists of two spaces: *total space* E and *base space* B, and a mapping π, called *projection*, of the total space onto the base. Space B has lower dimension than E, so many E points map to the same B point, as shown in Figure 1.

In our model of grayscale images the total space is R^3, the base is the image plane, and π gives us the location of each pixel in the image plane. There is no mapping that would give us the grayscale value of lightness for a pixel.

For each point $p \in B$ there is the so-called *fibre* (F_p in Figure 2) in E, consisting of all points that are sent to p by π (definition of fibre). We cannot compare the lightness of two points from different fibres because in the mathematical structure there is no mapping that would produce that lightness. Each fibre has its luminance coordinate, but luminances in different fibres are not related.

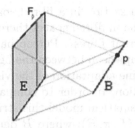

Fig. 1. Fibred space (E, π, B)

By definition, a section in a Fibred Space is a mapping f that sends points in B to E, and has the property $\pi(f(p)) = p$ for any $p \in B$. See Figure 2.

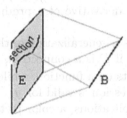

Fig. 2. Section in fibred space (E, π, B)

A section selects just one of the many points in each fibre. It defines one manifold (connected set of points) in total space E, with one point in E for each point in B. Intuitively it is "the closest we can get to the concept of function without defining a function".

A grayscale image is a section in a fibred image space (R^3, π, R^2). Since there is no projection onto z, there is no comparison between different pixels. As a result, change in image lightness and directional derivative at a point in image space is not defined. Pixels are simply records and come without interpretation. Luminance or pixel value is a perceptually meaningless coordinate.

2.4   Connections

In fibred spaces changes in the section (slopes of the section) are measured by the so called *connection*, or *covariant derivative* (instead of derivative). As the name suggests, connections show how fibres are "connected" or "glued together". Connections are used like derivatives to compare pixel values from different fibres. In Physics [3] the simplest example of such a field is the vector potential in Electrodynamics.

In order to introduce the definition of connection in a natural way, let us first consider the gradient when the image is defined traditionally as a function $f(x, y)$ on the image plane. The gradient is a vector $(\frac{\partial f}{\partial x}, \frac{\partial f}{\partial y})$ with two components that are functions of x, y.

If the image is defined as a section in a fibred space, the above definition of gradient does not work because in fibred spaces there is no concept of derivative or "comparison between different fibres". Perceptually the situation is similar. We do not have a sense of comparison between the lightness of different pixels in the image before assuming some adaptation of the visual system. Pixels are just "records" without interpretation. In order to compare pixels we need an additional structure. In our mathematical model this structure is called connection.

A *connection* on a bundle (E, π, B), where B denotes the image plane, is a mapping, or a rule, that for any section σ on E produces what is called the x and y components of the *covariant gradient* of that section. These components are also sections. This mapping has certain properties similar to the properties of the gradient. In order to come up with a natural definition, let's look again at the case of functions. If $f = f(x, y)$ and $s = s(x, y)$ are functions on B, the derivative of the product fs in direction x would be $\frac{\partial}{\partial x}(fs) = (\frac{\partial}{\partial x} f)s + f\frac{\partial}{\partial x} s$, which is known as the Leibniz rule for derivative of a product. A similar expression is valid for the y derivative.

The concept of connection is a generalization of the above Leibniz rule to the case of sections. By definition, if D is a connection, $D_x(f\sigma) = (\frac{\partial}{\partial x} f)\sigma + f D_x \sigma$. Note that the derivative $\frac{\partial}{\partial x}$ acts on a function, while the "derivative" acting on the section is D_x. Similar expression is valid for y.

In our image processing applications, a color picture is a section in a vector bundle, where each three dimensional fibre is a copy of the vector space of colors. A connection is "adapted (covariant) gradient of color", as perceived by the observer. In other words, it shows how the human visual system in a given state of adaptation perceives directional change of color.

Any section can be represented as a linear combination of a set of basis sections σ_i. In other words, $\sigma = \Sigma f^i \sigma_i$. Summation is assumed over $i = 1, 2, 3$, and the coefficients f^i are functions. These functions are referred to as color channels (Photoshop terminology).

By the above definition of connection, D_x and D_y would act on a section $\sigma = \Sigma f^i \sigma_i$ in the following way:

$$D_x \sigma = D_x \Sigma(f^i \sigma_i) = \Sigma((\frac{\partial}{\partial x} f^i)\sigma_i + f^i D_x \sigma_i) \tag{1}$$

$$D_y \sigma = D_y \Sigma(f^i \sigma_i) = \Sigma((\frac{\partial}{\partial y} f^i)\sigma_i + f^i D_y \sigma_i) \tag{2}$$

These expressions simply extend the Leibniz rule for the action of derivatives on functions to a Leibniz rule for sections. We don't know what the action on the basis section σ_i is, but we know that the result must be again a section, representable by the basis. So, it is $D_x \sigma_i = \Sigma A^j{}_{ix} \sigma_j$ where $A^j{}_{ix}$ is some matrix-valued function of x and y. Similar for D_y and $A^j{}_{iy}$.

$$D_x \Sigma(f^i \sigma_i) = \Sigma((\frac{\partial}{\partial x} f^i)\sigma_i + \Sigma f^i A^j{}_{ix} \sigma_j) \tag{3}$$

$$D_y \Sigma(f^i \sigma_i) = \Sigma((\frac{\partial}{\partial y} f^i)\sigma_i + \Sigma f^i A^j{}_{iy} \sigma_j) \tag{4}$$

As a matter of notation, often the basis σ_i is dropped, and we talk of the section as represented in terms of f^i. Then the action of the connection on f_i is:

$$D_x f^i = \frac{\partial}{\partial x} f^i + \Sigma A^i{}_{j_x} f^j. \tag{5}$$

$$D_y f^i = \frac{\partial}{\partial y} f^i + \Sigma A^i{}_{j_y} f^j. \tag{6}$$

This expression for the connection, as a replacement of the derivative, will be our main tool throughout this paper. The rule of thumb is that a connection D_x, D_y replaces the gradient $\frac{\partial}{\partial x}$, $\frac{\partial}{\partial y}$ according to the so called "minimal substitution":

$$\frac{\partial}{\partial x} \to D_x = \frac{\partial}{\partial x} + A_x. \tag{7}$$

$$\frac{\partial}{\partial y} \to D_y = \frac{\partial}{\partial y} + A_y. \tag{8}$$

The expression $\frac{\partial}{\partial x} + A_x$ and similar for y is called the *covariant derivative*, or *perceptual gradient*.

In color images A_x and A_y are matrix valued functions of x, y. In grayscale images A_x and A_y are functions.

Summary of the result to this point: In fibred spaces changes in the section are measured by a connection, instead of derivative. As the name indicates, connections show how we compare, or transfer pixel values from one fibre to another, in other words - how fibres are "connected". In Physics [3], connections are called covariant derivatives. A classical example of connection is the Electromagnetic field, represented by the vector potential **A**.

We would like to end this section with a perceptual example of how connections work in images. The image is a section in a fibre bundle, where we have no a priori comparison between pixel values in different fibres. As such, the image is a record without any interpretation. Adaptation, expressed as a connection, is what gives meaning to pixels, making comparisons possible in terms of lightness.

To make this all more intuitive, let's look at the example. The simultaneous contrast illusion, Figure 3 shows that humans do not perceive pixel values directly. (See [14, 15] for a general survey on lightness perception and examples of illusions.) In the figure there is a constant gray band surrounded by a variable background. Due to our visual system's adaptation, the band appears to vary in *lightness* in opposition to its surroundings. Pixel gradient is zero, but perceived or covariant gradient is not zero. The reason why we see change of lightness in the constant band is the nonzero covariant derivative by which we compare pixels.

Next we will be working with grayscale images, assuming the generalization to three color channels is straight forward.

2.5   Covariantly Constant Sections

Following formulas (7) and (8), we will be representing any section by the corresponding function, replacing gradients with covariant gradients. Since now we

Fig. 3. The central rectangle has constant pixel values

have a way to compare pixels and calculate derivatives, we can ask the question: When is a given section constant?

Any section $g(x, y)$ can be considered constant relative to appropriately chosen adaptation A_x, A_y, such that $(\frac{\partial}{\partial x} + A_x)g = 0$, and similar for y. The solution is:

$$A_x = -\frac{1}{g}\frac{\partial g}{\partial x} \qquad (9)$$

$$A_y = -\frac{1}{g}\frac{\partial g}{\partial y} \qquad (10)$$

We are considering Retinex-type adaptation of the visual system, in which the perceived gradient is the covariant derivative. In grayscale images it is described by a vector field $A_x, A_y)$. When the visual system is exactly adapted to the image in a given area, so that (9) and (10) are satisfied, we see constant gray image (or image matching the surrounding color). We call this state *complete adaptation* to the image. In practice, due to the unconscious motion of the eyes, a state of complete adaptation is very difficult to reach. Still, the idea of complete adaptation will be very useful in the following sections.

3   Test Case 1: Poisson Image Editing

3.1   Equations

It is well known that the Laplace equation $\triangle f = 0$ with Dirichlet boundary conditions is the simplest way to reconstruct (or inpaint) a defective area in an image. It can be used to remove scratches, wrinkles, or bigger unwanted objects. Let's write the derivatives in the Laplacian $\triangle$ explicitly:

$$\frac{\partial}{\partial x}\frac{\partial}{\partial x}f + \frac{\partial}{\partial y}\frac{\partial}{\partial y}f = 0, \qquad (11)$$

After performing the minimal substitution (7), (8), the Laplace equation (11) is converted into the *covariant Laplace equation*:

$$(\frac{\partial}{\partial x} + A_x)(\frac{\partial}{\partial x} + A_x)f + (\frac{\partial}{\partial y} + A_y)(\frac{\partial}{\partial y} + A_y)f = 0, \qquad (12)$$

which after performing the differentiation can be written as

$$\triangle f + f div \mathbf{A} + 2\mathbf{A} \cdot gradf + \mathbf{A} \cdot \mathbf{A}f = 0. \tag{13}$$

Here the vector function $\mathbf{A}(x,y) = (A_x(x,y), A_y(x,y))$ describes adaptation of the visual system, and $f(x,y)$ is the function that represents the grayscale image as a section. The minimal substitution above is equivalent to the transition from the conventional image model as a function to the new model of the image as a section on a fibre bundle. The Laplace equation is converted into the covariant Laplace equation, which is in fact closer to Poisson equation.

Next we assume $\mathbf{A}$ represents complete adaptation to a selected area where the image is a section defined by $g(x,y)$, translated. The solution of (13) would be smooth if observed with eyes adapted to $g(x,y)$, but the solution will look like having $g(x,y)$ "imprinted on it" if observed in some other more typical state of adaptation. Since state of complete adaptation is practically never achieved, solving (13) is a way of reconstructing some area with texture similar to g. At the same time this reconstruction is exact as a model of how the adapted visual system would "solve" the Laplace equation to fill in the selected region.

Notice that now $\mathbf{A}(x,y) = -\frac{gradg}{g}$ can be interpreted as playing the role of the "guidance field" in Poisson image editing [10]. Substituting in equation (13), we obtain the final form of the covariant Laplace equation:

$$\frac{\triangle f}{f} - 2\frac{gradf}{f} \cdot \frac{gradg}{g} - \frac{\triangle g}{g} + 2\frac{(gradg) \cdot (gradg)}{g^2} = 0. \tag{14}$$

Let's compare it with the Poisson equation used in [10]:

$$\triangle f = \triangle g \tag{15}$$

We see that the covariant Laplace equation is more complicated than (15). It can be viewed as a Poisson equation with a modified $\triangle g$ term on the "right hand side". The structure of the equation prescribed by our model is very specific. It prescribes the expression $2 gradf \cdot \frac{gradg}{g} + f\frac{\triangle g}{g} - 2f\frac{(gradg) \cdot (gradg)}{g^2}$ as the correct one to choose as a source term in the modified Poisson equation for seamless cloning. Equation (15) can be viewed as a simplified approximation.

3.2   Results

One of the practical results of this paper is that the new covariant equation (14) produces seamless cloning of better quality compared to Poisson editing. By simple differentiation we can see that (14) is equivalent to:

$$\triangle \frac{f}{g} = 0 \tag{16}$$

Equation (16) is easy to solve in 3 steps:

(1) Divide the image f by the texture image g, in which pixel value zero is replaced with a small number. This produces the first intermediate image $I_1(x,y)$.

$$I_1(x,y) = \frac{f(x,y)}{g(x,y)} \tag{17}$$

(2) Solve the Laplace equation for the second intermediate image

$$\triangle I_2(x,y) = 0, \tag{18}$$

with Dirichlet boundary conditions defined by $I_1(x,y)$ at the boundary of the reconstruction area.

(3) Multiply the result by the texture image $g(x,y)$

$$h(x,y) = I_2(x,y)g(x,y), \tag{19}$$

and substitute the original defective image $f(x,y)$ with the new image $h(x,y)$ in the area of reconstruction.

A multigrid approach to solving (18) with good performance is described in [11]. In practical terms, the tool works sufficiently fast for using it in interactive mode. For example, on a laptop running Windows XP with a 2 GHz Pentium 4 processor, applying a brush of radius 100 pixels takes less than 0.25 seconds to converge.

We apply the algorithm to fix a scratch in Figure 4. Figure 5 shows a zoom in, where the areas to clone from and to clone into are indicated.

Figure 6 (left) shows the result of Poisson Cloning by solving (15), and comparison with Covariant cloning based on the proposed method (right). The example was not selected in any special way. We see that the result is slightly better in terms of matching the contrast. This behavior is repeated consistently in other experiments, especially in areas of changing shadows/illumination. Sometimes the difference between the two methods is big, sometimes - small, but the covariant approach is always better.

Another example is taken from [16]. The authors use a version of Poisson cloning to fuse night and day images so that in a day image we can see clear

Fig. 4. Basilica San Marco, Venice

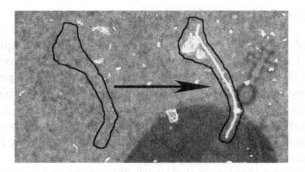

Fig. 5. Areas and direction of cloning

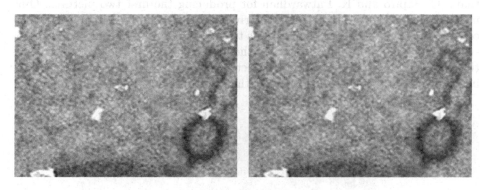

Fig. 6. Poisson cloning (left) and Covariant cloning (right)

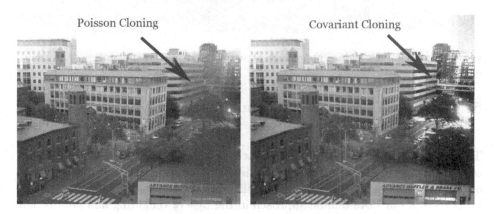

Fig. 7. Two methods of cloning from the night scene

representation of the night version of the same scene. In Figure 7 the right side of each image has been modified by cloning from the night image. We see that Poisson cloning looks blurry, while Covariant cloning looks better.

4   Test Case 2: Image Inpainting

The method of Inpainting [2] works similar to solving the Laplace equation
to reconstruct the selected area based on the boundaries. However, based on a
higher order PDE related to fluid dynamics the method is able to partially reconstruct "structure" inside the inpainted area by continuation of the surrounding
grayscale values into the inside. The behavior often resembles fluid flow and
sometimes is not exactly what we want. Later research attempts to also reconstruct the texture which is extracted from the surroundings using mathematical
results from functional analysis [17].

Figure 8 compares Inpainting (left) with "Structure and texture" Inpainting
[17] (middle) and our new method of Covariant Inpainting. We would like to
thank G. Sapiro and K. Patwardhan for producing the first two pictures. Our
method is equivalent to replacing the derivatives in conventional Inpainting with
covariant derivatives. As in the previous test case, the result is achieved in three
steps. (1) Divide the original image by the texture image. (2) Solve the PDE, in
this case the Inpainting PDE in the selected region. (3) Multiply by the texture
image. We see that our result is better than both previous methods.

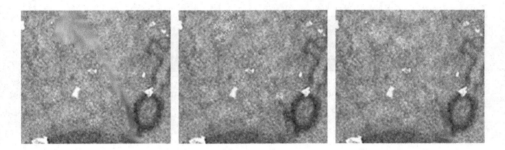

Fig. 8. From left to right: Inpainting, Structure and texture inpainting, Covariant
inpainting

5   Test Case 3: Gradient Domain High Dynamic Range Compression

This section will be a theoretical derivation of previous results. As in previous
sections, the value is in the new theoretical understanding and in showing that
our approach has a wide area of applicability. We will be looking at the invariance
properties of our fibre bundle approach in the case of relighting and adaptation
to the new illumination of the scene.

A central problem in dealing with high dynamic range images (HDR) is how
to display them on a low dynamic range device, like a monitor. Just like scratch
removal, the problem of HDR compression can be expressed in terms of relighting. As an example of how our method works, we will reproduce the results of
one of the best approaches [5] starting from first principles.

Here is a short review of the algorithm of [5]: Treat only the luminance, f. Calculate logarithm $F = \ln f$; find the gradient of it; attenuate big gradients to reduce dynamic range; then integrate back to get a real image in log space; and finally take the exponent to produce the output luminance.

The logarithm of luminance is used simply because human visual system is approximately logarithmic, and not based on theoretical reasons. Our approach will provide theoretical justification of the use of logarithm.

The authors minimize the following energy written in log-space

$$\int (\frac{\partial}{\partial x}F - A_x)^2 + (\frac{\partial}{\partial y}F - A_y)^2 dx dy \tag{20}$$

to produce the Poisson equation

$$\triangle F = div\mathbf{A} \tag{21}$$

for the logarthm of luminance, where $\mathbf{A}$ is the attenuated gradient of the log of the input. "Integrate back" in the above algorithm means "solve (21)". Without attenuation, (21) would produce seamless cloning from any image g if $\mathbf{A} = \frac{grad g}{g}$. We can also write $G = \ln g$ and then

$$\triangle F = \triangle G. \tag{22}$$

Now, let's do the same with our approach. The energy expression is written based on requirements for adaptation invariance. In other words, a multiplicative shadow/relighting g on the source image produces an additive to A_μ term in such a way that the new output image is multiplied by the same shadow/relighting. This simple requirement for energy invariance produces the result (21), (22), automatically placed in log-space. The transforms are:

$$f \to gf \tag{23}$$

$$\mathbf{A} \to \mathbf{A} - \frac{grad g}{g}. \tag{24}$$

The simplest energy expression that has the above invariance can easily be written using covariant derivatives:

$$\int \frac{((\frac{\partial}{\partial x} + A_x)f)^2 + ((\frac{\partial}{\partial y} + A_y)f)^2}{f^2} dx dy. \tag{25}$$

If we substitute $\mathbf{A}$ with $-\frac{grad g}{g}$, the Euler-Lagrange equation for this energy would be:

$$\triangle \ln f = \triangle \ln g, \tag{26}$$

which is exactly (22). In this way, we have found an invariant under (23), (24) energy expression that reproduces the results of [5].

Because of the logarithm in our result, we reproduce exactly (22), the same as [5]. What is the difference in our approach? We did not depend on intuition to motivate this use of log space; instead, it comes directly from our mathematical model based on first principles. This can be seen as theoretical motivation for using log space in any visual system.

Note that **A** is adaptation vector field, and it can be more general than gradient of a function. We adapt to what we see, and not to the pixel values of energy illuminating the retina. Due to these adaptation effects, what we see is not always representable in pixels or as a picture. In other words, the human visual system can produce internally things that can not possibly be represented as a picture (on a monitor or other device).

6   Other Test Cases and Future Research

As future research we are looking into more rigorous application of our approach to color images, which are naturally represented as sections in vector bundles. For example, the above Gradient Domain High Dynamic Range Compression [5] has been applied only on a grayscale image (or the luminance channel), and it would be useful to see what modifications could we bring with the fibre bundle approach.

Another test case would be the Bilateral [13] and Trilateral [4] filters, which are treating Image Space in the spirit of Bundles, filtering both in 'Domain' (image plane) direction and in 'Range' (pixel value) direction. This type of filtering can be captured in the mathematical formalism of Jet Bundles [12].

But the main idea of our current paper was that we need to use expressions for the energy based on connections (covariant derivatives) acting on images as sections, not functions. This could be done in relation to any PDE or other image processing algorithm, not just the Laplace equation and Inpainting, and this defines a wide area of research.

References

1. Adobe Systems: Photoshop 7.0 User Guide. Adobe Systems, San Jose, 2002.
2. M. Bertalmio, G. Sapiro, V. Castelles, C. Ballester, "Image Inpainting," Proceedings of ACM SIGGRAPH 2000, pp. 417-424, ACM Press, 2000.
3. Y. Choquet-Bruhat, C. DeWitt-Morette, Analysis, Manifolds and Physics, Amsterdam, North-Holland, 1982.
4. P. Choudhury, J. Tumblin, "The Trilateral Filter for High Contrast Images and Meshes," Proceedings of the 2003 Eurographics Symposium on Rendering, pp.186-196, 2003.
5. R. Fattal, D. Lischinski, M. Werman, "Gradient Domain High Dynamic Range Compression," Proceedings of ACM SIGGRAPH 2002, pp. 249-256, 2002.
6. B. Horn, "Determining Lightness from an Image," Computer Graphics and Image Processing, 3, pp. 277-299, 1974.
7. J. Koenderink, A. van Doorn, "Image Processing Done Right," Proceedings of ECCV 2002, pp. 158-172, Springer, 2002.
8. E. Land, J. McCann, "Lightness and Retinex Theory," Journal of the Optical Society of America, v. 61, no. 1, pp. 1-11, 1971.

9. L. Mangiarotti, G. Sardanashvily, Gauge Mechanics, World Scientific, North-Holland, 1998.
10. P. Prez, M. Gangnet, A. Blake, "Poisson Image Editing," Proceedings of ACM SIGGRAPH 2003, pp. 313-318, 2003.
11. W. Press, S. Teukolsky, W. Vetterling, B. Flannery, Numerical Recipes in C, Cambridge University Press, 1992.
12. D. Saunders, The Geometry of Jet Bundles, Cambridge University Press, 1989.
13. C. Tomasi, R. Manduchi, "Bilateral Filtering for Gray and Color Images." Proceedings IEEE Int. Conf. on Computer Vision, pp. 836-846, 1998.
14. M. Gazzaniga, The New Cognitive Neurosciences, MIT Press, Cambridge, MA, 2000, pp. 339-351.
15. A. Seckel, The Art of Optical Illusions, Carlton Books, 2000.
16. R. Raskar, A. Ilie, J. Yu, "Image Fusion for Enhancing Context in Images and Video." ACM Nonphotorealistic Animation and Rendering (NPAR) 2004.
17. M. Bertalmio, L. Vese, G. Sapiro, S. Osher, "Simultaneous Structure and Texture Image Inpainting." CVPR (2) 2003, pp. 707-712
18. J. Petitot, "The neurogeometry of pinwheels as a sub-Riemannian contact structure." Journal of Physiology - Paris 97, 2003, pp. 265-309.

Retexturing Single Views
Using Texture and Shading

Ryan White[1] and David Forsyth[2]

[1] University of California, Berkeley
ryanw@cs.berkeley.edu
[2] University of Illinois, Urbana Champaign
daf@cs.uiuc.edu

Abstract. We present a method for retexturing non-rigid objects from
a single viewpoint. Without reconstructing 3D geometry, we create realistic video with shape cues at two scales. At a coarse scale, a track of the
deforming surface in 2D allows us to erase the old texture and overwrite
it with a new texture. At a fine scale, estimates of the local irradiance
provide strong cues of fine scale structure in the actual lighting environment. Computing irradiance from explicit correspondence is difficult and
unreliable, so we limit our reconstructions to screen printing — a common printing techniques with a finite number of colors. Our irradiance
estimates are computed in a local manner: pixels are classified according
to color, then irradiance is computed given the color. We demonstrate
results in two situations: on a special shirt designed for easy retexturing
and on natural clothing with screen prints. Because of the quality of the
results, we believe that this technique has wide applications in special
effects and advertising.

1 Overview

We describe a novel image-based rendering technique to retexture fast-moving,
deforming objects in video while preserving original lighting. Our method uses
simple correspondence reasoning to recover texture coordinates, and color reasoning to recover a detailed, dense irradiance estimate. Our retextured images
have textures that appear to be stable on the surface, at spatial scales that cannot, in fact, be recovered. We believe that our high quality irradiance estimate
is a significant component of the sense of shape that is produced.

Retexturing starts with [3], who demonstrate a method based on shape from
texture. The method is not notably successful, and does not use irradiance estimates. Fang and Hart show that, in static images, a local shape from shading
estimate of normals is sufficient to retexture an image patch satisfactorily [2]:
they do not need to estimate irradiance for synthesis because they combine images multiplicatively. The shape estimate is very weak (shape from shading is
notoriously inaccurate [4, 12]), but sufficient for good results. Several methods
have been proposed to track nonrigid motion [10, 9]. Pilet et al [9] describe a
method to detect the surface deformation using wide-baseline matches between

A. Leonardis, H. Bischof, and A. Pinz (Eds.): ECCV 2006, Part IV, LNCS 3954, pp. 70–81, 2006.
© Springer-Verlag Berlin Heidelberg 2006

a frontal view and the image to estimate a transformation smoothed using surface energy. This method cannot stabilize texture for three reasons. First, there are few reliable keypoints in the texture we consider, especially in oblique views. Second, by using keypoints, the method does not track boundaries — and oscillations in the boundary conditions are noticeable in their videos. Third, the rigid smoothing using surface energy makes their method stiff, and limited in scope. In addition, they cannot obtain an irradiance estimate — small errors in their correspondence would make it impossible.

Irradiance estimation is now common in the image-based rendering community [1, 7, 11], usually relying on objects of known geometry and albedo. More recently, Lobay and Forsyth showed that a good irradiance estimate is available from a repeating texture [7].

Applications: Retexturing is a useful and pleasing image level utility. Retexturing clothing has a variety of applications if it can be done cleanly. First, one could sell the advertising space on the back of a sports-player's shirt multiple times — different adverts could be retextured for different television markets. Second, one could change the clothing of figures in legacy images or footage to meet modern tastes.

Conceptual advances: A growing theme of modern computer vision is the number of useful applications that are possible with little or no shape information. We show that high quality images can be rendered in realistic lighting conditions without 3D geometry (Figures 2, 5, 9 and 10). This can be achieved without high accuracy in localization. Furthermore, we adduce evidence suggesting that good irradiance estimates may be very useful indeed in sustaining a perception of 3D shape.

Procedure: Our method builds a non-parametric regression estimate of irradiance (Section 2). We then use quite simple correspondence reasoning to obtain texture coordinates (Section 3) from either a frontal view of the texture or a known, engineered pattern. This information is then composited using a new texture map to produce output frames. There is no elastic model of the material and no dynamical model of correspondence — the video is handled frame by frame.

2 Lighting Replacement: Modeling Irradiance

Careful estimates of irradiance are very useful, and appear to create a powerful impression of shape. Their significance for renderings of clothing is probably due to *vignetting*, an effect which occurs when a surface sees less light than it could because other surfaces obstruct the view. The most significant form for our purposes occurs locally, at the bottom of gutters where most incoming light is blocked by the sides of the gutters. This effect appears commonly on clothing and is quite distinctive [5, 6]. It is due to small folds in the cloth forming gutters and shadows and could not be represented with a parametric irradiance model unless one had a highly detailed normal map.

Fig. 1. Many common textured articles are made using *screen printing* — where each color is printed in a separate pass. Often, this method is cheaper than using a full color gamut. Screen printing is widespread: many T-shirts, advertisements, and corporate logos are composed of a small number of solid colors. Recovering irradiance is easier in this setting: correspondence to a frontal view of the pattern is not required. Instead, each color can be detected independently in order to recover irradiance. Because screen print items are composed of large regions of uniform color, they are robust to motion blur.

However, we do not have and cannot get a detailed normal map or depth map. Furthermore, as we shall see in Section 3, the estimates of material coordinates are of limited accuracy. As a result, irradiance estimates that use the material coordinates are inaccurate, especially in regions where the albedo changes quickly. A single pixel error in position on the texture map can, for example, mean that an image location produced by a dark patch on the shirt is ascribed

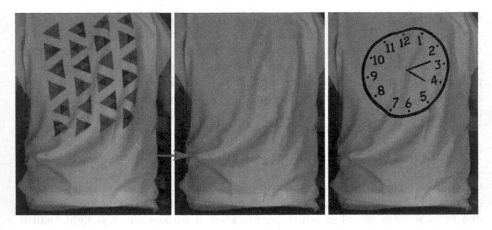

Fig. 2. Lighting cues provide a strong sense of shape — with or without a new texture. **Left**, an image from a video sequence taken directly from our video camera. **Middle**, we remove the texture items by estimating the irradiance and smoothing. **Right**, a retextured image. Notice that irradiance estimates capture shape at two scales: the large folds in the cloth that go through the middle (starting at the arrow, follow the fold up and to the right) and the finer creases.

to a light patch on the shirt resulting in a catastrophically inaccurate irradiance estimate. These errors probably explain why correspondence tracking methods ([9]) do not estimate irradiance or use it to retexture — the correspondence is not pixel accurate, meaning that irradiance estimation would probably fail.

What we do have is an assumption that the clothing pattern is screen-printed, using a small set of highly colored dyes in regions of constant color. In this case, we do not need a formal estimate of irradiance. Instead, at any point in the image, we need an estimate of what the reference (background) color would look like, if it appeared at this point. By taking this view, we avoid difficulties with scaling between pixel values and radiance, for example. We can obtain this estimate in three steps. First, we build a table that indicates, for each of the dyes in the screen print, what the reference color looks like in illumination that produces a given set of image R, G and B values from the dye. Second, at each image pixel, we determine what (if any) dye is present and use the look-up table to estimate the appearance of the reference color at that point. Third, we smooth the resulting field.

2.1   Regressing the Effects of Irradiance

We do not require irradiance: It is sufficient to know what a white patch would look like when a given dye patch has an observed appearance. This information can be obtained by regressing from observations. We build one table for each dye, using the following approach. We use our color classifier (below) to identify pixels from that dye that lie next to pixels produced by white patches. It is reasonable to assume that, if the pixels are sufficiently close, they undergo the same irradiance. We now have a series of examples, linking image RGB of the dye to image RGB of white. The number of examples is enormous; one might have 10^5 or even 10^6 pixel pairs in a given video. However, some examples may be inconsistent, and some image RGB values may have no entry.

We obtain a consistent entry for each image RGB value that occurs by identifying the mode of the examples. We now have a table with some missing entries (where there were no examples). We use a version of Parzen windows to smooth this table by interpolation.

2.2   What Dye Is Present?

We determine which dye is present with a classifier that quantizes the color of each pixel to a pre-determined finite set (determined by the user) based on the pixel's component colors. The classifier is a set of one-vs-all logistic regressions on first and second order powers of RGB and HSV. To classify pixels, the maximal response from the array of classifiers is selected, except when all classifiers respond weakly, in which case the pixel is labeled as ambiguous. We do not attempt to classify pixels close to color boundaries, because blur effects in the camera can lead to classifier errors. At present, we require the user to click on each color to train the classifier, but believe that clustering could remove this step of user intervention.

2.3   Interpolating, Smoothing, and Blending

We now take the pool of relevant pixels, determine what dye is present and do a dye specific table lookup using the RGB values as indices. The result is a representation of what the image would look like at that pixel if the dye had been white. However, this is not available at every pixel — the classifier might refuse to classify or the pixel might be close to a color boundary and dangerous to classify. Missing pixels are interpolated using a Gaussian weight to sum up nearby pixels, with the variance corresponding to the distance to the nearest pixel. Our irradiance estimates often have slight errors in color. Observing that color variations in lighting tend to be low frequency, we heavily smooth the hue and saturation of the recovered irradiance. (Figure 3). Finally, using the domain of the texture map (derived below), we combine our lighting estimate with the original pixels to get a 'blank' surface. We replace pixels in the textured region, blend nearby pixels, then use the original image pixels for the rest of the image (Figure 2).

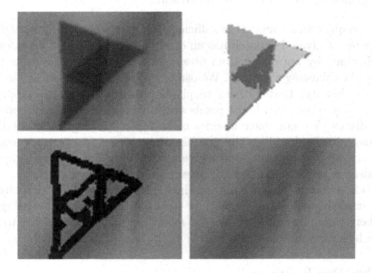

Fig. 3. We estimate lighting for each dye independently, throwing away confusing pixels and boundary regions. **Upper left**, an un-altered image of a triangle in our pattern contains strong lighting cues. However, the boundary regions yield conflicting cues: boundary colors change in somewhat unpredictable ways, hiding the strong lighting cues. **Upper right**, the output of our color classifier, run on a per pixel basis. As noted, colors at edges can be confusing (indicated in gray) or misclassified (notice the blue pixels at the right tip). **Lower left**, after eroding each colored region, we extract lighting cues for each pixel independently. At this stage, there are two problems in our lighting model: gaps in the irradiance estimates and slight chromatic aberrations. In the **lower right**, we interpolate regions using a Gaussian of varying width. To smooth out chromatic aberrations, we convert to HSV and heavily smooth both hue and saturation.

3   Texture Replacement: Computing a Deformation

We need to compute a set of texture coordinates (or, equivalently, material coordinates) from our observed image. There are two possible strategies. First, we could engineer a pattern that worked like a map; it would be easy to determine where a particular color lies in the map, and so we could use the color classifier outputs to determine which point on the map corresponds to a particular pixel in the image. Second, we could — at the expense of less precise estimates of texture coordinates — compare the image to a frontal view of the texture. Both methods are successful.

3.1   Using a Map

We use a custom printed pattern composed of colored triangles to create high quality texture mappings. The pattern is designed to ensure that neighborhoods are unique and easily discriminable. As a result, our method for computing the planar transformation is essentially local: for each region of image, we compute a map to the source image, then stitch together these neighborhoods to compute a complete mapping using nearby transformations to fill in gaps.

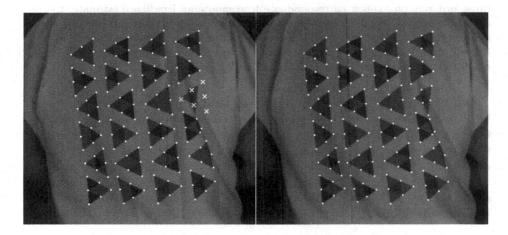

Fig. 4. A custom color-printed pattern provides more accurate deformation models. Our custom pattern is not screen printed, but follows the same model: a discrete number of colors composed in uniform colored blobs. This pattern creates a grid like structure over the image and allows us to track many more points than the deforming models we use on natural textures. Our transformations are computed locally — triangles are individually detected, colors classified, and correspondences computed. Missing correspondences can cause artifacts in video. On the **left** a single triangle is not detected. We interpolate the location of the triangle using a linear estimate based on the locations of the other triangles (shown as white Xs). In the next frame (**right**), the corresponding triangle is detected with a substantially different position — causing a pop in the video sequence.

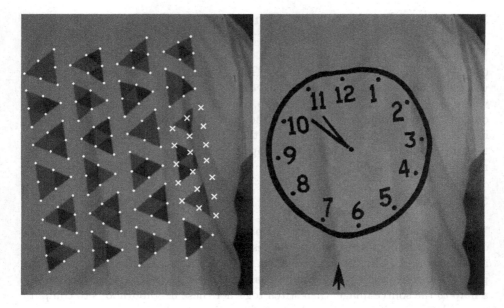

Fig. 5. In some cases, our estimate of the transformation is poor. On the **left**, vertex locations for missed triangles were approximated inaccurately. Because our method **does not** rely on explicit correspondence to compute an irradiance estimate, the reconstructed image on the **right** does not contain obvious artifacts. While the image appears plausible, the re-textured surface is not physically plausible — the texture and lighting cues disagree. Again, we point out that irradiance captures shape at multiple scales: fine creases (follow the black arrow) and larger folds.

Our neighborhood maps are encoded using uniquely colored triangles: we detect triangles independently, use the color to determine the triangle's identity, then use a deformable model to localize the vertices — creating an accurate transformation between domains. When triangles are detected and correspondences computed properly, this process is very accurate: experiments indicate that typical errors are less than a third of a pixel. Figures 4 and 6 show two sample frames with point locations. We now obtain detailed texture coordinates by a bilinear interpolate within each triangle.

3.2 Using Frontal Appearance

While the pattern detection approach in Section 3.1 is compelling, it is somewhat specific to the custom printed pattern. For arbitrary screen print textures, localization becomes a problem. Instead, we adopt a top-down method to fit the texture: first, search for the rough shape (Figure 7) then refine the mapping (Figure 8). We use a triangle mesh to represent the mapping, splitting triangles as the mapping is refined.

This method has several advantages. First, no region of the pattern needs to be particularly discriminative; only the pattern as a whole has to be unique. Second, highly oblique views still exhibit the overall shape and can be detected.

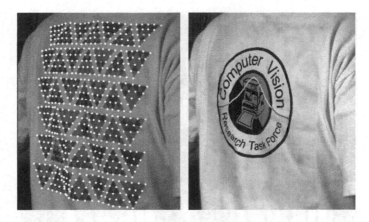

Fig. 6. Specialized patterns make it possible to track very large numbers of points. However, such large numbers are not necessary and can even be slightly detrimental: irradiance estimation becomes difficult because more pixels are classified as edge pixels. In comparison to Figure 2, the irradiance estimates here are visually less accurate.

Fig. 7. Our method requires a frontal view of the texture (**top row**) and a target image (**bottom row**). We quantize the colors using a color classifier, then compute a 4×4 color histogram, with separate bins for each color channel. In this case, with three colors (black, orange and yellow), our descriptor is 4×4×3. We visualize this descriptor by reconstructing the colors and normalizing appropriately (**right**). A search for the descriptor in a subsampled version of the target image reveals the closest match (**bottom right**).

Fig. 8. Our method refines estimates of texture location over scale. Starting with the output of initialization step (figure 7), we have an axis aligned box that corresponds roughly to the location. We use gradient descent on blurred versions of the color quantized image to improve the transformation. Iteratively, we refine the number of vertices (and correspondingly the number of triangles) while reducing the blur to get a better match. Our final model contains only 16 triangles.

Third, edges are powerful cues in this model: they provide a constraint that is not easily recorded using point feature correspondences. Fourth, in contrast to surface energy methods, this method does not have many of the common stiffness properties. However, the disadvantages of a top-down approach are not insignificant: it is not robust to occlusions and subject to local minima. Practically, this means that partial views of the surface may not be retextured properly.

Estimating an Initial Correspondence: Our method of fitting proceeds in two steps: first, estimate the rough location and scale of the logo, then refine the estimate. Because the quantized image has fewer lighting effects, both stages are performed on the output of our color classifier, not the original image. To detect the rough location of the object we use a color histogram with 16 spatial bins (arranged in a 4×4 grid) and the same number of color bins as colors in the texture, resulting in a histogram of size $4 \times 4 \times C$. Following other work with histograms [8], we normalize the values, suppress values above 0.2, then re-normalize. Using the descriptor from the frontal image as a query, we perform a combinatorial search over scale, location and aspect ratio in a downsampled version of the target image.

Refining the Transformation: Once the rough transformation has been computed, we refine over scales (Figure 8). At each stage in the refinement, we implement the same algorithm: blur the color quantized image (giving each quantized color its own channel), then run gradient descent over the locations of the vertices using the sum of squared distances between the transformed frontal texture and the blurred target image. Our model of the transformation is coarse: we start with a 4 vertex 2 triangle model, then refine to 9 vertices and 8 triangles, and finally 13 vertices and 16 triangles.

4   Results and Discussion

We have demonstrated the power of retexturing using irradiance on several videos of deforming non-rigid surfaces, including t-shirts and plastic bags. In general, results using a map are better: large numbers of correspondences provide a better replacement texture (Figures 2 and 9). However, our irradiance estimation is robust — meaning that irradiance estimates are correct even when the texture map is coarse (Figure 10). This is important because irradiance estimates are a powerful cue to surface shape. As a result, denser maps do not provide better estimates of irradiance (Figure 6). Different background colors do not present a problem: we show results on a shirt with a dark albedo as well (Figure 11).

Our results suggest several areas for future work. First, the local method does not interpolate missing triangles well, implying that a hybrid approach may be more effective. Second, our method of interpolating irradiance can be improved: we believe that using texture synthesis could provide more realistic results.

We interpret our results to indicate that surface energy terms may be unnecessary for retexturing. Furthermore, a model that reflects the underlying mechanics poorly can result in significant correspondence errors. A 2D elastic model has difficulty managing the very large apparent strains created by folds and occlusions. However, a model that uses the image data itself (without surface energy), such as the model presented in this paper, is enough to retexture.

Fig. 9. Retexturing is not limited to static images — here we retexture with a ticking clock. (there are 4 frames between each image) On the left, the white arrow points to a strong folds that pierces the middle of the clock — giving a strong cure about surface shape.

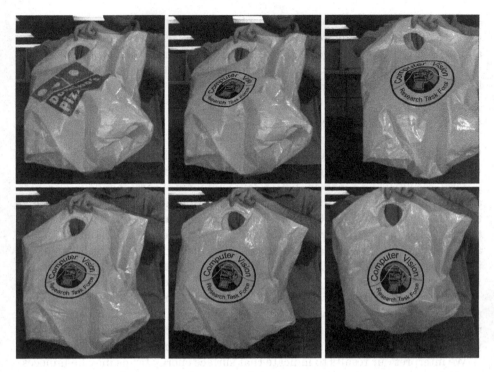

Fig. 10. Retexturing is not limited to clothing. This plastic bag exhibits a significantly different type of motion from textiles. Since our model does not include a surface deformation term, our detection method continues to work well. In addition, our lighting model can even account for the highlights due to specular reflection.

Fig. 11. Dark albedos present a challenge for our irradiance estimation. The range of intensities is smaller and there is more noise. Our irradiance estimates are smooth and have a distinctly different appearance (look closely at the lower left of the logo). However, the rendered surface is also dark, making errors harder to spot.

References

1. Paul Debevec. Rendering synthetic objects into real scenes: Bridging traditional and image-based graphics with global illumination and high dynamic range photography. In *Proceedings of SIGGRAPH 98*, Computer Graphics Proceedings, Annual Conference Series, pages 189–198, July 1998.
2. Hui Fang and John C. Hart. Textureshop: texture synthesis as a photograph editing tool. *ACM Trans. Graph.*, 23(3):354–359, 2004.
3. D.A. Forsyth. Shape from texture without boundaries. In *Proc. ECCV*, volume 3, pages 225–239, 2002.
4. D.A. Forsyth and A.P. Zisserman. Reflections on shading. *IEEE T. Pattern Analysis and Machine Intelligence*, 13(7):671–679, 1991.
5. J. Haddon and D.A. Forsyth. Shading primitives. In *Int. Conf. on Computer Vision*, 1997.
6. J. Haddon and D.A. Forsyth. Shape descriptions from shading primitives. In *European Conference on Computer Vision*, 1998.
7. Anthony Lobay and D.A. Forsyth. Recovering shape and irradiance maps from rich dense texton fields. In *Proceedings of Computer Vision and Pattern Recognition (CVPR)*, 2004.
8. D.G. Lowe. Distinctive image features from scale-invariant keypoints. *IJCV*, 60(2):91–110, November 2004.
9. Julien Pilet, Vincent Lepetit, and Pascal Fua. Real-time non-rigid surface detection. In *The IEEE Conference on Computer Vision and Pattern Recognition (CVPR)*, 2005.
10. Leonid V. Tsap, Dmitry B. Goldgof, and Sudeep Sarkar. Nonrigid motion analysis based on dynamic refinement of finite element models. *IEEE Trans. Pattern Anal. Mach. Intell.*, 22(5):526–543, 2000.
11. Yizhou Yu, Paul Debevec, Jitendra Malik, and Tim Hawkins. Inverse global illumination: Recovering reflectance models of real scenes from photographs from. In Alyn Rockwood, editor, *Siggraph99, Annual Conference Series*, pages 215–224, Los Angeles, 1999. Addison Wesley Longman.
12. Ruo Zhang, Ping-Sing Tsai, James Edwin Cryer, and Mubarak Shah. Shape from shading: A survey. *IEEE Transactions on Pattern Analysis and Machine Intelligence*, 21(8):690–706, 1999.

Feature Points Tracking: Robustness to Specular Highlights and Lighting Changes

Michèle Gouiffès[1], Christophe Collewet[2],
Christine Fernandez-Maloigne[1], and Alain Trémeau[3]

[1] SIC, University of Poitiers, 86962 Futuroscope, France
gouiffes@sic.sp2mi.univ-poitiers.fr
[2] IRISA/INRIA Rennes 35042 Rennes cedex, France
[3] LIGIV, University Jean Monnet 42000 Saint Etienne, France

Abstract. Since the precise modeling of reflection is a difficult task, most feature points trackers assume that objects are lambertian and that no lighting change occurs. To some extent, a few approaches answer these issues by computing an affine photometric model or by achieving a photometric normalization. Through a study based on specular reflection models, we explain explicitly the assumptions on which these techniques are based. Then we propose a tracker that compensates for specular highlights and lighting variations more efficiently when small windows of interest are considered. Experimental results on image sequences prove the robustness and the accuracy of this technique in comparison with the existing trackers. Moreover, the computation time of the tracking is not significantly increased.

1 Introduction

Since many algorithms rely on the accurate computation of correspondences between two frames through an image sequence, feature tracking has proved to be an essential component of vision systems. Indeed, many high level tasks can depend highly on it, such as 3D reconstruction, active vision or visual servoing for example. Nevertheless, robust feature tracking is still a problem to be addressed. It becomes far more complicated when no mark (edges or lines for example), can be extracted from the observed object, such as in natural environment [1]. In such a context, only points, among other possible features, are likely to be easily detectable. However, tracking a point into an image sequence is not a trivial task since the only available information is the luminance of the point and of its neighboring pixels. The seminal works in this domain are due to Lucas and Kanade [5,9] who assume the conservation of the point luminance during the image sequence [3]. The measure of a correlation function between two successive frames determines the translation motion undergone by the point. Thereafter, some more robust tracking approaches have been proposed [8,10]. However, such methods still assume that the luminance remains constant between two successive frames, which is often wrong. Indeed, most surfaces are not Lambertian and lighting conditions are mostly variable during an image sequence. To solve this problem, Hager and Belhumeur [2] acquire an image data

A. Leonardis, H. Bischof, and A. Pinz (Eds.): ECCV 2006, Part IV, LNCS 3954, pp. 82–93, 2006.

base of the scene under several illuminations and use these data to improve the tracking. This method is efficient but requires a prior learning step, which can be seen as too restrictive. An easier way to cope with illumination changes is to achieve a photometric normalization as in [10] for example. In [4], the tracking task compensates for affine illumination changes by computing the contrast and illumination variations during the whole image sequence. These two methods will be detailed in Section 3.

In this paper, we propose a new feature point tracking algorithm, based on the study of reflection models, which is robust to specular highlights occurrence and lighting changes. In addition, we show clearly on which assumptions the approaches mentioned above are based. Besides, we will see that the proposed algorithm provides a more appropriate model of the illumination changes, particularly for specular surfaces.

This article is structured as follows. Section 2 focuses on the modeling of luminance changes, especially in cases of specular reflections and lighting variations. Section 3 details some of the existing tracking approaches: the Shi-Tomasi-Kanade tracker [5,9,8], the normalized one [10] and the tracker with an affine illumination compensation [4]. Thereafter, section 4 describes the proposed tracking method. To finish, section 5 shows experimental results, in order to compare the different tracking techniques according to their robustness and accuracy. In addition, this section will prove the efficiency of our approach.

2   Modeling of Luminance Changes

Suppose f and f' to be respectively the images of an object acquired at two different times. A point P of this object projects in image f to p of coordinates (x_p, y_p) and to p' of coordinates (x'_p, y'_p) in the image f' after a relative motion between the camera and the scene. The luminance at p depends on the scene geometry. Fig.1 describes the vectors and the angles used in this paper. $\mathbf{V}$ and $\mathbf{L}$ are respectively the viewing and the lighting directions, which form the angles θ_r and θ_i with the normal $\mathbf{n}$ in P. $\mathbf{B}$ is the bisecting line between $\mathbf{V}$ and $\mathbf{L}$, it forms an angle ρ with the normal $\mathbf{n}$. According to the most widely used reflection models, such as the Torrance-Sparrow [11] and the Phong [7] ones, the luminance at p can be described as follows

$$f(p) = K_d(p)a(p)\cos\theta_i(P) + h_f(p) + K_a \tag{1}$$

where K_a is the intensity of ambient lighting and K_d a diffuse coefficient corresponding to the direct lighting intensity. These values depend also on the gain of the camera. The term $a(p)$ is related to the *albedo*[1] in P. The function h_f expresses the contribution of the specular reflection, which vanishes in case of a pure diffuse reflection, that is for Lambertian objects. Consequently, with such objects and for a given lighting direction $\mathbf{L}$, the luminance at p remains constant

---

[1] The albedo is the ratio of the amount of light reflected by a small surface in P to the amount of incident light. It depends only on the material and its texture.

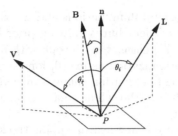

Fig. 1. Vectors and angles involved in the reflection description

whatever the viewing direction **V** is. Phong describes in [7] the specular reflection as a cosine function of ρ

$$h_f(p) = K_s(p) \cos^n(\rho(P)) \tag{2}$$

where n is inversely proportional to the roughness of the surface and K_s is the specular coefficient of the direct lighting. Torrance-Sparrow [11] describes h_f by an exponential function depending on ρ and on the surface roughness ς. For each model, h_f reaches a maximum value for $\rho(P) = 0$, that is when **B** coincides with **n**. Let us also notice that the specular reflection depends on the roughness, the lighting and the viewing directions.

After a relative motion between the camera and the scene, when no lighting change occurs, θ_i, K_d and K_a are constant at P during the time. In the same way, the albedo is constant at P leading to $a(p') = a(p)$. However, the specular component h_f, which depends on the viewing direction, may vary strongly during the motion of the camera. In those conditions, the luminance f' is given by

$$f'(p') = K_d(p)a(p) \cos \theta_i(P) + h_{f'}(p') + K_a \tag{3}$$

where $h_{f'}$ is the specular function.

Now, let us consider that some lighting shifts ΔK_a, ΔK_d and $\Delta \theta_i$ are respectively provoked on K_a, K_d and θ_i. Thus, the luminance can be expressed as

$$f'(p') = K_d'(p)a(p) \cos \theta_i'(P) + K_a' + h_{f'}(p') \tag{4}$$

with $K_d'(p) = K_d(p) + \Delta K_d(p)$, $\theta_i'(P) = \theta_i(P) + \Delta \theta_i(P)$ and $K_a' = K_a + \Delta K_a$. The specular term $h_{f'}(p')$ includes the intensity change of the specular coefficient K_s if necessary. From (4), the next section will clearly show the assumptions on which the most widely used tracking methods are based.

3   Analysis of Existing Tracking Methods According to Their Robustness to Illumination Changes

Let be m a point located in a window of interest $\mathcal{W}$ of size $\mathcal{N} \times \mathcal{N}$ centered around p. Point m is the projection of a physical point M in f and m' is its projection in f'. The tracking process consists in computing a motion model

δ parameterized by a vector $\mathbf{A}$ between f and f'. According to the tracking method, the assumptions about the photometric model are different. By eliminating $a(m)$ between (1) and (4), it yields to the following relationship between two images of the same sequence $f'(m') = \lambda(m)f(m) + \eta(m)$. This relationship is found in [6] in an optical flow context, but λ and η are supposed to be constant locally. According to our analysis based on the reflection models, $\lambda(m)$ and $\eta(m)$ are expressed by:

$$\lambda(m) = \frac{(K_d(m) + \Delta K_d(m))\cos(\theta_i(M) + \Delta\theta_i(M))}{K_d(m)\cos\theta_i(M)} \tag{5}$$

$$\eta(m) = -(h_f(m) + K_a)\lambda(m) + h_{f'}(m') + K_a + \Delta K_a \tag{6}$$

From these relations we deduce the assumptions on which the classical trackers are based.

The classical approach. The classical point feature tracker [5, 9, 8] assumes a perfect conservation of luminance at point M during the sequence: $f'(m') = f(m)$, $\forall m \in \mathcal{W}$ and $\forall\mathcal{W}$. Owing to (5) and (6), that implies $\lambda(m) = 1$ and $\eta(m) = 0$ $\forall m \in \mathcal{W}$, which is correct when no lighting change occurs ($\Delta\theta_i(M) = 0$, $\Delta K_d(m) = 0$ $\forall m \in \mathcal{W}$) and when objects are strictly lambertian ($h_f(m) = h_{f'}(m') = \Delta K_a = 0$, $\forall m \in \mathcal{W}$ and $\forall\mathcal{W}$). Because of noise and because of the strong assumptions considered on the motion and photometric models, it is more suitable to minimize the following criterion

$$\epsilon_1(\mathbf{A}) = \sum_{m \in \mathcal{W}} (f(m) - f'(\delta(m, \mathbf{A})))^2 \tag{7}$$

This approach leads to good results in most cases but can suffer from lighting changes and specular highlights occurrence. In order to cope with this problem, a photometric normalization can be performed.

Use of an affine photometric model. In [4] the authors propose a tracking method in order to compensate for contrast and intensity changes by computing the parameters of the following criterion

$$\epsilon_2(\mathbf{A}, \lambda, \eta) = \sum_{m \in \mathcal{W}} (\lambda f(m) - f'(\delta(m, \mathbf{A})) - \eta)^2. \tag{8}$$

According to (5), $\lambda(m)$ is supposed to be constant at each point of $\mathcal{W}$. That is correct for any surface curvature (and then $\forall\Delta\theta_i$ and $\forall\theta_i$) and for any lighting ($\forall K_d$ and $\forall\Delta K_d$) only if each function $\Delta\theta_i$, θ_i, ΔK_d, K_d is constant in $\mathcal{W}$. Then, it assumes that $\eta(m)$ is constant at each point of $\mathcal{W}$, which is correct for any surface curvature and for any roughness when both $h_{f'}(m)$ and $h_f(m)$ are constant at each point of $\mathcal{W}$.

As a conclusion, this technique assumes that the illumination changes are the same at each point of $\mathcal{W}$. Practically, that can be a coarse assumption when the surface projected onto $\mathcal{W}$ is non planar.

The photometric normalization approach. This approach is based on the minimization of the criterion $\epsilon_2(\mathbf{A})$ except that λ and η are measured at each step of the minimization process instead of being computed simultaneously with the motion parameter $\mathbf{A}$. Their values are $\lambda = \frac{\sigma_{f'}}{\sigma_f}$ and $\eta = \mu_{f'} - \frac{\sigma_{f'}\mu_f}{\sigma_f}$, where μ_f and $\mu_{f'}$ are the average values respectively of f and f' in $\mathcal{W}$ and σ_f, $\sigma_{f'}$ are the standard deviations. λ and η are supposed to be constant at each point m of $\mathcal{W}$, so that the same assumptions as the previous technique hold. Indeed, in those conditions, the values μ_f and σ_f are given by

$$\begin{cases} \mu_f = K_d \cos(\theta_i)\mu_a + K_a + h_f \\ \sigma_f = K_d \cos(\theta_i)\sigma_a \end{cases} \qquad (9)$$

where μ_a is the average value of a and σ_a its standard deviation. Consequently, $f(m) - \mu_f$, $a(m) - \mu_a$ and $f'(m') - \mu_{f'}$ are invariant to highlights occurrence. Finally we show easily that the following ratios are also invariant to ambient and direct lighting changes, and to gain variation

$$(f(m) - \mu_f)/\sigma_f = (a(m) - \mu_a)/\sigma_a = (f'(m') - \mu_{f'})/\sigma_{f'}, \; \forall m \in \mathcal{W}. \qquad (10)$$

Nevertheless, these properties are true only if the specular reflection and the lighting changes are the same at each point of $\mathcal{W}$, as it as been mentioned above. In some cases, these assumptions are not realistic, particularly when W is the projection of a non planar surface of the scene. In addition, these values can be ill-defined when $\sigma_a \approx 0$, that is when the intensities almost saturate or more generally when they are almost homogeneous in $\mathcal{W}$.

Our method is described in the next section. It states the assumption that the illumination changes can be approximated by a continuous function on $\mathcal{W}$.

4   The Proposed Approach

It has been shown in section 2 how each kind of illumination changes can be expressed. By considering (1) and (4), we immediately obtain the relationship between f' and f

$$f'(\delta(m, \mathbf{A})) = f(m) + \psi(m) \qquad (11)$$

In the general case the photometric change is written

$$\begin{aligned} \psi(m) = a(m)(K_d'(m) \cos(\theta_i(M) + \Delta\theta_i(M)) - K_d(m) \cos\theta_i(M)) + \\ h_{f'}(\delta(m, \mathbf{A})) - h_f(m) + \Delta K_a \end{aligned} \qquad (12)$$

When the lighting (or the gain of the camera) does not vary, the total temporal change ψ in the specular component at a fixed scene point m is equal to

$$\psi(m) = h_{f'}(\delta(m, \mathbf{A})) - h_f(m) \qquad (13)$$

According to the most widely used reflection models (see (2) for example), the function ψ is variable on $\mathcal{W}$ since it depends on the viewing and lighting angles and therefore on the normal **n** at each point of $\mathcal{W}$. When lighting changes are caused, it depends also on the albedo. We suppose that this function can be approximated by a continuous and derivable function ϕ on $\mathcal{W}$. In that case, a Taylor series expansion can be performed at m in a neighborhood of p leading to the following expression for $\phi(m)$ by neglecting the higher order terms

$$\phi(m) = \phi(p) + \left.\frac{\partial\phi}{\partial x}\right|_p (x - x_p) + \left.\frac{\partial\phi}{\partial y}\right|_p (y - y_p). \tag{14}$$

Finally, by using (14) in (11) with $m = (x, y)^T$ and noting $\alpha = \left.\frac{\partial\phi}{\partial x}\right|_p$, $\beta = \left.\frac{\partial\phi}{\partial y}\right|_p$ et $\gamma = \phi(p)$, the proposed tracker consists in computing the motion parameter **A** and the reflection parameters $\mathbf{B} = (\alpha, \beta, \gamma)^T$ by minimizing the following criterion:

$$\epsilon_3(\mathbf{A}, \mathbf{B}) = \sum_{m \in \mathcal{W}} \left(f(m) - f'(\delta(m, \mathbf{A})) - \mathbf{U}^T \mathbf{B} \right)^2 \tag{15}$$

where $\mathbf{U} = (x - x_p, y - y_p, 1)^T$. Contrary to the previous approaches, this method does not make assumptions about the scene. In particular, the incident angle θ_i, the viewing angle θ_r, the parameter K_s and the roughness n (or ς) can vary. Therefore, specular highlights and lighting changes can be different at each point of $\mathcal{W}$. However, when lighting changes occur, the method assumes that the values of the albedo can be approximated by a polynomial of first degree in $\mathcal{W}$. Only in that case, the proposed approach is more adapted for small windows of interest $\mathcal{W}$. In the next section, the different tracking methods are compared through experiments.

5   Experimental Results

In the following experiments, the tracking methods are based on the computation of an affine motion model between the first frame and the current one. The tracking algorithm integrates an outlier rejection module, based on the analysis of the residues convergence ϵ_i, $i = 1 \ldots 3$. A point is rejected of the tracking process as soon as its residues become greater than a threshold $S_{conv} = \mathcal{N}^2 E_{ave}^2$, where E_{ave} is the tolerated intensity variation for each point in $\mathcal{W}$ between f and f'. In these experiments, $E_{ave} = 15$. We consider some sizes from $\mathcal{N} = 9$ to $\mathcal{N} = 13$. In each case, the sequence is played from the first image to the last one and then from the last image to the first one, in order to evaluate the symmetry of the residuals and photometric curves. To compare the trackers we compute several criteria: 1) the *robustness* of the tracking, that is to say the number of points that have been tracked during the whole sequence; 2) the *accuracy* of the tracking: we compute the average of the residuals for all the points that have been tracked during the whole sequence by the considered method. This criterion provides information about the relevance of the photometric model. The lower the residues are, the better the illumination variations are compensated for; 3) the reflection parameters α, β and γ, computed by the parametric method. We will also compare the computation time and the conditioning of the matrices

used in the minimization algorithm. Moreover, simulations results compare the
accuracy of the tracking in terms of position estimation. In order to simplify
the explanations of results, we introduce the following notations: C (classical
approach), J (affine model compensation), T (photometric normalization) and
P (proposed approach).

First, the tracking algorithms are tested on scenes showing specular highlights.
For each image sequence, the scene (objects and lighting) is motionless, only the
camera moves. The scenes are lighted by a direct and an ambient lighting.

• **Experiment *Book*.** The first sequence (see Fig. 2a) shows a book. The
motion of the camera leads to specular highlights which appear and disappear
during the sequence. A number of 97 points has been selected in the first frame
but 11 points are lost because they are occluded by the book or because they
get out of the camera field of view. The number of points correctly tracked is

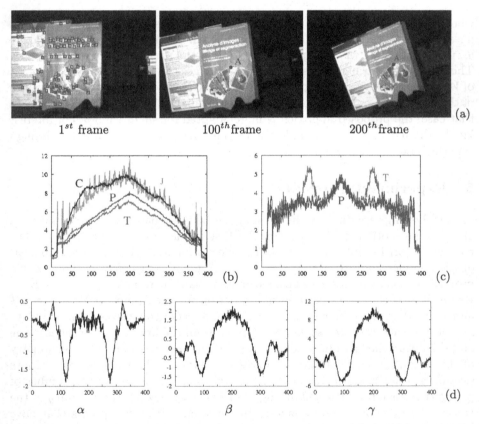

Fig. 2. Experiment *Book* (a) Three images of the sequence. (b) and (c): Residuals
for $\mathcal{N}=9$, (b) is the average of the residual computed on all the points tracked and
(c) the average of the residuals for the points that are correctly tracked by T et P
simultaneously. (d) Illumination parameters computed with the proposed approach.

counted in table 1a. These results prove that the proposed approach (P) is far more robust than the existing ones $(C, J$ and $T)$ since the number of tracked points is always much larger. Fig. 2b compares the average residuals obtained by the trackers during the sequence for $\mathcal{N} = 9$. Until the 100th frame, P obtains the lowest convergence residuals: the proposed photometric model fits best to the specular occurrence. After the 100th frame, the residuals of T become lower than the P ones. However, these values are computed by averaging the residuals of 33 points for T and 68 points for P. In order to compare correctly these two approaches, let us consider Fig. 2c, which shows the average residuals computed only on the few points that are correctly tracked by T and P simultaneously. Here, the residuals are lower for the proposed approach. That shows the good adequacy of the local model proposed to compensate for specular highlights. Let us notice that J is less convincing than T even though these two methods are based on the same photometric assumptions. As it will be shown later on, this is due to the ill-conditioning of J. Fig. 2d depicts the behavior of the photometric parameters that have been computed by P. Let us notice that these curves are perfectly symmetric, in agreement with the symmetry of the sequence and therefore with the symmetry of the illumination changes.

• **Experiment *Marylin*.** The image sequence *Marylin* (see Fig. 3a) shows different specular objects, planar or not, lighted by the daylight and the spotlights of the room. Different types of material are considered (ceramic, glass, glossy paper, metal). This sequence is particularly noisy since the camera used has an interlaced scan mode. Besides, we can see some specular reflections especially on the glass of the photograph. A total number of 56 points has been selected in the first frame, but a large number of points (20 points) is lost because of occlusions and noise. Table 1b collects the number of points that have been tracked until the end of the sequence by each technique. Contrary to the previous sequence, T is less powerful than J, which could mean that T is less robust to noise than J. P tracks a larger number of points in each case. As it can be seen from the residuals obtained on the points that have been tracked by the whole of the approaches (see Fig. 3b), this technique is also more accurate.

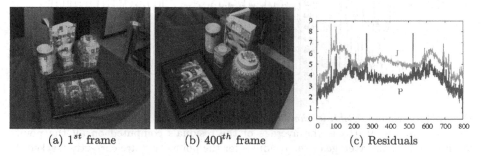

(a) 1st frame   (b) 400th frame   (c) Residuals

Fig. 3. Experiment *Marilyn* (a) and (b) Two images of the sequence. (c) Average of the residuals for $\mathcal{N}=9$ obtained by J and P.

Now, let us compare the techniques on a sequence showing lighting changes.

• **Experiment** *Lighting changes.* The scene consists of a specular planar object lighted by the daylight and by one direct spotlight (see Fig. 4a). Strong variations are produced on the direct lighting intensity since it varies periodically, from a minimum value to a maximum one each 10 frames. Table 1c collects the number of points that have been tracked, on 58 points selected initially. Obviously, the proposed method provides a better robustness of the tracking since the whole of the points are tracked. Fig. 4b shows the average residuals obtained. For this kind of illumination changes, P and T are the most accurate techniques and obtain quite similar residuals. However, Fig. 4c, compares the average residuals computed for the points that have been tracked by the two techniques simultaneously. P gets the lowest residuals. The temporal evolution

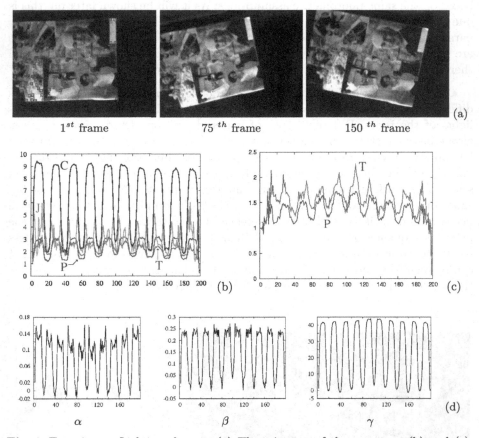

Fig. 4. Experiment *Lighting changes.* (a) Three images of the sequence. (b) and (c) Residuals for $\mathcal{N}=9$, (b) is the average of the residuals computed on all the points tracked and (c) the average of the residuals for the points that are correctly tracked by T et P at the same time. (d) Illumination parameters of point A computed with the proposed method.

of the illumination parameters is depicted on Fig. 4d. Their periodical variations correspond to the lighting changes that have been provoked.

Accuracy of the tracking. In order to evaluate the accuracy of the points positioning, we use a software that simulates the appearence of an object lighted by an ambient light and a direct spotlight, by using a Phong model (see (2)). In the simulated sequence from Fig.5a and 5b, a motionless cylinder is viewed by a moving camera. The direct light is moved, inducing some specular highlights changes. A point is rejected as soon as its error (the euclidian distance between the real position of the point, computed by the software, and its estimated position by the tracker) is greater than 0.5 pixel. 13 points are initially selected, the method C loses 13 points, T 7 points, J 6 points and P loses no point. The figure 5c shows the evolution of the average of positioning errors obtained by each technique. P obtains the lowest errors all along the sequence and the number of points that are correctly tracked is higher.

Discussions. As expected, the classical tracker is not robust neither to specular highlights occurrence nor to lighting variations. A large number of points are lost, sometimes the whole of the points. Obviously, the tracking with photometric normalization and the approach with an affine compensation roughly improve the results. Besides, their efficiency increases for large windows of interest. Indeed, for small windows, the computation of σ_f, σ_g and λ are sensitive to noise. Because these values are multiplied or divided by the luminance values f, an error caused on these parameters have a huge influence, and can yield to the computation of an incorrect motion parameter $\mathbf{A}$. On the other hand, it could seem surprising that J and T behave differently although they are based on the same photometric assumptions. Actually, J suffers from a bad convergence for small windows. As an example, table 2 contains the ratios CN given by the ratio of the Condition Number of the tracker to the Condition Number of the classical tracker (or the T approach since it has the same condition number), computed on 10 points of the sequence *Book* and for different sizes of window. It collects the maximum (Max), the minimum (Min) and the average values (Ave) obtained. These values show clearly that J is less well-conditioned than the other approaches included ours. To finish, the method P tracks a larger number of points than the other methods. It

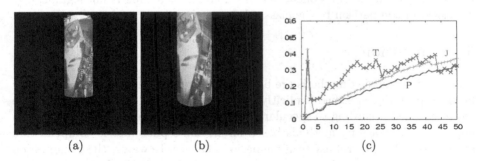

| (a) | (b) | (c) |

Fig. 5. Simulation. (a) and (b) Images of the sequence. (c) Average of the positioning errors (in pixels).

Table 1. Number of points tracked during the whole sequence versus $\mathcal{N}$

(a) *Book* (86 points to track)   (b) *Marylin* (36 points)   (c) *Lighting changes* (58 points)

Tracker	$\mathcal{N}$=9	$\mathcal{N}$=11	$\mathcal{N}$=13
C	27	20	16
T	33	49	53
J	15	25	48
P	68	68	69

Tracker	$\mathcal{N}$=9	$\mathcal{N}$=11	$\mathcal{N}$=13
C	0	0	0
T	1	3	7
J	4	8	15
P	23	21	21

Tracker	$\mathcal{N}$=9	$\mathcal{N}$=11	$\mathcal{N}$=13
C	37	29	23
T	45	51	53
J	39	48	51
P	58	58	58

Table 2. Conditioning number on 10 points selected on sequence *Book*. Maximum (Max), minimum (Min) and average value (Ave).

Tracker	Max	Min	**Ave**
J	9	1	**3.5**
P	2	0.5	**1.4**

really compensates for the variability of specular reflection and lighting variations on $\mathcal{W}$, which proves the relevance of the modeling of ψ by (14). However, let us notice that the difference of performance between the three methods (P, J and T) is less significant when lighting changes are caused than when only specular highlights occur, in particular for large windows of interest. J and T are well adapted to contrast changes, and not to specular highlights, which are generally not constant in $\mathcal{W}$. However, let us note once again that J is less efficient because of its ill-conditioning. The proposed method is perfectly adapted to specular highlights since their variations in $\mathcal{W}$ is well modeled. In case of lighting variations, the albedo must be approximated by a polynomial of first degree. However this approximation is satisfying for small windows of interest.

Up to now, we did not compare the computation time of the methods. For example, in sequence *Book*, the average tracking time of one point is 1.3ms for classical method, 1.7ms for the J technique, 4.6ms for the T one (let us note that the computation of the means and standard deviations are costly) and 1.4ms for our approach [2]. As a conclusion, the computation time is not significantly increased in comparison to the classical approach.

6   Conclusion

The existing tracking methods are based on several assumptions that had never been, or partially, specified explicitly before. In this paper, the analysis of these methods is led according to specular reflection models. Contrary to the classical approach, the tracking methods based on an affine photometric compensation are, to some extent, robust to illumination changes. However, the illumination parameters are assumed to be constant around the point to be tracked. This

---

[2] With a processor Pentium III, 1.8GHz, 512Mo RAM.

can be incorrect when the surfaces are non planar or when specular highlights occur. Our approach overcomes these issues. We assume that an illumination change can be approximated by a continuous and derivable function around the points to be tracked. This model is well adapted for small windows of interest, since it improves the robustness of the tracking against highlights occurrence and lighting changes. The computation duration of this method is not significantly increased in comparison with the classical technique and the accuracy of tracking is improved. In addition, its convergence properties are more satisfying than the technique involving an affine model since better conditioning numbers have been obtained. Our future work will focus on a more appropriate modeling of illumination changes for larger windows of interest.

References

1. F.X. Espiau, E. Malis, and P. Rives. Robust features tracking for robotic applications: towards 2d1/2 visual servoing with natural images. In *IEEE Int. Conf. on Robotics and Automation, ICRA'2002*, Washington, USA, May 2002.
2. G. D. Hager and P. N. Belhumeur. Efficient region tracking with parametric models of geometry and illumination. *IEEE Trans. on Pattern Analysis and Machine Intelligence*, 20(10):1025–1039, 1998.
3. K.P. Horn and B. G. Schunck. Determinig optical flow. *Artificial Intelligence*, 7:185–203, 1981.
4. H. Jin, S. Soatto, and P. Favaro. Real-time feature tracking and outlier rejection with changes in illumination. In *IEEE Int. Conf. on Computer Vision*, pages 684–689, Vancouver, Canada, July 9-12, 2001.
5. B.D. Lucas and T. Kanade. An iterative image registration technique. In *IJCAI'81*, pages 674–679, Vancouver, British Columbia, August 1981.
6. S. Negahdaripour. Revised definition of optical flow:integration of radiometric and geometric cues for dynamic scene analysis. *IEEE Transactions on Pattern Analysis and Machine Intelligence*, 20(9):961 – 979, September 1998.
7. B-T Phong. Illumination for computer generated images. *Communications of the ACM*, 18(6):311–317, June 1975.
8. J. Shi and C. Tomasi. Good features to track. In *IEEE Int. Conf. on Computer Vision and Pattern Recognition, CVPR'94*, pages 593–600, Seattle, Washington, USA, June 1994.
9. C. Tomasi and T. Kanade. Detection and tracking of point features. Technical report CMU-CS-91-132, Carnegie Mellon University, April 1991.
10. T. Tommasini, A. Fusiello, E. Trucco, and V. Roberto. Improving feature tracking with robust statistics. *Pattern Analysis & Applications*, 2:312–320, 1999.
11. K.E. Torrance and E.M. Sparrow. Theory for off-specular reflection from roughened surfaces. *Journal of the Optical Society of America*, 57(9), September 1967.

A General Framework for Motion Segmentation: Independent, Articulated, Rigid, Non-rigid, Degenerate and Non-degenerate*

Jingyu Yan and Marc Pollefeys

Department of Computer Science,
The University of North Carolina at Chapel Hill,
Chapel Hill, NC 27599
{yan, marc}@cs.unc.edu

Abstract. We cast the problem of motion segmentation of feature trajectories as linear manifold finding problems and propose a general framework for motion segmentation under affine projections which utilizes two properties of trajectory data: geometric constraint and locality. The geometric constraint states that the trajectories of the same motion lie in a low dimensional linear manifold and different motions result in different linear manifolds; locality, by which we mean in a transformed space a data and its neighbors tend to lie in the same linear manifold, provides a cue for efficient estimation of these manifolds. Our algorithm estimates a number of linear manifolds, whose dimensions are unknown beforehand, and segment the trajectories accordingly. It first transforms and normalizes the trajectories; secondly, for each trajectory it estimates a local linear manifold through local sampling; then it derives the affinity matrix based on principal subspace angles between these estimated linear manifolds; at last, spectral clustering is applied to the matrix and gives the segmentation result. Our algorithm is general without restriction on the number of linear manifolds and without prior knowledge of the dimensions of the linear manifolds. We demonstrate in our experiments that it can segment a wide range of motions including independent, articulated, rigid, non-rigid, degenerate, non-degenerate or any combination of them. In some highly challenging cases where other state-of-the-art motion segmentation algorithms may fail, our algorithm gives expected results.

1 Introduction

Motion segmentation of trajectory data has been an essential issue in understanding and reconstructing dynamic scenes. Dynamic scene consists of multiple moving objects with a static or moving camera. The objective is to segment the feature trajectories according to the motions in the scene.

Ever since Tomasi and Kanade[17] introduced the factorization method based on the idea that trajectories of a general rigid motion under affine projection

* The support of the NSF ITR grant IIS-0313047 is gratefully acknowledged.

A. Leonardis, H. Bischof, and A. Pinz (Eds.): ECCV 2006, Part IV, LNCS 3954, pp. 94–106, 2006.
© Springer-Verlag Berlin Heidelberg 2006

span a 4-dimensional linear manifold, this geometric constraint has been used extensively in motion segmentation, especially for independently moving objects whose trajectories have a nice property that they are from independent subspaces. Most notably, Costeria and Kanade[2] constructs a shape interaction matrix from this fact and uses the zero product between independent trajectories as a segmentation criteria. More recently, Yan and Pollefeys[21], Tresadern and Reid[22] studied articulated motions, another paradigm of dynamic scenes, and drew a conclusion that the motions of linked parts are dependent and their subspaces are intersecting on 1 or 2 dimensions depending on whether the link is a joint or an axis. Besides rigid motions, Bregler et al.[3] and Brand[4] showed that non-rigid motions like human facial motion etc. can be approximated using a higher dimensional linear subspace.

To sum up, motion segmentation of a dynamic scene that consists of multiple motions, either independent, articulated, rigid, non-rigid, degenerate or non-degenerate, can be casted as a linear manifold finding problem. The challenges are from the unknowns like dimensionality and dependency of these linear manifolds.

We propose a general framework for motion segmentation under affine projections. Our algorithm estimates a number of linear manifolds of different dimensions and segment the trajectories accordingly. It first estimates a local linear manifold for each trajectory by local sampling; then it derives an affinity matrix based on principal angles between each pair of estimated linear manifolds; spectral clustering is then applied to the matrix and segments the data. Our algorithm is general without restriction on the number of linear manifolds or their dimensionalities. So it can segment a wide range of motions including independent, articulated, rigid, non-rigid, degenerate, non-degenerate or any combination of them.

Due to the large volume of works of motion segmentation, we need to draw the distinction between our work and the previous ones. Most of the previous works assume independency between motion subspaces (Boult and Brown [8], Gear[9], Costeria and Kanade[2], Kanatani[11], Ichimura[10]) while our goal is to deal with a mixture of dependent and independent motions in a unified way.

Zelnik-Manor and Irani[12] addresses the dependency problem between motion subspaces and deals with it using a method with the same nature as [2] but an elevated perspective from Weiss[14] to derive an affinity matrix, followed by the technique of [11] to separate the dependent motions. In their case, the angle between every pair of vectors, expressed by a dot product, are used as the affinity measurement. However, unlike the independent motion subspace cases, angles, or any other distance measurement between the data, do not reflect the true geometric constraints, the subspace constraints, that we use to segment the data. Instead, our method uses the distance between two locally estimated subspaces of each data, expressed by subspace principal angles, as the affinity measurement. This new affinity measurement reflects the true nature of the constraint for segmentation and leads to more accurate results, which is confirmed by our experiments.

Vidal et al.[18][19][20] propose an algebraic framework called GPCA that can deal with dependent and independent subspaces with unknown dimensionality uniformly. It models a subspace as a set of linear polynomials and a mixture of n subspaces as a set of polynomials of degree n. Given enough sample points in the mixture of subspaces, the coefficients of these high degree polynomials can be estimated. By differentiating at each data point, the normals of each data can be estimated. Then it also uses standard methods like principal angles and spectral clustering to segment the data. However, because GPCA first brings the problem to a high degree nonlinear space and then solves it linearly, the number of sample points required by GPCA to estimate the polynomial coefficients becomes its Achilles' heel, which grows exponentially with the number of subspaces and the dimensions ($\bigcirc((d+1)^n)$, d is the dimension of the largest underlying subspace and n is the number of subspaces). In practice, the number of trajectories can hardly satisfy GPCA's requirement for it to handle more than 3 subspaces. And for non-rigid motion subspaces whose dimensions are more than 4, the situation gets even worse. Our method requires $\bigcirc(d \times n)$ trajectories which makes it practical to handle not only multiple motions but also non-rigid motions that have a higher dimension.

Our approach has not been attempted in motion segmentation. Under a different context [13] uses local sampling and clustering to identify discrete-time hybrid systems in piecewise affine form. We need to point out the differences: first, motion data is not in piecewise form; second, the first step of our approach that projects motion data onto a sphere is important in order to "localize" data of the same underlying subspace while [13] assumes that the data is piecewise beforehand. Our approach is motivated and derived independently, specifically aiming at motion segmentation.

The following sections are organized as followed: Section 2, detailed discussion of motion subspaces of all kinds; Section 3, the algorithm and its analysis; Section 4, experimental results; Section 5, conclusions and future work.

2   The Motion Subspaces

We are going to show that the trajectories of different kinds of motions lie in some low-dimensional linear manifolds under affine projection which models weak and paraperspective projection.

- For rigid motions, the trajectories of a rigid object forms a linear subspace of dimensions no more than 4 ([17]).

$$M_{2f \times p} = [R_{2f \times 3} | T_{2f \times 1}] \begin{bmatrix} S_{3 \times p} \\ 1_{1 \times p} \end{bmatrix} \tag{1}$$

f is the number of frames and p, the number of feature trajectories.
- For independent motions, $[R_i | T_i]$ is independent for each motion i, so each motion $M_i = [R_i | T_i] \begin{bmatrix} S_i \\ 1 \end{bmatrix}$ lies in an independent linear subspace of dimension no more than 4 ([2]).

– For articulated motions ([21][22]),
  • If the link is a joint, $[R_1|T_1]$ and $[R_2|T_2]$ must have $T_1 = T_2$ under the same coordinate system. So M_1 and M_2 lie in different linear subspaces but have 1-dimensional intersection.
  • If the link is an axis, $[R_1|T_1]$ and $[R_2|T_2]$ must have $T_1 = T_2$ and exactly one column of R_1 and R_2 being the same under a proper coordinate system. So M_1 and M_2 lie in different linear subspaces but have 2-dimensional intersection.
– The trajectories of a non-rigid object can be approximated by different weighings of a number of key shapes ([3][4][5]) and, as shown below, lie in a linear subspace of dimension no more than $3k + 1$.

$$M = \begin{bmatrix} c_1^1 R_{2\times3}^1|...|c_k^1 R_{2\times3}^1|T_{2\times1}^1 \\ ... \\ c_1^f R_{2\times3}^f|...|c_k^f R_{2\times3}^f|T_{2\times1}^f \end{bmatrix} \begin{bmatrix} S_{3\times1}^1 \\ ... \\ S_{3\times p}^k \\ 1_{1\times p} \end{bmatrix} \tag{2}$$

$c_j^i \ (1 \leq i \leq f, 1 \leq j \leq k).$

To sum up, the trajectories of a mixture of motions lie in a mixture of linear manifolds of different dimensions. If we can estimate these underlying linear manifolds accurately enough, we can segment the trajectories accordingly.

3   The Algorithm

In this section, we first outline our algorithm and discuss the details of each step. In the end, we will discuss the issue of outliers.

Our algorithm first transforms the trajectory data; then it estimates a local linear manifold for each trajectory by local sampling; it derives an affinity matrix based on principal subspace angles between each pair of local linear manifolds; spectral clustering is applied to the matrix and gives the segmentation result.

3.1   Motion Data Transformation

Given a motion matrix $W_{2f\times p}$, decompose W into $U_{2f\times K}, D_{K\times K}$ and $V_{K\times p}^T$ by SVD, assuming $rank(W)$ is K (A practical algorithm for rank detection is described in (Section 3.5)). Normalize each column of $V(:, 1:K)^T$. Each column unit vector $v_i(i = 1...p)$ becomes the new representation of the corresponding trajectory.

This transformation is an operator that projects a $\mathbf{R^{2f}}$ vector w_i(the ith column of W) onto the $\mathbf{R^K}$ unit sphere which preserves the subspace property, which is that any subset of $w_i(i = 1...p)$ spans a subspace of the same rank of the corresponding subset of $v_i(i = 1...p)$.

The purposes of transforming the trajectories into a unit sphere are:

– Dimension reduction. Notice each trajectory is a $2f \times 1$ vector. Most of the dimensions are redundant and can be effectively reduced by linear transformations.

- Normalization of the data.
- Preparation for the local sampling in the next step. Locality of trajectory data in our algorithm is not defined in the image coordinate space, i.e. proximity in images, but defined on the sphere which has simple geometric meanings.

We are going to perform the segmentation on these unit vectors. It is equivalent to state that we are trying to find a set of R^t spheres $(1 \leq t < K)$ whose union is the R^K sphere. And each vector is grouped according to this set of spheres unless it lies at the intersection of some spheres, in which case it can be grouped to either of these intersecting spheres (Fig. 1).

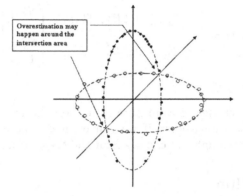

Fig. 1. There are two underlying subspaces of dimension 2 for the data which are transformed onto the $\mathbf{R^3}$ unit sphere. The empty dots represent a group of transformed data belonging to one subspace and the black dots represent another. Due to noise, the dots may not lie exactly on the $\mathbf{R^2}$ spheres. And the intersection area is where "overestimation" may happen, by which we mean that local sampling results in a local subspace estimation that crosses different underlying subspaces.

3.2   Subspace Estimation by Local Sampling

In the transformed space (e.g. see Fig. 1), most points and their closest neighbors lie on the same underlying subspace, which allows us to estimate the underlying subspace of a point α by local samples from itself and its n closest neighbors, i.e. computing the subspace of $[\alpha, \alpha_1, ..., \alpha_n]_{K \times (n+1)}$. This can be easily achieved using SVD (See Section 3.5 for rank detection). Because all the points lie in a $\mathbf{R^K}$ unit sphere, we can use either the Euclidean distance $\|\alpha - \beta\|_2 \in [0, 2]$ or the angle $\arccos(\alpha^T \beta \in [0, \pi]$ to find the n closest neighbors. Our algorithm is not very sensitive to the choice of n as long as $n + 1$ must not be less than the dimension of its underlying subspace.

Two naturally raised questions: what happens to a point near an intersection of subspaces, whose neighbors are from different subspaces (Fig. 1). Secondly, what if a point and its n neighbors do not span the whole underlying subspace? We will discuss these two important situations in the following section after introducing the concept of distance between subspaces.

The subspace constraint of the points is a reliable geometric property for segmentation while the "distance" between the points is not. Most previous works, e.g. [2][10][11][12], use the dot product of the trajectories or some normalized form as the affinity measurement for clustering. The dot product actually measures the angle between the trajectories and is a "distance" in essence. They assume that points of the same subspace are closer in "distance". This assumption mostly stems from works for independent motions [2], in which the dot product is always 0. But for dependent motions whose subspaces intersect like in Fig. 1, this assumption is invalid. Our affinity definition, which is the distance between two local estimated subspaces described by principal angles in the next section, reliably base the segmentation on the criteria of subspace constraint that the points conform to.

3.3 Principal Angles Between Local Subspaces

The distance between two subspaces can be measured by principal angles. The principal angles between two subspaces P and Q are defined recursively as a series of angles $0 \leq \theta_1 \leq,...,\leq \theta_M \leq \pi/2$ (M is the minimum of the dimensions of P and Q):

$$\cos(\theta_m) = max_{u \in S^1, v \in S^2} u^T v = u_m^T v_m$$

where

$$\|u\| = \|v\| = 1$$
$$u^T u_i = 0 \quad i = 1,...,m-1$$
$$v^T v_i = 0 \quad i = 1,...,m-1$$

We define the affinity of two points, α and β, as the distance between their estimated local subspaces denoted $S(\alpha)$ and $S(\beta)$.

$$a(\alpha, \beta) = e^{-\sum_{i=1,...,M} sin^2(\theta_i)}$$

where $\theta_1,...,\theta_M$ are the principal angles. Thus, we can build an affinity matrix for spectral clustering described in the following section.

Before we proceed to the next section, let us take a closer look at the two scenarios pointed out at the end of Section 3.2.

– When an estimated local subspace crosses different underlying subspaces, which happens to points near an intersection as shown in Fig. 1 (this usually happens to the trajectories of features very close to or at an articulated axis or joint), we call this estimation "overestimated". An overestimated subspace is usually distanced from the underlying subspaces that it crosses because it has dimensions from other underlying subspace(s). However, points near an intersection are usually small in amount compared to the total. So overestimated subspaces do not have a dominant effect for clustering. Besides, which cluster a point near an intersection may be classified to relies on which underlying subspaces have a larger portion of its overestimated subspace. So in the end it tends to cluster the point to its real underlying subspace. If not, it results in a misclassification. Our experiments show that if there are misclassifications, mostly it happens to points that are close to an intersection.

– When the estimated local subspace is a subspace of the underlying subspace, we call this estimation "underestimated" since it only estimates a part of it. This occurs when the local neighbors may not span the whole underlying subspace. However, this will not affect the effectiveness of the segmentation introduced in the following section. To explain why, we use an example in rigid motions and allow other cases. Suppose two underlying subspaces of dimension 4 having a 2-dimension intersection. This happens when two articulated parts are linked by an axis [21][22]. The total dimension is 6. The two underlying subspaces, S^1 and S^2, and their underestimated subspaces, A, B, C and D, E, F, of dimension 3 (2 is rare because the features corresponding to the point and its neighbors need to be exactly on a line for that to happen) are as follows.

Subspace \ Dimensions	1	2	3	4	5	6
S^1		X	X	X	X	
A		X	X	X		
B			X	X	X	
C		X		X	X	
S^2				X	X	X X
D				X	X	X
E					X	X X
F				X		X X

$$(3)$$

The number of non-zero principal angles between these subspaces and their underestimated subspaces are shown as follows.

Subspaces	S^1	A	B	C	S^2	D	E	F
S^1	0	0	0	0	2	1	2	2
A	0	0	1	1	2	2	3	2
B	0	1	0	1	1	1	2	2
C	0	1	1	0	1	1	2	2
S^2	2	2	1	1	0	0	0	0
D	1	2	1	1	0	0	1	1
E	2	3	2	2	0	1	0	1
F	2	2	2	2	0	1	1	0

$$(4)$$

Generally, intra-subspaces have smaller number of non-zero principal angles compared to inter-subspaces. So expectedly, an underestimated subspace tends to be closer to all possible estimated subspaces of its underlying subspace than to those of another underlying subspace.

3.4   Spectral Clustering

We can apply spectral clustering, e.g.[16][15], to the affinity matrix and retrieve N clusters. We advocate recursive 2-way clustering detailed in [16]. Thus we can re-estimate the local subspaces within the current clusters so that points belonging to different clusters will not affect each other any more. Secondly, recursive 2-way clustering gives a more stable result because k-way clustering like [15] depends on k-means which in turn depends on some random initialization. The recursive 2-way clustering is as follows, given N is the total number of underlying subspaces:

- Compute the affinity matrix using the approach in Section 3.2 and 3.3 above and segment the data into two clusters $\{C_1, C_2\}$ by spectral clustering.
- While $NumOfClusters\{C_1, ..., C_n\} < N$, compute the affinity matrix for each cluster C_i ($i = 1, ..., n$) from the points within the cluster; divide C_i into two clusters, C_i^1 and C_i^2; evaluate the Cheeger constant[15] of each pair of C_i^1 and C_i^2 and decide the best subdivision, C_J^1 and C_J^2 ($1 \leq J \leq n$); replace C_J with them.

3.5   Effective Rank Detection

In practice, a data matrix may be corrupted by noise or outliers and thus has a higher rank. We may use a model selection algorithm inspired by a similar one in [20] to detect an effective rank.

$$r_n = \arg \min_r \frac{\lambda_{r+1}^2}{\sum_{k=1}^r \lambda_k^2} + \kappa\, r$$

with λ_i, the ith singular value of the matrix, and κ, a parameter. If the sum of all λ_i^2 is below a certain threshold, the effective rank is 0. The higher the noise level is, the larger κ we should set.

For rank detection of local estimated subspaces, due to small number of samples, noise level is higher, so we prefer a larger κ.

3.6   Outliers

In practice, the trajectories may have some outliers. We are going to discuss their effects under the context of our algorithm.

First of all, an outlier will be classified to one of the segments, which depends on its locally estimated subspace. We suggest that outliers can be better dealt with after the segmentation because the segmented subspace offers less freedom for outliers and makes it easier to detect and reject them.

Second, an outlier will corrupt the estimation of local subspaces of a nearby point. However, this bad effect will not propagate under our algorithm and only remains on those points whose neighbors include the outlier. Misclassification may happen to these points. But as long as the outliers are not dominant in number, our algorithm is robust.

4   Experiments

We test our approach in various real dynamical scenes with 2 to 6 motions and a combination of independent, articulated, rigid, non-rigid, degenerate and non-degenerate motions.

For the experiments, we choose $\kappa = 10^{-6}$ to 10^{-5} for trajectory rank estimation depending on the noise level of the trajectories, and $\kappa = 10^{-3}$ for local subspace rank estimation (See Section 3.5 for more detail). We let $n = d$ where n is the number of neighbors for local sampling and d is the highest possible dimension of the underlying subspaces. That is 4 for rigid motions and 7 for non-rigid motions in our experiments.

Miscalssification errors vs. total number of trajectories and the number of outliers vs. total number of trajectories for the experiments is summaried in Table 1. Outliers may be clustered to any segments and are not counted as misclassification errors.

Table 1. A comparison between our method, GPCA and trajectory angle based method

Experiment	Our Method	GPCA	Angle based	Outliers
Truck	0/83	5/83	16/83	0/83
Head and Body	1/99	10/99	9/99	6/83
Booklet	0/38	2/38	2/38	1/38
Two bulldozers	1/94	4/94	24/94	8/94
One bulldozers	4/85	6/85	11/85	9/85
Dancing	21/268	not enough samples[1]	78/268	7/268

The first experiment is from a scene with non-degenerate data of an articulated object with a rotating axis. The detected rank of the trajectories is 6. The segmentation result is shown in Fig. 2. The ranks of the segmented trajectories are both 4.

The second experiment is from a scene of 2 non-degenerate motions of an articulated body with a joint. The detected rank of the trajectories is 7. There are one misclassification, the red dot on the left shoulder. The other red dot on the left arm is an outlier. The segmentation result is shown in Fig. 3. The ranks of the segmented trajectories are both 4.

The third experiment is from a scene of 2 degenerate shapes of an articulated object. Two pages of a booklet is being opened and closed. The detected rank of the trajectories is 4. The segmentation result is shown in Fig. 4. The ranks of the segmented trajectories are both 3.

---

[1] For the last experiment of 6 motions, GPCA requires a huge number of trajectories for it to work. Roughly, it needs $O((d+1)^6)$. d is the dimension of the largest subspace. For non-degenerate rigid motions, $d = 5$ [18]; for non-rigid motions, d is even larger. That many number of trajectories are normally not available in practice.

Fig. 2. (*left and middle*) A sequence of a truck moving with the shovel rotating around an axis. The color of a dot, red or green, shows the segmentation result. (*right*) The affinity matrix of local estimated subspaces is shown. The row and columns are rearranged based on the segmentation.

Fig. 3. (*left and middle*) A sequence of a person moving with his head rotating around the neck. The color of a dot, red or green, shows the segmentation result. There is one misclassification, the red dot on the left shoulder. The other red dot on the left arm is an outlier. (*right*) The affinity matrix of locally estimated subspaces is shown. The row and columns are rearranged based on the segmentation.

Fig. 4. (*left and middle*) A sequence of a booklet whose two pages are being opened and closed around an axis. The color of a dot, red or green, shows the segmentation result. There is no misclassification error. The green dot on the rotating axis can be grouped to either page. (*right*) The affinity matrix of local estimated subspaces is shown. The row and columns are rearranged based on the segmentation.

The fourth experiment has 3 motions. It comes from a scene of 2 independently moving bulldozers, one of which has an articulated arm rotating around an axis. Only the side of the articulated arm can be seen so it is a degenerate shape. The detected rank of the trajectories is 8 before the first segmentation. Both of the segments have rank 4. The next subdivision is automatically detected (See Section 3.4) for points from the right bulldozer and the segmented trajectories are of rank 3. The segmentation result is shown in Fig. 5.

The fifth experiment has **3** motions. It comes from a scene with an articulated object of 3 parts. The bulldozer has its forearm and upper-arm moving articulately rotating around two axes. The detected rank of the trajectories is 6 before

Fig. 5. (*left 2*)A sequence of two bulldozers moving independently, one of which moves articulately with its arm rotating around an axis. The color of a dot, red, blue or yellow, shows the segmentation result. There is one misclassification error which is the red dot on the forearm near the axis. Besides that, there are several outliers. (*right 2*) The affinity matrices for 2-stage segmentations are shown. The row and columns are rearranged based on the segmentation.

Fig. 6. A sequence of a bulldozer with its upper-arm and forearm moving articulately around some axis. The color of a dot, red, blue or yellow, shows the segmentation result. There are 4 misclassification errors. Two are the yellow dots on the forearm and two are the red dots on the upper-arm. All of them are near the axis connecting both arms. Besides these, there are several outliers in the trajectories and they are clustered to one of the segments.

Fig. 7. (*top*) A sequence of a person dancing with his upper body, his head and both of his upper arms and forearms moving. His mouth motion is non-rigid. The color of a dot shows the segmentation result. Besides outliers, there are about 8% misclassifications.

the first segmentation. The segmented trajectories have a rank 3 and 4. The rank-4 cluster gets subdivided into 2 rank-3 clusters. There are outliers in this experiment. They have been clustered to one of the segments. Besides outliers, there are 4 misclassifications, two of which are the yellow dots on the forearm and two of which are the red dots on the upper-arm and all of which are near the axis. The segmentation result is shown in Fig. 6.

The final experiment has 6 motions. It comes from a scene with a person dancing with his upper body, his head and both of his upper arms and forearms moving. Besides, his mouth movement generates a non-rigid motion. This is a highly challenging case not only because of the total number of motions but also because of the dependency between these articulated motions and the non-rigid kind of motion on the person's face. The detected rank of the trajectories is 12 before the first segmentation. Both of the segmented rank-7 and rank-6 clusters get subdivided into rank-6 and -3 clusters, and rank-4 and -3 clusters repectively. In the end, the rank-4 cluster gets subdivided into two rank-3 subspaces. There are outliers and there are about 8% misclassifications, most of which are near the articulated axes or joints. Interestingly, the green dots on the head are those features not turning as the head turns. Instead, they move like the features on the upper body. And indeed, our algorithm classifies them to those features on the upper body. A second interesting observation is the misclassification of the dark blue dots near the joint between the body and the person's right arm. Though they are far away from the left upper arm of the person, they are actually very close to the intersection between the motion subspaces of the left and right upper arms because they both are linked to the body. The segmentation result is shown in Fig. 7.

4.1 Comparisons

We compare our method with GPCA[18] and trajectory angle based approach, e.g. [12] except for that we use spectral clustering to segment the affinity matrix (Table 1). The numbers in the table are misclassification errors vs. the total number of trajectories and outliers vs. trajectories. Outliers are not counted as misclassification.

5 Conclusions and Future Work

We propose a general framework for motion segmentation of a wide range of motions including independent, articulated, rigid, non-rigid, degenerate and non-degenerate. It is based on local estimation of the subspace to which a trajectory belongs through local sampling and spectral clustering of the affinity matrix of the these subspaces. We demonstrate our approach in various situations. In some highly challenging cases where other state-of-the-art motion segmentation algorithms may fail, our algorithm gives expected results.

We plan to reconstruct complex dynamical scenes with a variety of objects and motions. An especially interesting case is human motion. Our algorithm can provide a good initialization for a follow-up EM algorithm to improve the segmentation and reject outliers.

References

1. M. A. Fischler, R. C. Bolles. Random Sample Consensus: A Paradigm for Model Fitting with Applications to Image Analysis and Automated Cartography. Comm. of the ACM, Vol 24, pp 381-395, 1981.
2. J.P. Costeira, T. Kanade, "A Multibody Factorization Method for Independently Moving Objects", *IJCV*, Vol. 29, Issue 3 pp. 159-179, 1998.

3. C. Bregler, A. Hertzmann, H. Biermann, "Recovering Non-Rigid 3D Shape from Image Streams", Proceedings of the IEEE Conference on Computer Vision and Pattern Recognition (CVPR '00), June 2000.
4. M. Brand, "Morphable 3D models from video", CVPR, pp. II:456-463, 2001.
5. J. Xiao, J. Chai, and T. Kanade, "A closed-form solution to non-rigid shape and motion recovery", Proceedings of the European Conference on Computer Vision, 2004.
6. Ullman, S. 1983. Maximizing rigidity: The incremental recovery of 3D structure from rigid and rubbery motion. Technical Report A.I. Memo No. 721, MIT.
7. Sinclair, D. 1993. Motion segmentation and local structure. In Proceedings of the 4th International Conference on Computer Vision.
8. Boult, T. and Brown, L. 1991. Factorization-based segmentation of motions. In Proceedings of the IEEE Workshop on Visual Motion.
9. Gear, C.W. 1994. Feature grouping in moving objects. In Proceedings of the Workshop on Motion of Non-Rigid and Articulated Objects, Austin, Texas
10. N. Ichimura. Motion segmentation based on factorization method and discriminant criterion. In Proc. IEEE Int. Conf. Computer Vision, pages 600605, 1999.
11. K. Kanatani. Motion segmentation by subspace separation and model selection:model selection and reliability evaluation. Intl. J. of Image and Graphics, 2(2):179197, 2002.
12. L. Zelnik-Manor and M. Irani. Degeneracies, dependencies and their implications in multi-body and multi-sequence factorizations. In Proc. IEEE Computer Vision and Pattern Recognition, 2003.
13. G. Ferrari-Trecate, M. Muselli, D. Liberati, and M. Morari. A clustering technique for the identification of piecewise affine and hybrid systems. Automatica, 39:205–217, 2003.
14. Y. Weiss. Segmentation using eigenvectors: A unifying view. In International Conference on Computer Vision, pages 975982, Corfu, Greece, September 1999.
15. A. Ng, M. Jordan, and Y. Weiss. On spectral clustering: analysis and an algorithm. In Advances in Neural Information Processing Systems 14. MIT Press, 2002.
16. J. Shi and J. Malik, Normalized Cuts and Image Segmentation, IEEE Transactions on Pattern Analysis and Machine Intelligence (PAMI), 2000.
17. C. Tomasi, T. Kanade, "Shape and motion from image streams under orthography: a factorization method", IJCV, Vol. 9, Issue 2 pp. 137-154, 1992.
18. R. Vidal and R. Hartley. Motion Segmentation with Missing Data using PowerFactorization and GPCA. IEEE Conference on Computer Vision and Pattern Recognition, 2004
19. R. Vidal, Y. Ma and S. Sastry, "Generalized Principal Component Analysis (GPCA) ", Proceedings of the IEEE Conference on Computer Vision and Pattern Recognition (CVPR'03), June 2003.
20. R. Vidal, Y. Ma and J. Piazzi, "A New GPCA Algorithm for Clustering Subspaces by Fitting, Differentiating and Dividing Polynomials", Proceedings of the IEEE Conference on Computer Vision and Pattern Recognition (CVPR'04), June 27 - July 02, 2004.
21. J. Yan, M. Pollefeys, A Factorization-based Approach to Articulated Motion Recovery, IEEE Conf. on Computer Vision and Pattern Recognition, 2005
22. P. Tresadern and I. Reid, Articulated Structure From Motion by Factorization, Proc IEEE Conf on Computer Vision and Pattern Recognition, 2005
23. Multiple View Geometry in Computer Vision, Richard Hartley and Andrew Zisserman, Cambridge University Press, 2002
24. G. Golub and A. van Loan. Matrix Computations. Johns Hopkins U. Press, 1996

Robust Visual Tracking for Multiple Targets

Yizheng Cai, Nando de Freitas, and James J. Little

University of British Columbia, Vancouver, B.C., Canada, V6T 1Z4
{yizhengc, nando, little}@cs.ubc.ca

Abstract. We address the problem of robust multi-target tracking within the application of hockey player tracking. The particle filter technique is adopted and modified to fit into the multi-target tracking framework. A rectification technique is employed to find the correspondence between the video frame coordinates and the standard hockey rink coordinates so that the system can compensate for camera motion and improve the dynamics of the players. A global nearest neighbor data association algorithm is introduced to assign boosting detections to the existing tracks for the proposal distribution in particle filters. The mean-shift algorithm is embedded into the particle filter framework to stabilize the trajectories of the targets for robust tracking during mutual occlusion. Experimental results show that our system is able to automatically and robustly track a variable number of targets and correctly maintain their identities regardless of background clutter, camera motion and frequent mutual occlusion between targets.

1 Introduction

Tracking multiple targets, although has its root in control theory, has been of broad interest in many computer vision applications for decades as well. A visual-based multi-target tracking system should be able to track a variable number of objects in a dynamic scene and maintain the correct identities of the targets regardless of occlusions and any other visual perturbations. As it is a very complicated and challenging problem, extensive research work has been done. In this work, we address the problem of robust multi-target tracking within the application of hockey player tracking.

Particle filtering was first introduced to visual tracking by Isard and Blake in [1]. Pérez et al. [2, 3] extended the particle filter framework to track multiple targets. Okuma et al. [4] further extended it [3] by incorporating a boosting detector [5] into the particle filter for automatic initialization of a variable number of targets. However, as their system did not have explicit mechanisms to model mutual occlusions between targets, it loses the identities of the targets after occlusions. On the other hand, various approaches have been taken to solve the occlusion problem in tracking. Kang et al. [6] tried to resolve the ambiguity of the locations of the targets by registering video frames from multiple cameras. Zhao et al. [7] also rectified video frames to the predefined ground plane and model the targets in the 3D space with a body shape model. A static camera was used and background subtraction was applied as well in their work. Explicit

A. Leonardis, H. Bischof, and A. Pinz (Eds.): ECCV 2006, Part IV, LNCS 3954, pp. 107–118, 2006.
© Springer-Verlag Berlin Heidelberg 2006

target shape modelling can help resolving the likelihood modelling and data association problems during occlusions. The approach is often used within static scenes [8, 9, 10]. However, in our application, camera motion makes it difficult to separate target motion or perform background subtraction. Players with drastic pose changes are difficult to be captured by any explicit shape models.

In order to build a tracking system that can correctly track multiple targets regardless of camera motion and mutual occlusion, we propose four improvements on the previous systems. Firstly, a rectification technique is employed to compensate for camera motions. Secondly, a second order autoregression model is adopted as the dynamics model. Thirdly, a global nearest neighbor data association technique is used to correctly associate boosting detections with the existing tracks. Finally, the mean-shift algorithm is embedded into the particle filter framework to stabilize the trajectories of the targets for reliable motion prediction. Although similar work [11] has been done on combining mean-shift with particle filtering, our work is the first one that describes in detail the theoretical formulation of embedding mean-shift seamlessly into the particle filter framework for multi-target tracking. Consequently, although our system performs comparably to the system in [4], it significantly improves upon that system when occlusions happen, which is the main focus of this work.

2   Filtering

Particle filtering has been a successful numerical approximation technique for Bayesian sequential estimation with non-linear, non-Gaussian models. In our application, the fast motion of hockey players and the color model we adopt [12, 13] is highly non-linear and non-Gaussian. Therefore, particle filtering is the ideal model to be the basic skeleton of our tracking system.

The basic Bayesian filtering is a recursive process in which each iteration consists of a prediction step and a filtering step.

$$
\begin{aligned}
\textbf{prediction step:} \ & p(x_t|y_{0:t-1}) = \int p(x_t|x_{t-1})p(x_{t-1}|y_{0:t-1})dx_{t-1} \\
\textbf{filtering step:} \ & p(x_t|y_{0:t}) = \frac{p(y_t|x_t)p(x_t|y_{0:t-1})}{\int p(y_t|x_t)p(x_t|y_{0:t-1})dx_t}
\end{aligned}
\tag{1}
$$

where the process is initialized by the prior distribution $p(x_0|y_0) = p(x_0)$, $p(x_t|x_{t-1})$ is the target dynamics model, and $p(y_t|x_t)$ is the likelihood model. Particle filtering uses a set of weighted samples $\{x_t^{(i)}, w_t^{(i)}\}_{i=1}^{N_s}$ to approximate the posterior distribution in the filtering. The sample set is propagated by sampling from a designed proposal distribution $q(x_t|x_{t-1}, y_{0:t})$, which is called importance sampling. The importance weights of the particles are updated in each iteration as follows

$$
w_t^{(i)} \propto \frac{p(y_t|x_t^{(i)})p(x_t^{(i)}|x_{t-1}^{(i)})}{q(x_t^{(i)}|x_{t-1}^{(i)}, y_{0:t})} w_{t-1}^{(i)}, \sum_{i=1}^{N_s} w_t^{(i)} = 1.
\tag{2}
$$

Resampling of the particles is necessary from time to time in each iteration to avoid degeneracy of the importance weights.

One of the critical issues in keeping particle filtering effective is the design of the proposal distribution. The proposal distribution should be able to shift the particles to the regions with high likelihood if there is a big gap between the mode of the prior distribution and the mode of likelihood distribution. The boosted particle filter (BPF) [4] used a mixture of Gaussians model that combines both the dynamics prior and the Adaboost detections [5]

$$q_B^*(x_t|x_{t-1}, y_{0:t}) = \alpha q_{ada}(x_t|y_t) + (1 - \alpha)p(x_t|x_{t-1}), \qquad (3)$$

where α is the parameter that is dynamically updated according to the overlap between the Gaussian distribution of boosting detection and the dynamics prior. The issue of data association arises here. Details about how to correctly assign boosting detections to the existing tracks will be discussed later. In addition, the original BPF work by Okuma et al. [4] is based on the mixture of particle filter structure (MPF) [3], which has a fixed number of particles for all the targets. As a result, new targets have to steal particles from existing tracks and reduce the accuracy of the approximation. The merge and split of particle clouds in the MPF structure also cause the loss of the correct identities of the targets during occlusions. Therefore, we adopt the boosted particle filter as the basic filtering framework in our application. However, instead of using the MPF structure, we use an independent particle set for each target to avoid the two inherent disadvantages of MPF.

3   Target Dynamics Modelling

In visual tracking systems, accurate modelling of the target dynamics can improve the prediction of the locations of the targets while visual support is insufficient due to occlusion. However, because of the camera motion in our application, the image coordinate system changes over time with respect to the hockey rink coordinates. Therefore, target motion modelling and prediction in the image coordinates are difficult. We adopt the approach by Okuma et al. [14] to map the locations of the targets from the image coordinates to the standard hockey rink coordinate system which is consistent over time. Therefore, according to the physical law of inertia, the motions of the players in hockey games are better predicted with a constant velocity autoregressive model.

3.1   Rectification

Homography is defined by Hartley and Zisserman in [15] as an invertible mapping h between two planes. Images recorded by cameras are 2D projections of the real world. For any plane in the world, its images from a camera, which can pan, tilt, zoom or even move, are exactly modelled by a homography as long as there is no noticeable lens distortion. As the hockey players are always moving in the plane formed by the hockey rink, their locations on the rink are in the same plane both in the real world and the image space. Therefore, it is possible to project their locations between the two planes.

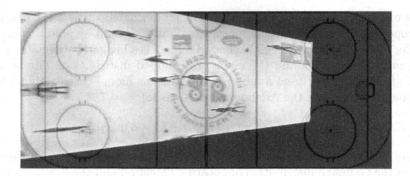

Fig. 1. This shows a projected video frame blended with the standard hockey rink

The work by Okuma et al. [14] is able to automatically compute the homography between video frames and the hockey rink. Figure 1 shows how the video frames are mapped to the standard rink with the homography. With this homography, the hidden states of the targets are represented in the rink coordinates and particle filtering is performed in the rink coordinates as well. Hidden states will be mapped to the image coordinates when evaluating the likelihood of the observation.

3.2   Autoregressive Dynamics Model

An autoregressive process is a time series modelling strategy which takes into account the historical data to predict the current state value. In this model, the current state $\mathbf{x}_t$ only depends on the previous states with a deterministic mapping function and a stochastic disturbance.

As the particle filtering process is performed in the standard rink coordinates, the motions of the players on the rink are separated from the camera motion. Thus, the modelling is much easier. In hockey games, because of the effect of inertia, a constant velocity model is suitable to model the motion of the players. It is best described by the following second order autoregressive model

$$\mathbf{x}_t = A\mathbf{x}_{t-1} + B\mathbf{x}_{t-2} + C\mathcal{N}(0, \Sigma) \tag{4}$$

where $\{A, B, C\}$ are the autoregression coefficients, $\mathcal{N}(0, \Sigma)$ is a Gaussian noise with zero mean and standard deviation of 1.

4   Data Association

In a standard Bayesian filtering framework, data association is performed to pair the observations and tracks for the evaluation of the likelihood function $p(y_t^m | x_t^n)$. With proper estimation of segmentation and shape of the targets [10], the observation can be assigned to tracks in a globally optimal way. However, as we do not have an explicit shape model for the targets, the particle filter framework in our application handles this level of data association locally in an implicit way. Because the boosting detections are used to improve the proposal distribution in particle filters as in shown in Equation 3, we perform data association at this level to assign boosting detections to the existing tracks.

4.1   Linear Optimization

The assignment problem can be best represented by an assignment matrix shown in Table 1. Each entry in the table is the cost or gain of pairing the corresponding track and observation. In our application, the values of all the entries in the assignment matrix are defined to be the distance between the observations and the tracks in the rink coordinates. Assignments that are forbidden by gating are denoted by $\times$ in the corresponding entries. Observations that are forbidden by the gating to be associated to any track are considered as a new track in our application.

Table 1. Example of the assignment matrix for the assignment problem

	Observations			
Tracks	O1	O2	O3	O4
T1	a_{11}	a_{12}	$\times$	$\times$
T2	a_{21}	$\times$	$\times$	a_{24}
T3	a_{31}	$\times$	$\times$	a_{34}

Such assignment problems stem from economic theory and auction theory as well. The objective is to minimize the cost or maximize the gain subject to a set of constraints. Given the assignment matrix shown in Table 1, the objective is to find a set $X = \{x_{ij}\}$, which are binary indicators, that maximizes or minimizes the objective function $C = \sum_{i=1}^{n} \sum_{j=1}^{m} a_{ij} x_{ij}$ subject to some linear constrains. Linear programming was initially used to solve this problem. Later on, it was found that the auction algorithm [16] is the most efficient method so far to reach the optimal solution or sub-optimal one without any practical difference.

The extended auction algorithm [17] is able to solve the rectangular matrix problems with the constraint that one observation can only be assigned to one target while a target can have at least one observations. However, in our application, it is very likely that some tracks do not have any observation due to the mis-detection of the boosting detector. Therefore, even if there are some observations within the gate of that track, it is still possible that none of the observations belongs to the track. Hence, the constraints are formalized as

$$\begin{array}{l} \sum_{i=1}^{n} x_{ij} = 1, \forall j \\ \sum_{j=1}^{m} x_{ij} \geq 0, \forall i \end{array} \tag{5}$$

and the solution is

$$x_{i'j} = \begin{cases} 1 \text{ if } i' = \arg_i \min a_{ij} \\ 0 \text{ otherwise} \end{cases} \forall j \tag{6}$$

5 Mean-Shift Embedded Particle Filter

The motivation of embedding the mean-shift algorithm into the particle filter framework of our tracking system is to stabilize the tracking result. It is important for the dynamics model because stabilizing trajectories improves the accuracy of the computed velocity of targets, which is critical for improving the prediction of the location of the targets. It is also important for the likelihood model because accurate prediction leads sampling to more promising areas so that the influence from background clutter and mutual occlusion will be reduced.

5.1 Color Model

We adopted the color model in [13, 4] in our application because it is successful in tracking non-rigid objects with partial occlusion. The model is originally introduced by Comaniciu et al. [18] for the mean-shift based object tracking. The observation of the target is represented by an N-bin color histogram extracted from the region $R(\mathbf{x}_t)$ centered at the location $\mathbf{x}_t$. It is denoted as $Q(\mathbf{x}_t) = \{q(n; \mathbf{x}_t)\}_{n=1,\ldots,N}$, where

$$q(n; \mathbf{x}_t) = C \sum_{k \in R(\mathbf{x}_t)} \delta[b(k) - n] \tag{7}$$

where δ is the Kronecker delta function, C is a normalization constant, k is any pixel within the region $R(\mathbf{x}_t)$. By normalizing the color histogram, $Q(\mathbf{x}_t)$ becomes a discrete probabilistic distribution.

The similarity between the current observation $Q(\mathbf{x}_t)$ and the reference model Q^*, which is constructed at the initialization step, is evaluated based on the Bhattacharyya coefficient

$$d(\mathbf{x}_t, \mathbf{x}_0) = \sqrt{1 - \rho[Q(\mathbf{x}_t), Q^*]}, \rho[Q(\mathbf{x}_t), Q^*] = \sum_{n=1}^{N} \sqrt{q(n; \mathbf{x}_t) q^*(n; \mathbf{x}_0)} \tag{8}$$

In order to encode the spatial information of the observation, a multi-part color model [13, 4] is employed, which splits the targets vertically into two parts. The color histogram of the two parts are constructed separately and concatenated in parallel as a new histogram. The likelihood is then evaluated as

$$p(\mathbf{y}_t|\mathbf{x}_t) \propto e^{-\lambda d^2(\mathbf{x}_t, \mathbf{x}_0)}. \tag{9}$$

5.2 Mean-Shift

Mean-shift is a nonparametric statistical method that seeks the mode of a density distribution in an iterative procedure. It was first generalized and analyzed by Cheng in [19] and later developed by Comaniciu et al. in [20]. The objective of the mean-shift algorithm is to iteratively shift the current location $\mathbf{x}$ to a new location $\mathbf{x}'$ according to the following relation

$$\mathbf{x}' = \frac{\sum_{i=1}^{M} a_i w(a_i) k \left(\left\| \frac{a_i - \mathbf{x}}{h} \right\|^2 \right)}{\sum_{i=1}^{M} w(a_i) k \left(\left\| \frac{a_i - \mathbf{x}}{h} \right\|^2 \right)} \tag{10}$$

where $\{a_i\}_{i=1}^M$ are normalized points within the region $R(\mathbf{x})$ around the current location $\mathbf{x}$, $w(a_i)$ is the weight associated to each pixel a_i, and $k(x)$ is a kernel profile of kernel K that can be written in terms of a profile function $k : [0, \infty) \to R$ such that $K(\mathbf{x}) = k(\|\mathbf{x}\|^2)$. According to [19], the kernel profile $k(x)$ should be nonnegative, nonincreasing, piecewise continuous, and $\int_0^\infty k(r)dr < \infty$.

The theory guarantees that the mean-shift offset at location $\mathbf{x}$ is in the opposite direction of the gradient direction of the convolution surface

$$C(x) = \sum_{i=1}^M G(a_i - \mathbf{x})w(a_i) \qquad (11)$$

where kernel G is called the shadow of kernel K and profile $k(x)$ is proportional to the derivative of profile $g(x)$.

In order to utilize mean-shift to analyze a discrete density distribution, i.e., the color histogram, an isotropic kernel G with a convex and monotonically decreasing kernel profile $g(\mathbf{x})$ is superimposed onto the candidate region $R(\mathbf{x}_t)$ to construct such a convolution surface. Therefore, the new color model can be rewritten as

$$q(n; \mathbf{x}_t) = C_h \sum_{i=1}^{M_h} g\left(\left\|\frac{a_i - \mathbf{x}_t}{h}\right\|^2\right) \delta[b(a_i) - n] \qquad (12)$$

where C_h is also a normalization constant that depends on h, and h is the bandwidth that determines the scale of the target candidate. It should be noted that in our application, scale of the targets is separated from the state space of the targets and smoothly updated, on per particle basis, using the adaptive scaling strategy in [12]. The weight in the mean-shift update for the color feature is shown below.

$$w(a_i) = \sum_{n=1}^N \sqrt{\frac{q^*(n; \mathbf{x}_0)}{q(n; \mathbf{x})}} \delta[b(a_i) - n]. \qquad (13)$$

The Epanechnikov profile [12] is chosen to be the kernel profile of kernel G in our application. Because it is linear, the kernel K becomes a constant and the kernel term in Equation 13 can be omitted.

5.3   Mean-Shift Embedded Particle Filter

Applying the mean-shift algorithm directly to the tracking output only gives one deterministic offset at each step. It might not be able to capture the true location of the targets due to background clutter or mutual occlusion between targets in the image. Embedding it into the particle filter framework brings uncertainty to the deterministic method so that the statistical property can improve the robustness of the algorithm. In our application, the mean-shift operation biases all the particles right after the sampling from the mixture of Gaussians proposal distribution and before the resampling step in the particle filter framework. Although similar work [11] has been done for tracking, it was only for single target and the proper way of updating the particle weights after the mean-shift bias was not addressed clearly.

However, embedding the mean-shift algorithm seamlessly into the particle filter framework without introducing bias is non-trivial. Directly biasing sampled particles from the old proposal distribution will change the overall posterior distribution. This makes updating the weight of the particles without bias extremely difficult. Although the mean-shift bias is a deterministic mapping so that it can be seen as a change of variable, it is not applicable in practice. On one hand, because the mean-shift bias is a multiple to one mapping, it is not invertible. On the other hand, because it is difficult to write the mean-shift bias in an analytical expression for differentiation even in a piecewise manner, it is difficult to compute the Jacobian matrix in the variable change.

We take an alternative approach in our application. Mean-shift biases the samples $\{\hat{\mathbf{x}}_t^{(i)}\}_{i=1,...,N}$ that are propagated by the old proposal distribution to a new particle set $\{\tilde{\mathbf{x}}_t^{(i)}\}_{i=1,...,N}$. We denote mean-shift searching with function $\varphi(\cdot)$ such that $\tilde{\mathbf{x}}_t = \varphi(\hat{\mathbf{x}}_t)$. Finally, a Gaussian distribution is superimposed on the biased particles to sample new particles. Therefore, the mean-shift bias with a superimposed Gaussian distribution combined with the old proposal distribution can be considered as a new proposal distribution $\breve{q}(\mathbf{x}_t|\mathbf{x}_{t-1},\mathbf{y}_t)$. For the new proposal distribution, the weight is updated as follows:

$$\breve{w}_t^{(i)} \propto \frac{p(\mathbf{y}_t|\breve{\mathbf{x}}_t^{(i)})p(\breve{\mathbf{x}}_t^{(i)}|\mathbf{x}_{t-1}^{(i)})}{\breve{q}(\breve{\mathbf{x}}_t^{(i)}|\mathbf{x}_{t-1}^{(i)},\mathbf{y}_t)} w_{t-1}^{(i)} \tag{14}$$

where $\breve{q}(\breve{\mathbf{x}}_t^{(i)}|\mathbf{x}_{t-1}^{(i)},\mathbf{y}_t) = \mathcal{N}(\breve{\mathbf{x}}_t^{(i)}|\tilde{\mathbf{x}}_t^{(i)},\Sigma)$. Here, Σ is a diagonal 2×2 matrix and the value of the two entries are chosen to be the same, which is 0.3, in our application. Note that we use a sample $\breve{\mathbf{x}}_t^{(i)}$ instead of the biased particle $\tilde{\mathbf{x}}_t^{(i)}$. This ensures that the sequential importance sampler remains unbiased and valid.

The following pseudo-code depicts the overall structure of our tracking system, which includes all the contributions in our work.

- **Initialization:** $t = 0$
    - Map boosting detections to the rink coordinates to get $\{\mathbf{x}_{k,0}\}_{k=1,...,M_0}$.
    - Create particle set $\{\mathbf{x}_{k,0}^{(i)}, \frac{1}{N}\}_{i=1}^N$ by sampling from $p(\mathbf{x}_{k,0})$.
- **For** $t = 1,...,T$,
    1. Targets addition and removal
        - Remove targets with large particle set variance.
        - Map boosting detections from the video frame to the rink.
        - Data association
            * Create a particle set for each new target.
            * Associate boosting detections to the existing tracks to construct Gaussian mixture proposal distribution $q(\mathbf{x}_{k,t}|\mathbf{x}_{k,t-1},\mathbf{z}_{k,t})$, where $\mathbf{z}_{k,t}$ is boosting detection.
    2. For all particles in each track
        - Importance sampling
            * For all particles in each track, sample $\hat{\mathbf{x}}_{k,t}^{(i)} \sim q(\mathbf{x}_{k,t}|\mathbf{x}_{k,t-1}^{(i)},\mathbf{z}_{k,t})$.

- Mean-shift biasing
  * Bias the particles as $\tilde{\mathbf{x}}_{k,t}^{(i)} = \varphi(\hat{\mathbf{x}}_{k,t}^{(i)})$.
  * Sample $\breve{\mathbf{x}}_{k,t}^{(i)} \sim \breve{q}(\mathbf{x}_{k,t}|\tilde{\mathbf{x}}_{k,t}^{(i)})$
- Weight update
  * Update weights $\breve{w}_{k,t}^{(i)}$ according to Equation 14 and normalize.

3. Deterministic resampling
   - For each track, resample particles to get new sample set $\{\mathbf{x}_{k,t}^{(i)}, \frac{1}{N}\}_{i=1}^{N}$.

4. Output
   - For each track, $E(\mathbf{x}_{k,t}) = \sum_{i=1}^{N} w_{k,t}^{(i)} \mathbf{x}_{k,t}^{(i)}$.

6 Experimental Results

Figure 2 shows the comparison between the tracking results of the system in [4] and our system. Subfigure (a) is the key frame in the same tracking sequence that shows the overall view of the tracking results. Subfigures (b-e) and (f-i) are the close-up views of the rectangular region labelled in (a). Each player has a unique color box assigned to it. The color of the same player may not necessarily the same across results of the two systems. According to the results, we can see from Subfigures (b-e) that the trackers merge together when they get close and a new track is created when they split. Meanwhile, our system can maintain correct identities during occlusion.

Subfigures (j-u) in Figure 2 shows the particle representation of the tracking results of our system. In the pseudo-code in Section 5.3, the evolution of particle sets in each iteration of propagation can be divided into three steps: before the mean-shift bias, after the bias, and after the deterministic resampling. The last three rows in the figure compare the difference between the particle sets after each step. Generally, the mean-shift algorithm moves particles from different locations around the target to locations in the neighborhood that are most similar to the reference model in the color space. Therefore, particle sets appear more condensed after the mean-shift bias. The difference between Subfigure (p) and (q) in Figure 2 indicates that mean-shift might move particles to some other targets because of the similarity between the two targets in the color space. However, such particles will be assigned low weights because of the regularization of the dynamics model. As a result, those particles will have much fewer or no children after the resampling stage. For the same reason, particles that are biased to regions without any target, as are shown in Subfigure (n) and (o), will be penalized as well. In summary, both the mean-shift algorithm and the dynamics model penalize erroneous particle hypotheses and improve the robustness of the overall tracking system.

Figure 3 shows more tracking results from three different sequences. All of them are able to correctly maintain the identities of the players regardless of partial of complete occlusions.

(a) Frame 1

(b) Frame 30   (c) Frame 39   (d) Frame 50   (e) Frame 58

(f) Frame 30   (g) Frame 39   (h) Frame 50   (i) Frame 58

(j) Frame 30   (k) Frame 39   (l) Frame 50   (m) Frame 58

(n) Frame 30   (o) Frame 39   (p) Frame 50   (q) Frame 58

(r) Frame 30   (s) Frame 39   (t) Frame 50   (u) Frame 58

Fig. 2. Each row is a close-up view of the rectangular region in (a). Subfigures (b-e) show the tracking results of the system in [4]. Subfigures (f-i) show the tracking results of our system. Subfigures (j-u) show the particle representation of each target during the tracking process. Different targets are labelled with rectangles of different colors.

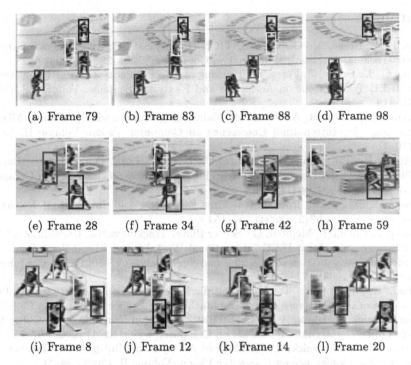

(a) Frame 79   (b) Frame 83   (c) Frame 88   (d) Frame 98

(e) Frame 28   (f) Frame 34   (g) Frame 42   (h) Frame 59

(i) Frame 8   (j) Frame 12   (k) Frame 14   (l) Frame 20

Fig. 3. Each row in the figure shows the tracking results of three different sequences where the top one is the same sequence as the one shown in Figure 2

7 Conclusions

In this paper, we devote our endeavors to building a tracking system that is able to robustly track multiple targets and correctly maintain their identities regardless of background clutter, camera motions and mutual occlusion between targets.

The new particle filter framework is more suitable for tracking a variable number of targets. The rectification technique compensates for the camera motion and make the motion of targets easier to predict by the second order autoregression model. The linear optimization algorithm achieves the global optimal solution to correctly assign boosting detections to the existing tracks. Finally, the mean-shift embedded particle filter is able to stabilize the trajectory of the targets and improve the dynamics model prediction. It biases particles to new locations with high likelihood so that the variance of particle sets decreases significantly.

Acknowledgements

This work has been supported by grants from NSERC, the GEOIDE Network of Centres of Excellence and Honeywell Video Systems.

References

1. Isard, M., Blake, A.: CONDENSATION-Conditional Density Propagation for Visual Tracking. Internatinal Journal on Computer Vision **29**(1) (1998) 5–28
2. Hue, C., Le Cadre, J., Pèrez, P.: Tracking Multiple Objects with Particle Filtering. In: IEEE Transactions on Aerospace and Electronic Systems. Volume 38. (2003) 313–318
3. Vermaak, J., Doucet, A., Pèrez, P.: Maintaining Multi-modality through Mixture Tracking. In: Internatinal Conference on Computer Vision. Volume II. (2003) 1110–1116
4. Okuma, K., Taleghani, A., de Freitas, J., Little, J., Lowe, D.: A Boosted Particle Filter: Multitarget Detection and Tracking. In: European Conference on Computer Vision. Volume I. (2004) 28–39
5. Viola, P., Jones, M.: Robust Real-Time Face Detection. Internatinal Journal on Computer Vision **57**(2) (2004) 137–154
6. Kang, J., Cohen, I., Medioni, G.: Soccer Player Tracking across Uncalibrated Camera Streams. In: Joint IEEE International Workshop on Visual Surveillance and Performance Evaluation of Tracking and Surveillance (VS-PETS) In Conjunction with ICCV. (2003) 172–179
7. Zhao, T., Nevatia, R.: Tracking Multiple Humans in Complex Situations. IEEE Transactions on Pattern Analysis and Machine Intelligence **26**(9) (2004) 1208–1221
8. MacCormick, J., Blake, A.: A Probabilistic Exclusion Principle for Tracking Multiple Objects. Internatinal Journal on Computer Vision **39**(1) (2000) 57–71
9. Isard, M., MacCormick, J.: BraMBLe: A Bayesian Multiple-Blob Tracker. In: Internatinal Conference on Computer Vision. Volume II. (2001) 34–41
10. Rittscher, J., Tu, P., Krahnstoever, N.: Simultaneous estimation of segmentation and shape. In: CVPR05. Volume II. (2005) 486–493
11. Shan, C., Wei, Y., Tan, T., Ojardias, F.: Real Time Hand Tracking by Combining Particle Filtering and Mean Shift. In: International Conference on Automatic Face and Gesture Recognition. (2004) 669–674
12. Comaniciu, D., Ramesh, V., Meer, P.: Kernel-based Object Tracking. IEEE Transactions on Pattern Analysis and Machine Intelligence **25**(5) (2003) 564–577
13. Pèrez, P., Hue, C., Vermaak, J., Gangnet, M.: Color-Based Probabilistic Tracking. In: European Conference on Computer Vision. Volume I. (2002) 661–675
14. Okuma, K., Little, J., Lowe, D.: Automatic Rectification of Long Image Sequences. In: Asian Conference on Computer Vision. (2004)
15. Hartley, R., Zisserman, A.: Multiple View Geometry in Computer Vision. Cambridge University Press (2000)
16. Blackman, S., Popoli, R.: Design and Analysis of Modern Tracking Systems. Artech House, Norwood (1999)
17. Bertsekas, D.: Linear Network Optimization: Algorithms and Codes. The MIT Press, Cambridge (1991)
18. Comaniciu, D., Ramesh, V., Meer, P.: Real-time tracking of non-rigid objects using mean shift. In: International Conference on Computer Vision and Pattern Recognition. (2000) 2142–2149
19. Cheng, Y.: Mean Shift, Mode Seeking, and Clustering. IEEE Transactions on Pattern Analysis and Machine Intelligence **17**(8) (1995) 790–799
20. Comaniciu, D., Meer, P.: Mean Shift: A Robust Approach Toward Feature Space Analysis. IEEE Transactions on Pattern Analysis and Machine Intelligence **24**(5) (2002) 603–619

Multivalued Default Logic for Identity Maintenance in Visual Surveillance*

Vinay D. Shet, David Harwood, and Larry S. Davis

Computer Vision Laboratory, University of Maryland, College Park, MD 20742
{vinay, harwood, lsd}@umiacs.umd.edu

Abstract. Recognition of complex activities from surveillance video requires detection and temporal ordering of its constituent "atomic" events. It also requires the capacity to robustly track individuals and maintain their identities across single as well as multiple camera views. Identity maintenance is a primary source of uncertainty for activity recognition and has been traditionally addressed via different appearance matching approaches. However these approaches, by themselves, are inadequate. In this paper, we propose a prioritized, multivalued, default logic based framework that allows reasoning about the identities of individuals. This is achieved by augmenting traditional appearance matching with contextual information about the environment and self identifying traits of certain actions. This framework also encodes qualitative confidence measures for the identity decisions it takes and finally, uses this information to reason about the occurrence of certain predefined activities in video.

1 Introduction

The primary goal of a visual surveillance system is to help ensure safety and security by detecting the occurrence of activities of interest within an environment. This typically requires the capacity to robustly track individuals not only when they are within the field of regard of the cameras, but also when they disappear from view and later reappear. Figure 1 shows an individual marked X appearing in the scene with a bag, dropping it off in the corridor, and disappearing from view through a door. Subsequently it shows individual Y appearing in the scene through the same door and picking up the bag.

If $individual(X) = individual(Y)$, the activity by itself, is probably not of interest from a security viewpoint. However, if $individual(X) \neq individual(Y)$, the activity observed could possibly be a theft. This example captures the general problem of automatically inferring whether two individuals observed in the video are equal or not. This problem is significant not only for camera setups where individuals routinely disappear into and reappear from pockets of the world not observed by the cameras, but also within a single field of view when tracking is lost due to a variety of reasons.

Traditionally in surveillance, the problem of identity maintenance has been addressed by appearance matching. Matching of appearances can be based on a person's color distribution and shape [1], gait [2], face [3] and other physical

---

* We thank the U.S.Government for supporting the research described in this paper.

A. Leonardis, H. Bischof, and A. Pinz (Eds.): ECCV 2006, Part IV, LNCS 3954, pp. 119–132, 2006.

Fig. 1. Sequence of images showing individual X appearing in the scene with a bag, depositing it on the ground and disappearing from view. Subsequently, individual Y appears in the scene, picks up the bag and leaves.

characteristics. However, all of these approaches are considered weak biometrics and, by themselves, are inadequate for maintaining identities for recognizing complex activities.

The objectives of this paper are to provide a framework

1. **that supports reasoning about identities of individuals observed in video.** We do this by augmenting traditional appearance matching with (a) contextual information about the world and (b) self identifying traits associated with actions. In addition to stating whether or not two individuals are equal, we also qualitatively encode our confidence in it.
2. **that facilitates using this information on identities to recognize activities.** We also propagate our confidence in the identity statements to activities to which they contribute.

In the example above, if the door through which individual X disappeared leads into a closed world (a world with no other exit), we could, under some circumstances, infer that individual Y coming out of that door at a later time had to be equal to individual X (with a high degree of confidence), regardless of whether or not he appeared similar to X.

In this work, we encode contextual information about the world and our common sense knowledge about self-identifying actions as rules in a logic programming language. Furthermore, we observe that since these rules reflect actions taking place in a real world, they can never be definite and completely correct. We therefore employ default logic as the language to specify these rules, which provides our framework the important property of nonmonotonicity (the property of retracting or disbelieving old beliefs upon acquisition of new information). We also employ a bilattice based multivalued representation that encodes our confidence in various rules and propagates these confidence values to the identity statements and subsequently to the activities themselves. We then use prioritization over these default rules to capture the fact that different cues could provide us with different amounts of information. Finally, we use this information about identities of individuals to reason about the occurrence of activities in the video.

2   Motivation

Our primary motivation is to build a visual surveillance system that draws heavily upon human reasoning. While humans are very skillful in matching appearances, even we commit mistakes in this process. However, we possess the capacity to employ context and non-visual cues to aid us in recovering from these errors.

Example 1. *Upon observing an individual, from the back and walking away from us, based on his gait and possibly body type, we tentatively conclude that the individual is Tom, a colleague at work. However, if we suddenly remember that Tom called in sick earlier in the day, we may decide that it cannot be Tom. Later still, if we observe that individual enter a Black BMW, a type of car we know Tom owns, we might conclude more strongly this time that it has to be Tom. However, before entering the car, if the individual turns around to face us and we realize that it is a person we have never seen before, we may definitely conclude that it is not Tom.*

The example demonstrates how humans employ common sense to reason about identities. Human reasoning is characterized, among other things, by [4]

1. Its ability to err and recover − This is important because when dealing with uncertain input, decisions or analysis made might have to be retracted upon acquisition of new information. In Example 1, we retracted our belief of the person being Tom or not several times,

2. Its qualitative description of uncertainty − A qualitative gradation of belief permits us to encode our confidence in decisions we make. In Example 1, our degree of belief in whether or not the person was Tom moved from slightly sure to definitely sure.

3. Prioritization − It is important to have a sense of how reliable our thread of reasoning is. In Example 1, based on appearance we were only slightly sure, based on vehicle information we were more sure, based on face recognition we were definitely sure etc.

3   Related Work

Identity maintenance in surveillance has typically only employed some form of appearance matching. [1] uses a SVM based approach to recognize individuals in indoor images based on color and shape based features. [2] employs gait as a characteristic to identify individuals while [3] performs face recognition from video. Microsoft's *EasyLiving* project [5] employs two stereo cameras to track up to 3 people in a small room while [6] describes a multi-camera indoor people localization in a cluttered environment. Activity recognition has traditionally been performed using statistical approaches. Hidden Markov Models have been used to recognize primitive actions in [7] and also complex behaviors in [8]. Bayesian networks are also widely used [9] [10]. Non statistics based approaches have also been used to recognize activities. [11], proposes an approach based on declarative models of activities and defines scenarios for *Vandalism, Access forbidden and Holdup* and uses a hierarchy of facts ranging from abstract to concrete to recognize these situations. [12] investigates the use of qualitative spatio-temporal representations and abduction in an architecture for Cognitive Vision. [13] employs a context representation scheme for surveillance systems. [14] uses *scenarios* to declare spatio-temporal knowledge in vision applications.

4   Reasoning Framework

Logic programming systems employ formulae that are either facts or rules to arrive at inferences. In visual surveillance, rules can be used to define various activities of interest [15] as well as intermediate inferences such as that of equality of individuals. Rules are of the form "$A \leftarrow A_0, A_1, \cdots, A_m$" where each A_i is called an atom and ',' represents logical conjunction. Each atom is of the form $p(t_1, t_2, \cdots, t_n)$, where t_i is a term, and p is a predicate symbol of arity n. Terms could either be variables (denoted by upper case alphabets) or constant symbols (denoted by lower case alphabets). The left hand side of the rule is referred to as the head and the right hand side is the body. Rules are interpreted as "if body then head". Facts are logical rules of the form "$A \leftarrow$" (henceforth denoted by just "A") and correspond to the input to the inference process. These facts are the output of the computer vision algorithms, and include "atomic" events detected in video (entering/exiting a door, picking up a bag) and data from background subtraction and tracking. Finally, '$\neg$' represents negation such that $A = \neg\neg A$.

4.1   Default Logic

Automatic visual surveillance systems need to function effectively under conditions of high uncertainty. As humans, we possess the ability to reason effectively under such circumstances using what is termed "common sense reasoning". Default logic [16] is an attempt to formalize common sense reasoning using default rules. Default logic expresses rules that are "true by default" or "generally true" but could be proven false upon acquisition of new information in the future. This property of default logic, where the truth value of a proposition can change if new information is added to the system, is called nonmonotonicity.

Definition 1 (Default Theory). *A default theory Δ is of the form $\langle W, D \rangle$, where W is a set of traditional first order logical formulae (rules and facts) also known as the definite rules and D is a set of default rules of the form $\frac{\alpha : \beta}{\gamma}$, where α is known as the precondition, β is known as the justification and γ is known as the inference or conclusion.*

A default rule of this form expresses that if the precondition α is known to be true, and the justification β is consistent with what is currently in the knowledge base, then it is possible to conclude γ. Such a rule can be also written as $\gamma \leftarrow \alpha, not(\neg\beta)$. 'not' represents the negation by "failure to prove" operator and the consistency check for β is done by failure to prove its negation.

Example 2. *Assume the following set of rules and facts:*

$$\neg equal(P_1, P_2) \leftarrow distinct(P_1, P_2). \in W$$
$$equal(P_1, P_2) \leftarrow appear\_similar(P_1, P_2), not(\neg equal(P_1, P_2)) \in D$$
$$\{appear\_similar(a, b)\}_t$$
$$\{appear\_similar(a, b), distinct(a, b)\}_{t+1}$$

where $\{\cdots\}_t$ *indicates the set of facts at time t and distinct(a, b) indicates that a and b appear as two separate and distinct individuals at some point of time.*

In this example, at time t, given the rules and the set of facts, the system concludes that since it cannot prove $\neg equal(a, b)$ and $appear\_similar(a, b)$ is true, therefore $equal(a, b)$ is true. However, at time t+1, it is now possible to prove $\neg equal(a, b)$ because $distinct(a, b)$ is true and therefore the system now can no longer conclude $equal(a, b)$ (the default rule is blocked by the definite rule) and concludes $\neg equal(a, b)$ instead.

While the property of a conclusion blocking another default rule is desirable since it bestows nonmonotonicity upon the system, it can also create a problem.

Example 3. *Assume the following set of rules and facts:*

$$\neg equal(P_1, P_2) \leftarrow distinct(P_1, P_2), not(equal(P_1, P_2)). \in D$$
$$equal(P_1, P_2) \leftarrow appear\_similar(P_1, P_2), not(\neg equal(P_1, P_2)) \in D$$
$$\{appear\_similar(a, b), distinct(a, b)\}_t$$

In Example 3, the rule for inferring that two individuals are not equal if they appear distinct is now made a default rule[1]. In this case, given the set of facts, at time t, depending on the order in which the default rules are applied, different sets of conclusions can be produced. If the first default is applied first, it blocks the second default and we conclude $\neg equal(a, b)$; but if the second default is applied first, it blocks the first and we conclude $equal(a, b)$. The different sets of conclusions that can be derived by applying defaults in different orders are called extensions.

Evidence from different extensions can be combined in an information theoretic manner to give us a single solution using Multivalued Default Logic. In this approach, various rules in the system are regarded as different sources of information concerning the truth value[2] of a given proposition. These sources contribute different amounts of information to the decision making process and consequently our degree of belief in these propositions mirrors their information content. E.g. default rules are not always correct and could be proven wrong by definite rules. Therefore, in this approach, definite rules provide more information than default rules. We now seek a representation that combines the truth value of a proposition with the information content of its sources.

4.2 Bilattice Theory

Bilattices [17] provide an elegant and convenient formal framework in which the information content from different sources can be viewed in a truth functional manner. Truth values assigned to a given proposition are taken from a set structured as a bilattice. A lattice is a set L equipped with a partial ordering $\leq$ over

---

[1] This default rule captures the fact that if there exists a mirror in the world, it could be possible for a single person to appear as two distinct individuals.

[2] Truth value here means our degree of belief in the veracity or falsity of a given proposition and not the actual truth value of the proposition in the real world.

the elements of L, a greatest lower bound (glb) and a lowest upper bound (lub) and is denoted by the triple (L,glb,lub). Informally a bilattice is a set, B, of truth values composed of two lattices $(B, \wedge, \vee)$ and $(B, \cdot, +)$ each of which is associated with a partial order $\leq_t$ and $\leq_k$ respectively. The $\leq_t$ partial order indicates how true or false a particular value is, with f being the minimal and t being the maximal. The $\leq_k$ partial order indicates how much is known about a particular sentence. The minimal element here is u (completely unknown) while the maximal element is $\perp$ (representing a contradictory state of knowledge where a sentence is both true and false). The glb and the lub operators on the $\leq_t$ partial order are $\wedge$ and $\vee$ and correspond to the usual logical notions of conjunction and distinction, respectively. The glb and the

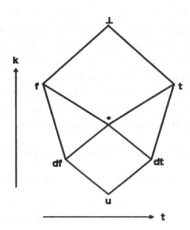

Fig. 2. Bilattice for default logic

lub operators on the $\leq_k$ partial order are $\cdot$ and $+$, respectively, where $+$ corresponds to the combination of evidence from different sources or lines of reasoning while $\cdot$ corresponds to the consensus operator. A bilattice is also equipped with a negation operator $\neg$ that inverts the sense of the $\leq_t$ partial order while leaving the $\leq_k$ partial order intact.

Properties of Bilattices: Figure 2 shows a bilattice corresponding to classical default logic. The set B of truth values contains, in addition to the usual definite truth values of t and f, dt and df corresponding to true-by-default (also called "decided-true") and false-by-default (also called "decided-false"), u corresponding to "unknown", * corresponding to "undecided" (indicating contradiction between dt and df) and $\perp$ corresponding to "contradiction" (between t and f). The t-axis reflects the partial ordering on the truth values while the k-axis reflects that over the information content. This bilattice provides us with a correlation between the amount of information and our degree of belief in a source's output. Procuring more information about a proposition, indicated by rising up along the k-axis, causes us to move away from the center of the t-axis towards more definitive truth values. The only exception to this being in case of a contradiction, we move back to the center of the t-axis. Negation corresponds to reflection of the bilattice about the $\perp -u$ axis. It is also important to note the this bilattice is distributive with respect to each of the four operators. Based on this framework, we can define the truth tables for each of the four operators.

4.3   Inference

Given a declarative language L, a truth assignment is a function $\phi : L \rightarrow B$, where B is a bilattice on truth values. The semantics of a bilattice system is given by a definition of closure. If $\mathcal{K}$ is the knowledge base and ϕ is a truth assignment labelling each sentence $k \in \mathcal{K}$ with a truth value then the closure of ϕ, denoted $cl(\phi)$, is the truth assignment that labels information entailed by $\mathcal{K}$. For example, if ϕ labels sentences $\{p, q \leftarrow p\} \in \mathcal{K}$ as true; i.e. $\phi(p) = T$ and $\phi(q \leftarrow p) = T$, then $cl(\phi)$ should also label q as true as it is information entailed by $\mathcal{K}$. Entailment is denoted by the symbol '$\models$' ($\mathcal{K} \models q$).

If $S \subset L$ is a set of sentences entailing q, then the truth value to be assigned to the conjunction of elements of S is $\bigwedge_{p \in S} cl(\phi)(p)$. This term represents the conjunction of the closure of the elements of S. It is important to note that this term is merely a contribution to the truth value of q and not the actual truth value itself. The reason it is merely a contribution is because there could be other sets of sentences S that entail q representing different lines of reasoning (or, in our case, different rules). The contributions of these sets of sentences need to be combined using the + operator. Also, if the term above evaluates to false, then its contribution to the value of q should be "unknown" and not "false". These arguments suggest that the closure over ϕ of q is

$$cl(\phi)(q) = \sum_{S \models q} u \vee [\bigwedge_{p \in S} cl(\phi)(p)] \tag{1}$$

We also need to take into account the set of sentences entailing $\neg q$. Since $\phi(\neg q) = \neg \phi(q)$, aggregating this information yields the following expression

$$cl(\phi)(q) = \sum_{S \models q} u \vee [\bigwedge_{p \in S} cl(\phi)(p)] + \neg \sum_{S \models \neg q} u \vee [\bigwedge_{p \in S} cl(\phi)(p)] \tag{2}$$

For more information on the properties and logical inference based on bilattice theory see [17].

Example 4 (Inference example).

$$\phi[\neg equal(P_1, P_2) \leftarrow distinct(P_1, P_2)] = DT$$
$$\phi[equal(P_1, P_2) \leftarrow appear\_similar(P_1, P_2)] = DT$$
$$\phi[appear\_similar(a, b)] = T \qquad \phi[distinct(a, b)] = T$$

$$cl(\phi)(equal(a, b)) = [U \vee (T \wedge DT)] + \neg[U \vee (T \wedge DT)]$$
$$= [U \vee DT] + \neg[U \vee DT] = DT + DF = *$$

In Example 4, we encode our belief that the two rules are only true in general and do not always hold by assigning a truth value of DT to them. We record our belief in the facts as T and apply equation 2 to compute the truth value of $equal(a, b)$. Note in Example 3, we obtained two extensions with $equal(a, b)$ being true in one and $\neg equal(a, b)$ being true in another. Using the multivalued approach we collapse these extensions and combine the two conclusions to obtain $DT + DF = *$ or "undecided".

4.4   Belief Revision and Prioritized Defaults

In classical AI, belief revision is the process of revising a proposition's belief state upon acquisition of new data. In the bilattice framework presented above, these revisions should only occur if the new data source promises more information than that which triggered the current truth value assignment. Note that the belief combination operator, + is a lub operator on the k-axis, meaning it will only choose a sentence with maximum information.

However, this poses a problem for our current theory. Since default rules could be contradicted by other default rules, it is possible that many propositions will suffer from a DT, DF contradiction and will settle in the * or undecided state. According to our current theory, only a rule with more information, the definite rules, can release it from this state. Unfortunately in visual surveillance, most rules are default rules and therefore it might be the case that there may be no definite rules to rescue a proposition once it gets labelled "undecided".

This problem arises because thus far we are assuming that all the default rules provide us the same amount of information, causing them to contradict each other and force a proposition into the * state. However, suppose, instead we assume that different defaults could provide different amounts of information and consequently could alter our belief state by different degrees. It turns out that the bilattice structure very elegantly generalizes to accommodate this assumption. Figure 3 shows a bilattice for a prioritized default theory with 3 priorities. Formally a prioritized default theory $\Delta_<$ is of the form $\langle W, D, < \rangle$ [18] where W and D are as defined in Definition 1 and $<$ is a strict partial ordering on D. The semantics of the bilattice on the new set of truth values stays the same as before.

5   Reasoning About Identities

Our system primarily employs four identifying cues or traits for reasoning about identities. These cues are based on the individuals possessions, closed world activity, knowledge and appearance. In addition to these cues, we also employ equality axioms of reflexivity, transitivity, and symmetry.

Identity can be verified on basis of a person possessing something that only he can possess. For example, if we know that a vehicle belongs to an individual and later we observe another individual entering that vehicle using a key, we can conclude that they must be equal. An individual can be identified on the basis of certain closed world activities, examples of which we will see below. One can also verify identity on the basis of the knowledge we think an individual possesses. For example, if there is a combination lock on a door controlling access to a office and we observe an individual successfully entering the code and opening the door to enter the room, we can conclude that he must be the owner of that office. Finally appearance based cues help identify individuals based on appearance. We employ a color histogram based appearance matching algorithm. Without loss of generality, we assume three levels or priorities of defaults. Figure 3 shows the resultant bilattice employed in our system. In the remainder of this section we will give English descriptions of various rules employed in our system, and note their priority levels.

Priority Level 1: Appearance based identification states that if two individuals appear similar to each other then they are equal to each other. On the other hand, if two individuals do not appear similar to each other, then they are not equal. These set of rules are required in situations where we are forced to compare individuals in the absence of any contextual information. Assume an individual disappears from view into an open world (a world with no constraints on the movements of that individual or others) and another person reappears. Since the person reappearing could potentially be anyone in the world, there is significant uncertainty associated with making an identity decision. Therefore,

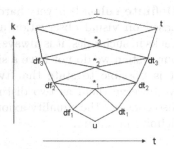

Fig. 3. Prioritized bilattice employed in our system

these rules provide us with least information compared to any approach that augments appearance matching with context. We therefore assign to it priority level 1.

Priority Level 2: If a number of individuals are observed entering a closed world and later reappearing, the uncertainty associated with performing appearance matching as before on that limited group of people is significantly lesser than in the previous case. Therefore, this rule, which reduces the space of possible matches via a closed world assumption, provides more information than pure appearance matching and we assign to it priority level 2.

Priority Level 3: Most of the rules based on possession and knowledge fall in this category as they cause us to depart from comparing groups of individuals to comparing just two individuals. For example, if we observe an individual arrive in the scene in a vehicle, disappear from view and subsequently another individual appears in the scene and uses a key to enter the vehicle, we can conclude, provided they appear similar, that they must be equal. Here we are comparing just two individuals the one who arrived in the vehicle and the one departing in it. Similar reasoning can be applied to offices which require a key or a combination number to enter[3]. Since the comparisons here involve an even more reduced set than the previous case, we assign to this set of rules priority level 3.

Another set of rules that fall in this prioritization are purely closed world based rules such as an individual entering a closed world that we believe to be empty and subsequently exiting it such that no other individual is observed entering or exiting the closed world in between. Here, since there exists the possibility of the individual changing their attire inside the closed world (taking off a jacket), appearance matching is not a strong cue. Other rules in this category are rules that state that if we observe an individual enter a closed world and if, while we believe he is still inside, we observe another individual elsewhere in the scene, then they cannot be equal to each other. Closed world rules such as these clearly have more information than rules with priority levels 1 and 2; however it isn't clear that they have more or less information than the knowledge and possession based rules mentioned above. Therefore we assign to these set of rules priority level 3.

---

[3] Provided we have reason to believe that the office usually has only one occupant.

Definite rules: It is very hard to state that two individuals are definitely equal based on visual observation alone. Irrespective of how much information one packs in such rules, it is always possible to find ways to defeat them. Therefore, in our system we do not have a single rule that definitely infers equality. However, it is possible to state that two individuals are not equal. We do that when we observe them as two distinct individuals at the same instant of time. We also consider the equality axioms of reflexivity, transitivity and symmetry to be definite in nature.

6   Activity Recognition

We can now use inferences made regarding equality of individuals to reason about the occurrence of various activities in the input video. Moreover we can propagate our degree of belief in the identity statement to the activities that it contributes to. We define three such activities and list some sample rules[4].

Theft: We define theft as the activity of an individual possessing a package that does not belong to him. A package does not belong to an individual P_1 at time T_1 if it belonged to another individual P_2 at some time $T_2 < T_1$ such that $\neg equal(P_1, P_2)$. Formally,

$$theft(P_1, B, T_1) \leftarrow human(P_1), bag(B), possess(P_1, B, T_1), \neg belongs(B, P_1, T_1).$$
$$\neg theft(P_1, B, T_1) \leftarrow human(P_1), bag(B), possess(P_1, B, T_1), belongs(B, P_1, T_1).$$

A package does not belong to an individual P_1 at time T_1 if it was originally possessed by individual P_2 at some time $T_2 < T_1$ such that $\neg equal(P_1, P_2)$.

$$\neg belongs(B, P_1, T_1) \leftarrow original\_possessor(P_2, B, T_2), T_2 < T_1, \neg equal(P_1, P_2).$$
$$belongs(B, P_1, T_1) \leftarrow original\_possessor(P_2, B, T_2), T_2 < T_1, equal(P_1, P_2).$$

Entry Violation: Assuming an identity card reader controls access to a building entrance, we define entry violation as the activity of an individual entering the building without scanning his card. Formally,

$$\neg entry\_violation(P_1) \leftarrow enter(P_1, T_1), scancard(P_2, T_2), T_2 < T_1, equal(P_1, P_2).$$
$$entry\_violation(P_1) \leftarrow enter(P_1, T_1), scancard(P_2, T_2), T_2 < T_1, \neg equal(P_1, P_2).$$

Unattended Package: We define a package to be unattended if we observe an individual drop off a package and then cease to be in its vicinity. This is captured by the following rules

$$\neg unattended(B, T_1) \leftarrow in\_vicinity(P_1, B, T_1), dropoff(P_2, B, T_2), equal(P_1, P_2).$$
$$unattended(B, T_1) \leftarrow not(\neg unattended(B, T_1)).$$

---

[4] Note, due to space constraints, rules listed in this paper are only those pertinent to the scenarios described in the next section and represent a small (modified for ease of understanding) subset of the rules encoded in the system. Typically for any predicate p, there exist multiple rules deriving p and/or $\neg p$ depending on how we want the system to behave under various scenarios.

Propagation of belief states from equality statements to these activities is done using equation 2.

7   Experiments

Our system has been implemented as a multi-threaded, C++ application capable of handling multiple cameras. A Prolog reasoning engine has been embedded within this C++ application. Multivalued default reasoning is implemented using meta-predicates provided by Prolog. As currently implemented, this application runs at frame rate while taking input from up to three cameras.

The application consists of two kinds of threads: the (possibly multiple) camera thread(s) which take input from the camera(s) and detect "atomic" events (like entering a door or picking up a bag) and a single reasoning thread responsible for the high level multivalued default reasoning. For each camera connected to the system, we create a camera thread that first performs background subtraction and tracking on the video. It then detects "atomic" events and syntactically structures them as Prolog facts. The reasoning thread, when first created, starts the Prolog engine and initializes it by inserting into its knowledge base all the predefined rules from the default theory. The reasoning thread is subsequently evoked every few seconds. Every time it runs, it assimilates Prolog facts generated by the camera threads and inserts them into the Prolog engine's knowledge base. Also, for every human observed in the video, it reasons about their identity by applying all applicable equality rules. Finally, equality statements, along with their qualitative confidence values, are used to reason about the occurrence of predefined activities using the rules listed in section 6. If any of the activities can be proven with belief states of DT_1, DT_2, DT_3 or T then the reasoning thread generates an alert. The tool we have built also allows the user to manually click on the image, while setting up the system, to mark and label regions (as 'closed world', 'hand-off region', 'card reader' etc.), in the scene. These regions, as seen in Fig 4 and 5 provide the system with information about the scene structure and properties and also helps the system to recognize a richer set of "atomic" events that log the interactions of individuals with the environment.

We demonstrate our system in action on a multi-camera surveillance setup. We employ cameras that have disjoint fields of view and label certain regions within the scene as hand-off regions. Hand-off regions are areas within an image where individuals disappear and reappear between cameras. We encode simple rules that state that if an individual disappears from the hand-off region in one camera and within a certain time interval appears within a specific hand-off region of another camera and the two individuals appear similar, then they must be equal. These rules as well as the belief states assigned to them are clearly setup specific. We now describe a few scenarios that were used to test the system.

Scenario 1 (Theft-See Figure 4). *Vehicle 1_0 enters the scene and individual 1_1 appears from it and disappears from the view of camera 1 from the right hand-off region. He appears in view of camera 2 from its hand-off region as 2_0,*

Frame 0397   Frame 0817   Frame 1131   Frame 1411   Frame 1682

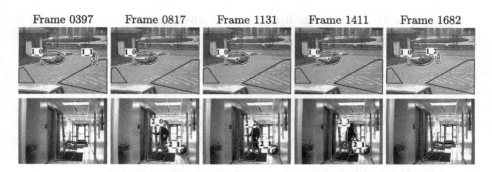

Fig. 4. Figure depicting scenario 1. Top row Camera 1 and bottom row Camera 2.

drops a bag, 2_1, in the corridor and enters a room (closed world). He is followed by another individual 2_2 (who appears from around the corner) into the room. Subsequently an individual 2_3 exits the room, picks up the bag and exits the view of camera 2 through the hand-off region. He appears in the hand-off region of camera 1 as 1_2 and enters the vehicle using a key and drives away.

In this scenario, the system correctly identifies human 2_0 as being equal to 1_1 due to the hand-off rules encoded for this camera setup. When human 2_3 exits the room, the system attempts to apply the closed world and appearance matching (default priority 2) set of rules mentioned in section 5. However, it turns out 2_3 appears similar to both 2_0 and 2_2, and therefore the system derives both $\phi[equal(2\_3, 2\_0)] = DT_2$ and $\phi[equal(2\_3, 2\_2)] = DT_2$. Note the system can also prove $\phi[equal(2\_0, 2\_2)] = DF_3$ which is inconsistent if we attempt to establish the transitivity relation. The system therefore is forced to assign $\phi[equal(2\_3, 2\_0)] = *_2$ and $\phi[equal(2\_3, 2\_2)] = *_2$ which represents the undecided state. When 2_3 picks up the bag left behind by 2_0, the system tries to prove whether or not a theft has taken place, however, it can only prove $\phi[theft(2\_3, 2\_1, 1415)] = *_2$ due to the uncertainty involved in the equality statement that contributes to it. The system continues on to correctly conclude that human 2_3 is equal to human 1_2. However, when 1_2 uses a key and enters the vehicle, it can now prove $\phi[equal(1\_1, 1\_2)] = DT_3$. By transitivity, the system is then able to revise its belief of $\phi[equal(2\_3, 2\_0)]$ from $*_2$ to DT_3 and consequently revise its belief of $\phi[theft(2\_3, 2\_1, 1415)]$ from $*_2$ to DF_3, i.e. no theft has occurred with high confidence.

In the next scenario, we assume there exists a card reader controlling access to a building.

Scenario 2 (Entry Violation). Individual 2 approaches the card reader and swipes her card while 1 is at the phone. Individuals 1 and 2 momentarily occlude each other causing the tracker to lose track of the individuals. Subsequently when the two individuals separate out again, tracking is resumed and human 3 enters the building.

In this scenario, after tracking is lost and resumed, the system needs to ascertain whether the person who entered the building is the one who swiped the

Frame 1197   Frame 1404   Frame 1408

Fig. 5. Figure depicting scenario 2

card. However due to a lack of any context based cues, it is forced to resort to appearance matching (priority level 1) rules. Based on those rules, the system concludes $\phi[equal(2,3)] = DT_1$ and $\phi[entry\_violation(3)] = DF_1$, i.e. no entry violation has taken place with low confidence.

Scenario 3 (Unattended Package). *Human 2_16 drops a bag 2_17 in the corridor and enters an empty room (closed world). Subsequently 2_18 exits the room.*

In this scenario, the event of 2_16 entering the room, triggers the unattended package alert as the bag's owner is no longer in its vicinity. However, when 2_18 appears, based on the closed world (priority level 3) rules, the system is able to conclude $\phi[equal(2\_16, 2\_18)] = DT_3$ and therefore it also concludes $\phi[unattended(2\_17, 1783)] = DF_3$, i.e. the bag is not unattended with high confidence.

8   Summary

The problem of identity maintenance is a very important problem in visual surveillance. Many activities that we wish to recognize in surveillance video depend, in some ways, upon the identities of the individuals involved, and therefore have to account for the uncertainty in reasoning about them. Traditionally, identity maintenance has relied solely on appearance matching, however it is extremely important to take into account context and cues provided by certain self-identifying actions to augment reasoning. This work is an attempt to provide a framework to do just that. The development of this framework has been heavily influenced by human reasoning. We believe human reasoning is characterized, among other things, by nonmonotonicity, qualitative belief gradation and prioritization. We have attempted to capture these traits in the proposed theory.

References

1. Nakajima, C., Pontil, M., Heisele, B., Poggio, T.: Full-body person recognition system. Pattern Recognition **36**(9) (2003) 1997–2006
2. BenAbdelkader, C., Cutler, R., Davis, L.: Motion-based recognition of people in eigengait space. In: Proc of Intl. Conf. on Auto Face and Gesture Recogtn. (2002)

3. Zhou, S., Krueger, V., Chellappa, R.: Probabilistic recognition of human faces from video. Comput. Vis. Image Underst. **91**(1-2) (2003) 214–245
4. McCarthy, J.: Artificial intelligence, logic and formalizing common sense. Philosophical Logic and Artificial Intelligence (1989)
5. Krumm, J., Harris, S., Meyers, B., Brumitt, B., Hale, M., Shafer, S.: Multi-camera multi-person tracking for easyliving. Proc. Intl Wkshp on Visual Surveil. (2000)
6. Wei, G., Petrushin, V., Gershman, A.: Multiple-camera people localization in a cluttered environment. The 5th Intl Workshop on Multimedia Data Mining (2004)
7. Starner, T., Pentland, A.: Real-time american sign language recognition from video using hidden markov models. In: Proc of the Intl Sym on Computer Vision. (1995)
8. Ivanov, Y.A., Bobick, A.F.: Recognition of visual activities and interactions by stochastic parsing. IEEE Trans. Pattern Anal. Mach. Intell. **22**(8) (2000) 852–872
9. Buxton, H., Gong, S.: Advanced Visual Surveillance using Bayesian Networks. In: International Conference on Computer Vision, Cambridge, Massachusetts (1995)
10. Intille, S.S., Bobick, A.F.: A framework for recognizing multi-agent action from visual evidence. In: Proceedings of the sixteenth NCAIIAAI. (1999) 518–525
11. Rota, N.A., Thonnat, M.: Activity recognition from video sequences using declarative models. 14th ECAI 2000 Berlin Germany (2000)
12. Cohn, A.G., Magee, D., Galata, A., Hogg, D., Hazarika, S.M.: Towards an architecture for cognitive vision using qualitative spatio-temporal representations and abduction. In: Spatial Cognition III, Springer (2002)
13. Bremond, F., Thonnat, M.: A context representation for surveillance systems. In: ECCV Worshop on Conceptual Descriptions from Images. (1996)
14. Vu, V., Bremond, F., Thonnat, M.: Automatic video interpretation: A novel algorithm for temporal scenario recognition. The Eighteenth IJCAI '03 (2003)
15. Shet, V., Harwood, D., Davis, L.: VidMAP: Video Monitoring of Activity with Prolog. IEEE Intl. Conf. on Advanced Video and Signal based Surveillance (2005)
16. Reiter, R.: A logic for default reasoning. Readings in nonmonotonic reasoning (1987) 68–93
17. Ginsberg, M.L.: Multi-valued logics: a uniform approach to reasoning in artificial intelligence. Computational Intelligence **4** (1988) 265–316
18. Brewka, G.: Adding priorities and specificity to default logic. In: JELIA '94: Proc. of the European Wkshp on Logics in Artificial Intelligence. (1994) 247–260

A Multiview Approach to Tracking People in Crowded Scenes Using a Planar Homography Constraint

Saad M. Khan and Mubarak Shah

University of Central Florida, USA

Abstract. Occlusion and lack of visibility in dense crowded scenes make it very difficult to track individual people correctly and consistently. This problem is particularly hard to tackle in single camera systems. We present a multi-view approach to tracking people in crowded scenes where people may be partially or completely occluding each other. Our approach is to use multiple views in synergy so that information from all views is combined to detect objects. To achieve this we present a novel planar homography constraint to resolve occlusions and robustly determine locations on the ground plane corresponding to the feet of the people. To find tracks we obtain feet regions over a window of frames and stack them creating a space time volume. Feet regions belonging to the same person form contiguous spatio-temporal regions that are clustered using a graph cuts segmentation approach. Each cluster is the track of a person and a slice in time of this cluster gives the tracked location. Experimental results are shown in scenes of dense crowds where severe occlusions are quite common. The algorithm is able to accurately track people in all views maintaining correct correspondences across views. Our algorithm is ideally suited for conditions when occlusions between people would seriously hamper tracking performance or if there simply are not enough features to distinguish between different people.

1 Introduction

Tracking multiple people accurately in dense crowded scenes is a challenging task primarily due to occlusion between people. If a person is visually isolated (i.e. neither occluded nor occluding another person in the scene) it is much simpler to perform the tasks of detection and tracking. This is because the physical attributes of the person's foreground blob like color distribution, shape and orientation remain largely unchanged as he/she moves. With increasing density of objects in the scene inter object occlusions increase. A foreground blob is no longer guaranteed to belong to a single person and may in fact belong to several people in the scene. Even worse, a person might be completely occluded by other people. Under such conditions of limited visibility and clutter it might be impossible to detect and track multiple people using only a single view. The logical step is to try and use multiple views of the same scene in an effort to recover information that might be missing in a particular view. In this paper

A. Leonardis, H. Bischof, and A. Pinz (Eds.): ECCV 2006, Part IV, LNCS 3954, pp. 133–146, 2006.
© Springer-Verlag Berlin Heidelberg 2006

Fig. 1. Four views of a scene containing a crowd of nine people. The ground plane is clear and visible from each view. Notice the occlusions. The scene is so crowded that no person is visually isolated in every view. In fact most people are either occluded or occluding other people in every view. There are also cases of near total occlusion in views on the top row.

we propose a multi-view approach to detecting and tracking multiple people in crowded scenes. We are interested in situations where the crowds are sufficiently dense that partial or total occlusions are very common and it can not be guaranteed that any of the people will be visually isolated. Figure 1 shows four views of a crowded scene from one of our experiments that will be used to illustrate our method. Notice that no single person is viewed in isolation in all four images and there are cases of near total occlusion.

In our approach we do not use color models or shape cues of individual people. Our method of detection and occlusion resolution is based on geometrical constructs and only requires the distinction of foreground from background. At the core of our method is a novel planar homography constraint that combines foreground likelihood information (probability of a pixel in the image belonging to the foreground) from different views to resolve occlusions and determine ground plane locations of people. The homography constraint implies that only pixels corresponding to the ground plane locations of people (i.e, the feet) will consistently warp (under homographies of the ground plane), to foreground regions in every view. The reason we use foreground likelihood maps instead of binary foreground images is to delay the thresholding step to the last possible stage. Warping foreground likelihood maps from all views onto a reference view and multiplying them out, the pixels pertaining to feet of the people are segmented out. To track these regions we obtain feet blobs over a window of frames and stack them together creating a space time volume. Feet regions belonging to the same person form contiguous spatio-temporal regions that are clustered using a graph cuts segmentation approach. Each cluster is the track of a person and a slice in time of this cluster gives the tracked location.

It should be noted that we neither detect nor track objects from any single camera, or camera pair; rather evidence is gathered from all the cameras into a synergistic framework and detection and tracking results are propagated back to each view. We assume the ground plane homography between cameras is available which requires that the ground plane is visible in each view. This is a reasonable assumption in typical surveillance installations monitoring people in busy crowded places. Usually the ground plane occupies a large enough image region to be automatically detected and aligned using robust methods of locking onto the dominant planar motion (e.g via one of the 2D parametric estimation techniques such as [1, 2]). We do not assume that the camera calibration information is known.

The rest of the paper is structured as follows. In Section 2 we discuss related work. Section 3 details the observation and theory behind the homography constraint. In section 4 we present our algorithm that uses the homography constraint to segment out pixels representing ground locations of people in the scene. Section 5 describes our tracking methodology. Section 6 details our experiments and results providing insight into the utility and efficiency of our method. We conclude this paper in section 7.

2   Related Work

There is extensive literature on single-camera detection and tracking algorithms, almost all of which suffer from the difficulties of tracking multiple objects under occlusions. Zhao and Nevatia [3] presented a method for tracking multiple people in a single camera. They used 3D shape models of people that were projected back in image space to aid in segmentation and resolving occlusions. Each human hypothesis was then tracked in 3D with a Kalman filter using the objects appearance constrained by its shape. Okuma et al. [4] propose an interesting combination of Adaboost for object detection and particle filters for multiple-object tracking. The combination of the two approaches leads to fewer failures than either one on its own, as well as addressing both detection and consistent track formation in the same framework. Leibe et al. [5] present a pedestrian detection algorithm for crowded scenes. Their method operates in a top-down fashion, iteratively aggregating local and global patterns for better segmentation. These and other similar algorithms [6, 7, 8] are challenged by occluding and partially occluding objects, as well as appearance changes. Connected foreground regions may not necessarily correspond to one object, but might have parts from several of them.

Some researchers have developed multi-camera detection and tracking algorithms in order to overcome these limitations. Orwell et al. [9] present a tracking algorithm to track multiple objects in multiple views using 'color' tracking. They model the connected blobs obtained from background subtraction using color histogram techniques and use them to match and track objects. Cai and Aggarwal [10] extend a single-camera tracking system by starting with tracking in a single camera view and switching to another camera when the system predicts that the current camera will no longer have a good view of the subject. Krumm et al. [11] use stereo cameras and combine information from multiple stereo cameras in 3D space. They perform background subtraction and then detect human-shaped blobs in 3D space. Color histograms are created for each person and are used to identify and track people. Mittal et al. [12] use a similar method to combine information in pairs of stereo cameras. Regions in different views are compared with each other and back-projection in 3D space is done in a manner that yields 3D points guaranteed to lie inside the objects.

Even though these methods attempt to resolve occlusions, the underlying problem of using features that might be corrupted due to occlusions remains. The scene shown in figure 1 would be difficult to resolve for any of these methods. Not only are there cases of near total occlusion, the people are dressed in very similar colors. Using blob shapes or color distributions for region matching across cameras would lead to incorrect segmentations and detections.

The homography constraint we present in this paper and its application to localize people on a ground plane can also be interpreted as a visual hull intersection process. The difference is that unlike traditional visual hull intersection algorithms [13, 14, 15], our method uses only 2D constructs and dose not require camera calibration. This is because the homography constraint effectively performs visual hull intersection on a plane.

3   Homography Constraint

We begin with the basic notions of planar homographies. Let $p = (x, y, 1)$ denote the image location (in homogeneous coordinates) of a 3D scene point in one view and let $p' = (x', y', 1)$ be its coordinates in another view. Let H denote the homography of the plane Π between the two views and H_3 be the third row of H. When the first image is warped toward the second image using the homography H, then the point p will move to p_w in the *warped image*:[1]

$$p_w = (x_w, y_w, 1) = \frac{Hp}{H_3 p}.$$

For 3D points on the plane Π, $p_w = p'$. For 3D points off Π, $p_w \neq p'$. The misalignment $p_w - p'$ is called the plane parallax. Geometrically speaking warping pixel p from the first image to the second using the homography H amounts to projecting a ray from the camera center through pixel p and extending it till it intersects the plane Π at the point often referred to as the 'piercing point' of pixel p with respect to plane Π. The ray is then projected from the piercing point

---

[1] For the remainder of this paper we will use only Hp to denote this operation.

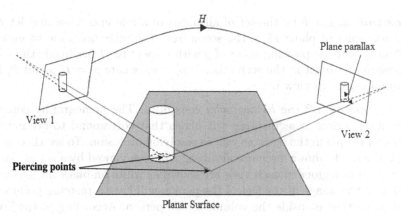

Fig. 2. The figure shows a cylinderical object standing on top a planar surface. The scene is being viewed by two cameras. H is the homography of the planar surface from view 1 to view 2. Warping a pixel from view 1 with H amounts to projecting a ray on to the plane at the piercing point and extending it to the second camera. Pixels that are image locations of scene points off the plane have plane parallax when warped. This can be observed for the red ray in the figure.

onto the second camera. The point in the image plane of the second camera that the ray intersects is p_w. In effect p_w is where the image of the piercing point is formed in the second camera. As can be seen in figure 2, 3D points on the plane Π have no plane-parallax while those off the plane have considerable plane-parallax.

Suppose a scene containing a ground plane is being viewed by a set of wide-baseline stationary cameras. The background models in each view are available and when an object appears in the scene it can be detected as foreground in each view using background difference. Any 3D point lying inside the foreground object in the scene will be projected to a foreground pixel in every view. The same is the case for 3D points inside the object that lie on the ground plane, except however that the projected image locations in each view will be related by homographies of the ground plane. Now we can state the following proposition:

Proposition 1. If $\exists P \in \mathbf{R}^3$ such that it lies on plane Π and is inside the volume of a foreground object then, the image projections of the scene point P given by $p_1, p_2, \ldots, p_n$ in any n views satisfy both of the following:

- $\forall_i$, if Ψ_i is the foreground region in view i then, $p_i \in \Psi_i$,
- $\forall_{i,j} p_i = H_{i,j} p_j$, where $H_{i,j}$ is the homography of plane Π from view j to view i.

As discussed earlier warping a pixel from one image to another using a homography of the ground plane amounts to projecting a ray through the pixel onto the piercing point and then projecting it to the second camera center. If the ray projected through a pixel in a view intersects the ground plane inside a foreground object in the scene, it follows from proposition 1 that the pixel will warp to foreground regions in all views. This can be formally stated as follows:

Proposition 2. Let Φ be the set of all pixels in a reference view and let H_i be the homography of plane Π in the scene from the reference view to view i. If $\exists p \in \Phi$ such that the piercing point of p with respect to Π lies inside the volume of a foreground object in the scene then $\forall_i p_i' \in \Psi_i$, where $p_i' = H_i p$ and Ψ_i is the foreground region in view i.

We call proposition 2 the *homography constraint*. The homography constraint has the dual action of segmenting out pixels that correspond to ground plane positions of people in the scene as well as resolving occlusion. To see this consider figure 3. Figure 3a shows a scene containing a person viewed by a set of cameras. The foreground regions in each view are shown as white on black background. A pixel that is the image of the feet of the person will have a piercing point on the ground plane that is inside the volume of the person. According to the homography constraint such a pixel will be warped to foreground regions in all views. This can be seen for the pixel in view 1 of figure 3a that has a blue ray projected through it. Foreground pixels that do not satisfy the homography constraint are images of points off the ground plane. Due to plane parallax they are warped to background regions in other views. This can be seen for the pixel with the red ray projected through it. Figure 3b shows how the homography constraint would resolve occlusions. The blue person is occluding the green person in view 1. This is apparent by the merging of their foreground blobs. In such a case there will be two sets of pixels in view 1 that satisfy the homoraphy constraint. The first set will contain pixels that are image locations of blue person's feet (same as in figure 3a). The other set of pixels are those that correspond to the blue person's torso region but are occluding the feet of the green person. Even though these pixels are image locations of points off the ground plane, they have

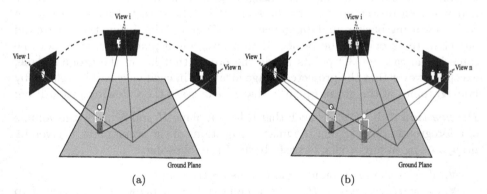

(a)   (b)

Fig. 3. The figure shows people viewed by a set of cameras. The views show the foreground detected in each view. For figure (a) the blue ray shows how the pixels that satisfy the homography constraint warp correctly to foreground in each view, while others have plane parallax and warp to background. Figure (b) demonstrates how occlusion is resolved in view 1. Foreground pixels that belong to the blue person but are occluding the feet region of the green person satisfy the homography constraint (the green ray). This creates seemingly a see through effect where the feet of the occluded person can be detected.

piercing points inside a foreground object which in this case happens to be the green person. This process creates a seemingly see thorough effect detecting feet regions even if they are completely occluded by other people. It is obvious that having more people between the blue and the green person will not affect the detection of the green person.

It should be noted that the homography constraint is not limited to the ground plane and depending on the application any plane in the scene could be used. In the context of localizing people the ground plane is used and finding pixels in all views that satisfy the homography constraint will give us the locations of people's feet (location on ground). In the next section we develop an operator that does exactly this.

4   Using the Homography Constraint to Locate People

Let $\Phi_1, \Phi_2, \ldots, \Phi_n$ be the images of the scene obtained from n uncalibrated cameras. Let Φ_1 be a reference image. H_i is homography of the ground plane between the reference view Φ_1 and any other view i. Using homography H_i, a pixel p in the reference image is warped to pixel p_i' in image Φ_i. Let $x_1, x_2 \ldots, x_n$ be the observations in images $\Phi_1, \Phi_2, \ldots \Phi_n$ at locations $p_1', p_2' \ldots, p_n'$ respectively i.e $x_i = \Phi_i(p_i')$. Let X be the event that pixel p has a piercing point inside a foreground object (i.e. p represents the ground location of a foreground object in the scene). Given $x_1, x_2 \ldots, x_n$, we are interested in finding the probability of event X happening, i.e $P(X \mid x_1, x_2 \ldots, x_n)$.

Using Bayes law:

$$P(X \mid x_1, x_2 \ldots, x_n) \propto P(x_1, x_2 \ldots, x_n \mid X)P(X). \tag{1}$$

The first term on the right hand side of equation 1 is the likelihood of making observation $x_1, x_2 \ldots, x_n$ given event X happens. By conditional independence we can write this term as:

$$P(x_1, x_2 \ldots, x_n \mid X) = P(x_1 \mid X) \times P(x_2 \mid X) \times \ldots \times P(x_n \mid X). \tag{2}$$

Now the homography constraint states that if a pixel has a piercing point inside a foreground object then it will warp to foreground regions in every view. Therefore it follows that:

$$P(x_i \mid X) \propto L(x_i), \tag{3}$$

where $L(x_i)$ is the likelihood of observation x_i belonging to the foreground. Plugging (3) into (2) and back into (1) we get:

$$P(X \mid x_1, x_2 \ldots, x_n) \propto \prod_{i=1}^{n} L(x_i). \tag{4}$$

Pixel p is classified as image of ground location of an object to be tracked if $P(X \mid x_1, x_2 \ldots, x_n)$ given by equation 4 is above a threshold. In the case foreground objects are people, pixel p will correspond to the feet of a person in the

scene. Since pixel p and its warped locations in other views $p'_1, p'_2 \ldots, p'_n$ all have
the same piercing point, they all correspond to the same location on the ground
plane. Therefore by finding pixel p in the reference view that satisfies the homography constraint, we have in fact, determined the image locations in all views of
a particular person's feet i.e $p'_1, p'_2 \ldots, p'_n$. This strategy also implicitly resolves
the issue of correspondences across views. Note that it is irrelevant which view
is chosen as the reference view. The results will be equivalent if some view other
than Φ_1 was chosen as the reference. In the following subsection we outline our
algorithm for finding the feet locations of people in the scene.

4.1   Algorithm

Our algorithm for locating people is quite straight forward. First we obtain
the foreground likelihood maps in each view. This is done by modelling the
background using a mixture of gaussians [16] and finding the probability for
each pixel belonging to the foreground. In the second step instead of warping
every pixel in the reference image to every other view we perform the equivalent
step of warping the foreground likelihood maps from all the other views on to
the reference view. These warped foreground likelihood maps are then multiplied
according to equation 4 to produce what we call a 'synergy map'. A threshold
is then applied to the synergy map to obtain pixels in the reference view that
represent ground plane locations of people in the scene. This image is warped
back from the reference view to every other view to obtain ground locations of
people in each view. Following are the steps in our algorithm:

1. Obtain the foreground likelihood maps $\Psi_1, \Psi_2 \ldots, \Psi_n$.
2. Warp likelihood maps to a reference view using homographies of the ground
   plane. Warped likelihood maps are $\Psi'_1, \Psi'_2 \ldots, \Psi'_n$.
3. Multiply the warped likelihood maps to obtain the synergy map: $\theta_{synergy} = \prod_i \Psi'_i$
4. Threshold the synergy map. For all pixels p in $\theta_{synergy}$
   - if $\theta_{synergy}(p) > T$ then return 1
   - else return 0
5. Warp thresholded image to every other view.

Figure 4 shows the algorithm applied to the scene shown in figure 1. The foreground likelihood maps are warped into view 4 (bottom right image of figure 1)
which was chosen as the reference view. Multiplying the warped views together
we obtain the synergy map which clearly highlights the feet regions of all the
people in the scene. The threshold T does not need to be precise as the values
at the correct locations in the synergy map are typically several magnitudes
higher than the rest. This is a natural consequence of the multiplication in step
3 and can be seen in figure 5. Notice how occlusions are resolved and the ground
locations of people are detected. For the purpose of tracking the binary image
obtained after thresholding is rectified with the ground plane. The rectified image is an accurate picture of the relative ground locations of the people in the
scene.

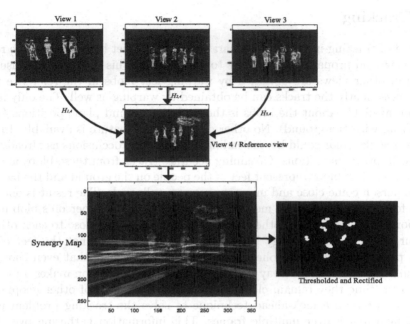

Fig. 4. The four smaller images are foreground likelihood maps obtained from the background model (mixture of gaussians) on the images shown in figure 1. In all images in the figure the colormap used assigns a hotter palette to higher values. View 4 was chosen as the reference view. The image on the bottom is the synergy map obtained by warping views 1, 2, and 3 onto view 4 and multiplying them together. The pixels representing the ground locations of the people are segmented out by applying an appropriate threshold. The binary image shown is the result of applying the threshold and rectifying with the ground plane (the white regions corresponding to the feet).

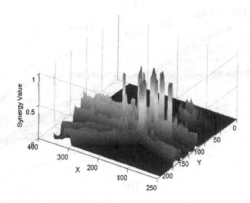

Fig. 5. A surface plot of the synergy map shown in figure 4. The peaks are the ground plane locations of the people in the scene.

5   Tracking

Instead of tracking in each view separately we track feet blobs only in the reference view and propagate the results to other views. This is simply because feet blobs in other views are obtained by warping feet blobs in the reference view and consequently the tracks can be obtained by warping as well. The only information available about the blobs is their relative ground plane positions (after rectifying with the ground). No other distinguishing feature is available. In fact a features like color could be misleading in the case of occlusions as already discussed in previous sections. Obtaining accurate tracks from these blobs is not a trivial task. The blobs represent feet of the people on the ground and the feet of a single person come close and move away every walk cycle. The result is one person's feet blob splitting and merging with itself. In fact one person's blob might temporarily merge with another person's if they come too close to each other.

Our tracking methodology is based on the observation that the feet of the same person are spatially coherent in time. That is to say that even though a person's feet might move away from each other, (as the person makes a forward step) over time they remain closer to each other than feet of other people. We therefore propose a look-ahead technique to solve the tracking problem using a sliding window over multiple frames. This information gathering over time for systems simulating the cognitive processes is supported by many researchers in both vision and psychology (e.g., [17], [18], [19]). Neisser [19] proposed a model according to which the perceptual processes continually interact with the incoming information to verify hypotheses formed on the basis of available

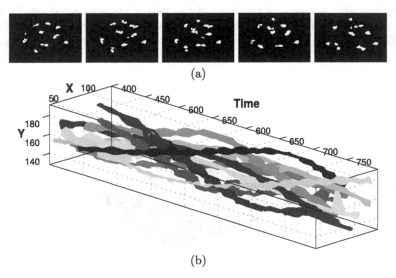

(a)

(b)

Fig. 6. Figure (a) shows a sequence of frames with feet blobs obtained using our algorithm. Stacking them in time the feet blobs form spatially coherent 'worms' that can be seen in figure (b). Different worms clustered out are colored differently to help in visualization. The spiralling pattern of the worms is only a coincidence. This resulted because the people were walking in circles in this particular sequence.

information up to a given time instant. Marrs principle of least commitment [18] states that any inference in a cognitive process must be delayed as much as possible. Many existing algorithms use similar look-ahead strategies or information gathering over longer intervals of time (for example, by backtracking) [20, 21].

For a window of size w using the algorithm described in the previous section we obtain the blobs for all frames in the window. Stacking them together in a space time volume, blobs belonging to the same person will form spatially coherent clusters that appear like 'worms'. Figure 6b shows an example of worms formed from the sequence shown in figure 1. Each worm is in fact the track of a person's feet as he moves in time. To segment out worms belonging to different people from this space time volume we use graph cuts to obtain the tightest clusters in this space time volume. Each blob pixel in the space time volume forms a node of a completely connected graph. Edge weights are assigned using the image distance (euclidean) between pixels connected by the edge. Using normalized cuts [22] on this graph we obtain the optimum clustering of blob pixels in the volume into worms. A slice in time of the worms give the ground plane locations of each person in the scene at that particular time. These are warped back to each view to obtain the image locations of each person's feet in different views.

6   Results and Discussions

To evaluate our approach we conducted several experiments with increasing number of people and varying the number of active cameras. The attempt was to increase the density of people till the algorithm broke down and to study the breakdown thresholds and other characteristics. Each sequence was roughly 750 frames long. The people were constrained to move in an area of approximately 5 meters by 5 meters to maintain the density of the crowd.

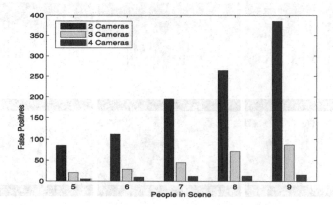

Fig. 7. A plot of false positives reported in our experiments. Each sequence was 500 frames long and contained between 5 and 9 people that were constrained to move in an area of 5x5 meters to simulate different densities of crowds. We varied the number of active cameras in different runs of the experiments to assess the effect of increasing and decreasing view points.

To negate a spot on the ground plane as a candidate location for a person, it must be visible as part of the background in atleast one view. If the spot is not occupied by a person but is occluded in each view (by the people in the scene), our algorithm will trigger a *false positive* at that spot. Note that this is not a limitation of the homography constraint, which states that the region should project to foreground in *all* (every possible) view. Therefore by increasing the number of views of the scene we can effectively lower false positives. This trend can be observed in figure 7, that summarizes the performance of our algorithm for crowds of various densities with increasing number of cameras.

In figure 8 we show track results from the densest sequence we tested our algorithm on. Note that the tracking windows do not imply that all pixels of the people were segmented (only the pixels representing feet blobs are known). The purpose of the track windows is to aid in visualization. The width of each track window is set as the horizontal spread of the feet blobs. The height is calculated by starting from the feet pixels and moving up the connected foreground region

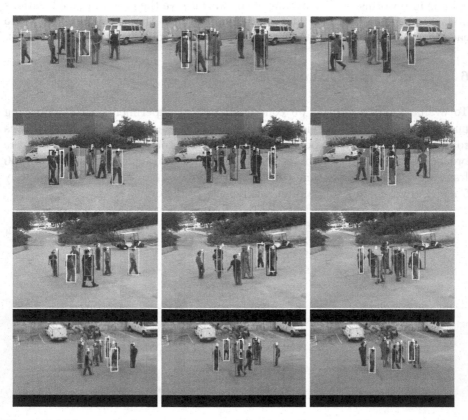

Fig. 8. Tracking results for a sequence containing 9 people captured from 4 view points. Top to bottom the rows correspond to views 1, 2, 3 and 4. Left to right the columns correspond to frames 100, 300 and 500 in the respective views. Track windows are color coded and numbered to show the correspondences that our algorithm accurately maintains across views.

before background is encountered. The sequence contained nine people and was captured from four different view points encircling the scene. Due to the density of the crowd occlusions were quite severe and abundant. An interesting thing to notice is the color similarity of the people in the scene. Naturally a method that uses color matching across views would perform poorly in such a situation whereas our method performs quite well.

One of the limitations of our method is its susceptibility to shadows. Currently the scheme incorporated in our method to handle shadows is to use HSV rather than RGB color space in background subtraction. This is sufficient for scenes like the one in figure 8 where the shadows are small and diffused. But with hard shadows our current implementation has increased false detections. We are working on several strategies to tackle this problem. One of the directions is to use an imaginary plane parallel to but higher than the ground plane in the homography constraint. This will cause foreground due to shadows to have plane parallax thus filtering them out.

7   Conclusions

In this paper we have presented a novel approach to tracking people in crowded scenes using multiple cameras. The major contribution of our work is the detection of ground plane locations of people and the resolution of occlusion using a planar homography constraint. Combining foreground likelihoods from all views into a reference view and using the homography constraint we segment out the blobs that represent the feet of the people in the scene. The feet are tracked by clustering them over time into spatially coherent worms. In the future we plan to investigate the use of multiple planes to handle shadows as well as complete segmentation of the people.

Acknowledgment. This material is based upon the work funded in part by the U.S. Government. Any opinions, findings and conclusions or recommendations expressed in this material are those of the authors and do not necessarily reflect the views of the U.S. Government.

References

1. Irani, M., Rousso, B. and Peleg, S. 1994. Computing Occluding and Transparent Motions. IJCV, Vol. 12, No. 1.
2. Gurdjos, P. and Sturm, P. Methods and Geometry for Plane-Based Self-Calibration. CVPR, 2003.
3. Zhao, T. and Nevatia, T. 2004. Tracking Multiple Humans in Complex Situations, IEEE PAMI, 2004.
4. Okuma, K., Taleghani, A., Freitas, N., Little, J.J., and Lowe, D.G. 2004. A Boosted Particle Filter: Multitarget Detection and Tracking., ECCV 2004.
5. Leibe, B., Seemann, E., and Schiele, B. 2005. Pedestrian Detection in Crowded Scenes, CVPR 2005.
6. McKenna, S.J., Jabri, S., Duric, Z., Rosenfeld, A. and Wechsler, H. 2000. Tracking Groups of People, CVIU 2000.

7. Rosales, R., and Sclaroff, S. 1999. 3D Trajectory Recovery for Tracking Multiple Objects and Trajectory Guided Recognition of Actions, CVPR 1999.
8. Sidenbladh, H., Black, M.J., Fleet, D.J. 2000. Stochastic Tracking of 3D Human Figures Using 2D Image Motion, ECCV 2000.
9. Orwell, J., Massey, S., Remagnino, P., Greenhill, D., and Jones, G.A. 1999. A Multi-agent framework for visual surveillance, ICIP 1999.
10. Cai, Q. and Aggarwal, J.K. 1998. Automatic tracking of human motion in indoor scenes across multiple synchronized video streams, ICCV 1998.
11. Krumm, J., Harris, S., Meyers, B., Brumitt, B., Hale, M., and Shafer, S. 2000. Multi-camera multi-person tracking for easy living, IEEE International Workshop on Visual Surveillance.
12. Mittal, A., Larry, S.D. 2002. M2Tracker: A Multi-View Approach to Segmenting and Tracking People in a Cluttered Scene. IJCV, 2002.
13. Laurentini, A., 1994. The Visual Hull Concept for Silhouette Based Image Understanding, IEEE PAMI 1994.
14. Franco, J., Boyer, E., 2005. Fusion of Multi-View Silhouette Cues Using a Space Occupancy Grid, ICCV 2005.
15. Cheung, K.M., Kanade, T., Bouguet, J.-Y. and Holler, M., 2000. A real time system for robust 3d voxel reconstruction of human motions, CVPR 2000.
16. Stauffer, C., Grimson, W.E.L. 1999. Adaptive background mixture models for real-time tracking, CVPR 1999.
17. Gibson, J.J. The Ecological Approach to Visual Perception. Boston: Houghton Mifflen 1979.
18. Marr, D. 1982. Vision: A Computational Investigation into the Human Representation and Processing of Visual Information. New York: W.H. Freeman.
19. Neisser, U. 1976. Cognition and Reality: Principles and Implications of Cognitive Psychology. San Francisco: W.H. Freeman.
20. Poore, A.B. 1995 Multidimensional Assignments and Multitarget Tracking. Proc. Partitioning Data Sets; DIMACS Workshop 1995.
21. Reid, D.B. 1979. An Algorithm for Tracking Multiple Targets. IEEE Trans. Automatic Control 1979.
22. Shi, J., Malik, J. 2000. Normalized Cuts and Image Segmentation, IEEE PAMI 2000.

Uncalibrated Factorization Using a Variable Symmetric Affine Camera

Kenichi Kanatani[1], Yasuyuki Sugaya[2], and Hanno Ackermann[1]

[1] Department of Computer Science, Okayama University, Okayama 700-8530, Japan
[2] Department of Information and Computer Sciences,
Toyohashi University of Technology, Toyohashi, Aichi 441-8480, Japan
{kanatani, sugaya, hanno}@suri.it.okayama-u.ac.jp

Abstract. In order to reconstruct 3-D Euclidean shape by the Tomasi-Kanade factorization, one needs to specify an affine camera model such as orthographic, weak perspective, and paraperspective. We present a new method that does not require any such specific models. We show that a minimal requirement for an affine camera to mimic perspective projection leads to a unique camera model, called *symmetric affine camera*, which has two free functions. We determine their values from input images by linear computation and demonstrate by experiments that an appropriate camera model is automatically selected.

1 Introduction

One of the best known techniques for 3-D reconstruction from feature point tracking through a video stream is the Tomasi-Kanade *factorization* [10], which computes the 3-D shape of the scene by approximating the camera imaging by an affine transformation. The computation consists of linear calculus alone without involving iterations [5]. The solution is sufficiently accurate for many practical purposes and is used as an initial solution for more sophisticated iterative reconstruction based on perspective projection [2].

If the camera model is not specified, other than being affine, the 3-D shape is computed only up to an affine transformation, known as *affine reconstruction* [9]. For computing the correct shape (*Euclid reconstruction*), we need to specify the camera model. For this, *orthographic*, *weak perspective*, and *paraperspective* projections have been used [7]. However, the reconstruction accuracy does not necessarily follow in that order [1]. To find the best camera models in a particular circumstance, one needs to choose the best one *a posteriori*. Is there any method for automatically selecting an appropriate camera model?

Quan [8] showed that a generic affine camera has three intrinsic parameters and that they can be determined by self-calibration if they are fixed. The intrinsic parameters cannot be determined if they vary freely. The situation is similar to the *dual absolute quadric constraint* [2] for upgrading projective reconstruction to Euclidean, which cannot be imposed unless something is known about the camera (e.g., zero skew).

In this paper, we show that minimal requirements for the general affine camera to mimic perspective projection leads to a unique camera model, which we call a

A. Leonardis, H. Bischof, and A. Pinz (Eds.): ECCV 2006, Part IV, LNCS 3954, pp. 147–158, 2006.

symmetric affine camera, having two free functions of motion parameters; specific choices of their function forms result in the orthographic, weak perspective, and paraperspective models.

However, we need not specify such function forms. We can determine their values directly from input images. All the computation is linear just as in the case of the traditional factorization method, and an appropriate model is automatically selected.

Sec. 2 summarizes fundamentals of affine cameras, and Sec. 3 summarizes the metric constraint. In Sec. 4, we derive our symmetric affine camera model. Sec. 5 describes the procedure for 3-D reconstruction using our model. Sec. 6 shows experiments, and Sec. 7 concludes this paper.

2   Affine Cameras

Consider a camera-based XYZ coordinate system with the origin O at the projection center and the Z axis along the optical axis. *Perspective projection* maps a point (X, Y, Z) in the scene onto a point with image coordinates (x, y) such that

$$x = f\frac{X}{Z}, \qquad y = f\frac{Y}{Z}, \tag{1}$$

where f is a constant called the *focal length* (Fig. 1(a)).

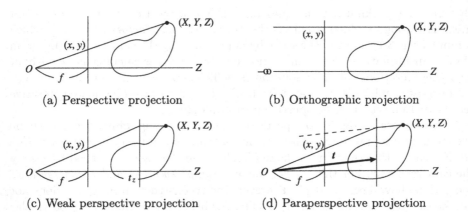

(a) Perspective projection   (b) Orthographic projection

(c) Weak perspective projection   (d) Paraperspective projection

Fig. 1. Camera models

Consider a world coordinate system fixed to the scene, and let t and $\{i, j, k\}$ be its origin and the orthonormal basis vectors described with respect to the camera coordinate system. We call t the *translation*, the matrix $R = (i\ j\ k)$ having $\{i, j, k\}$ as columns the *rotation*, and $\{t, R\}$ the *motion parameters*.

If (i) the object of our interest is localized around the world coordinate origin t, and (ii) the size of the object is small as compared with $\|t\|$, the imaging can be approximated by an *affine camera* [9] in the form

$$\begin{pmatrix} x \\ y \end{pmatrix} = \begin{pmatrix} \Pi_{11} & \Pi_{12} & \Pi_{13} \\ \Pi_{21} & \Pi_{22} & \Pi_{23} \end{pmatrix} \begin{pmatrix} X \\ Y \\ Z \end{pmatrix} + \begin{pmatrix} \pi_1 \\ \pi_2 \end{pmatrix}. \tag{2}$$

We call the 2×3 matrix $\boldsymbol{\Pi} = (\Pi_{ij})$ and the 2-D vector $\boldsymbol{\pi} = (\pi_i)$ the *projection matrix* and the *projection vector*, respectively; their elements are "functions" of the motion parameters $\{t, R\}$. The intrinsic parameters are *implicitly* defined via the functional forms of $\{\boldsymbol{\Pi}, \boldsymbol{\pi}\}$ on $\{t, R\}$, e.g., as coefficients. Typical affine cameras are

Orthographic projection. (Fig. 1(b))

$$\boldsymbol{\Pi} = \begin{pmatrix} 1 & 0 & 0 \\ 0 & 1 & 0 \end{pmatrix}, \qquad \boldsymbol{\pi} = \begin{pmatrix} 0 \\ 0 \end{pmatrix}. \tag{3}$$

Weak perspective projection. (Fig. 1(c))

$$\boldsymbol{\Pi} = \begin{pmatrix} f/t_z & 0 & 0 \\ 0 & f/t_z & 0 \end{pmatrix}, \qquad \boldsymbol{\pi} = \begin{pmatrix} 0 \\ 0 \end{pmatrix}. \tag{4}$$

Paraperspective projection. (Fig. 1(d))

$$\boldsymbol{\Pi} = \begin{pmatrix} f/t_z & 0 & -ft_x/t_z^2 \\ 0 & f/t_z & -ft_x/t_z^2 \end{pmatrix}, \qquad \boldsymbol{\pi} = \begin{pmatrix} ft_x/t_z \\ ft_y/t_z \end{pmatrix}. \tag{5}$$

Suppose we track N feature points over M frames. Identifying the frame number κ with "time", let t_κ and $\{i_\kappa, j_\kappa, k_\kappa\}$ be the origin and the basis vectors of the world coordinate system at time κ (Fig. 2(a)). The 3-D position of the αth point at time κ has the form

$$r_{\kappa\alpha} = t_\kappa + a_\alpha i_\kappa + b_\alpha j_\kappa + c_\alpha k_\kappa. \tag{6}$$

Under the affine camera of eq. (2), its image coordinates $(x_{\kappa\alpha}, y_{\kappa\alpha})$ are given by

$$\begin{pmatrix} x_{\kappa\alpha} \\ y_{\kappa\alpha} \end{pmatrix} = \tilde{t}_\kappa + a_\alpha \tilde{i}_\kappa + b_\alpha \tilde{j}_\kappa + c_\alpha \tilde{k}_\kappa, \tag{7}$$

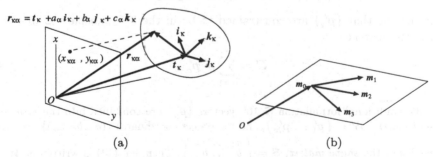

(a)   (b)

Fig. 2. (a) Camera-based description of the world coordinate system. (b) Affine space constraint.

where $\tilde{t}_\kappa$, $\tilde{i}_\kappa$, $\tilde{j}_\kappa$, and $\tilde{k}_\kappa$ are 2-D vectors defined by

$$\tilde{t}_\kappa = \Pi_\kappa t_\kappa + \pi_\kappa, \quad \tilde{i}_\kappa = \Pi_\kappa i_\kappa, \quad \tilde{j}_\kappa = \Pi_\kappa j_\kappa, \quad \tilde{k}_\kappa = \Pi_\kappa k_\kappa. \quad (8)$$

Here, Π_κ and π_κ are the projection matrix and the projective vector, respectively, at time κ. The motion history of the αth point is represented by a vector

$$p_\alpha = \begin{pmatrix} x_{1\alpha} \; y_{1\alpha} \; x_{2\alpha} \; y_{2\alpha} \cdots x_{M\alpha} \; y_{M\alpha} \end{pmatrix}^\top, \quad (9)$$

which we simply call the *trajectory* of that point. Using eq. (7), we can write

$$p_\alpha = m_0 + a_\alpha m_1 + b_\alpha m_2 + c_\alpha m_3, \quad (10)$$

where m_0, m_1, m_2, and m_3 are the following $2M$-dimensional vectors:

$$m_0 = \begin{pmatrix} \tilde{t}_1 \\ \tilde{t}_2 \\ \vdots \\ \tilde{t}_M \end{pmatrix}, \quad m_1 = \begin{pmatrix} \tilde{i}_1 \\ \tilde{i}_2 \\ \vdots \\ \tilde{i}_M \end{pmatrix}, \quad m_2 = \begin{pmatrix} \tilde{j}_1 \\ \tilde{j}_2 \\ \vdots \\ \tilde{j}_M \end{pmatrix}, \quad m_3 = \begin{pmatrix} \tilde{k}_1 \\ \tilde{k}_2 \\ \vdots \\ \tilde{k}_M \end{pmatrix}. \quad (11)$$

Thus, all the trajectories $\{p_\alpha\}$ are constrained to be in the 3-D affine space $\mathcal{A}$ in $\mathcal{R}^{2M}$ passing through m_0 and spanned by m_1, m_2, and m_3 (Fig. 2(b)). This fact is known as the *affine space constraint*.

3   Metric Constraint

Since the world coordinate system can be placed arbitrarily, we let its origin coincide with the centroid of the N feature points. This implies $\sum_{\alpha=1}^{N} a_\alpha = \sum_{\alpha=1}^{N} b_\alpha = \sum_{\alpha=1}^{N} c_\alpha = 0$, so we have from eq. (10)

$$\frac{1}{N} \sum_{\alpha=1}^{N} p_\alpha = m_0, \quad (12)$$

i.e., m_0 is the centroid of the trajectories $\{p_\alpha\}$ in $\mathcal{R}^{2M}$. It follows that the deviation p'_α of p_α from the centroid m_0 is written as[1]

$$p'_\alpha = p_\alpha - m_0 = a_\alpha m_1 + b_\alpha m_2 + c_\alpha m_3, \quad (13)$$

which means that $\{p'_\alpha\}$ are constrained to be in the 3-D subspace $\mathcal{L}$ in $\mathcal{R}^{2M}$. Hence, the matrix

$$C = \sum_{\alpha=1}^{N} p'_\alpha p'^\top_\alpha \quad (14)$$

---

[1] In the traditional formulation [7, 10], vectors $\{p'_\alpha\}$ are combined into the *measurement matrix*, $W = \begin{pmatrix} p'_1 \cdots p'_N \end{pmatrix}$, and the object coordinates $\{(a_\alpha, b_\alpha, c_\alpha)\}$ are combined into the *shape matrix*, $S = \begin{pmatrix} a_1 \cdots a_N \\ b_1 \cdots b_N \\ c_1 \cdots c_N \end{pmatrix}$. Then, eq. (13) is written as $W = MS$, where M, the *motion matrix*, is defined by the first of eqs. (16).

has rank 3, having three nonzero eigenvalues. The corresponding unit eigenvectors $\{u_1, u_2, u_3\}$ constitute an orthonormal basis of the subspace $\mathcal{L}$, and m_1, m_2, and m_3 are expressed as a linear combination of them in the form

$$m_i = \sum_{j=1}^{3} A_{ji} u_j. \tag{15}$$

Let M and U be the $2M \times 3$ matrices consisting of $\{m_1, m_2, m_3\}$ and $\{u_1, u_2, u_3\}$ as columns:

$$M = \begin{pmatrix} m_1 \ m_2 \ m_3 \end{pmatrix}, \qquad U = \begin{pmatrix} u_1 \ u_2 \ u_3 \end{pmatrix}. \tag{16}$$

From eq. (15), M and U are related by the matrix $A = (A_{ij})$ in the form[2]:

$$M = UA. \tag{17}$$

The rectifying matrix $A = (A_{ij})$ is determined so that m_1, m_2 and m_3 in eq. (11) are projections of the orthonormal basis vectors $\{i_\kappa, j_\kappa, k_\kappa\}$ in the form of eqs. (8). From eq. (8), we obtain

$$\begin{pmatrix} \tilde{i}_\kappa \ \tilde{j}_\kappa \ \tilde{k}_\kappa \end{pmatrix} = \Pi_\kappa \begin{pmatrix} i_\kappa \ j_\kappa \ k_\kappa \end{pmatrix} = \Pi_\kappa R_\kappa, \tag{18}$$

where R_κ is the rotation at time κ. If we let $m^\dagger_{\kappa(a)}$ be the $(2(\kappa-1)+a)$th column of the transpose $M^\top$ of the matrix M in eqs. (16), $\kappa = 1, ..., M$, $a = 1, 2$. The transpose of both sides of eq. (18) is

$$R_\kappa^\top \Pi_\kappa^\top = \begin{pmatrix} m^\dagger_{\kappa(1)} \ m^\dagger_{\kappa(2)} \end{pmatrix}. \tag{19}$$

Eq. (17) implies $M^\top = A^\top U^\top$, so if we let $u^\dagger_{\kappa(a)}$ be the $(2(\kappa-1)+a)$th column of the transpose $U^\top$ of the matrix U in eqs. (16), we obtain

$$m^\dagger_{\kappa(a)} = A^\top u^\dagger_{\kappa(a)}. \tag{20}$$

Substituting this, we can rewrite eq. (19) as

$$R_\kappa^\top \Pi_\kappa^\top = A^\top \begin{pmatrix} u^\dagger_{\kappa(1)} \ u^\dagger_{\kappa(2)} \end{pmatrix}. \tag{21}$$

Let $U_\kappa^\dagger$ the 3×2 matrix having $u^\dagger_{\kappa(1)}$ and $u^\dagger_{\kappa(2)}$ as columns:

$$U_\kappa^\dagger = \begin{pmatrix} u^\dagger_{\kappa(1)} \ u^\dagger_{\kappa(2)} \end{pmatrix}. \tag{22}$$

---

[2] In the traditional formulation [7,10], the measurement matrix W is decomposed by the singular value decomposition into $W = U\Lambda V^\top$, and the motion and the shape matrices M and S are set to $M = UA$ an $S = A^{-1}\Lambda V^\top$ via a nonsingular matrix A.

From eq. (21), we have $U_\kappa^{\dagger\top} AA^\top U_\kappa^\dagger = \Pi_\kappa R_\kappa R_\kappa^\top \Pi_\kappa^\top$. Since R_κ is a rotation matrix, we have the generic *metric constraint*

$$U_\kappa^{\dagger\top} T U_\kappa^\dagger = \Pi_\kappa \Pi_\kappa^\top, \tag{23}$$

where we define the *metric matrix* T as follows:

$$T = AA^\top. \tag{24}$$

Eq. (23) is the generic metric constraint given by Quan [8]. If we take out the elements on both sides, we have the following three expressions:

$$(u_{\kappa(1)}^\dagger, T u_{\kappa(1)}^\dagger) = \sum_{i=1}^{3} \Pi_{1i\kappa}^2, \qquad (u_{\kappa(2)}^\dagger, T u_{\kappa(2)}^\dagger) = \sum_{i=1}^{3} \Pi_{2i\kappa}^2,$$

$$(u_{\kappa(1)}^\dagger, T u_{\kappa(2)}^\dagger) = \sum_{i=1}^{3} \Pi_{1i\kappa} \Pi_{2i\kappa}. \tag{25}$$

These correspond to the *dual absolute quadric constraint* [2] on the homography that rectifies the basis of projective reconstruction to Euclidean.

We focus on the fact that *at most two* time varying unknowns of the camera model can be eliminated from eqs. (25). We show that (i) we can restrict the camera model without much impairing its descriptive capability so that it has *two* free functions and (ii) we can redefine them in such a way that the resulting $2M$ unknowns are *linearly* estimated.

4   Symmetric Affine Cameras

We now seek a concrete form of the affine camera by imposing minimal requirements that eq. (2) mimic perspective projection.

Requirement 1. *The frontal parallel plane passing through the world coordinate origin is projected as if by perspective projection.*

This corresponds to our assumption that the object of our interest is small and localized around the world coordinate origin (t_x, t_y, t_z). A point on the plane $Z = t_z$ is written as (X, Y, t_z), so Requirement 1 implies

$$\begin{pmatrix} fX/t_z \\ fY/t_z \end{pmatrix} = \begin{pmatrix} \Pi_{11} & \Pi_{12} \\ \Pi_{21} & \Pi_{22} \end{pmatrix} \begin{pmatrix} X \\ Y \end{pmatrix} + t_z \begin{pmatrix} \Pi_{13} \\ \Pi_{23} \end{pmatrix} + \begin{pmatrix} \pi_1 \\ \pi_2 \end{pmatrix}. \tag{26}$$

Since this should hold for arbitrary X and Y, we obtain

$$\Pi_{11} = \Pi_{22} = \frac{f}{t_z}, \quad \Pi_{12} = \Pi_{21} = 0, \quad t_z \Pi_{13} + \pi_1 = 0, \quad t_z \Pi_{23} + \pi_2 = 0, \tag{27}$$

which reduces eq. (2) to

$$\begin{pmatrix} x \\ y \end{pmatrix} = \frac{f}{t_z} \begin{pmatrix} X \\ Y \end{pmatrix} - (t_z - Z) \begin{pmatrix} \Pi_{13} \\ \Pi_{23} \end{pmatrix}, \tag{28}$$

where f, Π_{13} and Π_{23} are arbitrary functions of $\{t, R\}$. In order to obtain a more specific form, we impose the following requirements:

Requirement 2. *The camera imaging is symmetric around the Z-axis.*

Requirement 3. *The camera imaging does not depend on $\boldsymbol{R}$.*

Requirement 2 states that if the scene is rotated around the optical axis by an angle θ, the resulting image should also rotate around the image origin by the same angle θ, a very natural requirement. Requirement 3 is also natural, since the orientation of the world coordinate system can be defined arbitrarily, and such indeterminate parameterization should not affect the actual observation.

Let $\mathcal{R}(\theta)$ be the 2-D rotation matrix by angle θ:

$$\mathcal{R}(\theta) = \begin{pmatrix} \cos\theta & -\sin\theta \\ \sin\theta & \cos\theta \end{pmatrix}. \tag{29}$$

Requirement 2 is written as

$$\mathcal{R}(\theta)\begin{pmatrix} x \\ y \end{pmatrix} = \frac{f}{t_z}\mathcal{R}(\theta)\begin{pmatrix} X \\ Y \end{pmatrix} - (t_z - Z)\begin{pmatrix} \Pi_{13}' \\ \Pi_{23}' \end{pmatrix}, \tag{30}$$

where Π_{13}' and Π_{23}' are the values of the functions Π_{13} and Π_{23}, respectively, obtained by replacing t_x and t_y in their arguments by $t_x\cos\theta - t_y\sin\theta$ and $t_x\sin\theta + t_y\cos\theta$, respectively; by Requirement 3, the arguments of Π_{13} and Π_{23} do not contain $\boldsymbol{R}$. Multiplying both sides of eq. (28) by $\mathcal{R}(\theta)$, we obtain

$$\mathcal{R}(\theta)\begin{pmatrix} x \\ y \end{pmatrix} = \frac{f}{t_z}\mathcal{R}(\theta)\begin{pmatrix} X \\ Y \end{pmatrix} - (t_z - Z)\mathcal{R}(\theta)\begin{pmatrix} \Pi_{13} \\ \Pi_{23} \end{pmatrix}. \tag{31}$$

Comparing eqs. (30) and (31), we conclude that the equality

$$\begin{pmatrix} \Pi_{13}' \\ \Pi_{23}' \end{pmatrix} = \mathcal{R}(\theta)\begin{pmatrix} \Pi_{13} \\ \Pi_{23} \end{pmatrix} \tag{32}$$

should hold identically for an arbitrary θ. According to the theory of invariants [3], this implies

$$\begin{pmatrix} \Pi_{13} \\ \Pi_{23} \end{pmatrix} = c\begin{pmatrix} t_x \\ t_y \end{pmatrix}, \tag{33}$$

where c is an arbitrary function of $t_x^2 + t_y^2$ and t_z. Thus, if we define

$$\zeta = \frac{t_z}{f}, \qquad \beta = -\frac{ct_z}{f}, \tag{34}$$

eq. (28) is written as

$$\begin{pmatrix} x \\ y \end{pmatrix} = \frac{1}{\zeta}\left(\begin{pmatrix} X \\ Y \end{pmatrix} + \beta(t_z - Z)\begin{pmatrix} t_x \\ t_y \end{pmatrix}\right). \tag{35}$$

The corresponding projection matrix $\boldsymbol{\Pi}$ and the projection vector $\boldsymbol{\pi}$ are

$$\boldsymbol{\Pi} = \begin{pmatrix} 1/\zeta & 0 & -\beta t_x/\zeta \\ 0 & 1/\zeta & -\beta t_y/\zeta \end{pmatrix}, \qquad \boldsymbol{\pi} = \begin{pmatrix} \beta t_x t_z/\zeta \\ \beta t_y t_z/\zeta \end{pmatrix}, \tag{36}$$

where ζ and β are arbitrary *functions* of $t_x^2 + t_y^2$ and t_z. We observe:

- Eq. (35) reduces to the paraperspective projection (eq. (5)) if we choose

$$\zeta = \frac{t_z}{f}, \qquad \beta = \frac{1}{t_z}. \tag{37}$$

- Eq. (35) reduces to the weak perspective projection (eq. (4)) if we choose

$$\zeta = \frac{t_z}{f}, \qquad \beta = 0. \tag{38}$$

- Eq. (35) reduces to the orthographic projection (eq. (3)) if we choose

$$\zeta = 1, \qquad \beta = 0. \tag{39}$$

Thus, eq. (35) includes the traditional affine camera models as special instances and is the *only possible form* that satisfies Requirements 1, 2, and 3.

However, we need not define the functions ζ and β in any particular form; we can regard them as *time varying unknowns* and determine their values by self-calibration. This is made possible by the fact that *at most two* time varying unknowns can be eliminated from the metric constraint of eqs. (25).

5   Procedure for 3-D Reconstruction

3-D Euclidean reconstruction using eq. (35) goes just as for the traditional camera models (see [6] for the details):

1. We fit a 3-D affine space $\mathcal{A}$ to the trajectories $\{p_\alpha\}$ by least squares. Namely, we compute the centroid m_0 by eq. (12) and compute the unit eigenvectors $\{u_1, u_2, u_3\}$ of the matrix C in eq. (14) for the largest three eigenvalues[3].
2. We eliminate time varying unknowns from the the metric constraint of eqs. (25) and solve for the metric matrix T by least squares. To be specific, substituting eqs. (36) into eqs. (25), we have

$$(u_{\kappa(1)}^\dagger, T u_{\kappa(1)}^\dagger) = \frac{1}{\zeta_\kappa^2} + \beta_\kappa^2 \tilde{t}_{x\kappa}^2, \qquad (u_{\kappa(2)}^\dagger, T u_{\kappa(2)}^\dagger) = \frac{1}{\zeta_\kappa^2} + \beta_\kappa^2 \tilde{t}_{y\kappa}^2$$

$$(u_{\kappa(1)}^\dagger, T u_{\kappa(2)}^\dagger) = \beta_\kappa^2 \tilde{t}_{x\kappa} \tilde{t}_{y\kappa}, \tag{40}$$

where $\tilde{t}_{x\kappa}$ and $\tilde{t}_{y\kappa}$ are, respectively, the $(2(\kappa-1)+1)$th and the $(2(\kappa-1)+2)$th components of the centroid m_0. Eliminating ζ_κ and β_κ, we obtain

$$A_\kappa(u_{\kappa(1)}^\dagger, T u_{\kappa(1)}^\dagger) - C_\kappa(u_{\kappa(1)}^\dagger, T u_{\kappa(2)}^\dagger) - A_\kappa(u_{\kappa(2)}^\dagger, T u_{\kappa(2)}^\dagger) = 0, \tag{41}$$

where $A_\kappa = \tilde{t}_{x\kappa}\tilde{t}_{y\kappa}$ and $C_\kappa = \tilde{t}_{x\kappa}^2 - \tilde{t}_{y\kappa}^2$. This is a linear constraint on T, so we can determine T by solving the M equations for $\kappa = 1, ..., M$ by least squares. Once we have determined T, we can determine ζ_κ and β_κ from eqs. (40) by least squares.

---

[3] This corresponds to the singular value decomposition $W = U \Lambda V^\top$ of the measurement matrix W in the traditional formulation [7, 10].

3. We decompose the metric matrix T into the rectifying matrix A in the form of eq. (24), and compute the vectors m_1, m_2, and m_3 from eq. (15).
4. We compute the translation t_κ and the rotation R_κ at each time. The translation components $t_{x\kappa}$ and $t_{y\kappa}$ are given by the first of eqs. (8) in the form of $t_{x\kappa} = \zeta_\kappa \bar{t}_{x\kappa}$ and $t_{y\kappa} = \zeta_\kappa \bar{t}_{y\kappa}$. The three rows $r_{\kappa(1)}$, $r_{\kappa(2)}$, and $r_{\kappa(3)}$ of the rotation R_κ are given by solving the linear equations

$$
\begin{aligned}
r_{\kappa(1)} && -\beta_\kappa t_{x\kappa} r_{\kappa(3)} &= \zeta_\kappa m^\dagger_{\kappa(1)}, \\
r_{\kappa(2)} -\beta_\kappa t_{y\kappa} r_{\kappa(3)} &= \zeta_\kappa m^\dagger_{\kappa(2)}, \\
\beta_\kappa t_{x\kappa} r_{\kappa(1)} +\beta_\kappa t_{y\kappa} r_{\kappa(2)} &&+r_{\kappa(3)} &= \zeta^2_\kappa m^\dagger_{\kappa(1)} \times m^\dagger_{\kappa(2)}.
\end{aligned}
\tag{42}
$$

The resulting matrix $\left(r_{\kappa(1)}\ r_{\kappa(2)}\ r_{\kappa(3)} \right)$ may not be strictly orthogonal, so we compute its singular value decomposition $V_\kappa \Lambda_\kappa U^\top_\kappa$ and let $R_\kappa = U_\kappa V^\top_\kappa$ [4].
5. We recompute the vectors m_1, m_2, and m_3 in the form of eqs. (11) using the computed rotations $R_\kappa = \left(i_\kappa\ j_\kappa\ k_\kappa \right)$.
6. We compute the object coordinates $(a_\alpha, b_\beta, c_\beta)$ of each point by least-squares expansion of p'_α in the form of eq. (13). The solution is given by $M^- p_\alpha$, using the pseudoinverse M^- of M.

However, the following indeterminacy remains:

1. Another solution is obtained by multiplying all $\{t_\kappa\}$ and $\{(a_\alpha, b_\alpha, c_\alpha)\}$ by a common constant.
2. Another solution is obtained by multiplying the all $\{R_\kappa\}$ by a common rotation. The object coordinates $\{(a_\alpha, b_\alpha, c_\alpha)\}$ are rotated accordingly.
3. Each solution has its mirror image solution. The mirror image rotation R'_κ is obtained by the rotation R_κ followed by a rotation around axis $(\beta_\kappa t_{x\kappa}, \beta_\kappa t_{y\kappa}, 1)$ by angle 2π. At the same time, the object coordinates $\{(a_\alpha, b_\alpha, c_\alpha)\}$ change their signs.
4. *The absolute depth t_z of the world coordinate origin is indeterminate.*

Item 1 is the fundamental ambiguity of 3-D reconstruction from images, meaning that a large motion of a large object in the distance is indistinguishable from a small motion of a small object nearby. Item 2 reflects the fact that the orientation of the world coordinate system can be arbitrarily chosen. Item 3 is due to eq. (24), which can be written as $T = (\pm AQ)(\pm AQ)^\top$ for an arbitrary rotation Q. This ambiguity is inherent of all affine cameras [8, 9].

Item 4 is due to the fact that eq. (35) involves only the *relative depth* of individual point from the world coordinate origin t_κ. The absolute depth t_z is determined only if ζ and β are given as *specific functions of t_z*, as in the case of the traditional camera models. Here, however, we do not specify their functional forms, directly determining their values by self-calibration and leaving t_z unspecified.

6　Experiments

Fig. 3 shows four simulated image sequences of 600×600 pixels perspectively projected with focal length $f = 600$ pixels. Each consists of 11 frames; six decimated frames are shown here. We added Gaussian random noise of mean 0 and standard deviation 1 pixel independently to the x and y coordinates of the feature points and reconstructed their 3-D shape (the frames in Fig. 3(a), (b) are merely for visual ease).

From the resulting two mirror image shapes, we choose the correct one by comparing the depths of two points that are known be close to and away from the camera. Since the absolute depth and scale are indeterminate, we translate the true and the reconstructed shapes so that their centroids are at the coordinate origin and scaled their sizes so that the root-mean-square distance of the feature points from the origin is 1. Then, we rotate the reconstructed shape so that root-mean-square distances between the corresponding points of the two shapes is minimized. We adopt the resulting residual as the measure of reconstruction accuracy.

We compare three camera models: the weak perspective, the paraperspective, and our symmetric affine camera models. The orthographic model is omitted, since evidently good results cannot be obtained when the object moves in the depth direction. For the weak perspective and paraperspective models, we need to specify the focal length f (see eqs. (4) and (5)). If the size of the reconstructed shape is normalized as described earlier, the choice of f is irrelevant for the weak perspective model, because it only affects the object size as a whole. However, the paraperspective model depends on the value of f we use.

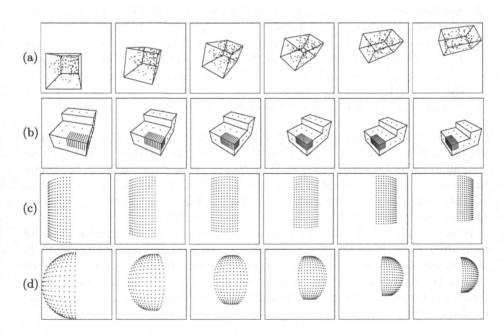

(a)

(b)

(c)

(d)

Fig. 3. Simulated image sequences (six decimated frames for each)

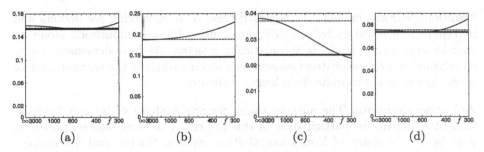

Fig. 4. 3-D reconstruction accuracy for the image sequences of Fig. 3(a)~(d). The horizontal axis is scaled in proportion to $1/f$. Three models are compared: The dashed line: weak perspective (dashed lines), paraperspective (thin solid lines), and our generic model (thick solid lines).

Fig. 4 plots the reconstruction accuracy vs. the input focal length f; the horizontal axis is scaled in proportion to $1/f$. The dashed line is for weak perspective, the thin solid line is for paraperspective, and the thick solid line is for our model. We observe that the paraperspective model does not necessarily give the highest accuracy when f coincides with the focal length (600 pixels) of the perspective images. The error is indeed minimum around $f = 600$ for Fig. 4(a), (d), but the error decreases as f increases for Fig. 4(b) and as f decreases for Fig. 4(c).

We conclude that our model achieves the accuracy comparable to paraperspective projection given an appropriate value of f, which is unknown in advance. This means that our model automatically chooses appropriate parameter values without any knowledge about f.

We conducted many other experiments (not shown here) and observed similar results. We have found that *degeneracy* can occur in special circumstances; the matrix A becomes rank deficient so that the resulting vectors $\{m_i\}$ are linearly dependent (see eq. (15)). As a result, the reconstructed shape is "flat" (see eq. (13)). This occurs when the smallest eigenvalue of T computed by least squares is negative, while eq. (24) requires T to be positive semidefinite. In the computation, we replace the negative eigenvalue by zero, resulting in degeneracy.

This type of degeneracy occurs for the traditional camera models, too. In principle, we could avoid it by parameterizing T so that it is guaranteed to be positive definite [8]. However, this would require nonlinear optimization, and the merit of the factorization approach (i.e., linear computation only) would be lost. Moreover, if we look at the images that cause degeneracy, they really look as if a planar object is moving. Since the information is insufficient in the first place, any methods may not be able to solve such degeneracy.

7   Conclusions

We showed that minimal requirements for an affine camera to mimic perspective projection leads to a unique camera model, which we call "symmetric affine camera", having two free functions, whose specific choices would result in the traditional camera models. We regarded them as time varying parameters and determined their values by self-calibration, using linear computation alone, so that an appropriate model is automatically selected. We have demonstrated by simulation that the reconstruction accuracy is comparable to the paraperspective model given an appropriate focal length estimate.

Acknowledgments. The authors thank Seitaro Asahara of Recruit Staffing, Co., Ltd., Japan, for participating in this project. This work was supported in part by the Ministry of Education, Culture, Sports, Science and Technology, Japan, under a Grant in Aid for Scientific Research C (No. 17500112).

References

1. K. Deguchi, T. Sasano, H. Arai, and H. Yoshikawa, 3-D shape reconstruction from endoscope image sequences by the factorization method, *IEICE Trans. Inf. & Syst.*, *E79-D-9* (1996-9), 1329–1336.
2. R. Hartley and A. Zisserman, *Multiple View Geometry in Computer Vision*, Cambridge University Press, Cambridge, U.K., 2000.
3. K. Kanatani, *Group-Theoretical Methods in Image Understanding*, Springer-Verlag, Berlin, Germany, 1990.
4. K. Kanatani, *Geometric Computation for Machine Vision*, Oxford University Press, Oxford, U.K., 1993.
5. K. Kanatani and Y. Sugaya, Factorization without factorization: complete recipe, *Mem. Fac. Eng. Okayama Univ.*, **38**-1/2 (2004-3), pp. 61-72.
6. K. Kanatani, Y. Sugaya and H. Ackermann, Uncalibrated factorization using a variable symmetric affine camera, *Mem. Fac. Eng. Okayama Univ.*, **40** (2006-1), pp. 53–63.
7. C. J. Poelman and T. Kanade, A paraperspective factorization method for shape and motion recovery, *IEEE Trans. Patt. Anal. Mach. Intell.*, *19*-3 (1997-3), 206–218.
8. L. Quan, Self-calibration of an affine camera from multiple views, *Int. J. Comput. Vision*, **19**-1 (1996-7), 93–105.
9. L. S. Shapiro, A. Zisserman, and M. Brady, 3D motion recovery via affine epipolar geometry, *Int. J. Comput. Vision*, **16**-2 (1995-10), 147–182.
10. C. Tomasi and T. Kanade, Shape and motion from image streams under orthography—A factorization method, *Int. J. Comput. Vision*, *9*-2 (1992-10), 137–154.

Dense Photometric Stereo by Expectation Maximization*

Tai-Pang Wu and Chi-Keung Tang

Vision and Graphics Group,
The Hong Kong University of Science and Technology,
Clear Water Bay, Hong Kong

Abstract. We formulate a robust method using Expectation Maximization (EM) to address the problem of dense photometric stereo. Previous approaches using Markov Random Fields (MRF) utilized a dense set of noisy photometric images for estimating an initial normal to encode the matching cost at each pixel, followed by normal refinement by considering the neighborhood of the pixel. In this paper, we argue that they had not fully utilized the inherent data redundancy in the dense set and that its full exploitation leads to considerable improvement. Using the same noisy and dense input, this paper contributes in learning relevant observations, recovering accurate normals and very good surface albedos, and inferring optimal parameters in an unifying EM framework that converges to an optimal solution and has no free user-supplied parameter to set. Experiments show that our EM approach for dense photometric stereo outperforms the previous approaches using the same input.

1 Introduction

Woodham [1] first introduced photometric stereo for Lambertian surfaces, in which three images are used to solve the reflectance equation for recovering surface gradients and albedos of a Lambertian surface. Since [1], extensive research on more robust techniques for photometric stereo have been reported:

More than three images. Four images were used in [2] and [3] so that inconsistent observation due to shadows or highlight can be discarded by majority vote. A larger number of images (about 20) were used in [4] where two algorithms were investigated. More recently, [5] used structure from motion and photometric stereo in an iterative framework.

Model-based approaches. In [6], an m-lobed reflective map was derived by considering diffuse and non-Lambertian surfaces. This was extended in [7] in which nonlinear regression was applied to a larger number of input images. The Torrance-Sparrow model was used in [3]. In [8], a hybrid reflectance model was used to recover surface gradients and the parameters of the reflectance model.

---

* This work was supported by the Research Grant Council of Hong Kong Special Administrative Region, China, under grant # 62005.

A. Leonardis, H. Bischof, and A. Pinz (Eds.): ECCV 2006, Part IV, LNCS 3954, pp. 159–172, 2006.

Reference objects. The use of a reference object was first introduced in [9]. In [10], surface orientations and reflectance properties are computed by using a reference object.

Despite that significant advancement has been made in photometric stereo by previous approaches, they still suffer from one or more of the following limitations:

- light directions must be very accurate. The use of uncalibrated lights require additional constraints [11].
- accurate normals and albedos cannot be recovered in the presence of highlight and cast shadows, and severe violations to the Lambertian assumption.
- in certain model-based approaches, the problem formulation is very complex, making them susceptible to numerical instability.

Recently, two Markov Random Field (MRF) inference algorithms [12, 13] were developed independently to recover normals by dense photometric stereo using a dense set of noisy photometric images conveniently captured by a simple setup. These two methods were based on similar MRF formulation but different distribution models, and made use of the neighborhood information to improve the results. For high precision normal reconstruction, the graph-cut algorithm [13] converges in a few iterations. The tensorial message passing was proposed in [12] for efficient belief propagation. In both cases, estimated normal maps are very good (certain subtle geometry can be reasonably reconstructed) despite the presence of highlight, shadows and complex geometry. Albeit this, several issues remain unaddressed:

- Albedo is not recovered in [12, 13].
- The data redundancy inherent in the dense set has not been fully utilized. Specifically, linear plane fitting was used to estimate an initial normal at each pixel based on the assumption that sufficient linear Lambertian observations are present. However, each observation, regardless of Lambertian or otherwise, is equally weighted during the plane fitting process.
- The MRF is introduced in [12, 13] to improve the results. However, the introduction implies the surface smoothness assumption. Despite the use of a discontinuity-preserving metric, [12, 13] apply the MRF refinement globally as in other MRF methods. Very fine details such as subtle texture bumps and surface imperfections will inevitably be lost after the process.
- As with other MRF processes, a user-supplied parameter is required to control the influence of neighborhood. The optimal parameter is different for different scenes and has to be determined empirically but not automatically.

In this paper, we propose a unifying framework based on the Expectation Maximization (EM) algorithm to address all the above seven issues. We shall show that considerable improvement are made by our EM approach, using the same noisy dense set as input. The organization of the paper is as follows. Section 2 reviews dense photometric stereo and describes the above issues in detail in order to motivate our work. Section 3 describes our unified EM framework. Finally, results are presented in Section 4 and we conclude our paper in Section 5.

2   Review of Dense Photometric Stereo

Given a dense set of images captured at a fixed viewpoint with their corresponding light directions, the goal of dense photometric stereo is to find the optimal
normal N_s and albedo ρ_s at each pixel s. In [13], a simple capture device was
proposed for obtaining a dense but noisy set of photometric images. By utilizing
the redundancy inherent in the captured data, a dense matching cost was derived
and used as the local evidence at each observation node in the MRF network. The
capture process is simple [13] compared with other previous approaches whereas
the methods in [12, 13] produced some of most accurate normal reconstruction to
date despite the presence of severe shadows, highlight, transparencies, complex
geometry, and inaccurate estimation in light directions.

2.1   Data Acquisition

Shown in Fig. 1(a) is the simple capture system consisting of a digital video
camera (DV), a handheld spotlight and a mirror sphere which is used to give
the light direction. The location of the brightest spot on the mirror sphere indicates the light direction which can be calculated easily [13]. Note however that
the set of estimated light directions is scattered and very noisy, as shown in
Fig. 1(c). Uniform resampling on a light direction sphere, based on icosahedron
subdivision, was performed in [13], which is also adopted in this work. The inaccurate light directions and the contaminated photometric images both make
the reconstruction problem very challenging.

(a)   (b)   (c)

Fig. 1. (a) Data capture. (b) Typical captured image. (c) A typical trajectory of the
estimated light directions shows that they are scattered and very noisy.

2.2   The MRF Formulation

Given a set of photometric images with the corresponding estimated light directions, the surface normals are estimated by maximizing the following posterior
probability [12, 13]:

$$P(X|Y) \propto \prod_s \varphi_s(x_s, y_s) \prod_s \prod_{t \in \mathcal{N}(s)} \varphi_{st}(x_s, x_t) \qquad (1)$$

where $X = \{x_s\}$, $Y = \{y_s\}$, x_s is the hidden variable (i.e. the normal to be
estimated) at pixel location s, y_s is the observed normal at s, $\mathcal{N}(s)$ is a set of
first order neighbors of s, and $\varphi_s(x_s, y_s)$ is the *local evidence* at the observation
node and $\varphi_{st}(x_s, x_t)$ is the *compatibility function*. To maximize (1), tensorial
belief propagation was used in [12] while graph-cut was used in [13].

2.3   Issues in Deriving Local Evidences

In [12, 13] the local evidence and initial normals are derived by least-square plane fitting, assuming that sufficient Lambertian observations are present and that non-Lambertian observations are noises. The reflectance at each pixel can then be described by $\rho(\mathbf{N}_s \cdot \mathbf{L})$, where ρ is the surface albedo, $\mathbf{N}_s$ is the initial normal and $\mathbf{L}$ is the light direction at the pixel s. Let T be the total number of sampled images. To eliminate ρ, we divide $T-1$ sampled images by a chosen image called *denominator image* to obtain $T-1$ *ratio images*. Let I_d be the denominator image. Each pixel in a ratio image is therefore expressed by $\frac{I_t}{I_d} = \frac{\mathbf{N}_s \cdot \mathbf{L}_t}{\mathbf{N}_s \cdot \mathbf{L}_d}$. By using no less than three ratio images, we produce a local estimation of the normal at each pixel:

$$A_t x + B_t y + C_t z = 0 \tag{2}$$

where $A_t = I_t l_{d,x} - I_d l_{t,x}$, $B_t = I_t l_{d,y} - I_d l_{t,y}$, $C_t = I_t l_{d,z} - I_d l_{t,z}$, $\mathbf{L}_t = (l_{t,x}, l_{t,y}, l_{t,z})^T$ is the light direction at time $t = 1 \cdots T$, $\mathbf{N}_s = (x, y, z)^T$ is the normal to be estimated. Note that an ideal denominator image is one that satisfies the Lambertian model and is minimally affected by shadows and specular highlight, which is difficult if not impossible to obtain. On the other hand, the use of least-square plane fitting to estimate $\mathbf{N}_s$ has several problems:

- The albedo is canceled out to produce ratio images.
- Least-square plane fitting is incapable of rejecting non-Lambertian observations. Outliers significantly affect the result of the fitting.
- If the denominator contains a non-Lambertian observation, the whole set of ratio images becomes garbage thus leading to unpredictable results.

Different alternatives of selecting the denominator image from the dense set have been proposed. Fig. 2(a) shows the normal map produced by [13]. Problems can be observed on the "ground" in the bottom part of the teapot image because only a *single* image is used which is chosen using simple criteria. Fig. 2(b) shows another initial normal map produced by [12]. The result is very noisy because in [12] *different* images were used as denominators for different pixels. Severe orientation jittering is resulted in the estimated normal map due to the non-Lambertian properties and the quantization errors of the intensities of the denominator image.

So the first question we ask is: *can we identify or learn the relevant Lambertian observations automatically?*

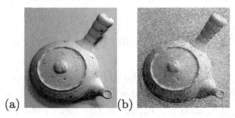

(a)   (b)

Fig. 2. Local evidence (initial normals) produced by (a) [13] and (b) [12]

2.4   Issues in Defining Compatibility Functions

In [12, 13] the noises due to non-Lambertian observations and inaccurate estimation in light directions that cannot be handled by plane fitting are addressed by the MRF refinement process which assumes that the underlying surface is locally smooth. Although discontinuity-preserving functions are used, the smoothing effect is applied globally because we have no prior knowledge which regions should be smoothed. If the variation in global and local surface orientation do not match, over-smoothing will occur. Therefore, fine details such as surface imperfections and texture bumps are inevitably lost. Thus, in [12, 13] and other MRF algorithms, a free parameter should be supplied by the user to control the degree of smoothness. The parameters are empirically obtained and varies with different scenes.

So, the second question we ask is: *how can we obtain the set of optimal parameters automatically?*

3   Normal and Albedo Estimation by Expectation Maximization

In this paper, a unified EM algorithm is proposed which identifies relevant Lambertian observations automatically by fully exploiting the data redundancy inherent in the dense and noisy data. Our results show significant improvement without any MRF smoothing refinement and thus the setting of MRF parameters is no longer an issue. In fact, by using our EM algorithm, *all* parameters can be optimized alternately within the same framework, making the robust method free of any user-supplied parameters.

In this section, we formulate our EM algorithm to estimate the surface albedos and normals from a set of dense and noisy measurement captured as described in the previous section. In [12, 13], the simple least-square plane fitting is used for initial normal estimation. No special handling is performed for unreliable data or outliers generated by non-Lambertian phenomena such as specular highlight and shadows. In real cases, however, these observations occupy a significant proportion in the captured data due to the restrictive Lambertian model and the diversity of surface geometry and material.

Suppose that the measurement error for each observation is known. We could perform *weighted* least-square plane fitting to weaken the contribution of defective data. However, given the simple data capture system, it is very difficult to estimate such measurement errors. In this paper we propose a data-driven approach to estimate the weight of each observation by utilizing useful information inherent in the dense set although it consists of scattered and noisy data.

3.1   Overview

While the albedo is problematic and canceled out in [12, 13], in this paper we use the albedo as one of the contributing factors in estimating the weight of each observed intensity. The idea is as follows. Consider a pixel location i.

Suppose the albedo ρ_i is known, given the observed intensity I_{it} at time t and the corresponding light direction $\mathbf{L}_{it}$, we model the probability of the intensity I_{it} generated by the Lambertian model without shadow and specular highlight to be inversely proportional to:

$$||I_{it} - \rho_i \mathbf{N}_i \cdot \mathbf{L}_{it}|| \qquad (3)$$

where $\mathbf{N}_i$ is the normal at pixel i. Thus, if the albedo is known, more information concerning the observations can be extracted.

However, albedo derivation alone is a difficult problem. In this paper, we demonstrate how the albedo and surface normal can be estimated *simultaneously* using an EM framework to obtain accurate results.

While we argue that plane fitting without a proper contribution weight for each observation is not a good solution, some useful lesson can still be learnt from [12, 13]. Suppose that each image is a candidate of the denominator image. If we have T different observations for a pixel location, in total, we can produce T different planes by using all images successively as the denominator. For the denominators consisting of non-Lambertian observations, the orientations of the fitted planes are arbitrary because the denominator intensity interacts with all other intensity samples when ratio images are derived during plane fitting and thus the whole data set is contaminated. For the other denominators whose observations are explained by the Lambertian model, however, the orientations of the produced planes should cluster themselves together. Despite that such estimated planes are not error-free because of the presence of outliers, the cluster limits the solution space for the optimal surface orientation at the pixel.

3.2   The Objective Function

The main reason of using the EM approach is that the above-mentioned cues are not given but are inherent within the data itself. Alternating optimization approaches such as EM allow for the simultaneous estimation of the cues and the solution. In this section, we define our objective function which forms the basis of our EM algorithm.

Without confusion, in the rest of this section, the index of pixel location i will be dropped to simplify the notation, since the algorithm is applied individually at each pixel location.

We define $\mathbf{O} = \{o_t\}$ to be the set of observations, where $t = 1..T$ and T is the total number of captured images, $o_t = \{I_t, \mathbf{n}_t\}$, I_t (a 3-vector in RGB space) is the observed intensity at time t, and $\mathbf{n}_t$ is the normal obtained after plane fitting with image t as the denominator image.[1]

To encode the clustering of $\{\mathbf{n}_t\}$, a 3×3 covariance matrix $\mathbf{K}$ that stores the second-order moment collection is used since it represents the orientation distribution. The optimal normal is the direction that gives the largest variance in $\mathbf{K}$.

---

[1] Note that we only use the highest 50% intensities as numerators to perform plane fitting because dark pixels tend to be affected by shadows and the presence of a large number of outliers will affect the accuracy of the estimated normal. The aforementioned number of samples provides sufficient redundancy for robust estimation.

Our goal is to find the optimal albedo ρ (a 3-vector in RGB space) and the covariance matrix $\mathbf{K}$ given the pixel observations. In other words, we want to estimate the following:

$$\Theta^* = \arg\max_{\Theta} P(\mathbf{O}, \mathbf{S}|\Theta) \tag{4}$$

where $P(\mathbf{O}, \mathbf{S}|\Theta)$ is the complete-data likelihood we want to maximize, $\Theta = \{\mathbf{K}, \rho, \alpha, \sigma\}$ is a set of parameters to be estimated and $\mathbf{S} = \{s_t\}$ is a set of hidden states indicating which observation is generated by the Lambertian model. $s_t = 1$ if o_t is generated by Lambertian model, $s_t = 0$ otherwise. α and σ are respectively the proportion of Lambertian observations and the standard deviation of Eqn. 3, which are the parameters that help us to find the solution and will be described.

Our EM algorithm estimates Eqn. 4 by finding the expected value of the complete-data log-likelihood $\log P(\mathbf{O}, \mathbf{S}|\Theta)$ w.r.t. $\mathbf{S}$ given the observation $\mathbf{O}$ and the current estimated parameters:

$$Q(\Theta, \Theta') = \sum_{\mathbf{S} \in \varphi} \log P(\mathbf{O}, \mathbf{S}|\Theta) P(\mathbf{S}|\mathbf{O}, \Theta') d\mathbf{S} \tag{5}$$

where Θ' are current parameters and φ is a space containing all $\mathbf{S}$ of size T.

3.3 Expectation Estimation

In this section, we address how to estimate the marginal distribution $p(s_t|o_t, \Theta')$ so that we can maximize the expectation Q defined by Eqn. 5 by proceeding to the next iteration given the current parameters.

If s_t is known, the observation o_t that is generated by the Lambertian model minimizes Eqn. 3 and $\mathbf{n}_t^T \mathbf{K}^{-1} \mathbf{n}_t$. Suppose that the noise distribution of Eqn. 3 and the jittering distribution of $\mathbf{n}_t$ are Gaussian distributions, and that the existence of non-Lambertian observations follow a uniform distribution. The observation probability of o_t is:

$$p(o_t|s_t, \Theta') \propto \begin{cases} \exp(-\frac{||I_t - \rho \mathbf{n}_t \cdot \mathbf{L}_t||^2}{2\sigma^2}) \exp(-\frac{1}{2}\mathbf{n}_t^T \mathbf{K}^{-1}\mathbf{n}_t), & \text{if } s_t = 1; \\ \frac{1}{C}, & \text{if } s_t = 0. \end{cases} \tag{6}$$

Base on the uniform distribution assumption, the choice of C should be $max\{I_t - \rho \mathbf{n}_t \cdot \mathbf{L}_t\}$. However, in real case, the assumption can be violated seriously. To lower the chance of wrong classification, we choose $C = C_m = mean\{I_t - \rho \mathbf{n}_t \cdot \mathbf{L}_t\}$ because smaller C trends to classify more observations to $s_t = 0$. This lowers the probability of the non-Lambertian samples in obtaining wrong labels while we still have sufficient redundancy for estimation robustness. To calculate C, we choose ρ to be the color has median gray-level intensity. Indeed, C needs not to be precise. In all of our experiments, varying C, $C_m \leq C \leq 2C_m$ produces very similar results and thus this constant is not critical.

Let α be the proportion of the observation generated by the Lambertian model. Then we have a mixture probability of the observations:

$$p(s_t = 1) = \alpha \tag{7}$$

So, given Θ' only, we have

$$p(o_t|\Theta') \propto \alpha \, \exp(-\frac{||I_t - \rho \mathbf{n}_t \cdot \mathbf{L}_t||^2}{2\sigma^2}) \exp(-\frac{1}{2}\mathbf{n}_t^T \mathbf{K}^{-1} \mathbf{n}_t) + \frac{1-\alpha}{C} \qquad (8)$$

Let w_t be the probability of o_t being generated by the Lambertian model. Then:

$$
\begin{aligned}
w_t = p(s_t = 1|o_t, \Theta') &= \frac{p(o_t, s_t = 1|\Theta')}{p(o_t|\Theta')} \\
&= \frac{\alpha \, \exp(-\frac{||I_t - \rho \mathbf{n}_t \cdot \mathbf{L}_t||^2}{2\sigma^2}) \exp(-\frac{1}{2}\mathbf{n}_t^T \mathbf{K}^{-1}\mathbf{n}_t)}{\alpha \, \exp(-\frac{||I_t - \rho \mathbf{n}_t \cdot \mathbf{L}_t||^2}{2\sigma^2}) \exp(-\frac{1}{2}\mathbf{n}_t^T \mathbf{K}^{-1}\mathbf{n}_t) + \frac{1-\alpha}{C}}
\end{aligned} \qquad (9)
$$

Hence, in the E-step of our EM algorithm, we compute w_t for all $t = 1 \cdots T$.

3.4 Maximization

In this section, we maximize the likelihood (Eqn. 4) given the marginal distribution w_t computed in the E-Step.

Since we only have two states $\{0,1\}$ for each s_t, the Q function (Eqn. 5) is:

$$
\begin{aligned}
Q(\Theta, \Theta') &= \sum_t \log p(o_t, s_t = 1|\Theta)w_t + \sum_t \log p(o_t, s_t = 0|\Theta)(1 - w_t) \\
&= \sum_t \log(\alpha \frac{1}{\sigma\sqrt{2\pi}} \exp(-\frac{||I_t - \rho\mathbf{n}_t \cdot \mathbf{L}_t||^2}{2\sigma^2}))w_t \\
&\quad + \sum_t \log(\frac{1}{|\mathbf{K}|^{\frac{1}{2}}(2\pi)^{\frac{3}{2}}} \exp(-\frac{1}{2}\mathbf{n}_t^T \mathbf{K}^{-1}\mathbf{n}_t))w_t \\
&\quad + \sum_t \log(\frac{1-\alpha}{C})(1 - w_t)
\end{aligned} \qquad (10)
$$

To maximize (10), we set the first derivative of Q w.r.t. α, σ, ρ and $\mathbf{K}$ respectively equals to zero and obtain the following:

$$
\begin{aligned}
\alpha &= \frac{1}{T}\sum_t w_t \\
\sigma &= \frac{\sum_t ||I_t - \rho \mathbf{n}_t \cdot \mathbf{L}_t||^2 w_t}{\sum_t w_t} \\
\rho &= \frac{1}{\sum_t (\mathbf{n}_t \cdot \mathbf{L}_t)^2 w_t} \sum_t I_t(\mathbf{n}_t \cdot \mathbf{L}_t)w_t \\
\mathbf{K} &= \frac{1}{\sum_t w_t} \sum_t \mathbf{n}_t \mathbf{n}_t^T w_t
\end{aligned} \qquad (11)
$$

which constitutes the parameter updating rule for Θ and thus the M-Step of our EM algorithm. The E-Step and M-Step are executed alternately until the process converges. The convergence of EM was well established [14].

Upon convergence, we apply eigen-decomposition on **K** to obtain the optimal normal direction. The eigenvector corresponding to the largest eigenvalue gives the normal direction.

In addition, using our method, we produce not only surface normals but also surface albedo ρ and the weights w_t indicating the degree an observation o_t is consistent with the Lambertian model. Such inferred information is very useful in parameter estimation for fitting analytic reflectance models to real and noisy observations.

4   Experimental Results

In this section, we first demonstrate the considerable improvement by comparing our method with [13] using the same input data. The synthetic case we use is *Three Spheres* and the real examples are *Teapot*, *Rope* and *Toy Car*. After the comparison, we apply our method to reconstruct albedos and normals on selected complex objects to examine the robustness and efficacy of our method. The running time of all the examples are tabulated in Table 1.

Three Spheres. Fig. 3(a)–(b) show two input synthetic images of *Three Spheres*. The depicted object is generated by the Phong illumination model. Fig 3(e) and (f) shows respectively the normal map produced by [13] and by our EM method. Note that they are rendered using the Lambertian model ($\mathbf{N} \cdot \mathbf{L}$) for clarity of display. The ground truth is shown in Fig. 3(c). Our estimated albedo is shown in Fig. 3(d). Qualitatively, the appearance of (c), (e) and (f) are very similar. On the other hand, the image difference show the clear improvement of our method in terms of accuracy. Fig. 3(g) is the image difference between (c) and (e), while Fig. 3(h) is the image difference between (c) and (f). Notice the presence of three halos in Fig. 3(g) which are brighter than those observed in Fig. 3(h), which is nearly totally black. We measure the mean angular error of the recovered normals to evaluate both methods quantitatively. Using *Three Spheres*, the mean error of the result produced by [13] is 4.041 degree while the error of our EM result is only 1.5065 degree.

Teapot. Our method shows very significant improvement in the presence of a large amount of noises in the representative case of *Teapot*, which is one of the most difficult examples in [13] where the geometry and texture are very complex.

Table 1. Summary of running times. The experiments were run on a shared CPU server with 4 Opteron(TM) 844 CPU at 1.8GHz with 16GB Memory.

Data set	Three Spheres	Teapot	Toy Car	Rope	Face	Hair
Number of images	305	282	287	265	195	189
Image Size	256x256	188x202	181x184	171x144	216x225	224x298
Running Time	3m04s	4m24s	4m37s	4m09s	4m45s	3m25s

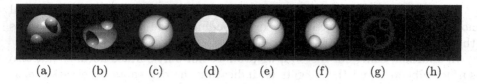

(a)   (b)   (c)   (d)   (e)   (f)   (g)   (h)

Fig. 3. *Three Spheres*: (a)–(b) Two typical noisy input images. (c) The ground truth normal map. (d) The albedo ρ produced by our EM method. (e) The normal map produced by [13]. (f) The normal map produced by our EM method. (g) The image difference between (c) and (e). (h) the image difference between (c) and (f). Note that (c), (e) and (f) are rendered using the pure Lambertian model ($\mathbf{N\cdot L}$) with $\mathbf{L} = (0, 0, 1)^T$.

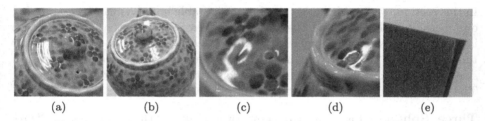

(a)   (b)   (c)   (d)   (e)

Fig. 4. Detail of the *Teapot*: (a)–(b) The specular reflection depicts the concentric ripple-shaped structures on the lid. (c) The specular reflection depicts a smooth but shallow *dent* near the hole of the lid. (d) A small *bump* at the center of a deep-colored flower pattern. (e) A black cardboard with a lot of *surface imperfections*, which is the plane where the teapot is placed for image capturing.

To better illustrate how our result has been improved, let us study in detail the geometry of the *Teapot* using Fig. 4. The selected close-up views of the teapot reveal fine surface details and subtle geometry.

The complete set of the result shown in Fig. 5. Fig. 5(a) and (b) show two sample input images which are contaminated by highlight and shadows. To show the overall smoothness, Fig. 5(c) depicts the color coded normal map produced by our EM method where $(R, G, B) = (\frac{x+1}{2}, \frac{y+1}{2}, z)$ and $\mathbf{N} = (x, y, z)^T$. Fig. 5(d) is the albedo ρ image produced by our EM method. Fig. 5(e) shows the local evidence of [13] which consists of the initial normals produced by the plane fitting method reviewed in Section 2 or described in [13]. Fig. 5(g) is the final result produced by [13] where all surface details are smoothed out. For clarity of display, Fig. 5(f) and (h) show the same normal map produced by our EM method, which are rendered using the Lambertian model ($\mathbf{N \cdot L}$) illuminated at two different light directions.

It is evident that, although Fig. 5(g) demonstrates a visually smoother appearance, all the fine details described in Fig. 4 are lost due to the MRF refinement process. However, Fig. 5(e) show that if MRF process is not applied in [13], due to the complexity of the texture and the geometry, the surface normals produced are unsatisfactory and severe artifacts can be observed. On the other hand, our method preserves all important fine details of the *Teapot* illustrated and revealed in the close-up views of Fig. 4.

Fig. 5. *Teapot*: (a)–(b) Two captured images. (c) The color coded normal map produced by our EM method. (d) The albedo ρ estimated by our EM method. (e) The local evidence of [13]. (g) The final normal map in [13]. (f) and (h) are the same normal map produced by our EM method. Note that the normal maps in (e)– (h) are rendered using the pure Lambertian model $(\mathbf{N} \cdot \mathbf{L})$ where the light directions in (e), (g) and (h) are respectively $\mathbf{L} = (\frac{1}{\sqrt{3}}, \frac{1}{\sqrt{3}}, \frac{1}{\sqrt{3}})^T$ and in (f) is $\mathbf{L} = (0, 0, 1)^T$. Please see the electronic version for higher resolution display.

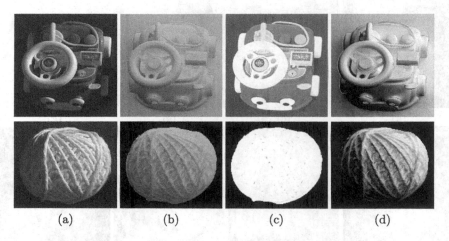

Fig. 6. Toy Car (first row) / Rope (second row) : (a) One of the input images. (b) The color coded normal map produced by our EM method. (c) The albedo ρ estimated by our EM method. (e) The normal map produced by our EM method rendered by the pure Lambertian model $(\mathbf{N} \cdot \mathbf{L})$ where the light direction $\mathbf{L} = (\frac{1}{\sqrt{3}}, \frac{1}{\sqrt{3}}, \frac{1}{\sqrt{3}})^T$.

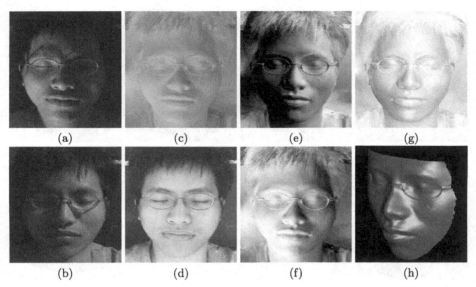

(a)   (c)   (e)   (g)

(b)   (d)   (f)   (h)

Fig. 7. *Face*: (a)–(b) Two captured images. (c) The color coded normal map produced by our EM method. (d) The albedo ρ estimated by our EM method. (e)–(g) The normal map produced by our EM method rendered using the Lambertian model ($\mathbf{N} \cdot \mathbf{L}$) where the light direction in (e), (f) and (g) are $\mathbf{L} = (\frac{1}{\sqrt{3}}, \frac{1}{\sqrt{3}}, \frac{1}{\sqrt{3}})^T$, $\mathbf{L} = (-\frac{1}{\sqrt{3}}, -\frac{1}{\sqrt{3}}, \frac{1}{\sqrt{3}})^T$ and $\mathbf{L} = (0, 0, 1)^T$ respectively. (h) The reconstructed surface.

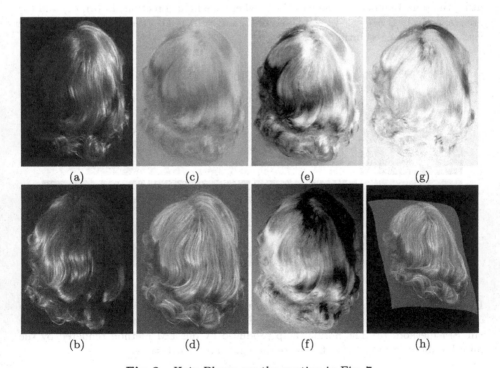

(a)   (c)   (e)   (g)

(b)   (d)   (f)   (h)

Fig. 8. *Hair*: Please see the caption in Fig. 7

Toy Car and Rope. We applied our method to two existing data sets and the results are shown in Fig. 6. Our method works very well in estimating the surface albedos and surface normals. Hardly any shading is left in the albedo image of *Toy Car*. For *Rope*, only some small spots of shadow artifact are left in the albedo image because these regions were always under shadow due to the complex mesostructure. Besides, the surface normal maps obtained are more accurate than the maps obtained in [13].

Face and Hair. Human face and hair reconstruction are receiving more attention in the area of computer vision and computer graphics. Both human features consist of complex geometry and fine details and are non-Lambertian.

Fig. 7 shows our result on *Face*. The normal map (Fig. 7(e)–(g)) shows that our method retains the subtle geometry such as the pimple and other facial imperfections. Fig. 7(d) shows the estimated albedo image. Fig. 7(h) depicts the reconstructed surface by [15] using our normal map as input.

Fig. 8 shows our result on *Hair*. The normal map (Fig. 8(e)–(g)) shows that our method preserves the curvilinearity and the meso-structural details of the hair. Observe that some structure information are left in the albedo image (Fig. 8(d)). There are two reasons. First, although the sampled light directions are very dense, some pixels are always occluded and thus under shadows due to the complexity of the hair geometry. Besides, the Lambertian model is not sufficient to describe human hairs and so Lambertian samples are rare even dense measurement is available. These two problems make the estimation process extremely challenging; yet our method still produces very good result in normal estimation.

5   Conclusion

In this paper we propose a robust method for dense photometric stereo reconstruction using the Expectation Maximization (EM). By exploiting useful information inherent in the dense and noisy set of photometric images, this paper contributes in identifying relevant observations, recovering very good normals and albedos, and estimating optimal parameters in an automatic EM framework that has no free user-supplied parameter to set. The convergence of the EM method has been well established. Very good results have been obtained, showing that our EM approach is robust in the presence of severe shadows, highlight, complex and subtle geometry, and inaccurate light directions. Our future work focuses on the use of adaptive MRF refinement to further improve the accuracy and applicability of our EM technique for photometric stereo.

References

1. Woodham, R.: Photometric method for determining surface orientation from multiple images. OptEng **19**(1) (1980) 139–144
2. Coleman, Jr., E., Jain, R.: Obtaining 3-dimensional shape of textured and specular surfaces using four-source photometry. CGIP **18**(4) (1982) 309–328

3. Solomon, F., Ikeuchi, K.: Extracting the shape and roughness of specular lobe objects using four light photometric stereo. PAMI **18**(4) (1996) 449–454
4. Lee, K., Kuo, C.: Shape reconstruction from photometric stereo. In: CVPR92. (1992) 479–484
5. Lim, J., Ho, J., Yang, M., Kriegman, D.: Passive photometric stereo from motion. In: ICCV05. (2005)
6. Tagare, H., deFigueiredo, R.: A theory of photometric stereo for a class of diffuse non-lambertian surfaces. PAMI **13**(2) (1991) 133–152
7. Kay, G., Caelly, T.: Estimating the parameters of an illumination model using photometric stereo. GMIP **57**(5) (1995) 365–388
8. Nayar, S., Ikeuchi, K., Kanade, T.: Determining shape and reflectance of hybrid surfaces by photometric sampling. IEEE Trans. on Robotics and Automation **6**(4) (1990) 418–431
9. Horn, B., Woodham, R., Silver, W.: Determining shape and reflectance using multiple images. In: MIT AI Memo. (1978)
10. Hertzmann, A., Seitz, S.: Shape and materials by example: a photometric stereo approach. In: CVPR03. (2003) I: 533–540
11. Drbohlav, O., Sara, R.: Unambiguous determination of shape from photometric stereo with unknown light sources. In: ICCV01. (2001)
12. Tang, K., Tang, C., Wong, T.: Dense photometric stereo using tensorial belief propagation. In: CVPR2005. Volume 1. (2005) 132–139
13. Wu, T., Tang, C.: Dense photometric stereo using a mirror sphere and graph cut. In: CVPR2005. Volume 1. (2005) 140–147
14. Bilmes, J.: A gentle tutorial on the EM algorithm and its application to parameter estimation for Gaussian mixture and hidden Markov models. Technical Report ICSI-TR-97-021, ICSI (1997)
15. Kovesi, P.: Shapelets correlated with surface normals produce surfaces. In: ICCV05. (2005)

Space-Time-Scale Registration of Dynamic Scene Reconstructions

Kemal E. Ozden[1], Kurt Cornelis[1], and Luc Van Gool[1,2]

[1] ESAT/PSI, Computer Vision Lab., K.U. Leuven, Belgium
{Egemen.Ozden, Kurt.Cornelis, Luc.Vangool}@esat.kuleuven.be
http://www.esat.kuleuven.be/psi/visics/
[2] BIWI, ETH, Zurich, Switzerland
vangool@vision.ee.ethz.ch
http://www.vision.ee.ethz.ch/

Abstract. The paper presents a method for multi-dimensional registration of two video streams. The sequences are captured by two hand-held cameras moving independently with respect to each other, both observing one object rigidly moving apart from the background. The method is based on uncalibrated Structure-from-Motion (SfM) to extract 3D models for the foreground object and the background, as well as for their relative motion. It fixes the relative scales between the scene parts within and between the videos. It also provides the registration between all partial 3D models, and the temporal synchronization between the videos. The crux is that not a single point on the foreground or background needs to be in common between both video streams. Extensions to more than two cameras and multiple foreground objects are possible.

1 Introduction

Structure-from-Motion (SfM) techniques have made impressive progress in the last two decades [11]. They can compute 3D models and camera motion out of image sequences coming from a single moving camera. However, most of these methods can only cope with static scenes and this limitation is one of the biggest challenges for applying SfM in real life, with its many dynamic elements. Nevertheless, some SfM techniques for dynamic scenes are around [2, 3, 6, 9] and the subject is getting more and more attention.

A subtle issue with uncalibrated SfM is that scenes can only be reconstructed up to an unknown scale between the independently moving objects. This does not only have an impact on the relative sizes of the objects, but actually also on the shape of their trajectories with respect to the background. Typical approaches to solve this problem, explicitly or implicitly, make assumptions about the object motion, e.g. [13, 15, 1]. Here we propose an alternative solution. It requires multiple cameras but it works with generic object motions and without any corresponding features between the video streams. Not only does it allow to determine the relative scales, the videos are also synchronized and the resulting 3D extracted from each stream is spatially registered.

A. Leonardis, H. Bischof, and A. Pinz (Eds.): ECCV 2006, Part IV, LNCS 3954, pp. 173–185, 2006.

Obviously, this is far from the first work using multiple cameras in a SfM context. Here we only mention the most related work. In [7], the relative displacement between the cameras of a stereo rig is computed using several motions of the rig. In [24], a self-calibration method for a moving rig is presented where the rig itself does not need to be rigid, however some constraints on the camera orientations are still required. In [25], a non-rigid scene is reconstructed with static orthographic stereo cameras. All of the above work has the common advantage of being correspondence-free, i.e. there are no stereo correspondences between the cameras.

Here, we use two (hand-held) cameras moving completely independently with respect to each other, still not assuming knowledge of any correspondences. The price to pay for this freedom is that at least one moving and rigid object ought to be observed by both cameras as the information from the background itself is not enough to solve the problem. The fact that the object should move the same way with respect to the background in both sequences is the trivial but key observation exploited by the algorithm. It can thereby fix the scales of the object and the background, bring their partial 3D reconstructions into registration, and even synchronize - i.e. temporally align - the two videos.

Video synchronization in combination with (partial) camera calibration has also been studied by several researchers, and the exploitation of moving objects in particular as well. For example, Caspi et al. [4] use point trajectories to find a suitable transformation to spatio-temporally align image sequences. Sinha and Pollefeys [18] also combine camera calibration with synchronization, but they use fixed cameras. These papers still require the visibility of the same points at the same time. Caspi et al. [5] could lift this restriction by using moving cameras with the same optical center. The views were aligned in space (through a homography) and in time.

2   Problem

In this paper we consider two hand-held cameras which move independently with respect to each other. Furthermore, we consider a single object moving independently against a static background. The cameras may view the moving object from totally different directions, so it is well possible that there are no common feature points between the video sequences both for the background and the foreground. However it is required that the cameras see the same rigidly moving object, though possibly different parts thereof.

In order to reconstruct such a scene the first step is to segment the foreground object from the background for which several solutions are available (e.g. [6, 12, 16, 20, 21]), though currently we are doing it manually. This then allows a typical uncalibrated SfM algorithm [11] to be applied to the object and background segments in each of the videos. This results in four 3D point clouds and four sets of camera matrices (trajectories relative to the capturing camera). These cannot be readily integrated however, not even for the object and background data derived from the same camera. Several parameters need to be determined first.

Three of those parameters come from the fact that uncalibrated SfM is defined only up to a scale factor, i.e. the scene reconstructed from a single moving camera has a scale ambiguity for every independently moving object. This scale ambiguity is not a serious problem in the case of an entirely rigid scene, since then everything has correct relative scales and only the absolute scale is missing. However, for independently moving objects the correct relative scale with respect to the background is also unknown and may result in unrealistic reconstructions. This is a problem that cannot be resolved through hard geometric constraints among the frames of a single video. As a matter of fact, there is an entire one-dimensional family of relative scales + corresponding trajectories for the object with respect to the background, which are all *fully* compatible with all image data within the sequence [13, 15]. Many special effects in movies are based on this fact. When seeing a car driving on a road it could actually also be a miniature car close to the camera with a motion quite different from that of an actual car.

In the case of monocular input this ambiguity can be lifted by assuming that the object is following a plausible motion constraint [13, 15]. Here it is shown that the use of two cameras allows the objects to move arbitrarily. We will have to determine the 3D similarity transformation between the reconstructed backgrounds in the two videos, as well as the relative scales of the foreground in each video with respect to its background. This will require the synchronization of the two videos.

Suppose we fix the scale for the background in one video. We will have to determine the correct relative scale of the foreground in the same video, as well as the scales which then have to be applied to the foreground and the background in the other video. Therefore, two unknown relative scales and one inter-camera scale ambiguity count for the three scale parameters we have to solve for. Obviously, there is also an Euclidean transformation (defined by six parameters) between the reconstructions coming from the different cameras. So in total we have to solve for nine parameters. The wrong choice for these parameters will result in a different object motion for each different video stream which actually must be identical. Our goal is to search for those parameters which will make the object motions for both sequences identical or if stated in a different way, which will make the overall object motion the most rigid since if the objects motions as seen from both cameras are identical, the related foreground point clouds must move rigidly.

3   Notation and Basic Formulation

The two cameras are arbitrarily labeled as the first and the second camera. Applying SfM to the first sequence yields the following object transformation matrices:

$$\mathbf{M}^i = \mathbf{T}^i \mathbf{M} = \begin{bmatrix} \mathbf{R}^i_o & \mathbf{t}^i_o \\ \mathbf{0} & 1 \end{bmatrix} \mathbf{M} \tag{1}$$

which describe the motion of a 3D homogeneous point $\mathbf{M}$, which is a fixed point in the object coordinate system. $\mathbf{M}^i$ is the position of point $\mathbf{M}$ at frame index

i in the world coordinate system. Typically the camera pose of the first frame is chosen as the world coordinate system, which is also the case here. $\mathbf{R}_o^i$ is a 3×3 rotation matrix and $\mathbf{t}_o^i$ is a 3×1 translation vector. It is very important to note that $\mathbf{T}^i$ is computed by multiplying the inverse of the related background motion matrix with the relative motion matrix of the foreground, both of which are direct outputs of the SfM algorithm (see [13, 15]).

However, due to unknown relative scales, there exists a one-parameter family of solutions [13, 15] for these object transformation matrices because:

$$\mathbf{t}_o^i = m \left(\mathbf{t}_{of}^i - \mathbf{t}_c^i \right) + \mathbf{t}_c^i \tag{2}$$

where $\mathbf{t}_{of}^i$ is a particular solution for the object translation and $\mathbf{t}_c^i$ is the position of the optical center in the world coordinate system, which are both returned by SfM. The one-parameter family is described by scale factor m. To give an intuitive explanation we can interpret Eq (2) as a set of 3D lines which pass through the optical center at each frame index i. Consequently, every point on these lines project to the same location in the same image given any value m.

The world coordinate system will be different for both image sequences since the camera poses for the first frame will differ. However, a similarity transformation exists which aligns the world coordinate systems of both sequences:

$$\mathbf{M}^i = \mathbf{X}\mathbf{M}'^i \text{ with } \mathbf{X} = \begin{bmatrix} k\mathbf{R} & \mathbf{t} \\ \mathbf{0} & 1 \end{bmatrix} \tag{3}$$

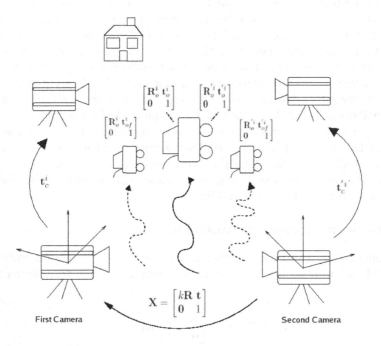

Fig. 1. A depiction of the transformations. Due to the relative scale ambiguity, different cameras see arbitrarily scaled objects and ambiguous object translations.

where $\mathbf{M}^{'i}$ is a point in the second image sequence which corresponds to point $\mathbf{M}^i$ in the first sequence. Here, it is important to stress that $\mathbf{X}$ is a transformation between the 3D reconstruction reference frames, and not between the moving cameras. Therefore, $\mathbf{X}$ is constant throughout the sequence but the transformation between the camera local coordinate systems is allowed to change freely.

The aforementioned transformations are all illustrated in Fig. 1 in which the superscript $'$ accompanies the symbols related to the second sequence.

4 Solution

Combining Eq. (1) and Eq. (3) for both sequences, we arrive at:

$$\begin{bmatrix} \mathbf{R}_o^i & \mathbf{t}_o^i \\ 0 & 1 \end{bmatrix} = \mathbf{X} \begin{bmatrix} \mathbf{R}_o^{'i} & \mathbf{t}_o^{'i} \\ 0 & 1 \end{bmatrix} \mathbf{X}^{-1} \tag{4}$$

which is a different form of the famous hand-eye calibration problem. A common technique in hand-eye calibration is to solve for the rotation part first:

$$\mathbf{R}_o = \mathbf{R}\mathbf{R}_o^{'}\mathbf{R}^T \tag{5}$$

and subsequently solve for the translation part:

$$\mathbf{t}_o = -\mathbf{R}_o\mathbf{t} + k\mathbf{R}\mathbf{t}_o^{'} + \mathbf{t} \tag{6}$$

where the frame indices have been dropped for ease of notation. We will follow the same approach. As to the solution of Eq. (5) it is known that every rotation matrix has an axis which remains unaffected under that particular rotation. Let $\mathbf{n}$ be that axis for $\mathbf{R}_o$ and $\mathbf{n}^{'}$ be that axis for $\mathbf{R}_o^{'}$. It can be derived and intuitively understood that after alignment of the world coordinate systems of both sequences the axes of the related rotations must be identical:

$$\mathbf{n} = \mathbf{R}\mathbf{n}^{'} \tag{7}$$

Many solutions have been proposed to solve the above equation, e.g. [8, 17, 19]. We chose the unit quaternion approach by Faugeras and Hebert [8] which is also detailed in Horaud and Dornaika [10]. Unit quaternions are 4-parameter imaginary representations of rotations in 3D. Since their length is one, their degree of freedom is three as expected from a rotation representation. The operation of a rotation matrix on other rotation matrices and 3D vectors can be easily represented as quaternion multiplications. The rotation of a 3D vector $\mathbf{n}$ with the rotation matrix $\mathbf{R}$ can be written as:

$$\mathbf{q} * \mathbf{n}_q^{'} * \overline{\mathbf{q}} = \mathbf{R}\mathbf{n}^{'} \tag{8}$$

where $\mathbf{q}$ is the quaternion representation of $\mathbf{R}$, $\overline{\mathbf{q}}$ is the conjugate of $\mathbf{q}$, $\mathbf{n}_q^{'}$ is the quaternion representation of the vector $\mathbf{n}^{'}$ and $*$ is quaternion multiplication.

As we have many frames and noisy data, it is practically impossible to find a perfect solution to Eq. (7) so we should minimize an error criterion. The one used here is the total 3D squared distance between the corresponding rotation axes after the application of rotation **R** which can be written as:

$$E_1 = \sum_{i=1}^{\#frames} \left| \mathbf{n}_q^i - \mathbf{q} * \mathbf{n}_q'^i * \bar{\mathbf{q}} \right|^2 \tag{9}$$

Since quaternions are of unit length, the statement inside the summation can be written as :

$$\left| \mathbf{n}_q^i - \mathbf{q} * \mathbf{n}_q'^i * \bar{\mathbf{q}} \right|^2 = \left| \mathbf{n}_q^i - \mathbf{q} * \mathbf{n}_q'^i * \bar{\mathbf{q}} \right|^2 |\mathbf{q}|^2 \tag{10}$$

$$= \left| \mathbf{n}_q^i * \mathbf{q} - \mathbf{q} * \mathbf{n}_q'^i \right|^2 \tag{11}$$

$$= \mathbf{q}^T \mathbf{A}^i \mathbf{q} \tag{12}$$

where $\mathbf{A}^i$ is a 4×4 matrix whose elements are computed from $\mathbf{n}^i$ and $\mathbf{n}'^i$ [8, 10]. In the end we have a minimization of the form :

$$E_1 = \mathbf{q}^T \mathbf{A} \mathbf{q} \tag{13}$$

where $\mathbf{A} = \sum_{i=1}^{\#frames} \mathbf{A}^i$. When we try to minimize Eq. (13) with the constraint that quaternions are of unit length, the quaternion turns out to be the eigenvector of A corresponding to the minimum eigen-value.

Now that the rotation parameters are computed, we can proceed to solve Eq. (6) for the translation and the scale parameters. Inserting Eq.(2) for both sequences into Eq.(6) results in:

$$\mathbf{t}_c = (\mathbf{t}_c - \mathbf{t}_{of}) m + (\mathbf{I} - \mathbf{R}_o) \mathbf{t} + \left(\mathbf{R} \mathbf{t}_c' \right) k + \left(\mathbf{R} \mathbf{t}_{of}' - \mathbf{R} \mathbf{t}_c' \right) k m' \tag{14}$$

which is a linear equation in terms of $\mathbf{t}$, k,m and km' . In a typical scenario, we would have redundant equations so a simple linear least squares scheme is applicable here.

Since the rotation is estimated separately from other parameters, it is desirable to minimize an error criterion which handles all parameters simultaneously. We must also note that our final aim is to come up with a solution where the foreground objects as reconstructed from both sequences move as rigidly as possible with respect to each other. However, a minimization in transformation space does not necessarily result in the best rigid motion for the foreground objects since it minimizes an algebraic error rather than a geometric one. A good way to express rigidity is by stating that distances between points remain the same. Therefore, the current solution is used as an initialization of a non-linear iterative refinement technique like Levenberg-Marquardt with the following error criterion:

$$E_2 = \sum_{k=1}^{6} F\left(\mathbf{p}_k \right) \tag{15}$$

$$F\left(\mathbf{p}\right) = \sum_{i=1}^{\#frames} \left|\mathbf{T}^i\mathbf{p} - \mathbf{X}\mathbf{T}^{'i}\mathbf{X}^{-1}\mathbf{p}\right|^2 \qquad (16)$$

where $\mathbf{T}^i$ and $\mathbf{T}^{'i}$ are euclidean transformation matrices describing the object motion in the ith frame for the first and the second camera. F is an error measure between the paths of a 3D point when the motion matrices computed for the first and the second image sequence are applied separately and $\mathbf{p}_k$ is a specific point in the object coordinate system of the first camera. As to the choice for $\mathbf{p}_k$, we followed some guidelines. First of all, a 3D Euclidean transformation is defined by the motion of at least 3 non-linear points, so the number of points must be more or equal to three and they must be non-linear. Secondly as the SfM measurements are valid only around the reconstructed object, the points may not be far away from the 3D point cloud of the object but also may not be very close to each other in order not to degenerate to a single point. So in order to satisfy all these criteria, we decided to take the PCA transform of the point cloud and choose the end points of the computed axes which result in six points in total.

So far we implicitly assumed that both video streams are synchronized in time. However, with hand-held cameras this is usually not the case. To overcome this difficulty, researchers proposed different techniques, e.g. [4, 18, 25], and the problem of time synchronization becomes more and more popular.

In our case, Eq.(5) and Eq.(6) give a geometric relationship between two frames and we would expect that these equations do not hold when two frames do not correspond to each other in time, just like any other geometric relationship like the fundamental matrix etc. So the technique we propose for time synchronization is to shift the video sequences with respect to each other within a reasonable range and compute the residual of the solution to Eq. (15). We expect that the correct time shift corresponds to the lowest residual. After a rough discrete shift value is found, the residual graph can be interpolated to search for the solution at sub-frame accuracy. To achieve this, a sub-frame time shift parameter λ is incorporated into Eq. (16) which results in:

$$F_{sub}\left(\mathbf{p}\right) = \sum_{i=1}^{\#frames} \left|\lambda\mathbf{T}^{i+shift}\mathbf{p} + \left(1 - \lambda\right)\mathbf{T}^{i+1+shift}\mathbf{p} - \mathbf{X}\mathbf{T}^{'i}\mathbf{X}^{-1}\mathbf{p}\right|^2 \qquad (17)$$

where λ is restricted to be between 0 and 1 and $shift$ is the rough discrete time-shift value. This equation basically introduces linear interpolation to the paths defined by the principal points.

5   Experiments

We conducted two different experiments to demonstrate the effectiveness of the proposed technique. In the first experiment, a person is pushing a dolly on which a pile of boxes are placed. The person and the background are recorded by two freely moving hand-held cameras whose viewing angles are quite different so it

Views

Time

Fig. 2. Samples from the original image sequence. Each row belongs to a separate camera, each column is related to a different time instant.

is hard to find common photometric features between the two image sequences. Some example frames from the first and the second camera can be seen in Fig. 2. The careful reader might notice that although the set-up is very wide-baseline, there are still some common feature points. However those points will only be used for *verification* of the computed registration parameters. Although our algorithm does not require their existence, it helps us to demonstrate that the algorithm works well.

The sequence is 180 frames long (image size is 720×576) and the dolly passes through different poses. Both sequences are segmented beforehand as foreground and background sequences, are reconstructed separately using SfM and subsequently fed to our algorithm. The time-shift between the sequences is approximately known to be 5 frames which is quite close to 5.13, the value computed by the algorithm.

Fig. 3 shows the background reconstructions from two different cameras which are registered together. It can be clearly seen that the corresponding ground planes and walls are aligned quite well. To give a different view of the result we manually chose three common features from the first sequence, computed their 3D positions and projected them in the second sequence using the registration parameters we computed. In Fig. 4, the black circles denote the actual position of the feature points and the white squares nearby depict the the reprojection of the corresponding 3D points of the second sequence after transfer to the second sequence. The average pixel error is 6 pixels. but we must note that this error value highly depends on the image we use to reproject into. If we have a good registration, we also expect the foreground motions to be the same. So in order to test the latter, we chose a 3D point from the foreground object of the first sequence and computed its 3D path according to the motion parameters from the first sequence and also according to the *registered* motion parameters computed from the second sequence. Fig. 5 demonstrates such a registration for an arbitrary 3D point. The circles and the triangles correspond to point paths computed with

Fig. 3. A top and a side view of the reconstruction. Notice how well the walls and the ground planes are registered.

Fig. 4. Manually tracked features from one image sequence are projected into the other image sequence. In the region of interest, the original features are depicted by black circles, whereas their reprojections are depicted by white squares.

object motions from the two different video streams. The error measure, which is the average distance between the corresponding point positions divided by the path length, is 0.8% which is quite low as expected.

As for the second experiment, we recorded a 330 frames-long (image size is 720×576) sequence where a person himself is carrying boxes on a staircase and is moving arbitrarily but rigidly. Fig. 6 show some example frames. The cameras are also moving freely and view the scene from quite different angles. We computed the reconstructions and registration parameters in the same way as

Fig. 5. Different views on the resulting path of an arbitrary 3D point on the foreground in the first image sequence when displaced by object transformations coming from the first sequence (circles) and the second sequence (triangles) after registration

Fig. 6. Samples from another image sequence. Each row belongs to a separate camera, each column is related to a different time instant.

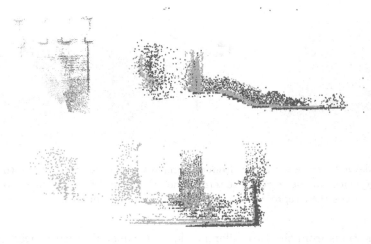

Fig. 7. A top, side and front view of the registered reconstructions. Notice the good registration of the stairs, the ground plane, the right wall and the pillars.

the previous experiment. Fig. 7 shows the registered background reconstructions. As can be seen, the ground plane, the stairs, the walls and the pillars are very well registered. Fig. 8 demonstrates the reprojection of some common feature points having an average pixel error of 15, but as mentioned earlier this error

Fig. 8. Just like the previous experiment, manually selected features from one image sequence are projected into the other image sequence

Fig. 9. Different views on the resulting path of an arbitrary 3D point on the foreground in the first image sequence when displaced by object transformations coming from the first sequence (circles) and the second sequence (triangles) after registration

value highly depends on the image chosen for reprojection. Fig. 9 demonstrates the 3D point paths computed from the object motions from two different video-sets. The error measure, which is the average distance between the corresponding point positions divided by the path length, is 0.4% which is quite low as expected.

6   Conclusion and Discussion

In this paper, we presented a novel technique which finds the space-time-scale parameters between two reconstructions of a scene coming from two independently moving hand-held cameras. Rather than matching photometric features like points, lines etc., it tries to find a consistent transformation which results in the most similar motion for the independently moving foreground object. As a consequence, the cameras are free to observe the scene from totally different angles with the restriction that at least one rigidly moving foreground object is required. Although we presented our initial results here, there are still open questions and possible improvements. As an initial improvement, the basic approach can easily be extended to scenarios which contain more than two cameras and multiple rigidly moving foreground objects. Although we have not used common feature points we can find such features much more easily after an initial registration and use them as well in a global optimization. As an interesting fact, such features need not be simultaneously visible in both cameras which is a necessity in many multicamera systems. Another interesting remark would be how to determine which part of the segmented scene correspond to the background and which to the foreground. Upto now, we assumed this to be known apriori. This, however, can be achieved automatically in several ways, e.g. with a typical

assumption that the biggest object is the background, or with a more elabo-
rate technique [14] if the foreground motion complies to a certain constraint.
However, our framework itself is also capable of identifying the corresponding
segmentation parts between the two sequences, since a wrong choice would result
in a higher error value after the final minimization.

Unfortunately, the proposed technique can not handle certain foreground object motions which are degenerate cases. As to the solution of the Eq. (5), it is
known that the existence of at least two rotation axes is necessary and as the
number of axes increase the solution becomes more stable. We also noticed a
certain degeneracy when the foreground object motion is a pure rotation around
a single point. However, we expect that the existence of multiple moving objects
would significantly decrease such problems.

Acknowledgments

The authors gratefully acknowledge support by the KULeuven Research Council
GOA project 'MARVEL' and the Flemish Fund for Scientific Research FWO.

References

1. Avidan, S., Shashua, A. Trajectory triangulation: 3D reconstruction of moving
   points from a monocular image sequence. PAMI Vol. 22(4) pages 348-357 (2000)
2. Brand, M. Morphable 3d models from video. CVPR, Vol.2, pages 456-463, (2001)
3. Bregler, C., Hertzmann, A., Biermann, H. Recovering non-rigid 3d shape from
   image streams. CVPR, pages 2690-2696, (2000)
4. Caspi, Y., Irani, M. Spatio-temporal Alignment of Sequences. PAMI, Vol 24(11),
   pages 1409- 1424, (2002)
5. Caspi, Y., Irani, M. Alignment of Non-Overlapping Sequences. ICCV, pages 76-83,
   (2001)
6. Costeira, J., Kanade, T. A Multi-Body Factorization Method for Motion Analysis.
   ICCV, pages 1071-1076, (1995)
7. Dornaika, F., Chung, R. Self-calibration of a stereo rig without stereo correspondence. Vision Interface, pages 264-271, (1999)
8. Faugeras, O.D.,Hebert,M. The representation, recognition and locating of 3D objects. International Journal of Robotics Research, Vol 5(3), pages 27-52 (1986)
9. Fitzgibbon, A.W., Zisserman, A. Multibody structure and motion: 3-D reconstruction of independently moving objects. ECCV, pages 891-906, (2000)
10. Horaud, R., Dornaika, F. Hand-Eye Calibration. International Journal of Robotics
    Research, Vol 14(3), pages 195-210, (1995)
11. Hartley, R., Zisserman A. *Multiple View Geometry*. Cambridge University Press
    (2000)
12. Machline, M., Zelnik-Manor, L., Irani, M. Multi-body segmentation: Revisiting
    motion consistency. ECCV Workshop on Vision and Modeling of Dynamic Scenes,
    Copenhagen (2002)
13. Ozden, K. E., Cornelis, K., Van Eycken, L., Van Gool ,L. Reconstructing 3D inde-
    pendent motions using non-accidentalness. CVPR, Vol. 1, pages 819-825, (2004)
14. Ozden, K. E., Van Gool ,L. Background recognition in dynamic scenes with motion
    constraints. CVPR, Vol. 1, pages 250-255 (2005)

15. Ozden, K. E., Cornelis, K., Van Gool ,L. Reconstructing 3D trajectories of independently moving objects using generic constraints. CVIU, pages 453-471, December 2004.
16. J. Shi, J. Malik. Motion segmentation and tracking using normalized cuts. ICCV, 1154-1160, (1998)
17. Shiu,Y.C.,Ahmad,S. Calibration of wrist mounted robotic sensors by solving homogenous transform equations of the form AX=XB. IEEE J. Robot. Automation 5(1), pages 16-19 (1989)
18. Sinha, S.N., Pollefeys, M. Synchronization and Calibration of Camera Networks from Silhouettes. ICPR, Vol. 1, pages 116-119 (2004)
19. Tsai, R.Y. A versatile camera calibration technique for high accuracy 3D machine vision metrology using off-the-shelf TV cameras and lenses. IEEE J. Robot. Automotion RA-3(4), pages 323-344 (1987)
20. Torr, P. H. S. Geometric motion segmentation and model selection. Phil. Trans. Royal Society of London A, 356(1740):1321-1340 (1998)
21. Vidal, R., Soatto, S., Ma, Y., Sastry, S. Segmentation of dynamic scenes from the multibody fundamental matrix. ECCV Workshop on Vision and Modeling of Dynamic Scenes, Copenhagen (2002)
22. Vidal, R., Soatto, S., Ma, Y., Sastry, S. A Factorization Method for 3D Multi-body Motion Estimation and Segmentation. Technical Report, (2002).
23. Wolf, L.,Shashua, A.. On projection matrices $P^k \rightarrow P^2$, k=3,...,6, and their applications in computer vision. ICCV, pages 412-419, (2001)
24. Wolf, L., Zomet, A. Sequence-to-Sequence Self Calibration. ECCV Vol 2., pages 370-382, (2002)
25. Wolf, L., Zomet, A. Correspondence-free synchronization and reconstruction in a non-rigid scene. ECCV Workshop on Vision and Modeling of Dynamic Scenes, Copenhagen (2002)

Self-calibration of a General Radially Symmetric Distortion Model

Jean-Philippe Tardif[1], Peter Sturm[2], and Sébastien Roy[1]

[1] DIRO, Université de Montréal, Canada
{tardifj, roys}@iro.umontreal.ca
[2] INRIA Rhône-Alpes, 38330 Montbonnot St Martin, France
Peter.Sturm@inrialpes.fr

Abstract. We present a new approach for self-calibrating the distortion function and the distortion center of cameras with general radially symmetric distortion. In contrast to most current models, we propose a model encompassing fisheye lenses as well as catadioptric cameras with a view angle larger than 180°.

Rather than representing distortion as an image displacement, we model it as a varying focal length, which is a function of the distance to the distortion center. This function can be discretized, acting as a general model, or represented with e.g. a polynomial expression.

We present two flexible approaches for calibrating the distortion function. The first one is a plumbline-type method; images of line patterns are used to formulate linear constraints on the distortion function parameters. This linear system can be solved up to an unknown scale factor (a global focal length), which is sufficient for image rectification. The second approach is based on the first one and performs self-calibration from images of a textured planar object of unknown structure. We also show that by restricting the camera motion, self-calibration is possible from images of a completely unknown, non-planar scene.

The analysis of rectified images, obtained using the computed distortion functions, shows very good results compared to other approaches and models, even those relying on non-linear optimization.

1 Introduction

Most theoretical advances in geometric computer vision make use of the pin-hole camera model. One benefit of such a model is the linearity of the projection which simplifies multi-view constraints and other structure-from-motion computations. Unfortunately in many cases, this model is a poor representation of how the camera samples the world, especially when dealing with wide angle cameras where radial distortion usually occurs. In addition to these cameras, catadioptric devices (i.e. cameras pointed at a mirror) also admit a very large field of view. Their image distortion can also be seen as a type of radial distortion, although, in general, it cannot be modeled with traditional models. This is because the view angle of these cameras can be larger than 180°, which is not compatible with the usual *image-displacement* approach. The effect of radial distortion is

A. Leonardis, H. Bischof, and A. Pinz (Eds.): ECCV 2006, Part IV, LNCS 3954, pp. 186–199, 2006.
© Springer-Verlag Berlin Heidelberg 2006

that straight lines in the scene are not in general projected onto straight lines in the image, contrary to pin-hole cameras. Many calibration algorithms can deal with distortion, but they are usually tailor-made for specific distortion models and involve non-linear optimization.

In this paper, we introduce a general distortion model, whose main feature is to consider radially symmetric distortion. More precisely, we make the following assumptions on the camera projection function:

- the aspect ratio is 1,
- the distortion center is aligned with the principal point[1],
- the projection function is radially symmetric (around the distortion center),
- the projection is central, i.e. projection rays pass through a single (effective) optical center.

Given the quality of camera hardware manufacturing, it is common practice to assume an aspect ratio of 1. As for the second and third assumptions, they are made to ensure our model is consistent with both catadioptric devices and regular fisheye cameras. Finally, a central projection is assumed for simplicity even for very large field of view cameras [1, 23] in which a non-single viewpoint might be induced by the lens [3], or by a misaligned mirror [18].

Our full camera model consists therefore of the position of the distortion center and the actual distortion function that maps distance from the distortion center to focal length. This model, together with the above assumptions, fully represents a camera projection function. It is a good compromise between traditional low-parametric camera models and fully general ones, modeling one projection ray per pixel [10, 17], in terms of modeling power and ease and stability of calibration. The model is indeed general enough to represent cameras of different types and with very different view angles.

Problem statement. In this paper, we intend to solve the proposed model relying on images of collinear points in space. Our algorithm makes no assumption on the distortion function and on the distortion center position. Only a rough initial value of the latter is needed.

Organization. A short review of the most popular distortion models is presented in the first section. The model we adopt is presented in §3. In §4 we propose a plumbline method for calibrating our model using images of collinear points. Based on this, we propose a plane-based self-calibration approach, in §5. Finally, the performance of our methods is analyzed and compared to another similar approach [6].

2 Related Work

As the field of view of a camera lens increases, the distortion occurring in the captured images becomes more and more important. Traditionally, researchers have sought new models with more degrees of freedom and complexity. These

---

[1] We will see that this constraint may be dropped in some cases.

models include the traditional polynomial model [11] (which can be combined with a field of view model (FOV) [6]), division [7] and rational [5]. Most of the time the models are calibrated using non-linear optimization of either a full projection model from points located on a calibration object [24] or a homography mapping from a planar grid [5]. Recent papers have also shown that radial distortion models can be calibrated linearly from a calibration grid [12] of by feature point matching between images [7, 5, 20, 21].

Other approaches focus only on calibrating the distortion function by imposing either that a straight line in space should appear straight in the image [4, 6] or that spherical objects should appear circular [16].

The aforementioned models all apply to cameras with a field of view smaller than 180° since the distortion is *image-based*. They fail to handle data captured by a camera with a view angle larger than 180°, typical for catadioptric devices. Different models and algorithms have been specifically designed to address these cases [9, 14] and their parameters have an explicit geometric interpretation rather than expressing distortion directly.

Finally, only few attempts were made to find models able to deal with both dioptric systems (including radial distortion) and catadioptric ones [23, 2, 19]. The model we propose fits in this category with the benefit that its distortion function can be general.

3   Camera Model

We describe the camera model that corresponds to the assumptions explained in the introduction. Consider a camera with canonical orientation, i.e. the optical axis is aligned with the Z-axis and image x and y-axes are parallel to world X and Y-axes respectively. Our camera model is then fully described by the position of a distortion center $(c_x, c_y)^\top$ and a distortion "function" $f : \mathcal{R} \to \mathcal{R}$, such that an image point $(x, y)^\top$ is back-projected to a 3D line spanned by the optical center and the point at infinity with coordinates:

$$\left[x - c_x, y - c_y, f(r), 0 \right]^\top , \ r = \sqrt{(x - c_x)^2 + (y - c_y)^2}$$

The distortion function (it should actually be called "undistortion function", but we did not find this very elegant) can for example be chosen as a polynomial with even powers of r, in which case we have the division model, as used in [7, 20]. The model also subsumes fisheye models [8, 15] and cameras of the 'unified central catadioptric model' [9].

In this paper, we use two representations for the distortion function. The first one is a polynomial of a degree d to be fixed, like in the division model, however including odd powers:

$$f(r) = \sum_{i=0}^{d} \lambda_i r^i. \tag{1}$$

The second one is a discrete representation, consisting of a lookup table of the distortion function values at a set of discrete values for r (in practice, we use one sample per step of one pixel). We denote these values as:

$$f(r) = f_r. \tag{2}$$

Note that a constant function f allows the representation of a pinhole camera with f's value as focal length. From the above back-projection equation, it is easy to deduce equations for distortion correction, also called rectification in the sequel. This can for example be done by re-projecting the points at infinity of projection rays into a pinhole camera with the same optical center and orientation as the original camera. As for the intrinsic parameters of the (virtual) pinhole camera, we usually also adopt an aspect ratio of 1 and zero skew; if the distortion center is to have the same coordinates in the rectified image as in the original one, and if g denotes the rectified image's focal length, then the homogeneous coordinates of the rectified point are:

$$\begin{bmatrix} g & 0 & c_x \\ 0 & g & c_y \\ 0 & 0 & 1 \end{bmatrix} \begin{bmatrix} x - c_x \\ y - c_y \\ f(r) \end{bmatrix}.$$

In the following, we introduce a few geometric notions that will be used in this paper. A **distortion circle** is a circle in the image, centered in the distortion center. Projection rays of points lying on a distortion circle span an associated circular **viewing cone** in space. In our model, all cones have the same axis (the optical axis) and vertex (the optical center).

Each cone can actually be understood as an individual pinhole camera, with $f(r)$ as focal length (r being the distortion circle's radius). Geometrically, this is equivalent to virtually moving the image plane along the optical axis, according to the distortion function. This situation is depicted in fig. 1. In the case of a camera with a view angle larger than 180°, the focal length becomes equal or smaller than zero. In the zero case, the cone is actually the **principal plane**,

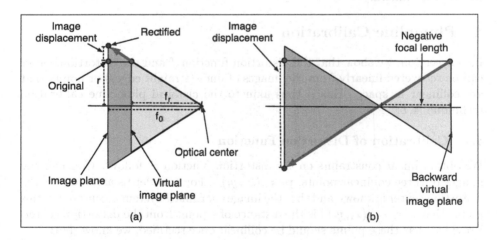

Fig. 1. Distortion circles are associated with cones in space. Theoretically, any point of the image can be projected into a single plane. a) Pixel from a cone looking forward, b) one from a cone looking backward.

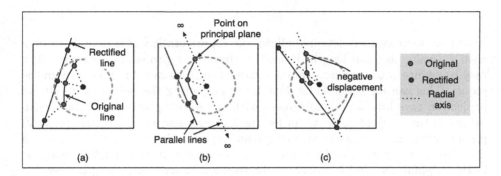

Fig. 2. Situations where three points are rectified into collinear positions. **a)** Three points corresponding to forward cones. **b)** One point located on principal distortion circle, i.e. scene point on principal plane. **c)** Two points on forward cones and one on a backward cone.

i.e. the plane containing the optical center and that is perpendicular to the optical axis. Let us call the associated distortion circle **principal distortion circle**. A negative $f(r)$ is equivalent to a camera with positive focal length, looking backward and whose image is mirrored in x and y. Typical situations for rectification are depicted in fig. 2.

Rectification for cameras with a view angle larger than 180° cannot be done as usual: the above rectification operation is no longer a bijection (two points in the original image may be mapped to the same location in the rectified one) and points on the principal distortion circle are mapped to points at infinity (fig. 2b). It is still possible to rectify individual parts of the image correctly, by giving the virtual pinhole camera a limited field of view and allowing it to rotate relative to the true camera.

4   Plumbline Calibration

In this section, we show that the distortion function f and the distortion center can be recovered linearly from the images of lines (straight edges) or points that are collinear in space. This is thus akin to the classical plumbline calibration technique [4, 6].

4.1   Calibration of Distortion Function

We obtain linear constraints on the distortion function as follows. Consider the images of three collinear points, $\mathbf{p}_i = (x_i, y_i)^\top$. For now, let us assume that the distortion center is known and that the image coordinate system is centered in this point. Hence, $r_i = \|(x_i, y_i)\|$ is the distance of a point from the distortion center. Provided that these points should be collinear once rectified, we know that:

$$\begin{vmatrix} x_0 & x_1 & x_2 \\ y_0 & y_1 & y_2 \\ f(r_0) & f(r_1) & f(r_2) \end{vmatrix} = 0 \tag{3}$$

which can be written explicitly as a linear constraint on the $f(r_i)$'s:

$$f(r_0)\begin{vmatrix} x_1 & x_2 \\ y_1 & y_2 \end{vmatrix} + f(r_1)\begin{vmatrix} x_2 & x_0 \\ y_2 & y_0 \end{vmatrix} + f(r_2)\begin{vmatrix} x_0 & x_1 \\ y_0 & y_1 \end{vmatrix} = 0. \tag{4}$$

If f is of the form (1) or (2), then this equation gives a linear constraint on its parameters λ_i respectively f_r.

Constraints can be accumulated from all possible triplets of points that are projections of collinear points in space. We thus obtain a linear equation system of the form $A\mathbf{x} = \mathbf{0}$, where $\mathbf{x}$ contains the parameters of f (the λ_i's or the f_r's). Note that constraints from triplets where two or all three image points lie close to one another are not very useful and hence can be neglected in order to reduce the number of equations. Solving this system to least squares yields parameters that maximize the collinearity of the rectified points[2]. Note that the equation system is homogeneous, i.e. the distortion parameters are only estimated up to scale. This is natural, as explained below; a unique solution can be guaranteed by setting $\lambda_0 = 1$ as is usually done for the division model, or by setting one f_r to a fixed value.

4.2   Calibration of Distortion Center

So far, we have assumed a known distortion center. In this section, we show how it can be estimated as well, in addition to the actual distortion function. A first idea is to sample likely positions of the distortion center, e.g. consider a regular grid of points in a circular region in the image center, and compute the distortion function for each of them using the above method. We then keep the point yielding the smallest residual of the linear equation system as the estimated distortion center. This approach is simple and not very elegant, but is fully justified and works well in practice. Its downside is that the computation time is proportional to the number of sampled points.

Therefore, we investigate a local optimization procedure, as opposed to the above brute force one. Let (c_x, c_y) be the unknown distortion center. Equation (3) now becomes:

$$\begin{vmatrix} x_0 - c_x & x_1 - c_x & x_2 - c_x \\ y_0 - c_y & y_1 - c_y & y_2 - c_y \\ f(\left\| \begin{bmatrix} x_0 - c_x \\ y_0 - c_y \end{bmatrix} \right\|) & f(\left\| \begin{bmatrix} x_1 - c_x \\ y_1 - c_y \end{bmatrix} \right\|) & f(\left\| \begin{bmatrix} x_2 - c_x \\ y_2 - c_y \end{bmatrix} \right\|) \end{vmatrix} = 0. \tag{5}$$

First, this constraint cannot be used directly for the discretized version of the distortion function. Second, if we use the polynomial model, the constraint is highly non-linear in the coordinates of the distortion center.

We thus consider an approximation of (5): we assume that a current estimate of the distortion center is not too far away from the true position ($\|(c_x, c_y)\|$ is small), so that f can be approximated with $(c_x, c_y) = \mathbf{0}$ and

---

[2] However, it is not optimal in terms of geometric distance.

$$f(\left\|\begin{bmatrix} x \\ y \end{bmatrix}\right\|) \approx f(\left\|\begin{bmatrix} x - c_x \\ y - c_y \end{bmatrix}\right\|).$$

Equation (5) thus simplifies to:

$$\begin{vmatrix} x_0 - c_x & x_1 - c_x & x_2 - c_x \\ y_0 - c_y & y_1 - c_y & y_2 - c_y \\ f(\left\|\begin{bmatrix} x_0 \\ y_0 \end{bmatrix}\right\|) & f(\left\|\begin{bmatrix} x_1 \\ y_1 \end{bmatrix}\right\|) & f(\left\|\begin{bmatrix} x_2 \\ y_2 \end{bmatrix}\right\|) \end{vmatrix} = 0 \tag{6}$$

which is linear in c_x and c_y. Once again, combining many constraints leads to an over-determined linear equation system. The recovered distortion center may not be optimal because the points are expressed relative to the approximate center and because of the simplification of (5). Hoping that the previous assumptions are applicable, this new center should nevertheless improve our rectification. This estimation is used in a local optimization scheme of alternation type:

0. Initialize the distortion center with e.g. the center of the image.
1. Fix the distortion center and compute the distortion function (§4.1).
2. Fix the distortion function and update the distortion center (§4.2).
3. Go to step 1, unless convergence is observed.

Instead of using the least-squares cost function based on the algebraic distance (3), we also consider a more geometric cost function to judge convergence in step 3. Consider a set of image points belonging to a line image. From the current values of distortion center and function, we compute their projection rays and fit a plane as follows: determine the plane that contains the optical center and that minimizes the sum of (squared) angles with projection rays. The residual squared angles, summed over all line images, give the alternative cost function.

4.3   Discussion

The estimation of distortion center and function is based on an algebraic distance expressing collinearity of rectified image points. Better would be of course to use a geometric distance in the original images; this is possible but rather involved and is left for future work.

We briefly describe what the calibration of the distortion function amounts to, in terms of full metric calibration. First, recall that the distortion function can be computed up to scale only from our input (see §4.1). This is natural: if we have a distortion function that satisfies all collinearity constraints, then multiplying it by a scale factor results in a distortion function that satisfies them as well. This ambiguity means that once the distortion function is computed (up to scale) and the image rectified, the camera can be considered as equivalent to a pinhole camera with unknown focal length, with the difference that the field of view is potentially larger than 180°. Any existing focal length calibration or self-calibration algorithm designed for pinhole cameras can be applied to obtain a full metric calibration. A direct application of such algorithms can probably use only features that lie inside the principal distortion circle, but it should be possible to adapt them so as to use even fields of view larger than 180°. At this step, the second assumption of §1 can also be relaxed if desired: a full pinhole model, i.e. not only focal length, can in principle be estimated from rectified images.

5 Self-calibration

We now develop a plane-based self-calibration approach that is based on the plumbline technique of the previous section. Consider that the camera acquires two images of a textured plane with otherwise unknown structure. We suppose that we can match the two images densely; the matching does not actually need to be perfectly dense, but assuming it simplifies the following explanations. This is discussed below in more details.

We now describe how dense matches between two images of a planar scene allow the generation of line images and hence to apply the plumbline technique. Consider any radial line (line going through the distortion center) in the first image; the projection rays associated with the points on that line are necessarily coplanar according to our camera model. Therefore, the scene points that are observed along that radial line must be collinear: they lie on the intersection of the plane of projection rays, with the scene plane. Due to the dense matching, we know the projections of these collinear scene points in the second image. By considering dense matches of points along n radial lines in one image, we thus obtain n line images in the other image, and vice versa. In addition, these line images usually extend across a large part of the image, bringing about strong constraints.

We now simply stack all plumbline constraints (4) for all pairs of images, and solve for the distortion parameters as in §4. Here, we have assumed the knowledge of the distortion center (in order to define radial lines); the distortion center can of course also be estimated, using e.g. the exhaustive approach of §4.2. Moreover, the input, once rectified, can be given to a classical plane-based self-calibration algorithm to obtain a full metric calibration, using e.g. [22].

Dense Matching. Dense matching can be achieved rather straightforwardly. If the camera acquires a continuous image sequence, most existing optical flow algorithms can be applied for successive frames and their results propagated in order to obtain a dense matching between two images with a substantial motion between them. In addition, the fact that a planar scene is observed eliminates the occlusion problem. If the scene is not sufficiently textured, but only allows to extract and track sparse interest points, then we proceed as follows. We extract dominant lines in each image using a Hough transform of the extracted interest points, and only keep the lines passing near the current distortion center estimate. These are almost radial lines. An example is shown in fig. 3a,b. The rest of the self-calibration is as above.

Constrained Camera Motions. Another way to obtain line images without the need for linear features in the scene is to acquire images under constrained camera motions. A first possibility is to carry out pure rotations about the

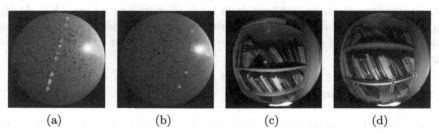

| (a) | (b) | (c) | (d) |

Fig. 3. (a)+(b) Two images of a planar scene. a) shows interest points lying on a radial line in the first image and b) corresponding points in the second image. **(c)+(d)** Two images of a general scene, taken with pure translation. c) shows two interest points in the first image and d) their paths, accumulated in the last image.

optical center, as suggested also by [20]. The scene can then be assimilated to a plane, and the above self-calibration method can be directly applied. A second possibility is to perform pure translations (with e.g. a tripod) and to track image points across several images. In this case, any point track constitutes a line image (an example is shown in fig. 3c,d).

6   Results and Analysis

We tested our algorithm with data acquired from real and simulated cameras. An 8.0mm lens, a 3.5mm fisheye lens and a para-catadioptric camera were used. We also simulated ten cameras featuring distortions from small to very large.

6.1   Convergence Analysis of the Distortion Center Detection

Two aspects of convergence of the plumbline method were evaluated. First, evaluating if the minimization of the constraints given by (6) instead of (5) leads to similar results. This is not critical though, as the path of the optimizer needs not be the same to ensure convergence. On the other hand, if the paths are similar, it suggests that the convergence pace is not penalized too much with the simplified cost function. We proceeded as follows. For samples of distortion center positions in a box around the initial position, we computed the two cost functions and found their minima (fig. 4a,b). We see that the functions' general shapes are almost identical, as well as the positions of their respective minima. Another evaluation consists in initializing the distortion center randomly around the optimal one and finding the minima of the two cost functions. Figure 4c shows the average distance between these minima, as a function of the distance of the given distortion center from the optimal one. It is generally small, suggesting that both cost functions may lead to similar optimization paths.

Secondly, the overall convergence was tested with simulated and real data. In the first case, three criteria were considered: the number of lines images given as input, the amount of noise added to the data and the distance of the given initial distortion center from the true one. For each simulated camera, up to 11

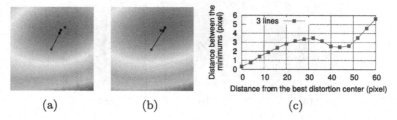

Fig. 4. Plots of cost functions and optimization paths associated with **(a)** eq. (5) and **(b)** eq. (6). **(c)** Distance between minima of these two cost functions, with respect to distance of current estimate of distortion center from optimal one. Data from the 3.5mm fisheye lens.

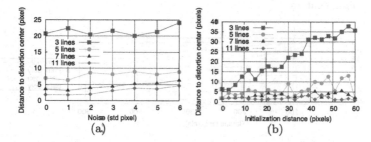

Fig. 5. Precision of the recovered distortion center on simulated data w.r.t. **a)** noise and number of lines, **b)** number of lines and initialization distance.

line segments were generated randomly, Gaussian noise of standard deviation 0 to 6 pixels was added to image point coordinates and these were then quantized to pixel precision. For every camera, 50 initial values for the distortion center were randomly chosen in a circle of 60 pixels radius around the true position (for images of size 1000 × 1000) and given as input to the algorithm. This a realistic test considering that for our real cameras, we found that the estimated distortion center converged to around 30 pixels from the initial value (image center) in the worst case. The results in fig. 5 show that the number of lines has a much larger impact on the quality of the recovered distortion center than the noise and the initialization distance. This is especially true when the number of line is larger than 7.

6.2 Plumbline Calibration

We acquired images of lines with our real cameras, calibrated the distortion and then performed rectification. Once again, we tested the convergence and also the quality of the rectification by checking the collinearity of rectified line images. Convergence was really good, especially for the two dioptric lenses (fig. 6). Even with a really bad initialization of the distortion center, resulting in a poor initial estimate of the distortion function, the algorithm converged surprisingly fast (fig. 8). The distortion functions for our real cameras are shown in fig. 7 as well as rectified images in fig. 9 (images not used for the calibration). We compared

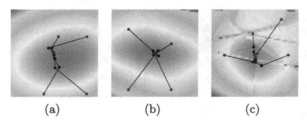

(a)   (b)   (c)

Fig. 6. Convergence examples of the algorithm for **a)** the 8.0 mm, **b)** the 3.5 mm fisheye, **c)** the para-catadioptric. The density plots show the value of the cost function explained at the end of §4.2, with f computed using distortion center positions (c_x, c_y) in a box of 60 × 60 pixels around the final distortion centers. In dark-green, different initializations of the algorithm; in black, the centers at each step of the algorithm; in purple, the final centers.

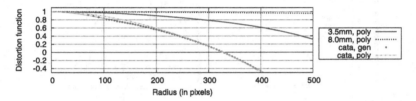

Fig. 7. Calibrated distortion functions for our real cameras. *poly* refers to (1) and *gen* to (2). For the 8.0 and 3.5mm, both representations lead to virtually identical results (details at table 1).

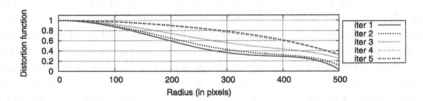

Fig. 8. The distortion function of the fisheye lens, at different iterations of the calibration algorithm for an initial center very far from the true position (200,400). The final estimate of (512,523) was found in only 5 iterations (image of size 1000 × 1000 pixels). Subsequent steps were only minor improvements.

our approach with the one presented in [6], run on the same data. Since that approach performs non-linear optimization, it can easily incorporate different distortion models. Results for different models are shown in table 1; we initialized the distortion centers with the one that was estimated with our approach and the distortion function as a constant.

Details are given in fig. 10 for the catadioptric cameras. We observe that a polynomial function did not give satisfying results. Using higher degrees (up to 10) and changing the distortion function did not give much better results. On

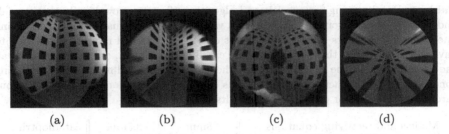

Fig. 9. Rectification examples. **a,b)** A 3.5mm fisheye original and rectified images. **c,d)** a catadioptric image. The radius of the principal distortion circle was estimated as 329 pixels, so circles of radius 0 to 320 pixels were rectified.

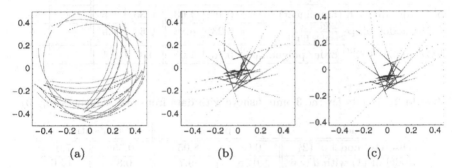

Fig. 10. Line images used as input of the algorithms and rectification results for the catadioptric camera (with principal distortion circle found at 329 pixels). **a)** Input (only shown for radius smaller than 315 pixels), **b)** Rectification with a traditional model of degree 6 (model as in third row of table 1), **c)** with the polynomial distortion function (1) and $d = 6$ (the discrete model of (2) gave almost identical results).

the other hand, we see that a division function is very well suited to model the distortion in the image.

6.3   Self-calibration from Real Sequences

Two sequences were tested. In the first one, points were tracked from a flat surface (our laboratory floor) with a hand-held camera. In the second case, a tripod was used and the camera was translated in constant direction. Overall, the results were satisfying although not as precise as with the direct plumbline technique using images of actual linear features. Results are summarized in table 2; values shown were computed like explained in table 1 and using images of actual lines. The distortion center detection was also not as precise. The algorithm converged as usual, but not exactly to the best distortion center. In fact, it was much closer to the image center. This is explained by the fact that towards the image border, features are much more difficult to track: they are smaller and blurry. In this case, they are usually dropped by the tracking algorithm resulting in less data for large radiuses, where the distortion is the worst.

Table 1. Results using our models and algorithm (first two rows) and other models and the non-linear algorithm of [6]. Shown values refer to residual distances for fitting lines to rectified points (average and worst case). The rectified images were scaled to have the same size as the original. For the catadioptric camera, our approach used all the points, whereas the others used only the points corresponding to forward viewing cones (they failed otherwise). "—" means the algorithm did not converge without careful initialization or gave very bad results.

Models and rectifying equations	8mm		3.5mm		catadioptric	
Discrete model of (2)	0.16	1.03	**0.35**	**3.7**	**0.51**	**7.6**
Model of (1) with $d = 6$	0.16	1.12	0.35	5.5	**0.47**	**6.3**
6th order polynomial $\mathbf{p}(1 + \lambda_1\|\mathbf{p}\| + ... + \lambda_6\|\mathbf{p}\|^6)$	0.16	1.08	0.42	7.0	1.5	14.4
6th order division (non-linear)	0.16	1.08	0.36	5.6	—	—
FOV-model [6]: $\mathbf{p}\frac{\tan(\omega\|\mathbf{p}\|)}{2\tan(\frac{\omega}{2})\|\mathbf{p}\|}$	0.23	4.86	0.54	7.9	—	—
FOV-model + 2nd order polynomial	0.16	1.06	0.37	6.1	—	—

Table 2. Results for the 3.5mm fisheye with data from real sequences (fig. 3)

Models	plane		translation	
Discrete model of (2)	0.68	8.05	0.55	7.0
Model of (1) with $d = 6$	0.58	9.7	0.85	14.6

Consequently, the distortion is a little bit under-evaluated and the distortion center less well constrained.

7 Conclusion

We presented flexible calibration methods for a general model for radial distortion, one plumbline type method and one for plane-based self-calibration. The methods were applied for simulated and real images of different cameras (fisheye and catadioptric). Results are satisfying, in terms of convergence basin and speed, precision as well as accuracy.

The most closely related works are [20, 21]. There, elegant though rather more involved procedures are proposed. These start with an even more general camera model than here, that does not enforce radial symmetry; only after computing and exploiting multi-view relations for that model, radial symmetry is enforced in order to compute distortion parameters. Our methods are much simpler to implement, use radial symmetry directly and can work with fewer images (two for plane-based self-calibration). Future work will mainly concern improving the tracking for the self-calibration method and investigating the optimization of reprojection based cost functions.

References

1. S. Baker, S.K. Nayar. A Theory of Single-Viewpoint Catadioptric Image Formation. IJCV, 35(2), 1–22, 1999.
2. J.P. Barreto, K. Daniilidis. Unifying image plane liftings for central catadioptric and dioptric cameras. OMNIVIS 2004.
3. M. Born and E. Wolf. Principles of Optics, Pergamon Press, 1965.
4. D.C. Brown. Close-Range Camera Calibration. Photogrammetric Engineering, 37(8), 855-866, 1971.
5. D. Claus, A.W. Fitzgibbon. Rational Function Model for Fish-eye Lens Distortion CVPR 2005.
6. F. Devernay, O. Faugeras. Straight lines have to be straight: Automatic calibration and removal of distortion from scenes of structured environments. MVA 2001.
7. A.W. Fitzgibbon. Simultaneous linear estimation of multiple view geometry and lens distortion. CVPR 2001.
8. M.M. Fleck. Perspective Projection: The Wrong Imaging Model. TR 95–01, University of Iowa, 1995.
9. C. Geyer, K. Daniilidis. Catadioptric Camera Calibration. ICCV 1999.
10. M.D. Grossberg, S.K. Nayar. A general imaging model and a method for finding its parameters. ICCV 2001.
11. R. Hartley, A. Zisserman. Multiple View Geometry in Computer Vision Cambridge University Press 2000.
12. R. I. Hartley, S. B. Kang. Parameter-free Radial Distortion Correction with Centre of Distortion Estimation. ICCV 2005.
13. Intel Open Source Computer Vision Library. http://www.intel.com/research/mrl/research/opencv/
14. B.Micusik, T.Pajdla. Autocalibration & 3D Reconstruction with Non-central Catadioptric Cameras. CVPR 2004.
15. S. Shah, J.K. Aggarwal. Intrinsic Parameter Calibration Procedure for A (High-Distortion) Fish-Eye Lens Camera with Distortion Model and Accuracy Estimation. Pattern Recognition, 29(11), 1775-1788, 1996.
16. D.E. Stevenson, M.M. Fleck. Nonparametric correction of distortion. TR 95–07, University of Iowa, 1995.
17. P. Sturm, S. Ramalingam. A Generic Concept for Camera Calibration. ECCV 2004.
18. R. Swaminathan, M. Grossberg, S. Nayar. Caustics of catadioptric cameras. ICCV 2001.
19. J.-P. Tardif, P. Sturm, Calibration of Cameras with Radially Symmetric Distortion. OMNIVIS'2005.
20. S. Thirthala, M. Pollefeys. The Radial Trifocal Tensor. A tool for calibrating the radial distortion of wide-angle cameras. CVPR 2005.
21. S. Thirthala, M. Pollefeys. Multi-View Geometry of 1D Radial Cameras and its Application to Omnidirectional Camera Calibration. to appear, ICCV 2005.
22. B. Triggs. Autocalibration from Planar Scenes. ECCV 1998.
23. X. Ying, Z. Hu Can We Consider Central Catadioptric Cameras and Fisheye Cameras within a Unified Imaging Model. ECCV 2004.
24. Z. Zhang. A Flexible New Technique for Camera Calibration. PAMI, 22(11), 1330-1334, 2000.

A Simple Solution to the Six-Point Two-View Focal-Length Problem

Hongdong Li

RSISE, The Australian National University, National ICT Australia

Abstract. This paper presents a simple and practical solution to the 6-point 2-view focal-length estimation problem. Based on the *hidden-variable* technique we have derived a 15th degree polynomial in the unknown focal-length. During this course, a simple and constructive algorithm is established. To make use of multiple redundant measurements and then select the best solution, we suggest a kernel-voting scheme. The algorithm has been tested on both synthetic data and real images. Satisfactory results are obtained for both cases. For reference purpose we include our Matlab implementation in the paper, which is quite concise, consisting of 20 lines of code only. The result of this paper will make a small but useful module in many computer vision systems.

1 Introduction

This paper considers the problem of estimating a constant unknown focal-length from six corresponding points of two semi-calibrated views. By *semi-calibration* we mean that all camera intrinsic parameters but a fixed focal-length are known. This scenario is quite common (not restrictive) in daily camera use. For example, except for the case where the camera lens is allowed to zoom continuously, it is often practical to assume that its focal-length is constant across multiple views. In fact, all *other* camera intrinsic parameters (such as principal point and aspect ratio) can be considered fixed and known for a certain camera. In other words, the only user-adjustable (therefore variable) camera intrinsic parameter is the focal-length. Yet still, the focal-length is often kept constant over two successive image shoots [7][8].

It is well known that five points of two fully-calibrated views are possible to recover the essential matrix E between the two views. Since an essential matrix is a faithful representation of the camera motion (up to an unknown scale), namely, $E = [t]_\times R$, it therefore has five degrees of freedom. So, from five points it is possible to estimate the camera motion—this is exactly what the five-point algorithm does [11].

Now consider a semi-calibrated case where only a fixed focal-length f is unknown. For this case, it is shown that six points (in general position) are enough to estimate the camera motion as well as the unknown focal-length. This can be easily seen by the following reasoning. Compared to the fully-calibrated five-point case, the one extra point correspondence will provide one more constraint on the camera intrinsic matrix. Consequently, a single unknown focal-length, as well as the relative camera motion, can be computed from it.

The above conclusion can also be approached from the other direction. If the two camera views are uncalibrated, then seven points are the minimal requirement to compute a fundamental matrix F. Since a fundamental matrix has seven degrees of freedom,

A. Leonardis, H. Bischof, and A. Pinz (Eds.): ECCV 2006, Part IV, LNCS 3954, pp. 200–213, 2006.

it provides two more constraints on the camera intrinsics, besides the camera motion encoded by an essential matrix. These two extra constraints are essentially the two Kruppa equations. Therefore, if the two views are only partially calibrated in that all camera intrinsics but *two* possibly different focal-lengths f and f' are known, then seven points are enough to estimate the relative camera motion and the two unknown focal-lengths [2]. Now, if we have only seven less one points, and the two focal-lengths are assumed identical, then it is possible to recover the single unknown focal-length as well as the camera motion from six corresponding points.

For the first time, Stewénius et al have proposed a concrete algorithm to solve the 6-point focal-length problem [1]. They have utilized a special mathematical tool—the Gröbner basis technique. The idea behind the Gröbner basis is to construct a complete and algebraically-closed polynomial system (an *ideal*) by adding in some newly *generated* compatible equations. By this tool they show that there are at most 15 solutions to the six-point algorithm. The Gröbner basis is a mathematically elegant technique for handling polynomial system. However, since it originates from a special mathematical field (i.e. *computational commutative algebra and algebraic geometry*), some readers may find it not fully-comfortable to follow, let alone to actually implement it and use it.

Why Six Points? Traditionally, the focal-length problem is solved through the fundamental matrix which itself can be computed from seven points. Moving from seven points to six points provides some benefits. The first benefit lies in its theoretic value. Compared with its non-minimal counterpart, the minimal algorithm offers a deeper theoretical understanding to the problem itself. For example, both the five-point algorithms [11] and the six point algorithm all better exploit the constraints provided by the epipolar equations and the Kruppa equations (cf. [14][15]); Secondly, effective techniques developed during the course of deriving the six-point algorithm are very useful for other similar vision problems too (e.g. [11]); Thirdly, for the task of focal-length estimation itself, it is demonstrated by experiments that the six-point algorithm sometimes offers even better performance than the seven-point algorithm; In addition, as shown in [11], six-point algorithm has less degenerate configurations than the seven-point algorithm; Moreover, when combine a minimal solver with the RANSAC scheme using six points (rather than seven) allows significant reduction in computation [5].

1.1 Main Contributions

This paper provides an alternative yet much simpler and practical solution to the 6-point focal-length problem, compared to the one originally proposed in [1].

We will show that to solve the 6-point problem there is *no* need to generate new equations. The original equations system, which includes the six epipolar conditions, one singularity condition and two Kruppa equations, already provides sufficient and algebraically-closed constraints to the problem. As a result, in the real domain $\mathbb{R}$ it is already enough to solve the six-point problem using 10 *rigidity equations*—equivalent to the above equations—without resorting to the Gröbner basis technique. For reference purposes we provide our implementation in the appendix of the paper, which is very concise and consists of 20 lines of general Matlab code only.

Paper [1] tested its algorithm mainly on noise-free simulation data. In this paper, we go beyond such an idealized scenario. We have tested the performance of our algorithm on both synthetic and real images (with different levels of noise). We demonstrate our results by the accuracy of focal-length estimation *per se*, rather than by the errors in the reprojected fundamental matrix.

In the root-selection stage (whose purpose is to single-out the best root from multiple solutions), we propose a *kernel-voting* scheme, as an alternative to the conventionally adopted RANSAC. We show by experiments that our scheme is suitable for the particular problem context, and there is no need to wait until the reprojected fundamental matrix error is obtained.

2   Theoretic Backgrounds

Consider a camera, with constant intrinsic parameters denoted by a matrix $K \in \mathbb{R}^{3 \times 3}$, observing a static scene. Two corresponding image points m and m' are related by a fundamental matrix $F \in \mathbb{R}^{3 \times 3}$:

$$m'^T F m = 0. \tag{1}$$

A valid fundamental matrix must satisfy the following singularity condition:

$$\det(F) = 0. \tag{2}$$

This is a cubic equation. Remember that the 3×3 fundamental matrix is only defined up to a scale, it therefore has 7 degrees of freedom in total. Consequently, seven corresponding points are sufficient to estimate the F.

If the camera is fully-calibrated, then the fundamental matrix is reduced to an *essential matrix*, denoted by E, and the relationship between them reads as:

$$K^{-T} E K^{-1} = F. \tag{3}$$

Since an essential matrix E is a faithful representation of the relative camera motion (translation and rotation, up to a scale), it has only five degrees of freedom. Consequently, to be a valid essential matrix E, it must further satisfy two more constraints, which are characterized by the following theorem.

Theorem-1: A real 3×3 *matrix* E is an essential matrix *if and only if* it satisfies the following condition

$$2 E E^T E - \text{tr}(E E^T) E = 0. \tag{4}$$

This gives 9 equations in the elements of E, but only two of them are algebraically independent. The above theorem, owing to many researchers (e.g, Kruppa, Demazure, Maybank, Huang, Trivedi, Faugeras, etc, just name a few, cf. [6][5][15]), is an important result in geometric vision.

For the semi-calibrated case considered here, since only one focal-length is unknown, without loss of generality we can assume the intrinsic camera matrix is: $K = \begin{bmatrix} f & 0 & 0 \\ 0 & f & 0 \\ 0 & 0 & 1 \end{bmatrix}$, where f is the focal-length. Define a matrix $Q = w^{-1} \begin{bmatrix} 1 & 0 & 0 \\ 0 & 1 & 0 \\ 0 & 0 & w \end{bmatrix}$, where $w = f^{-2}$.

Write down the epipolar relations Eq. (1) for six points m_i and m'_i,

$$m'^T_i F m_i = 0, \tag{5}$$

for $i = 1, \cdots, 6$. Using the six points we get a linear representation of the fundamental matrix:

$$F = x\mathbf{F}_0 + y\mathbf{F}_1 + z\mathbf{F}_2, \tag{6}$$

where x, y, z are three unknown scalars to be estimated, and $\mathbf{F}_0, \mathbf{F}_1, \mathbf{F}_2$ are the bases of the null-space of the *epipolar design matrix*, which can be readily computed from the six points (cf. [5]).

Substituting this F into Eq.(3) and Eq.(4), we get the following equations in the unknown set $\{w, x, y, z\}$.

$$2FQF^TQF - \text{tr}(FQF^TQ)F = 0. \tag{7}$$

This is a group of nine equations, and they provide sufficient conditions to find the unknown $\{w, x, y, z\}$ (up to an unknown scalar). If we somehow solve these equations, then the task of estimating the focal-length is accomplished. The above reasoning basically follows [1].

3   Review the Previous Algorithm

Stewénius et al proposed a clever algorithm based on the Gröbner basis technique [1]. More precisely, it is a variant of the classical Gröbner technique [4]. The key steps of their algorithm are briefly reviewed below.

Given six corresponding image points in general position, write down Eq.(7) and Eq.(2). Rearrange them in such a way that a 10×33 matrix equation $A\mathbf{X} = 0$ is obtained, where A is a 10×33 coefficient matrix, and $\mathbf{X}$ a vector containing 33 terms of monomials of the unknowns. Now we have a polynomial system of 10 equations. This system is then ported into a finite field $\mathbb{Z}_p$ (p is a large *prime number*), and is solved using the Gröbner basis elimination procedure. This procedure is stopped when the whole system becomes an algebraically-closed *ideal generator set* of the original system. So far, a minimal solver (for $\mathbb{Z}_p$) has been built up.

The next step is to apply the same solver (i.e, the same sequence of elimination) to the original problem. One then obtains an enlarged polynomial system containing $n \times 33$ ($n > 10$) monomial terms. Finally, a generalized eigen-decomposition is employed to solve the polynomial system, for which there are 15 solutions. In order to improve numerical stability, a pivoted Gauss-Jordan elimination is used.

An important detail of the algorithm is that the arbitrary scale factor of the fundamental matrix is parameterized by setting one unknown to an arbitrary scalar. Thereby the number of unknowns is reduced by one, which simplifies the later derivation. By contrast, in this paper we avoid such scale parametrization in order to keep the homogeneity of some unknowns of the equation system. The reason will be explained later.

Limitations. The main mathematical device adopted by [1] is the Gröbner basis technique. The Gröbner basis is an elegant and powerful technique[3] [4]. Many commercial or free mathematical software packages include it as a standard module (for instance, in Maple and Mathematica etc). In many cases, to use it the user is not assumed to have specialized knowledge of it, and thus can simply apply it in a black-box manner, as also claimed by [1]. However, using a tool in a black-box manner is not always a safe way.

Whenever a program runs into trouble, it would be nicer if the user could understand its internal mechanism. Moreover, due to its special origin (*computational commutative algebra and algebraic geometry*), not every reader finds it easy to follow. Furthermore, paper [1] did not test its algorithm extensively on more realistic case. It experimented on perfect simulated data only. No result on real images was given there.

Finally, the *root-selection* procedure (i.e., single-out the best root from the possibly multiple solutions) is not addressed by paper [1], because it deals with simulated cases only, and thereby assumes the ground-truth data is available. However, in a real-world problem an efficient root-selection mechanism is necessary. It is in fact a common requirement for various minimal solvers (see for example [11] and [8]), where one often obtains multiple and maybe complex roots. The RANSAC is a good scheme to find the best solution from multiple candidates. In this paper, we propose an alternative *kernel-voting* scheme which is suitable for the particular context.

4   Our New Six-Point Algorithm

In this paper, we propose a new method for solving the six-point focal-length problem, using the *hidden variable* technique which is probably the best known technique for algebra elimination.

We claim that the recommended *hidden variable* technique is *not yet-another* specialized mathematical technique (which otherwise would be equally unfamiliar and uncomfortable to readers), but it follows very straightforward principle and procedures. It is so transparent and simple to the end-user that is almost self-explained. As will be described later, to better apply this technique to the problem, we introduce a small trick that is to keep the homogeneity of some unknowns of the equation system.

Hidden Variable Technique. The Hidden-Variable technique (also known as the *Dialytic Elimination*) is possibly one of the best known *resultant* techniques in algebraic geometry [4]. It is used to eliminate variables from a multivariate polynomial equation system. The basic idea is as follows.

Consider a system of M homogeneous polynomial equations in N variables, say, $p_i(x_1, x_2, ..., x_N) = 0$, for $i = 1, 2, ..., M$. If we treat one of the unknowns (for example, x_1) as a *parameter* (in the conventional terms, we *hide* the variable x_1), then by some simple algebra we can re-write the equation system as a matrix equation

$$C(x_1)\mathbf{X} = 0,$$

where the coefficient matrix C will depend on the *hidden variable* x_1, and the $\mathbf{X}$ is a vector space consisting of the homogeneous monomial terms of all other N-1 variables (say, $x_2, x_3, \cdots, x_N$).

If the number of equations equals the number of monomial terms in the vector $\mathbf{X}$ (i.e. the matrix C is square), then one will have a *resultant equation* defined on x_1, say, $\det(C(x_1)) = 0$ *if and only if* the equation system has non-trivial solutions. By such procedure, one thus successfully eliminates N-1 variables from the equation system all at once. Solving the resulting resultant equation for x_1 and back-substituting it, one thus eventually solves the whole system.

4.1 Algorithm Derivation

Remember that Eq.(2) and Eq.(7) are the main equations we are to use. Notice that they are ten cubic equations in the four unknowns $\{w, x, y, z\}$. A careful analysis will show that within the real domain $\mathbb{R}$, Eq.(7) already implies Eq.(2). However, we would keep all these ten equations together in our derivation, and the reason will become clear soon.

Now we treat the unknown w as the hidden variable, and collect a coefficient matrix (denoted by $C(w)$) with respect to the other three variables $\{x, y, z\}$. Here we do not replace one variable with an arbitrary scalar. Rather, we keep the homogeneous forms in the monomials formed by $[x, y, z]$. These are all cubic monomials which actually span a vector space:

$$\mathbf{X} = [xyz, x^2z, xy^2, xz^2, y^2z, yz^2, x^3, y^3, x^2y, z^3]^T \qquad (8)$$

To give a more close examination of the coefficient matrix C, we list it element-wise:

	0	1	2	3	4	5	6	7	8	9
	xyz	x^2z	xy^2	xz^2	y^2z	yz^2	x^3	y^3	x^2y	z^3
0	s_0	s_1	s_2	s_3	s_4	s_5	s_6	s_7	s_8	s_9
1	$[w]_{10}$	$[w]_{11}$	$[w]_{12}$	$[w]_{13}$	$[w]_{14}$	$[w]_{15}$	$[w]_{16}$	$[w]_{17}$	$[w]_{18}$	$[w]_{19}$
2	$[w]_{20}$	$[w]_{21}$	$[w]_{22}$	$[w]_{23}$	$[w]_{24}$	$[w]_{25}$	$[w]_{26}$	$[w]_{27}$	$[w]_{28}$	$[w]_{29}$
3	$\cdots$	$\cdots$		$\cdots$		$\cdots$	$\cdots$	$\cdots$	$\cdots$	$\cdots$
$\cdots$	$\cdots$	$\cdots$	$[w]_{i-1,j}$	$\cdots$		$\cdots$	$\cdots$	$\cdots$	$\cdots$	$\cdots$
$\cdots$	$\cdots$	$[w]_{i,j-1}$	$[w]_{i,j}$	$[w]_{i,j+1}$	$\cdots$	$\cdots$	$\cdots$	$\cdots$	$\cdots$	$\cdots$
$\cdots$	$\cdots$		$[w]_{i+1,j}$	$\cdots$		$\cdots$	$\cdots$	$\cdots$	$\cdots$	$\cdots$
8	$\cdots$	$\cdots$	$\cdots$	$\cdots$	$\cdots$	$\cdots$	$\cdots$	$\cdots$	$\cdots$	$\cdots$
9	$[w]_{90}$	$[w]_{91}$	$[w]_{92}$	$[w]_{93}$	$[w]_{94}$	$[w]_{95}$	$[w]_{96}$	$[w]_{97}$	$[w]_{98}$	$[w]_{99}$

Here, elements in the first row are some scalars, $C(i, j) = s_j$, for $i = 0$, computed from the singularity constraint Eq.(2). Elements of all other rows are quadratic in w, computed from the nine rigidity constraints Eq.(4). More precisely, it is in the form of $C(i, j) = [w]_{ij} \doteq a_{ij}w^2 + b_{ij}w + c_{ij}$, for $1 \leqslant i \leqslant 9$.

As the monomial vector has been kept homogenous, the equation $C(w)\mathbf{X} = 0$ will have non-trivial solutions of $\{x, y, z\}$ if and only if the determinant of the coefficient matrix vanishes. That is:

$$\boxed{\det(C(w)) = 0.} \qquad (9)$$

This determinant is better known as a *hidden-variable-resultant*, which is an univariate polynomial of the hidden variable, w.

By observing the elements of C, one would expect that its determinant is an 18th degree polynomial. However, a more close inspection reveals that: it is actually a 15th degree polynomial, because terms of degree greater than 15 precisely cancel out. As a result, from a group of six points we will eventually obtain a **15th** degree polynomial in the single unknown w. More importantly, since the vector $\mathbf{X}$ is homogenous in $\{x, y, z\}$, and during the above construction we did not *generate* any extra equations besides the original ten, we are therefore safe to conclude that there are indeed at most 15 solutions to the six-point two-view focal-length problem. This result accords precisely with [1], but we achieve this via a different and more transparent approach.

Another benefit of keeping the homogeneity of $\mathbf{X}$ is that: estimating the fundamental matrix corresponding to the computed w is also made much easier than by [1]. Notice that the null-space $\mathbf{X} = \mathbf{null}(\mathbf{C}(w))$ is homogenous in $\{x, y, z\}$. Therefore, computing x, y, z is also made simple, thanks to the symmetric structure of the vector $\mathbf{X}$. As a result, the fundamental matrix $\mathbf{F}$ can be directly found using Eq. (6). By contrast, the back-substitution sequences used in [1] is more *ad hoc* and heuristic.

5   Implementation

5.1   Minimal Solver

Using the above construction, one can compute a hidden-variable resultant (i.e. a univariate polynomial equation) from every six points. Solving the hidden-variable resultant for the unknown w, one then finds the focal-length f. In general there are multiple *candidate* solutions. By *candidate* we mean that they have real positive values. To give a flavor we show below an example of such a 15th degree resultant polynomial and the corresponding real positive roots of f:

$$poly = -9.3992319e^{-14}w^{15} - 4.7922208e^{-17}w^{14} + 8.7010404e^{-22}w^{13}$$
$$+7.4700030e^{-25}w^{12} + 4.5342426e^{-29}w^{11} + 1.1095702e^{-33}w^{10}$$
$$+9.3596284e^{-39}w^9 - 9.8528519e^{-44}w^8 - 1.3185972e^{-48}w^7$$
$$+1.3420899e^{-53}w^6 - 2.6216189e^{-59}w^5 - 1.0514824e^{-64}w^4$$
$$+5.5394855e^{-70}w^3 - 9.1789042e^{-76}w^2 + 6.0294511e^{-82}w - 1.2914421e^{-88}$$
$$f_{cand} = 1/\sqrt{w} = [1536.38, 1104.52, 600.01, 593.99, 521.99, 83.74].$$

For this example we knew the ground-truth solution is $f_{true} = 600$ pixels.

There exist many (*global*) approaches to solving a univariate polynomial equation. Popular options include the *companion matrix* technique, or Sturm sequence bi-section technique [4]. The former can find *all roots* of a univariate polynomial, and the later can find *all real roots*. After solving the resultant equation, we only keep the real positive ones as the *candidate roots*, and then feed them into a second stage—root-selection.

5.2   Root Selection

From six point correspondences, one may get multiple candidate focal-lengths. Therefore a root-selection stage is required to single out a unique best root. In general, this stage is possible if only we have more than six points. In other words, it is the redundant measurements that provides extra information to resolve the multi-root ambiguity.

Paper [1] did not address the issue of root-selection, because it only deals with synthetic data with known ground-truth. RANSAC scheme is a good choice to fulfil such root-selection task. In the following we propose a kernel-voting scheme, which can be used as an alternative to the RANSAC, and which we think is suitable for the underlying problem.

6   Kernel Voting: Combining Multiple Measurements

To resolve the multiple roots ambiguity, the classical way is to use multiple measurements to eliminate those inconsistent solutions.

Given N ($N \gg 1$) groups of data, we will have a system of N simultaneous polynomial equations in one unknown. Any attempt to solve such an over-determined equation system strictly (exactly) is doomed to fail, because the inevitable noise in input will almost always make the equation system inconsistent (i.e, *co-prime*).

Alternatively, one could exploit the *least square* idea. For example, one might think of using a global cost function by summing up the square of each individual resultant equations Eq.(9) and then apply the bundle adjustment. However, experiments show that this simple idea does not work, because the summation has cancelled many of the convexities of the individual polynomials, leading to a cost function which is less likely to converge to global minima [13] [9].

RANSAC has been proposed as a successful approach to disambiguate the multiple roots problem, e.g, in *five-point relative-orientation* problem [11]. It is a good option here to resolve the ambiguity. However, in this paper, we suggest an alternative scheme based on the kernel-voting idea [10], which we believe is quite useful for certain situations.

The basic strategy is to keep the form of *minimal solver* for each individual data group (of six points), and use a *voting* scheme to choose the *best root* afterward. By the *best root* we mean that it is agreed by the majority of the the input measurements. This technique is therefore also immune to outliers.

6.1   Kernel Voting

The purpose of kernel-voting ([10]) is to single out the best real root from multiple candidate solutions. We fulfil this by a "soft" voting scheme, where the *votes* are the candidate roots that each polynomial Eq.(9) produces.

Because Eq.(9) is a high-degree polynomial, it is very sensitive to noise. A small perturbation in the input point coordinates may cause large changes in the polynomial coefficients. And this may significantly distort the resultant equation, as well as its roots. However, By experimentations we found: although noise affects the high-order basic equations *individually*, the obtained roots mostly surround the genuine root (this is also because a polynomial is a continuous function). The statistical distribution of all roots computed from the multiple measurements displays a peak shape. So long as a sufficiently large number of measurements, an asymptotically correct root will be eventually found. That is, the position that receives the maximal numbers of votes will eventually win.

In spirit, our voting scheme is similar to the Hough transform. However, their operations are differences. In the Hough transform the voting space is tessellated into discrete cells, while the voting space of ours is the continuous real axis. In addition, since we only receive votes at rather sparse and isolated positions (of the real roots), our search can be performed more efficiently. In order to smooth the voting space, we introduce a kernel density estimator (KDE) to estimate the distribution of the candidate roots. Then the peak position, corresponding to the (globally) maximal (peak) probability, is identified as the output of the best root. In this sense, it works like a Maximal-Likelihood Decision-Maker. Compared with the RANSAC, our kernel-voting scheme turns to make a *collective* decision, rather than depending on one *individual* decision.

Given multiple independent observations of a random variable, the KDE at point x is defined as

$$\hat{f}_h(x) = \sum_{i=1}^{n} \frac{\mathcal{K}(x_i - x)}{h} \tag{10}$$

where $\mathcal{K}()$ denotes the kernel function, and h the bandwidth. Here we choose a Gaussian Kernel with fixed bandwidth, and simply set the bandwidth as the estimation precision that we expect (e.g, 0.5%–1% of the focal-length).

7 Experiments

Thanks to the simplicity of the *hidden variable* technique, we implemented our six-point algorithm economically. The program language used is Matlab (with Symbolic-Math toolbox, which is essentially a subset of Maple). For reference purposes we include our Matlab program in the appendix of the paper. The central part of the program consists of 20 lines of code only, most being general (Matlab and Maple) functions. No hidden code is used. Only for demonstration purpose, a Maple function `solve` is applied in one step, which itself is indeed a long implementation. However, since that step is only used to solve a univariate equation, the reader can change it to any suitable solver.

We test our algorithm on both synthetic data (with various levels of noise and outliers) and real images. Some results are reported below.

7.1 Test on Synthetic Data

To resemble the real case, the size of synthetic image is 512×512. We tested different values for f, but found that they do not affect the final accuracy. So, in what follows we always use a ground-truth focal-length of 600 pixels. The camera motions between two views are drawn randomly. No special attention has been paid to avoid the *degenerate* motions (for focal-length estimation [7]). Gaussian noise was introduced to the raw image coordinates. It is noteworthy that the Hartley's normalization ([5]) is *not* essential for our six-point algorithm.

Our first experiment aimed at testing the focal-length estimation accuracy versus different image noises. From six points our algorithm is already able to output real focal length. However, in order to obtain a statistically robust estimation, fifty feature points were used to extract three 9-dimensional null-space vectors. After applying the procedures, we choose the best root as the nearest one to the ground-truth, and repeat this procedure 100 times. The following curves (fig-1) show the distribution of relative errors (percentage) in focal-length under different levels of noise. Our second experiment was used to test the performance of the root-selection based on the proposed kernel-voting scheme. From 50 point correspondences, we randomly drew 50 six-point data-groups, and apply our six-point algorithm to them. After performing a kernel-voting on all the obtained candidate focal-lengths, we plot the curves of root distribution and pick up the peak position. Some example curves are shown in figure-2. These curves show that the estimated focal-lengths are quite accurate.

We also test the cases where there are outliers in inputs and where there are errors in some of the camera intrinsics. From the voting curves shown in fig-3 we see that

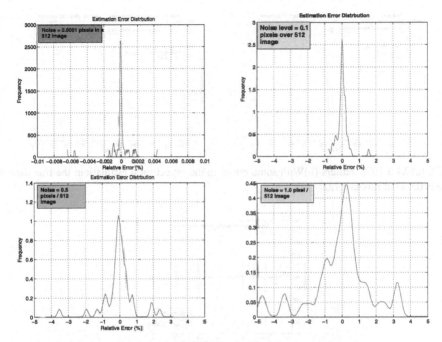

Fig. 1. Distribution of relative errors in focal-length estimation, for noise levels at (a) 0.0001 pixels, (b) 0.1 pixels and(c) 0.5 pixels (d) 1.0 pixels in a 512 size synthetic image. Note that even when the noise level is at 1.0 pixels, the relative errors are mainly less than 5%.

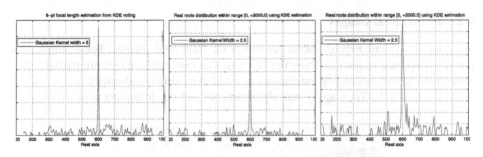

Fig. 2. Kernel-voting results, for noise level at (a)0.0001 pixels, (b)0.1 pixels and (c)1.0 pixels in a 512 size image. From the peak position we get the focal-length estimation $f \approx 600$.

the proposed method is robust to outliers, and not sensitive to the errors in some intrinsics. To quantitatively evaluate the estimation accuracy, we repeat the experiment 100 times, and plot the error-bar curve (mean value and standard deviation versus noise) in fig-4. Remember that the camera motions are drawn randomly (i.e. we did not intentionally avoid the degenerate motion). We also conducted experiments for comparing the numerical performances between our algorithm and ([1]), but no significant difference was found. This makes sense as both algorithms use essentially the same formulation.

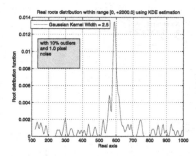
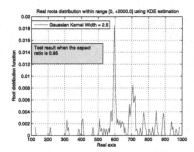

Fig. 3. (a)With 10% outliers (b)With some errors in the aspect ratio estimation: the true aspect-ratio is 0.95 but mis-use 1.00

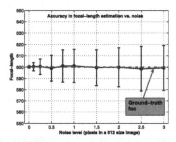

Fig. 4. Error bars (mean value and standard deviations) of focal-length estimation under different levels of noise

7.2   Test on Real Images

We have tested our new six-point algorithm on some real images. For example, we test the Valbonne sequences shown in fig-5(a). The two input images are partially calibrated using the calibration information provided by other authors[9]: $[\alpha, u_0, v_0] = [1.0, 258.8, 383.2]$. Then apply our algorithm, we get the following root distribution

(a) Two Valbonne images and some corresponding points.

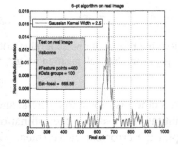

(b) Real roots distribution.

Fig. 5. Test on real images: Valbonne sequences

curve shown in figure-5(b), from which we can read the focal-length is about 670 pixels, which is close to the estimation of 699 pixels given by [9]. We also test some other standard image sequences. We find that as long as the two cameras are not in degenerate configurations ([8]) the estimated focal-length is close to the ground-truth data (obtained from other calibration procedure).

8   Discussion

Even when there are more than six points available in image, there are still advantages of using the *six-point* algorithm. Indeed, it is a good strategy of keep using such a *minimal-solver* even when extra data are available. The reason is explained in [11] and [1], showing that minimal-solver often offers better performance than the non-minimal ones. At first sight this is a bit surprise. However, a careful analysis will reveal the reason. That is, the minimal solver has better exploited all available inherent constraints of the problem (both linear and nonlinear), while many other conventional algorithms (e.g, 8pt algorithm) only use the extra measurements to get a better linear null-space estimation [5].

Our algorithm will fail when the *degenerate cases*(for focal-length estimation, cf. [8]) is met, for example, when the two optical axes intersect at equal distances, or when the camera underwent a pure translation. As this is a general difficulty for any focal-length algorithm, we do not intend to overcome it here. However, it is our conjecture that because the six-point algorithm has better exploited the nonlinear constraints it might have better conditioning near some degenerate configurations (including the critical surfaces and singular motions). To justify this, more critical experiments and theoretical analysis are yet to be done. The author believes that how to mitigate the degenerate surfaces problem in motion-and-structure computation is a topic worth researching.

9   Conclusions

We have provided a practical algorithm to solve the six-point focal-length problem. The most appealing feature is its simplicity and transparency. Besides its theoretical contribution, we hope the six-point algorithm will make a small and useful module in many vision systems.

We believe that the proposed algorithm is not an individual success of the powerful hidden-variable technique. It can have wider applications in similar problems, for example, five-point relative-orientation and three-point absolute-orientation etc. These can be future work.

Acknowledgments. NICTA is funded through the Australian Government's Backing Australia's Ability Initiative, in part through the ARC. The author wishes to thank Richard (H) for inspiration, guidance and invaluable support, to Fredrik (K) for many illuminating discussions, to Fred (S) for introducing me to UAG [4] and for the mug, and to the three anonymous reviewers for their suggestions that much improve the paper.

References

1. H.Stewénius, D.Nistér, F.Kahl, F.Schaffalitzky, A minimal solution for relative pose with unknown focal length, in Proc. IEEE-CVPR-2005, 2005.
2. R.I.Hartley, Estimation of Relative Camera Positions for Uncalibrated Cameras, In Proc.2nd ECCV, 1992.
3. S.Petitjean, Algebraic geometry and computer vision: Polynomial systems, real and complex roots, Journal of Mathematical Imaging and Vision,10:191-220,1999.
4. D.Cox, J.Little and D.O'shea, *Using Algebraic Geometry*, 2nd Edition, Springer, 2005.
5. R.Hartley, A.Zisserman, Mutiview Geometry in computer vision, 2nd Edition, Cambridge University Press, 2004.
6. O.Faugeras, Q.Luong, *The geometry of multiple images*, The MIT Press, 2001.
7. P.Sturm, On focal-length calibration from two views, In Proc.CVPR-2001, December, 2001.
8. P.Sturm,et al, Focal length calibration from two views:method and alaysis of singular cases, Computer Vision and Image Understanding,Vol 99, No.1,2005.
9. A.Fusiello, et al, Globally convergent autocalibration using interval analysis, IEEE T-PAMI 26(12), 2004.
10. Hongdong Li, Richard Hartley, A Non-iterative Method for Correcting Lens Distortion from Nine-Point Correspondences, In Proc. OmniVision'05, ICCV-workshop,2005.
11. D.Nistér, An efficient solution to the five-point relative pose problem, in Proc. IEEE CVPR-2003,Vol-2, pp. 195-202, 2003.
12. R.Hartley, F.Schaffalitzky, L-inf minimization in geometric reconstruction problems, In Proc. CVPR-2004, 2004.
13. F.Kahl, D.Henrion, Globally optimal estimes for geometric reconstruction problems, In Proc. ICCV-2005, Beijing, 2005.
14. O. Faugeras and S. Maybank, Motion from Point Matches:Multiplicity of Solutions, IJCV,vol.4,pp.225-246,1990.
15. A. Heyden, and G. Sparr, Reconstruction from Calibrated Cameras A New Proof of the Kruppa-Demazure Theorem, J. Math. Imag. and Vis., vol.10, pp.1-20, 1999.

Appendix

Program 1 . The six-point focal-length algorithm

```
%%%%%%%%%%%%%%%%%%%%%%%%%%%%%%%%%%%%%%%%%%%%%%%%%%%%%%%%%%%%%%%%%
%% This is a simple 6-pt focal-length algorithm.          %%%
%% Use Matlab-7.0(6.5)with SymbolicMath Toolbox.          %%%
%% The "Matches" is a 6x4 matrix containing six points.   %%%
%% For example,                                           %%%
Matches = [ 93.3053,    59.9312, -420.3770, -773.9141;
           -141.9589,  -50.1980, -386.7602, -471.0662;
           -174.0883, -157.0080, -489.9528, -259.9091;
            -57.6271 , -12.2055 , -394.5345, -466.4747;
           -115.7769,  154.4320, -172.2640, -461.6882;
            134.6858,   -4.0822, -575.1835, -855.5145]
%% For this example the ground truth is foc = 600.  %%%%%%%%%
%% Output: all computed focal-lengths in foc. %%%%%%%%%%%%%%%
%%%%%%%%%%%%%%%%%%%%%%%%%%%%%%%%%%%%%%%%%%%%%%%%%%%%%%%%%%%%%%%%%
function foc = SixPtFocal(Matches)

  syms F f x y z w equ Res Q C
  Q = [1, 0 ,0 ; 0 ,1 ,0; 0, 0, w];
  q  = [ Matches(:,1), Matches(:,2)] ;
  qp = [ Matches(:,3), Matches(:,4)] ;
  M = [qp(:,1).*q(:,1), qp(:,1).*q(:,2), qp(:,1), ...
       qp(:,2).*q(:,1), qp(:,2).*q(:,2), qp(:,2), ...
       q(:,1), q(:,2), ones(6,1)] ;

  N = null(M) %%% compute the null-space
  f = x*N(:,1) + y*N(:,2) + z*N(:,3); %% form the FM
  F = transpose(reshape(f,3,3));
  FT =transpose(F);
  equ(1)    = det(F);
  equ(2:10) = expand(2*F*Q*FT*Q*F-trace(F*Q*FT*Q)*F);

  for i =1:10
   %Note:Be careful with MATLAB delimiter for string, 'or'?
    equ(i) = maple('collect',equ(i),'[x,y,z]','distributed');
    for j =1:10
       oper = maple('op', j, equ(i)) ;
       C(i,j) = maple('op',1,oper);
    end
  end
  disp('Compute Det(C),need a while,please wait,,,');
  Res = maple('evalf', det(C))%%Hidden-variable resultant
  foc = 1.0./sqrt(double([solve( Res)]))
  disp('Ground-truth focal-length = 600.0000');
```

Iterative Extensions of the Sturm/Triggs Algorithm: Convergence and Nonconvergence

John Oliensis[1] and Richard Hartley[2],*

[1] Department of Computer Science, Stevens Institute of Technology,
Castle Point on Hudson, Hoboken, NJ 07030
[2] Australian National University and National ICT Australia

Abstract. We show that SIESTA, the simplest iterative extension of the Sturm/Triggs algorithm, descends an error function. However, we prove that SIESTA does not converge to usable results. The iterative extension of Mahamud et al. has similar problems, and experiments with "balanced" iterations show that they can fail to converge. We present CIESTA, an algorithm which avoids these problems. It is identical to SIESTA except for one extra, simple stage of computation. We prove that CIESTA descends an error and approaches fixed points. Under weak assumptions, it converges. The CIESTA error can be minimized using a standard descent method such as Gauss–Newton, combining quadratic convergence with the advantage of minimizing in the projective depths.

1 Introduction

The Sturm/Triggs (**ST**) algorithm [9] is a popular example of the factorization strategy [10] for estimating 3D structure and camera matrices from a collection of matched images. The factorization part of the algorithm needs starting estimates of the *projective depths* λ_n^i, which [9] obtained originally from image pairs. After [9], researchers noted that the λ_n^i can be taken equal or close to 1 for important classes of camera motions [11][1][5]. For these motions, the algorithm becomes almost a direct method, since it computes the structure/cameras directly from the λ_n^i whose values are approximately known.

To improve the results of **ST**, several researchers proposed iterative extensions of the method which: initialize the λ_n^i (typically) at 1, estimate the structure/cameras, use these estimates to recompute the λ_n^i, use the new λ_n^i to recompute the structure/cameras, etc. [11][1][5][8][4]. One common use is for initializing bundle adjustment [4]; for example, a few iterations can extend an affine estimate computed via Tomasi/Kanade [10] to a projective initialization. The iteration often gives much faster initial convergence than bundle adjustment does [2]. Variant iterative extensions include [1][5][8][4]. Notably, [4] recommends adding a "balancing" step [9] following the computation of the λ_n^i to readjust

---

* National ICT Australia is funded by the Australian Government's Department of Communications, Information Technology and the Arts And the Australian Research Council through Backing Australia's Ability And the ICT Research Centre of Excellence programs.

A. Leonardis, H. Bischof, and A. Pinz (Eds.): ECCV 2006, Part IV, LNCS 3954, pp. 214–227, 2006.

their values toward 1. This keeps the λ_n^i near the correct values (for many classes of motions) and also reduces the bias of the estimates [4].

This paper discusses the convergence of these iterations. Our theorems and experiments show that the versions without balancing do not converge sensibly and that the balanced iteration [4] can fail to converge. We propose CIESTA, a simple algorithm which avoids these problems. We prove that CIESTA descends an error function, that it iterates toward a "best achievable" estimate, and that these "best" estimates are stationary points of the error. CIESTA extends **ST** to a sound iteration, replacing balancing with regularization. Since CIESTA descends a known error function, it can be replaced by a standard descent method such as Gauss–Newton, combining quadratic convergence with the advantage of minimizing in the projective depths.

Notation. Given N quantities ζ_a indexed by a, we use $\{\zeta\} \in \Re^N$ to denote the column vector whose ath element is ζ_a. if $A \in \Re^{M \times N}$ is a matrix, we define $\{A\} \in \Re^{MN}$ as the column vector obtained by concatenating the columns of A.

For multiview geometry, we use the notation of [4]. Let $\mathbf{X}_n \equiv \left(X_n; Y_n; Z_n; 1 \right) \in \Re^4$ represent the homogenous coordinates of the nth 3D point (we use ';' to indicate a column vector), with $n = 1, 2, \ldots, N_p$, and let $\mathbf{x}_n^i \equiv \left(x_n^i; y_n^i; 1 \right) \in \Re^3$ be its homogenous image in the ith image, for $i = 1, \ldots N_I$. Let $M^i \in \Re^{3 \times 4}$ be the ith *camera matrix*, and let $\mathcal{M} \in \Re^{3N_I \times 4}$ consist of the M^i concatenated one on top of the other. Define the *structure matrix* $\mathcal{X} \in \Re^{4 \times N_p}$ so that its nth column $\mathcal{X}_n$ is proportional to $\mathbf{X}_n$. Neglecting noise, we have $\lambda_n^i \mathbf{x}_n^i = M^i \mathcal{X}_n$, where the constants λ_n^i are the *projective depths*. We use $\lambda \in \Re^{N_I N_p}$ to denote the vector of all the projective depths ordered in the natural way. Let $\mathcal{W} = \mathcal{W}(\lambda) \in \Re^{3N_I \times N_p}$ be the scaled data matrix consisting of the $\mathbf{x}_n^i$ multiplied by the projective depths, with $\mathcal{W}_n^{(3i-2):3i} = \lambda_n^i \mathbf{x}_n^i$. **ST** exploits the fact that, for known λ_j^i and zero noise, the matrix $\mathcal{W}$ has rank ≤ 4 and factors into a camera matrix times a structure matrix.

2 Simplest Iterative Extension of the ST Algorithm

Let $\hat{\mathcal{W}}(\lambda)$ be a matrix with rank ≤ 4 that gives the best approximation to $\mathcal{W}(\lambda)$ under the Frobenius norm: $\hat{\mathcal{W}}(\lambda) \equiv \arg\min_{\text{rank}(Y) \leq 4} \|\mathcal{W}(\lambda) - Y\|$. Given the SVD $\mathcal{W}(\lambda) = UDV^T$, we have the standard result $\hat{\mathcal{W}}(\lambda) = U\hat{D}V^T$, where $\hat{D}$ is obtained from D by zeroing all but the first four diagonal entries.

SIESTA repeatedly adjusts the λ_n^i to make the scaled data matrix $\mathcal{W}$ closer to rank 4. Let $\lambda^{(k)}$ and $\mathcal{W}^{(k)} \equiv \mathcal{W}\left(\lambda^{(k)}\right)$ give the estimates of the λ_n^i and $\mathcal{W}$ in the the the kth iteration. The algorithm is:

- **Initialize** the λ_n^i. By default we set all the $\lambda_n^{i(0)}$ to 1.
- **Iteration k, stage 1:** Given the scaled data matrix $\mathcal{W}^{(k-1)} \equiv \mathcal{W}\left(\lambda^{(k-1)}\right)$, compute its best rank ≤ 4 approximation $\hat{\mathcal{W}}$. Set $\hat{\mathcal{W}}^{(k-1)} = \hat{\mathcal{W}}$.
- **Iteration k, stage 2:** Given $\hat{\mathcal{W}}^{(k-1)}$, choose $\lambda^{(k)}$ to give the closest matrix of the form $\mathcal{W}(\lambda^{(k)})$, that is, $\lambda^{(k)} = \arg\min_\lambda \|\mathcal{W}(\lambda) - \hat{\mathcal{W}}^{(k-1)}\|$.

Remark 1. The SIESTA algorithm has a simple interpretation if one thinks of the $\mathcal{W}^{(k)}$ and $\hat{\mathcal{W}}^{(k)}$ as points in $\Re^{3N_I N_p}$. For fixed image points $\mathbf{x}_n^i$, the set of all $\{\mathcal{W}(\lambda)\}$ is a linear subspace of $\Re^{3N_I N_p}$ which has dimension $N_I N_p$ since its points are indexed by the $N_I N_p$ projective depths. We denote it by $\mathcal{L}^{N_I N_p}$. Let $\hat{\Omega}$ denote the set of all points $\{\hat{\mathcal{W}}\}$ in $\Re^{3N_I N_p}$ coming from matrices $\hat{W} \in \Re^{3N_I \times N_p}$ of rank ≤ 4. The SIESTA iteration can be rewritten as:

- **Stage 1:** Given $\{\mathcal{W}^{(k-1)}\}$, find the closest point $\{\hat{\mathcal{W}}^{(k-1)}\}$ from the set $\hat{\Omega}$.
- **Stage 2:** Given $\{\hat{\mathcal{W}}^{(k-1)}\}$, find the closest point $\{\mathcal{W}^{(k)}\}$ from $\mathcal{L}^{N_I N_p}$.

Next we show that each SIESTA iteration "improves" the reconstruction.

Definition 1. *Define $E(\mathcal{W}, Y) \equiv \|W - Y\|/\|W\|$ and*

$$\hat{E}(\lambda) \equiv \min_{\text{rank}(Y) \leq 4} E(\mathcal{W}(\lambda), Y) = E(\mathcal{W}, \hat{W}) \quad \text{(SIESTA error)}.$$

The SIESTA error $\hat{E}$ measures the fractional size of the non-rank 4 part of $\mathcal{W}$.

Proposition 1. *The SIESTA error $\hat{E}\left(\lambda^{(k)}\right)$ is nonincreasing with k.*

Proof (sketch). Let $\theta^{(k)} \equiv \theta(\mathcal{W}^{(k)}, \hat{\mathcal{W}}^{(k)})$ give the angle between the matrices $\mathcal{W}^{(k)}$ and $\hat{\mathcal{W}}^{(k)}$ considered as vectors in $R^{3N_I N_p}$. Its sine relates to the error $\hat{E}$:

$$\sin^2(\theta^{(k)}) = \left|\{\mathcal{W}^{(k)}\} - \{\hat{\mathcal{W}}^{(k)}\}\right|^2 / \left|\{\mathcal{W}^{(k)}\}\right|^2 = \hat{E}\left(\lambda^{(k)}\right). \quad (1)$$

SIESTA starts with a point in $\mathcal{L}^{N_I N_p}$, finds the closest point from $\hat{\Omega}$, finds the closest point to this from $\mathcal{L}^{N_I N_p}$, etc. Since it computes the best approximation each time, the angle between the two latest estimates from $\hat{\Omega}$ and $\mathcal{L}^{N_I N_p}$ is nonincreasing, so $\theta^{(k)}$ and $\hat{E}$ are nonincreasing. ∎

Discussion. Our result justifies the practice of applying a few iterations of SIESTA to extend an affine estimate based on $\lambda_n^i = 1$ to a projective one, which can be used to start bundle adjustment. Although we show below that SIESTA does not converge correctly, this is not be a fatal flaw, since the drift away from good estimates is extraordinarily slow and hence correctable.

3 Convergence Problems for Iterative Factorization

3.1 SIESTA Fails to Converge

Trivial minima. We begin by describing trivial minima. If we choose the λ_n^i zero except in four columns, the matrix $\mathcal{W}(\lambda)$ will have all columns but four composed of zeros. Then $\mathcal{W}(\lambda)$ will have rank ≤ 4, and the error $\hat{E}(\lambda) = E(\mathcal{W}(\lambda), \hat{W}(\lambda)) = 0$ because $\mathcal{W}(\lambda)$ and its closest rank ≤ 4 matrix $\hat{W}(\lambda)$ are equal.

This set of λ_n^i gives a *trivial minimum* of the SIESTA error. Choosing all the λ_n^i zero except in one row also gives a trivial minimum. Trivial minima are of no interest, since they don't give reasonable interpretations of the data. Unfortunately, the proposition below shows that unless a non-trivial solution exists with exactly zero error (meaning that the data admits a noise-free solution), then the SIESTA algorithm must approach a trivial minimum, or possibly, in rare circumstances, a saddle point of the error. Experiments on small problems show that the algorithm approaches trivial minima, though extremely slowly.

Proposition 2. *Every local minimum of the SIESTA error $\hat{E}$ is a global minimum with zero error.*

Proof. We can assume without loss of generality that every 3D point has nonzero λ_n^i in some images, since otherwise we can eliminate these points and apply the argument below to the remaining set of points.

We suppose that the SIESTA error $\hat{E}$ has a local minimum at λ. Let $\mathcal{W} = \mathcal{W}(\lambda)$ be the corresponding scaled data matrix. By the assumption just above, $\mathcal{W}$ has no columns consisting entirely of zeros. Under these two conditions, we will show that the error equals zero or, equivalently, that $\mathcal{W}$ has rank ≤ 4.

Consider a transformation that perturbs a matrix by multiplying its n-th column by a value s. We denote this transformation by $\tau_{n\kappa}$ where $\kappa = s^2 - 1$. The reason for introducing the variable κ is that the subsequent computations simplify when expressed in terms of κ. For $\kappa = 0$, the transformation $\tau_{n\kappa}$ is the identity transformation and leaves the original matrix unchanged. It is evident that applying $\tau_{n\kappa}$ to the matrix $\mathcal{W} = \mathcal{W}(\lambda)$ is equivalent to multiplying the nth column of the projective depths λ_n^i by s, so we can write $\tau_{nk}(\mathcal{W}) = \mathcal{W}(\lambda^{\tau nk})$, where $\lambda^{\tau nk}$ equals λ except for the appropriate scaling of the nth column.

For the remainder of the proof, we write simply $\mathcal{W}$, omitting the dependence on λ. We denote $\tau_{n\kappa}(\mathcal{W})$ by $\mathcal{W}^\tau$, and the nearest[1] rank ≤ 4 matrix to $\mathcal{W}^\tau$ by $\widehat{\mathcal{W}^\tau}$. Recall that, similarly, $\hat{\mathcal{W}}$ is the closest matrix to $\mathcal{W}$ having rank ≤ 4. We may also apply the transformation $\tau_{n\kappa}$ to $\hat{\mathcal{W}}$, resulting in a matrix $(\hat{\mathcal{W}})^\tau = \tau_{n\kappa}(\hat{\mathcal{W}})$. This matrix has the same rank as $\hat{\mathcal{W}}$ for $s \neq 0$ and hence has rank ≤ 4, but, as we shall see, it is in general distinct from $\widehat{\mathcal{W}^\tau}$. It is important to understand the difference between $(\hat{\mathcal{W}})^\tau$ and $\widehat{\mathcal{W}^\tau}$.

As a first step, we show (under our assumptions above) that *any* $\kappa \neq 0$ gives

$$\hat{E}(\mathcal{W}^\tau) \equiv E(\mathcal{W}^\tau, \widehat{\mathcal{W}^\tau}) \leq E(\mathcal{W}^\tau, (\hat{\mathcal{W}})^\tau) = E(\mathcal{W}, \hat{\mathcal{W}}) \equiv \hat{E}(\mathcal{W}) . \qquad (2)$$

The inequality in (2) follows simply from the definition of the error E and the fact that $\widehat{\mathcal{W}^\tau}$ is the closest matrix to $\mathcal{W}^\tau$ having rank ≤ 4. Consider the equality $E(\mathcal{W}^\tau, (\hat{\mathcal{W}})^\tau) = E(\mathcal{W}, \hat{\mathcal{W}})$. Noting that $\mathcal{W}$ and $\mathcal{W}^\tau$ differ only in the overall scale of their nth columns, we may compute

$$E(\mathcal{W}^\tau, (\hat{\mathcal{W}})^\tau) = (\kappa|\mathcal{R}_n|^2 + \|\mathcal{R}\|^2)/(\kappa|\mathcal{W}_n|^2 + \|\mathcal{W}\|^2), \qquad (3)$$

where $\mathcal{R} = \mathcal{W} - \hat{\mathcal{W}}$, and $\mathcal{R}_n$ and $\mathcal{W}_n$ are the nth columns of $\mathcal{R}$ and $\mathcal{W}$. Under our assumption that $\mathcal{W}$ gives a local minimum, the derivative of this expression

---

[1] The nearest matrix need not be unique.

with respect to κ must be zero. Computing the derivative at $\kappa = 0$, and setting the numerator to zero leads to $\|\mathcal{W}\|^2 |\mathcal{R}_n|^2 - \|\mathcal{R}\|^2 |\mathcal{W}_n|^2 = 0$, which gives

$$|\mathcal{R}_n|^2/|\mathcal{W}_n|^2 = \|\mathcal{R}\|^2/\|\mathcal{W}\|^2, \tag{4}$$

i.e., the left–hand ratio has the same value for any n. After substituting in (3),

$$E(\mathcal{W}^\tau, (\hat{\mathcal{W}})^\tau) = \|\mathcal{R}\|^2/\|\mathcal{W}\|^2 = E(\mathcal{W}, \hat{\mathcal{W}}) \tag{5}$$

for all values of κ, as required. This proves (2).

Suppose we could make the inequality in (2) strict for arbitrarily small values of κ. In fact, we cannot do this, since if we could the error $\hat{E}$ would be strictly decreasing at λ and $\mathcal{W}(\lambda)$ rather than having a local minimum as assumed. Therefore, for all κ less than some small value, we have the equality $E(\mathcal{W}^\tau, \widehat{\mathcal{W}^\tau}) = E(\mathcal{W}^\tau, (\hat{\mathcal{W}})^\tau)$. This means that $(\hat{\mathcal{W}})^\tau$ is a closest rank ≤ 4 matrix to $\mathcal{W}^\tau$ for all sufficiently small κ, regardless of which column n is scaled by the transform. We will prove the proposition by showing that this can hold only if $\mathcal{W}$ already has rank ≤ 4. First, we need a lemma.

Lemma 1. *If a matrix $\hat{\mathcal{W}}$ is a closest matrix having rank $\leq r$ to a matrix $\mathcal{W}$, then $\mathcal{R}^\top \hat{\mathcal{W}} = \mathcal{R} \hat{\mathcal{W}}^\top = 0$, where $\mathcal{R} = \mathcal{W} - \hat{\mathcal{W}}$.*

Proof (sketch). Write $\hat{\mathcal{W}} = AB$, where A has r columns, take derivatives of $\|\mathcal{W} - AB^\top\|^2$ with respect to the entries of A or B, and set them to zero.

We return to the proof of the proposition. Since $\hat{\mathcal{W}}$ is a closest rank ≤ 4 matrix to $\mathcal{W}$, the lemma gives $\mathcal{R}\hat{\mathcal{W}}^\top = 0$. As argued above, we can choose $\kappa \neq 0$ small enough so that $(\hat{\mathcal{W}})^\tau$ is a closest rank ≤ 4 matrix to $\mathcal{W}^\tau$, regardless of what n we choose for τ_{nk}. For such κ, the lemma gives $\mathcal{R}^\tau (\hat{\mathcal{W}})^{\tau\top} = 0$, where $\mathcal{R}^\tau = \mathcal{W}^\tau - (\hat{\mathcal{W}})^\tau$, and it follows that $\mathcal{R}\hat{\mathcal{W}}^\top - \mathcal{R}^\tau (\hat{\mathcal{W}})^{\tau\top} = 0$. Since $\mathcal{W}$ and $\mathcal{W}^\tau$, and similarly $\mathcal{R}$ and $\mathcal{R}^\tau$, differ only in the scaling of their n-th columns, we may easily compute the matrix $\mathcal{R}\hat{\mathcal{W}}^\top - \mathcal{R}^\tau (\hat{\mathcal{W}})^{\tau\top}$: Its (p,q)-th entry equals $\kappa \mathcal{R}_n^p \mathcal{W}_n^q$. Since $\kappa \neq 0$ and our arguments hold regardless of the n we choose for τ_{nk}, we have $\mathcal{R}_n^p \mathcal{W}_n^q = 0$ for all values of n, p, and q.

We assumed that $\mathcal{W}$ has no columns consisting entirely of zeros. Thus, each column n of $\mathcal{W}$ contains a non-zero entry $\mathcal{W}_n^q$, so for each n we must have $\mathcal{R}_n^p = 0$ for all p, which means that column n of $\mathcal{R}$ is zero. Hence $\mathcal{R} = 0$ and $\mathcal{W}$ gives zero error, which is what we set out to prove.   ∎

Remark 2. Intuitively, Proposition 2 holds because the trivial minima are so destabilizing that one can always reduce the error by moving toward one.

SIESTA can be useful despite our result. (5) suggests that the error can be very flat and SIESTA's descent to a trivial minimum extremely slow. In trials on realistic data, the SIESTA error drops quickly from its start at $\lambda_n^i = 1$ but never approaches a trivial minimum; in fact, it descends so slowly after a few hundred iterations (with $\Delta \hat{E} \leq O(10^{-11})$) that one can easily conclude wrongly that it has converged. What seems to happen is that SIESTA approaches an almost minimum—a saddle point that would be a minimum if it weren't destabilized by the trivial minima—and then slows, usually still with $\lambda_n^i \approx 1$.

All this suggests that the destabilization from the trivial minima is weak, only becoming important at small error values. If we can compensate for it, e.g., by 'balancing', this might turn the saddles into minima giving correct estimates. In trials, SIESTA does give good estimates once it slows. Although its error has no usable minima, the saddle points may serve as useful 'effective minima.'

3.2   Other Iterative Extensions of ST

Mahamud et al. [7][8] proposed an iteration similar to SIESTA that differs by maintaining a normalization constraint on the columns of $\mathcal{W}$.[2] The first stage of the iteration is the same as in SIESTA, and the second stage is:

-   **Iteration k, stage 2:** Given $\hat{\mathcal{W}}^{(k-1)}$, choose new projective depths $\lambda^{(k)}$ so that $\mathcal{W}(\lambda^{(k)})$ optimally approximates $\hat{\mathcal{W}}^{(k-1)}$ subject to the N_p columns constraints $|\mathcal{W}_n| = 1$, $n \in \{1 \ldots N_p\}$.

With the constraints, the SIESTA error $\hat{E}$ reduces in effect to $\|\mathcal{W} - \hat{\mathcal{W}}\|^2$. It is easy to show that the iteration descends this error [8]. The constrained error possibly does have nontrivial minima, but we argue below that it does not have usable minima corresponding to good structure/camera estimates.

[1][5] proposed a SIESTA variant roughly dual to [8] but did not give an error for it. A similar iteration that descends an error is SIESTA with a new stage 2:

-   **Iteration k, stage 2:** Given $\hat{\mathcal{W}}^{(k-1)}$, choose new projective depths $\lambda^{(k)}$ so that $\mathcal{W}(\lambda^{(k)})$ optimally approximates $\hat{\mathcal{W}}^{(k-1)}$ subject to the N_I image constraints $\|\mathcal{W}^{(3i-2):3i}\| = 1$, where each matrix $\mathcal{W}^{(3i-2):3i} \in \Re^{3 \times N_p}$ gives the three rows of $\mathcal{W}$ for image i.

This iteration also descends the error $\|\mathcal{W} - \hat{\mathcal{W}}\|^2$. We have not analyzed its convergence, but we expect that it has the same problems as the previous one. **Convergence analysis for the iteration of [7][8].**[2]

Our results are weaker than for SIESTA, so we just summarize them.

As for SIESTA, we start by considering a transformation that scales the λ_n^i toward a trivial minimum (see Remark 2). We define the transform so that it first scales all the projective depths for the kth image by s, and then scales the column of projective depths for each 3D point to maintain the norm constraints on the columns of $\mathcal{W}$. As before, we apply the same transform to $\hat{\mathcal{W}}$ as for $\mathcal{W}$. Assuming that λ gives a stationary point of the error, our transform must also give a stationary point at λ, and this leads to constraints on $\mathcal{W}$ and $\hat{\mathcal{W}}$ analogous to (4). Exploiting these constraints, we try to modify the transform so that it strictly decreases the error at λ.

This is much harder than for SIESTA. The initial transform τ_{nk} for SIESTA gave an error that was *constant* at a stationary point, so we could make the error

---

[2] Mahamud et al. [7] also proposed a different iteration that minimizes alternately with respect to the camera and structure matrices. This approach loses the advantage of minimizing in the λ_n^i—it cannot exploit prior knowledge that the λ_n^i are near one.

decrease, establishing the stationary point as a saddle, by an arbitrarily small change in τ_{nk}. For the algorithm of [8], the error at a stationary point usually has a minimum under our initial transform. We need a *large* change in the transform to make the error decrease, so this may not always be possible. However, we argue that we can make the error decrease at "desirable" stationary points, where the estimates of the structure/cameras are roughly correct and $\lambda_n^i \approx 1$.

We now describe how to modify the inital transform described above. Let $\hat{\mathcal{W}} = \hat{M}\hat{X}^T$ be the rank 4 factoring that comes from the SVD of $\mathcal{W}$. We modify the initial transform of $\hat{\mathcal{W}}$ by transforming $\hat{X}$ linearly before scaling it, where we choose this linear transform to minimize the error's second derivative with respect to the transform at the stationary point. We have derived upper bounds on the resulting second derivatives. We will argue that these are negative at a "desirable" stationary point, so such stationary points are saddles.

Define $\mathbf{w}_n^i \equiv [\mathcal{W}]_n^{(3i-2):3i}$ and $\hat{\mathbf{w}}_n^i \equiv \left[\hat{\mathcal{W}}\right]_n^{(3i-2):3i}$ and the residual $\mathbf{r}_n^i \equiv \mathbf{w}_n^i - \hat{\mathbf{w}}_n^i$; all are vectors in $\Re^3$. Without loss of generality, take the columns of $\hat{M}$ orthogonal and define $\hat{m}^i \equiv \hat{M}^{(3i-2):3i} \in \Re^{3\times4}$. Let $\hat{\mu}_a^i$ be the ath singular value of $\hat{m}^i$ and let $\hat{\mathbf{m}}_a^i \in \Re^3$ be the ath column of $\hat{m}^i$. Choose image k so

$$\left\langle |\hat{\mathbf{m}}^k|^2 \right\rangle \geq \left\langle |\mathbf{w}^k|^2 \right\rangle, \tag{6}$$

where we use $\langle \cdot \rangle$ to denote the average, taken over the omitted index. Such an image always exists, since our normalizations give

$$1 = \sum_{i=1}^{N_I}\sum_{a=1}^{4} |\hat{\mathbf{m}}_a^i|^2/4 = \sum_{i=1}^{N_I}\left\langle |\hat{\mathbf{m}}^i|^2 \right\rangle = \sum_{i=1}^{N_I}\left\langle |\mathbf{w}^i|^2 \right\rangle = \sum_{i=1}^{N_I}\sum_{n=1}^{N_p} |\mathbf{w}_n^i|^2/N_P.$$

Our upper bound on the second derivative for the modified transform is

$$2\left(\sum_{n=1}^{N_p} |\mathbf{r}_n^k|^2\right)\left(2\max_{n=1\ldots N_p} \left| |\mathbf{w}_n^k|^2 - \left\langle |\mathbf{w}^k|^2 \right\rangle \right| - \frac{4}{3}\frac{|\hat{\mu}_3^k|^2}{\left\langle |\hat{\mu}^k|^2 \right\rangle}\left\langle |\mathbf{w}^k|^2 \right\rangle\right) \tag{7}$$

for the chosen image k. In practice, [4][9] recommend normalizing the homogenous image points to a unit box before applying **ST**. Then, assuming a "desirable" stationary point with all λ_n^i near 1, the $|\mathbf{w}_n^k|^2$ will be approximately constant in k and n. If the singular values $\hat{\mu}_a^k$ all have roughly the same size, then $|\hat{\mu}_3^k|^2/\left\langle |\hat{\mu}^k|^2 \right\rangle \approx 1$, and our bound is likely to be negative.

In our experiments on real sequences, the apparent convergence points of the Mahamud et al. iteration [7][8] always have $\left(\hat{\mu}_3^k\right)^2/\left\langle |\hat{\mu}^k|^2 \right\rangle \approx 1$, and they almost always give a negative value of the bound (7), which rules out these "convergence points" as local minima. Note that the bound is conservative; in practice, we expect cancellations to reduce the second derivative below (7).

Why is the ratio $\left(\hat{\mu}_3^k\right)^2/\left\langle |\hat{\mu}^k|^2 \right\rangle$ typically near 1? One contributing factor is that, after the standard scaling to a unit box, the image submatrix $w^i \equiv$

$\left[\mathbf{w}_1^i, \mathbf{w}_2^i, \ldots, \mathbf{w}_{N_P}^i \right] \in \Re^{3 \times N_P}$ typically has three singular values of the same order. Another cause is the following. Write the SVD of the scaled data matrix as $\mathcal{W} = UDV^T$. Writing the singular values $\hat{\mu}_a^k$ in terms of the image data gives

$$\left(\hat{\mu}_a^k \right)^2 = N_I^{-1} \sum_{n=1}^{N_p} \left| \mathbf{s}_a^{kT} w^k V_n \right|^2 / \left\langle |wV_n|^2 \right\rangle,$$

where $\mathbf{s}_a^k \in \Re^3$ represent the ath left singular vector of $\hat{m}^k$ and V_n denotes the nth column of V. The average in the denominator is over all images i. Thus, $\left(\hat{\mu}_a^k \right)^2$ is proportional to a sum of projections of the (homogeneous) image data normalized by their average values. If the camera positions are spaced roughly uniformly, as they are in many sequences, the kth image is often close to "average," so the singular values $\hat{\mu}_a^k$ all have similar sizes. One can get $\hat{\mu}_3^k \ll \hat{\mu}_1^k$ if, for example, most of the camera positions cluster together but one is very far from the others.

We have also derived a second bound whose size is easier to estimate. Choose image k such that $\left\| w^k - \hat{w}^k \right\|^2 \leq \hat{E} \left\| w^k \right\|^2$, which is always possible since one can show that $\sum_i \left\| w^i - \hat{w}^i \right\|^2 = \hat{E} \sum_i \left\| w^i \right\|^2$. Denote the ath singular value of w^k by d_a^k and the ath singular value of $\mathcal{W}$ by D_a. Our new bound is

$$2 \left(\sum_{n=1}^{N_p} |\mathbf{r}_n^k|^2 \right) \left(2 \max_{n=1\ldots N_p} \left| \, |\mathbf{w}_n^k|^2 - \left\langle |\mathbf{w}^k|^2 \right\rangle \, \right| - \left(d_3^k / \left\| w^k \right\| - \hat{E}^{1/2} \right)^2 \frac{N_p}{D_1^2} \left\langle |\mathbf{w}^k|^2 \right\rangle \right).$$

(8)

After the standard scaling of the image data to a unit box, we expect $d_3^k / \left\| w^k \right\| \approx 3^{-1/2} \approx 0.58$. Even if the scene is planar, the first three singular values of $\mathcal{W}$ are usually substantial, causing $N_p/D_1^2 > 1$. Experimentally, we find $d_3^k / \left\| w^k \right\| \approx 0.3$ and $N_p/D_1^2 \approx 1.3$. Substituting the experimental values, and assuming $\mathcal{W}$ is close to a rank ≤ 4 matrix so $\hat{E} \ll 1/3$, we can approximate the bound as

$$2 \left(\sum_{n=1}^{N_p} |\mathbf{r}_n^k|^2 \right) \left(2 \max_{n=1\ldots N_p} \left| \, |\mathbf{w}_n^k|^2 - \left\langle |\mathbf{w}^k|^2 \right\rangle \, \right| - 0.13 \left\langle |\mathbf{w}^k|^2 \right\rangle \right).$$

(9)

Table 1 shows results for the Mahamud et al. algorithm on real image sequences, see Figure 1. We obtained these by running the algorithm for 1000 iterations, after which the error was changing so slowly that the algorithm seemed to have converged. In all but one case, we found negative values for the bounds (8) and (9), proving the algorithm had not converged to a minimum. In the exceptional case, the trivial minima had produced small λ_n^i for a few points. Repeating the experiment without these points gave a negative bound. We have verified our upper bounds experimentally on several thousand synthetic sequences. We also used a standard nonlinear minimization routine (LSQNONLIN from MATLAB) to minimize the error for the Mahamud et al. algorithm. The routine converged to a trivial minimum in all cases. These results indicate that the convergence of the Mahamud et al. algorithm is problematic at best. [2]

Table 1. The bounds (7), (8) for five real sequences (Fig. 1). 'Ox0–10' is for 11 images; other 'Ox' rows are for image pairs. 'Ox0&8*' is for images 0 and 8, with 3 points subtracted. The 'μ ratio' column gives the least $|\hat{\mu}_3^k|^2 / \langle |\hat{\mu}^k|^2 \rangle$ over k satisfying (6).

	Est. Range λ	First Bound	Least μ ratio	$\hat{E}^{1/2}$ ($\times 10^{-3}$)	Range for $\max_n$ $\left\| \frac{\|\mathbf{w}_n\|^2}{\langle \|\mathbf{w}\|^2 \rangle} - 1 \right\|$	$\frac{N_p}{D_1^2}$	$\max_k$ $\frac{d_3^2}{\|w\|^2}$	Second Bound
Ox0-10	0.79–1.15	−0.06	0.40	1.6	0.01–0.37	1.3	0.08	−0.09
Ox0&10	0.83–1.14	−0.24	0.78	1.8	0.29–0.31	1.3	0.10	0.44
Ox0&8	0.14–1.40	0.52	0.73	8.2	0.98–1.08	1.3	0.09	1.9
Ox0&8*	0.85–1.13	−0.28	0.78	1.6	0.24–0.25	1.3	0.09	0.37
Ox0&1	0.97–1.03	−0.46	0.75	0.5	0.04–0.04	1.3	0.12	−0.07
Rock	0.90–1.09	−0.07	0.46	6.0	0.03–0.20	1.4	0.08	0.01
Puma	0.99–1.01	−0.05	0.50	1.7	0.01–0.06	1.5	0.14	−0.21
MSTea	0.97–1.03	−0.43	0.75	0.7	0.05–0.05	1.5	0.16	−0.14
MSPlane	0.91–1.10	−0.13	0.44	0.6	0.05–0.13	1.5	0.18	−0.17

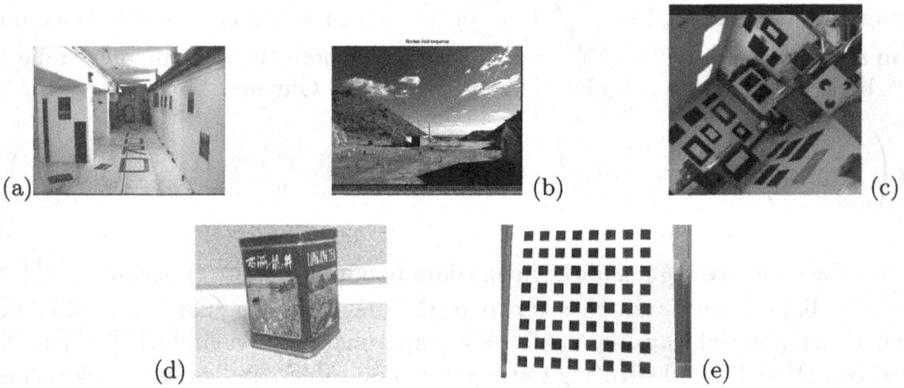

(a) (b) (c)

(d) (e)

Fig. 1. Images from the five real sequences. (a) Oxford corridor; (b) Rocket–Field [3]; (c) PUMA [6]; (d) Microsoft tea [12]; (e) Microsoft Plane calibration [12].

3.3 Balancing

[4] modifies SIESTA by adding a third "balancing" stage [11] following stage 2 that rescales the λ_n^i to make them close to 1. This lessens the algorithm's bias and helps to steer it away from trivial minima. The balancing can be done in two passes, by first scaling $\lambda_n^i \longrightarrow \alpha^i \lambda_n^i$ for each image i so that $\sum_{n=1}^{N_p} |\lambda_n^i|^2 = N_I$, and then scaling $\lambda_n^i \longrightarrow \beta_n \lambda_n^i$ for each point so $\sum_{i=1}^{N_I} |\lambda_n^i|^2 = N_p$. Optionally, this can be repeated several times or iterated to convergence. Unfortunately, it seems likely that the rescaling conflicts with the error minimization in stages 1 and 2, and that the balanced iteration need not converge. To exaggerate this potential conflict and make it more observable, we implemented SIESTA with a balancing stage that iterates to near convergence, with up to 10 rounds of first balancing the rows and then the columns of λ_n^i. In one of our experiments, this algorithm apparently converged to a limit cycle which repeatedly passed through

three different values for λ with three different values of the error $\hat{E}(\lambda)$. For this strong version of balancing, it seems that an iteration of SIESTA–plus–balancing does not guarantee improvement in the projective–depth estimates.

Nevertheless, occasional balancing may serve as a useful "mid–course correction" that compensates for SIESTA's drift toward trivial minima.

4   CIESTA

An alternative to balancing is regularization. We define a new iteration CIESTA that descends the error $\hat{E}_{\text{reg}}(\lambda)$, where

$$\hat{E}_{\text{reg}}(\lambda) \equiv \min_{\text{rank}(Y) \leq 4} E_{\text{reg}}, \quad E_{\text{reg}}(\lambda, Y) \equiv E(\mathcal{W}(\lambda), Y) + \mu \sum_{i=1}^{N_I} \sum_{n=1}^{N_p} |\mathbf{x}_n^i|^2 (1 - \lambda_n^i)^2,$$
(10)

and $\mu > 0$ is the regularization constant. The algorithm is the same as SIESTA except for a new third stage in the iteration.

Let $\lambda^{(k)} \in \Re^{N_I N_p}$ and $\mathcal{W}^{(k)} \equiv \mathcal{W}(\lambda^{(k)})$ now denote the output of the kth CIESTA iteration, and let $\lambda^{(0)}$ and $\mathcal{W}^{(0)}$ give the initialization. As before, let $\hat{\mathcal{W}}^{(k)}$ be the best approximation of rank ≤ 4 to $\mathcal{W}^{(k)}$. Define the constants

$$C_0 = \mu \sum_{i=1}^{N_I} \sum_{n=1}^{N_p} |\mathbf{x}_n^i|^2, \quad C_1^{(k)} \equiv \mu \sum_{i=1}^{N_I} \sum_{n=1}^{N_p} \mathbf{x}_n^i \cdot \hat{\mathbf{w}}_n^{i(k)},$$
(11)

$$C_2^{(k)} \equiv \mu \sum_{i=1}^{N_I} \sum_{n=1}^{N_p} \frac{\left(\mathbf{x}_n^i \cdot \hat{\mathbf{w}}_n^{i(k)}\right)^2}{|\mathbf{x}_n^i|^2}, \quad C_3^{(k)} = \mu \sum_{i=1}^{N_I} \sum_{n=1}^{N_p} |\hat{\mathbf{w}}_n^{i(k)}|^2,$$

and $z^{(k)} \equiv C_3^{(k)} C_0 / C_2^{(k)}$. Define the function

$$b_+^{(k)}(a) \equiv a^{1/2} / \left(a^2 C_0 + 2a C_1^{(k)} + C_2^{(k)}\right)^{1/2},$$
(12)

which is obtained as an intermediate result while minimizing $E_{\text{reg}}(\lambda, \hat{\mathcal{W}}^{(k)})$ in λ.

Remark 3. One can show that CIESTA gives the following constraints:

1. $C_0 > 0, \quad C_3^{(k)} \geq C_2^{(k)}, \quad C_2^{(k)} > 0.$
2. $\mathcal{Q}^{(k)} \equiv a^2 C_0 + 2a C_1^{(k)} + C_2^{(k)} > 0, \quad z^{(k)} > 0$

From the second line we see that b_+ is finite. CIESTA's new third stage is:

– **CIESTA** (iteration k, stage 3): With $\kappa \equiv k - 1$, compute the roots of $P^{(\kappa)}(a)$

$$\equiv C_0 a^6 - \left(C_0^2 - 2C_1^{(\kappa)}\right) a^5 - \left(2C_0 C_3^{(\kappa)} - C_2^{(\kappa)}\right) a^4 - \left(4C_1^{(\kappa)} C_3^{(\kappa)} - 2C_2^{(\kappa)} C_0\right) a^3$$

$$+ \left(C_0 C_3^{(\kappa)2} - 2C_2^{(\kappa)} C_3^{(\kappa)}\right) a^2 + \left(2C_1^{(\kappa)} C_3^{(\kappa)2} - C_2^{(\kappa)2}\right) a + C_2^{(\kappa)} C_3^{(\kappa)2}.$$
(13)

Choose a root $a > 0$ such that: For $z^{(\kappa)} \neq 1$, the quantity $\bar{a} \equiv a(C_0/C_2^{(\kappa)})^{1/2}$ and $z^{(\kappa)}$ lie on the same side of 1; For $z^{(\kappa)} = 1$, when there is a choice, take either of the choices with $\bar{a} \neq 1$. Redefine $\lambda^{(k)} \longrightarrow \lambda^{(k)} = \left(a + \lambda^{(k)}\right) b_+^{(\kappa)}(a)$.

The four propositions below address the convergence of CIESTA (proofs omitted). Let $\hat{E}_\infty$ be the greatest lower bound of the errors $\hat{E}_{\text{reg}}(\lambda^{(k)})$, and let $\mathcal{A}$ be the set of accumulation points of the sequence $\lambda^{(k)}$.

Assumption 1 (μ condition). *CIESTA starts with all $\lambda_n^i = 1$, and*

$$\mu\|\mathcal{W}^{(0)}\|^2 > \|\mathcal{W}^{(0)} - \hat{\mathcal{W}}^{(0)}\|^2/\|\mathcal{W}^{(0)}\|^2, \tag{14}$$

which is equivalent to $C_0^2 > \left(C_0 + C_3^{(0)} - 2C_1^{(0)}\right)$.

Remark 4. Our results below don't require that CIESTA start at $\lambda_n^i = 1$; we assume this just to simplify the theorems and proofs. The Assumption specifies how much regularization is needed to guarantee CIESTA's performance. Taking μ large enough rules out the trivial minima.

Proposition 3. *Suppose Assumption 1 holds. The errors $\hat{E}_{\text{reg}}\left(\lambda^{(k)}\right)$ are non-increasing with k and converge monotonically in the limit $k \to \infty$.*

Proposition 4. *Suppose Assumption 1 holds. Then: 1) Every $\lambda_{\mathcal{A}} \in \mathcal{A}$ has $\hat{E}_{\text{reg}}(\lambda_{\mathcal{A}}) = \hat{E}_\infty$; 2) For any $\epsilon > 0$, there exists a K such that $k > K$ implies $\left|\lambda^{(k)} - \lambda_{\mathcal{A}}\right| \leq \epsilon$ for some $\lambda_{\mathcal{A}} \in \mathcal{A}$.*

Proposition 5. *Suppose Assumption 1 holds. Let $\lambda_{\mathcal{A}} \in \mathcal{A}$. Let the fourth singular value of $\mathcal{W}(\lambda_{\mathcal{A}})$ be strictly greater than the fifth, and $z^{\mathcal{A}} \neq 1$, where $z^{\mathcal{A}}$ is the constant from (11) evaluated at $\lambda_{\mathcal{A}}$. Then $\lambda_{\mathcal{A}}$ is a fixed point of CIESTA and a stationary point of the error $\hat{E}_{\text{reg}}$ (not necessarily a minimum).*

Proposition 6. *Suppose the assumptions of Proposition 5 hold for some $\lambda_{\mathcal{A}} \in \mathcal{A}$. Proposition 5 states that $\hat{E}_{\text{reg}}$ has a stationary point at $\lambda_{\mathcal{A}}$. If in fact $\hat{E}_{\text{reg}}$ has a strict local minimum at $\lambda_{\mathcal{A}}$, then CIESTA converges uniquely to $\lambda_{\mathcal{A}}$.*

Propositions 3 and 4 show that CIESTA "converges" in a certain sense (discussed below). Proposition 5 states that its end results are sensible, that is, they are stationary points of the error. Proposition 6 shows that under weak assumptions CIESTA converges in a strict sense to a unique result.

The proof of Prop. 4 is easy and the proof of Prop. 3 is a calculation. The proof of Proposition 5 is more technical: We need to show that E_{reg} has a unique global minimum and that the output of stage 3 depends continuously on its input.

Discussion. Like balancing, CIESTA favors $\lambda_n^i \approx 1$, but it guarantees improved estimates with lower error. The error $\hat{E}_{\text{reg}}$ shows explicitly how CIESTA weights its preference for $\lambda_n^i \approx 1$ versus the data error $\hat{E}$. The extra computation of stage 3 is small: it just requires finding the eigenvalues of a 6×6 matrix.

We have not shown that CIESTA converges to a single λ (except under the assumptions of Prop. 6), and it is not clear whether this always happens. But our results have the same practical implications as a convergence proof.

A convergence proof would amount to the following guarantee: by iterating enough times, one can bring the algorithm as close as desired to a "best achievable result," i.e., to a λ with the lowest error reachable from its starting point. This does not forbid other equally good estimates with the same error as the "best result," though the algorithm happens not to converge to them.

Proposition 4 provides essentially the same guarantee: by iterating enough times, we can bring CIESTA arbitrarily close to a "best achievable result." The difference is that the nearest "best result" may change from iteration to iteration. This doesn't matter since all are good and we may choose any one as CIESTA's final output. Under the conditions of Prop. 6, we do have strict convergence.

One can minimize $\hat{E}_{reg}$ using a traditional quadratically convergent technique such as Gauss–Newton instead of CIESTA.

4.1 CIESTA Experiments

Table 2 shows results obtained using a standard quadratically convergent nonlinear minimization routine (from MATLAB) to minimize $\hat{E}_{reg}$ for the real image sequences of Figure 1. The algorithm always converged to a nontrivial minimum with $\lambda_n^i \approx 1$, though we used a value for μ that permitted some of the λ_n^i to go to zero. The value of μ was twice that needed to avoid $\lambda = 0$.

The iterative extensions of ST, including SIESTA, CIESTA, and the balanced iterations, all give similar results in practice, and iterating them to convergence (or apparent convergence) gives better results than a single iteration does. To illustrate this, we compared their results against ground truth on one synthetic and two real sequences, see Table 3. (We generated the synthetic OxCorr sequence in Table 3 using the Oxford Corridor ground truth structure and random translations and rotations. For OxDino, we extracted 50 points tracked over 6 images from the Oxford Dinosaur sequence and computed the ground truth by bundle adjustment.)

In all three cases: SIESTA gave the best agreement with the ground truth; the result at "convergence" improved on that obtained after a single iteration; the results of the "balanced" iteration did not depend on the number of rounds

Table 2. Results of using MATLAB's LSQNONLIN to minimize the CIESTA error $\hat{E}_{reg}$. Results show the values at convergence. The f values do not equal 1 exactly.

Sequence	μ/Bound	λ range	f	C_0	C_2	C_3
Rock	2	0.90–1.08	1	1.9786	1.9785	1.9785
PUMA	2	0.98–1.01	1	1.9954	1.9954	1.9954
Ox0&1	2	0.98–1.02	1	1.9993	1.9993	1.9993
Ox0&8	2	0.71–1.09	1	1.9358	1.9355	1.9357
Ox0&10	2	0.82–1.13	1	1.9770	1.9770	1.9770
Ox0-10	2	0.79–1.13	1	1.9844	1.9844	1.9844
MSTea	2	0.98–1.02	1	1.9993	1.9993	1.9993
MSPlane	2	0.90–1.09	1	1.9958	1.9958	1.9958

Table 3. Fractional errors $\sum_n |P_n^{\text{calc}} - P_n^{\text{GT}}|^2 / \sum_n |P_n^{\text{GT}}|^2$ ($\times 10^4$) for the structure after "convergence." We compute $P_n^{\text{calc}} \in \Re^3$ from the calculated homogeneous structure by applying a projective transform to minimize the error. SIESTA1 gives results after one iteration; other results are after 1000 iterations or convergence (CIESTA). Ball and 10 results are obtained using a single round or 10 rounds of column/row balancing in each iteration.

Sequence	SIESTA1	SIESTA	Ball	Ball10	CIESTA
OxCorr	4.8	2.8	3.0	3.0	2.9
PUMA	0.97	0.47	0.47	0.47	0.48
OxDino	1.48	0.39	0.49	0.49	0.54

of balancing; and CIESTA (using μ computed as in Table 2) performed as well as the balanced iterations.

5 Conclusion

We showed that SIESTA, the simplest iterative extension of ST, descends an error function: Each iteration "improves" the estimates. However, we proved that the SIESTA doesn't converges to useful results. We showed that another proposed extension of **ST** [7] shares this problem.[2] [4] advocate "balancing" to improve convergence. Our experiments show that balancing need not yield a convergent algorithm.

We proposed CIESTA, a new iterative extension of ST, which avoids these problems. CIESTA replaces balancing by regularization. The algorithm is identical to SIESTA except for one additional and still simple stage of computation. We proved that CIESTA descends an error function and approaches nontrivial fixed points, and that it converges under weak assumptions.

CIESTA, like other iterative extensions of **ST**, has the advantage of minimizing in the λ_n^i, whose values are often known to be near one a priori. Thus, it often shows fast initial convergence toward estimates that are approximately correct. Like other iterative extensions, CIESTA has the disadvantage that it converges linearly. A quadratically convergent method such as Gauss–Newton will be faster near a fixed point or in narrow valleys of the error function. Using such a method instead of CIESTA can combine quadratic convergence with the advantage of minimizing in the λ_n^i. A hybrid strategy that uses CIESTA initially and then switches to a second–order method, or full bundle adjustment, can combine the speed advantages of both [2].

Unlike bundle adjustment, CIESTA needs regularization. This allows the user to incorporate a realistic preference for projective depth values near 1 but can bias the final estimate. However, our experiments indicate that just a small amount of regularization suffices to stabilize the error minima. CIESTA's regularization and SIESTA's trivial convergence generally do not have a big effect on the estimates obtained once the algorithms slow their progress.

References

1. R. Berthilsson, A. Heyden, G. Sparr, "Recursive Structure and Motion from Image Sequences Using Shape and Depth Spaces," *CVPR* 444–449, 1997.
2. A. Buchanan and A. Fitzgibbon, "Damped Newton Algorithms for Matrix Factorization with Missing Data," *CVPR* 2005.
3. R. Dutta, R. Manmatha, L.R. Williams, and E.M. Riseman, "A data set for quantitative motion analysis," *CVPR*, 159-164, 1989.
4. R. Hartley and A. Zisserman, *Multiple View Geometry in Computer Vision*, Cambridge, 2000.
5. A. Heyden, R. Berthilsson, G. Sparr, "An iterative factorization method for projective structure and motion from image sequences," **IVC** 17 981–991,1999.
6. R. Kumar and A.R. Hanson, "Sensitivity of the Pose Refinement Problem to Accurate Estimation of Camera Parameters," *ICCV*, 365-369, 1990.
7. S. Mahamud, M. Hebert, Y. Omori, J. Ponce, "Provably-Convergent Iterative Methods for Projective Structure from Motion," *CVPR* I:1018-1025, 2001.
8. S. Mahamud, M. Hebert, "Iterative Projective Reconstruction from Multiple Views," *CVPR* II 430-437, 2000.
9. P. Sturm and B. Triggs, "A factorization based algorithm for multi–image projective structure and motion," *ECCV* II 709–720, 1996.
10. C. Tomasi and T. Kanade, "Shape and motion from image streams under orthography: A factorization method," **IJCV** 9, 137-154, 1992.
11. B. Triggs, "Factorization methods for projective structure and motion," *CVPR* 845–851, 1996.
12. Zhengyou Zhang, "A Flexible New Technique for Camera Calibration," **PAMI** 22:11, 1330-1334, 2000 and Microsoft Technical Report MSR-TR-98-71, 1998.

An Efficient Method for Tensor Voting Using Steerable Filters

Erik Franken[1], Markus van Almsick[1], Peter Rongen[2],
Luc Florack[1,*], and Bart ter Haar Romeny[1]

[1] Department of Biomedical Engineering, Technische Universiteit Eindhoven,
P.O. Box 513, 5600 MB Eindhoven, The Netherlands
{E.M.Franken, M.v.Almsick, L.M.J.Florack,
B.M.terHaarRomeny}@tue.nl
[2] Philips Medical Systems, Best, The Netherlands
peter.rongen@philips.com

Abstract. In many image analysis applications there is a need to extract curves in noisy images. To achieve a more robust extraction, one can exploit correlations of oriented features over a spatial context in the image. Tensor voting is an existing technique to extract features in this way. In this paper, we present a new computational scheme for tensor voting on a dense field of rank-2 tensors. Using steerable filter theory, it is possible to rewrite the tensor voting operation as a linear combination of complex-valued convolutions. This approach has computational advantages since convolutions can be implemented efficiently. We provide speed measurements to indicate the gain in speed, and illustrate the use of steerable tensor voting on medical applications.

1 Introduction

Tensor voting (TV) was originally proposed by Guy and Medioni [1], and later presented in a book by Medioni et al. [2]. It is a technique for robust grouping and extraction of lines and curves from images. In noisy images, local feature measurements, i.e. measurements of local edges or ridges, are often unreliable, e.g. the curves are noisy and interrupted. TV aims at making these local feature measurements more robust by making them consistent with the measurements in the neighborhood. To achieve this, local image features strengthen each other if they are consistent according to a model for smooth curves.

TV is a an interesting and powerful method because of its simplicity and its wide applicability. However, the method exhibits some ad hoc concepts, namely the way the input data are encoded into a sparse tensor field representation, and the voting field model that is used. In this paper we focus on another problem: the current implementation is rather cumbersome in mathematical terms. A better mathematical formulation will help to better understand the method, and we will show that it also leads to a more efficient implementation.

---

* The Netherlands Organisation for Scientific Research (NWO) is gratefully acknowledged for financial support.

A. Leonardis, H. Bischof, and A. Pinz (Eds.): ECCV 2006, Part IV, LNCS 3954, pp. 228–240, 2006.

This paper starts with a description of the "traditional" tensor voting method. We will redefine the operational definition of tensor voting in a neater way. Subsequently we will show that using steerable filter theory [3], we can create an implementation of tensor voting that consists of ordinary complex-valued convolutions. This is more efficient, since no algebraic calculations or interpolations are necessary anymore. We will evaluate the advantages of the new approach, show some examples, and finally we will draw conclusions.

2 Tensor Voting

2.1 Data Representation

In 2D tensor voting, local image features are encoded into a tensor field $\mathbf{H} : \Omega \to \mathbf{T}_2(\mathbb{R}^2)$, where $\Omega \subset \mathbb{R}^2$ is the image domain, and $\mathbf{T}_2(\mathbb{R}^2)$ denotes the set of symmetric, positive semidefinite tensors of tensor rank 2 (i.e., rank-2 tensors) on $\mathbb{R}^2$.

In the following, we shall denote the cartesian basis vectors in the image space by $\mathbf{e}_x$ and $\mathbf{e}_y$, respectively. Unless stated otherwise, all vectors and tensors will be expressed in this basis. In this basis, each tensor $\mathbf{A} \in \mathbf{T}_2(\mathbb{R}^2)$ can be written as a positive semidefinite symmetric 2×2 matrix. We call this the *matrix representation* of the tensor. We can decompose such matrix into its eigenvectors and eigenvalues

$$\mathbf{A} = \begin{pmatrix} a_{xx} & a_{xy} \\ a_{xy} & a_{yy} \end{pmatrix} = \lambda_1 \, \mathbf{e}_1 \, \mathbf{e}_1^{\mathrm{T}} + \lambda_2 \, \mathbf{e}_2 \, \mathbf{e}_2^{\mathrm{T}}, \tag{1}$$

where λ_1 and λ_2 are nonnegative eigenvalues ($\lambda_1 \geq \lambda_2 \geq 0$), and $\mathbf{e}_1$ and $\mathbf{e}_2$ are the orthonormal eigenvectors. A graphical illustration of such a tensor is an ellipse, see Figure 1a. In this representation, the following three properties become apparent

$$\text{Orientation} \quad \beta[\mathbf{A}] = \arccos(\mathbf{e}_1 \cdot \mathbf{e}_x) = \frac{1}{2} \arg(a_{xx} - a_{yy} + 2i\, a_{xy}), \tag{2}$$

$$\text{Stickness} \quad s[\mathbf{A}] = \lambda_1 - \lambda_2 = \sqrt{\mathrm{tr}(\mathbf{A})^2 - 4 \det \mathbf{A}}, \tag{3}$$

$$\text{Ballness} \quad b[\mathbf{A}] = \lambda_2 = \frac{1}{2}\left(\mathrm{tr}(\mathbf{A}) - \sqrt{\mathrm{tr}(\mathbf{A})^2 - 4 \det \mathbf{A}}\right). \tag{4}$$

Each tensor $\mathbf{A}$ is uniquely determined by these three scalars β (mod π, since the tensor has a 180° symmetry), $s \in \mathbb{R}^+ \cup \{0\}$, and $b \in \mathbb{R}^+ \cup \{0\}$. The stickness s is interpreted as a measure for the *orientation certainty* or a measure of anisotropy of the ellipse in orientation β. The ballness b is interpreted as a measure for the *orientation uncertainty* or isotropy.

There are two special cases for the positive semidefinite tensors: a *stick tensor* is a tensor with $b = 0$ and $s > 0$, and a *ball tensor* is an isotropic tensor, i.e. $s = 0$.

There are many ways to generate an input tensor field $\mathbf{H}$ from an input image. Medioni et al. assume that the input tensor field $\mathbf{H}$ is sparse, i.e. that most of the tensors in $\mathbf{H}$ are zero and therefore do not play any role. The way to generate a sparse tensor field (or in other words, a sparse set of tokens) out of an image is currently application-specific, but it is considered important to come to a more generic approach for generating tokens [4]. In this work, we assume that the obtained input field $\mathbf{H}$ is dense, to make

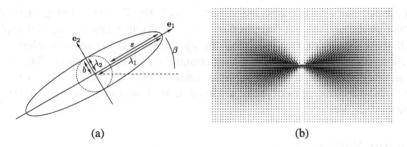

Fig. 1. (a) Graphical representation of a rank-2 symmetric positive semidefinite tensor. (b) Example of a stick voting field. Gray scale indicates stickness value (darker mean higher value) and line segments indicate orientation.

the algorithms we develop generically applicable for both sparse and dense data, which is desirable as long as we do not have a well-justified method to sparsify our data.

As an example, a dense input tensor field could be obtained by creating feature images $\beta(\mathbf{x})$ and $s(\mathbf{x})$ by applying any type of orientation-selective filter with a 180° symmetry on the image data and taking the orientation with maximum filter response. The ballness $b(\mathbf{x})$ could be obtained by any isotropic filter on the image data. A tensor is uniquely determined by these three features, so we can now construct a tensor field $\mathbf{H}(\mathbf{x})$.

2.2 Voting Fields

TV uses a *stick tensor voting field* to incorporate the continuation of line structures. This voting field is a tensor field $\mathbf{V} : \Omega \to \mathbf{T}_2(\mathbb{R}^2)$, consisting entirely of stick tensors, in which the stickness of the tensors describes the likelihood that a feature at position $\mathbf{x}$ belongs to the *same* line structure as the feature positioned in the center $(0,0)$ of the voting field with reference orientation 0°. The orientation of the tensor at $\mathbf{x}$ describes the most probable orientation of a feature at that position. Rotated versions of $\mathbf{V}$ will be denoted by $\mathbf{V}^\alpha$, where α denotes the rotation angle

$$\mathbf{V}^\alpha(\mathbf{x}) = \mathbf{R}_\alpha \mathbf{V}(\mathbf{R}_\alpha^{-1}\mathbf{x})\mathbf{R}_\alpha^{-1}, \tag{5}$$

where

$$\mathbf{R}_\alpha = \begin{pmatrix} \cos\alpha & -\sin\alpha \\ \sin\alpha & \cos\alpha \end{pmatrix}. \tag{6}$$

Medioni et al. [2] claim in their work that TV is model-free and that there is only one involved parameter, viz. scale. We, however, consider the voting field as the *model* used in tensor voting. Medioni's fundamental stick voting field is a model based on some assumptions on curves in images, but it is definitely not the only possible choice. One alternative voting field is discussed in Section 4. Figure 1b shows an example of a typical stick voting field.

2.3 Tensor Voting Operation

The idea of the TV operation is to let tensors *communicate* with each other by adding up contributions of neighboring tensors, resulting in a context-enhanced tensor field $\mathbf{U}$.

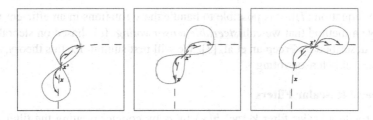

Fig. 2. Illustration of context communication within TV: the tensors communicate with each other using the stick voting field, which is indicated by the "8-shaped" contour. In this way the tensors strengthen each other.

Figure 2 illustrates the way the voting field is used on input data consisting of stick tensors. For each (nonzero) tensor $\mathbf{H}(\mathbf{x}')$, the voting field $\mathbf{V}^\alpha$ is centered at position $\mathbf{x}'$, aligned with the local orientation $\beta(\mathbf{H}(\mathbf{x}'))$: $\mathbf{V}^{\beta(\mathbf{H}(\mathbf{x}'))}(\mathbf{x}-\mathbf{x}')$. Then, to all tensors in a certain neighborhood (determined by the scale of the voting field), a weighted contribution (called a *vote*) $s(\mathbf{H}(\mathbf{x}'))\mathbf{V}^{\beta(\mathbf{H}(\mathbf{x}'))}(\mathbf{x}-\mathbf{x}')$ is added, where $\mathbf{x}$ is the position of the tensor that receives the vote. In other words, each tensor *broadcasts* contributions to the neighbors by appropriate alignment and rotation of the voting field. This results in the following operational definition for TV

$$\mathbf{U}(\mathbf{x}) = \int_\Omega s(\mathbf{H}(\mathbf{x}'))\,\mathbf{V}^{\beta(\mathbf{H}(\mathbf{x}'))}(\mathbf{x}-\mathbf{x}')\,d^2\mathbf{x}', \qquad (7)$$

where the output is a tensor field $\mathbf{U}(\mathbf{x})$ with context-enhanced measures for orientation, stickness, and ballness. Note that in practice, the integral symbol in the previous equation amounts to a summation on a discrete grid.

Note that ballness b is not used in (7). The original TV formulation also incorporates *ball voting* [2], used to generate orientation estimates for β. Since we obtain estimates for β using local orientation-selective filters, we will not consider ball voting, hence the ballness b of all tensors in input tensor field $\mathbf{H}$ will be assumed to be zero.

2.4 Related Work

When using a dense input tensor field, the representation shows similarity with the well known *structure tensor*, and especially with the hour-glass smoothing filter extension described in [5], which shows resemblance with the tensor voting field. The difference is that the structure tensor is always constructed from the gradient of the image, while in tensor voting the input tensor field is considered a free choice. Also, the smoothing kernel used to smooth the structure tensor field is scalar-valued, while our voting field is tensorial. Tensor voting also shows resemblance with non-linear structure tensors [6], where anisotropic non-linear diffusion is applied on tensor images.

3 Steerable Tensor Voting

A technical difficulty in tensor voting is the alignment of the voting field with the orientation of a tensor, which needs to be done at every position. Since TV is a linear operation (equation (7)), it is possible to handle these rotations in an efficient way. We will derive a method that we call *steerable tensor voting*. It is based on steerable filter theory as described by Freeman et al. [3]. We will first summarize this theory, and then explain steerable tensor voting.

3.1 Steerable Scalar Filters

One can rotate a scalar filter kernel $h(\mathbf{x})$ by α by counter rotating the filter domain: $h^\alpha(\mathbf{x}) = h(\mathbf{R}_\alpha^{-1}\mathbf{x})$. If we write the function in polar coordinates, denoted by $\tilde{h}(r, \phi)$, such that $\tilde{h}(r, \phi) = h(\mathbf{x})$ with $\mathbf{x} = (r\cos\phi, r\sin\phi)$, rotation becomes $\tilde{h}^\alpha(r, \phi) = \tilde{h}(r, \phi - \alpha)$.

Here we introduce the *spatial-angular Fourier decomposition* of a function $h : \mathbb{R}^2 \to \mathbb{C}$, which is given by

$$\tilde{h}_{m_s}(r) = \frac{1}{2\pi} \int_0^{2\pi} \tilde{h}(r, \phi)\, e^{-im_s\phi} d\phi, \tag{8}$$

and its inverse, the spatial composition, is

$$\tilde{h}(r, \phi) = \sum_{m_s \in \mathbb{Z}} \tilde{h}_{m_s}(r)\, e^{im_s\phi}. \tag{9}$$

A filter h is *steerable* if its spatial-angular Fourier composition (9) is a finite sum, i.e., there must be a finite number of nonzero Fourier coefficients $\tilde{h}_{m_s}(r)$. If a desired filter can be accurately approximated with a finite sum, we also call the filter steerable.

We write a steerable filter as $\tilde{h}(r, \phi) = \sum_{m_s=-M}^{M} f_{m_s}(r)e^{im_s\phi}$, where $M < \infty$ is the highest angular frequency of the filter kernel. Rotation of the steerable filter becomes

$$h^\alpha(\mathbf{x}) = \sum_{m_s=-M}^{M} \underbrace{e^{-im_s\alpha}}_{k_{m_s}(\alpha)} \underbrace{\tilde{h}_{m_s}(r)e^{im_s\phi}}_{h_{m_s}(\mathbf{x})}, \tag{10}$$

where $k_{m_s}(\alpha)$ are the linear coefficients as function of rotation angle α.

The filter response u^α of a filter h^α in orientation α is obtained by $u^\alpha(\mathbf{x}) = (f * h^\alpha)(\mathbf{x})$ where f is an image and "*" indicates convolution. If we substitute h^α by (10) in this equation and interchange sum and convolution, we get

$$u^\alpha(\mathbf{x}) = \sum_{m_s=-M}^{M} k_{m_s}(\alpha)\, (f * h_{m_s})(\mathbf{x}). \tag{11}$$

Hence, we can first convolve an image f with the $2M + 1$ component functions h_{m_s} and then calculate the filter response for any orientation α, by simply taking the linear combination with coefficients $k_{m_s}(\alpha)$. This leads to an efficient method for oriented filtering if M is sufficiently small.

3.2 Rotation of 2-Tensors

A rank-2 symmetric tensor $\mathbf{A}$ can be rotated over an angle α as follows.

$$\mathbf{A}^\alpha = \mathbf{R}_\alpha \mathbf{A}\, \mathbf{R}_\alpha^{-1} \quad \text{with } \mathbf{R}_\alpha = \begin{pmatrix} \cos\alpha & -\sin\alpha \\ \sin\alpha & \cos\alpha \end{pmatrix}. \tag{12}$$

It is more convenient to rewrite tensor $\mathbf{A}$ as a 3-tuple and to perform the tensor rotation with a single 3×3 matrix. That is, if we write $\overrightarrow{\mathbf{A}} = \begin{pmatrix} a_{xx} \\ a_{xy} \\ a_{yy} \end{pmatrix}$ then one can verify that

$$\overrightarrow{\mathbf{A}}^{\alpha} = \begin{pmatrix} \frac{1}{2}(1+\cos(2\,\alpha)) & -\sin(2\,\alpha) & \frac{1}{2}(1-\cos(2\,\alpha)) \\ \frac{1}{2}\sin(2\,\alpha) & \cos(2\,\alpha) & -\frac{1}{2}\sin(2\,\alpha) \\ \frac{1}{2}(1-\cos(2\,\alpha)) & \sin(2\,\alpha) & \frac{1}{2}(1+\cos(2\,\alpha)) \end{pmatrix} \overrightarrow{\mathbf{A}}. \tag{13}$$

It is a special property of the 2D rotation group that one can diagonalize the rotation matrix for all α by applying a similarity transformation $\mathbf{S}$

$$\overrightarrow{\mathbf{A}}^{\alpha} = \underbrace{\frac{1}{4}\begin{pmatrix} 2 & 1 & 1 \\ 0 & i & -i \\ 2 & -1 & -1 \end{pmatrix}}_{S^{-1}} \underbrace{\begin{pmatrix} 1 & 0 & 0 \\ 0 & e^{-2i\,\alpha} & 0 \\ 0 & 0 & e^{2i\,\alpha} \end{pmatrix}}_{R'_{\alpha}} \underbrace{\begin{pmatrix} 1 & 0 & 1 \\ 1 & -2i & -1 \\ 1 & 2i & -1 \end{pmatrix}}_{S} \overrightarrow{\mathbf{A}}. \tag{14}$$

So if we transform a tensor $\overrightarrow{\mathbf{A}}$ as

$$\overrightarrow{\mathbf{A}}' = \begin{pmatrix} A_0 \\ A_2 \\ A_{-2} \end{pmatrix} = \mathbf{S}\,\overrightarrow{\mathbf{A}} = \begin{pmatrix} 1 & 0 & 1 \\ 1 & -2i & -1 \\ 1 & 2i & -1 \end{pmatrix} \begin{pmatrix} a_{xx} \\ a_{xy} \\ a_{yy} \end{pmatrix}, \tag{15}$$

we obtain components A_0, A_2, and A_{-2}, which are the tensor components in rotation-invariant subspaces. These components are rotated by a simple complex phase factor: $A_{m_a}^{\alpha} = e^{-im_a\alpha}A_{m_a}$ ($m_a = 0, -2, 2$), which directly follows from (14). Henceforth we will call these components the m_a-components of the tensor, and the transformation of (15) is called the *orientation-angular Fourier decomposition* of the tensor.

Note that the properties β, s, b defined in equations (2) to (4) can be easily described in terms of A_0, A_{-2} and A_2 using (15)

$$\beta = \frac{1}{2}\arg A_{-2} \qquad s = \sqrt{A_{-2}A_2} = |A_2| = |A_{-2}| \qquad b = \frac{1}{2}(A_0 - |A_2|). \tag{16}$$

Note also that $A_2 = \overline{A_{-2}}$ where $\overline{A_{-2}}$ is the complex conjugate of A_{-2}.

3.3 Steerable Tensor Filters

The concept of steerable filters can also be applied to tensor fields and to the voting field in particular, which rotates according to $\mathbf{V}^{\alpha}(\mathbf{x}) = \mathbf{R}_{\alpha}\mathbf{V}(\mathbf{R}_{\alpha}^{-1}\mathbf{x})\mathbf{R}_{\alpha}^{-1}$. In the previous subsection we showed how to decompose tensors in orientation-angular Fourier components and how to rotate them. For the voting field we get $V_{m_a}^{\alpha}(\mathbf{x}) = e^{-im_a\alpha}V_{m_a}(\mathbf{R}_{\alpha}^{-1}\mathbf{x})$ for $m_a = -2, 0, 2$. These three V_{m_a} functions are of the form $\mathbb{R}^2 \to \mathbb{C}$ and can be made steerable in the same way as scalar filters. So, a voting field is steerable if for all m_a-components ($m_a = 0, -2, 2$) of the tensor field we can write $V_{m_a}(\mathbf{x}) = \sum_{m_s=-M}^{M} \tilde{V}_{m_a m_s}(r)e^{im_s\phi}$. Rotation becomes

$$V_{m_a}^{\alpha}(\mathbf{x}) = \sum_{m_s=-M}^{M} e^{-i(m_a+m_s)\alpha} \underbrace{\tilde{V}_{m_a m_s}(r)\,e^{im_s\phi}}_{V_{m_a m_s}(\mathbf{x})}, \tag{17}$$

where $V_{m_a m_s}(\mathbf{x})$ are the basis filters and $e^{-i(m_a+m_s)\alpha}$ are the linear coefficient functions of rotation angle α. Filling the previous equation into (7), and writing $\mathbf{U}$ in its m_a-components according to (15) results in

$$U_{m_a}(\mathbf{x}) = \int_\Omega s(\mathbf{H}(\mathbf{x}'))\, V_{m_a}^{\beta(\mathbf{H}(\mathbf{x}'))}(\mathbf{x} - \mathbf{x}')d\mathbf{x}'$$

$$= \int_\Omega s(\mathbf{H}(\mathbf{x}')) \left(\sum_{m_s=-M}^{M} e^{-i(m_a+m_s)\beta(\mathbf{H}(\mathbf{x}'))}\, V_{m_a m_s}(\mathbf{x} - \mathbf{x}') \right) d\mathbf{x}'$$

$$= \sum_{m_s=-M}^{M} \int_\Omega \left(s(\mathbf{H}(\mathbf{x}'))\, e^{-i(m_a+m_s)\beta(\mathbf{H}(\mathbf{x}'))} \right) V_{m_a m_s}(\mathbf{x} - \mathbf{x}')d\mathbf{x}'$$

$$= \sum_{m_s=-M}^{M} \left(\left(s(\mathbf{H})\, e^{-i(m_a+m_s)\beta(\mathbf{H})} \right) * V_{m_a m_s} \right)(\mathbf{x}). \tag{18}$$

This important result states that, as opposed to non-steerable TV, we can apply TV simply by calculating $2 \cdot (M+1)$ convolutions, viz. for each m_a component we need $M+1$ m_s-terms, since all odd m_s components are zero for 180°-symmetric voting fields. Furthermore, taking into account that $U_2(\mathbf{x}) = \overline{U_{-2}(\mathbf{x})}$ we see that we only have to calculate and $U_0(\mathbf{x})$ and $U_2(\mathbf{x})$. Notice also that the convolutions involve relatively large kernels, meaning that they can possibly be done more efficiently via the Fourier domain, i.e. $A * B = \mathcal{F}^{-1}[\mathcal{F}[A] \cdot \mathcal{F}[B]]$, where $\mathcal{F}$ denotes the spatial Fourier transform.

4 Voting Fields

The stick voting field can be freely chosen in tensor voting. In this section we will treat two different voting fields and state some qualitative differences between them.

4.1 Medioni's Voting Field

Medioni et al. [2] assume that the best connection between two points with one orientation imposed is a circular arc. If one point is horizontally oriented and the angle of the vector connecting the two points is ϕ, then the angle at the other point is 2ϕ. This *cocircularity model* is encoded in a tensor field consisting of stick tensors with $\lambda_1 = 1$ (and $\lambda_2 = 0$) as $\mathbf{c}\mathbf{c}^T$ with $\mathbf{c} = \begin{pmatrix} \cos 2\phi \\ \sin 2\phi \end{pmatrix}$ (cf. (1)).

To obtain a locally confined voting field the cocircularity pattern is modulated with a function that decays with radius curve length and curvature. This yields the following voting field

$$\tilde{\mathbf{V}}(r, \phi) = e^{-\left(\frac{\phi r}{\sigma_{\mathrm{ctx}} \sin \phi}\right)^2 - p\left(\frac{2\sigma_{\mathrm{ctx}} \sin \phi}{r}\right)^2} \begin{pmatrix} 1+\cos(4\phi) & \sin(4\phi) \\ \sin(4\phi) & 1-\cos(4\phi) \end{pmatrix} \tag{19}$$

where σ_{ctx} is the scale of the voting field, p is a dimensionless constant describing the relative weight of the curvature. In practice, points above an below the diagonals $\phi = \pm\pi/4 \mod \pi$ in the field are considered too unlikely to belong to the same structure as the point in the center of the field, so the field is truncated for these values of ϕ.

There are two drawbacks of this voting field concerning steerable tensor voting. First, there is no simple analytic expression for the components $V_{m_a m_s}(\mathbf{x})$, so one should calculate the steerable components of this kernel numerically. Second, the field has an infinite number of m_s-components, so we have to cut the sum over m_s such that we get a reasonable approximation. Therefore, in the next subsection we propose a different voting field, which is more suitable for steerable tensor voting.

4.2 Bandlimited Voting Field

Here we propose a bandlimited voting field, which is especially useful for steerable tensor voting, since it has a limited number of spatial-angular Fourier components. The decay function is similar to the one for instance used in [7].

Similar to Medioni's voting field, we assume that the best connection between two points with one orientation imposed is a circular arc. Now we modulate the cocircularity pattern with a function that decays with radius r. We choose a Gaussian decay as function of r. To penalize high-curvature arcs, we must also account for some periodic modulation that reaches its maximum at $\phi = 0 \mod \pi$ and minimum for $\phi = \pi/2 \mod \pi$. This is achieved with the term $\cos^{2n} \phi$, where $n \in \mathbb{N}$ is a parameter specifying the speed of decay of the field as function of ϕ. The voting field now becomes, expressed in spatial polar coordinates

$$\tilde{\mathbf{V}}(r, \phi) = \frac{1}{G} e^{\frac{-r^2}{2\sigma_{\text{ctx}}^2}} \cos^{2n}(\phi) \begin{pmatrix} 1+\cos(4\phi) & \sin(4\phi) \\ \sin(4\phi) & 1-\cos(4\phi) \end{pmatrix}, \tag{20}$$

where $\sigma_{\text{ctx}} \in \mathbb{R}^+$ is the scale of the voting field. The factor G is a normalization factor. This voting field is depicted in Figure 1b. In the following, to get simpler equations, we will use $G = 1/16$ and $n = 2$.

We apply orientation-angular (15) and spatial-angular (8) Fourier decomposition to this voting field. The spatial-angular Fourier decomposition is trivial if we first replace all trigonometric functions by exponentials and expand these exponentials.

$$\begin{pmatrix} \tilde{V}_0(r,\phi) \\ \tilde{V}_2(r,\phi) \\ \tilde{V}_{-2}(r,\phi) \end{pmatrix} = e^{-\frac{r^2}{2\sigma_{\text{ctx}}^2}} \begin{pmatrix} e^{-i4\phi}+4e^{-i2\phi}+6+4e^{i2\phi}+e^{i4\phi} \\ e^{-i8\phi}+4e^{-i6\phi}+6e^{-i4\phi}+4e^{-i2\phi}+1 \\ 1+4e^{i2\phi}+6e^{i4\phi}+4e^{i6\phi}+e^{i8\phi} \end{pmatrix} \tag{21}$$

For every m_a-component we have effectively 5 m_s-components. We can now write this filter in the steerable form cf. (17)

$$\begin{pmatrix} V_0^\alpha(\mathbf{x}) \\ V_2^\alpha(\mathbf{x}) \\ V_{-2}^\alpha(\mathbf{x}) \end{pmatrix} = \begin{pmatrix} 0 & 0 & e^{4i\alpha} & 4e^{2i\alpha} & 6 & 4e^{-2i\alpha} & e^{-4i\alpha} & 0 & 0 \\ e^{6i\alpha} & 4e^{4i\alpha} & 6e^{2i\alpha} & 4 & e^{-2i\alpha} & 0 & 0 & 0 & 0 \\ 0 & 0 & 0 & 0 & e^{2i\alpha} & 4 & 6e^{-2i\alpha} & 4e^{-4i\alpha} & e^{-6i\alpha} \end{pmatrix} \begin{pmatrix} w_{-8}(\mathbf{x}) \\ w_{-6}(\mathbf{x}) \\ \vdots \\ w_6(\mathbf{x}) \\ w_8(\mathbf{x}) \end{pmatrix} \tag{22}$$

where the matrix contains the linear coefficients as function of rotation, and the vector at the right side contains the basis filters. The basis filters are defined by $\tilde{w}_{m_s}(r, \phi) = e^{-\frac{r^2}{2\sigma_{\text{ctx}}^2}} e^{im_s\phi}$. In cartesian coordinates they are given by

$$w_{m_s}(\mathbf{x}) = e^{-\frac{x^2+y^2}{2\sigma_{\text{ctx}}^2}} \left(\frac{x+iy}{\sqrt{x^2+y^2}} \right)^{m_s}, \quad \text{for } \mathbf{x} \neq (0,0). \tag{23}$$

Using (18) we can implement steerable tensor voting for this voting field, as follows. The filter kernels $w_{m_s}(\mathbf{x})$ are tabulated for $m_s = 0, 2, 4, 6, 8$ (note that $w_{-m_s} = \overline{w_{m_s}}$). Given the stickness s and orientation β of tensors in $\mathbf{H}$, we need to calculate a number of complex-valued feature images $c_{m_s}(\mathbf{x}) = s(\mathbf{H}(\mathbf{x})) \, e^{-im_s\beta(\mathbf{H}(\mathbf{x}))}$ for $m_s = 0, 2, 4, 6$. Now, we can calculate the resulting $m_a = -2$ part by

$$U_{-2}(\mathbf{x}) = (w_0 * \overline{c_2}) + 4(w_2 * c_0) + 6(w_4 * c_2) + 4(w_6 * c_4) + (w_8 * c_6), \tag{24}$$

where $\overline{c_2}$ denotes complex conjugate and $\overline{c_2} = c_{-2}$. The $m_a = 2$ part does not need to be calculated explicitly, because it is simply the complex conjugate of the $m_a = -2$ part. The $m_a = 0$ part can be calculated by

$$U_0(\mathbf{x}) = (\overline{w_4} * \overline{c_4}) + 4(\overline{w_2} * \overline{c_2}) + 6(w_0 * c_0) + 4(w_2 * c_2) + (w_4 * c_4)$$
$$= \mathrm{Re}\big(6(w_0 * c_0) + 8(w_2 * c_2) + 2(w_4 * c_4)\big). \tag{25}$$

So TV with this voting field requires 8 convolutions. In the resulting context-enhanced tensor field $\mathbf{U}$, we are interested in the orientation, stickness, and ballness. These measures are calculated using (16).

5   Computational Efficiency

In this section we compare three different versions of tensor voting:

- *Normal TV*: "Normal" tensor voting where the stick voting field is calculated algebraically at every position;
- *Steerable TV spatial*: Steerable tensor voting using spatial convolutions;
- *Steerable TV FFT*: Steerable tensor voting using FFT.

5.1   Computational Complexity

A typical TV implementation scans through the entire image, and collects or broadcasts information from or to the neighborhood of every tensor. If our image is square with a size of $s \times s$ pixels and the voting field kernel has a size $k \times k$, then $s^2 k^2$ tensor additions need to take place. The order of this algorithm is thus $\mathcal{O}(s^2 k^2)$. Steerable tensor voting consists of a sum of complex-valued 2D convolutions. If they are implemented in the spatial domain, the order is $\mathcal{O}(s^2 k^2)$ as well. However, if the convolutions are implemented through the Fourier domain using a 2D FFT implementation, the order is reduced to $\mathcal{O}(s^2 \log s)$.

5.2   Speed Comparison

To give an impression of the differences in speed we did some speed measurements. All algorithms were implemented in C++, and compiled using Microsoft Visual C++. To make the comparison fair, all 3 variants use the bandlimited voting field of Subsection 4.2, implying that they all give the same results. We use the FFTW library for the FFT (see http://www.fftw.org/). All numbers are stored using data type "double". For normal TV and steerable TV spatial the kernel has a pixel size of $\frac{1}{4}$ times the size of the image, i.e. the scale of the kernel scales proportionally to the image size. The steerable TV implementation uses a voting field with 9 steerable components. We use random dense stickness and orientation maps as input, since the speed of the algorithms is not dependent on the contents of the input data if the input data is dense.

Figure 3 shows computation times as function of image size, measured on an AMD Athlon 64 X2 4400+ running on Windows XP at 2.3 GHz. It is clear that steerable TV FFT performs fastest, followed by steerable TV spatial. The normal TV version is much slower. As example to show the large differences, on a 512×512 image, steerable TV

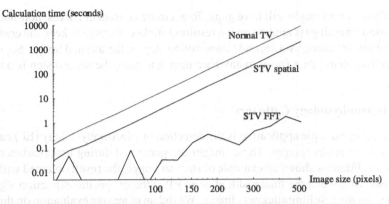

Fig. 3. Speed measurements of three different TV algorithms as function of image size. STV = Steerable tensor voting. See Subsection 5.2 for details.

FFT takes 1.05 seconds, while steerable TV spatial takes 1980 seconds, and normal TV takes 8803 seconds. Since the graph is a log-log plot, the slope of the curves indicates the computational complexity of the algorithm. As expected, steerable TV with FFT has a smaller slope. The latter curve shows an irregular trajectory, due to some technicalities of the FFT algorithm. The FFT implementation is more efficient if the data size is a power of 2 a product of small prime factors. The normal TV implementation is slower because of the analytic calculations that are required for every vote[1].

Convolutions and FFT's only involve multiplications, additions, and memory accesses in a very regular fashion. These operations are therefore very suitable for efficient implementations exploiting cache memory and parallelism. A graphical processing unit (GPU) might be suitable to host an extremely fast implementation of steerable tensor voting [8].

As final remark, note that if the tensor field is very sparse, steerable TV may perform worse since it does not benefit from the possibility to skip zero-valued tensors during the voting process.

6   Examples of 2D Steerable Tensor Voting

Steerable tensor voting is a new computational method for tensor voting, which yields the same result as normal tensor voting if exactly the same voting field is used. Therefore, in this section we do not perform comparison of results of the two methods, but only show two applications that require computationally efficient algorithms.

In the examples, our approach for the curve extraction process is as follows. The input stickness s and the orientation β are constructed using first order (for edges) or second order (for ridges) Gaussian derivatives. To enhance these data, a steerable tensor voting step is performed according to (18). Spurious responses caused by noise in the image cause that the resulting stickness image is not sufficiently enhanced: for instance,

---

[1] Alternatively, one could also precalculate the voting field in one or a limited number of orientations and then interpolate. However, this will lead to discretization errors and irregular memory accesses, and therefore possible caching problems on typical computer systems.

the resulting curves might still have gaps. To get more consistent curves, non-maximum suppression (thinning) is applied on the resulting stickness image to keep the centerlines of the curves, followed by a second tensor voting step on the thinned image. So, the first TV step is on dense data (prior to any hard decision step), the second step is on sparse data.

6.1 Electrophysiology Catheters

An interesting example application is the detection of Electrophysiology (EP) catheters in X-ray fluoroscopy images. These images are generated during heart catheterization procedures. Figure 4 shows an example of such an image, the result obtained with steerable tensor voting and the final result after an EP-catheter specific extraction algorithm is applied on the resulting stickness image. We did an extensive evaluation on this medical application, and clearly our extraction performance increased using tensor voting compared to not using tensor voting. More details can be found in [9].

6.2 Ultrasound Kidney

Figure 5 shows the results on the ultrasound image of a kidney. The line segment extraction in subimages (c) en (f) is achieved by applying thinning, and extraction of strings of

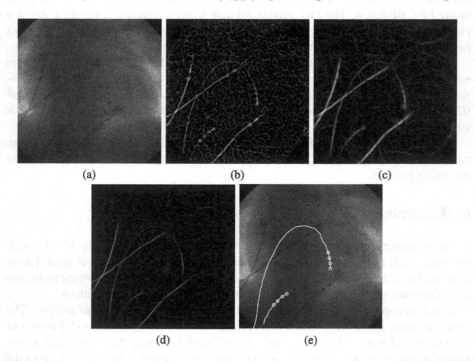

(a)   (b)   (c)

(d)   (e)

Fig. 4. Electrophysiology catheter extraction example. (b) Original noisy image, used as input for this example. Size 512×512 pixels. (b) Local ridgeness image (i.e. the largest eigenvalue of Hessian constructed using 2nd order Gaussian derivatives with scale $\sigma = 3.4$ pixels). (c) Result of first tensor voting step with $\sigma_{ctx} = 15$. (d) Result of a second tensor voting step with $\sigma_{ctx} = 7.5$. (e) Final extraction result using EP-catheter specific extraction algorithm.

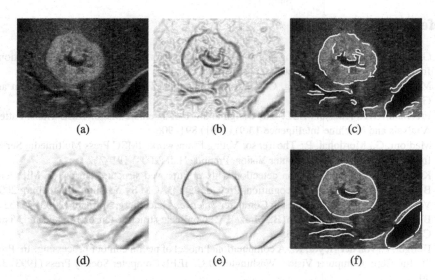

Fig. 5. Example of tensor voting on an ultrasound image of a kidney. (a) Original image, size 345×260 pixels. (b) Gradient magnitude with $\sigma = 3$ pixels. (c) Extracted line segments using (b). (d) Result after first tensor voting step with $\sigma_{ctx} = 15$. (e) Result after second tensor voting step with same settings. (f) Extracted line segments using image (e). In both (c) and (f), 1250 pixels were extracted for the sake of comparison.

connected pixels starting from the pixel with highest value that is not yet extracted, until a predefined number of pixels is extracted. The contours are more enhanced after tensor voting, which can be seen if we compare the extracted contours with and without the use of tensor voting. Clearly, tensor voting helps to extract longer and smoother contours.

7   Conclusion

The main conclusion of this paper is that tensor voting can be made steerable. We are able to write tensor voting as a summation of a number of complex-valued convolutions. We showed that two-dimensional steerable tensor voting is computationally more efficient on dense tensor fields. The highest speed gain is achieved if we implement steerable tensor voting using FFT. A GPU implementation might lead to an even faster implementation.

Another point we made is that the voting field of Medioni is not the only possible voting field. We proposed the bandlimited voting field as alternative. The voting field could also be made more application-specific by gathering statistics on curves in a specific application. Or it can be made as generic as possible by only using the random walker prior, leading to the stochastic completion field [10, 11].

Our examples show that the method is especially feasible for applications where thin noisy line-structures must be detected. These kind of problems often arise in the field of medical image analysis.

Tensor voting and related methods are promising methods for robust extraction of line-like structures in images. There are still a lot of challenges to be faced, such as 3D steerable tensor voting and multi-scale tensor voting.

References

1. Guy, G., Medioni, G.: Inferring global perceptual contours from local features. International Journal of Computer Vision **20**(1–2) (1996) 113–33
2. Medioni, G., Lee, M.S., Tang, C.K.: A Computational Framework for Segmentation and Grouping. Elsevier (2000)
3. Freeman, W.T., Adelson, E.H.: The design and use of steerable filters. IEEE Trans. Pattern Analysis and Machine Intelligence **13**(9) (1991) 891–906
4. Medioni, G., Mordohai, P.: The Tensor Voting Framework. IMSC Press Multimedia Series. In: Emerging Topics in Computer Vision. Prentice Hall (2004) 191–252
5. Köthe, U.: Edge and junction detection with an improved structure tensor. In Michaelis, B., Krell, G., eds.: Pattern Recognition, Proc. of 25th DAGM Symposium, Magdeburg 2003. Volume 2781 of Lecture Notes in Computer Science., Heidelberg, Springer (2003) 25–32
6. Brox, T., Weickert, J., Burgeth, B., Mrázek, P.: Nonlinear structure tensors. Image and Vision Computing **24**(1) (2006) 41–55
7. Heitger, F., von der Heydt, R.: A computational model of neural contour processing. In: Proc. 4th Int. Conf. Computer Vision, Washington D.C.: IEEE Computer Society Press (1993) 32–40
8. Moreland, K., Angel, E.: The FFT on a GPU. In: SIGGRAPH/Eurographics Workshop on Graphics Hardware. (2003) 112–119
9. Franken, E., van Almsick, M., Rongen, P., ter Haar Romeny, B.: Context-enhanced detection of electrophysiology catheters in X-ray fluoroscopy images. Conference Poster, European Conference of Radiology (ECR) (2005) http://www.ecr.org/.
10. Williams, L.R., Jacobs, D.W.: Stochastic completion fields: a neural model of illusory contour shape and salience. Neural Comput. **9**(4) (1997) 837–858
11. Almsick, M.A., Duits, R., Franken, E., ter Haar Romeny, B.: From stochastic completion fields to tensor voting. In Fogh Olsen, O., Florack, L., Kuijper, A., eds.: Deep Structure Singularities and Computer Vision. Volume 3753 of Lecture Notes in Computer Science., Springer-Verlag (2005) 124–134

Interpolating Orientation Fields: An Axiomatic Approach

Anatole Chessel[1], Frederic Cao[2], and Ronan Fablet[1]

[1] IFREMER/LASAA, BP 70, Technopole Brest-Iroise, 28280, Plouzane, France
{achessel, rfablet}@ifremer.fr
[2] IRISA/VISTA, Campus de Beaulieu, 35041, Rennes, France
fcao@irisa.fr

Abstract. We develop an axiomatic approach of vector field interpolation, which is useful as a feature extraction preprocessing step. Two operators will be singled out: the curvature operator, appearing in the total variation minimisation for image restoration and inpainting/disocclusion, and the Absolutely Minimizing Lipschitz Extension (AMLE), already known as a robust and coherent scalar image interpolation technique if we relax slightly the axioms. Numerical results, using a multiresolution scheme, show that they produce fields in accordance with the human perception of edges.

1 Introduction

Given a set of edgels (*i.e.* a set of points with an assigned direction), what are the most invariant and stable ways to reconstruct an orientation field in the whole plan? Because orientation live on the unit circle, an everywhere smooth interpolation is not always possible, due to global topological arguments. However, if we now use local arguments, a analysis similar to [1, 2] is possible and leads also to similar necessary conditions, showing that only very few differential operators have good properties. Since the functions that will be considered in this paper are vector valued or have values in the unit circle, only little is known about existence, uniqueness or classification of the singularities of the solutions to equations we single out. This contribution is an insight of what could be those results and their interest from a low-level vision point of view.

Detecting what we intuitively call "edges" is a first step towards low level feature extraction and integration and has been the focus of a lot of work since the beginning of computer vision. But as noted by psycho-visual experiment and models [3], that concept has appeared to be more difficult to define than simply "contrasted image part". Psychovision experiments by the Gestaltists [3, 4] has given us an acute and unified framework to analyse those effects, and many grouping laws are often involved in the recognition of what we call an edge. The so-called subjective contour effect in particular let us see edges which are strictly speaking not even actually present. It uses amodal completion (reconstruction of occluded edges due to the 2D projection of a 3D world) and modal completion (leading to *illusory contour*, where the object and the background have the same color). In both cases it rely on a curve interpolation process of unknown data according to the input.

A. Leonardis, H. Bischof, and A. Pinz (Eds.): ECCV 2006, Part IV, LNCS 3954, pp. 241–254, 2006.

The main origin for those subjective contours is the good continuation principle, which states that if two edgels (edge elements, i.e. a collection of points together with the orientation of the curve which should pass through it) are not too far apart and have compatible directions, we tend to see the curve to which they are both tangent as an edge. Many studies have aimed at computationally implementing this phenomenon. To this end, it is generally assumed that a filter has given us an image of edgels from which we want to extract the curves. Two classical approaches are the curve detector of Parent and Zucker [5], which uses a discrete co-circularity measure to extract potentially interesting point, and Sha'ashua and Ullman saliency network [6], where dynamic programming is used to exhaustively search for the "best" curves under curvature minimisation and length maximisation constraints. More recently, interesting approaches are Medioni's tensor voting [7, 8], where curves emerge from votes of sparse edgels, and Zweck and al. stochastic completion fields [9], an Euclidean group invariant implementation of the advection-diffusion model of Mumford [10].

Related problems include image inpainting and restoration, and the operators described here are also applied in those cases. In particular, recent developpement extended them to the case of non-scalar image (vector or tensor valued images) [11, 12, 13]. The aim however is not exactly the same, as this work does not seek to recover the image itself, but an orientation field that would capture its geometrical features.

The good continuation principle states conditions on tangent vectors, and most of the approaches mentioned earlier rely, explicitly or not, on vector or orientation fields. The present work aims at finding out the most invariant interpolation methods based on partial differential equations (PDE). Experiments will be shown using artificial and natural images.

Section 2 states some generalities about interpolating angle, and in particular that singularities are often unavoidable. Section 3 is devoted to the actual axiomatic approach. The last two sections present in more details the two singled out operators, along with experiments. All the proofs are omitted and are given in [14].

2   Interpolating Angles

Let $\Omega \subset \mathbb{R}^2$ and $\partial\Omega$ its boundary. Let S^1 be the unit circle of $\mathbb{R}^2$. We consider the *extension problem*: knowing $I = (I_1, I_2) : \partial\Omega \to S^1 \subset \mathbb{R}^2$, how to extend I to the whole domain Ω? The circle represents angular data modulo 2π. In addition, we may also consider the directions of unoriented lines (*i.e.* angles modulo π). All the argumentation below will also apply to this case.

2.1   Topological Restriction

The first problem we encounter when extending vectors as opposed to scalars, is that singularities in the field may be unavoidable. Given a data to be interpolated when can we hope for a singularity free extension? A necessary and sufficient condition is the following.

Proposition 1. *Let f be a continuous vector field over $\partial\Omega$. There exists a continuous extension of f to Ω if and only if f satisfies condition C.*

$$\exists\alpha \in S^1, \ \alpha \notin f(\partial\Omega), \tag{C}$$

that is to say only if f is not surjective.

These topological results mean that a singularity free extension is impossible for orientation field when the bounding data cover the whole unit circle. This classical result is equivalent to the Brouwer fixed point theorem [15].

2.2 A Fundamental Ambiguity

Another problem arising in orientation interpolation (compared to scalar interpolation) is that, due to the periodicity of the data (hence the absence of a total ordering) there are always two manners to interpolate between two fixed values. For instance, on Fig. 1, one goes through zero, while the other goes through $\frac{\pi}{2}$.

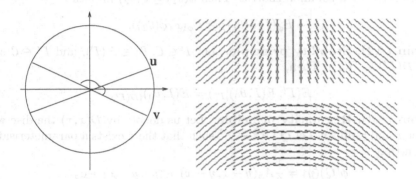

Fig. 1. Ambiguity of interpolation between two directions (modulo π in the present figure). Left: there are two ways of going from u to v. Right: example when $u - v = \pi/2$.

For a singularity free (non-surjective) field, at least one value is excluded hence only one of the two possibilities is available. The operators we study are numerically solved by iterative methods, hence, in absence of uniqueness result on the solution of the stationary problem, the final result may depend on the initialisation. Moreover, the topological condition (C) might not be fulfilled in practice for the whole domain but only in sub-domains. This could lead to instabilities that do not exist in the scalar case. A possible workaround is a multiresolution scheme, which will be detailed in a forthcoming work [14].

3 Axiomatic Approach

This section details the axiomatic approach exploited to defined operators for the interpolation of orientation field.

Let Γ be a continuous Jordan curve bounding a simply connected domain Ω. We look for an extension operator E, which associates with each directional data $\theta_0 : \Gamma \to S^1$ a unique extension $E(\Gamma, \theta_0)$. Throughout all the discussion to follow, it is assumed that θ_0 satisfies the global condition (C). The set of all those functions will be denoted by $\mathcal{F}(\Gamma)$. It is necessary to parameterise S^1, to be able to deal with numerical functions. A slight difficulty will arise, since it is not possible to describe the whole circle by a unique chart. Let ϕ be such a local parameterisation, that is to say, a bijective function $U \to V$, where U is an open subset strictly included in S^1 and V an open subset of $\mathbb{R}$. Let us now consider the extension operator E_ϕ interpolating real valued boundary data u, defined by $E_\phi(\Gamma, u) = \phi \circ E(\Gamma, \phi^{-1} \circ u)$. Since $E_\phi(\Gamma, u)$ is a numerical function, it is easier to formulate conditions on the operator E_ϕ. However, since the parameterization ϕ is arbitrary, the result should be independent on the parametrisation and condition on E_ϕ should stand for any ϕ.

Following [2], we ask that E_ϕ satisfies the following axioms:

Axiom (A1): Comparison principle. Let $\theta_1, \theta_2 \in \mathcal{F}(\Gamma)$ such that they can be described by a common chart ϕ. Then $\phi(\theta_1) \geq \phi(\theta_2)$ implies

$$E_\phi(\Gamma, \phi(\theta_1)) \geq E_\phi(\Gamma, \phi(\theta_2)). \tag{1}$$

Axiom (A2): Stability principle. Let $\Gamma \in \mathcal{C}$, $\theta_0 \in \mathcal{F}(\Gamma)$, and $\Gamma' \in \mathcal{C}$ such that $D(\Gamma') \subseteq D(\Gamma)$. Then,

$$E(\Gamma', E(\Gamma, \theta_0)|_{\Gamma'}) = E(\Gamma, \theta_0)|_{D(\Gamma')} \tag{2}$$

Axiom (A3): Regularity principle. Let us denote by $D(x, r)$ the disc with center x and radius r. Let $Q : \mathbb{R}^2 \to S^1$ such that there exists a parameterisation ϕ such that

$$\phi(Q)(y) = \frac{1}{2} A_\phi(y - x, y - x) + (p_\phi, y - x) + c_\phi$$

where $A_\phi \in SM(2)$ the set of two dimensional symmetric matrices, $p_\phi \in \mathbb{R}^2 \backslash \{0\}$, $x \in \mathbb{R}^2$ and $c_\phi \in \mathbb{R}$. Then there exists a continuous function $F : SM(2) \times \mathbb{R}^2 \backslash \{0\} \times \mathbb{R} \times \mathbb{R}^2$, independent of ϕ such that

$$\lim_{r \to 0^+} \frac{\phi(E(\partial D(x, r), Q|_{\partial D(x,r)}))(x) - \phi(Q)(x)}{r^2/2} \to F(A_\phi, p_\phi, c_\phi, x). \tag{3}$$

Axiom (A4): Translation invariance. Let $\tau_h \theta_0(x) = \theta_0(x - h)$, $\theta_0 : \mathbb{R}^2 \to S^1$, $h \in \mathbb{R}^2$. Then for all h,

$$E(\Gamma - h, \tau_h \theta_0) = \tau_h E(\Gamma, \theta_0). \tag{4}$$

Axiom (A5): Domain rotation invariance. For any plane rotation R,

$$E(R\Gamma, \theta_0 \circ R^{-1}) = E(\Gamma, \theta_0) \circ R^{-1}. \tag{5}$$

Axiom (A6): Zoom invariance. Let $H_\lambda \theta_0(x) = \theta_0(\lambda x)$, for $\lambda > 0$. Then,

$$E(\lambda^{-1} \Gamma, H_\lambda \theta_0) = H_\lambda E(\Gamma, \theta_0). \tag{6}$$

Once the parametrisation is taken care of, all result obtained in the scalar case are extended to orientation fields. This extension is nearly straightforward, complete proof can be found in [2].

Theorem 1. *Assume that the interpolation operator E satisfies (A1)-(A3). Then $F(A, p, x, c)$ does not depend on c. Moreover, if $\theta_0 \in \mathcal{F}(\Gamma)$, then $\phi(E(\Gamma, \theta_0))$ is a viscosity solution of*

$$\begin{cases} F(D^2 u, Du, x) = 0 \ in \ D(\Gamma) \\ u = \phi(\theta_0) \ on \ \Gamma. \end{cases} \tag{7}$$

Remark 1. In the scalar case [2], grey scale shift invariance is assumed to prove this result. Of course, it does not make sense since angles do not add. However, since the result must be invariant with respect to the parameterisation, we get an equivalent property for free.

Theorem 2. *Assume that E satisfies axioms (1)-(6) and that F is differentiable at 0. Then, for all parameterisation ϕ, $\phi(E(\Gamma, \theta_0))$ is solution of*

$$\begin{cases} D^2 u(Du^\perp, Du^\perp) = 0 \ in \ D(\Gamma). \\ u = \phi(\theta_0) \ on \ \Gamma. \end{cases} \tag{8}$$

Remark that this operator is the curvature of the level lines of u, up to a $|Du|^3$ factor. These level lines are independent of the parameterisation, which makes the result possible. Indeed, the independence with respect to parameterisation implies that, for all admissible ϕ and ψ,

$$E(\Gamma, \theta_0) = \phi^{-1} \circ E_\phi(\Gamma, \phi \circ \theta_0) = \psi^{-1} \circ E_\psi(\Gamma, \psi \circ \theta_0).$$

By noting $u = \phi \circ \theta_0$ and $g = \psi \circ \phi^{-1}$, this equation becomes

$$g \circ E_\phi(\Gamma, u) = E_\psi(\Gamma, g \circ u).$$

This condition is closely related to invariance with respect to contrast change for scalar data, and the arguments developed in [1] indeed apply.

As noted in disocclusion experiments [16], this operator interpolates the level lines of the data with straight lines. A well known problem is that the solution of this equation may be not unique, and we will see in the next section that if it manages to keep the discontinuities structuring the image, it fails to give a field smooth enough to recover subjective contour. Thus we may drop the full independence over parameterisation and slightly relax Axioms (1) and (3).

Proposition 2. *Assume that Axioms (1) and (3) only holds for parameterisation that are Euclidean, up to a multiplicative factor. Then $\phi(E(\Gamma, \theta_0))$ is solution of*

$$aD^2 u(Du, Du) + bD^2 u(Du, Du^\perp) + cD^2 u(Du^\perp, Du^\perp) = 0, \tag{9}$$

where $ac - b^2 \geq 0$.

The condition $ac - b^2 \geq 0$ ensures that the equation is elliptic, and that the maximum principle can hold. As expected, a solution of (9) is invariant with respect to an affine reparameterisation of the circle, but not to any general parameterisation.

Among all those operators, the case $b = c = 0$ is the Absolutely Minimizing Lipschitz Extension (AMLE)

$$\begin{cases} D^2u(Du, Du) = 0 \text{ in } D(\Gamma), \\ u|_\Gamma = \phi(\theta_0) \text{ on } \Gamma, \end{cases} \tag{10}$$

for which existence and uniqueness of viscosity solution is known. It gives continuous oscillation free solution. It will be studied in more detail in Sect. 5.

4   Angle Interpolation with the Curvature Operator

As a result of the previous section, the only operator satisfying the given axioms is the curvature operator. It is well known in the computer vision community as a scalar restoration operator via total variation minimisation and has been used for scalar interpolation to solve the disocclusion problem [16, 17, 18].

The argumentation above gives the equation which is locally satisfied by the orientation of the vector field. An alternate formulation [19] is to consider the variational problem

$$\min_{W^{1,p}(\Omega)} \int \|DI\|^p,$$

under the constraint $|I| = 1$. In this case $I = (I_1, I_2)$ and $|I|$ is the Euclidean norm $|I| = \sqrt{I_1^2 + I_2^2}$ and $\|DI\| = \sqrt{|DI_1|^2 + |DI_2|^2}$. Inspired by the scalar case, we can compute the Euler-Lagrange equations for the energy above by setting $I = \frac{u}{|u|}$ so that the constraint is automatically satisfied. Careful calculations lead to a system of the two coupled PDEs

$$\operatorname{div}\left(\|DI\|^{p-2}DI_i\right) + I_i\|DI\|^p = 0, \quad 1 \leq i \leq 2. \tag{11}$$

It is worth noticing that $\|DI\|^p$ may be interpreted as the Lagrange multiplier of the constraint $|I| = 1$. The case $p = 1$, corresponding to the total variation, leads to

$$\operatorname{div}\left(\frac{DI_i}{\|DI\|}\right) + I_i\|DI\| = 0, \quad 1 \leq i \leq 2. \tag{12}$$

As a sanity check, elementary calculations lead to the following result, which holds thanks to the particular choice of norm $\|DI\|$.

Proposition 3. *Let* $I = (I_1, I_2) \in C^2(\Omega, \mathbb{R}^2)$ *with* $|I| = 1$ *everywhere. Let* θ *such that* $I = (\cos(\theta), \sin(\theta))$. *Then*

$$\operatorname{div}\left(\frac{DI_i}{\|DI\|}\right) + I_i\|DI\| = 0, \quad 1 \leq i \leq 2. \iff \frac{1}{|D\theta|}D^2\theta\left(\frac{D\theta^\perp}{|D\theta|}, \frac{D\theta^\perp}{|D\theta|}\right) = 0. \tag{13}$$

Fig. 2. Interpolation with the curvature operator on Lena. The initialization is orthogonal to the gradient orientation field decimated using a Canny-Deriche filter. A general observation is that T-junctions are preserved.

4.1   Numerical Resolution

Experiments (not detailed here) show that the numerical solutions of the two outlined methods are indeed the same. Hence in the following we use the parametrized to S^1 equation. To compute a numerical solution, we will use the associated evolution problem

$$\frac{\partial \theta}{\partial t} = D^2\theta \left(\frac{D\theta^\perp}{|D\theta|}, \frac{D\theta^\perp}{|D\theta|} \right), \tag{14}$$

and let $t \to \infty$.

   To solve this equation, we used a non-linear over relaxation scheme (NLOR) similar to the one found in [2] implemented in Megawave2 [20]. As noted in [21] and [22], we took some special numerical attention to work with angles modulo 2π and circumvent the problem caused by the discontinuities at $2k\pi, k \in \mathbb{N}$. Moreover, as noted above, a multiresolution scheme was used to take care of the initialisation, see [14].

4.2   Experiments on the Curvature Operator

Geometrically, the curvature extension operator tries to extend the level lines of the boundary data by straight lines. Obviously, there are cases for which that approach does not apply [16]. In particular it fails to compute any solution for the simple artificial cases we will see in the next section (see figure 3).

   However, experiments carried out for larger images with a larger set of boundary points yields interesting results. Figure 2, displays an example with the Lena image. We visualise the field via its field line, using Line Integral Convolution (LIC) [23]. The initial field is given by the orientation of the tangents to the level lines (the orthogonal to the gradient) decimated with a thresholded Canny-Deriche edge filter [24]. As expected, the curvature operator keeps discontinuities, as at the top of Lena's hat. Interestingly enough, it also manages to keep singularities adequately. In particular, *T-junctions* are preserved, which is particularly relevant in a perceptual point of view. Not only singularities that are present on the boundary data are preserved, but they can also be created in the interpolated area in a suitable way (see for instance at the interface of the cheek and the hair).

   To sum up, the curvature operator is (as in the scalar case) able to preserve singularities when necessary. It may be considered as a drawback when the smoothest solution is sought. Moreover, there is no existence and uniqueness result in the general case.

5   AMLE on Angle

In this section, we will provide more insight to the AMLE extension. A more detailed presentation can be found in [2, 25, 26] We know that a non surjective data can be smoothly interpolated inside a single parameterisation, and that AMLE is independent of affine change of parametrisation.

AMLE was introduced in [27]. It was proved (see [25, 26] and references therein) that it can be equivalently defined, in the scalar case, as

- the extension in Ω of a data defined on $\partial\Omega$ whose Lipschitz constant is minimal in any $\Omega' \subset \Omega$.
- the viscosity solution of the PDE $D^2u(Du, Du) = 0$.
- the limit for $p \to \infty$ of *p-harmonic maps*, defined as the minimization of the *p-harmonic energy*

$$\min_{W^{1,p}(\Omega)} \int |Du|^p.$$

Those results heavily rely on a maximum principle (eventually proved by Jensen [26]), which guarantees in particular that the solution has no oscillation inside the domain. More importantly, it yields the existence and uniqueness of the solution.

5.1 Equivalence of AMLE on Angle and AMLE on Vector Restricted to S^1

Again, we can link the intrinsic formulation on angle used until now and the $\mathbb{R}^2$ restricted to S^1 one. Let us consider (11) again and let p go to $+\infty$. We formally obtain the two coupled equations

$$\sum_{i=1}^{2} D^2I_i(DI_i, DI_j) = 0 \quad j = 1, 2. \tag{15}$$

The definition of a solution of this system is, to the best of our knowledge, an open problem. However, we point out the two following interesting facts.

Proposition 4. *Let* $I = (I_1, I_2) \in C^2(\Omega, \mathbb{R}^2)$ *with* $|I| = 1$ *everywhere. Let* θ *such that* $I = (\cos(\theta), \sin(\theta))$. *Then*

$$\sum_{i=1}^{2} D^2I_i(DI_i, DI_j) = 0 \quad j = 1, 2 \iff D^2\theta(D\theta, D\theta) = 0. \tag{16}$$

This means that I is a vector AMLE on the circle if its argument is a scalar AMLE.

The second point is that the term corresponding to the constraint $|I| = 1$ has vanished from (11) to (15). Now, a method to solve the stationary problem (15) is to solve the corresponding evolution system

$$\frac{\partial I_j}{\partial t} = \sum_{i=1}^{2} D^2I_i(DI_i, DI_j) \quad j = 1, 2. \tag{17}$$

If I is a continuous solution of (17) such that $|I| = 1$ everywhere at time $t = 0$, does it remain true for $t > 0$? At this step, we cannot tell, but we have the following hint.

Lemma 1. *Let* I *be a a* C^2 *vector field with* $|I| = 1$ *everywhere. Then the vector with coordinates* $\sum_{i=1}^{2} D^2I_i(DI_i, DI_j)$ *is everywhere normal to* I.

5.2   Numerical Resolution

Again we can numerically check for the equivalence of the two formulation, and we used the simpler parametrized to S^1 one. It is proved, in the scalar case, that when $t \to \infty$ the solution of the evolution problem

$$\frac{\partial \theta}{\partial t} = D^2\theta(D\theta, D\theta), \tag{18}$$

tends to the solution of the stationary problem, because this solution is unique. In the vector case, we do not have such a result, but we display experiments showing that this is still reasonable. We used a multiresolution NLOR scheme similar to the one used for the curvature operator (see Sect. 4.1).

5.3   Experiments

Figure 3 shows numerical results on artificial data. The first one simply consists of two vectors. The interpolated vector field is as expected tangent to the curve with which we would like to connect the two vectors, something close to Euler elastica [10]. The next two figures show the same mechanism with more complex curves: a circle and a tube. The interpolated field is perceptually sound.

As asserted by Prop. 1, we do find singularities in the center of the circle and the extension is there somewhat chaotic, as we are looking for a Lipschitz function where it cannot even be continuous. The situation below the tube (Fig. 3, last experiment) is interesting as it is an example of the ambiguity of Sect. 2.2: a smooth extension do exist, but due to the lack of information the algorithm extended the orientation field the other way round and put a singularity.

We see Fig. 4 an experiment on Lena. The initial field is again the orientation of the tangents to the level lines (the orthogonal to the gradient) decimated with a thresholded Canny-Deriche edge filter [24]. The interpolation field is again tangent to the edges as requested. On the other hand, there is no control on the position of the unavoidable singularities. Moreover, singularities are smoothed out, which can be expected, regarding the properties of the AMLE in the scalar case.

Nonetheless, the AMLE is a good candidate for an interpolation operator as we have a complete theory in the scalar case stating existence and uniqueness of solution. Moreover, it gives smooth solution from which extracting subjective contour as curves is possible. Compared to the curvature however, it tend to lack the ability to keep discontinuities in the fields it produce.

5.4   Conclusion

An axiomatic approach of orientation field interpolation has been presented to define extension operators. There is a unique operator satisfying a small set of axioms including geometrical invariance and stability: the curvature operator. This operator is able to preserve singularities. On the other hand, one may require a smoother solution. Moreover, an existence and uniqueness of a solution are not well established. If the independence of the interpolation with respect

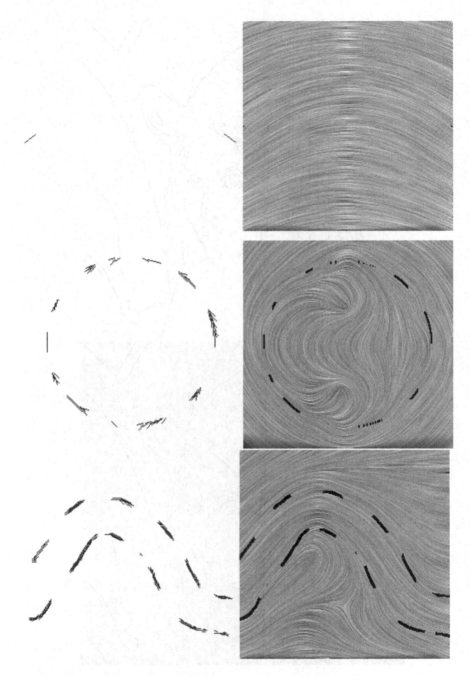

Fig. 3. Three artificial geometric tests, initial orientation field on the left, AMLE extension visualised with LIC on the right. As expected, where we would put a curve it do find the tangent to that curve. It's behaviour is less predictable where there is no information.

Fig. 4. Test with the Lena image, initialised with the orthogonal to the gradient orientation field decimated using a Canny-Deriche filter. Notice that the recovered field is tangent to the edges, in particular at the top of the hat, on the strands of hair around the face and on Lena's jaw and chin.

to reparameterisation of the unit circle is relaxed, another operator becomes interesting: the AMLE. Existence and uniqueness holds in the scalar case. The AMLE is, to some extent, dual to the curvature operator (it minimizes the L^∞ norm of the gradient, while the curvature minimizes the norm L^1), and somehow smoothes out the singularities.

The proposed extension operators provides the required basis for the extraction of meaningful curves in images as curves tangent to the orientation field: for instance using Fast Marching approaches [28]. Other obvious applications include LIC-based interpolation or restoration [23, 29]. The operators above are the more natural popping out from the required axioms. However, if some of them are relaxed or more prior knowledge from the image is introduced, some variations of these operators may lead to new types of interpolation model.

References

1. Alvarez, L., Guichard, F., Lions, P.L., Morel, J.: Axioms and fondamental equations of image processing. Arch. Rational Mechanics and Anal. **16** (1993) 200–257
2. Caselles, V., Morel, J., Sbert, C.: An axiomatic approach to image interpolation. IEEE Trans. Image Processing **7** (1998) 376–386
3. Kaniza, G.: La grammaire du voir. Diderot (1996)
4. Wertheimer, M.: Untersuchungen zur Lehre der Gestalt II. Psychologische Forschung **4** (1923) 301–350
5. Parent, P., Zucker, W.: Trace inference, curvature consistency, and curve detection. IEEE Transactions on Pattern Analysis and Machine Intelligence **11** (1989)
6. Sha'ashua, A., S.Ullman: Structual saliency: The detection of globally salient structures using a locally connected network. In: Second Int. Conf. Comp. Vision, Tarpon Springs, FL. (1988) 321–327
7. Medioni, G., Lee, M.: Grouping .,-,-¿ into regions, curves, and junctions. Computer Vision and Image Understanding **76** (1999) 54–69
8. Medioni, G., Lee, M., Tang, C.: A computational framework for segmentation and grouping. Elsevier Science (2000)
9. Zweck, J., Williams, L.: Euclidian group invariant computation of stochastic completion fields using shiftable-twistable basis function. J. Math. Imaging and Vision **21** (2004) 135–154
10. Mumford, D.: Elastica and computer vision. In Bajaj, C., ed.: Algebraic Geometry and Its Applications. Springer-Verlag (1994)
11. Ballester, C., Caselles, V., J.Verdera: Disocclusion by joint interpolation of vector fields and gray levels. Multiscale Modelling and Simulation **2** (2003) 80–123
12. Kimmel, R., Sochen, N.: Orientation diffusion or how to comb a porcupine. Journal of Visual Communication and Image Representation **13** (2002) 238–248
13. Osher, S., Sole, A., Vese, L.: Image decomposition and restoration using total variation minimization and the H^1 norm. Multiscale Modeling and Simulation **1** (2003) 349–370
14. Chessel, A., Cao, F., Fablet, R.: Orientation interpolation : an axiomatic approach. Technical report, IRISA (in preparation)
15. Granas, A., Dugundji, J.: Fixed point theory. Springer-Verlag (2003)
16. Masnou, S., Morel, J.: Level-line based disocclusion. IEEE ICIP (October 1998)
17. Rudin, L.I., Osher, S., Fatemi, E.: Nonlinear total variation bsaed noise removal algorithms. Phisica D **60** (1992) 259–268

18. Chan, T., Shen, J.: Local inpainting model and TV inpainting. SIAM J. Appl. Math. **62** (2001) 1019–1043
19. Tang, B., Sapiro, G., Caselles, V.: Diffusion of general data on non-flat manifolds. Int. J. Computer Vision **36** (2000) 149–161
20. Froment, J.: Megawave2. (http://www.cmla.ens-cachan.fr/Cmla/Megawave/)
21. Perona, P.: Orientation diffusion. IEEE Trans. Image Processing **7** (1998) 457–467
22. Cecil, T., Osher, S., Vese, L.: Numerical methods for minimization problems constrained to S^1 and S^2. J. of Computational Physics **198** (2004) 567–579
23. Cabral, B., Leedom, L.: Imaging vector field using line integral convolution. Computer Graphics Proceedings (1993) 263–270
24. Deriche, R.: Using canny's criteria to derive a recursively implemented optimal edge detector. Int. J. Computer Vision **1** (1987) 167–187
25. Aronsson, G., Crandall, M.G., Juutinen, P.: A tour of the theory of absolutely minimizing functions. Bull. Amer. Math. Soc. **41** (2004) 439–505
26. Jensen, R.: Uniqueness of lipschitz extentions: minimizing the sup norm of gradient. Arch. Rational Mechanics and Anal. **123** (1993) 51–74
27. Aronsson, G.: Extention of function satisfying lipschtiz conditions. Ark. Mat. **6** (1997) 551–561
28. Sethian, J.: Level Set Methods and Fast Marching Methods. Cambridge University Press (1999)
29. Tschumperlé, D.: LIC-based regularization of multi-valued images. In: ICIP 05, Genoa, Italy. (2005)

Alias-Free Interpolation

C.V. Jiji, Prakash Neethu, and Subhasis Chaudhuri

Indian Institute of Technology Bombay, Mumbai, India
{jiji, neethu, sc}@ee.iitb.ac.in

Abstract. In this paper we study the possibility of removing aliasing in a scene from a single observation by designing an alias-free upsampling scheme. We generate the unknown high frequency components of the given partially aliased (low resolution) image by minimizing the total variation of the interpolant subject to the constraint that part of unaliased spectral components in the low resolution observation are known precisely and under the assumption of sparsity in the data. This provides a mathematical basis for exact reproduction of high frequency components with probability approaching one, from their aliased observation. The primary application of the given approach would be in super-resolution imaging.

1 Introduction

Images with high spatial resolution are always a necessity in computer vision applications. Resolution enhancement using interpolation techniques is of limited application because of the aliasing present in the low resolution (LR) image. Hence researchers have been working in the field of *super-resolution* (SR) where a high-resolution (HR) image is reconstructed using one or more LR observations. In general, super-resolution involves deblurring, denoising and alias-removal. There are, in general, two classes of super-resolution techniques: reconstruction-based and learning-based [1]. In reconstruction-based SR techniques several LR images are used to reconstruct the super-resolved image. In learning-based methods proposed in the literature, one or more LR observations are used, but they make use of a database of several HR images to estimate the HR image corresponding to the given LR image.

All existing papers claim that they have been able to generate additional high frequency components through the use of multiple exposures or learning from the database. But there has been no mathematical proof or studies to show that the generated high frequency components are, indeed, the correct ones! For example, even a bilinear interpolation will generate (spurious) high frequency components. Unlike all previous work, we provide a mathematical basis based on which the correctness of the generated high frequency components can be established. In this paper we study only one specific aspect of SR, the alias removal part, at an exact theoretical level. We deal with a very specific case-only a single LR observation, no multiple view collation and no learning from a database. In effect, we show how much additional information can be extracted from a single observation through alias removal alone.

A. Leonardis, H. Bischof, and A. Pinz (Eds.): ECCV 2006, Part IV, LNCS 3954, pp. 255–266, 2006.

The super-resolution idea was first proposed by Tsai and Huang[2]. Their frequency domain approach reconstructs an HR image from a sequence of several LR undersampled images by exploiting the relationship between the continuous and the discrete Fourier transforms of the undersampled frames. A different approach to the super-resolution restoration problem was suggested by Irani *et al.* [3] based on the iterative back projection method. A maximum *aposteriori* (MAP) estimator with Huber-Markov random field prior is described by Schultz and Stevenson in [4]. Elad and Feuer [5] proposed a unified methodology for super-resolution restoration from several geometrically warped, blurred, noisy and down-sampled images by combining maximum likelihood, MAP and projection onto convex sets approaches. Nguyen *et al.* proposed circulant block preconditioners to accelerate the conjugate gradient descent method while solving the Tikhonov-regularized super-resolution problem [6].

In all the above methods, the quality of the super-resolved image is measured either by means of visual inspection or using a PSNR check. It can be easily shown that the PSNR measure is heavily biased towards the lower part of the spectrum due to the fact that most of the energy is contained in this region. Hence the PSNR may not be a good measure to evaluate the performance of an SR scheme. The issue that the reconstructed components are really the high frequency components has not really been investigated so far. Our work in this paper is a study in this direction. In [7], Lin and Shum determine the quantitative limits of reconstruction-based super-resolution algorithms and obtain the upsampling limits from the conditioning analysis of the coefficient matrix. But it is restricted to a perturbation analysis and not on spectral resolvability. Shahram and Milanfar in [8] study how far beyond the classical Rayleigh limit of resolution one can reach at a given signal to noise ratio using statistical analysis. Here the authors do not study the system performance in the presence of aliasing.

Rajan *et al.* have analyzed the possibility of alias-free upsampling of images in [9] through the use of a generalized interpolation. They have shown the conditions under which such an interpolation is possible. However, it requires several observations and the knowledge of a non-linear transform to achieve this. We study the issue of alias-free interpolation at a more fundamental level and restrict ourselves to using a single observation. Our work is motivated by the work of Candes *et al.* [10] where the authors address the problem of exact signal reconstruction from incomplete frequency information. We build on the theorem developed by them to derive a method for exact removal of aliasing while interpolating an image.

The reminder of the paper is organized as follows. We discuss the LR image formation process in section 2. We also define the problem here. A relevant theorem which we make use of in solving the problem is stated in 3. Some useful corollaries are also given. Section 4 explains our alias-free interpolation technique. In section 5 we discuss the computational scheme to solve the problem. We present experimental results on different types of images in section 6, and the paper concludes in section 7.

2   Aliasing in LR Image

It is assumed that the observed low resolution image is produced from a single high resolution image under the following generative model. Let $\bar{z}$ represent the lexicographically ordered high resolution image of $K^2 \times 1$ pixels. If $\bar{g}$ is the $N^2 \times 1$ lexicographically ordered vector containing pixels from the low resolution observation, then it can be modeled as

$$\bar{g} = DA\bar{z} \tag{1}$$

where D is the decimation matrix, size of which depends on the decimation factor and A is the blur matrix, assumed to be an identity matrix in this paper for the specific task of studying the alias-removal property.

The LR image formed through the above process will, in general, be aliased. The aliasing mechanism is illustrated in Figure 1. The spectrum of a continuous-time 1-D signal $x_c(t)$ band limited to B is shown in Figure 1(a). The spectrum of the sampled signal $x(n)$ sampled at a rate $F < 2B$ is shown in Figure 1(b). Of course the spectrum will be aliased since the signal is sampled at a rate less than the Nyquist rate. The resultant aliased spectrum of the sampled signal is shown in Figure 1(c). As can be noted from Figure 1(c) the portion of the spectrum $F - B \leq \omega \leq B$ will be aliased and the rest will be alias-free. A similar form of aliasing takes place in low resolution images unless the blur matrix A in equation (1) is quite severe. The knowledge about the portion of the spectrum $0 \leq \omega \leq F - B$ will be used as a constraint, as these components are free from aliasing, in the proposed method to recover the high frequency components.

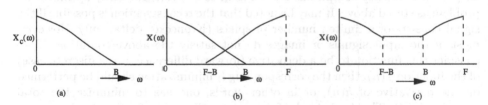

Fig. 1. Illustration of the aliasing process: (a) Spectrum of a continuous-time signal $x_c(t)$, (b) components of the spectrum of the sampled signal $x(n)$, and (c) resultant spectrum of $x(n)$

Having explained the aliasing process, we now define our problem in terms of alias-free interpolation: Given an LR image $g(x, y)$ of size $N \times N$ whose spectrum is *partially* aliased, generate an interpolated image $z(x, y)$ of size $2N \times 2N$ which is *completely* alias-free under the assumption that the image consists of piece-wise constant intensity regions. The significance of the assumption will be explained in the next section.

3   A Relevant Theorem by Candes *et al.*

Theorem 1: Consider a discrete-time 1-D signal $f \in C^N$ and a randomly chosen set of frequencies Ω of mean size $\tau N, 0 < \tau < 1$. Then for each $\zeta > 0$, suppose that f obeys

$$\#\{n, f(n) \neq 0\} \leq \alpha(\zeta) \cdot (\log N)^{-1} \cdot \#\Omega, \tag{2}$$

then with probability at least $1 - O(N^{-\zeta})$, f can be reconstructed exactly as the solution to the l_1 minimization problem

$$\min_h \sum_{n=0}^{N-1} |h(n)| \quad s.t. \quad H(\omega) = F(\omega) \ \forall \omega \in \Omega \tag{3}$$

where $H(\omega)$ and $F(\omega)$ are the discrete Fourier transforms of $h(n)$ and $f(n)$ respectively and $\#$ refers to the count.

Here ζ is an accuracy parameter in the term $O(N^{-\zeta})$ and $\alpha(\zeta)$ has been shown to be equal to $(1+o(1))/(29.6(\zeta+1))$ under certain conditions in [10]. In a simple language it means that as one selects more spectral components compared to the number of non-zero elements in $f(n)$, one is likely to recover the true function $f(n)$ with a higher accuracy. Proof of the theorem can be found in [10]. This is typically known as data sparsity problem [11], one such common example of which is inpainting [12] where one is required to reconstruct the missing data. An interesting reference to this work is by Chan *et al.* [13] where the authors investigate the reverse problem, i.e., how much loss in data can be tolerated for a faithful reconstruction of a signal as opposed to what Candes *et al.* [10] has studied.

According to the theorem the discrete-time signal f can be reconstructed from its partial frequency samples as the solution to the constrained l_1 optimization problem as stated above. It may be noted that the reconstruction is possible if the signal consists of a limited number of spikes (Kronecker delta) only. However, most of the input signals or images do not satisfy the above condition. If we consider this function to be a derivative (forward difference in the discrete case) of the function $f(n)$, then the corresponding l_1 minimization should be performed on the derivative of $h(n)$, or in other words, one has to minimize the total variation (TV). This leads to the following corollary.

Corollary 1: A piecewise constant object can be reconstructed from incomplete frequency samples provided the number of discontinuities satisfy the above condition 2, as the solution to the minimization problem

$$\min_h \sum_{n=0}^{N-1} |h(n) - h(n-1)| \quad s.t. \quad H(\omega) = F(\omega) \ \forall \omega \in \Omega \tag{4}$$

Corollary 2: If $f(x, y)$ is a two-dimensional object, it can be reconstructed from its incomplete frequency samples as the solution to the minimization problem

$$\min_h \sum\sum (|h_x| + |h_y|) \quad s.t. \quad H(\omega) = F(\omega) \ \forall \omega \in \Omega \tag{5}$$

where $h_x(x,y) = h(x,y) - h(x-1,y)$ and $h_y(x,y) = h(x,y) - h(x,y-1)$. This is similar to minimizing the total variation norm of $h(x,y)$. But this is not rotationally symmetric.

It may be noted that the same solution was proposed in 1981 by Levy and Fullagar [14] in connection with the reconstruction of geophysical data. Also see the reference [15] for a similar work. Candes et $al.$ have provided a theoretical footing of the existing solution. It may be noted that total variation-based image interpolation methods are also proposed in [16] and [17]. But the authors do not specifically address the issue of alias removal. For a detailed review of TV, readers are referred to [18].

4   Alias-Free Interpolation

The problem addressed in [10] is a restoration problem where the discrete-time signal is reconstructed from its incomplete Fourier samples such as in computed tomography. However, they do not consider the effect of aliasing on the sampled data. But our problem is a signal interpolation one, where only one LR observation g is available, which is the decimated version of the unknown HR image z as explained in section 2. Of course, g will be aliased. We wish to remove this aliasing completely while interpolating the image assuming the aliasing to be only partial. It may be noted that without the interpolation (use of a denser grid to represent the data), one cannot recover the aliased components. To apply the above theorem to our problem, a partial knowledge about $Z(\omega)$ should be available. We now explain how a partial knowledge of $Z(\omega)$ can be obtained from the given observation $G(\omega)$. Our alias-free interpolation procedure is illustrated in Figure 2 with respect to a given 1-D LR sequence $g(n)$ of length N. Note that unlike in theorem 1, we are dealing with real valued function $g(n)$ and hence the spectrum is always conjugate symmetric and one has to consider only one half of the spectral components. Figure 2(a) shows the partially aliased spectrum of the LR sequence $g(n)$ of length N. We assume that $G(\omega)$ in $0 \leq \omega \leq M$ is free from aliasing and the remaining portion is aliased. This corresponds to the assumption that the continuous signal $g_c(t)$ is band limited to the normalized frequency $(1 - M/N)$, where $0 \leq M \leq N/2$. The smaller the value of M, the larger is the amount of aliasing. Figure 2(b) shows the spectrum of the HR sequence $z(n)$ of

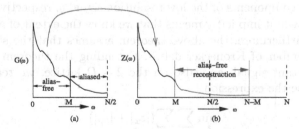

Fig. 2. Illustration of (a) partially aliased spectrum of the LR sequence $g(n)$, and (b) spectrum of the HR sequence $z(n)$ to be estimated. Note that only half of the spectrum is shown due to conjugate symmetry.

length $2N$ to be estimated. The alias-free interpolation method should recover the frequency components in the region $M \leq \omega \leq N - M$ in $Z(\omega)$ as shown in Figure 2 (b). From the figure, note that we have

$$Z(i) = qG(i) \text{ for } 0 \leq i < M \tag{6}$$

$$Z(i) = 0 \text{ for } N - M < i \leq N \tag{7}$$

and using the property of aliasing (wrapping around of frequencies)

$$Z(i) + Z(N - i) = qG(i) \text{ for } M \leq i \leq N/2 \tag{8}$$

Hence the alias-free reconstruction of the high resolution signal involves recovering the spectrum $Z(\omega)$ given equations (6-8). Clearly, this cannot be done without additional constraints. Note that one needs the scale factor q (equal to 2 in this study) to satisfy the energy relationship (Parseval's theorem). In order to recover $z(n)$, we need state the following theorem.

Theorem 2: Given a discrete-time partially aliased 1- D signal $g \in R^N$, and two distinct spectral intervals $\Omega_f = \{0 \leq \omega < M\}$ and $\Omega_a = \{M \leq \omega \leq N/2\}$ and another discrete-time signal $z \in R^{2N}$ satisfying Nyquist criterion with three distinct spectral intervals $\Omega_f' = \Omega_f$, $\Omega_a' = \{M \leq \omega \leq N - M\}$ and $\Omega_0' = \{N - M < \omega \leq N\}$, under conditions very similar to those defined in theorem 1, z can be recovered exactly from g as a solution to the l_1 minimization problem

$$\min_z \sum_{n=0}^{2N-1} |z(n)| \tag{9}$$

subject to the constraints

$$Z(\omega) = 2G(\omega) \ \forall \omega \in \Omega_f' \tag{10}$$

$$Z(\omega) + Z(N - \omega) = 2G(\omega) \ \forall \omega \in \Omega_a \tag{11}$$

$$Z(\omega) = 0 \ \forall \omega \in \Omega_0' \tag{12}$$

One can follow arguments similar to those in [10] except that the partitions are deterministic and hence it will lead to different values of the parameters α and ζ. It may be noted that the partitions Ω_f and Ω_a correspond to the alias-free and the aliased components of the low resolution signal g, respectively. Since the partition is known, it implicitly means that we know the extent of aliasing in the observation. Furthermore, the above theorem assumes that the signal consists of a limited number of Kronecker deltas. Extending the theorem to deal with piece-wise constant signal, and also on the $2 - D$ lattice, we realize that we should minimize the expression

$$\min_z \sum \sum (|z_x| + |z_y|) \tag{13}$$

instead of equation (9) to recover the high resolution image z. (The multiplication factor q in equations (10) and (11) should be replaced by $q^2 = 4$ due to the extension to $2 - D$.) It may be noted that if z is, indeed, piecewise constant then it cannot ideally be band limited, and hence the partition Ω_f will not be completely free from aliasing.

Now we look at the issue of the choice of the value of M for alias removal. It is assumed in theorem 2, that M is known. This is tantamount to assuming the highest frequency component present in z is known apriori. However, one would not know M in practical super-resolution applications. We suggest that one solves the problem for different values of M and then compare the results. However, as the value of M is lowered from $N/2$ toward 0, the cardinality of the set Ω_f reduces and the reconstruction would be progressively more unreliable. It also leads to the following observation that one cannot use an interpolation factor q greater than 2 as this would mean $M = 0$, implying a several fold aliasing when $\Omega_f = \{\emptyset\}$ and hence reconstruction would be very unreliable.

5   Computational Method

Theorem 2 provides a theoretical basis for obtaining the alias-free interpolated image z. We now provide the computational tool to solve this. We obtain the solution to the above optimization problem using linear programming (LP). The objective function for the LP problem is the total variation cost as given in equation (13). The equality constraints are obtained using equations (10), (11) and (12). The equality constraints corresponding to equation (10) can be written in the form

$$T_f \bar{z} = \bar{G}_f \qquad (14)$$

where T is the $2N \times 2N$ DFT matrix with elements $T(m, n) = [e^{-j\pi/N}]^{mn}$ and T_f represents the top M rows of T. Thus T_f is an $M \times 2N$ matrix. Similarly $\bar{G}$ is the DFT of the observation $qg(n)$ and $\bar{G}_f$ corresponds to the top M elements of $\bar{G}$. The equality constraints corresponding to equation (11) can be written as

$$T_a \bar{z} = \bar{G}_a \qquad (15)$$

where T_a is an $(N/2 - M + 1) \times 2N$ matrix whose each row is obtained by summing the corresponding two rows of the DFT matrix T_f as per the indices shown in equation (8). $\bar{G}_a$ corresponds to the spectral components $(M + 1)$ to $(N/2 - M)$ in $\bar{G}$. Similarly equation (12) can be written as a linear equality

$$T_0 \bar{z} = \bar{0} \qquad (16)$$

where T_0 consists of the $(N - M + 1)$ to N rows of the DFT matrix T and $\bar{0}$ is a null vector. All the above three linear equations can now be compactly written as

$$\begin{bmatrix} T_f \\ T_a \\ T_0 \end{bmatrix} \bar{z} = \begin{bmatrix} \bar{G} \\ \bar{0} \end{bmatrix} \qquad (17)$$

which is of the form $C\bar{z} = \bar{d}$. We also know that $z(n) \geq 0\ \forall n$ as $z(n)$ corresponds to an image. Also note that the above equation is meant for the first half of the spectrum. One would get an equivalent constraint for the other half based on the conjugate symmetry. Hence equations (9) and (17) constitute a standard LP problem. We have explained the problem with respect a $1 - D$ signal and it should be suitably changed to handle $2 - D$ images.

To solve the l_1 minimization using LP equation (13) should be written as

$$\min_z \sum \sum ((z_x^+ + z_x^-) + (z_y^+ + z_y^-)) \tag{18}$$

where $z_x^+ = \max(z_x, 0)$ and $z_x^- = -\min(z_x, 0)$, etc. Unfortunately, this increases the dimensionality of the unknown variables by five fold, increasing the computation significantly. Further the constraint equations involve complex numbers when the relationships have to be split into real and imaginary parts separately, increasing the computation further. We generate the appropriate constraint matrix and solve using the *linprog* routine in Matlab. But, even for a 128×128 image, the computational resources required are very large. Unfortunately, Matlab fails to allocate the necessary memory even for a small sized image. A typical option in LP is to utilize the possible sparseness properties of C matrix in equation (17). Unfortunately again, C does not have any sparseness as the DFT matrix T is not a sparse one. So we solve it as a sequential 1-D problem taking first the rows and then the columns. Hence the results obtained by this method for images in this paper are all sub-optimal.

6   Experimental Results

In this section we present the results of alias-free interpolation obtained using the proposed approach. All the LR images are of size 64×64. All the results shown in this section are for interpolation factor of 2 for the reason described in section 4. Since the amount of aliasing M is not known, we show results for various choices of M.

First we show the applicability of the proposed method on a simulated $1 - D$ data. Figure 3 (a) shows a low resolution rectangular pulse train and the corresponding spectrum is shown in Figure 3 (b). The signal shown in Figure 3 (a) is superimposed with three high frequency components corresponding to the normalized frequencies $35/64, 36/64$ and $37/64$ to obtain the signal shown in Figure 3 (c). Clearly, these three spectral components are aliased ones. Figure 3 (d) shows the spectrum of the aliased signal. One cannot find that the signal is aliased either from Figures 3 (c) or 3 (d). Figure 3 (e) shows the interpolated signal using the proposed method and its spectrum is shown in Figure 3 (f). One can see that there are spectral components at locations beyond the normalized frequency $32/128$. These components match quite well with the introduced high frequency components. We have used $M = 26$ in this example. To further see the gain arising out of the proposed method, one can note that the spectrum of the rectangular pulse train (without the additional high frequency components) shown in Figure 3 (b) compares very favorably with the spectrum of the interpolated signal till the normalized frequency of $32/128$. On

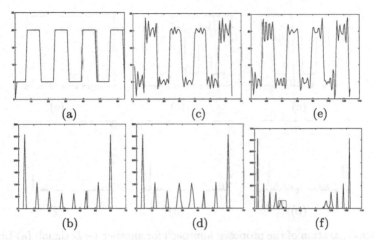

Fig. 3. Demonstration of the proposed approach for a $1 - D$ signal: (a) alias-free LR signal, (b) spectrum of (a), (c) aliased LR signal, (d) spectrum of (c), (e) interpolated signal using the proposed approach and (f) spectrum of (e)

comparing the interpolated signal in Figure 3 (e) with the low resolution signal in Figure 3 (c), one can clearly see that Figure 3 (e) cannot be obtained by the linear or cubic interpolation of the original signal. (see the highlighted spectral components in Figure 3 (f)). This confirms the utility of the proposed method. Further, to illustrate the capability of our method we compare the results of our alias free interpolation with spline interpolation in Figure 4. Figure 4 (a) shows a low resolution rectangular pulse train and the corresponding spectrum is shown in Figure 4 (b). The spline interpolated result and the corresponding spectrum are shown in Figures 4 (c) and (d) respectively. The alias free interpolated signal and its spectrum are shown in Figures 4 (e) and (f), respectively. As can be observed, the alias free interpolated signal is almost free from overshoot and ripples as compared to the spline interpolated one.

Figure 5 (a) shows a partially aliased low resolution Lena image of size 64×64. Figure 5 (b) shows the bicubic interpolated image for comparison to the proposed method. Figures 5 (c-e) show the alias-free interpolation results obtained using the sub-optimal linear programming method. Figure 5 (c) corresponds to the result where 10% ($M = 29$), additional high frequency components are generated. Here we assume that the aliasing in the LR image is small, only 10% of the entire spectrum. If we assume that the aliasing in the LR observation is about 20%, the corresponding alias-free interpolated image is shown in Figure 5 (d). This corresponds to the choice of $M = 26$. Figure 5 (e) shows the alias-free interpolated image where we attempt to generate 30% additional high frequency components assuming that 30% of the spectrum of the LR image is aliased. As can be observed from Figures 5 (c-e), there is a gradual reduction in the quality of the reconstructed image as the aliasing in the LR image is assumed to have increased from 10% to 30%. This is due to the fact that only a smaller subset of spectral components are known exactly. In comparison to

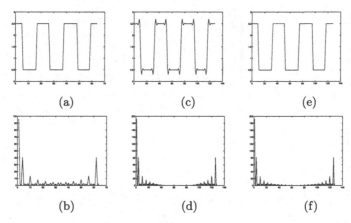

(a)   (c)   (e)

(b)   (d)   (f)

Fig. 4. Demonstration of the proposed approach for another $1-D$ signal: (a) LR signal, (b) spectrum of (a), (c) spline interpolated signal, (d) spectrum of (c), (e) interpolated signal using the proposed approach and (f) spectrum of (e)

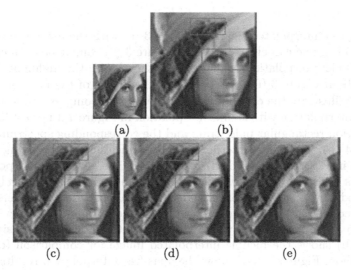

(a)   (b)

(c)   (d)   (e)

Fig. 5. (a) A low resolution Lena image, (b) bicubic interpolated image. Interpolated images using the proposed approach generating additional (c) 10%, (d) 20% and (e) 30% high frequency components.

the bicubic interpolated image, the result using the proposed approach is much sharper. Observe the eyes, hair strands, etc. in Figure 5 (d). Some of the regions are highlighted in the figure. We have observed that the reconstruction becomes poor when the aliasing present in the LR image is assumed to be more than 20 to 30%. Now we perform the experiments on a severely aliased randomly textured image. The purpose of this experiment is to demonstrate that one does not get any improvement during interpolation if the signal is highly aliased. The LR observation is shown Figure 6 (a). The interpolated images using the proposed

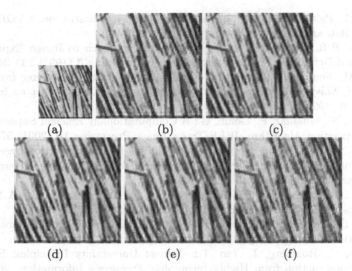

(a)   (b)   (c)

(d)   (e)   (f)

Fig. 6. (a) A severely aliased low resolution texture image, (b) bicubic interpolated image. Interpolated images using the proposed approach generating (c) 10%, (d) 20% and (e) 30% high frequency components, (f) Interpolated image when the LR image is fully aliased.

approach are shown in Figures 6 (c-e) assuming 10%, 20% and 30% aliasing, respectively, in the given LR image. As the aliasing present in the LR image is very high, the proposed method does not give a significant edge over bicubic interpolation as can be observed from Figures 6 (c-e). Now we assume that the entire spectrum is aliased, ie,$\Omega_f = \{\emptyset\}$ in theorem 2 (M=1). Figure 6 (f) shows the corresponding interpolated result. We observe that the reconstruction is quite inferior as we do not have any of the spectral components known exactly.

7   Conclusion

In this paper we have presented a method for alias-free interpolation from a partially aliased low resolution image. We have provided a theoretical basis on how an alias-free upsampling can be achieved. In order to interpolate the given LR image we generate the exact additional high frequency components assuming a knowledge of the nature of aliasing in the spectrum of the LR observation and assuming a piecewise constant intensity image. The alias-free interpolation is achieved by solving the l_1 optimization. A sub-optimal computational procedure using linear programming is also presented.

References

1. Chaudhuri, S., Joshi, M.V.: Motion-Free Super-Resolution. Springer (2005)
2. Tsai, R.Y., Huang, T.S.: Multiframe Image Restoration and Registration. In: Advances in Computer Vision and Image Processsing. JAI Press Inc. (1984) 317–339

3. Irani, M., Peleg, S.: Improving Resolution by Image Registration. CVGIP: Graphical Models and Image Processing **53** (1991) 231–239
4. Schultz, R.R., Stevenson, R.L.: A Bayesian Approach to Image Expansion for Improved Definition. IEEE Trans. on Image Processing **3** (1994) 233–242
5. Elad, M., Feuer, A.: Restoration of a Single Superresolution Image from Several Blurred, Noisy and Undersampled Measured Images. IEEE Trans. on Image Processing **6** (1997) 1646–1658
6. Nguyen, N., Milanfar, P., Golub, G.: A Computationally Efficient Super-resolution Reconstruction Algorithm. IEEE Trans. Image Processing **10** (2001) 573–583
7. Lin, Z., Shum, H.Y.: Fundamental Limits of Reconstruction-Based Super-Resolution Algorithms under Local Translation. IEEE Trans. on Pattern Analysis and Machine Intelligence **26** (2004) 83–97
8. Shahram, M., Milanfar, P.: Imaging Below the Diffraction Limit: A Statistical Analysis. IEEE Trans. on Image Processing **13** (2004) 677–689
9. Rajan, D., Chaudhuri, S.: Generalized Interpolation and its Applications in Super-Resolution imaging. Image and Vision Computing **19** (2001) 957–969
10. Candes, E., Romberg, J., Tao, T.: Robust Uncertainty Principles: Exact Signal Reconstruction from Highly Incomplete Frequency Information (2004) http://www.acm.caltech.edu/ ~ emmanuel/publications.html.
11. Donoho, D.L., Elad, M.: Maximal sparsity Representation via l_1 Minimization. the Proc. Nat. Aca. Sci. **100** (2003) 2197–2202
12. Bertalmio, M., G. Sapiro, V.C., Ballester, C.: Image Inpainting. In: Proc. SIGGRAPH, New Orleans, USA (2000)
13. Chan, T., Kang, S.H.: Error Analysis for Image Inpainting. UCLA CAM report 04-72 (2004)
14. Levy, S., Fullagar, P.K.: Reconstruction of a sparse spike train from a portion of its spectrum and application to high-resolution deconvolution. GEOPHYSICS **46** (1981) 1235–1243
15. Santosa, F., Symes, W.W.: Linear inversion of band-limited reflection seismograms. SIAM J. Sci. Statist. Comput. **7** (1986) 1307–1330
16. Guichard, F., Malgouyres, F.: Total Variation Based Interpolation. In: Proc. European Signal Processing Conference. (1998) 1741–1744
17. Malgouyres, F., Guichard, F.: Edge Direction Preserving Image Zooming: A Mathematical and Numerical Analysis. SIAM J. Numerical Analysis **39** (2001) 1–37
18. Rudin, L., Osher, S., Fatemi, E.: Nonlinear total variation based noise removal algorithms. PHYSICA D **60** (1992) 259–268

An Intensity Similarity Measure
in Low-Light Conditions

François Alter[1,*], Yasuyuki Matsushita[2], and Xiaoou Tang[2]

[1] CMLA, École Normale Supérieure de Cachan
[2] Microsoft Research Asia
francois.alter@mines.org, {yasumat, xitang}@microsoft.com

Abstract. In low-light conditions, it is known that Poisson noise and quantization noise become dominant sources of noise. While intensity difference is usually measured by Euclidean distance, it often breaks down due to an unneglible amount of uncertainty in observations caused by noise. In this paper, we develop a new noise model based upon Poisson noise and quantization noise. We then propose a new intensity similarity function built upon the proposed noise model. The similarity measure is derived by maximum likelihood estimation based on the nature of Poisson noise and quantization process in digital imaging systems, and it deals with the uncertainty embedded in observations. The proposed intensity similarity measure is useful in many computer vision applications which involve intensity differencing, e.g., block matching, optical flow, and image alignment. We verified the correctness of the proposed noise model by comparisons with real-world noise data and confirmed superior robustness of the proposed similarity measure compared with the standard Euclidean norm.

1 Introduction

Noise is inevitable in any imaging device. A digital imaging system consists of an optical system followed by a photodetector and associated electrical filters. The photodetector converts the incident optical intensity to a detector current, or photons to electrons. During the process, the true signals are contaminated by many different sources of noise. In fact, the true signal itself has fluctuations in time due to the discrete nature of photons; the arrival of photons is not a steady stream and obeys the Poisson law [1]. It implies that no matter how accurately a computer vision experiment is performed, temporal fluctuation in intensity exists. The fluctuation becomes significant especially in low-light conditions where the number of incoming photons is limited, i.e., photon-limited conditions. In photon-limited conditions, quantization noise also becomes dominant due to the lack of intensity resolution in the limited dynamic range. Besides these noise sources, reset noise, dark current noise and read-out noise also become significant, and it is known that they can also be approximated by the Poisson noise model. Read-out noise is sometimes modelled by Gaussian noise; however, Gaussian noise with variance σ^2 and mean σ^2 is nearly identical to Poisson noise with

---

* This work is done while the first author was visiting Microsoft Research Asia.

A. Leonardis, H. Bischof, and A. Pinz (Eds.): ECCV 2006, Part IV, LNCS 3954, pp. 267–280, 2006.
© Springer-Verlag Berlin Heidelberg 2006

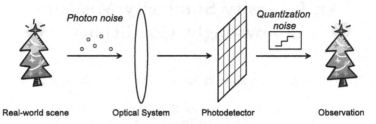

Fig. 1. Sources of noise in imaging process in low-light conditions. In low-light conditions, photon noise and quantization noise become dominant. In addition to them, there exist reset noise, dark current noise and readout noise that also cannot be ignored. It is known that they can be approximated by a Poisson distribution.

mean σ^2 if σ is sufficiently large. Read-out noise satisfies this condition when operating a camera at room temperature and with a high read-out frequency.

Important low-light vision applications include night vision, medical imaging, underwater imaging, microscopic imaging and astronomical imaging. Even in daily situations, Poisson noise often becomes significant in high-speed imaging. In these situations, uncertainty in observations increases significantly due to Poisson noise and quantization noise. Particular operations under these conditions, such as template matching [8, 6, 12] and edge detection [5, 4, 2, 10], have been widely studied for many applications in fields such as object recognition and motion estimation. Image restoration is also one of the central problems since photon-limited images are usually severely degraded. Statistical methods [15, 14, 11, 13, 7], such as maximum likelihood (ML) estimation, are found to be effective since they can account for the special properties of the Poisson distribution. All of these techniques are found useful in low-light conditions; however, one fundamental question still remains open; *what is the similarity between two intensity observations with uncertainty?*

Intensity distance is often measured in many computer vision algorithms, and it is usually computed by Euclidean distance. Let k, l be two intensity measurements. The Euclidean distance $d_E(k, l)$ is given by $d_E^2(k, l) = (k-l)^2$. It is correct for measuring the intensity distance between two signals when intensity noise is negligible, or a non-biased distribution of noise is assumed. However, they do not hold in photon-limited conditions where a significant amount of biased noise is added to the signal. Therefore, it is important to establish a new intensity similarity function which deals with the uncertainty embedded in observations.

In this paper, we describe a new noise model for low-light conditions and propose a new intensity similarity measure based upon the noise model. This paper has two primary contributions.

– **Poisson-quantization noise model:** A realistic noise model in low-light conditions is derived. The new noise model is built upon two inevitable noise sources: Poisson noise and quantization noise. We call the combined model of these two noise sources the Poisson-quantization noise, or PQ-noise in short. The proposed noise model is able to account for the uncertainty caused by the nature of photon arrival and digitizing process. The correctness of the proposed noise model is confirmed by experiments with real-world data.

- **A new intensity similarity measure:** A new intensity similarity measure is proposed based on our noise model, which deals with the uncertainty caused by PQ-noise. The proposed similarity measure is useful in many computer vision applications which involve intensity differencing, e.g., block matching, stereo, optical flow and image alignment. The key advantage of the similarity function is that it can easily take place of existing intensity distance functions based on Euclidean distance. We compare the performance of the new intensity similarity function with the Euclidean distance function in order to verify the robustness of the proposed method against noise.

The outline of the paper is as follows: In Section 2, we briefly review the Poisson noise model and quantization noise model, and derive the PQ-noise model. Section 3 formalizes the intensity similarity function which measures the likelihood of two observations. The correctness and effectiveness of the PQ-noise model and the intensity similarity measure are verified with experiments described in Section 4.

2   Poisson-Quantization Noise Model

In this section, we first briefly review Poisson noise and quantization noise in Sections 2.1 and 2.2. We then formalize the Poisson-quantization noise model in Section 2.3.

2.1   Poisson Noise Model

Poisson noise is modelled by a Poisson distribution defined as follows.

Definition 2.1: *A Poisson distribution [9] with parameter λ is defined for all $k \in \mathbb{N}$ by the probability*

$$p(k, \lambda) = \frac{\lambda^k}{k!} e^{-\lambda}, \tag{1}$$

with the mean E and variance V defined as follows.

$$E(\lambda) = \sum_{k=0}^{\infty} kp(k, \lambda) = \lambda, \quad V(\lambda) = \sum_{k=0}^{\infty} k^2 p(k, \lambda) - E^2 = \lambda. \tag{2}$$

2.2   Quantization Noise Model

Quantization noise is the uncertainty caused by rounding observation amplitudes to discrete levels which occurs due to the finite amplitude resolution of any digital system. In analog-to-digital conversion, the signal is assumed to lie within a predefined range. Suppose the minimum number of electrons which is necessary to raise one level of observed intensity is q, and e_q is the quantization noise. The count of electrons is proportional to the number of photons by the factor of the photon-electron conversion efficiency (the quantum efficiency of the sensor). A simple model of quantization noise can be described as

$$e_q = \frac{N}{q} - \left\lfloor \frac{N}{q} \right\rfloor, \tag{3}$$

where N is the number of electrons which are generated by the measurement. For a more detailed quantization error analysis in computer vision, readers are referred to [3].

2.3 Poisson-Quantization Noise Model

Now we formalize the PQ-noise model, which is the combination of Poisson noise and quantization noise.

Definition 2.2: *A Poisson distribution with parameter λ and quantization $Q = \{q_0 = 0, \ldots, q_k, \ldots, q_{n+1} = \infty\}$ is defined for all $k \in \{0, \ldots, n\}$ by the probability $p(k, \lambda, Q)$ as*

$$p(k, \lambda, Q) = \sum_{i=q_k}^{q_{k+1}-1} \frac{\lambda^i}{i!} e^{-\lambda}. \tag{4}$$

The quantization parameter q_k represents the minimum number of electrons which produces intensity level k.

Suppose the simple case where the quantization interval is constant, i.e., $q_k = kq$, and the observations are far from saturation. The quantization interval is defined as the range of input values assigned to the same output level. With this simple model, we first observe the different behavior of PQ-noise from that of the Poisson noise model. We later relax the assumption to fit to a more realistic model. In this condition, the mean $E(\lambda, q)$ and variance $V(\lambda, q)$ of the PQ-noise model are given by[1]:

$$E(\lambda, q) = \frac{\lambda}{q} - \frac{1}{2} + \frac{1}{2q} + \frac{1}{q} \sum_{k=1}^{q-1} \frac{e^{\lambda(e^{\frac{2\pi i k}{q}} - 1)}}{1 - e^{-\frac{2\pi i k}{q}}}, \tag{5}$$

$$V(\lambda, q) = \frac{\lambda}{q} + \frac{1}{12} - \frac{1}{12q^2} - \frac{2\lambda}{q^2} \sum_{k=1}^{q-1} \frac{e^{\frac{2\pi i k}{q}} e^{\lambda(e^{\frac{2\pi i k}{q}} - 1)}}{1 - e^{-\frac{2\pi i k}{q}}} + \frac{2}{q^2} \sum_{k=1}^{q-1} \frac{e^{-\frac{2\pi i k}{q}} e^{\lambda(e^{\frac{2\pi i k}{q}} - 1)}}{(1 - e^{-\frac{2\pi i k}{q}})^2}$$

$$+ \frac{1}{q} \sum_{k=1}^{q-1} \frac{e^{\lambda(e^{\frac{2\pi i k}{q}} - 1)}}{1 - e^{-\frac{2\pi i k}{q}}} - \frac{1}{q^2} \left(\sum_{k=1}^{q-1} \frac{e^{\lambda(e^{\frac{2\pi i k}{q}} - 1)}}{1 - e^{-\frac{2\pi i k}{q}}} \right)^2. \tag{6}$$

As seen in the above equations and in Fig. 2, oscillation with an exponential decay $e^{-\lambda(1-cos(\frac{2\pi}{q}))}$ is observed in both mean and variance. The minimum intensity level of the linear range corresponds to $\lambda \propto \frac{1}{1-cos(\frac{2\pi}{q})} \approx \frac{q^2}{2\pi^2}$.

---

[1] The derivation of the mean and variance is detailed in Appendix A.

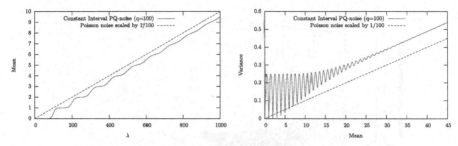

Fig. 2. The mean and variance properties of PQ-noise. Due to quantization noise, strong oscillations are observed. Left: Evolution of the mean with respect to λ with $q = 100$. Right: Evolution of the variance with respect to the mean with $q = 100$.

Fig. 2 illustrates the difference between the ordinary Poisson noise model and the PQ-noise model. As shown in the figures, PQ-noise has oscillations due to the quantization noise component.

In practice, q_1 does not equal to q due to the shift of the function caused by the offset voltage. Here we consider the more realistic model of the PQ-noise model with the following conditions: $q_0 = 0$ and $q_k = q_1 + (k-1)q$. It is possible to derive $E(\lambda, q)$ and $V(\lambda, q)$ for this condition by the same derivation used for Eqs. (5) and (6). When $E(\lambda, q)$ is reasonably high, i.e., $E(\lambda, q) \gg \frac{q}{2\pi^2}$, the following relationship[2] between $E(\lambda, q)$ and $V(\lambda, q)$ holds in the linear range.

$$V(E, q, q_1) = \frac{E}{q} + \frac{q^2 + 12q_1 - 6q - 7}{12q^2}. \tag{7}$$

This model has two unknown parameters q and q_1. These unknown parameters can be calibrated by fitting the observed noise data to Eq. (7).

3   Derivation of Intensity Similarity Measure

Given two intensity observations k and l, what can we tell about the similarity between them? Usually, the similarity is measured by Euclidean distance with an assumption that k and l are *true* signals, or the noise model is non-biased. However, they do not hold in low-light conditions. We develop a new intensity similarity measure which is based upon the probability that two intensity observations come from the same source intensity. In this section, we first derive the intensity similarity measure for the Poisson noise case in order to make the derivation clear. We then develop the intensity similarity measure for the PQ-noise model. In fact, the Poisson noise model can be considered as the special case of the general PQ-model with the quantization parameter $q = q_1 = 1$.

3.1   Poisson Noise Case

In the Poisson noise model, the case where two observed intensities arise from the same intensity distribution is equivalent to their sharing the same parameter

---

[2] The derivation of Eq. (7) is detailed in Appendix B.

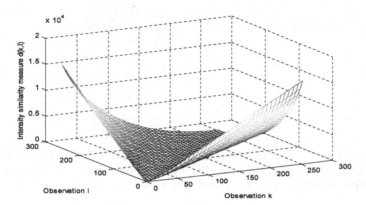

Fig. 3. The intensity similarity function defined in Eq. (10)

λ. If we assume that two intensity observations have the same parameter λ, the probability of obtaining two observations k and l is

$$P(k, l, \lambda) = p(k, \lambda)p(l, \lambda) = \frac{\lambda^{k+l}}{k!l!}e^{-2\lambda}. \tag{8}$$

This is obviously not sufficient to produce the actual probability because of the unknown parameter λ. However, the best case where λ maximizes the probability gives the measure which maximizes the similarity between k and l. Indeed, this approach corresponds to the ML estimation of the observation of the pair (k, l). Therefore, the optimal $\hat{\lambda}$ can be obtained by putting the first derivative $\frac{\partial P}{\partial \lambda} = 0$, and we obtain

$$\hat{\lambda} = \frac{k + l}{2}, \tag{9}$$

which maximizes the probability defined in Eq. (8). In this way, the intensity similarity function can be defined as

$$d(k, l) = -\ln(P(k, l, \hat{\lambda})) = (k + l)\left(1 - \ln\left(\frac{k + l}{2}\right)\right) + \ln(k!) + \ln(l!). \tag{10}$$

Note that this similarity measure does not agree with the exact definition of distance because $d(k, k) > 0$ if $k > 0$, but it produces the similarity between two observations.

Fig. 3 shows the intensity similarity function defined in Eq. (10). The function has a similarity to the l^2 norm when two observed intensity levels are high. In fact, when k and l are sufficiently big, $d(k, l)$ has a connection to the squared l^2 norm. This can be shown by rewriting Eq. (10) with the approximation $\ln(k!) \approx k \ln(k) - k$:

$$d(k, l) \approx k \ln(k) + l \ln(l) - (k + l) \ln\left(\frac{k + l}{2}\right) \tag{11}$$

$$= f(k) + f(l) - 2f\left(\frac{k + l}{2}\right) \approx \frac{f''(\frac{k+l}{2})(k - l)^2}{4} \approx \frac{(k - l)^2}{2(k + l)}.$$

3.2   Poisson-Quantization Noise Case

Using the derivation in the previous section, we formalize the intensity similarity function for the PQ-noise model. We first define the joint probability P; the probability of observing k and l having parameters λ_k and λ_l respectively with the quantization Q by

$$P(k, l, \lambda_k, \lambda_l, Q) = p(k, \lambda_k, Q)p(l, \lambda_l, Q). \tag{12}$$

We are seeking $\hat{\lambda}$ $(= \lambda_k = \lambda_l)$ which maximizes the probability P. This is equivalent to maximizing the probability that two intensity observations share the same intensity source $\hat{\lambda}$. We denote $P(k, l, \lambda, Q) = P(k, l, \lambda_k, \lambda_l, Q)$ when $\lambda_k = \lambda_l$. The optimal $\hat{\lambda}$ always exists since the logged probability $-\ln P$ is convex.[3]

1. If $k = l$, the maximum of $P(k, k, \lambda, Q)$ is given by[4]

$$\hat{\lambda} = (q_k...(q_{k+1} - 1))^{\frac{1}{q_{k+1} - q_k - 1}}. \tag{13}$$

2. If $k \neq l$, we can obtain the optimal $\hat{\lambda}$ by minimizing the convex function $-\ln(P)$. Here we describe a simple algorithm for finding the optimal $\hat{\lambda}$ with a dichotomic search over the first derivative of P.

Algorithm. for finding the optimal $\hat{\lambda}$
Input are $k, l, q_k, q_{k+1}, q_l, q_{l+1}$ and n_{iter}.
Set $\lambda_{min} = 0$ and λ_{max} sufficiently big, and $n = 0$,
While $n < n_{iter}$ and $P' \neq 0$
do
  Set $\lambda \leftarrow \frac{\lambda_{min} + \lambda_{max}}{2}$ and $n \leftarrow n + 1$.
  Compute $P' = -\frac{\partial \ln(P(k,l,\lambda,Q))}{\partial \lambda}$
  If $P' < 0$ set $\lambda_{min} \leftarrow \lambda$.
  If $P' > 0$ set $\lambda_{max} \leftarrow \lambda$.
done
Set $\hat{\lambda} \leftarrow \lambda$.

The sign of P' can be determined by computing the sign of

$$\left(\frac{\lambda^{q_{k+1}-1}}{(q_{k+1} - 1)!} - \frac{\lambda^{q_k-1}}{(q_k - 1)!} \right) \sum_{i=q_l}^{q_{l+1}-1} \frac{\lambda^i}{i!} + \left(\frac{\lambda^{q_{l+1}-1}}{(q_{l+1} - 1)!} - \frac{\lambda^{q_l-1}}{(q_l - 1)!} \right) \sum_{i=q_k}^{q_{k+1}-1} \frac{\lambda^i}{i!}.$$

To find the optimal $\hat{\lambda}$, other descent methods such as gradient descent, Newton-Raphson, etc. can also be used alternatively.

---

[3] The convexity is proved in Appendix C.
[4] It can be derived from the first derivation of the function described in Appendix C.

In the above way, the optimal $\hat{\lambda}$ is determined. The intensity similarity function is finally determined by plugging in the optimal $\hat{\lambda}$ into the following function using Eqs. (4) and (12):

$$d(k,l,Q) = \min_{\lambda}\{-\ln(P(k,l,\lambda,Q))\} = -\ln(P(k,l,\hat{\lambda},Q)) \qquad (14)$$

$$= -\ln\left\{e^{-2\hat{\lambda}}\left(\sum_{i=q_k}^{q_{k+1}-1}\frac{\hat{\lambda}^i}{i!}\right)\left(\sum_{j=q_l}^{q_{l+1}-1}\frac{\hat{\lambda}^j}{j!}\right)\right\}.$$

4   Experiments

In order to confirm our theoretical results, we performed experiments with real-world noise datasets. Our interests are 1) verifying the correctness of the proposed PQ-noise model and 2) confirming the superiority of the proposed intensity similarity measure over the standard l^2 norm.

In order to obtain datasets, we mounted a video camera at a fixed position and captured an image sequence of a static scene in a low-light condition. Therefore, the only fluctuation in an image sequence is caused by noise. The images captured under the severe low-light conditions are almost totally black to human eyes, but they still contain intensity information. Fig. 4 shows one of such scenes used for the experiment. We captured raw image sequences by a Point Grey Dragonfly^{TM} camera, and the intensities observed in the green channel are used for the entire experiment. For the illumination source, a DC light source is used to avoid intensity oscillations. We also used a small aperture and a short shutter speed to produce a low-light environment.

PQ-noise model. To verify the correctness of the PQ-noise model, we compared the mean-variance distribution of the real-world data with our analytic model described in Sec. 3.2. For the experiment, we have captured 1000 images of a static scene in a low-light condition. The unknowns q and q_1 are both estimated by least squares fitting to the linear range of the PQ-noise model described in Eq. (7). Fig. 5 shows the plot of observations and the analytic model with estimated q and q_1. As shown in the figure, our analytic model well fits the actual observations, especially in the low intensity levels where the oscillation is observed clearly. The root mean-square error of observations from the theoretic curve is 0.0090 in Fig. 5.

Intensity similarity measure. To evaluate the robustness of the proposed similarity measure against noise, block matching is applied to the image sequences; if the block stays at the original position, the measure is not affected by noise. The same test is performed using the l^1 and l^2 norms over the same datasets, and we compared the outcomes of these norms with that of the proposed intensity similarity measure. We denote the l^1 and l^2 norm measure and our intensity similarity measure described in Eq. (14) as d_{l^1}, d_{l^2} and d_{PQ} respectively. The parameters for d_{PQ}, i.e., q and q_1, are calibrated beforehand by curve fitting as done in the previous experiment. The parameters q and q_1 are estimated as $q = 67$ and $q_1 = 168$ in our experiment.

Fig. 4. One of the scenes used for the experiment. Left: The original input image in a low-light condition. Right: The left image is linearly scaled by 60.

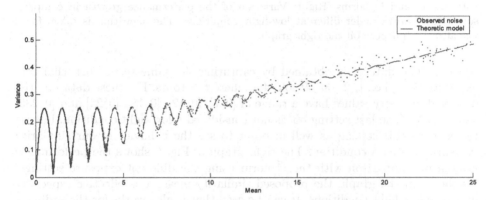

Fig. 5. Evolution of the variance with the mean. The dotted line is the theoretical result with the calibrated parameters, $q = 67$ and $q_1 = 168$. The dots are the measured noise which is obtained from 1000 images of a static scene under a low-light condition.

In the left image of Fig. 6, the performance growth obtained by our similarity measure in comparison with the l^1 and l^2 norm is shown. Our major interest is the comparison with the l^2 norm; however, a comparison with the l^1 norm is also given since the l^1 norm is often used in practice because of its simplicity. In the left graph, 0% indicates the same performance as the l^1 or l^2 norm. The performance growth from the l^2 norm, for example, is computed by $\frac{N_c(d_{PQ}) - N_c(d_{l^2})}{N_c(d_{l^2})}$ where $N_c(d_{PQ})$ and $N_c(d_{l^2})$ are the number of correct matches with d_{PQ} and d_{l^2} respectively. The same computation is applied for the l^1 norm case to obtain the performance improvement analysis as well. We can observe that our similarity measure significantly exceeds the l^1 and l^2 measures, especially when the block size is small. In fact, when the number of pixels in a block is large, the averaging of error reduces the biased property of the Poisson-quantization distribution. Therefore, the l^2 norm which is adapted to Gaussian noise becomes effective as well.

In order to analyze the performance variation in different low-light conditions, we performed the same experiment over image sequences with different exposure

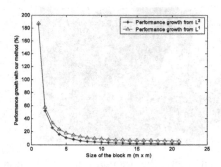 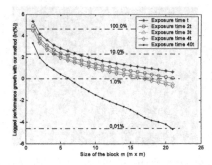

Fig. 6. Performance evaluation the proposed intensity similarity measure. Left: Performance growth of block matching using our intensity similarity measure in comparison with the l^1 and l^2 norms. Right: Variation of the performance growth in comparison with l^2 norm under different low-light conditions. The logarithm is taken for a visualization purpose on the right graph.

settings. The dataset is obtained by capturing the same scene with changing exposure time, i.e., t, $2t$, $3t$, $4t$ and $40t$ where $t = 15ms$. For these datasets, the observed intensity values have a range of $[0, 7]$, $[0, 12]$, $[0, 18]$, $[0, 24]$ and $[0, 235]$ respectively. The last setting $40t$ is not considered a low-light condition, but we tested with this setting as well in order to see the behavior of our similarity measure in such a condition. The right graph of Fig. 6 shows the performance growth in comparison with the l^2 norm using the different exposure settings. As shown in the graph, the proposed similarity measure is effective especially in severe low-light conditions. It can be seen that it also works for the ordinary condition (the $40t$ setting), although the performance improvement from the l^2 norm is almost zero.

5   Conclusion

In this work, we have proposed a new intensity similarity measure which is useful for low-light conditions where Poisson noise and quantization noise become significant. The intensity similarity measure is derived from the Poisson-quantization noise model which we develop as the combination of the Poisson noise model and the quantization noise model.

The correctness of the proposed PQ-noise model is verified by comparison with real-world noise data. The proposed intensity similarity measure is robust against Poisson-quantization noise, and is therefore effective in low-light conditions. The robustness is compared with the l^2 norm using block matching, and we confirmed that the proposed method largely exceeds the performance of the l^2 norm especially when the block size is small. Our intensity similarity measure is capable of achieving more accurate matching, especially in situations where large blocks cannot be used. The proposed noise model and intensity similarity measure are useful for many computer vision applications which involve intensity/image matching in photon-limited conditions.

References

1. N. Campbell. Discontinuities in light emission. *Proc. Cambridge Phil. Soc.*, 15:310–328, 1909.
2. M. Das and J. Anand. Robust edge detection in noisy images using an adaptive stochastic gradient technique. In *Proc. of International Conference on Image Processing*, volume 2, pages 23–26, 1995.
3. B. Kamgar-Parsi and B. Kamgar-Parsi. Evaluation of quantization error in computer vision. *IEEE Trans. Pattern Anal. Mach. Intell.*, 11(9):929–940, 1989.
4. A. Kundu. Robust edge detection. In *Proc. of Computer Vision and Pattern Recognition*, pages 11–18, 1989.
5. L. Liu, B.G. Schunck, and C.R. Meyer. Multi-dimensional robust edge detection. In *Proc. of Computer Vision and Pattern Recognition*, pages 698–699, 1991.
6. S.B. Lowen and M.C Teich. Power-law shot noise. *IEEE Trans. Information Theory*, 36:1302–1318, 1990.
7. H. Lu, Y. Kim, and J.M.M. Anderson. Improved poisson intensity estimation: Denoising application using poisson data. *IEEE Trans. on Image Proc*, 13(8), 2004.
8. G.M. Morris. Scene matching using photon limited images. *Journal of Opt. Soc. Am. A*, pages 482–488, 1984.
9. A. Papoulis. *Probability, Random Variables, and Stochastic Processes*, pages 554–576. McGraw-Hill, New York, 2nd edition, 1984.
10. P. Qiu and S.M. Bhandarkar. An edge detection technique using local smoothing and statistical hypothesis testing. *Pattern Recognition Lett.*, 17:849–872, 1996.
11. W.H. Richardson. Bayesian-based iterative method of image restoration. *Journal of Opt. Soc. of Am.*, 62:55–59, 1972.
12. R.E. Sequira, J. Gubner, and B.E.A. Saleh. Image detection under low-level illumination. *IEEE Trans. on Image Processing*, 2(1):18–26, 1993.
13. K.E. Timmermann and R.D. Nowak. Multiscale modeling and estimation of poisson processes with application to photon-limited imaging. *IEEE Trans. on Inform. Theory*, 45:846–862, 1999.
14. G.M.P. van Kempen, H.T.M. van der Voort, J.G.J. Bauman, and K.C. Strasters. Comparing maximum likelihood estimation and constrained tikhonov-miller restoration. *IEEE Engineering in Medicine and Biology Magazine*, 15:76–83, 1996.
15. Y. Vardi, L.A. Shepp, and L. Kaufman. A statistical model for positron emission tomography. *Journal of Amer. Statist. Assoc.*, 80:8–37, 1985.

Appendix A

We derive the mean and variance for a PQ-distribution described in Eqs. (5) and (6). We begin with the following theorem about quantization.

Theorem 1. *Let $X \in \mathbb{Z}$ be a discrete random variable which has a characteristic function $\phi(t) = \mathbb{E}(e^{itX})$. Its quantized version X_q can be defined by $X_q = \lfloor \frac{X}{q} \rfloor$. The characteristic function ϕ_q of X_q is given by*

$$\phi_q(t) = \frac{1 - e^{-it}}{q} \sum_{k=0}^{q-1} \frac{\phi(\frac{t+2\pi k}{q})}{1 - e^{-i\frac{t+2\pi k}{q}}}.$$

Proof. Let p_n be $p_n = P(X = n)$. The characteristic function ϕ_q of X_q is

$$\phi_q(t) = \sum_{n=-\infty}^{\infty} p_n e^{i\lfloor \frac{n}{q} \rfloor t} = \sum_{n=-\infty}^{\infty} p_n e^{i\frac{n}{q}t} e^{i(\lfloor \frac{n}{q} \rfloor t - \frac{n}{q}t)}.$$

The function $f : \begin{cases} \mathbb{Z} & \mapsto \mathbb{C} \\ n & \to e^{i(\lfloor \frac{n}{q} \rfloor t - \frac{n}{q}t)} \end{cases}$ is q-periodic, therefore it can be written

by a trigonometric polynomial $\sum_{k=0}^{q-1} a_k e^{\frac{2\pi i k n}{q}}$. Using a discrete Fourier transformation, we obtain:

$$a_k = \frac{1}{q}\sum_{j=0}^{q-1} f(j)e^{-\frac{2\pi i j k}{q}} = \frac{1}{q}\sum_{j=0}^{q-1} e^{-i\frac{j}{q}t}e^{-\frac{2\pi i j k}{q}} = \frac{1}{q}\sum_{j=0}^{q-1} e^{-j\frac{i(t+2\pi k)}{q}}$$

$$= \frac{1 - e^{-i(t+2\pi k)}}{q(1 - e^{-i\frac{t+2\pi k}{q}})} = \frac{1 - e^{-it}}{q(1 - e^{-i\frac{t+2\pi k}{q}})}.$$

Therefore,

$$\phi_q(t) = \sum_{n=-\infty}^{\infty} p_n e^{i\frac{n}{q}t} \sum_{k=0}^{q-1} a_k e^{\frac{2\pi i k n}{q}} = \sum_{k=0}^{q-1} \sum_{n=-\infty}^{\infty} p_n e^{in\frac{t+2\pi k}{q}} \frac{1 - e^{-it}}{q(1 - e^{-i\frac{t+2\pi k}{q}})}$$

$$= \sum_{k=0}^{q-1} \phi\left(\frac{t+2\pi k}{q}\right) \frac{1 - e^{-it}}{q(1 - e^{-i\frac{t+2\pi k}{q}})}.$$

QED

Corollary 1. *The mean E_q of X_q and variance V_q of X_q can be written by the mean E, the variance V, and the characteristic function ϕ of X:*

$$E_q = \frac{E}{q} - \frac{1}{2} + \frac{1}{2q} + \frac{1}{q}\sum_{k=1}^{q-1} \frac{\phi(\frac{2\pi k}{q})}{1 - e^{-\frac{2\pi i k}{q}}}$$

$$V_q = \frac{V}{q} + \frac{1}{12} - \frac{1}{12q^2} - \frac{2E}{q^2}\sum_{k=1}^{q-1} \frac{e^{\frac{2\pi i k}{q}}\phi(\frac{2\pi k}{q})}{1 - e^{-\frac{2\pi i k}{q}}} + \frac{2}{q^2}\sum_{k=1}^{q-1} \frac{e^{-\frac{2\pi i k}{q}}\phi(\frac{2\pi k}{q})}{(1 - e^{-\frac{2\pi i k}{q}})^2}$$

$$+ \frac{1}{q}\sum_{k=1}^{q-1} \frac{\phi(\frac{2\pi k}{q})}{1 - e^{-\frac{2\pi i k}{q}}} - \frac{1}{q^2}\left(\sum_{k=1}^{q-1} \frac{\phi(\frac{2\pi k}{q})}{1 - e^{-\frac{2\pi i k}{q}}}\right)^2.$$

These formulas are given by the computation of the derivatives of ϕ_q, using the fact that $E_q = -i\phi_q'(0)$ and $V_q = -\phi_q''(0) - E_q^2$.

Eqs. (5) and (6) are the result of the previous formulas with a Poisson distribution which has the characteristic function $\phi(t) = e^{\lambda(e^{it}-1)}$.

Remark 1. We can extend the previous result to the continuous random variable case. Let X be a random variable in $\mathbb{R}$, and $\phi_X(t)$ its characteristic function. Let $\lfloor X \rfloor$ be the quantized version of X. Using the Fourier series of the 1-periodic function defined over $\mathbb{R}$, i.e., $f(x) = e^{it(\lfloor x \rfloor - x)} = \sum_{n=-\infty}^{\infty} i \frac{e^{-i(t+2\pi n)} - 1}{t + 2\pi n} e^{2\pi i n x}$, we can show that the characteristic function $\phi_{\lfloor X \rfloor}$ of $\lfloor X \rfloor$ is

$$\phi_{\lfloor X \rfloor}(t) = \sum_{n=-\infty}^{\infty} i \frac{e^{-i(t+2\pi n)} - 1}{t + 2\pi n} \phi_X(t + 2\pi n),$$

where the summation has to be done by grouping terms of n and $-n$ together if it is not convergent. The mean $E_{\lfloor X \rfloor}$ can be simply derived by

$$E_{\lfloor X \rfloor} = E_X - \frac{1}{2} + \sum_{n \neq 0} \frac{\phi_X(2\pi n)}{2\pi n}.$$

This applies to any kind of distribution, for example, the mean of a Gaussian distribution can be derived as follows. Let X be a random variable following the Gaussian law $\mathcal{N}(\mu, \sigma^2)$. The characteristic function becomes $\phi_X(t) = e^{i\mu t - \frac{\sigma^2 t^2}{2}}$. Therefore,

$$E_{\lfloor X \rfloor} = \mu - \frac{1}{2} + \sum_{n \neq 0} \frac{e^{i\mu 2\pi n - \sigma^2 2\pi^2 n^2}}{2\pi n} = \mu - \frac{1}{2} + \sum_{n=1}^{\infty} \frac{\cos(2\pi n \mu) e^{-\sigma^2 2\pi^2 n^2}}{\pi n}$$

As the series on the right is decreasing exponentially with n, this gives a practical way to compute $E_{\lfloor X \rfloor}$.

Appendix B

We derive the PQ-noise model in the linear range described in Eq. (7). With an assumption that observed intensities are far enough from saturation, the approximation $n = \infty$ can be used. We use the previous theorem described in Appendix A and divide the problem into two cases.

1. If $q_1 \leq q$, let $X(\lambda)$ be a discrete random variable on the shifted Poisson distribution defined by

$$\forall k \geq q_1 - q, \; P(X(\lambda) = k) = \frac{\lambda^{k+q_1-q}}{(k+q_1-q)!} e^{-\lambda}.$$

   In this case, $\lfloor \frac{X(\lambda)}{q} \rfloor$ has the wanted PQ-distribution. It is straightforward to see that $E_{X(\lambda)} = \lambda + q_1 - q$, and $V_{X(\lambda)} = \lambda$.

2. If $q_1 > q$, let $X(\lambda)$ be a discrete random variable which satisfies

$$\begin{cases} P(X(\lambda) = 0) = \sum_{j=0}^{q_1-q} \frac{\lambda^j}{j!} e^{-\lambda}, \\ P(X(\lambda) = k) = \frac{\lambda^{k+q_1-q}}{(k+q_1-q)!} e^{-\lambda}. \quad \forall k \geq 1 \end{cases}$$

Then again, $\lfloor \frac{X(\lambda)}{q} \rfloor$ has the wanted PQ-distribution. When λ is big, the approximation $P(X = 0) \approx 0$ holds. Therefore, $E_{X(\lambda)} \approx \lambda + q_1 - q$, and $V_{X(\lambda)} \approx \lambda$ are deduced.

Using Corollary 1 and the remark, which shows $\lim_{\lambda \to \infty} \phi_{X(\lambda)}(2k\pi) = \lim_{\lambda \to \infty} \phi'_{X(\lambda)}(2k\pi) = 0$, we are able to deduce that $E(\lambda, q, q_1) = \frac{\lambda + q_1}{q} - \frac{1}{2} + \frac{1}{2q}$ and $V(\lambda, q, q_1) = \frac{\lambda}{q^2} + \frac{1}{12} - \frac{1}{12q^2}$ in the linear range. Therefore,

$$V(\lambda, q, q_1) = \frac{qE(\lambda, q, q_1) - q_1 + \frac{q}{2} - \frac{1}{2}}{q^2} + \frac{1}{12} - \frac{1}{12q^2} = \frac{E(\lambda, q, q_1)}{q} + \frac{q^2 + 12q_1 - 6q - 7}{12q^2}.$$

Appendix C

We show that the probability function $-\ln P$ in Eq. (12) is convex.

Proposition: $f : \lambda \mapsto -\ln \left(\sum_{i=m}^{n} \frac{\lambda^i}{i!} e^{-\lambda} \right)$ is convex.

Proof.

$$f'(\lambda) = \frac{-\sum_{i=m}^{n} \left(\frac{\lambda^{i-1}}{(i-1)!} - \frac{\lambda^i}{i!} \right) e^{-\lambda}}{\sum \frac{\lambda^i}{i!} e^{-\lambda}} = \frac{\frac{\lambda^n}{n!} - \frac{\lambda^{m-1}}{(m-1)!}}{\sum \frac{\lambda^i}{i!}}$$

$$f''(\lambda) = \frac{\sum_{i=m}^{n} \left(\frac{\lambda^{n-1}}{(n-1)!} - \frac{\lambda^{m-2}}{(m-2)!} \right) \frac{\lambda^i}{i!} - \left(\frac{\lambda^n}{n!} - \frac{\lambda^{m-1}}{(m-1)!} \right) \frac{\lambda^{i-1}}{(i-1)!}}{(\sum \frac{\lambda^i}{i!})^2}$$

$$= \frac{\sum_{i=m}^{n} \frac{\lambda^{n+i-1}}{n!i!}(n-i) + \frac{\lambda^{m+i-2}}{(m-1)!i!}(i-m+1)}{(\sum \frac{\lambda^i}{i!})^2} > 0.$$

Therefore f is convex.

QED

Direct Energy Minimization for Super-Resolution on Nonlinear Manifolds

Tien-Lung Chang[1,2], Tyng-Luh Liu[1], and Jen-Hui Chuang[2]

[1] Institute of Information Science, Academia Sinica, Taipei 115, Taiwan
liutyng@iis.sinica.edu.tw
[2] Dept. of Computer Science, National Chiao Tung University, Hsinchu 300, Taiwan

Abstract. We address the problem of single image super-resolution by exploring the manifold properties. Given a set of low resolution image patches and their corresponding high resolution patches, we assume they respectively reside on two non-linear manifolds that have similar locally-linear structure. This manifold correlation can be realized by a three-layer Markov network that connects performing super-resolution with energy minimization. The main advantage of our approach is that by working directly with the network model, there is no need to actually construct the mappings for the underlying manifolds. To achieve such efficiency, we establish an energy minimization model for the network that directly accounts for the expected property entailed by the manifold assumption. The resulting energy function has two nice properties for super-resolution. First, the function is convex so that the optimization can be efficiently done. Second, it can be shown to be an upper bound of the reconstruction error by our algorithm. Thus, minimizing the energy function automatically guarantees a lower reconstruction error— an important characteristic for promising stable super-resolution results.

1 Introduction

In this work *super-resolution* specifically means the technique to estimate a high-resolution (HR) image from one or more low-resolution (LR) instances taken of the same scene by some imaging processes. One reason for looking into such an issue is due to the quality constraints on many existing imaging devices, especially on nowadays *digital* imaging systems. Although a large portion of them are suitable for most imaging applications, the current resolution levels by the affordable price still can not satisfy certain common needs. Take, for example, the ubiquitous security surveillance systems. To completely monitor the whole area of interest, lots of cameras are often needed. However, the quality of these cameras is generally not good enough for providing useful information. While it is always possible to physically increase the quality of sensors by investing more budgets, image processing techniques such as super-resolution provide a reasonable solution, and have been studied for years.

Super-resolution has lately become an active topic in vision research. Its application ranges from medical imaging to image compression. An extensive number of useful approaches have thus been proposed to address the problem with different aspects of consideration [1], [3], [5], [6], [7], [10], [12], [13], [15], [17], [18],

A. Leonardis, H. Bischof, and A. Pinz (Eds.): ECCV 2006, Part IV, LNCS 3954, pp. 281–294, 2006.
© Springer-Verlag Berlin Heidelberg 2006

[19], [20], [21]. By the underlying models, these methods can be roughly divided into two categories [1], [19]: *reconstruction-based* and *recognition-based*. Typically a reconstruction-based technique tries to accomplish super-resolution with an ML or a MAP formulation [5], [10], [17], [18], [20]. To avoid causing an underdetermined system, some kind of prior information needs to be imposed for regularizing the results of super-resolution and for adding more high frequencies. On the other hand, the recognition-based methods, e.g., [1], [7], [19], often first resize an LR image into the desirable size of a target HR one, and then add the appropriate high frequencies from the training set to improve the quality of the resized image. While the reconstruction-based methods assume a more realistic model, which simulates the process that we produce an LR image and can be solved by standard optimization algorithms, the recognition-based methods indeed provide more feasible results, especially for the case that the number of given LR images is rather small.

Different from previous approaches for super-resolution, we are motivated by investigating the manifold property of LR and HR image patches, with an emphasis on the assumption that for each pair of corresponding LR and HR image patches their local neighborhoods on some proper nonlinear manifolds would be *similar*. Specifically, our method deals with the single (LR) image super-resolution problem, and uses a three-layer Markov network to realize the manifold assumption. The key contribution of the proposed approach is to explore the connection between the LR and HR manifolds without the need to explicitly construct the respective manifolds. We achieve such efficiency by establishing an energy minimization model that *directly* accounts for the expected property entailed by the implicit manifold structure. It therefore results in an optimization-based algorithm for super-resolution, and requires only a training set consisting of a small number of pairwise LR and HR image patches.

2   Previous Work

For convenience we always denote an LR image by L, and an HR image by H. The task of single image super-resolution is therefore to find a *best H* of a specified higher resolution, from which the given L can be reasonably reproduced. Indeed over the years there are many attempts to address the problem, including, e.g., direct interpolation, or frequency-domain reconstruction [12]. Our discussion here focuses only on more recent super-resolution techniques, sorted according to the following two classes.

Reconstruction-Based. Methods of this kind typically assume an observation model that describes how one can get L from H. If L and H are represented in the form of column vectors, the observation model can often be written out in a linear form:

$$L = TH + Z, \tag{1}$$

where T can be thought of as some underlying imaging system transforming H to L, and Z is the additive zero-mean Gaussian noise. As an example to illustrate, suppose H is of size $\mathcal{X}_H$ pixels and L is of size $\mathcal{X}_L$ pixels. Then the observation model in the work of Elad et al. [5] can be stated as

$$L = DBH + Z, \tag{2}$$

where B is a blur matrix of size $\mathcal{X}_H$-by-$\mathcal{X}_H$, and D is a downsampling operator of size $\mathcal{X}_L$-by-$\mathcal{X}_H$. Notice that we have omitted the geometric motion matrix and the indices of image frames in [5] owing to that in our case there is only one LR image, namely L, as the input. With equation (1), the derivation of H can be readily casted as solving an ML (maximum likelihood) or a MAP (maximum a posteriori) problem, e.g., [5], [10], [17], [18], [20].

Still the huge dimensional characteristic of the super-resolution problem like (1) or (2) can be a challenging factor. A simple and effective technique has been proposed by Irani and Peleg [13] that approximates a *solution* of (2) based on *iterative back projection* (IBP). Their method starts with an initial guess H_0 for the HR image, projects the temporary result H_k by the same process for producing an LR image, and then updates H_k into H_{k+1} according to the projection error. These steps can be summarized by

$$H_{k+1} = H_k + B'U(L - DBH_k), \tag{3}$$

where U is now an upsampling matrix and B' is another blur matrix distributing the projection error. The IBP scheme given by (3) is intuitive and fast. However, it has no unique solution due to the ill-posed nature of equation (2), and cannot be effectively extended to include prior information on H for regularizing the solution. The concern of adding the prior information is necessary in that for the single image super-resolution problem the matrix T in (1) is inherently singular. Consequently, without using appropriate prior information on H, a reconstruction-based method for (1) could yield super-resolution results containing appreciable artifacts. Alternatively, the *projection onto convex sets* (POCS) approach [5], [20] applies set theories to the super-resolution problem, and allows constraints on additional prior information. The main disadvantages of POCS-based methods include non-uniqueness of solution, slow convergence, and high computational cost.

The ill-posedness of super-resolution noticeably hinders the performance of reconstruction-based methods, and could yield jaggy or ringing artifacts, e.g., as in the results of [19]. While adding some prior may alleviate the problem, it is generally too simple for simulating the real world texture. In fact regularizing super-resolution with prior information mostly smooths out small derivatives. When carefully done, it could produce *good* edges. However, the scheme may also suppress useful details, and is insufficient for representing complex textures.

Recognition-Based. To more naturally retain good image characteristics for super-resolution, the recognition-based techniques [1], [3], [7], [11], [19] resort to a training set of LR and HR image patches. The main idea is to use the actual HR patches to construct the results of super-resolution. Such methods usually carry out super-resolution by the following steps: divide the given LR image into small (overlapping) patches, compare them with LR image patches in the training set, and replace them with the corresponding HR patches. In [1], Baker and Kanade discuss the limits of reconstruction-based approaches, and also establish a recognition-based super-resolution technique. Freeman et al. [7] propose a Markov model, in which overlapping patches are used to enhance the spatial continuity. However, in most of the recognition-based algorithms, the recognition of each LR patch gives a hard assignment to a specific HR counterpart in the training set. The mechanism could cause blocky effect, or oversmoothness—if image processing is performed to eliminate the blocky effect [3].

With the exception of [19], the above-mentioned recognition-based methods are restricted by the class of their collected training sets. Indeed Sun et al. [19] only replace the patches of detected primal sketches, and then apply IBP [13] to ensure the reconstruction constraint. Though the primal-sketch scheme is useful for processing a wide range of LR images, its super-resolution results may contain artifacts induced by the back projection scheme. More recently, Chang et. al [3] consider neighbor components in generating the HR image patches so that the size of the training set can be dramatically reduced.

There are some attempts to integrate the two concepts, reconstruction-based and recognition-based, for establishing a super-resolution technique that has low reconstruction error, and meanwhile enriches a resulting HR image with complex priors learned from training patches. For example, Pickup et al. [15] include the learned image prior into a MAP model for super-resolution. The way they define the image prior on an image pixel is to assume a Gaussian distribution with the mean obtained by searching the set of training patches, finding the patch most similar to the neighborhood region around this image pixel, and identifying the value from the central pixel of the resulting patch. To feasibly optimize the formulation, Pickup et al. assume that small perturbations of the neighborhood region will not affect the searching result, an assumption that is not necessary the case. In some ways the method of Sun et al. [19] also has the advantages of the two types of approaches, but it is in essence an IBP algorithm with a better initial guess (learned from the training set).

3   Manifold Ways for Super-Resolution

Given a single LR image L, which can be thought of being derived by blurring and then downsampling some HR image of a real scene, the task of super-resolution is then to approximate a high-resolution H that is similar to the original scene. In our formulation we shall split L into n overlapping patches $\{\ell_i\}_{i=1}^{n}$. Intuitively, for each LR patch ℓ_i, the corresponding site i on H should have an HR patch h_i that is closely related to the appearance of ℓ_i (see Figure 1a).

Note that the site correlation between ℓ_i and (a desired) h_i does not imply it needs a training set, denoted as Ω, comprising numerous pairs of LR and HR patches to construct a reasonable H. The supporting evidence could come from investigating the properties of natural image statistics. One key conclusion related to our application is that although images are typically represented as high dimensional data, the natural images are actually distributed over a relatively

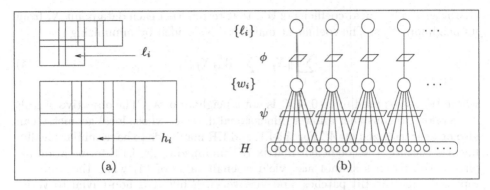

Fig. 1. (a) The corresponding low- and high-resolution patches ℓ_i and h_i (highlighted in red). (b) The 1-D illustration for the 3-layer Markov model. Note that in the output layer for describing the resulting HR image H each node represents an image pixel.

low dimensional manifold. For example, Lee et al. [14] find that the state space of natural image patches of size 3-by-3 pixels is indeed very sparse.

We assume that, among our training data, the set of HR patches and the set of corresponding LR patches respectively reside on two different nonlinear manifolds, but with similar locally-linear structure. In other words, the linear neighborhood relation of ℓ_i on the LR manifold can be used as a hint to correlate h_i and its neighbors on the HR manifold. The same assumption has been made in Chang et al. [3], and shown to produce stable super-resolution performance. Nonetheless, we emphasize a crucial difference that in [3] the locally-linear structure of the LR manifold is approximated exclusively with information from the LR patches in Ω. And each patch of the resulting HR image is independently determined via a hard assignment by imposing a similar locally-linear structure on the HR manifold. For each pixel covered by different overlapping HR patches, the average of these different values is assigned to resolve inconsistency. Such a tactic sometimes introduces oversmoothness in the results [3].

Even though our discussion so far has indicated that the proposed super-resolution algorithm involves learning two different manifolds from the training data Ω, it turns out to be more a conceptual idea. In practice there is no need to explicitly construct the LR and HR manifolds as we are only interested in exploring their underlying locally-linear property. Later in the next section we will explain how to use a Markov network to *conform* the two manifolds without knowing their structure. For now we shall give more discussions on the assumption that the two manifolds have similar locally-linear structure.

3.1   Locally Linear Assumption

Locally linear embedding (LLE) [16] is a way to map high dimensional data into a low dimensional space with the useful property of maintaining the neighborhood relationship. LLE assumes that each data point X_i and its neighbors lie on (or close to) a locally-linear patch of the manifold. This local geometry can be characterized by linear coefficients W_{ij} that reconstruct each data point X_i from its neighbors X_j's. The coefficient matrix W is decided by minimizing

$$\sum_i \|X_i - \sum_j W_{ij} X_j\|^2, \tag{4}$$

where W_{ij} is required to be 0 if X_j is not a neighbor of X_i. The objective of LLE is therefore to construct a lower dimensional data set whose local geometry can also be characterized by W. For the LR and HR manifolds to have similar locally-linear structure, the coefficient matrix W^* minimizing the LLE formulation (4) on the HR patches should also yield a small value of (4) when the data are replaced with the LR patches, and vice versa. While it is non-trivial to verify the property analytically, the linear model (1) relating an HR image H with its corresponding LR image L suggests the assumption is indeed a reasonable one.

4   The Energy Minimization Model

We now describe how super-resolution on nonlinear manifolds can be done with the convenience of skipping constructing the manifolds. Suppose we have a pair of LR and HR image patches, respectively denoted as ℓ and h. (Each image patch will hereafter be represented as a column vector.) Let P and Q be two matrices with the same number of columns. In particular, the columns of P are ℓ's neighbors in the training set Ω, and those of Q are h's neighbors in Ω. By the similar locally-linear structure of the LR and HR manifolds, we can find a reconstruction coefficient vector w satisfying

$$\begin{bmatrix} \ell \\ h \end{bmatrix} = \begin{bmatrix} P \\ Q \end{bmatrix} w + \begin{bmatrix} \epsilon \\ \delta \end{bmatrix}, \tag{5}$$

where ϵ and δ are Gaussian noise terms. Clearly equation (5) is the mathematical interpretation for the adopted manifold assumption, and it also nicely connects pivotal *elements* in solving the single image super-resolution problem.

To realize the manifold concept embodied in (5), we consider a three-layer Markov network, shown in Figure 1b. In the input layer of the network, each node represents an LR patch, say, ℓ_i from the ith site of the given LR image L. Each node of the second (hidden) layer is a coefficient vector w_i, stating how ℓ_i and the corresponding patch h_i from the ith site of the approximated HR image H can be reconstructed from their neighbors in the training set Ω. Note that each node of the output layer consists of only one pixel of H. In the network each node ℓ_i is connected to the reconstruction coefficient vector w_i, and w_i is further connected to those nodes (image pixels) in the ith site of H. The output layer itself is a fully-connected graph, i.e., a big clique.

With (5) and the Markov network described above, we are in a position to define the energy function F for the network by

$$F(W, H; L) = \sum_i \phi(\ell_i, w_i) + \lambda_1^2 \sum_i \sum_{j \in \text{site } i} \psi(w_i, H^j) + \lambda_2^2 \zeta(H), \tag{6}$$

where there are in turn three kinds of potential functions, namely ϕ, ψ, and ζ to be specified, $W = [w_1 \cdots w_n]$ is the coefficient matrix, λ_1 and λ_2 are parameters to weigh the contributions of the three terms, and H^j denotes the jth pixel of H. We next give the definitions for each of the three potential functions. To begin with, for each LR patch ℓ_i and the connected node w_i, the network is designed to maximize the joint probability of ℓ_i and w_i. Thus, from (5), we arrive at the following definition:

$$\phi(\ell_i, w_i) = \|\ell_i - P_i w_i\|^2. \tag{7}$$

Suppose H^j is the kth pixel on site i of H (i.e. h_i). Then the potential function ψ for w_i and H^j can be defined by

$$\psi(w_i, H^j) = \|e_k^T h_i - e_k^T Q_i w_i\|^2, \tag{8}$$

where e_k is the kth coordinate vector. Notice that, from (5), minimizing the summation $\sum_{j \in \text{site } i} \psi(w_i, H^j)$ is equivalent to maximizing the joint probability of h_i and w_i. Finally, the potential function ζ in (6) is to add appropriate image prior for super-resolution, and is defined on the big clique of the whole H:

$$\zeta(H) = \|SH\|^2, \tag{9}$$

where we shall discuss the matrix S later, and here we simply treat S as the zero matrix. With (7), (8), and (9) so defined, the energy function F in (6) is convex to w_i and H. Hence the super-resolution output H^* by the Markov network can be achieved by minimizing F with respect to w_i and H, respectively and iteratively. The proposed super-resolution algorithm is summarized in Algorithm 1. (Notice that the computation of H described in line 5 of Algorithm 1 is for the convenience of presentation. Owing to the structure of the Markov network, we can indeed compute H pixelwise for a more efficient implementation.)

Algorithm 1. Direct Energy Minimization for Super-Resolution

   Input   : An inpute LR image L, and a training set Ω.
   Output: An HR image H^*.

1 Split L into n overlapping LR image patches, $\{\ell_i\}_{i=1}^n$.
2 For each ℓ_i, find its K nearest LR neighbors in Ω, and form P_i as in (5).
3 For each P_i, take the corresponding K HR patches in Ω to form Q_i as in (5).
4 For each i, compute the initial w_i based on P_i and ℓ_i.
  Repeat
5 | For each i, compute h_i from (5), given w_i and Q_i.
6 | For each i, compute w_i from (5), given ℓ_i, h_i, P_i, and Q_i.
  Until *Convergence*

4.1 Bound the Reconstruction Error

Besides being convex for the ease of optimization, the energy function F defined in (6) can be shown to be an upper bound of the reconstruction error yielded by our algorithm. That is, since our approach is to minimize F, a resulting super-resolution result H^* by Algorithm 1 would have a small reconstruction error (bounded by the minimal energy F^*). Thus the proposed direct energy minimization method not only possesses the convenience for not constructing the manifolds explicitly but also produces stable super-resolution results.

With (2) and a given LR image L, the reconstruction error of H^* derived by Algorithm 1 can be expressed in the following matrix form

$$\|DBH^* - L\|^2, \tag{10}$$

where B is a symmetric blur matrix and D is the downsampling matrix. We now explain why the reconstruction error in (10) will be lower than F in (6). Let B' and D' be the corresponding blur and downsampling matrices on the HR patches. It can be shown that there exists a (mask) matrix M to extract a central region within an LR patch such that $M\ell_j = MD'B'h_j$ for any pair of patches ℓ_j and h_j in Ω. We split the input L into overlapping $\{\ell_i\}_{i=1}^n$. For each ℓ_i we define M_i to select pixels from the central region defined by M such that L is a disjoint union of $\{\tilde{\ell}_i = M_i\ell_i\}_{i=1}^n$. The above procedure can be accomplished by splitting L into denser overlapping patches, or by adjusting M_i for each site i. The reconstruction error in (10) can then be rewritten as

$$\sum_i \|M_iD'B'h_i^* - M_i\ell_i\|^2 = \sum_i \|M_iD'B'(Q_iw_i + \delta_i) - M_i(P_iw_i + \epsilon_i)\|^2$$

$$= \sum_i \|M_iD'B'\delta_i - M_i\epsilon_i\|^2 \leq \sum_i (\|D'B'\delta_i\|^2 + \|\epsilon_i\|^2)$$

$$\leq \sum_i (\lambda_1^2\|\delta_i\|^2 + \|\epsilon_i\|^2) \leq F \tag{11}$$

The only restriction for (11) to be valid is that λ_1 should be larger than the downsampling ratio. One can see that F is not a tight bound for the reconstruction error. So in some cases the resulting reconstruction errors by our method are higher than those induced by the IBP. However, in our experiments the proposed algorithm often gives satisfactory results and lower reconstruction errors in fewer iteration steps than those required by IBP. (See Figure 2b.)

4.2   The Partial Gestalt Prior

We now discuss the use of prior information for super-resolution. Indeed those HR patches in the training set Ω can be considered as some kind of prior. However, due to the computation complexity, most super-resolution methods, including ours, can manage only small patches. Otherwise, the variances of image patches would cause Ω to grow into an infeasible size. Due to such limitation, there are some features of large scale as well as high frequencies cannot be recovered by techniques that work on small patches. One example can be seen in Figure 2c. To account for such artifacts, we adopt the concept of **Gestalt** [2], [4]. The Gestalt theory contains many rules to describe human visual perceptions, including symmetry, closeness, and good continuation, to name a few. In this

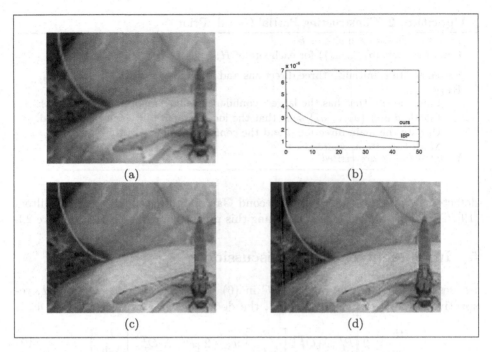

Fig. 2. Dragonfly. (a) The original low-resolution image. (b) Reconstruction errors of IBP and ours. (c) Our approach with $S = 0$. (d) Our approach with Gestalt prior.

work we adopt only the *good continuation* as the large-scale prior information for super-resolution in that properties such as symmetry are often well preserved in LR images, and can be recovered even by simple magnifying schemes.

One way to keep good continuation is to make H smoother along edges and ridges. Thus we choose to define the matrix S in (9) to be the directional derivative operator pixelwise according to the main (edge) direction multiplied by the confidence. More precisely, at pixel j, large confidence c_j means a high probability of having an edge around j in the main direction d_j. We model this claim as an attributed graph that is similar to a Gestalt field [9]. (A Gestalt field is actually a specific mixed Markov model [8] where each address node is connected to only one regular node.) In the generated attributed graph $G = (V, E)$, each node v represents a site on the desired H and has attributes $(d, c, \{a_1, ..., a_4\})$. The attributes d and c mean the main edge direction and the confidence of the patch, respectively. The attributes $\{a_1, ..., a_4\}$ are address variables whose values are neighbors of v (if an edge goes through them) or *nil*. Intuitively, d and c should be compatible with the neighbors of v in Ω as well as the neighbors indicated by $\{a_1, ..., a_4\}$ in the graph. We can therefore define two compatible functions. Like Guo et al. [9], we propose a greedy method to decide $(d, c, \{a_1, ..., a_4\})$. (See Algorithm 2.) However, we discrete the direction into 16 values, and specify the marching order to be the same as the decreasing order of confidence values. In Algorithm 2, the main directions and confidences of sampled HR patches are

---

Algorithm 2. Constructing Partial Gestalt Prior

Input : Q_i for each site of H.
Output: $(d, c, \{a_1, ..., a_4\})$ for each site of H.

For each site i, initialize three directions and a confidence c by referencing Q_i.
Repeat
    Find the site that has the largest confidence value c among unvisited sites.
    Decide d and $\{a_1, ..., a_4\}$ such that the local compatibility can be achieved.
    Update the main direction d and the confidence value c of this site.
    Mark this site as visited.
Until *All sites are visited*

---

detected by a set of the first and second Gaussian directional-derivative filters [19]. The improvement owing to adding this prior term can be seen in Figure 2d.

5   Implementation and Discussions

As described before, we optimize F in (6) with respect to w_i and to H, respectively and iteratively. Given H, the derivative of F with respect to w_i is

$$\frac{\partial F}{\partial w_i} = 2 \left[P_i^T, \lambda_1 Q_i^T \right] \begin{bmatrix} P_i \\ \lambda_1 Q_i \end{bmatrix} w_i - 2 \left[P_i^T, \lambda_1 Q_i^T \right] \begin{bmatrix} l_i \\ \lambda_1 h_i \end{bmatrix}. \tag{12}$$

Hence the optimization with respect to w_i can be achieved directly. Given w_i, the derivative of F with respect to H is

$$\frac{\partial F}{\partial H} = \lambda_1^2 [V_1, ..., V_{\chi_H}]^T + 2\lambda_2^2 S^T S H, \tag{13}$$

where

$$V_j = \sum_{i \in C_j} (-2 e_{g(j,i)}^T Q_i w_i + 2 H^j), \text{ for } j = 1, \ldots, \chi_H, \tag{14}$$

C_j means the set of sites that cover jth pixel of H, and $g(j, i)$ indicates the order of the jth pixel of H in site i. If S is the zero matrix or $\lambda_2 = 0$, optimizing F according to H can also be done in one step. Otherwise, $S^T S$ is a very large matrix and may be singular. In this case we implement a conjugate gradient algorithm as suggested in [21].

5.1   Experimental Results

Due to the fact that humans are more sensitive to changes in luminance channel, we only test our method on the luminance channel, and magnify the color channel to the desired size through bicubic interpolation. Thus, after being preserved only the luminance channel, the training images are blurred with a 5-by-5 Gaussian kernel, and then downsampled into one third of the original sizes. In all our experiments the LR patches are of size 4-by-4 and the HR patches are of size 8-by-8. The parameter λ_1 is set to be $\sqrt{(4 \times 4)/(8 \times 8)}$ to balance errors induced

(a)   (b)

Fig. 3. The two training sets used for the results reported in this work

by (7) and (8). The other parameter λ_2 is set as a relatively smaller number, $0.2\lambda_1$, because we believe that the information from the training set is more important. We have run our algorithm over two classes of images. To enrich the training set we shift the training images by 0 to 2 pixels in each direction before the training set generating process, and produce nine times more patch pairs. The experimental results can be seen in Figures 2 and 4. In each case we set K (the number of neighbors) to be 20, and carry out the algorithm for 30 iterations. For comparison, we also include the results by IBP and by Chang et al. [3] in Figure 4. Overall, the super-resolution results by our method are of satisfactory quality.

5.2   Discussions

We have proposed a new model for the single image super-resolution problem. Our approach is motivated by the manifold property of LR and HR image patches, and is fortified by the use of a three-layer Markov network. Through the proposed framework, we can directly use the information from the training data, and suppress the reconstruction error in the same time. The method thus has the advantages of both recognition-based and reconstruction-based approaches. Unlike [19], our direct energy minimization formulation guarantees reasonable reconstruction errors so there is no need to worry about that the learned information may be destroyed by depressing the reconstruction error. When compared with [15], the convex energy function, defined in (6), for the Markov network ensures better convergency property. The related work by Chang et al. [3] also starts at the manifold assumption. Suppose we use the same features to measure the distances between image patches. Then the super-resolution algorithm of [3] in fact does similar effects as those produced by our algorithm at the first iteration without using additional image prior.

A direct generalization of our method could be dealing with only primal sketch patches [19]. Furthermore, since we update the high-resolution image pixelwise,

(a)   (e)

(b)   (f)

(c)   (g)

(d)   (h)

Fig. 4. From top to bottom of both columns: the low-resolution images, the results by IBP, the results by Chang et al. [3], and the results by our method

the proposed approach can be more easily extended to handle multiple image super-resolution than other recognition-based methods.

Acknowledgements

This work is supported in part by grants NSC 94-2213-E-001-020 and 94-EC-17-A-02-S1-032.

References

1. S. Baker and T. Kanade, "Limits on Super-Resolution and How to Break Them," *IEEE Trans. Pattern Analysis and Machine Intelligence*, vol. 24, no. 9, pp. 1167–1183, September 2002.
2. F. Cao, "Good Continuations in Digital Image Level Lines," *International Conference on Computer Vision*, pp. 440–447, 2003.
3. H. Chang, D.Y. Yeung, and Y. Xiong, "Super-Resolution through Neighbor Embedding," *Proc. IEEE Conf. Computer Vision and Pattern Recognition*, pp. I: 275–282, 2004.
4. A. Desolneux, L. Moisan, and J. Morel, "Partial Gestalts," Tech. Rep., CMLA, 2001.
5. M. Elad and A. Feuer, "Restoration of a Single Superresolution Image from Several Blurred, Noisy, and Undersampled Measured Images," *IEEE Trans. Image Processing*, vol. 6, no. 12, pp. 1646–1658, December 1997.
6. S. Farsiu, M.D. Robinson, M. Elad, and P. Milanfar, "Fast and Robust Multiframe Super Resolution," *IEEE Trans. Image Processing*, vol. 13, no. 10, pp. 1327–1344, October 2004.
7. W. T. Freeman, T. R. Jones, and E. C. Pasztor, "Example-based super-resolution," *IEEE Computer Graphics and Applications*, vol. 22, no. 2, pp. 56–65, 2002.
8. A. Fridman, *Mixed Markov Models*, Ph.D. thesis, Department of Mathematics, Brown University, 2000.
9. C.E. Guo, S.C. Zhu, and Y.N. Wu, "Towards a Mathematical Theory of Primal Sketch and Sketchability," *International Conference on Computer Vision*, pp. 1228–1235, 2003.
10. R.C. Hardie, K.J. Barnard, and E.E. Armstrong, "Joint MAP Registration and High Resolution Image Estimation Using a Sequence of Undersampled Images," *IEEE Trans. Image Processing*, vol. 6, no. 12, pp. 1621–1633, December 1997.
11. A. Hertzmann, C. E. Jacobs, N. Oliver, B. Curless, and D.H. Salesin, "Image Analogies," *Proc. of ACM SIGGRAPH'01*, pp. 327–340, 2001.
12. T. S. Huang and R. Y. Tsai, "Multi-Frame Image Restoration and Registration," *Advances in Computer Vision and Image Processing*, vol. 1, pp. 317–339, 1984.
13. M. Irani and S. Peleg, "Improving Resolution by Image Registration," *GMIP*, vol. 53, pp. 231–239, 1991.
14. A.B. Lee, K.S. Pedersen, and D. Mumford, "The Nonlinear Statistics of High-Contrast Patches in Natural Images," *Int'l J. Computer Vision*, vol. 54, no. 1-3, pp. 83–103, August 2003.
15. L. C. Pickup, S. J. Roberts, and A. Zisserman, "A Sampled Texture Prior for Image Super-Resolution," *Advances in Neural Information Processing Systems 16*, 2004.

16. S.T. Roweis and L.K. Saul, "Nonlinear Dimensionality Reduction by Locally Linear Embedding," *Science*, vol. 290, pp. 2323–2326, 2000.
17. R.R. Schultz and R.L. Stevenson, "Extraction of High-Resolution Frames from Video Sequences," *IEEE Trans. Image Processing*, vol. 5, no. 6, pp. 996–1011, June 1996.
18. H. Stark and P. Oskoui, "High Resolution Image Recovery form Image-Plane Arrays, Using Convex Projections," *J. Opt. Soc. Am. A*, vol. 6, pp. 1715–1726, 1989.
19. J. Sun, N.N. Zheng, H. Tao, and H.Y. Shum, "Image Hallucination with Primal Sketch Priors," *Proc. IEEE Conf. Computer Vision and Pattern Recognition*, pp. II: 729–736, 2003.
20. D. C. Youla, "Generalized Image Restoration by the Method of Alternating Projections," *IEEE Trans. Circuits Syst.*, vol. CAS-25, pp. 694–702, 1978.
21. A. Zomet and S. Peleg, "Efficient Super-Resolution and Applications to Mosaics," *International Conference on Pattern Recognition*, pp. Vol I: 579–583, 2000.

Wavelet-Based Super-Resolution Reconstruction: Theory and Algorithm

Hui Ji and Cornelia Fermüller

Center for Automation Research, Department of Computer Science,
University of Maryland, College Park
{jihui, fer}@cfar.umd.edu

Abstract. We present a theoretical analysis and a new algorithm for the problem of super-resolution imaging: the reconstruction of HR (high-resolution) images from a sequence of LR (low-resolution) images. Super-resolution imaging entails solutions to two problems. One is the alignment of image frames. The other is the reconstruction of a HR image from multiple aligned LR images. Our analysis of the latter problem reveals insights into the theoretical limits of super-resolution reconstruction. We find that at best we can reconstruct a HR image blurred by a specific low-pass filter. Based on the analysis we present a new wavelet-based iterative reconstruction algorithm which is very robust to noise. Furthermore, it has a computationally efficient built-in denoising scheme with a nearly optimal risk bound. Roughly speaking, our method could be described as a better-conditioned iterative back-projection scheme with a fast and optimal regularization criteria in each iteration step. Experiments with both simulated and real data demonstrate that our approach has significantly better performance than existing super-resolution methods. It has the ability to remove even large amounts of mixed noise without creating smoothing artifacts.

1 Introduction

The problem of obtaining a *super-resolution* image from a sequence of low-resolution images has been studied by many researchers in recent years. Most super-resolution algorithms formulate the problem as a signal reconstruction problem. Essentially these algorithms differ in two aspects: one is in how the images of the sequence are aligned; the other is in how the high-resolution image is reconstructed from the aligned image frames. Both issues are critical for the success of the super-resolution reconstruction. In this paper we take a flow-based approach to image alignment ([1, 2, 3, 4]). The focus of the paper is on the later problem (Reconstructing HR from aligned LR images).

Iterative back-projection methods ([1, 5]) have been shown to be effective for high-resolution image reconstruction. It is known, however, that the deblurring process, which is part of this approach, makes it very sensitive to the noise. Thus, the requirement of very accurate image alignment estimates limits its practical use. Various regularization methods have been proposed to deal with the noise issue. However, these methods either are very sensitive to the assumed

A. Leonardis, H. Bischof, and A. Pinz (Eds.): ECCV 2006, Part IV, LNCS 3954, pp. 295–307, 2006.
© Springer-Verlag Berlin Heidelberg 2006

noise model (Tikhonov regularization) or are computationally expensive (Total-Variation regularization). See [6] for more details.

Our contributions in this paper are two-fold. First, we model the image formation procedure from the point of view of filter bank theory. Then based on this new formulation, we provide an analysis of the limits of the high-resolution reconstruction. The conclusion is that in general full recovery is not possible without enforcing some constraints on the recovered images. At best we could reconstruct the image convolved with a specific low-pass filter (namely $\frac{1}{4}(1,1) \otimes (1,1)$ for the case of the Box-type PSF).

Second, based on our new formulation, we present a robust wavelet-based algorithm to reconstruct the image. The iteration scheme in our algorithm is inherently more robust to noise than that of classic back-projection methods ([1,5]), since the projection matrix of our new back-projection scheme has a better condition number. We will show that, both in theory and experiments, it has better performance in suppressing the error propagation than other back-projection iteration schemes.

Furthermore, our algorithm allows us to include a wavelet-based denoising scheme in each iteration of the reconstruction which effectively removes the noise without creating smoothing artifacts. The advantage of our denoising scheme over regularization methods is that it is nearly optimal with respect to the risk bound. That is, it has the theoretical minimal error in removing noises of unknown models. Its effectiveness in removing mixed noises and relatively large amounts of noise is demonstrated in experiments. It is worth mentioning that our denoising scheme adds very little computational burden compared to other complicated regularization methods. Briefly, our method could be described as a generalized iterative back-projection method with a fast and optimal regularization criteria in each iteration step.

Wavelet theory has previously been used for image denoising and deblurring from static images ([7,9]). However, it has not been studied much with respect to the super-resolution problem. In recent work wavelet theory has been applied to this problem in this sector i [10], but only for the purpose of speeding up the computation. Our contribution lies in an analysis that reveals the relationship between the inherent structure of super-resolution reconstruction and the theory of wavelet filter banks. This relationship is fully exploited by using various techniques from wavelet theory in the iterations of the reconstruction.

2   Analysis of Super-Resolution Reconstruction

2.1   Formulation of High-to-Low Image Formation

We first formulate the high-to-low image formation process. To simplify the exposition, in the following we only discuss 1D signals with resolution enhancement by a factor 2. Later, without much difficulty, the analysis will be extended to the 2D case with arbitrary resolution increase. Using Farsiu's notation ([6]), the image formation process in the pixel domain can be modeled as

$$y = \sigma[H * X(F(t))] + N, \tag{1}$$

where t is the spatial variable, $X(t)$ is the continuous signal and y is the discrete signal. H is the blurring operator (either optical blurring or motion blurring or both), F is the geometric transform, N is the noise in the low-resolution image, σ is the decimation operator, and "$*$" is the convolution operator. Not considering the noise, the high-resolution (HR) signal x and low-resolution (LR) signal y can be defined as:

$$x = \sigma[X], \quad y = [\sigma[H * X(F(\cdot))]] \downarrow_2. \tag{2}$$

where $\downarrow_2$ is the downsampling operator with rate 2.

Next we derive the relation between the LR signal y and the HR signal x. Define the difference $E(t) = X(F(t)) - X(t)$, which is also called the *optical flow*. For the simplicity of notation, here we assume a constant flow model $E(t) = \epsilon$ with $0 \le \epsilon < 2$ on the denser grid of the HR image x. Thus, in the LR image the flow is a sub-pixel shift (Recall a 1-unit shift on the coarse grid of y equals a 2-unit shift on the fine grid of x). For the case of $0 \le \epsilon < 1$, the first-order Taylor approximation of Equation (2) can be written as

$$\begin{aligned}
y &= [\sigma[H * (X(t + \epsilon))]] \downarrow_2 = [\sigma[H * X + H * (\epsilon X')]] \downarrow_2 \\
&= [\sigma[H * X + \epsilon(H * X')]] \downarrow_2 = [\sigma[H * X + \epsilon(H' * X)]] \downarrow_2 \\
&= [\sigma[H * X]] \downarrow_2 + \epsilon[\sigma[H' * X]] \downarrow_2,
\end{aligned}$$

The expression above in the pixel domain is then

$$y = [a * x] \downarrow_2 + \epsilon[b * x] \downarrow_2, \tag{3}$$

where a, b are discrete versions of the convolution kernels H and H' respectively. For the case of $1 \le \epsilon < 2$, a similar argument yields

$$y = [a * x(\cdot + 1)] \downarrow_2 + (\epsilon - 1)[b * x(\cdot + 1)] \downarrow_2. \tag{4}$$

Thus for any LR signal y_k with general optical flow $E_k(t)$, we have the approximation of y_k as either in the form of:

$$y_k = [a * x] \downarrow_2 + \epsilon_k \cdot *[b * x] \downarrow_2$$

or in the form of:

$$y_k = [a * x(\cdot + 1)] \downarrow_2 + (\epsilon_k - 1) \cdot *[b * x(\cdot + 1)] \downarrow_2,$$

where $\cdot *$ denotes the component-wise multiplication operator (to denote general optic flow), and ϵ_k denotes the discrete sample of the optical flow $E_k(t)$. Having available the optical flow values ϵ_k for multiple low-resolution images y_k, we can extract the four components:

$$\begin{aligned}
&[a * x] \downarrow_2, \quad [a * x(\cdot + 1)] \downarrow_2 \\
&[b * x] \downarrow_2, \quad [b * x(\cdot + 1)] \downarrow_2.
\end{aligned} \tag{5}$$

As will be shown in the next subsection, the two filters a and b (which are determined by the blurring kernel H and its derivative H') characterize the super-resolution reconstruction.

Let us next look at some examples of filters a and b for different blurring kernels.

Example 1. Consider the box-type blurring kernel $H = \frac{1}{2n}\chi_{[-n,n]}$. Let $E(t) = \epsilon \leq 1$. Then we have

$$y(j) = \int_{-\infty}^{\infty} \chi(2j - t)X(F(t))dt = \frac{1}{2n}\int_{2j-n}^{2j+n} X(F(t))dt = \frac{1}{2n}\int_{2j-n}^{2j+n} X(t+\epsilon)dt.$$

Approximating the integration by quadrature rules, we obtain

$$y(j) = \frac{1}{2n}\left(\frac{1}{2}(1-\epsilon)x(2j-n) + \sum_{i=-n+1}^{n-1} x(2j-i) + \frac{1}{2}(1+\epsilon)x(2j+n)\right).$$

Or equivalently,

$$y = [a * x + \epsilon(b * x)] \downarrow_2, \tag{6}$$

where a and b are the following low-pass and high-pass filters respectively:

$$a = \frac{1}{4n}(1, 2, \cdots, 2, 1), \quad b = \frac{1}{4n}(-1, 0, \cdots, 0, 1).$$

Example 2. Consider a Gaussian-type blurring kernel H. Using the Cubic Cardinal B-spline $B(t)$ as approximation to the Gaussian function we have

$$y(j) = \int_{-\infty}^{\infty} B(2j - t)X(F(t))dt.$$

Again, by the quadrature rule, we have the approximation

$$y = \sum_i x(2j - i)(a(i) - \epsilon b(i)),$$

where $a = \frac{1}{96}(1, 8, 23, 32, 23, 8, 1)$, $b = \frac{1}{48}(3, 12, 15, 0, -15, -12, -3)$.

2.2   Analysis of the HR Reconstruction

Given multiple LR signals y_k with different motions ϵ_k, theoretically we can obtain two complete sequences $a * x$ and $b * x$. An interesting question arises. Without any assumption on the finite signal x, can we theoretically reconstruct the signal sequence x from these two sequences $a * x$ and $b * x$?

To answer this question, let us express the sequences in another form. Let us write the Z-transform of a signal sequence $x = \{x(i)\}$ as

$$x(z) = \sum_i x(i)z^{-i}.$$

Then with $a(z)$ and $b(z)$ being the Z-transforms of the filters a and b, the Z-transforms of $a * x$ and $b * x$ are $a(z)x(z)$ and $b(z)x(z)$ respectively. Now the question can be answered by investigating whether the polynomial equation

$$(a(z)x(z))u(z) + (b(z)x(z))v(z) = x(z), \tag{7}$$

is solvable for the two unknowns $u(z)$ and $v(z)$. Eliminating $x(z)$ from both sides of the equation (7) yields

$$a(z)u(z) + b(z)v(z) = 1. \tag{8}$$

From the theory of Diophantine equation we know that

Lemma 1. *Given two polynomials $a(z)$ and $b(z)$, Equation (8) is solvable if and only if the greatest common divisor of $a(z)$ and $b(z)$ is a scalar, that is, $a(z)$ and $b(z)$ are co-prime.*

It is observed that $a(z)$ and $b(z)$ in our two examples (Example 1 and 2): both have a common divisor

$$c(z) = (1 + z),$$

which can be seen from the fact that $a(-1) = b(-1) = 0$ and thus $z = -1$ is the root of both $a(z)$ and $b(z)$. Thus for these blurring kernels we cannot perfectly reconstruct $x(z)$ from $a(z)x(z)$ and $b(z)x(z)$. This conclusion holds true not only for our examples, but also for general blurring kernels, as we will show next.

We follow Baker's modeling of the blurring kernel H ([11]). The blurring kernel (Point spread function) is decomposed into two components:

$$H = \Omega * C,$$

where $\Omega(X)$ models the blurring caused by the optics and $C(X)$ models the spatial integration performed by the CCD sensor. Typically Ω is modeled by a Gaussian-type function and C is modeled by a Box-type function. Notice that

$$H' = \Omega' * C.$$

Thus we can express the corresponding discrete filters as:

$$a = \ell * c; \quad b = \tau * c,$$

where c is the discrete version of the spatial integration kernel C, and ℓ and τ are the discrete versions of H and H'. Since $a(z)$ and $b(z)$ have a common divisor $c(z)$, we cannot reconstruct $x(z)$ for general $x(z)$, unless C is a Dirac function, which generally is not true. Based on Lemma 1, we then have the following claim.

Claim 1. *Given multiple LR finite signals y_k, we can not perfectly reconstruct the HR finite signal x without any assumptions on x. At most we can reconstruct $c * x$ for some low-pass filter c. The corresponding Z-transform $c(z)$ of c is the greatest common divisor of $a(z)$ and $b(z)$, which includes the spatial integration filter.*

Notice that c is a low-pass FIR (finite impulse response) filter. To recover x from $c * x$, we have to apply a high-pass filter on $c * x$ and impose some boundary condition on the signal x. Such a deblurring process generally is sensitive to the noise. A reasonable strategy then is to modify our reconstruction goal during the intermediate iterative reconstruction process. Instead of trying to reconstruct x, we reconstruct $c * x$ in the iterative process, and we leave the recovery of x from $c * x$ to the last step after finishing the iterative reconstruction.

Thus the modified HR signal to be reconstructed becomes $\tilde{x} = c * x$. The corresponding equation for y_k and $\tilde{x}$ is then:

$$y_k = [\ell * \tilde{x}] \downarrow_2 + \epsilon_k \cdot [\tau * \tilde{x}] \downarrow_2 \tag{9}$$

or

$$y_k = [\ell * \tilde{x}(\cdot + 1)] \downarrow_2 + (\epsilon_k - 1) \cdot [\tau * \tilde{x}(\cdot + 1)] \downarrow_2,$$

where the Z-transform of ℓ and τ are $a(z)$ and $b(z)$ divided by their greatest common divisor $c(z)$.

It is worth mentioning that we model the blurring procedure from HR to LR by a first-order Taylor approximation. But our reasoning could easily be extended to the modeling by higher-order Taylor approximations, leading to the same conclusions.

3   Reconstruction Method

3.1   Reconstruction Based on PR Filter Banks

Introduction to PR filter banks. Before presenting our algorithm, we first give a brief introduction to 2-channel PR (*perfect reconstruction*) filter banks (see [12] for more details). A two-channel filter bank consists of two parts: an analysis filter bank and a synthesis filter bank. In our case, the signal $\tilde{x}$ is first convolved with a low-pass filter ℓ and a high-pass filter h and then subsampled by 2. In other words, we analyze the signal by an analysis filter bank. Then a reconstructed signal $\hat{x}$ is obtained by upsampling the signal by zero interpolation and then filtering it with a dual low-pass filter g and a dual high-pass filter q. In other words, we reconstruct the signal by synthesizing the output from the analysis bank with a synthesis filter bank. See Fig. 1 for an illustration.

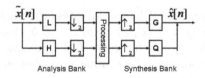

Fig. 1. Two-channel filter bank

Such a filter bank is called a PR filter bank if $\hat{x} = \tilde{x}$ for any input $\tilde{x}$. It is known that (see [12]) the synthesis filters $\{\ell, h\}$ of a perfect reconstruction filter bank have to satisfy the following condition:

$$\ell(z)h(-z) - \ell(-z)h(z) = z^m \text{ for some integer } m \tag{10}$$

and the corresponding synthesis filters amount to

$$g(z) = h(-z); \quad q(z) = -(\ell(-z)).$$

Thus, given any low-pass filter $\ell(z)$, we can find the corresponding high-pass filter $h(z)$ such that we have a PR filter by solving the linear system (10).

Iterative reconstruction scheme. We have available a number of signals y_k and the corresponding estimates of the optic flow values ϵ_k. We also have estimates of the convolution kernels ℓ and τ. Let then ℓ be the low pass filter of our PR filter bank, and we compute the corresponding h (Note h may be different from τ).

Recall that for each LR signal y_k, we have

$$y_k = [\ell * \widetilde{x}] \downarrow_2 + \epsilon_k \cdot *[\tau * \widetilde{x}] \downarrow_2 .$$

Thus $[\ell * \widetilde{x}] \downarrow_2$ amounts to

$$[\ell * \widetilde{x}] \downarrow_2 = y_k - \epsilon_k \cdot *[\tau * \widetilde{x}] \downarrow_2 . \tag{11}$$

Notice that the process of a signal $\widetilde{x}$ passing through a PR filter bank as shown in Fig. 1 can be expressed as:

$$\widetilde{x} = g * [(\ell * \widetilde{x}) \downarrow_2] \uparrow_2 + q * [(h * \widetilde{x}) \downarrow_2] \uparrow_2 . \tag{12}$$

Combining Equation (11) and (12), we obtain the iterative reconstruction of $\widetilde{x}$ from K LR signals y_k as follows: At step $n+1$

$$\widetilde{x}^{n+1} = q * [(h * \widetilde{x}^n) \downarrow_2] \uparrow_2 + g * \left(\frac{1}{K} \sum_{k=1}^{K} [y_k - \epsilon_k \cdot *(\tau * \widetilde{x}^n) \downarrow_2] \uparrow_2 \right). \tag{13}$$

Relation to other back-projection methods. Applying Equation (12), we can rewrite Equation (13) in the form

$$\widetilde{x}^{n+1} = (\widetilde{x}^n - g * [\ell * (\widetilde{x}^n) \downarrow_2] \uparrow_2 + g * \left(\frac{1}{K} \sum_{k=1}^{K} [y_k - \epsilon_k \cdot *(\tau * \widetilde{x}^n) \downarrow_2] \uparrow_2 \right)$$

$$= \widetilde{x}^n + g * \left(\frac{1}{K} \sum_{k=1}^{K} [y_k - (\ell * \widetilde{x}^n + \epsilon_k \cdot *(\tau * \widetilde{x}^n)) \downarrow_2] \uparrow_2 \right).$$

It can be seen that the iteration scheme presented here falls in the class of back-projection methods. But it has advantages over the usual back-projection iterations. Consider the well-known method by Irani and Peleg [1]. Its iteration can be described as:

$$x^{n+1} = x^n + \frac{1}{K} \sum_{k=1}^{K} T_k^{-1} \left(((y_k - [\ell * T_k(x^n)] \downarrow_2) \uparrow_2) * p \right), \tag{14}$$

where T_k is the geometric transform between y_k and $\widetilde{x}$, and the high-pass filter p is the deblurring kernel. Notice that the two methods differ in the deblurring kernel: one is g with $g(z) = h(-z)$ defined in Equation (10); the other is p in Equation (14), the approximate inverse filter of ℓ.

The requirement on p in (14) is

$$||\delta - \ell * p|| < 1, \qquad (15)$$

where δ is the ideal unit impulse response filter. In other words, p should be a good approximation for the inverse of ℓ. In comparison, g in our iteration only needs to satisfy:

$$\ell(z)g(-z) - \ell(-z)g(z) = z^m, \qquad (16)$$

that is, $\ell(z)g(-z)$ either has to have no odd-order components or no even-order components. Briefly, Iteration (14) requires a deblurring kernel p such that $\ell * p$ has small coefficients everywhere but the origin. In comparison, Iteration (13) only requires a kernel g with half the coefficients of $\ell * g$ being zero.

It is easy to see that the noise will be propagated exponentially as $O(\|p\|^n)$ in (14) and as $O(\|g\|^n)$ in (13). Generally the flexibility of $g(z)$ makes it possible to design a g that has much smaller norm than p. This leads to much better resistance to noise propagation. Here is an example: Consider $\ell = \frac{1}{4}(1,2,1)$. Then

$$g = (-1/8, -1/4, 3/4, -1/4, -1/8)$$

is a dual PR filter for ℓ with

$$\ell(z)g(-z) = -1 + 9z^{-2} + 16z^{-3} + 9z^{-4} - z^{-6}.$$

It is easy to check that $\|g\|_2$ is around 0.85. The minimum for the norm of all filters with the same length as g is around 1.1. The corresponding p is

$$p = (\frac{1}{2}, -\frac{2}{3}, \frac{4}{3}, -\frac{2}{3}, \frac{1}{2}).$$

This clearly indicates that our iteration scheme is more robust to noise than the usual back-projection scheme.

3.2   Algorithm on 2D Images with Denoising

Next we generalize the algorithm to 2D images. Furthermore we introduce a denoising process during the iterative reconstruction to suppress the noise in the optical flow estimation.

Extension to 2D image. All the previous analysis can be generalized using the tensor product. By an argument similar as for the 1D case, we approximate the LR image I^{LR} with the HR image I^{HR} as follows:

$$I^{LR} = [(a \otimes a) * I^{HR} + u \cdot *((a \otimes b) * I^{HR}) + v \cdot *((b \otimes a) * I^{HR})] \downarrow 2,$$

where "$\otimes$" is the Kronecker tensor product and (u, v) is the 2D optical flow vector. Then the 2D analysis bank is

Low-pass filter: $L = \ell \otimes \ell,$
High-pass filters: $H_1 = \ell \otimes h, H_2 = h \otimes \ell, H_3 = h \otimes h$

and the 2D synthesis filter bank is

Low-pass filter: $G = g \otimes g$,
High-pass filters: $G_1 = g \otimes q, G_2 = q \otimes g, G_3 = q \otimes q$.

It is easy to verify that the 2D filter bank defined above is a perfect reconstruction filter bank with the analysis filter bank $\{L, H_i\}$ and the reconstruction filter bank $\{G, Q_i\}$. Then generalizing (13), the iterative equation for the reconstruction of the HR image $\widetilde{I}$ from LR images I_k^{LR} amounts to:

$$\widetilde{I}^{n+1} = \sum_{i=1}^{3} Q_i * [(H_i * \widetilde{I}^{(n)}) \downarrow_2] \uparrow_2$$
$$+ G * \frac{1}{K} \left(\sum_k^K [\widetilde{I}_k^{LR} - u \cdot *((\ell \otimes \tau) * \widetilde{I}^n) \downarrow_2 - v \cdot *((\tau \otimes \ell) * \widetilde{I}^{(n)}) \downarrow_2] \uparrow_2 \right)$$

Recall that here $\widetilde{I}$ is the blurred version of the true I with $\widetilde{I} = (c \otimes c) * I$.

Modified algorithm with denoising process. There always is noise in the estimated flow u, v. However, the deconvolution operator could make the HR image reconstruction very sensitive to such noise. It is known that the noise variance of the solution will have hyperbolic growth when the blurring low-pass filter has zeros in the high frequencies. Thus, denoising is necessary in order to suppress the error propagation during the iterative reconstruction.

To suppress the noise, we introduce a wavelet denoising scheme which subtracts some high-frequency components from $\widetilde{I}^n$. Briefly, we first do a wavelet decomposition of the high-pass response, then apply a shrinkage of wavelet coefficients to the decomposition, and then reassemble the signal.

Our iteration scheme with built-in denoising operator amounts to

$$\widetilde{I}^{n+1} = \sum_{i=1}^{3} Q_i * [\Psi(H_i * \widetilde{I}^{(n)}) \downarrow_2] \uparrow_2$$
$$+ G * \frac{1}{K} \left(\sum_k^K [\widetilde{I}_k^{LR} - u \cdot *((\ell \otimes \tau) * \widetilde{I}^n) \downarrow_2 - v \cdot *((\tau \otimes \ell) * I^{(n)}) \downarrow_2] \uparrow_2 \right).$$

The denoising operator Ψ defined in the equation above is

$$\Psi(H_i * \widetilde{I}^n) = G * [(L * (H_i * \widetilde{I}^n)) \downarrow_2] \uparrow_2 + \sum_{i=1}^{3} [Q_i * (\Gamma[H_i * (H_i * \widetilde{I}^n)]) \downarrow_2] \uparrow_2,$$

where Γ is the thresholding operator. Here we use the following soft-denoising scheme ([12]):

$$\Gamma(\nu) = \begin{cases} Sign(\nu)(\nu - \mu) & \text{if } |\nu| > \mu \\ 0 & \text{Otherwise.} \end{cases}$$

Briefly the process of super-resolution is:

1. Compute the affine flow between every frame and the key frame.
2. Transform the affine flow to sub-pixel shifts on the finer grid of the HR image.
3. Apply the iteration process described above to the key frame to obtain the HR image.

The algorithm above could easily be adapted to different blur filters by modifying the corresponding dual filters G, Q_i. Also, here we only consider a resolution increase by a factor 2. Any other resolution increase could easily be achieved by changing the two-channel PR filter bank to an M-channel PR filter bank.

Relation to regularization methods. One popular denoising technique used for robust reconstruction is regularization ([13]). Recall that back-projection methods basically find $\tilde{x}$ by minimizing $\sum_k^K \|y_k - \tilde{y}_k(\tilde{x})\|_2^2$, where $\tilde{y}_k(\tilde{x})$ is the LR signals derived from our estimated $\tilde{x}$. Such a least square problem usually is ill-conditioned. One way to increase the stability is to enforce a regularization term and solve:

$$\min_{\tilde{x}} \sum_k^K \|y_k - \tilde{y}_k(\tilde{x})\|_2^2 + \alpha \|\Phi(\tilde{x})\|,$$

where Φ is some regularization function and α is some pre-defined smoothing factor. If the regularization is a least squares problem, we call it a Tikhonov-type regularization. The advantage is its simplicity and efficiency, the disadvantage is its relatively poor performance. A nonlinear diffusion regularization, like Total Variation regularization usually performs better, but is computational expensive.

Wavelet denoising is closely related to nonlinear diffusion regularization. [14] shows that a simple soft-denoising with Haar wavelets ($\ell = \frac{1}{2}(1,1), h = \frac{1}{2}(1,-1)$) is equivalent to Total Variation based nonlinear diffusion ($\Phi(\tilde{x}) = \|\tilde{x}\|_1$) for a two-pixel signal. Roughly speaking, the wavelet denoising process in our reconstruction is comparable to some nonlinear diffusion regularization schemes in its ability to suppress the error propagation. However it doesn't have the computational burden of most nonlinear diffusion regularizations, since it only needs a linear wavelet decomposition over one level. In comparison nonlinear regularizations need to solve a nonlinear optimization.

4   Experiments and Conclusion

We compare our algorithm's high-resolution reconstruction to standard methods using both simulated and real data.

Simulated data. We simulated 4 low-resolution images (16×16) from a high resolution image by shifting, blurring and downsampling. The blurring filter is

$$\ell = \frac{1}{16} \begin{pmatrix} 1 & 2 & 1 \\ 2 & 4 & 2 \\ 1 & 2 & 1 \end{pmatrix}.$$

Noise of three types of sources was simulated:

1. Error in motion estimation. It is modeled by local Gaussian white noise with parameter σ. The local covariance matrix is made up by the magnitudes of the image gradients.
2. Noise in pixel formation. We added a Gaussian white noise with parameter γ to the pixel values.

3. Error in PSF modeling. We also checked how error in the PSF modeling influences the performance. The approximated PSF $\hat{\ell}$ used in the reconstruction was

$$\hat{\ell} = \frac{1}{16} \begin{pmatrix} 1 & 1 & 1 \\ 1 & 8 & 1 \\ 1 & 1 & 1 \end{pmatrix}.$$

We compared our wavelet-based method to the popular "POCS" backprojection method ([8]) enforced by Tikhonov regularization (See Fig. 2). It is possible that enforcing Total Variation regularization would give a bit better results. However, it requires solving a nonlinear minimization over each iterative step during the reconstruction, which is very computational expensive. In our implementation, the regularization term is the 2-norm of the Laplacian smoothness constraint with parameter $\alpha = 1$.

Fig. 3 demonstrates how well the wavelet-based method performs for various noise settings. Performance is measured by the SNR (Signal-to-Noise ratio) of the reconstructed image to the true image, which is defined as: $SNR = 20 \log_{10} \frac{\|x\|_2}{\|x - \hat{x}\|_2}$, where $\hat{x}$ is the estimation for the true image x. Fig. 3 clearly indicates the advantage of our wavelet-based method in suppressing the noise. Especially when noise is large, the boost in performance is significant.

Real data. We used an indoor sequence with a paper box (Fig. 4) of 13 image frames. An interesting planar region was chosen manually. Fig. 5 and Fig. 6

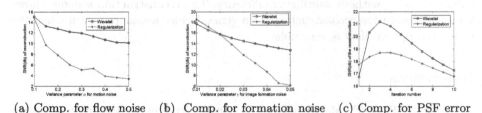

| (a) Original image | (b) Noisy LR image | (c) Wavelet | (d) Tikhonov |

Fig. 2. The HR images (c) and (d) are reconstructed from four LR images by five iterations. (c) is reconstructed by our method. (d) is reconstructed by POCS method with Tikhonov regularization. The motion noise is local Gaussian noise with $\sigma = 0.2$. The image formation noise is Gaussian noise with $\gamma = 0.01$. The approximation $\hat{\ell}$ is used in the reconstruction instead of the true PSF ℓ.

(a) Comp. for flow noise   (b) Comp. for formation noise   (c) Comp. for PSF error

Fig. 3. (a) and (b) Compare two methods for various amounts of motion noise and image formation noise. The reconstructed image is obtained by 5 iterations. The x-axis denotes the variance of the noise, the y-axis denotes the SNR of the reconstruction. (c) compares the performance of two methods over the iterations for PSF model error. The x-axis denotes the iteration number, the y-axis denotes the SNR of the reconstruction.

(a) Reference frame   (b) LR planar image region

Fig. 4. The reference image frame from the video and its selected region

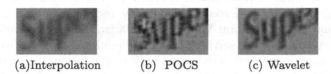

(a)Interpolation   (b) POCS   (c) Wavelet

Fig. 5. Comparison of one reconstructed HR region for various methods

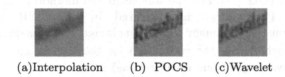

(a)Interpolation   (b) POCS   (c)Wavelet

Fig. 6. Comparison of another reconstructed HR region for various methods

show the comparisons of four different methods for different regions. Here the reconstructed HR images double the resolution of the LR images. The HR image in Fig. 5-6(a) were obtained by cubic interpolation from a single LR image. In Fig. 5-6(b) we used the POCS method, where the flow field is estimated by an affine motion model. Fig. 5-6(c) show the results from our reconstruction scheme. The difference can be visually evaluated. Clearly, there is large improvement from (b) to (c) in Fig. 5 and Fig. 6. The letters in Fig. 5(c) and Fig. 6(c) are the clearest, and there are minimal artifacts around the edges.

Summary. We have presented a theoretical analysis and a new algorithm for super-resolution problem based on wavelet theory. It has been demonstrated both in theory and experiments that the proposed method in this paper is very robust to noise without sacrificing efficiency. The reconstruction scheme allows for super-resolution reconstruction from general video sequences, even when the estimated optical flow is very noisy.

References

1. Irani, M., Peleg, F.: Motion analysis for image enhancement: Resolution, occlusion and transparency. Journal of Visual Comm. and Image Repr. 4 (1993) 324–335.
2. Eland, M., Feuer, A.: Restoration of a signal super-resolution image from several blurred, noisy and undersampled measured images. IEEE Transaction on Image Processing (1997) 1646–1658.
3. Bascle, B., Blake, A., Zisserman, A.: Motion deblurring and super-resolution from an image sequence. In: ECCV. Volume 2. (1996) 573–582.

4. Zhao, W., Sawhney, H.S.: Is super-resolution with optical flow feasible? In: ECCV. (2002) 599–613.
5. Tekalp, A., Ozkan, M., Sezan, M.: High-resolution image reconstruction from low-resolution image sequences and space-varying image restoration. In: ICASSP. (1992) 169–172.
6. Farsiu, S., Robinson, D., Elad, M., Milanfar, P.: Robust shift and add approach to super-resolution. In: SPIE. (2003).
7. Chambolle, A., Devore, R., Lee, N., Lucier, B.: Nonlinear wavelet image processing: variational problems, compression and noise removal through wavelets. IEEE Trans. Image Processing 7 (1998).
8. Youla, C.: Generalized image restoration by the method of alternating orthogonal projections IEEE Trans. Circuits Syst. 25 1978.
9. Chan, R., Chan, T., Shen, L., Shen, Z.: Wavelet deblurring algorithms for spatially varying blur from high-resolution image reconstruction. Linear algebra and its applications 366 (2003) 139–155.
10. Nguyen, N., Milanfar, N.P.: An wavelet-based interpolation-restoration method for superresolution. Circuits, Systems and Signal Processing 19 (2002) 321–338.
11. Baker, S., Kanade, T.: Limits on super-resolution and how to break them. In: CVPR. (2000) 372–379.
12. Mallat, S.: A wavelet tour of signal processing. Academic Press (1999).
13. Weickert, J.: Anisotropic Diffusion in Image Processing. ECMI Series, Teubner, Stuttgart, 1998.
14. Mrazek, P., Weickert, J., Steidl, G.: Correspondences between wavelet shrinkage and nonlinear diffusion. In: Scale-Space. (2003) 101–116.

Extending Kernel Fisher Discriminant Analysis with the Weighted Pairwise Chernoff Criterion

Guang Dai, Dit-Yan Yeung, and Hong Chang

Department of Computer Science, Hong Kong University of Science and Technology,
Clear Water Bay, Kowloon, Hong Kong
{daiguang, dyyeung, hongch}@cs.ust.hk

Abstract. Many linear discriminant analysis (LDA) and kernel Fisher discriminant analysis (KFD) methods are based on the restrictive assumption that the data are homoscedastic. In this paper, we propose a new KFD method called heteroscedastic kernel weighted discriminant analysis (HKWDA) which has several appealing characteristics. First, like all kernel methods, it can handle nonlinearity efficiently in a disciplined manner. Second, by incorporating a weighting function that can capture heteroscedastic data distributions into the discriminant criterion, it can work under more realistic situations and hence can further enhance the classification accuracy in many real-world applications. Moreover, it can effectively deal with the small sample size problem. We have performed some face recognition experiments to compare HKWDA with several linear and nonlinear dimensionality reduction methods, showing that HKWDA consistently gives the best results.

1 Introduction

In many classification applications in machine learning and pattern recognition, dimensionality reduction of the input space often plays an important role in reducing the complexity of the classification model and possibly leading to higher classification accuracy in the lower-dimensional feature space. This process is typically referred to as feature extraction or feature selection[1]. Linear discriminant analysis (LDA) is a classical linear dimensionality reduction method for feature extraction that has been used successfully for many classification applications. However, traditional LDA suffers from at least two limitations. First, the solution of LDA is optimal only when the data distributions for different classes are homoscedastic. In particular, the probability density functions of all classes are assumed to be Gaussian with identical covariance matrix. Second, for multi-class problems involving more than two classes, the linear transformation of traditional LDA tends to preserve the inter-class distances of well-separated classes in the input space at the expense of classes that are close to each other leading to significant overlap between them, so the overall discrimination ability is further degraded. To overcome the first limitation, the maximum likelihood

---

[1] Feature selection may be regarded as a special case of feature extraction in which each feature is either selected or not selected as a binary decision.

A. Leonardis, H. Bischof, and A. Pinz (Eds.): ECCV 2006, Part IV, LNCS 3954, pp. 308–320, 2006.
© Springer-Verlag Berlin Heidelberg 2006

approach [1] and mixture discriminant analysis [2] have been proposed. More recently, Loog et al. [3] proposed a heteroscedastic extension to LDA based on the Chernoff criterion. Some methods have also been proposed to overcome the second limitation. For example, [4, 5, 6] proposed using a monotonically decreasing weighting function based on Euclidean distance to balance the contribution of different class pairs to the total optimization criterion. Loog et al. [7] proposed an approximate pairwise accuracy criterion which defines the weighting function based on Bayesian error information of the class pairs. More recently, Qin et al. [8] proposed the weighted pairwise Chernoff criterion which combines the strengths of the earlier works of Loog et al. [3, 7] while it overcomes the two limitations above simultaneously. In fact, the methods in [4, 5, 6, 7] may be regarded as special cases of [8].

On the other hand, those LDA-based algorithms generally suffer from the so-called small sample size problem which arises in many real-world applications when the number of examples is smaller than the input dimensionality, i.e., the data are undersampled. A traditional solution to this problem is to apply PCA in conjunction with LDA, as was done for example in Fisherfaces [9]. Recently, more effective solutions, sometimes referred to as direct LDA (DLDA) methods, have been proposed [10, 11, 12, 13, 14]. All DLDA methods focus on exploiting the discriminatory information in the null space of the within-class scatter matrix where most discriminatory information that is crucial for classification exists.

While LDA-based methods perform well for many classification applications, their performance is unsatisfactory for many other classification problems in which nonlinear decision boundaries are necessary. Motivated by kernel machines such as support vector machine (SVM) and kernel principal component analysis (KPCA) [15], nonlinear extension of LDA called kernel Fisher discriminant analysis (KFD) by applying the "kernel trick" has been shown to improve over LDA for many applications [16, 17, 18, 19, 20, 21, 22, 23, 24]. The basic idea of KFD is to map each input data point $\mathbf{x}$ via a nonlinear mapping ϕ implicitly to a feature space $\mathcal{F}$ and then perform LDA there. Mika et al. [16] first proposed a two-class KFD algorithm which was later generalized by Baudat and Anouar [17] to give the generalized discriminant analysis (GDA) algorithm for multi-class problems. Subsequently, a number of KFD algorithms [18, 19, 20, 21, 22, 23, 24] have been developed. However, these KFD-based algorithms suffer from the small sample size problem a lot more than the LDA-based ones since the kernel-induced feature space is typically of very high or even infinite dimensionality. Many methods have been proposed to address this problem. Mike et al. [16] proposed adding a small multiple of the identity matrix to make the inner product matrix invertible. Baudat and Anouar [17] and Xiong et al. [18] used QR decomposition to avoid the singularity of the inner product matrix. Park et al. [19] proposed the KFD/GSVD algorithm by employing generalized singular value decomposition (GSVD). Yang [20] adopted the technique introduced in Fisherfaces [9], i.e., kernel Fisherfaces. Lu et al. [21] proposed the kernel direct discriminant analysis (KDDA) algorithm based on generalization of the LDA algorithm in [11]. Recently, [22, 23] presented a further enhanced method called the kernel generalized nonlinear discriminant analysis (KGNDA) algorithm which is based on the theoretical foundation established in [24]. More specifically, it attempts to exploit the crucial discriminatory information in the null space of the within-class scatter matrix in the feature space $\mathcal{F}$.

Similar to traditional LDA, however, most existing KFD-based algorithms, including KGNDA, are not optimal under the multi-class case as they tend to overemphasize the classes that are more separable and at the same time they are incapable of dealing with heteroscedastic data that are commonly found in real-world applications. In this paper, based on the idea of weighted pairwise Chernoff criterion proposed in [8], we further improve the overall discrimination ability of KGNDA by proposing a novel KFD algorithm called heteroscedastic kernel weighted discriminant analysis (HKWDA). We study the combination of the weighted pairwise Chernoff criterion and nonlinear techniques based on KFD directly, as the linear case can simply be seen as a special case when the mapping is linear, i.e., $\phi(\mathbf{x}) = \mathbf{x}$. Our method mainly focuses on improvement of the discriminatory information in the null space of the within-class scatter matrix, for two main reasons. First, this discriminatory information is crucial for improving the classification accuracy. Second, improving this discriminatory information is also the focus of other related works [10, 11, 12, 13, 14, 21, 22, 23, 24]. As a result, our proposed method has several appealing characteristics. First, like all kernel methods, it can handle nonlinearity efficiently in a disciplined manner. Second, by incorporating a weighting function that can capture heteroscedastic data distributions into the discriminant criterion, it can work under more realistic situations and hence can further enhance the classification accuracy in many real-world applications. Moreover, it can effectively deal with the small sample size problem. To demonstrate the efficacy of HKWDA, we compare it with several existing dimensionality reduction methods on face recognition where both the nonlinearity problem and the small sample size problem generally exist.

2   Existing Kernel Fisher Discriminant Analysis Algorithms

As discussed above, KFD algorithms essentially perform LDA in the feature space $\mathcal{F}$. Computation of the inner product of two vectors in $\mathcal{F}$ does not require applying the nonlinear mapping ϕ explicitly when the kernel trick is applied through using a kernel function $k(\mathbf{x}, \mathbf{y}) = \phi(\mathbf{x})^T \phi(\mathbf{y})$. We regard a matrix as an operator in the feature space $\mathcal{F}$ which is a Hilbert space. Moreover, for any operator $\mathbf{A}$ in a Hilbert space $\mathcal{H}$ (which may be the feature space $\mathcal{F}$), we let $\mathbf{A}(0)$ denote the null space of $\mathbf{A}$, i.e., $\mathbf{A}(0) = \{\mathbf{x} | \mathbf{A}\mathbf{x} = 0\}$, and $\mathbf{A}^{\perp}(0)$ denote the orthogonal complement space of $\mathbf{A}(0)$, i.e., $\mathbf{A}(0) \bigoplus \mathbf{A}^{\perp}(0) = \mathcal{H}$.

Let $\mathbf{x}_i$ $(i = 1, \ldots, N)$ denote N points in the training set $\mathcal{X}$. We partition $\mathcal{X}$ into c disjoint subsets $\mathcal{X}_i$, i.e., $\mathcal{X} = \bigcup_{i=1}^{c} \mathcal{X}_i$, where $\mathcal{X}_i$ consists of N_i points that belong to class i with $N = \sum_{i=1}^{c} N_i$. The between-class scatter operator $\mathbf{S}_b$, within-class scatter operator $\mathbf{S}_w$, and population scatter operator $\mathbf{S}_t$ can be expressed as follows [24]: $\mathbf{S}_b = \frac{1}{N} \sum_{i=1}^{c} N_i (\mathbf{m}_i - \mathbf{m})(\mathbf{m}_i - \mathbf{m})^T$, $\mathbf{S}_w =$

$\frac{1}{N} \sum_{i=1}^{c} \sum_{\mathbf{x}_j \in \mathcal{X}_i} (\phi(\mathbf{x}_j) - \mathbf{m}_i)(\phi(\mathbf{x}_j) - \mathbf{m}_i)^T$, and $\mathbf{S}_t = \mathbf{S}_b + \mathbf{S}_w = \frac{1}{N} \sum_{i=1}^{N} (\phi(\mathbf{x}_i) - \mathbf{m})(\phi(\mathbf{x}_i) - \mathbf{m})^T$, where $\mathbf{m}_i = \frac{1}{N_i} \sum_{\mathbf{x}_j \in \mathcal{X}_i} \phi(\mathbf{x}_j)$ denotes the sample mean of class i in $\mathcal{F}$ and $\mathbf{m} = \frac{1}{N} \sum_{i=1}^{N} \phi(\mathbf{x}_i)$ denotes the sample mean of all N points in $\mathcal{F}$. We maximize the following criterion function to find the optimal coefficients $\mathbf{w}$ for the discriminants:

$$J(\mathbf{w}) = \frac{\mathbf{w}^T \mathbf{S}_b \mathbf{w}}{\mathbf{w}^T \mathbf{S}_w \mathbf{w}}. \tag{1}$$

However, many algorithms [16, 17, 18, 19, 20, 21] presented for KFD have not effectively solved the small sample size problem with respect to (5) and they generally discard the intersection space $\mathbf{S}_w(0) \cap \mathbf{S}_b^{\perp}(0)$ which potentially contains useful discriminatory information that can help to improve the classification accuracy. Recently, KGNDA was proposed to solve this problem [22, 23, 24]. To prevent the loss of crucial discriminatory information, the procedure of computing optimal discriminant coefficients in $\mathcal{F}$, which essentially can be considered as a nonlinear extension of DLDA [10, 12, 13, 14], is applied in KGNDA. KGNDA is based on the assumption that discriminatory information in F can be obtained from the intersection space $\mathbf{S}_w(0) \cap \mathbf{S}_t^{\perp}(0)$, since the intersection space $\mathbf{S}_w(0) \cap \mathbf{S}_t^{\perp}(0)$ is equivalent to the intersection space $\mathbf{S}_w(0) \cap \mathbf{S}_b^{\perp}(0)$ in practice. To obtain $\mathbf{S}_w(0) \cap \mathbf{S}_t^{\perp}(0)$, KGNDA first computes $\mathbf{S}_t^{\perp}(0)$ by the eigenanalysis of $\mathbf{S}_t$ in $\mathcal{F}$ (which essentially performs KPCA), and then obtains this intersection space by the eigenanalysis of the projection of $\mathbf{S}_w$ in $\mathbf{S}_t^{\perp}(0)$. Since $\mathbf{S}_w(0) \cap \mathbf{S}_t^{\perp}(0)$ can be obtained, KGNDA computes the discriminant coefficients in this intersection space without discarding the useful discriminatory information there. Besides this crucial discriminatory information in $\mathbf{S}_w(0) \cap \mathbf{S}_t^{\perp}(0)$, KGNDA also obtains some other discriminatory information in $\mathbf{S}_w^{\perp}(0) \cap \mathbf{S}_t^{\perp}(0)$ at the same time. More details can be found in [22, 23, 24]. Since it is generally believed that the subspace $\mathbf{S}_w(0) \cap \mathbf{S}_b^{\perp}(0)$ or $\mathbf{S}_w(0) \cap \mathbf{S}_t^{\perp}(0)$ contains most discriminatory information for classification, many recently developed discriminant analysis algorithms [10, 11, 12, 13, 14, 21, 22, 23, 24, 25] actually mainly focus on this subspace.

3   Our Heteroscedastic Kernel Weighted Discriminant Analysis Algorithm

Since KFD is essentially LDA in the feature space $\mathcal{F}$, the two limitations of traditional LDA, i.e., data homoscedasticity assumption and overemphasis on well-separated classes, as discussed in Section 1 are still applicable here. In this section, we present our HKWDA algorithm based on the weighted pairwise Chernoff criterion, by incorporating into the discriminant criterion in $\mathcal{F}$ a weighting function that does not rely on the restrictive homoscedasticity assumption. The theoretical results outlined in this section can be proved by applying tools from functional analysis in the Hilbert space, but their proofs are omitted here due to space limitation.

Based on the multi-class Chernoff criterion presented in [3], we replace the conventional between-class scatter operator $\mathbf{S}_b$ by a positive semi-definite between-class operator $\mathbf{S}_o$ as defined below:

$$\mathbf{S}_o = \frac{1}{N^2} \sum_{i=1}^{c} \sum_{j=i+1}^{c} N_i N_j \mathbf{S}_w^{1/2} \{(\mathbf{S}_w^{-1/2}\mathbf{S}_{i,j}\mathbf{S}_w^{-1/2})^{-1/2}\mathbf{S}_w^{-1/2}(\mathbf{m}_i - \mathbf{m}_j) \times$$

$$(\mathbf{m}_i - \mathbf{m}_j)^T \mathbf{S}_w^{-1/2}(\mathbf{S}_w^{-1/2}\mathbf{S}_{i,j}\mathbf{S}_w^{-1/2})^{-1/2} + \frac{1}{\pi_i \pi_j}[\log(\mathbf{S}_w^{-1/2}\mathbf{S}_{i,j}\mathbf{S}_w^{-1/2}) -$$

$$\pi_i \log(\mathbf{S}_w^{-1/2}\mathbf{S}_i\mathbf{S}_w^{-1/2}) - \pi_j \log(\mathbf{S}_w^{-1/2}\mathbf{S}_j\mathbf{S}_w^{-1/2})]\}\mathbf{S}_w^{1/2}, \tag{2}$$

where $\pi_i = N_i/(N_i + N_j)$ and $\pi_j = N_j/(N_i + N_j)$ are the prior probabilities of classes i and j, respectively, $\mathbf{S}_{i,j} = \pi_i\mathbf{S}_i + \pi_j\mathbf{S}_j$, and $\mathbf{S}_i$ and $\mathbf{S}_j$ the covariance operators of classes i and j, respectively. The detailed derivation is omitted here but can be found in [3].

Although the multi-class Chernoff criterion can effectively handle heteroscedastic data, it still cannot overcome the second limitation mentioned above. Moreover, direct computation of $\mathbf{S}_o$ in $\mathcal{F}$ is inconvenient or even computationally infeasible. To overcome the second limitation, we introduce a weighting function to the discriminant criterion as in [4, 5, 7], where a weighted between-class scatter operator is defined to replace the conventional between-class scatter operator. To overcome both limitations and make the computation in $\mathcal{F}$ tractable simultaneously, we define a weighted between-class scatter operator $\mathbf{S}_B$ on the Chernoff distance measure in $\mathcal{F}$ based on the previous work in [3,4,5,7,8]:

$$\mathbf{S}_B = \frac{1}{N^2} \sum_{i=1}^{c-1} \sum_{j=i+1}^{c} N_i N_j w(d_{i,j})(\mathbf{m}_i - \mathbf{m}_j)(\mathbf{m}_i - \mathbf{m}_j)^T, \tag{3}$$

with the weighting function defined as $w(d_{i,j}) = \frac{1}{2d_{i,j}^2}\mathrm{erf}(\frac{d_{i,j}}{2\sqrt{2}})$, where $\mathrm{erf}(z) = \frac{2}{\sqrt{\pi}}\int_0^z e^{-t^2} dt$ is the pairwise approximated Bayesian accuracy and $d_{i,j} = \frac{\pi_i\pi_j}{2}(\mathbf{m}_i - \mathbf{m}_j)\mathbf{S}_{i,j}^{-1}(\mathbf{m}_i - \mathbf{m}_j) + \frac{1}{2}(\log|\mathbf{S}_{i,j}| - \pi_i\log|\mathbf{S}_i| - \pi_j\log|\mathbf{S}_j|)$ is the pairwise Chernoff distance measure between the means of classes i and j in $\mathcal{F}$. From the definition of the weighting function $w(d_{i,j})$, it can be seen that classes that are closer together in the feature space and thus can potentially impair the classification performance should be more heavily weighted in the input space. In addition, by considering the pairwise Chernoff distance, the heteroscedastic characteristic can be explicitly taken into account. One method for computing the Chernoff distance between two classes in the feature space has been presented in [26], which is based on the kernel extension of the probabilistic principal component analysis [27].

Based on the weighted between-class scatter operator $\mathbf{S}_B$ defined in (3), we define a new population scatter operator $\mathbf{S}_T = \mathbf{S}_B + \mathbf{S}_w$. Same as the traditional scatter operators, the new scatter operators satisfy the following properties.

Lemma 1. *Both the operators $\mathbf{S}_B$ and $\mathbf{S}_T$ are*

1. *bounded,*
2. *compact,*
3. *self-adjoint (symmetric), and*
4. *positive on the Hilbert space $\mathcal{F}$.*

From Lemma 1 and [24], we define our new kernel discriminant criterion as follows.

Definition 1. *The weighted pairwise Chernoff criterion in $\mathcal{F}$ is defined as*

$$J_1(\mathbf{w}) = \frac{\mathbf{w}^T \mathbf{S}_B \mathbf{w}}{\mathbf{w}^T \mathbf{S}_w \mathbf{w}} \qquad or \qquad J_2(\mathbf{w}) = \frac{\mathbf{w}^T \mathbf{S}_B \mathbf{w}}{\mathbf{w}^T \mathbf{S}_T \mathbf{w}}. \qquad (4)$$

From [21], both criteria are equivalent in that they should lead to the same solution. According to Lemma 1, Definition 1 and the recent work in [22, 23, 24], we assume the crucial discriminatory information with respect to $J_1(\mathbf{w})$ or $J_2(\mathbf{w})$ only exists in the intersection space $\mathbf{S}_w(0) \bigcap \mathbf{S}_B^{\perp}(0)$.

Lemma 2. *The space $\mathbf{S}_w(0) \bigcap \mathbf{S}_B^{\perp}(0)$ is equivalent to the space $\mathbf{S}_w(0) \bigcap \mathbf{S}_T^{\perp}(0)$.*

From Lemma 2, the crucial discriminatory information can also be obtained from the intersection space $\mathbf{S}_w(0) \bigcap \mathbf{S}_T^{\perp}(0)$.[2] However, it is intractable to compute this intersection space for two reasons. First, it is intractable to compute $\mathbf{S}_w(0)$ since the dimensionality of $\mathcal{F}$ may be arbitrarily large or even infinite. Second, it is intractable to compute $\mathbf{S}_T^{\perp}(0)$ by the eigenanalysis of $\mathbf{S}_T$, since $\mathbf{S}_T = \mathbf{S}_B + \mathbf{S}_w$. Fortunately, we note the following two lemmas.

Lemma 3. *The discriminant vectors with respect to $J_1(\mathbf{w})$ and $J_2(\mathbf{w})$ can be computed in the space $\mathbf{S}_T^{\perp}(0)$ without any loss of the discriminatory information.*

Lemma 4. *The space $\mathbf{S}_T^{\perp}(0)$ is equivalent to the space $\mathbf{S}_t^{\perp}(0)$.*

According to Lemma 3, it is more reasonable to first compute $\mathbf{S}_T^{\perp}(0)$. Moreover, from Lemma 4, we can use $\mathbf{S}_w(0) \bigcap \mathbf{S}_t^{\perp}(0)$ in place of $\mathbf{S}_w(0) \bigcap \mathbf{S}_T^{\perp}(0)$.

From KGNDA [22, 23, 24], we can compute the intersection space $\mathbf{S}_w(0) \bigcap \mathbf{S}_t^{\perp}(0)$ by the eigenanalysis of $\mathbf{S}_t$ and $\mathbf{S}_w$ in $\mathcal{F}$, as follows:

- **Eigenanalysis of $\mathbf{S}_t$ in $\mathcal{F}$:**
  To obtain $\mathbf{S}_t^{\perp}(0)$, we need to compute the orthonormal basis of $\mathbf{S}_t^{\perp}(0)$ which can be obtained by applying KPCA. Then, $\mathbf{S}_t$ in (4) can be rewritten as:

$$\mathbf{S}_t = \sum_{i=1}^{N} \bar{\phi}(\mathbf{x}_i) \bar{\phi}(\mathbf{x}_i)^T = \boldsymbol{\Phi}_t \boldsymbol{\Phi}_t^T, \qquad (5)$$

where $\bar{\phi}(\mathbf{x}_i) = \sqrt{1/N}(\phi(\mathbf{x}_i) - \mathbf{m})$ and $\boldsymbol{\Phi}_t = [\bar{\phi}(\mathbf{x}_1), \dots, \bar{\phi}(\mathbf{x}_N)]$. It is generally believed that direct computation of the orthonormal basis is intractable, since the order of the operator $\mathbf{S}_t$ is arbitrarily large or even infinite in $\mathcal{F}$. One solution is to compute the eigenvectors and eigenvalues of $N \times N$ matrix $\boldsymbol{\Phi}_t^T \boldsymbol{\Phi}_t$ [22, 23, 24, 26].

For all training examples $\{\phi(\mathbf{x}_i)\}_{i=1}^{N}$ in $\mathcal{F}$, we can define an $N \times N$ kernel matrix $\mathbf{K}$ as $\mathbf{K} = [k_{ij}]_{N \times N}$, where $k_{ij} = \phi(\mathbf{x}_i)^T \phi(\mathbf{x}_j)$. Hence, by the kernel trick, $\boldsymbol{\Phi}_t^T \boldsymbol{\Phi}_t$ can be expressed as

---

[2] In fact, direct computation of $\mathbf{S}_B^{\perp}(0)$ will lead to some loss of the crucial discriminatory information. See [23, 25] for analysis of KDDA [21].

$$\boldsymbol{\Phi}_t^T \boldsymbol{\Phi}_t = \frac{1}{N} \left[\mathbf{K} - \frac{1}{N}(\mathbf{K}1_{N\times N} + 1_{N\times N}\mathbf{K}) + \frac{1}{N^2}1_{N\times N}\mathbf{K}1_{N\times N} \right], \qquad (6)$$

where $1_{N\times N}$ is an $N\times N$ matrix with all terms being one. Let λ_i and $\mathbf{e}_i$ $(i = 1, \dots, m)$ be the ith positive eigenvalue and the corresponding eigenvector of $\boldsymbol{\Phi}_t^T \boldsymbol{\Phi}_t$, respectively. According to [22, 23, 24, 26], it is clear that $\mathbf{v}_i = \boldsymbol{\Phi}_t \mathbf{e}_i \lambda_i^{-1/2}$ $(i = 1, \dots, m)$ constitute the orthonormal basis of $\mathbf{S}_t^{\perp}(0)$.

- **Eigenanalysis of $\mathbf{S}_w$ in $\mathcal{F}$:**
  Projecting $\mathbf{S}_w$ onto the subspace spanned by $\mathbf{v}_i = \boldsymbol{\Phi}_t \mathbf{e}_i \lambda_i^{-1/2}$ $(i = 1, \dots, m)$, it is clear that the projection $\bar{\mathbf{S}}_w$ of $\mathbf{S}_w$ in this subspace can be expanded as

$$\bar{\mathbf{S}}_w = \mathbf{V}^T \mathbf{S}_w \mathbf{V} = \mathbf{E}^T \boldsymbol{\Xi}^T \boldsymbol{\Xi} \mathbf{E}. \qquad (7)$$

Here, $\mathbf{V} = [\mathbf{v}_1, \dots, \mathbf{v}_m]$, $\mathbf{E} = [\mathbf{e}_1 \lambda_1^{-1/2}, \dots, \mathbf{e}_m \lambda_m^{-1/2}]$, and $\boldsymbol{\Xi} = \mathbf{K}/N - 1_{N\times N}\mathbf{K}/N^2 - \mathbf{A}_{N\times N}\mathbf{K}/N + 1_{N\times N}\mathbf{K}\mathbf{A}_{N\times N}/N^2$, where $\mathbf{A}_{N\times N} = \mathrm{diag}(\mathbf{A}_1, \dots, \mathbf{A}_m)$ is a block-diagonal matrix with $\mathbf{A}_i$ being an $N_i \times N_i$ matrix with all its terms equal to $1/N_i$.

Let $\mathbf{P} = [\boldsymbol{\gamma}_1, \dots, \boldsymbol{\gamma}_l]$ be the corresponding eigenvectors of the zero eigenvalues of $\bar{\mathbf{S}}_w$. So it is clear that $\mathbf{S}_w(0) \cap \mathbf{S}_T^{\perp}(0)$ can be spanned by $\mathbf{VP}$. Then, the optimal discriminant vectors with respect to $J_1(\mathbf{w})$ or $J_2(\mathbf{w})$ can be computed in $\mathbf{S}_w(0) \cap \mathbf{S}_T^{\perp}(0)$ without the loss of crucial discriminatory information. From [22, 23, 24], since the between-class distance is equal to zero in $\mathbf{S}_w(0) \cap \mathbf{S}_T^{\perp}(0)$, the weighted pairwise Chernoff criterion in (9) can be replaced by $\hat{J}(\mathbf{w}) = \mathbf{P}^T \mathbf{V}^T \mathbf{S}_B \mathbf{PV}$. By the kernel trick, it can be expanded as:

$$\hat{J}(\mathbf{w}) = \mathbf{P}^T \mathbf{V}^T \mathbf{S}_B \mathbf{VP} = \mathbf{P}^T \mathbf{E}^T \left[\sum_{i=1}^{c-1} \sum_{j=i+1}^{c} \left(\frac{\sqrt{N_i N_j}}{N^{3/2}} w(d_{i,j}) \mathbf{Z}_{i,j}^T \mathbf{Z}_{i,j} \right) \right] \mathbf{EP},$$

$$(8)$$

where $\mathbf{P} = [\boldsymbol{\gamma}_1, \dots, \boldsymbol{\gamma}_l]$, $\mathbf{V} = [\mathbf{v}_1, \dots, \mathbf{v}_m]$, $\mathbf{E} = [\mathbf{e}_1 \lambda_1^{-1/2}, \dots, \mathbf{e}_m \lambda_m^{-1/2}]$, $\mathbf{Z}_{i,j} = \mathbf{KL}_i + \mathbf{HKL}_j - \mathbf{KL}_j - \mathbf{HKL}_i$, $\mathbf{H}$ is an $N \times N$ matrix with all terms being $1/N$, $\mathbf{L}_i$ is an $N \times 1$ matrix where the terms corresponding to class i are $1/N_i$ and the remaining terms are zero. It is clear that the matrix $\mathbf{P}^T \mathbf{V}^T \mathbf{S}_B \mathbf{VP}$ is a tractable $l \times l$ matrix. Let $\mathbf{z}_i$ $(i = 1, \dots, l)$ be the eigenvectors of $\mathbf{P}^T \mathbf{V}^T \mathbf{S}_B \mathbf{VP}$, sorted in descending order of the corresponding eigenvalues λ_i. According to [22, 23, 24], it is clear that $\mathbf{Y}_i = \mathbf{VP}\mathbf{z}_i$ $(i = 1, \dots, l)$ constitute the optimal discriminant vectors with respect to the weighted pairwise Chernoff criterion (4) in $\mathcal{F}$.

This gives the new HKWDA algorithm. For an input pattern $\mathbf{x}$, its projection onto the subspace spanned by $\boldsymbol{\Theta} = [\mathbf{Y}_1, \dots, \mathbf{Y}_l]$ can be computed as $\mathbf{z} = \boldsymbol{\Theta}^T \phi(\mathbf{x})$. This expression can be rewritten via the kernel trick as follows: $\mathbf{z} = \sqrt{\frac{1}{N}}(\mathbf{z}_1, \dots, \mathbf{z}_l)^T \mathbf{P}^T \mathbf{E}^T \mathbf{k}_x$, where $\mathbf{k}_x = (K(\mathbf{x}, \mathbf{x}_1) - \frac{1}{N}\sum_{i=1}^{N} K(\mathbf{x}, \mathbf{x}_i), \dots, K(\mathbf{x}, \mathbf{x}_N) - \frac{1}{N}\sum_{i=1}^{N} K(\mathbf{x}, \mathbf{x}_i))^T$.

Thus, HKWDA can give a low-dimensional representation with enhanced discriminating power on the whole. Moreover, this method also effectively addresses the nonlinearity problem and the small sample size problem.

4   Experimental Results

To assess the performance of the HKWDA algorithm proposed in this paper, we conduct some face recognition experiments to compare HKWDA with other dimensionality reduction methods. Note that typical face recognition applications suffer from the small sample size problem and require nonlinear methods, which are particularly suitable for demonstrating the strengths of HKWDA. In addition, real-world face image databases seldom satisfy the restrictive homoscedasticity assumption.

Our experiments are performed on two different data sets:

1. Mixed data set of 1545 images from 117 subjects which are obtained from four different image sources:
    − 47 subjects from the FERET database, with each subject contributing 10 gray-scale images.
    − 40 subjects from the ORL database, with each subject contributing 10 gray-scale images.
    − 20 subjects from the UMIST database, with a total of 575 gray-scale images.
    − 10 subjects from the YaleB database, with each subject contributing 10 gray-scale images.
2. A subset of the FERET database: 200 subjects each with four different images.

The gray-level and spatial resolution of all images in both data sets are 256 and 92×112, respectively. Since there exist large variations in illumination, facial expression and pose in both data sets, the distribution of the face image patterns is highly nonlinear, complex, and heteroscedastic.

Both data sets are randomly partitioned into two disjoint sets for training and testing, respectively. For the mixed data set, five images per subject are randomly chosen for training while the rest for testing; for the subset of the FERET database, three images per subject are randomly chosen from the four images available for each subject for training while the rest for testing. For each feature representation obtained by a dimensionality reduction method, we use a simple minimum distance classifier [24] with Euclidean distance measure to assess the classification accuracy. Each experiment is repeated 10 times and the average classification rates are reported. For the kernel methods, we use the RBF kernel function $k(z_1, z_2) = \exp(\|z_1 - z_2\|^2/\sigma)$ and polynomial kernel function $k(z_1, z_2) = (z_1^T z_2/\sigma + 1)^2$ where $\sigma = 10^9$.

To reveal the fact that HKWDA can better utilize the crucial discriminatory information in the null space of the within-class scatter operator, our first experiment compares HKWDA with the corresponding part of KGNDA

316   G. Dai, D.-Y. Yeung, and H. Chang

[22, 23, 24] and a special case of HKWDA, referred to as Euclidean KWDA (EKWDA), which can be seen as HKWDA where the weighting function is defined based on the Euclidean distance instead of the Chernoff distance in the feature space. It is obvious that EKWDA is based on the homoscedasticity assumption. In addition, to show the effectiveness of the nonlinear extension, we also compare the corresponding part of the DLDA method [10, 12, 13, 14] which may be seen as the linear special case of KGNDA. The experimental results shown in Fig. 1 reveal that, as expected, HKWDA outperforms KGNDA, EKWDA and DLDA for both kernel functions on the two different data sets. From the results of paired t-test with significance level 0.05, we can conclude that the results of HKWDA are significantly better than those of the other three methods. Since DLDA is a linear method, it cannot effectively extract nonlinear features and hence the classification rate is very low. Comparing HKWDA and EKWDA, we can see that relaxing the homoscedasticity assumption of the face image data can result in significant improvement in classification performance.

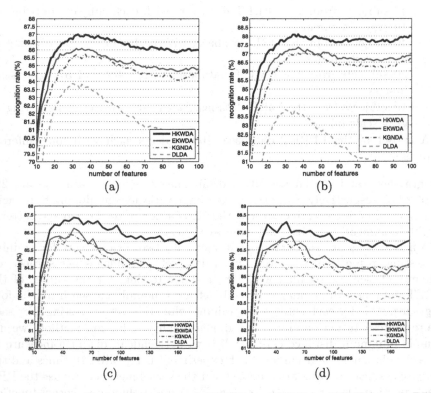

Fig. 1. Comparative performance of HKWDA, EKWDA, KGNDA and DLDA. (a) Polynomial kernel on the mixed data set; (b) RBF kernel on the mixed data set; (c) Polynomial kernel on the subset of FERET; (d) RBF kernel on the subset of FERET.

The second experiment compares HKWDA with several other kernel-based nonlinear dimensionality reduction methods, including KPCA [15], GDA [17], kernel Fisherfaces [20], KFD/QR [18], KFD/GSVD [19], and KDDA [21]. Previous works [22, 23, 24] also compare KGNDA with most of these methods in detail. Fig. 2 shows the classification rates for different methods based on the RBF kernel on both data sets. It can be seen that HKWDA is better than KPCA, GDA, kernel Fisherfaces, KFD/QR, KFD/GSVD and KDDA. In addition, we also compare different methods based on the average error percentage, which was originally proposed in [21] and can successfully evaluate the overall effectiveness of the proposed method compared with other methods. Specifically, in our experimental setting, the average percentage of the error rate of HKWDA over that of another method can be computed as the average of $(1-\alpha_i)/(1-\beta_i)$ $(i = 6, \ldots, J)$, where α_i and β_i are the recognition rates of HKWDA and another method, respectively, when i features are used. Using less than six features is not included in computing the average error percentages because the recognition rates are very low for all algorithms. Moreover, the value of J is set to 116 and 199,

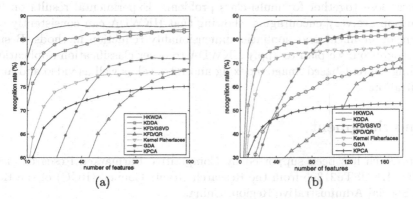

Fig. 2. Comparative performance of HKWDA and several other kernel methods based on the RBF kernel. (a) Mixed data set; (b) Subset of FERET.

Table 1. Average error percentages for different methods when compared with HKWDA

Algorithm	Mixed data set		Subset of FERET	
	Poly.	RBF	Poly.	RBF
DLDA [10, 12, 13, 14]	76.05%	67.85%	86.47%	82.31%
KPCA [15]	50.33%	45.19%	27.58%	26.38%
GDA [17]	71.17%	86.05%	33.13%	34.76%
Kernel Fisherfaces [20]	51.97%	53.01%	49.93%	27.80%
KFD/QR [18]	45.23%	39.98%	32.87%	58.79%
KFD/GSVD [19]	51.99%	51.87%	52.84%	58.79%
KDDA [21]	85.48%	81.63%	64.48%	63.35%
KGNDA [22, 23, 24]	90.57%	90.81%	91.11%	90.83%
EKWDA	93.39%	93.26%	91.42%	91.95%

respectively, for the mixed data set and the subset of FERET. The average error percentages for different methods are summarized in Table 1, showing that HKWDA is more effective than all other methods. We have performed more experiments but their results are not included in this paper due to space limitation. For example, we have performed similar experiments on another data set of 120 subjects selected from the AR database with each subject contributing 7 gray-scale images. All results consistently show that HKWDA outperforms other competing methods.

5   Conclusion

We have presented a new kernel Fisher discriminant analysis algorithm, called HKWDA, that performs nonlinear feature extraction for classification applications. By incorporating an appropriately chosen weighting function into the discriminant criterion, it can not only handle heteroscedastic data that are commonly found in real-world applications, but it can also put emphasis on classes that are close together for multi-class problems. Experimental results on face recognition are very encouraging, showing that HKWDA can consistently outperform other linear and nonlinear dimensionality reduction methods. Besides face recognition, we plan to apply HKWDA to other classification applications, including content-based image indexing and retrieval as well as video and audio classification.

Acknowledgment

This research has been supported by Competitive Earmarked Research Grant (CERG) HKUST621305 from the Research Grants Council (RGC) of the Hong Kong Special Administrative Region, China.

References

1. N. Kumar and A.G. Andreou. Heteroscedastic discriminant analysis and reduced rank HMMS for improved speech recognition. *Speech Communication*, 26:283–297, 1998.
2. T. Hastie and R. Tibshirani. Discriminant analysis by Gaussian mixture. *Journal of the Royal Statistical Society, Series B*, 58:155–176, 1996.
3. M. Loog and R.P.W. Duin. Linear dimensionality reduction via a heteroscedastic extension of LDA: the Chernoff criterion. *IEEE Transactions on Pattern Analysis and Machine Intelligence*, 26(6):32–739, June 2004.
4. Y.X. Li, Y.Q. Gao, and H. Erdogan. Weighted pairwise scatter to improve linear discriminant analysis. In *Proceedings of the 6th International Conference on Spoken Language Processing*, 2000.
5. R. Lotlikar and R. Kothari. Fractional-step dimensionality reduction. *IEEE Transactions on Pattern Analysis and Machine Intelligence*, 20(6):623–627, 2000.

6. J.W. Lu, K.N. Plataniotis, and A.N. Venetsanopoulos. Face recognition using LDA-based algorithms. *IEEE Transactions on Neural Networks*, 14:195–200, 2003.

7. M. Loog, R.P.W. Duin, and R. Haeb-Umbach. Multiclass linear dimension reduction by weighted pairwise Fisher criteria. *IEEE Transactions on Pattern Analysis and Machine Intelligence*, 23(7):762–766, July 2001.

8. A.K. Qin, P.N. Suganthan, and M. Loog. Uncorrelated heteroscedastic LDA based on the weighted pairwise Chernoff criterion. *Pattern Recognition*, 2005.

9. P.N. Belhumeur, J.P. Hespanha, and D.J. Kriegman. Eigenfaces vs. Fisherfaces: recognition using class specific linear projection. *IEEE Transactions on Pattern Analysis and Machine Intelligence*, 19:711–720, July 1997.

10. L.F. Chen, H.Y.M. Liao, M.T. Ko, J.C. Lin, and G.J. Yu. A new LDA-based face recognition system which can solve the small sample size problem. *Pattern Recognition*, 33:1713–1726, 2000.

11. H. Yu and J. Yang. A direct LDA algorithm for high-dimensional data with application to face recognition. *Pattern Recognition*, 34:2067–2070, 2001.

12. R. Huang, Q. Liu, H. Lu, and S. Ma. Solving the small size problem of LDA. In *Proceedings of the Sixteenth International Conference on Pattern Recognition*, volume 3, pages 29–32, August 2002.

13. J. Yang and J.Y. Yang. Why can LDA be performed in PCA transformed space? *Pattern Recognition*, 36:563–566, 2003.

14. H. Cevikalp, M. Neamtu, M. Wilkes, and A. Barkana. Discriminative common vectors for face recognition. *IEEE Transactions on Pattern Analysis and Machine Intelligence*, 27(1):4–13, 2005.

15. B. Schölkopf, A. Smola, and K.R. Müller. Nonlinear component analysis as a kernel eigenvalue problem. *Neural Computation*, 10:1299–1319, 1999.

16. S. Mika, G. Rätsch, J. Weston, B. Schölkopf, and K.R. Müller. Fisher discriminant analysis with kernels. In Y.H. Hu, J. Larsen, E. Wilson, and S. Douglas, editors, *Proceedings of the Neural Networks for Signal Processing IX*, pages 41–48, 1999.

17. G. Baudat and F. Anouar. Generalized discriminant analysis using a kernel approach. *Neural Computation*, 12:2385–2404, 2000.

18. T. Xiong, J.P. Ye, Q. Li, V. Cherkassky, and R. Janardan. Efficient kernel discriminant analysis via QR decomposition. In *Advances in Neural Information Processing Systems 17*, 2005.

19. C.H. Park and H. Park. Nonlinear discriminant analysis using kernel functions and the generalized singular value decomposition. *SIAM Journal on Matrix Analysis and Application*, to appear (http://www-users.cs.umn.edu/ hpark/pub.html).

20. M.H. Yang. Kernel eigenfaces vs. kernel Fisherfaces: face recognition using kernel methods. In *Proceedings of the Fifth IEEE International Conference on Automatic Face and Gesture Recognition*, pages 215–220, May 2002.

21. J.W. Lu, K.N. Plataniotis, and A.N. Venetsanopoulos. Face recognition using kernel direct discriminant analysis algorithms. *IEEE Transactions on Neural Networks*, 12:117–126, 2003.

22. G. Dai and Y.T. Qian. Modified kernel-based nonlinear feature extraction. In *Proceedings of the IEEE International Conference on Acoustics, Speech, and Signal Processing*, pages 17–21, 2004.

23. G. Dai and Y.T. Qian. Kernel generalized nonlinear discriminant analysis algorithm for pattern recognition. In *Proceedings of the IEEE International Conference on Image Processing*, pages 2697–2700, 2004.

24. J. Yang, A.F. Frangi, J.Y. Yang, D. Zhang, and Z. Jin. KPCA plus LDA: a complete kernel Fisher discriminant framework for feature extraction and recognition. *IEEE Transactions on Pattern Analysis and Machine Intelligence*, 27(2):230–244, 2005.
25. G. Dai and D.Y. Yeung. Nonlinear dimensionality reduction for classification using kernel weighted subspace method. In *Proceedings of the IEEE International Conference on Image Processing*, pages 838–841, 2005.
26. S.H. Zhou and R. Chellappa. From sample similarity to ensemble similarity. Technical Report SCR Technical Report (SCR-05-TR-774), Maryland University, 2005(http://www.umiacs.umd.edu/~shaohua/).
27. M.E. Tipping and C.M. Bishop. Probabilistic principal component analysis. *Journal of the Royal Statistical Society, Series B*, 61(3):611–622, 1999.

Face Authentication Using Adapted Local Binary Pattern Histograms

Yann Rodriguez and Sébastien Marcel

IDIAP Research Institute, Rue du Simplon 4, 1920 Martigny, Switzerland
{rodrig, marcel}@idiap.ch

Abstract. In this paper, we propose a novel generative approach for face authentication, based on a Local Binary Pattern (LBP) description of the face. A generic face model is considered as a collection of LBP-histograms. Then, a client-specific model is obtained by an adaptation technique from this generic model under a probabilistic framework. We compare the proposed approach to standard state-of-the-art face authentication methods on two benchmark databases, namely XM2VTS and BANCA, associated to their experimental protocol. We also compare our approach to two state-of-the-art LBP-based face recognition techniques, that we have adapted to the verification task.

1 Introduction

A *face authentication* (or *verification*) system involves confirming or denying the identity claimed by a person (one-to-one matching). In contrast, a *face identification* (or *recognition*) system attempts to establish the identity of a given person out of a closed pool of N people (one-to-N matching). Both modes are generally grouped under the generic *face recognition* term.

Authentication and identification share the same preprocessing and feature extraction steps and a large part of the classifier design. However, both modes target distinct applications. In authentication mode, people are supposed to cooperate with the system (the claimant wants to be accepted). The main applications are access control systems, such as computer or mobile devices log-in, building gate control, digital multimedia access. On the other hand, in identification mode, people are generally not concerned by the system and often even do not want to be identified. Potential applications include video surveillance (public places, restricted areas) and information retrieval (police databases, video or photo album annotation/identification).

Face recognition has been widely studied and is performing well in controlled lighting environment and on frontal faces. In real-world applications (unconstrained environment and non-frontal faces), face recognition does not yet achieve efficient results. Beside the pose of the subject, a major difficulty comes from the appearance variability of a given identity due to facial expressions, lighting, facial features (mustaches, glasses, make-up or other artefacts) or even the hair cut and skin color. The challenge of face recognition is then to extract relevant facial features which best discriminate individuals, in spite of the possible variations cited above.

A. Leonardis, H. Bischof, and A. Pinz (Eds.): ECCV 2006, Part IV, LNCS 3954, pp. 321–332, 2006.
© Springer-Verlag Berlin Heidelberg 2006

The problem of face authentication has been addressed by different researchers using various approaches. Thus, the performance of face authentication systems has steadily improved over the last few years. For a comparison of different approaches see [1]. These approaches can be divided mainly into *discriminative* approaches and *generative* approaches.

A *discriminative* approach takes a binary decision (whether or not the input face is a client) and considers the whole input for this purpose. Such *holistic* approaches are using the original gray-scale face image or its projection onto a Principal Component subspace (referred to as PCA or Eigenfaces [2]) or Linear Discriminant subspace (referred to as LDA or Fisherfaces [3]), or illumination-invariant features [4, 5] as input of a discriminative classifier such as Multi-Layer Perceptrons (MLPs) [6], Support Vector Machines (SVMs) [7] or simply a metric [8, 9]. Recently, it has been shown that *generative* approaches such as Gaussian Mixture Models (GMMs) [10] and Hidden Markov Models (HMMs) [11, 12] were more robust to automatic face localization than the above discriminative methods. A generative approach computes the likelihood of an observation (a holistic representation of the face image) or a set of observations (local observations of particular facial features) given a client model and compares it to the corresponding likelihood given an impostor model. Finally, the decision to accept or reject a claim depends on a score (distance measure, MLP output or Likelihood ratio) which could be either above (accept) or under (reject) a given threshold.

In this paper, we propose a novel generative approach for face authentication, based on a Local Binary Pattern (LBP) description of the face. A generic face model is considered as a collection of LBP-histograms. Then, a client-specific model is obtained by an adaptation technique from this generic model under a probabilistic framework.

In the next section, we introduce the reader to the Local Binary Pattern (LBP) operator and its use to represent a face. Then, we describe the proposed approach. Finally, we provide experimental results comparing the proposed approach to state-of-the-art face verification techniques as well as to state-of-the-art LBP-based face identification techniques, on two databases, namely XM2VTS and BANCA, associated to their experimental protocol.

2 Local Binary Patterns

2.1 The Local Binary Pattern Operator

The local binary pattern (LBP) operator is a non-parametric 3x3 kernel which summarizes the local spacial structure of an image. It was first introduced by Ojala et al. [13] who showed the high discriminative power of this operator for texture classification. At a given pixel position (x_c, y_c), LBP is defined as an ordered set of binary comparisons of pixel intensities between the center pixel and its eight surrounding pixels. The decimal form of the resulting 8-bit word (LBP code) can be expressed as follows (Figure 1):

$$LBP(x_c, y_c) = \sum_{n=0}^{7} s(i_n - i_c)2^n \tag{1}$$

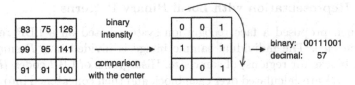

Fig. 1. The LBP operator

where i_c corresponds to the grey value of the center pixel (x_c, y_c), i_n to the grey values of the 8 surrounding pixels, and function $s(x)$ is defined as:

$$s(x) = \begin{cases} 1 & \text{if } x \geq 0 \\ 0 & \text{if } x < 0 . \end{cases} \tag{2}$$

Note that each bit of the LBP code has the same significance level and that two successive bit values may have a totally different meaning. Actually, The LBP code may be interpreted as a kernel structure index. By definition, the LBP operator is unaffected by any monotonic gray-scale transformation which preserves the pixel intensity order in a local neighbourhood.

Later, Ojala et al. [14] extended their original LBP operator to a circular neighbourhood of different radius size. Their $LBP_{P,R}$ notation refers to P equally spaced pixels on a circle of radius R. In [14], they also noticed that most of the texture information was contained in a small subset of LBP patterns. These patterns, called uniform patterns, contain at most two bitwise 0 to 1 or 1 to 0 transitions (circular binary code). 11111111, 00000110 or 10000111 are for instance uniform patterns. They mainly represent primitive micro-features such as lines, edges, corners. $LBP_{P,R}^{u2}$ denotes the extended LBP operator ($u2$ for only uniform patterns, labelling all remaining patterns with a single label).

Recently, new variants of LBP have appeared. For instance, Jin et al. [15] remarked that LBP features miss the local structure under certain circumstance, and thus they introduced the *Improved* Local Binary Pattern (ILBP). Huang et al. [16] pointed out that LBP can only reflect the first derivative information of images, but could not present the velocity of local variation. To solve this problem, they propose an *Extended* version of Local Binary Patterns (ELBP).

Due to its texture discriminative property and its very low computational cost, LBP is becoming very popular in pattern recognition. Recently, LBP has been applied for instance to face detection [15], face recognition [5, 4], image retrieval [17] or motion detection [18][1]. We finally point out that, approximately in the same time the original LBP operator was introduced by Ojala [13], Zabih and Woodfill [19] proposed a very similar local structure feature. This feature, called *Census Transform*, also maps the local neighbourhood surrounding a pixel. With respect to LBP, the *Census Transform* only differs by the order of the bit string. Later, the *Census Transform* has been extended to become the *Modified Census Transform* (MCT) [20]. Again, one can point out the same similarity between ILBP and MCT (also published at the same time).

---

[1] A more exhaustive list of applications can be found on Oulu University web site at: http://www.ee.oulu.fi/research/imag/texture/lbp/lbp.php

2.2   Face Representation with Local Binary Patterns

In [4], Ahonen proposed a face recognition system based on a LBP representation of the face. The individual sample image is divided into R small non-overlapping blocks (or regions) of same size. Histograms of LBP codes H^r, with $r \in \{1, 2, \ldots, R\}$ are calculated over each block and then concatened into a single histogram representing the face image. A block histogram can be defined as:

$$H^r(i) = \sum_{x,y \in block_r} I(f(x,y) = i), \ i = 1, ..., N, \tag{3}$$

where N is the number of bins (number of different labels produced by the LBP operator), $f(x,y)$ the LBP label [2] at pixel (x,y) and I the indicator function.

This model contains information on three different levels (Figure 2): LBP code labels for the local histograms (pixel level), local histograms (region level) and a concatened histogram which builds a global description of the face image (image level). Because some regions are supposed to contain more information (such as eyes), Ahonen propose an empirical method to assign weights to each region. For classification, a nearest-neighbour classifier is used with Chi square (χ^2) dissimilarity measure (see [4]).

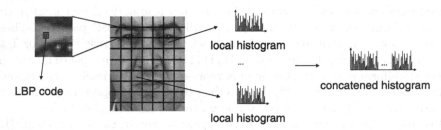

Fig. 2. LBP face description with three levels of information: pixel level (LBP code), region level (local histogram), image level (concatened histogram)

Following the work of Ahonen, Zhang et al. [5] underlined some limitations. First, the size and position of each region are fixed which limits the size of the available feature space. Second, the weighting region method is not optimal. To overcome these limitations, they propose to shift and scale a scanning window over pairs of images, extract the local LBP histograms and compute a dissimilarity measure between the corresponding local histograms. If both images are from the same identity, the dissimilarity measure are labelled as positive features, otherwise as negative features. Classification is performed with AdaBoost learning, which solves the feature selection and classifier design problem. Optimal position/size, weight and selection of the regions are then chosen by the boosting procedure. Comparative study with Ahonen's method showed similar results. Zhang et al.'s system uses however much less features (local LBP histograms).

---

[2] Note that $LBP(x,y)$, the LBP operator value, may not be equal to $f(x,y)$ which is the label assigned to the LBP operator value. With the $LBP_{P,R}^{u2}$ operator, for instance, all non-uniform patterns are labelled with a single label.

3   Proposed Approach

3.1   Model Description

In this paper, we propose a new generative model for face authentication, based on a LBP description of the face. Sample images are divided in R non-overlapping block regions of same size. This block by block basis is mainly motivated by the success of some recent works [21, 22, 12]. Similar to [4], a histogram of LBP codes is computed for each block. However, this histogram is not seen as a static observation. We instead consider it as a probability distribution. Each block histogram is thus normalized: $\sum_i H^r(i) = 1$, where $r \in \{1, 2, \ldots, R\}$.

Given a claim for client C, let us denote a set of independent features $X = \{x_r\}_{r=1}^R$, extracted from the given face image. If θ_C is the set of parameters to be estimated from sample X, we can define the likelihood of the claim coming from the true claimant C as:

$$P(X|\theta_C) = \prod_{r=1}^R p(x_r|\theta_C) \tag{4}$$

$$= \prod_{r=1}^R p(x_r|\theta_{C_1}, \ldots, \theta_{C_R}) \tag{5}$$

$$= \prod_{r=1}^R p(x_r|\theta_{C_r}), \tag{6}$$

assuming that each block is independent and that θ_C can be decomposed as a set of independent parameters per block $(\theta_{C_1}, \ldots, \theta_{C_R})$.

The next important step consists in choosing the function to estimate the likelihood functions $p(x_r|\theta_{C_r})$. We chose a very simple and computationally inexpensive non parametric model: histogram of LBP codes. $x_r = \{l_k\}_{k=1}^K$ is thus defined as a set of K labelled LBP code observations, where K is the maximum number of kernels which can be computed in the block by the LBP operator. This value is constant because all blocks have the same size. Assuming that each LBP code observation is independent, we can thus develop further:

$$P(X|\theta_C) = \prod_{r=1}^R p(x_r|\theta_{C_r}) \tag{7}$$

$$= \prod_{r=1}^R p(l_1, \ldots, l_K|\theta_{C_r}) \tag{8}$$

$$= \prod_{r=1}^R \prod_{k=1}^K p(l_k|\theta_{C_r}) \tag{9}$$

where $p(l_k|\theta_{C_r}) = H_C^r(l_k)$, then:

$$P(X|\theta_C) = \prod_{r=1}^R \prod_{k=1}^K H_C^r(l_k) \tag{10}$$

3.2   Client Model Adaptation

In face verification, the available image gallery set of a given client is usually very limited (one to five images). To overcome this lack of training data, adaptation methods have been proposed, first for speaker verification [23] and then adapted for face verification [22, 12]. They consist in starting from a generic model and then adapting it to a specific client. This generic model, referred to as *world model* or *universal background model*, is trained with a large amount of data, generally independent of the client set, but as representative as possible of the client population to model. The most used technique of incorporating prior knowledge in the learning process is know as *Maximum A Posteriori* (MAP) adaptation [24]. MAP assumes that the parameters θ_C of the distribution $P(X|\theta_C)$ is a random variable which has a prior distribution $P(\theta_C)$. The MAP principle states that one should select $\hat{\theta}_C$ such that it maximizes its posterior probability density, that is:

$$\hat{\theta}_C = \arg\max_{\theta_C} P(\theta_C|X)$$
$$= \arg\max_{\theta_C} P(X|\theta_C) \cdot P(\theta_C). \tag{11}$$

Moreover, one can simplify further without loss of performance by using a global parameter to tune the relative importance of the prior. The parameter updating can be described from the general MAP estimation equations using constraints on the prior distribution presented in [24]:

$$\hat{H}_C^r(l_k) = \alpha H_W^r(l_k) + (1-\alpha)H_C^r(l_k) \tag{12}$$

where $H_W^r(l_k)$ is the feature value (bin l_k of the histogram of block r) of the world model (prior), $H_C^r(l_k)$ is the current estimation (client training data) and $\hat{H}_C^r(l_k)$ is the updated feature value. The weighting factor α is chosen by cross-validation. The client model is thus a combination of parameters estimated from an independent world model and from training samples. After adaptation, each block histogram $\hat{H}_C^r$ is normalized to remain a probability distribution.

3.3   Face Verification Task

Let us denote θ_C the parameter set for client model C, θ_W the parameter set for the world model and a set of feature X. The binary process of face verification can be expressed as follows:

$$\Lambda(X) = \log P(X|\theta_C) - \log P(X|\theta_W) \tag{13}$$

where $P(X|\theta_C)$ is the likelihood of the claim coming from the true claimant and $P(X|\theta_W)$ is the likelihood of the claim coming from an impostor. Given a decision threshold τ, the claim is accepted when $\Lambda(X) \geq \tau$ and rejected when $\Lambda(X) < \tau$. $P(X|\theta.)$ is computed using Eq.10.

4   Experiments

There are two main face authentication benchmark databases, namely XM2VTS and BANCA, which we briefly describe in this section. We will also provide comparative experiments with Ahonen and Zhang systems introduced in Section 2.

4.1 Databases and Protocol

The XM2VTS database [25] contains synchronized video and speech data from 295 subjects, recorded during four sessions taken at one month intervals. The subjects were divided into a set of 200 training clients, 25 evaluation impostors and 70 test impostors. We performed the experiments following the *Lausanne Protocol Configuration I.*

The BANCA database [26] was designed to test multi-modal identity verification with various acquisition devices under several scenarios (controlled, degraded and adverse). In the experiments described here we used the face images from the English corpora, containing 52 subjects. Each subject participated in 12 recording sessions in different conditions and with different cameras. Each of these sessions contains two video recordings: one true client access and one impostor attack. Five frontal face images were extracted from each video recording.

Whereas XM2VTS database contains face images in well controlled conditions (uniform blue background), BANCA is a much more challenging database with face images recorded in uncontrolled environment (complex background, difficult lightning conditions). See Figure 3 for example images of each database. To assess verification performance, the Half Total Error Rate (HTER) is generally used:

$$\text{HTER}(\theta) = \frac{\text{FAR}(\theta) + \text{FRR}(\theta)}{2}. \tag{14}$$

where FAR if the false acceptance rate, FRR the false rejection rate and θ the decision threshold. To correspond to a realistic situation, θ is chosen *a priori* on the validation set at Equal Error Rate (EER).

(a) XM2VTS (controlled conditions): uniform background and lighting

(b) BANCA English (uncontrolled conditions): complex background and lighting variability

Fig. 3. Comparison of XM2VTS (1) and BANCA (2) face image conditions

4.2   Experimental Setup

For both XM2VTS and BANCA databases, face images are extracted to a size of 84×68 (rows × columns), according to the provided groundtruth eye positions. The cropped faces are then processed with the $LBP_{8,2}^{u2}$ operator ($N = 59$ labels). The resulting 80×64 *LBP* face images do not need any further lighting normalization, due to the gray-scale invariant property of LBP operators. In a block by block basis, the face images are decomposed in 8×8 blocks ($R = 80$ blocks). Histograms of LBP codes are then computed over each block r and normalized ($\sum_i H^r(i) = 1$, where $i \in \{1, 2, \ldots, N\}$).

For experiments on XM2VTS database, we use all available training client images to build the generic model. For BANCA experiments, the generic model was trained with the additional set of images, referred to as *world data* (independent of the subjects in the client database). For both set of experiments, the adaptation factor α of Eq. 12 (client model adaptation) is selected on the respective validation sets.

For comparison purpose, we implemented the systems of Ahonen [4] and Zhang [5], briefly described in Section 2.2. Similarly, we used a 8×8 block decomposition and computed LBP histograms for each block with the $LBP_{8,2}^{u2}$ operator.

4.3   Results on XM2VTS Database

Table 1 reports comparative results for Ahonen and Zhang systems, our proposed LBP/MAP histogram adaptation approach, as well as for two standard state-of-the-art methods. LDA/NC [27] combines Linear Discriminant Analysis with Normalized Correlation (holistic representation of the face), while DCT/GMM [12] is a generative approach based on a modified version of the Discrete Cosine Transform and Gaussian Mixture Models (local description of the face).

We first remark that our method obtains state-of-the-art results. The main advantage of LBP/MAP is its very simple training procedure (only one parameter, the map factor). Training PCA and LDA matrices takes time (several hours) and is not trivial (initial dataset, data normalization, % of variance). Training GMM's is neither straightforward (choice of number of gaussians, iteration, floor factor, etc). We also note that compared to LDA/NC or DCTmod2/GMM, LBP/MAP does not need any lighting normalization preprocessing.

Table 1. HTER performance comparison (in %) for two state-of-the-art methods (LDA/NC and DCT/GMM), Ahonen and Zhang systems and our proposed LBP/MAP histogram adaptation approach, on Configuration I of the XM2VTS database

Models	Test set
LDA/NC [27]	0.74
DCTmod2/GMM [12]	1.67
LBP Ahonen	3.40
LBP Zhang	3.94
LBP/MAP	1.42

Compared to the two other LBP methods, LBP/MAP performs clearly better. However, it must be noted that these methods have been originally designed for face identification task. We finally point out that as reported in [5] for identification, Ahonen and Zhang methods give similar results.

4.4 Results on BANCA Database

Table 2 reports results from the same systems than those in Table 1, but the LBP Zhang system. This is because Huang et al. [28] recently proposed an improved version of Zhang et al. system [5], based on a modified version of the boosting procedure called *JSBoost*, and provided results on BANCA. We then denote this method LBP/JSBoost. Unfortunately they only gave results with Protocol G.

Table 2. HTER performance comparison (in %) for two state-of-the-art methods (LDA/NC and DCT/GMM), Ahonen and LBP/JSBoost systems and our proposed LBP/MAP histogram adaptation approach, for Protocol Mc, Ud, Ua, P and G of the BANCA database. Boldface indicates the best result for a protocol.

Models	Protocols				
	Mc	Ud	Ua	P	G
LDA/NC [27]	**4.9**	16.0	20.2	**14.8**	5.2
DCTmod2/GMM [12]	6.2	23.7	**17.6**	18.6	-
LBP Ahonen	8.3	14.3	23.1	20.8	10.4
LBP/JSBoost [28]	-	-	-	-	10.7
LBP/MAP	7.3	**10.7**	22.6	19.2	**5.0**

Looking at the last three rows of Table 2, we notice again that our generative method performs better that the two other LBP-based methods for all conditions. On protocol G, where more client training data is available, LBP/MAP clearly outperforms the improved version of Zhang system (LBP/JSBoost).

The LDA/NC model obtains the best result in *matched* condition (Mc). For uncontrolled environment, LBP/MAP shows the best results in *degraded* condition (Ud). This is certainly due to the illumination invariant property of LBP features. Indeed, in controlled (Mc) and adverse (Ua) conditions, the lighting is almost uniform on the faces, whereas in degraded condition, the left part of most of the faces are illuminated.

In *adverse* condition, the recording camera was below the horizontal plan of the head. Moreover, people were not really looking at the camera, leading to a distorsion effect. The local representation of the face in the DCTmod2/GMM model can probably explain why this approach outperforms the other holistic models[3] Finally, it is interesting to notice that no single model appears to be the best one in all conditions.

---

[3] Although based on local histograms, all three LBP methods are holistic because of the concatened histogram representing the face.

5   Conclusion

In this paper, we proposed a novel generative approach for face authentication, based on a Local Binary Pattern (LBP) description of the face. A generic face model was considered as a collection of LBP-histograms. Then, a client-specific model was obtained by an adaptation technique from this generic model under a probabilistic framework. Experiments were performed on two databases, namely XM2VTS and BANCA, associated to their experimental protocol. Results have shown that the proposed approach performs better than state-of-the-art LBP-based face recognition techniques and is much faster than other state-of-the-art face verification techniques that perform similarly than the proposed approach.

Experimental results on BANCA database show that our method was performing well in uncontrolled lighting condition (Ud), due to the illumination invariance property of the LBP operator. However, our system was limited in the *adverse* condition (Ua), whereas the local approach (DCTmod2/GMM) was performing best. An interesting future work would be to investigate the use of LBP features with more appropriate Graphical Models, similar to the above GMM framework. This also motivated by the fact that local approaches have shown more robustness to non-perfect face localization than holistic approaches, which is particularly important for real-life automatic systems.

Acknowledgment

This research has been carried out in the framework of the Swiss NCCR project (IM)2. This publication only reflects the authors' views. All experiments were done using the *Torch3* library [29] and the *Torch3vision* package[4]. The authors would like to thank Samy Bengio for corrections and useful suggestions.

References

1. Messer, K., Kittler, J., Sadeghi, M., Hamouz, M., Kostyn, A., Marcel, S., Bengio, S., Cardinaux, F., Sanderson, C., Poh, N., Rodriguez, Y., Kryszczuk, K., Czyz, J., Vandendorpe, L., Ng, J., Cheung, H., Tang, B.: Face authentication competition on the BANCA database. In: Proceedings of the International Conference on Biometric Authentication (ICBA), Hong Kong (2004)
2. Turk, M., Pentland, A.: Eigenface for recognition. Journal of Cognitive Neuroscience 3(1) (1991) 70–86
3. Belhumeur, P., Hespanha, J.P., Kriegman, D.J.: Eigenfaces vs. Fisherfaces: Recognition using class specific linear projection. In: ECCV'96. (1996) 45–58 Cambridge, United Kingdom.
4. Ahonen, T., Hadid, A., Pietikäinen, M.: Face recognition with local binary patterns. In: Proc. 8th European Conference on Computer Vision (ECCV), Prague, Czech Republic. (2004) 469–481

---

[4] See: http://www.idiap.ch/~marcel/en/torch3/introduction.php

5. Zhang, G., Huang, X., Li, S., Wang, Y., Wu, X.: Boosting local binary pattern (LBP)-based face recognition. In: Proc. Advances in Biometric Person Authentication: 5th Chinese Conference on Biometric Recognition, SINOBIOMETRICS 2004Guangzhou, China. (2004) 179–186
6. Marcel, S.: A symmetric transformation for LDA-based face verification. In: Proceedings of the 6th International Conference on Automatic Face and Gesture Recognition, IEEE Computer Society Press (2004)
7. Jonsson, K., Matas, J., Kittler, J., Li, Y.: Learning support vectors for face verification and recognition. In: 4th International Conference on Automatic Face and Gesture Recognition. (2000) 208–213
8. Li, Y., Kittler, J., Matas, J.: On matching scores of LDA-based face verification. In Pridmore, T., Elliman, D., eds.: Proceedings of the British Machine Vision Conference BMVC2000, British Machine Vision Association (2000)
9. Kittler, J., Ghaderi, R., Windeatt, T., Matas, G.: Face verification via ECOC. In: British Machine Vision Conference (BMVC01). (2001) 593–602
10. Cardinaux, F., Sanderson, C., Marcel, S.: Comparison of MLP and GMM classifiers for face verification on XM2VTS. In: 4th International Conference on Audio- and Video-Based Biometric Person Authentication (AVBPA), Guilford, UK (2003) 911–920
11. Nefian, A., Hayes, M.: Face recognition using an embedded HMM. In: Proceedings of the IEEE Conference on Audio and Video-based Biometric Person Authentication (AVBPA). (1999) 19–24
12. Cardinaux, F., Sanderson, C., Bengio, S.: Face verification using adapted generative models. In: IEEE Conference on Automatic Face and Gesture Recognition (AFGR). (2004)
13. Ojala, T., Pietikäinen, M., Harwood, D.: A comparative study of texture measures with classification based on feature distributions. Pattern Recognition 29 (1996)
14. Ojala, T., Pietikäinen, M., Mäenpää, T.: Multiresolution gray-scale and rotation invariant texture classification with local binary patterns. IEEE Transactions on Pattern Analysis and Machine intelligence 24 (2002) 971–987
15. Jin, H., Liu, Q., Lu, H., Tong, X.: Face detection using improved LBP under bayesian framework. In: Proc. Third International Conference on Image and Graphics (ICIG), Hong Kong, China. (2004) 306–309
16. Huang, X., Li, S., Wang, Y.: Shape localization based on statistical method using extended local binary pattern. In: Proc. Third International Conference on Image and Graphics (ICIG), Hong Kong, China. (2004) 184–187
17. Takala, V., Ahonen, T., Pietikäinen, M.: Block-based methods for image retrieval using local binary patterns. In: Proc. 14th Scandinavian Conference on Image Analysis (SCIA), Joensuu, Finland. (2005) 882–891
18. Heikkilä, M., Pietikäinen, M., Heikkilä, J.: A texture-based method for detecting moving objects. In: Proc. the 15th British Machine Vision Conference (BMVC), London, UK. Volume 1. (2004) 187–196
19. Zabih, R., Woodfill, J.: A non-parametric approach to visual correspondence. IEEE Transactions on Pattern Analysis and Machine intelligence (1996)
20. Fröba, B., Ernst, A.: Face detection with the modified census transform. In: IEEE Conference on Automatic Face and Gesture Recognition (AFGR). (2004)
21. Lucey, S., Chen, T.: A GMM parts based face representation for improved verification through relevance adaptation. In: Proc. IEEE Int. Conf. on Computer Vision and Pattern Recognition (CVPR), Washington D.C., USA. (2004)
22. Sanderson, C., Paliwal, K.: Fast features for face authentication under illumination direction changes. Pattern Recognition Letters (2003) 2409–2419

23. Reynolds, D.A., Quatieri, T.F., Dunn, R.B.: Speaker verification using adapted gaussian mixture models. Digital Signal Processing 10(1–3) (2000)
24. Gauvain, J.L., Lee, C.H.: Maximum a posteriori estimation for multivariate gaussian mixture observation of markov chains. In: IEEE Transactions on Speech Audio Processing. Volume 2. (1994) 291–298
25. Messer, K., Matas, J., Kittler, J., Luettin, J., Maitre, G.: XM2VTSDB: The extended M2VTS database. In: Second International Conference on Audio and Video-based Biometric Person Authentication. (1999)
26. Bailly-Baillière, E., Bengio, S., Bimbot, F., Hamouz, M., Kittler, J., Mariéthoz, J., Matas, J., Messer, K., Popovici, V., Porée, F., Ruiz, B., Thiran, J.P.: The BANCA database and evaluation protocol. In: 4th International Conference on Audio- and Video-Based Biometric Person Authentication (AVBPA), Guilford, UK (2003)
27. Sadeghi, M., Kittler, J., Kostin, A., Messer, K.: A comparative study of automatic face verification algorithms on the banca database. In: 4th International Conference on Audio- and Video-Based Biometric Person Authentication (AVBPA), Guilford, UK (2003) 35–43
28. huang, X., Li, S.Z., Wang, Y.: Jensen-shannon boosting learning for object recognition. In: Proc. IEEE Int. Conf. on Computer Vision and Pattern Recognition (CVPR), San Diego, USA. (2005)
29. Collobert, R., Bengio, S., Mariéthoz, J.: Torch: a modular machine learning software library. Technical Report 02-46, IDIAP, Martigny, Switzerland (2002)

An Integrated Model for Accurate Shape Alignment

Lin Liang, Fang Wen, Xiaoou Tang, and Ying-qing Xu

Visual Computing Group, Microsoft Research Asia, Beijing 100080, China
{lliang, fangwen, xitang, yqxu}@microsoft.com

Abstract. In this paper, we propose a two-level integrated model for accurate face shape alignment. At the low level, the shape is split into a set of line segments which serve as the nodes in the hidden layer of a Markov Network. At the high level, all the line segments are constrained by a global Gaussian point distribution model. Furthermore, those already accurately aligned points from the low level are detected and constrained using a constrained regularization algorithm. By analyzing the regularization result, a mask image of local minima is generated to guide the distribution of Markov Network states, which makes our algorithm more robust. Extensive experiments demonstrate the accuracy and effectiveness of our proposed approach.

1 Introduction

Shape alignment is a fundamental problem in computer vision with applications in many areas, such as medical image processing [1], object tracking [2], face recognition and modeling [3], and face cartoon animation [4]. Accurate alignment of deformable shapes or contours depends on estimation of optimal deformable shape parameters such that the deformed shape model matches the image evidence collected from images or video.

A number of different shape models have been proposed for shape alignment. One approach is to postulate the deformation parameters by reducing the shape deformation correlations. The shape prior is then modeled by the distribution of the deformation parameters. The leading work of this approach is the active shape model (ASM) [5]. In light of this work, several improved methods have been developed. A Bayesian tangent shape model and an EM based searching algorithm are proposed in [6] to make the parameter estimation more accurate and robust. To alleviate the local minima problem, Liu et.al. [7] designed a hierarchical shape model and DDMCMC inference algorithm. To handle the nonlinear shape variance, a mixture of Gaussians [8] and kernel PCA [9] are used to model the distribution of deformation parameters. For optimization, these methods usually generate an observed shape by sampling each feature point independently from a local likelihood and then regularize it using the shape prior model. The main advantage of these methods is that the global regularization step based on a shape prior may help to assure an overall shape reasonably in line with the object. However, since each feature point is sampled without considering its relationship with neighbor points, the observed location

A. Leonardis, H. Bischof, and A. Pinz (Eds.): ECCV 2006, Part IV, LNCS 3954, pp. 333–346, 2006.

of each individual point is very sensitive to noise. To avoid the influence of the faraway outliers, some works such as [10] imposed a simple smoothness constraint between the neighbor points and used Dynamic Programming (DP) to find an observed optimal shape. Unfortunately, the observed shape optimized by DP was still directly regularized by the PCA shape model. The problem is that the regularized shape is usually placed at a mean position with the minimal sum of points distance to the observed optimal shape. Thus it cannot guide each "bad" point of observed shape to the accurate location. Moreover, it may even drag away the already accurately aligned points. Therefore, alignment accuracies of these methods are in general insufficient for many applications.

Recently, a different type of shape alignment method based on the Markov Random Field model has been proposed [11]. In this method, each feature point is considered as a node in a graph, and a link is set between each pair of feature points with the interaction energy designed to impose the local structure constraints between them. The benefit of such a model is that the shape prior is distributed in a Markov network of components and the image observation is still distributed by modeling the image likelihood of each individual component. The close interaction between the local image observation and structure constraints leads to far more accurate local shape estimation. The shortcoming of such an approach is that it models the shape only in a local neighborhood. Such a low level model cannot capture high level semantics in the shape. The lack of a global shape prior often leads the methods to nonstable results.

In this paper, by combining the advantages of the above two approaches, we propose an integrated model for accurate shape alignment. At the low level, the shape is modeled as a Markov Network with simple structure to effectively capture the local geometry constraints. At the high level, a global points distribution model based on PCA is adopted to regularize the inferred shape from the Markov Network. In order to avoid a decrease in accuracy during regularization, a constrained regularization algorithm is developed to keep the "good" point positions. The information from the global model is also fed back to the next Markov Network inference step by a mask image to guide the distribution of Markov Network states. This scheme effectively prevents the Markov Network from sticking to the local minima. The accuracy of the proposed approach has been demonstrated by extensive experiments.

2   A Two-Level Shape Model

In this section, we present a two-level model for shape alignment. The shape is split into a set of line segments and modeled as a Markov Network with simple structure to make the searching stage more effective and robust. At the same time, all the line segments are correlated through a global point distribution model to guarantee a globally reasonable shape.

2.1   Low Level Shape Model Based on Markov Network

Assuming that a shape $\mathbf{S}$ is described by N feature points (x_i, y_i) in the image, we can represent it by a $2N$-dimensional vector $\mathbf{S} = \{(x_i, y_i), i = 1, ..., N\}$.

We break the shape **S** into a set of line segments by the feature points. The parameters of each line segment $\mathbf{q}_i$ are the coordinates of its two endpoints $\mathbf{q}_i = [\mathbf{w}_i^s, \mathbf{w}_i^e]$. As shown in Figure 1 (a), these line segments are the nodes in the hidden layer of the graph. If two nodes are correlated, there will be an undirected link between them. For a deformable shape, we put a link between the connected line segments.

Assuming the Markovian property among the nodes, the shape prior can be modeled as $p(\mathbf{Q}), \mathbf{Q} = \{\mathbf{q}_0, \mathbf{q}_1, ..., \mathbf{q}_K\}$, which is a Gibbs distribution and can be factorized as a product of all the potential functions over the cliques in the graph:

$$p(\mathbf{Q}) = \frac{1}{Z} \prod_{c \in C} \psi_c(\mathbf{Q}_c) \tag{1}$$

where C is a collection of cliques in the graph and $\mathbf{Q}_c$ is the set of variables corresponding to the nodes in clique c, and Z is the normalization constant or the partition function.

In the context of deformable shapes, we adopt a pairwise potential function $\psi_{ij}(\mathbf{q}_i, \mathbf{q}_j)$ to present the constraint between two connected line segments. Thus we write the shape prior $p(\mathbf{Q})$ as:

$$p(\mathbf{Q}) = \frac{1}{Z} \prod_{(i,j) \in C^2} \psi_{ij}(\mathbf{q}_i, \mathbf{q}_j) \tag{2}$$

The pairwise potential function is defined by the constraints of the distance of two endpoints ($\mathbf{w}_i^e$ and $\mathbf{w}_j^s$) and the angle γ_{ij} between the two line segments, as illustrated in Figure 2:

$$\psi_{ij}(\mathbf{q}_i, \mathbf{q}_j) = G(d_{ij}; 0, \sigma_{ij}^d) \cdot G(A_{ij}; \mu_{ij}^A, \sigma_{ij}^A) \tag{3}$$

where $d_{ij} = |\mathbf{w}_i^e - \mathbf{w}_j^s|$ is the distance between $\mathbf{w}_i^e$ and $\mathbf{w}_j^s$, $A_{ij} = \sin(\gamma_{ij})$, and σ_{ij}^d and σ_{ij}^A are variance parameters that control the tightness of the connectivity constraint.

Given the image observation I, as shown in Figure 1 (a), each segment $\mathbf{q}_i$ is also associated with its image observation, denoted as Γ_i. Assuming the local observation is independent of other nodes given $\mathbf{q}_i$, the likelihood is factorized as:

$$p(I|\mathbf{Q}) = \prod_i p_i(\Gamma_i|\mathbf{q}_i) \tag{4}$$

Then the posterior can be factorized as:

$$p(\mathbf{Q}|I) \propto \frac{1}{Z} \prod_i p_i(\Gamma_i|\mathbf{q}_i) \prod_{(i,j) \in C^2} \psi_{ij}(\mathbf{q}_i, \mathbf{q}_j) \tag{5}$$

For a complex shape, such as the face that contains multiple parts (brows, eyes, etc.), only the connected line segments belonging to the same part are linked, as shown in Figure 1 (b). We do not add links between different parts. This will guarantee that the good parts (with strong local image observation) move to its accurate position while not being affected by other bad parts. Such a simple structure is also easy for inference. The global relationship between

336   L. Liang et al.

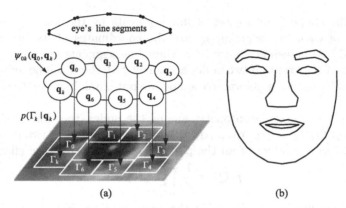

(a)   (b)

Fig. 1. The Markov Network for face. (a) The graph for the eye shape. (b) For the graph of face, the links are added within each black line.

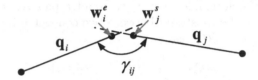

Fig. 2. The constraint of two connected line segments

different parts is constrained by a global shape model as explained in the following sections.

2.2   Global Shape Model Based on PCA

We adopt principal components analysis (PCA) to model the points distribution of a shape S as in [5]. To remove the shape variation caused by the global transformation, the shape is first aligned to the tangent space:

$$S = cR_\theta x + t \qquad (6)$$

where x is the tangent shape vector, c is the scaling parameter, R_θ is the rotation matrix and t is the translation parameter.

PCA is then adopted to find a set of main deformable modes. The deformable shape can be generated by a linear combination of these modes. Suppose r modes are retained in PCA, then:

$$x = \mu + \phi_r b + \varepsilon \qquad (7)$$

where μ is the mean shape, and ϕ_r consists the first r columns of the projection matrix. Each column of ϕ_r corresponds to a deformable mode. ε is an isotropic noise in the tangent space. b is a hidden variables vector to generate the shape. Each item of b is independent and b is distributed as a multivariate Gaussian:

$$p(b) = G(b; 0, \Lambda) \qquad (8)$$

where $\Lambda = diag(\lambda_1, ..., \lambda_r)$. λ_i is the ith eigenvalue.

Under such model, the global shape prior is modeled as $p(S) \sim p(b)$.

2.3   An Integrated Model

In our integrated model, a deformable shape is parameterized by the hidden variable $\mathbf{b}$, the pose parameters $\Theta = (c, \theta, \mathbf{t})$ and the positions of the line segments $\mathbf{Q} = \{\mathbf{q}_i\}$. Given an observation image I, we want to maximize the following posterior $p(\mathbf{b}, \Theta, \mathbf{Q}|I)$ to get the optimal shape. Notice that given $\mathbf{Q}$, $\mathbf{b}$ and Θ can be considered as independent of I, thus

$$p(\mathbf{b}, \Theta, \mathbf{Q}|I) \propto p(\mathbf{b}, \Theta|\mathbf{Q})p(\mathbf{Q}|I) \tag{9}$$

$p(\mathbf{Q}|I)$ is defined in Equation (5), and the likelihood and low level's shape prior are factorized in this part. The final shape $\mathbf{S}$ can be easily got from $\mathbf{Q}$ by setting the position of one point s_i as the average position of the connected segments' endpoints, which can be written as $\mathbf{S} = T\mathbf{Q}$, so $p(\mathbf{b}, \Theta|\mathbf{Q})$ can be evaluated as $p(\mathbf{b}, \Theta|T\mathbf{Q})$, which is:

$$p(\mathbf{b}, \Theta|\mathbf{Q}) \propto p(T\mathbf{Q}|\mathbf{b}, \Theta)p(\mathbf{b}) \tag{10}$$

Maximizing the posterior equation (9) is equal to minimizing the following energy:

$$E = \lambda E_p + E_{mn} \tag{11}$$

where

$$E_p = -\log p(\mathbf{b}, \Theta|\mathbf{Q}) \tag{12}$$

$$E_{mn} = -\log p(\mathbf{Q}|I) \tag{13}$$

λ is a weighting parameter to balance the strength of the global shape prior and the Markov Network.

Based on this integrated model, the local and global shape constraints are imposed by Markov Network and the global PCA model respectively. The local structure constraints make the feature points more consistent with the image observation and robust to the local noise, thus a more accurate result can be achieved. And the global shape constraint regularizes the globally unreasonable shape to obtain a more stable result.

Besides, in order to make the inference more efficient, we adopt a hierarchical shape model similar to [7]: the shape resolution changes from coarse to fine corresponding to a Gaussian pyramid of the image. The located coarse shape is used to initialize the search for a finer shape in the higher resolution image.

Hierarchical Shape Model. Suppose $\mathbf{S}_l$ is the shape at the resolution level l and $\mathbf{S}_{l+1}$ is the shape at the coarser resolution level $l+1$, we model the conditional distribution $p(\mathbf{S}_l|\mathbf{S}_{l+1})$ as a Gaussian, as in [7]. Given the located coarse shape $\mathbf{S}_{l+1}$, we initialize the finer shape $\mathbf{S}_l$ as:

$$\mathbf{S}_l^0 = \max_{\mathbf{S}_l} p(\mathbf{S}_l|\mathbf{S}_{l+1}). \tag{14}$$

3 Shape Alignment by the Two-Level Shape Model

To find the optimal shape which minimizes the energy Equation (11), we update the shape to minimize E_{mn} and E_p iteratively. To minimize E_p, the previous methods such as [5] usually place the regularized shape at a mean position with the minimal sum of points distance to the shape obtained in the E_{mn} minimization step. Thus some points that have already converged to the good positions will be dragged away by those "bad" points. Also, although some "bad" points are regularized in the E_p minimization step, they may fall into the same false positions again in the next E_{mn} minimization step.

In order to solve these problems, we propose a new iterative optimization strategy. To avoid a decrease of the accuracy during the E_p minimization step, a constrained regularization algorithm is proposed to detect and keep the "good" points. Also to prevent the search from falling into the same mistake twice, the information from the global shape model is fed back to the next E_{mn} minimization step by recording the "bad" areas. Such optimization strategy helps to achieve more accurate and robust alignment result.

3.1 Alignment Algorithm Overview

We design a multi-resolution iterative search strategy to find the optimal shape. For searching at resolution level l, the algorithm is summarized as follows:

1. Given a located coarse shape $\mathbf{S}_{l+1}$, initialize the finer shape $\mathbf{S}_l^0$ by Equation (14);
2. In the neighboring region of current shape $\mathbf{S}_l^t$, find the optimal line segments set $\mathbf{Q}_l^t$ to minimize the E_{mn} in Equation (13), see subsection 3.2;
3. Update the global shape and pose parameters $\{\mathbf{b}, \Theta\}$ to fit $\mathbf{Q}_l^t$ using constrained regularization algorithm, and try to find a better shape $\tilde{\mathbf{S}}_l^t$ with lower posterior energy in Equation (11), see subsection 3.3;
4. If a better shape $\tilde{\mathbf{S}}_l^t$ is found: $\mathbf{S}_l^t = \tilde{\mathbf{S}}_l^t$, and also create the mask image for guiding the distribution of Markov Network states. Else, $\mathbf{S}_l^t = T\mathbf{Q}_l^t$, and repeat until convergence, see subsection 3.4.

The algorithm is converged if the posterior energy of current step is larger than the previous step, i.e. $E(\mathbf{S}_l^t) > E(\mathbf{S}_l^{t-1})$, or the changing is small enough, i.e. $E(\mathbf{S}_l^t) - E(\mathbf{S}_l^{t-1}) < \delta$.

3.2 Local Search by Markov Network

Given the current shape $\mathbf{S}_l^t$, we first discretize the state space of the Markov Network in the neighbor of $\mathbf{S}_l^t$. Then for an open curve, such as the facial contour, we adopt DP to find the optimal solution which is very efficient. For a closed curve, such as the eye part, we use loopy belief propagation (BP) [12] which produces excellent empirical results for a graph containing loops [13].

To make the inference more efficient, we generate an efficient state set by pruning states according to the strength of the local likelihood, then generating new possible states based on the Markovian property.

In more details, as shown in Figure 3, inspired by ASM [5], we distribute the possible states along the profiles of $\mathbf{S}_l^t$. Then we select the states from coarse to fine: the line segments connecting the profile points sampled at a larger step are tested first and those with strong local likelihood are selected. Then we select stronger ones in the neighborhood of the kept line segments.

States pruning based on local likelihood does not consider the relationship between one node and its neighbors, thus some key states may be missed. As shown in Figure 3, if the two green states are selected for $\mathbf{q}_{i-1}$ and $\mathbf{q}_{i+1}$, but the red one of $\mathbf{q}_i$ connecting them is not selected, we cannot find a good solution. So we add new possible states based on the Markovian property: for a node $\mathbf{q}_i$, given the states of its neighbors, we add the connections with a large enough potential as the new states of $\mathbf{q}_i$. Based on the above states discretization mechanism, 15 states kept for each node are enough for inference, which makes the algorithm more efficient.

Local search by the Markov Network will make the algorithm more robust to local noise. As shown in Figure 4, in the previous approaches [5][6], each feature point is moved independently. The problem is that although some points have moved to good positions, the final shape will still be dragged to a bad position after the regularization because of those bad points, as shown in Figure 4 (b)

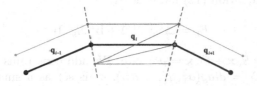

Fig. 3. Generate Markov Network states. The black line (most thick black line in printed version) is the current shape $\mathbf{S}_l^t$. $\mathbf{q}_i, \mathbf{q}_{i-1}, \mathbf{q}_{i+1}$ are linked Markov Network nodes. The pink line segments (3 line segments starting from the same point) are some candidate states of $\mathbf{q}_i$. If the two green line segments (line segments up the $\mathbf{q}_{i-1}$ and $\mathbf{q}_{i+1}$) are selected by $\mathbf{q}_{i-1}$ and $\mathbf{q}_{i+1}$, the red line segment (line segment up the $\mathbf{q}_i$) should be added to $\mathbf{q}_i$ for inference.

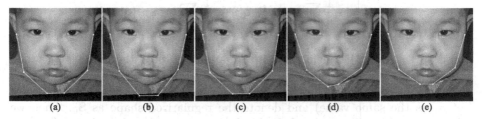

    (a)   (b)   (c)   (d)   (e)

Fig. 4. Comparing the result of one step local search by Markov Network with ASM's approach. The search is executed at the low resolution (64x64) level with a ±4 pixels search range along the shape profile for both methods. (a) The initial shape. (b) The result of ASM's approach. (c) The result of regularizing the shape of (b) with the shape model. (d) The result of local search by Markov Network. (e) The result of regularizing the shape of (d) in our constrained way.

and (c). As a result, a precise alignment result cannot be achieved. In our integrated model, by distributing the shape prior into the nodes of the Markov Network, the movement of one point is affected by the local image observation and the messages from its neighbors together, thus if the strength of the good points are strong enough, other points can be dragged away from the bad areas, as shown in Figure 4 (d) and (e). From our experiments, in many cases our algorithm can drag the shape out of local minima and generate a more precise result.

3.3   Constrained Regularization

Only minimizing E_{mn} can not guarantee a globally reasonable shape, especially when a strong edge appears nearby the ground truth, as shown in Figure 6 (a). Given the shape $\mathbf{S}^*$ obtained by Markov network inference, we expect the regularization of $\mathbf{S}^*$ will drag the "bad" points toward the better positions and maintain the positions of those "good" points. However, directly minimizing E_p as in ASM [5] does not meet this expectation. Some "good" points are dragged away as shown in Figure 6 (b). As a result, E_p is minimized but E_{mn} becomes much larger. To solve this problem we propose a constrained regularization algorithm . The key idea is to select some points of $\mathbf{S}^*$ that need to be fixed, then add these constraints during E_p minimization step.

We formulate Equation (12) more clearly:

$$E_p = \Delta^T \Sigma_l^{-1} \Delta + \mathbf{b}^T \Sigma_b^{-1} \mathbf{b} \tag{15}$$

where $\Delta = \mathbf{S}^* - (cR_\theta \mathbf{x} + \mathbf{t}), \mathbf{x} = \mu + \phi_r \mathbf{b}$. We add constrains by the likelihood variance matrix $\Sigma_l = diag(\sigma_1^2, \sigma_2^2, ..., \sigma_N^2)$. σ_i is set as a smaller value, if the corresponding point needs to be constrained. To find the optimal $\{\mathbf{b}, c, \theta, \mathbf{t}\}$, we adopt EM algorithm as [6].

To explain how we add constraints, we define the local energy of a feature point s_i first. Denoting $\{\mathbf{q}_k^i\}_{k=1}^n$ as the line segments connecting to point s_i, the local energy is defined as the mean of these line segments' likelihoods and their potentials:

$$e(s_i) = -\frac{1}{n} \sum_k \log p(\Gamma_k | \mathbf{q}_k^i) - \frac{1}{m} \sum_{k,j} \log \psi_{kj}(\mathbf{q}_k^i, \mathbf{q}_j^i) \tag{16}$$

Potential $\psi_{kj}(\mathbf{q}_k^i, \mathbf{q}_j^i)$ is defined as in Equation (3). m is the number of added potentials.

To add the constraints, we first minimize Equation (15) without any constraint (set σ_i as the same value) and denote the regularized shape as $\mathbf{S}_0$. Then we calculate the changing ratio of the local energy of each point: $\Delta e_i = (e(s_i^0) - e(s_i^*))/e(s_i^*)$. It's obvious that when $\Delta e_i <= 0$, the points are moved to a better location and need not to be constrained, while when $\Delta e_i > 0$, the points may be moved to a worse location, and the larger Δe_i is, the priority to constrain this point is higher. So we query those points with $\Delta e_i > 0$ in the order of Δe_i from large to small, then test which point to be constrained following this order.

To guarantee that the added constraint will drag the whole shape to a better location, we accept the constraint only when the shape's energy $E(\mathbf{S}_t)$ becomes lower, where $E(\cdot)$ is defined as Equation (11). If one constraint point is accepted, we re-order the points based on the local energy changes between current $\mathbf{S}_t$ and the Markov Network result $\mathbf{S}^*$. The algorithm is summarized in Figure 5.

Given the shape $\mathbf{S}^*$ from Markov Network, the minimal energy $E_{min} = E(\mathbf{S}^*)$, the optimal shape $\tilde{S} = \mathbf{S}^*$, the constraint marks of all points: $\{b_i = false\}$, the likelihood variance $\Sigma_l = diag(1, 1, ..., 1)$, v_k is the point index, $\{v_k\}$ is the points order.

1. Set Σ_l: $\sigma_i = 0.01$ if $b_i = true$, minimize Equation (15) to find an optimal shape $\mathbf{S}_t$
2. Evaluate the shape energy $E(\mathbf{S}_t)$.
   If $E(\mathbf{S}_t) < E_{min}$: set $\tilde{S} = \mathbf{S}_t, E_{min} = E(\mathbf{S}_t)$
   else: set $b_{v_k} = false, b_{v_{k+1}} = true$, goto 1.
3. Calculate the local energy changes: $\{\Delta e_i\}$, update the points order $\{v_k\}$,
   Set $b_{v_0} = true$, goto 1.
4. Repeat the above process, until the allowed maximum tested points number has achieved

---

Fig. 5. Constrained Regularization Algorithm

Figure 6 (b) and (c) shows the procedure of constrained regularization. Our algorithm can generate reasonable shape while keeping the positions of those good points.

3.4   Guiding the Distribution of Markov Network States

After the regularization, if a better shape $\tilde{\mathbf{S}}^t$ is found, this suggests that some parts of the Markov Network result $\mathbf{Q}^t$ is really bad to make the shape deviates the global shape prior. To prevent the Markov Network from getting stuck into the same mistake in the next local search step, we generate a mask image that

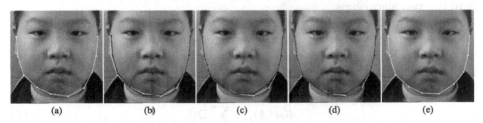

(a)   (b)   (c)   (d)   (e)

Fig. 6. The procedure of constrained regularization and guiding Markov Network states distribution. The yellow shape (white shape in printed version) is the result of Markov Network. The dark blue shape (black shape in printed version) is the result after regularization. (a) The result after one step Markov Network local search. (b) Regularization without constraints. (c) Regularization with constraints. (d) The states are forbidden to distribute in the red area (thick gray line in printed version). (e) After pruning the states in the blue area in (d), the result of Markov Network is much better.

points out the danger regions. Then we prune those states that mostly drop into the marked regions.

To mask the danger regions, we first calculate the distance of each line segment q_i^t to the better shape $\tilde{S}^t$. Then if one line segment's distance is much larger than the mean distance, which shows that its location is really bad, we will draw it as a line with a certain width on the mask image, as shown in Figure 6 (d). Since after the constrained regularization, the shape $\tilde{S}^t$ fits the good points quite well, detecting the bad line segments by this simple method is robust. By preventing the states from dropping into the detected wrong regions, the Markov Network will converge to the right position, see in Figure 6 (e).

4 Experiments

In this section, we apply the integrated shape model for face alignment and compare it with BTSM [6] and demonstrate that our algorithm improves accuracy greatly. The reason for comparing with BTSM is that it is an improvement of the classic ASM algorithm and extensive experiments have demonstrated its good performance in the context of face alignment.

To compare the accuracy of the two algorithms we use a set of child face images with size of 512×512 and divide the data set into 428 images for training and 350 images for testing. Each image contains a face with a size ranging from 270×270 to 330×330. A total of 87 feature points are manually labeled on each image for both the training and testing data sets. This data set contains the photos of children from 2 to 15 years old with different expressions. Thus the face shape variance is large. Consequently, although the images have good quality, the data set is still difficult for precise alignment.

In our hierarchical search scheme, a four-level Gaussian pyramid is built by repeated sub-sampling. For each image layer from coarse to fine, the corresponding face shape contains 28, 37, 57, 87 feature points respectively. For each test image, an initial shape is generated by randomly rotating (from $-20°$ to $20°$) and scaling (from 0.9 to 1.1) the mean shape of the training set, and it is fed into the two algorithms.

To quantitatively evaluate the accuracy of the algorithm, we calculate the estimation error by a curve difference measurement. Defining D_k as the distance of one point P_k of the searched shape to its corresponding ground true curve as explained in Figure 7(a), the estimation error is calculated as:

$$dist(A)_j = \sum_{k=1}^{N} D_k^A \tag{17}$$

where $dist(A)_j$ denotes the estimation error of algorithm A on the image j, and N is the number of feature points. For those closed sub-parts such as the eyes, brows and mouth, we break one closed contour into two open curves as shown in Figure 7(b). Comparing with the error measurement by summarizing the distance between searched point and annotated point, such a curve measurement

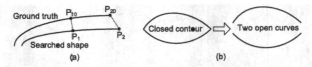

Fig. 7. Illustration for shape distance definition. (a) For the point P_1 of an open curve, D_1 is defined as the minimum distance $|P_1P_{10}|$. For the endpoint P_2, D_2 is defined as the distance between two endpoints $|P_2P_{20}|$. (b) The closed contour is broken into two open curves to calculate the error.

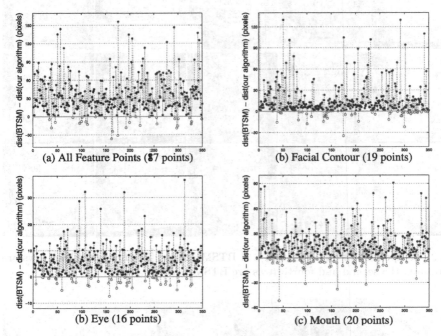

Fig. 8. Comparison of the accuracy of our algorithm and BTSM for the whole facial shape (a), facial contour (b), the eyes (c) and the mouth (d), respectively. The x-axis denotes the index j of test images and the y-axis denotes the difference of the estimation errors $dist(BTSM)_j - dist(our\ algorithm)_j$. Points above $y = 0$ (blue stars) denote images with better accuracy by our algorithm and points below $y = 0$ (red circles) are opposite.

is more reasonable for the comparison of alignment accuracy, because in many cases the fitted curves are almost the same although the positions of two sets of control points are different.

We have plotted $j \sim dist(BTSM)_j - dist(our\ algorithm)_j$ in Figure 8(a) for the whole face alignment. It is shown that on 320 of 350 (91.4%) images, the search results of our algorithm are better than that of BTSM. Since a human is more sensitive to the alignment accuracy for facial contour, eyes and mouth, we also compare the accuracy of these three parts respectively. For the facial contour, the eyes and the mouth, 308(88.0%), 309(88.3%), 289(82.6%) of 350

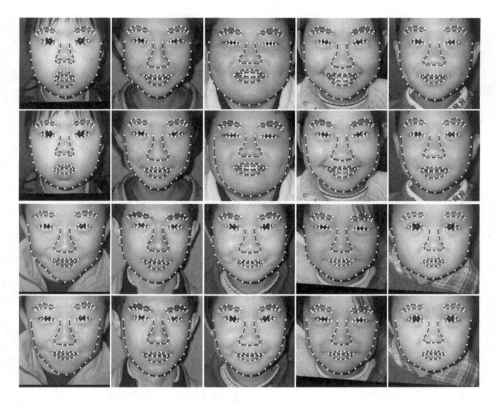

Fig. 9. Comparison of our algorithm and BTSM results. The first and third rows are our results, the second and fourth rows are BTSM results.

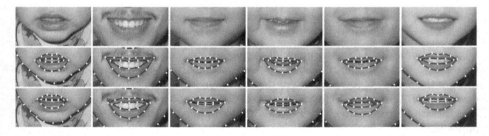

Fig. 10. Comparison of our algorithm and BTSM searching results for the mouth part. The first row is the mouth part cut from the test image, the second row is our results, and the third row is BTSM's results.

results of our algorithm are better than that of BTSM. As shown in Figure 8(b), 8(c) and 8(d), the improvement is distinct.

Figure 9 shows a set of searching results of our algorithm and BTSM. In the case that the facial contour or other facial sub-parts is largely variant from the average shape or there are wrinkles and shadings on the face, our algorithm can give more accurate results than BTSM. In many cases, BTSM can localize the

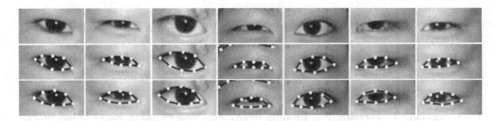

Fig. 11. Comparison of our algorithm and BTSM searching results for the eye part. First row is the eye part cut from the test image, the second row is our results, and the third row is BTSM's result.

whole face well, but when you look at each part closely, the results are often not accurate enough, as shown in Figure 10 and Figure 11, while our algorithm can get more accurate results.

5   Conclusion

In this paper, we present an integrated model for accurate shape alignment. The low level shape model based on a Markov Network serves to align the feature points to the image clues more accurately, while the global shape model based on PCA guarantees the shape to be globally reasonable. Constrained regularization and the mask image for guiding the distribution of Markov Network states make the algorithm more effective and robust. We have compared our algorithm with BTSM and demonstrated its greatly improved accuracy.

References

1. Thodberg, H.H., Rosholm, A.: Application of the active shape model in a commercial medical device for bone densitometry. In: BMVC, Manchester, UK (2001)
2. Zhang, T., Freedman, D.: Tracking objects using density matching and shape priors. In: ICCV, Nice, France (2003)
3. Hu, Y., Jiang, D., Yan, S., Zhang, L., Zhang, H.J.: Automatic 3d reconstruction for face recognition. In: FGR, Seoul, Korea (2004)
4. Liu, C., Zhu, S.C., Shum, H.Y.: Learning inhomogeneous gibbs model of faces by minimax entropy. In: IEEE Int'l Conf. on Computer Vision, Vancouver, Canada (2001)
5. Cootes, T.F., Taylor, C.J., Graham, J.: Active shape models – their training and application. Computer Vision and Image Understanding **61** (1995) 38–59
6. Zhou, Y., Gu, L., Zhang, H.J.: Bayesian tangent shape model: Estimating shape and pose parameters via bayesian inference. In: IEEE Conf. on Computer Vision and Pattern Recognition, Madison, WI (2003)
7. Liu, C., Shum, H.Y., Zhang, C.: Hierarchical shape modeling for automatic face localization. In: Enropean Conf. on Computer Vision. (2002) 687–703
8. Cootes, T.F., Taylor, C.: A mixture model for representing shape variation. Image and Vision Computing **17**(8) (1999) 567–574

9. Romdhani, S., Cong, S., Psarrou, A.: A multi-view non-linear active shape model using kernel pca. In: 10th British Machine Vision Conference, Nottingham, UK (1999)
10. Mitchell, S.C., Lelieveldt, B.P.F., van der Geest, R., Bosch, H.G., Reiber, J.H.C., Sonka, M.: Multistage hybrid active appearance model matching: Segmentation of left and right ventricles in cardiac mr images. IEEE Transactions on Medical Imaging **20**(5) (2001) 415–423
11. Coughlan, J., Ferreira, S.: Finding deformable shapes using loopy belief propagation. In: The Seventh European Conference on Computer Vision, Copenhagen, Denmark (2002)
12. Pearl, J.: Probabilistic Reasoning in Intelligent Systems: Networks of Plausible Inference. Morgan Kaufmann Publishers, San Mateo, California (1988)
13. Freeman, W., Pasztor, E., Carmichael, O.: Learning low-level vision. Int. J. Computer Vision **40**(1) (2000) 25–47

Robust Player Gesture Spotting and Recognition in Low-Resolution Sports Video

Myung-Cheol Roh[1], Bill Christmas[2], Joseph Kittler[2], and Seong-Whan Lee[1],*

[1] Center for Artificial Vision Research, Korea Univ., Seoul, Korea
{mcroh, swlee}@image.korea.ac.kr
[2] Center for Vision, Speech, and Signal Processing, Univ. of Surrey, Guildford, UK
{w.christmas, j.kittler}@surrey.ac.uk

Abstract. The determination of the player's gestures and actions in sports video is a key task in automating the analysis of the video material at a high level. In many sports views, the camera covers a large part of the sports arena, so that the resolution of player's region is low. This makes the determination of the player's gestures and actions a challenging task, especially if there is large camera motion. To overcome these problems, we propose a method based on curvature scale space templates of the player's silhouette. The use of curvature scale space makes the method robust to noise and our method is robust to significant shape corruption of a part of player's silhouette. We also propose a new recognition method which is robust to noisy sequences of data and needs only a small amount of training data.

1 Introduction

The development of high-speed digital cameras and video processing technology has attracted people's attention to automated video analysis such as surveillance video analysis, video retrieval, sports video analysis. Specifically, applying this technology to sports video has many potential applications: automatic summary of play, highlight extraction, winning pattern analysis, adding virtual advertizement, etc. There are interesting works on ball tracking, player tracking and stroke detection for tennis, baseball, soccer, American football, etc[2, 13, 14].

Although there has been much discussion in the literature on automatic sports video annotation and gesture recognition in restricted environment, there is little on player's gesture detection/recognition in standard off-air video, due to low resolution of the player's region, fast motion of the player and camera motion[11, 14].

In sports video, the player's region often has low resolution because the audience wants to watch a wide view of the scene in order to understand the persons' situation and relative position in the field. The same is often true in surveillance video where fixed cameras are used. Camera motion can also make tracking players and extracting players' silhouettes hard, and low resolution makes matching

---

* To whom all correspondence should be addressed.

A. Leonardis, H. Bischof, and A. Pinz (Eds.): ECCV 2006, Part IV, LNCS 3954, pp. 347–358, 2006.
© Springer-Verlag Berlin Heidelberg 2006

player's posture to trained models unstable. Then, because of unstable matched postures, recognition and detection of gestures can also be hard.

J. Sullivan et al. proposed a method for detecting tennis players' strokes, based on qualitative similarity that computes point to point correspondence between shapes by combinatorial geometric hashing. They demonstrated that specific human actions can be detected from single frame postures in a video sequence with higher resolution than that typically found in broadcast tennis video[11]. Although they presented interesting results from their video sequence, the method has some shortcomings. The outline of player will not be extracted accurately when the resolution is low. Often we can see only the player's back while playing, so that we cannot use information of the player's arm because of self occlusion. S. Kopf et al. proposed shape-based posture and gesture recognition using a new curvature scale space (CSS) method in a video sequence which was recorded by pan/tilt/zoom camera[5]. Their new CSS representation can describes convex segment of shape as well as concave. However, their test sequence is of good quality, with good resolution of the player. Also they recognized postures, rather than gesture which is a set of postures. To date, there is much literature in human gesture recognition using 3D, but these methods are difficult to apply to low-resolution video which shows mainly player's back posture; also they are not computationally efficient[9].

There are many sequence recognition and matching methods considering time information, and they have given interesting result in particular environments [3, 6]. But, in special cases such as broadcast sports video, we may not have enough data to train a recognizer such as an HMM. Some methods such as Dynamic Time Warping (DTW) which computes the distance between two time series of given sample rates, gives a similarity measure[10]. But it needs high computational cost and does not give probability measurement. An extension of DTW, Continuous Dynamic Programming (CDP) was proposed by Oka[8], which is our baseline algorithm for comparing with our proposed gesture matching/spotting algorithm.

J. Alon et al. proposed a gesture spotting CDP algorithm via pruning and sub-gesture reasoning . Their method shows an 18% increase in recognition accuracy over the CDP algorithm for video clips of two users gesturing the ten digits 0-9 in an office environment[1].

In this paper, we suggest a new type of feature to represent the player silhouette, together with a novel gesture spotting method. We found the combination to be efficient and robust to the problems of noise and low resolution we encountered using standard off-air video.

2   Sports Player Posture Matching and Gesture Spotting

Our system consists of four parts: foreground separation, silhouette feature extraction, player posture matching and gesture detection. Fig. 1 shows a diagram of our gesture spotting system. Foreground separation is to separate foreground objects from original frames using mosaicing. As a result of foreground separation, we get players' silhouette, ball silhouette and noise blobs roughly, and

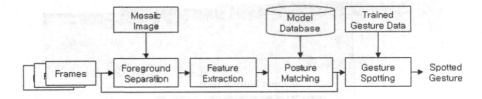

Fig. 1. Player's gesture annotation system

can track player's position using particle filter. Silhouette matching is to match player's silhouette which also includes wrong separated area, to trained silhouettes in database. Gesture detection is done using history of matched silhouettes and database, which is a function of time domain.

2.1 Foreground Separation

Background Generation. We assume a pan/tilt/zoom camera in this method, which is the situation in many sports events. It also makes feasible the use of a mosaicking technique: each frame is projected into a single coordinate system, and a mosaic is created by median filtering of the pixels, creating a background image.

Foreground Separation. By warping the mosaic to match the current frame, the foreground image is extracted simply by taking the difference between the frame and mosaic. Fig. 2 shows input frames, mosaic image and foreground images.

2.2 Silhouette Feature Extraction

We extract the silhouettes from the foreground image of the previous stage by identifying the two largest blobs. The silhouettes are used for matching a posture to posture models in a database, using the following steps.

Curvature Scale Space(CSS). [7] CSS is a well-established technique for shape representation used in image retrieval, and is one of the descriptors used in the MPEG-7 standard. We outline the method here, paraphrasing the description in [7]. The CSS image of a planar curve is computed by convolving a path-based parametric representation of the curve with a Gaussian function of increasing variance σ^2, extracting the zeros of curvature of the convolved curves, and combining them in a scale space representation for the curve. These zero curvature points are calculated continuously while the planar curve is evolving by the expanding Gaussian smoothing function. Let the closed planar curve r be represented by the normalized arc length parameter u:

$$r(u) = \{(x(u), y(u)|u \in [0, 1]\} \tag{1}$$

Then the evolved curve is represented by Γ_σ :

$$\Gamma_\sigma(u) = \{\chi(u, \sigma), \psi(u, \sigma)\} \tag{2}$$

350   M.-C. Roh et al.

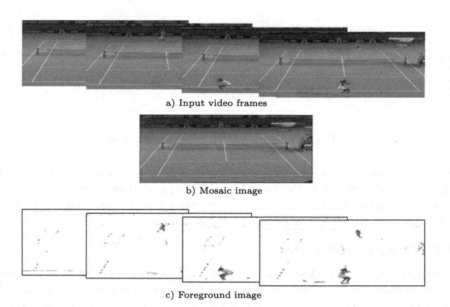

a) Input video frames

b) Mosaic image

c) Foreground image

Fig. 2. Mosaic image and foreground images separated from input frames

where

$$\chi(u,\sigma) = x(u) \otimes g(u,\sigma)$$

$$\psi(u,\sigma) = y(u) \otimes g(u,\sigma)$$

g denotes a Gaussian function of width σ, and $\otimes$ is the convolution operator.

$$g(u,\sigma) = \frac{1}{\sigma\sqrt{2\pi}}e^{-u^2/2\sigma^2}$$

Then curvature of Γ is defined as :

$$\kappa(u,\sigma) = \frac{\chi_u(u,\sigma) - \psi_{uu}(u,\sigma) - \chi_{uu}(u,\sigma) - \psi_u(u,\sigma)}{(\chi_u(u,\sigma)^2 + \psi_u(u,\sigma)^2)^{3/2}} \qquad (3)$$

where

$$\chi_u(u,\sigma) = \frac{\partial}{\partial u}(x(u) \otimes g(u,\sigma)) = x(u) \otimes g_u(u,\sigma)$$

$$\chi_{uu}(u,\sigma) = \frac{\partial^2}{\partial^2 u}(x(u) \otimes g(u,\sigma)) = x(u) \otimes g_{uu}(u,\sigma)$$

$$\psi_u(u,\sigma) = y(u) \otimes g_u(u,\sigma)$$

$$\psi_{uu}(u,\sigma) = y(u) \otimes g_{uu}(u,\sigma)$$

Then, CSS image I_c provides a multi-scale representation of zero crossing points by:

$$I_c = \{(u,\sigma)|\kappa(u,\sigma) = 0, u \in [0,1], \sigma \geq 0\} \qquad (4)$$

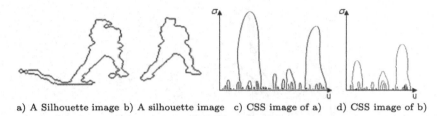

a) A Silhouette image b) A silhouette image   c) CSS image of a)   d) CSS image of b)

Fig. 3. Examples of foreground silhouette and CSS represented images

The CSS image representation is robust to a similarity transformation and (to a lesser extent) an affine transformation, so significant peaks in the CSS shape representation are considered as suitable features for similarity-based retrieval. But the drawback is the zero crossing points of CSS are not reliable features, if part of the shape is corrupted significantly. Fig. 3 (a) and (b) show examples of foreground silhouettes which are corrupted by noise blobs due to low-quality video sequence and a posture model to be matched, respectively. Fig. 3 (c) and (d) shows CSS images of foreground silhouette(a) and posture model(b). These two CSS images are not likely to be considered the same.

Proposed Feature Extraction. We propose a new feature which is based on CSS. Given threshold t, new feature set F of a curve is defined by:

$$F = \{(r(u), \sigma) | (u, \sigma) \in I_c^t\} \tag{5}$$

where

$$I_c^t = \{(u, \sigma) | \kappa(u, \sigma) = 0, u \in [0, 1], \sigma = t\}$$

Fig. 4 represents the processing of extracting features. Fig. 5 shows an example of the new feature set from silhouette images. In contrast to the CSS and the sampling method which is sampling some points on the contour with fixed number[12], the proposed feature is more robust to local noise and significant shape corruption of a part of silhouette and has low computational cost to match two shape images.

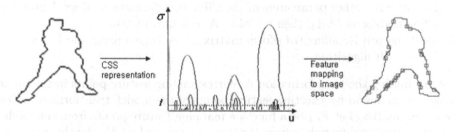

Fig. 4. Proposed feature extracting

Fig. 5. The proposed features based on CSS. The squares indicate feature locations.

2.3   Posture Matching

A posture model database using the proposed feature is constructed from a set of silhouette images of which are extracted manually from representative image sequences. We call silhouette images extracted from test frames *input images* and the silhouettes in the database *models* from now on. To match input image with models in the database and measure the difference, the transformation between them must be estimated. RANSAC algorithm is used for finding transformation of two sets of feature points because of its powerfulness and simplicity[4]. We considered affine transformations in this paper, but extensions to other geometric transformations can be made easily. Apart from the translation parameters, parameter values in the affine transform matrix are assumed to be small on the grounds that there are a sufficient number of images in the database to match shape and size variations. We assume that a large proportion of the shape of the input image is preserved well enough to be matched to one of the models.

The affine transform between model and input image is computed in two steps: firstly the translation is calculated, and secondly the remaining parameters of the affine transform are estimated. The algorithm for finding transformation is defined as follows:

1. Pick one feature point from the feature set of the input image and other feature point from the feature set of the model.
2. Calculate the translation $\mathbf{t}$.
3. Count the number of inliers between the input image and the model with the $\mathbf{t}$.
4. Repeat above steps k times and find $\mathbf{t}$ which has the biggest number of inliers.
5. Initialize the other parameters of the affine transformation : if we denote the affine matrix as $(\mathbf{A}|\mathbf{t})$, then initialise $\mathbf{A}$ as a unit matrix.
6. Find the precise affine transform matrix of the inliers using the Levenberg-Marquardt algorithm.

After finding the transformation $\mathbf{A}$, corresponding feature points in the input image can be found by selecting feature points of the model, transformed by the transform matrix. Let F_{mi} be a function mapping feature points from the model to their corresponding points from the input image, and let F_{im} be the converse. Then, we define D_{mi} as the mean distance between feature points from the model and their corresponding points from the input image, and similarly for D_{im}.

$M = D_{im} + D_{mi}$ is used as a measurement, and a matched model which has lowest M is selected. Fig. 7 shows some examples of input images and models matched to input images.

2.4 Gesture Spotting

We will introduce our Sequence Matching/spotting algorithm and the continuous dynamic programming(CDP) algorithm which is the baseline algorithm to which we compare our proposed algorithm.

Continuous Dynamic Programming. [8] CDP is an extension of the Dynamic Time Warping (DTW) algorithm. Let $f(t)$ and $Z(\tau)$ be variables to represent inputs which are functions of time t in the input image sequence space and time τ in the reference sequence space, respectively. Thus t is unbounded and $\tau \in \{1 \ldots T\}$, where T is the length of the reference pattern. The local distance is defined by $d(t, \tau) = |f(t) - Z(\tau)|$ and a minimum accumulated value of local distances $P(t, \tau)$ is initialized by $P(-1, \tau) = P(0, \tau) = \infty$. Then iteration $(t = 1, 2, \ldots)$ is :

for $\tau = 1$

$$P(t, 1) = 3 \cdot d(t, 1) \tag{6}$$

for $\tau = 2$

$$P(t, 2) = \min \begin{cases} P(t-2, 1) + 2 \cdot d(t-1, 2) + d(t, 2) \\ P(t-1, 1) + 3 \cdot d(t, 2) \\ P(t, 1) + 3 \cdot d(t, 2) \end{cases} \tag{7}$$

for $\tau \le 2$

$$P(t, 2) = \min \begin{cases} P(t-2, \tau-1) + 2 \cdot d(t-1, \tau) + d(t, \tau) \\ P(t-1, \tau-1) + 3 \cdot d(t, \tau) \\ P(t-1, \tau-2) + 3 \cdot d(t, \tau-1) + 3 \cdot d(t, \tau) \end{cases} \tag{8}$$

A section of an input sequence is "spotted" if the value of $A(t)$ gives a local minimum below a threshold value, where $A(t)$ is given by:

$$A(t) = \frac{1}{3 \cdot T} P(t, T) \tag{9}$$

How different a spotted sequence is from a reference sequence is dependent on the threshold value.

Proposed Sequence Matching Algorithm. We propose a new method of sequence matching which is simple and works with a small amount of training data. The need for a small amount of training data is clearly important, as the large training sets typically needed for the commonly used Neural Networks and Hidden Markov Models can be hard to come by. In this paper, we represent a gesture (which is a sequence of postures) as a curve in a 2D Cartesian space of reference time τ versus input image time sequence t. Let $D = \{g_1, g_2, \ldots, g_N\}$ represent a gesture ordered by time index. Thus the kth element g_k represents a member of a cluster of models which have same posture. Let the object $n \leq N$ is the model index of interest (the gesture models to be trained). Given a curve C, a re-aligned index D' can be represented by:

$$D' = \{h_1, h_2, \ldots, h_n, (h_n + g_{n+1}), \ldots, (h_n + g_N)\} \qquad (10)$$

where

$$h_i = C(g_i), \qquad i \leq n$$

If line equation, $C(g_k) = ag_k + b$, is used, then D' will be aligned linearly and only two parameters (a, b) need to be trained. Variances (a_σ, b_σ) and means (a_μ, b_μ) of a and b are trained on some training data and these are used for estimating the likelihood of the input sequence. Thus we can say the dimensionality of gesture is reduced to 2. Given the size l of interval, let v_s be an interval $v_s = [s, s+l]$ in the input sequence and s be a starting frame of a sliding window. For spotting, we estimate a' and b' such that $C'(g_j) = a'g_j + b'$ for each interval v_s where $g_j \in v_s$ and calculate the likelihoods L_a, L_b as follows:

$$L_a(a') = -\frac{1}{2\pi a_\sigma} e^{\frac{(a'-a_\mu)^2}{2a_\sigma^2}} \qquad (11)$$

$$L_b(b') = -\frac{1}{2\pi b_\sigma} e^{\frac{(b'-b_\mu)^2}{2b_\sigma^2}} \qquad (12)$$

Then, we define likelihood L of the interval for the trained curve as follows:

$$L(v_s) = L_a(a') \times L_b(b') \qquad (13)$$

Although the size of interval is fixed in implementation, various speed of gestures can be absorbed by the variance of b, which is determined from the training sequences. Finding maximum value of $L(v_s)$ for the interval where $L(v_s) > L_{threshold}$, we can spot gestures. The threshold value $L_{threshold}$ can be determined roughly because it does not affect the performance seriously. In our experiments on serve detection in tennis video, the difference of peaks of serve and non-serve gesture sequence was larger than 10^{-11} at least. For a robust estimation of C', we need to choose inliers of the estimated line parameters because there are mismatched postures in posture matching, although most of them are matched correctly. Simply, we use posture indexes which are of interest for estimating C' and ignore the indexes which are out of interest. Of course we can use other robust methods to reject outliers. If the number of interesting postures in the interval v_s is smaller than a given threshold, it means that the sequence in the interval has few information to be matched a gesture, in which case we can discard the interval. Fig. 6 shows examples of lines which are fitted from 2 sets of training data by a least square fitting method.

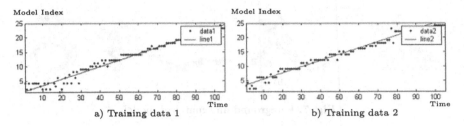

Fig. 6. Examples of line fitting to training data set

3   Experimental Results

3.1   Environment

To evaluate the performance of the proposed posture matching and gesture spotting, we used an off-air interlaced sequence from the 2003 Australian open tennis tournament video. We separated out the fields from the frames, due to player's fast motion; some examples are shown in Fig. 2. Our target player is the near (or bottom) player. Initialization of the player's location was achieved by using a simple background subtraction method. The average width and height of the player are 53 and 97 pixels, respectively. To create the posture model database, we chose one play shot from the whole collection of play shots, and extracted player's posture manually. A model in database is represented by the curve coordinates of silhouette, zero-crossing points' locations in the image space, and additionally, zero-crossing points' height in the curvature scale space. For training gestures, i.e. estimating line parameters, we used only three sequences of a gesture data.

3.2   Posture Matching

Posture matching is achieved by using our new CSS-based features. We extracted the feature set and compared the distance to the posture models in the database. Fig. 7 shows some examples of foreground extracted from the input frames and matched models. In Fig. 7(a-c), the contours (yellow) of the foregrounds are not extracted accurately because of shadows and white lines of the court. Nevertheless, we can see good matched results with our new features even though the contours are not good enough to match with the standard CSS matching method. Sometimes, matching are failed such as in Fig. 7(d), but in the 5 best matched models we could find proper model.

3.3   Serve Gesture Spotting

We tested using 50 sequences, of which some include a serve gesture, some do not. The sequences are also partitioned by the players' identity ('A' and 'B') and position of player on the court('Left' and 'Right'). Fig. 6 shows a sequence projected onto the time-model space for a serve gesture. For training, we use a

Fig. 7. Foreground and matched model

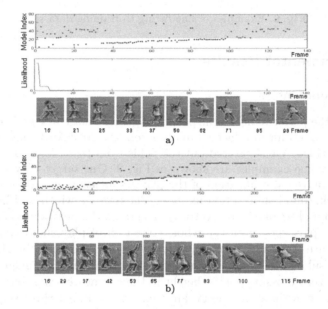

Fig. 8. Likelihood and some snapshots of spotted gesture for representative shots

single shot, of which one of the players is serving on the right-hand side of the court.

Fig. 8 shows postures plotted onto the time-model space (first rows), likelihood graph versus time (second rows) and some snap-shots of sequences which are detected as a serve gesture(third rows). The gray area in the first rows indicates the which model indices are outliers (do not contribute to calculating line parameters for matching serve gesture). The yellow contours in the third rows shows a matched posture model. We can see that gesture spotting is achieved successfully, even though posture matching sometime fails. In Fig. 8(a), the player is bouncing the ball for a while, so the serve gestures is spotted at the 16th frame. In Fig. 8(b), there are two serve sequences (starting from 1st and 548th frame) in a shot. The player served twice because the first serve was a fault. Table 1 shows results of serve gesture spotting. In the table, true positive(TP), true negative(TN), false positive(FP) and false negative(FN) indicate serve gesture detected in correct location, no serve gesture detected where there is no serve, serve gesture detected where there is no serve and serve gesture not detected where there is a serve, respectively. Our method generates 90%

Table 1. Gesture spotting result using CDP and the proposed method

		Player A		Player B		Total
		Left	Right	Left	Right	
CDP	TP	5/11	8/11	4/8	7/8	62% correct
	TN	7/12				
	FP	4/11	3/11	4/8	3/8	36.8% incorrect
	FN	6/11	3/11	4/8	1/8	
Proposed method	TP	8/11	11/11	7/8	7/8	90% correct
	TN	12/12				
	FP	0/11	0/11	0/8	0/8	5.2% incorrect
	FN	2/11	0/11	1/8	1/8	

correct result(TP+TN)and 5.2% incorrect result(FP+FN), while the results for the baseline algorithm, CDP, are 62% and 36.8%. The spotting results show that our method is substantially better than CDP.

4   Conclusions

In this paper, we presented a robust posture matching method and a gesture spotting method. For matching posture from low-resolution video frames, we proposed a feature based on CSS, which is robust to noise and significant shape corruption of the player's silhouette. For gesture spotting under a sequence of matched postures which may include mismatches, we calculate parameters for a curve of gestures plotted on the time-model space, and then estimate the likelihood using these trained parameters for spotting. According to our experiments, our spotting method generates 90% correct results and 5.2% incorrect results while the figures for the continuous dynamic programming algorithm are 62% and 36.8%, respectively. The proposed spotting method is robust to noise in the sequence data, with computational costs small enough to be calculated in real time.

Acknowledgements. This work was supported by the Korea Science and Engineering Foundation (KOSEF).

References

1. J. Alon, V. Athitsos, and S. Sclaroff, Accurate and Efficient Gesture Spotting via Pruning and Subgesture Reasoning, Proc. the IEEE Workshop on Human-Computer Interaction, Beijing, China, Oct. (2005) 189-198
2. W. J. Christmas, A. Kostin, F. Yan, I. Kolonias and J. Kittler. A System for The Automatic Annotation of Tennis Matches, Fourth International Workshop on Content-based Multimedia Indexing, Riga, June (2005)
3. A. Corradini, Dynamic Time Warping for Off-line Recognition of A Small Gesture Vocabulary, Proc. the IEEE ICCV Workshop on Recognition, Analysis, and Tracking of Faces and Gestures in Real-Time Systems, Vancouver, Canada (2001) 82-89

4. M. A. Fischler and R. C. Bolles, Random Sample Consensus: A Paradigm for Model Fitting with Applications to Image Analysis and Automated Cartography, Comm. of the ACM, Vol. 24 (1981) 381-395
5. S. Kopf, T. Haenselmann and W. Effelsberg, Shape-base Posture and Gesture Recognition in Videos, Electronic Imaging, 5682, San José, CA, January (2005) 114-124
6. H.-K. Lee and J. H. Kim, An HMM-Based Threshold Model Approach for Gesture Recognition, the IEEE Trans. on Pattern Analysis and Machine Intelligence, Vol. 21, No. 10 (1999) 961-973
7. F. Mokhtarian and M. Bober, Curvature Scale Space Representation: Theory, Applications & MPEG-7 Standardisation, Kluwer Academic (2003)
8. R. Oka, Spotting method for classification of real world data, The Computer Journal, Vol. 41, No. 8 (1998) 559-565
9. A.-Y. Park, and S.-W. Lee, Gesture Spotting in Continuous Whole Body Action Sequences Using Discrete Hidden Markov Models, Gesture in Human-Computer Interaction and Simulation, Lecture Notes in Computer Science, Vol. 3881 (2005) 100-111
10. L. Rabiner and B.-H. Juang, Fundamentals of Speech Recognition, Prentice-Hall (1993)
11. J. Sullivan and S. Carlsson, Recognising and Tracking Human Action, Proc. European Conf. on Computer Vision, Copenhagen, Denmark, May (2002) 629-644
12. B. J. Super, Improving Object Recognition Accuracy and Speed through Non-Uniform Sampling, Proc. SPIE Conf. on Intelligent Robots and Computer Vision XXI: Algorithms, Techniques, and Active Vision, Providence, RI (2003) 228-239
13. F. Yan, W. Christmas and J. Kittler, A Tennis Ball Tracking Algorithm for Automatic Annotation of Tennis Match, Proc. British Machine Vision Conference, Oxford, UK, Sep. (2005) 619-628
14. J. R. Wang and N. Parameswaran, Survey of Sports Video Analysis: Research Issues and Applications, Proc. Pan-Sydney Area Workshop on Visual Information Processing, Vol. 36, Sydney, Australia, Dec. (2004) 87-90

Recognition and Segmentation of 3-D Human Action Using HMM and Multi-class AdaBoost*

Fengjun Lv and Ramakant Nevatia

University of Southern California,
Institute for Robotics and Intelligent Systems,
Los Angeles, CA 90089-0273
{flv, nevatia}@usc.edu

Abstract. Our goal is to automatically segment and recognize basic human actions, such as stand, walk and wave hands, from a sequence of joint positions or pose angles. Such recognition is difficult due to high dimensionality of the data and large spatial and temporal variations in the same action. We decompose the high dimensional 3-D joint space into a set of feature spaces where each feature corresponds to the motion of a single joint or combination of related multiple joints. For each feature, the dynamics of each action class is learned with one **HMM**. Given a sequence, the observation probability is computed in each HMM and a weak classifier for that feature is formed based on those probabilities. The weak classifiers with strong discriminative power are then combined by the Multi-Class AdaBoost (**AdaBoost.M2**) algorithm. A dynamic programming algorithm is applied to segment and recognize actions simultaneously. Results of recognizing 22 actions on a large number of motion capture sequences as well as several annotated and automatically tracked sequences show the effectiveness of the proposed algorithms.

1 Introduction and Related Work

Human action recognition and analysis has been of interest to researchers in domains of computer vision [1] [2] [9] [3] [10] [12] for many years. The problem can be defined as: given an input motion sequence, the computer should identify the sequence of actions performed by the humans present in the video. While some approaches process the video images directly as spatio-temporal volumes [10] , it is common to first detect and track humans to infer their actions [3] [12]. For finer action distinction, such as picking up an object, it may also be necessary to track the joint positions. The methods may be further distinguished by use of 2-D or 3-D joint positions.

In this paper, we describe a method for action recognition, *given* 3-D joint positions. Of course, estimating such joint positions from an image sequence is a difficult task in itself; we do not address this issue in this paper. We use

---

* This research was supported, in part, by the Advanced Research and Development Activity of the U.S. Government under contract No. MDA904-03-C1786.

A. Leonardis, H. Bischof, and A. Pinz (Eds.): ECCV 2006, Part IV, LNCS 3954, pp. 359–372, 2006.
© Springer-Verlag Berlin Heidelberg 2006

data from a Motion Capture (*MoCap*) system[1]or from a video pose tracking system. It may seem that the task of action recognition given 3-D joint positions is trivial, but this is not the case, largely due to the high dimensionality (e.g. 67-D) of the pose space. The high dimensionality not only creates a computational complexity challenge but, more importantly, key features of the actions are not apparent, the observed measurements may have significant spatial and temporal variations for the same action when performed by different humans or even by the same person. Furthermore, to achieve continuous action recognition, the sequence needs to be segmented into contiguous action segments; such segmentation is as important as recognition itself and is often neglected in action recognition research. Our method attempts to solve both the problem of action segmentation and of recognition in presence of variations inherent in performance of such actions. Even though we assume that 3-D positions are given, we present results illustrating the effects of noise in the given data (for positions derived from videos).

Previously reported action recognition methods can be divided into two categories with respect to the data types that they use: those based on 2-D image sequences, e.g. [2] [9] [3] [10] [12] and those based on 3-D motion streams, e.g. [1] [7]. The above 2-D approaches can be further divided by the image features they use: those based on object contours [2] [12], those base on motion descriptor such as optical flow [3] or gradient matrix [10] and those base on object trajectories [9]. A 3-D approach has many advantages over a 2-D approach as the dependence on viewpoint and illumination has been removed. Nonetheless, many algorithms use a 2-D approach because of the easy availability of video inputs and difficulty of recovering 3-D information.

In the above 3-D approaches, [1] decomposes the original 3-D joint trajectories into a collection of 2-D projected curves. Action recognition is based on the distances to each of these curves. However, the predictors they use are static constructs as the correlation between 2-D curves are lost after projection. In [7], actions are represented by spatio-temporal motion templates, which correspond to the evolution of 3-D joint coordinates. As matching results can be affected by temporal scale change, each template is resampled and multiple-scale template matching is performed.

The approaches cited above (except for [7]) assume that the given sequence contains only one action performed throughout the length of the sequence; it is not clear how and whether they could be extended to segment a video containing sequence of actions and recognize the constituent actions. In [7] action segmentation is obtained to some extent by classifying action at each frame by considering a fixed length sequence preceding it; such segmentation is inaccurate at the boundaries and over-segmentation may occur. Explicit action segmentation is considered in the context of complex actions consisting of a sequence of simpler actions but only when a model of the sequence is available, such as in [5]. We consider a sequence of actions where such models are not

---

[1] Part of data comes from mocap.cs.cmu.edu, which was created with funding from NSF EIA-0196217.

known and actions may occur in any sequence (though some sequences may be eliminated due to kinematic constraints; we do not consider such constraints in this work).

Our approach is based on 3-D joint position trajectories. The actions we consider are *primitive* components that may be composed to form more complex actions. The actions are grouped according to the set of body parts that are related to the action. In our approach, the high dimensional space of 3-D joint positions is decomposed into a set of lower dimensional feature spaces where each feature corresponds to the motion of a single joint or combination of related multiple joints. For each feature, the dynamics of one action class is learned with one continuous Hidden Markov Model (HMM) with outputs modeled by a mixture of Gaussian. A weak classifier for that feature is formed based on the corresponding HMM observation probabilities. Weak classifiers of the features with strong discriminative power are then selected and combined by the Multi-Class AdaBoost (**AdaBoost.M2**) algorithm to improve the overall accuracy. A dynamic programming-based algorithm is applied to segment and recognize actions simultaneously in a continuous sequence.

To our knowledge, there has been little work done in computer vision that integrates HMM with AdaBoost. In [13], an integration called "boosted HMM" is proposed for lip reading. Their approach is different from ours in that they use AdaBoost first to select frame level features and then use HMM to exploit long term dynamics. This does not suit the action recognition problem well because the full body motion is much more complex than the lip motion. Without the dynamic information, the static features tend to cluster in the feature space and thus can not discriminate different actions well; their combination (using AdaBoost) is unlikely to alleviate the problem much. Another difference is that [13] works with pre-segmented sequences only.

We show the results of our system on a large collection of motion capture sequences with a large variety of actions and on some hand annotated as well as automatically tracked video sequences. The recognition results are very good and the method demonstrates tolerance to considerable amount of noise. We also compare performance with our earlier work [7] which was based on a simpler algorithm. Most importantly, the new approach can take a data stream containing a sequence of actions and then segment and recognize the component actions which is not possible with the earlier approach.

2   The Dataset and Feature Space Decomposition

We collected 1979 MoCap sequences consisting of 22 Actions from Internet. We also generated some sequences of 3-D joint position from a 3-D annotation software [6] and from an automatic 3-D tracking software [6]. The generated data are much less accurate compared with MoCap. They are used in testing only to show that our algorithm can work on real data and that training on MoCap data transfers to video sequences; we do not claim to have solved the tracking problem as well.

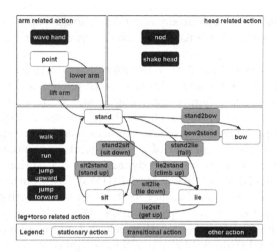

Fig. 1. Categorization of actions that need to be recognized

Actions in these videos can be grouped into 3 categories according to the involved primary body parts: {*leg+torso, arm, head*}. The categorization is illustrated in Fig.1. Actions in the same group are mutually exclusive to each other, but actions from different groups can be recognized simultaneously. This allows us to execute logical queries such as *find the sequence in which the subject is walking while his head is nodding.*

Actions can also be classified based on whether the primary body parts move or not. We view a *stationary* pose, *e.g. stand or sit (white blocks* in Fig.1) as a special type of action, with the constraint that duration of the action should be long enough (longer than some threshold). The *transitional* actions (*gray blocks*) transit from one stationary pose to another. The remainder (*black blocks*) consist of *periodic* actions (*e.g. walk, run*) and other actions.

Different joint configurations (i.e. number of joints/bones, joint names and joint hierarchy) are unified to one that consists of 23 joints. The joint positions are normalized so that the motion is invariant to the absolute body position, the initial body orientation and the body size.

Since there are 23 joints and each has 3 coordinates (only y coordinate is used for hip, the root joint), the whole body pose at each frame can be represented by a 67-D vector (called a *pose vector*). We performed some experiments to evaluate the effectiveness of using the 67-D pose vector on a simpler subset of action classes Walk, Run, Stand, Fall, Jump, Sit down. We first used a Bayesian network to classify static pose and found the classification accuracy to be less than 50%. Then, we trained and tested a 3-state continuous HMM (the same as one described in section 3.1) and found the accuracy to be still low (below 60%). These experiments do not conclusively prove that using the full pose vector is undesirable but it is reasonable to think that relevant information can get lost in the large pose vector.

Rather than enumerate all combinations of different components in the pose vector (as in [1]), we design feature vectors, called just *features* from now on, such that each feature corresponds to the pose of a single joint or combination of multiple joints. Following is the list of different types of features that are included.

Type 1: one coordinate of a joint, e.g. the vertical position of the hip
Type 2: coordinates of each non-root joint
Type 3: coordinates of 2 connected joints, e.g. neck and head
Type 4: coordinates of 3 connected joints, e.g. chest, neck and head
Type 5: coordinates of one pair of symmetric nodes, e.g. left hip and right hip
Type 6: coordinates of all leg and torso related joints
Type 7: coordinates of all arm related joints

Features are designed in this way based on our analysis of the actions and the features that can distinguish them. Different types characterize different levels of dynamics of an action. For example, Type 2,3 and 4 corresponds to joint position, bone position and joint angle, respectively. Type 5 features are useful for detecting periodic motions and type 6 and 7 features provide an overall guidance for recognition. In total we have 141 features.

3   Integrated Multi-class AdaBoost HMM Classifiers

We now describe our action recognition methodology. It consists of a combination of HMM classifiers, which are treated as *weak* classifiers in the AdaBoost terminology, and whose outputs are combined by a multi-class AdaBoost algorithm (**AdaBoost.M2**). We first describe the HMM classifiers and then their combination. The issue of segmenting the pose sequence into separate actions is addressed separately in section 4 later.

3.1   Learning Weak Classifiers Using HMMs

We choose a hidden Markov model (HMM) to capture the dynamic information in the feature vectors as experience shows them to be more powerful than models such as Dynamic Time Warping or Motion Templates. An HMM is defined by states, transition probabilities between them and probabilities of outputs given a state. Well known algorithms [8] are available to answer the following questions:

1. How to compute $P(O|\lambda)$, the probability of occurrence of the observation sequence $O=O_1O_2...O_T$ given model parameters λ? This problem can be solved by the **Forward-Backward** procedure.
2. How to select the best state sequence $I=i_1i_2...i_T$ such that $P(O,I|\lambda)$ is maximized? This problem can be solved by the **Viterbi** algorithm.
3. How to learn model parameters λ given O such that $P(O|\lambda)$ is maximized? This problem can be solved by the **Baum-Welch** algorithm.

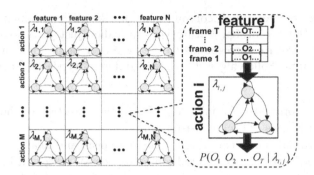

Fig. 2. The matrix of HMMs. Each HMM has 3 hidden states. Each state contains a 3-component mixture of Gaussian. Once $\lambda_{i,j}$, the parameters of $\text{HMM}_{i,j}$ is learned, the probability of the observation sequence $O_1O_2...O_T$ is computed using the **Forward** procedure. The action with the maximum probability in the same column is selected.

For the action classification problem, suppose there are M action classes and N features (feature classes). For the j-th feature ($j = 1,...,N$), we learn one HMM for each action class and the corresponding parameters λ_i, $i = 1,...,M$. Given one observation sequence O, we compute $P(O|\lambda)$ for each HMM using the **Forward-Backward** procedure. Action classification based on feature j can be solved by finding action class i that has the maximum value of $P(O|\lambda_i)$, as shown in Eq.1.

$$action(O) = \underset{i:i=1,...,M}{\arg\max}\left(P(O|\lambda_i)\right) \tag{1}$$

We call the set of these HMMs and the decision rule in Eq.1 as the weak classifier for feature j (a term used in boosting algorithm literature). These M action classes and N features form an $M \times N$ matrix of HMMs, as shown in Fig.2. We denote by $\text{HMM}_{i,j}$ the HMM of action i (i-th row) and feature j (j-th column) and its corresponding parameters is $\lambda_{i,j}$. The set of HMMs in column j correspond to the weak classifier for feature j.

Recall that there are three action groups based on involved body parts. Therefore, to recognize actions in a specific group, only related features need to be considered. In other words, a feature can only classify related actions. For example, feature $neck_{xyz}+head_{xyz}$ can only classify action "nod" and "shake head". Therefore, there are three matrices of HMMs, corresponding to three action groups. As HMMs in three groups are used in the same way; unless otherwise stated, we do not specify which group that they belong to.

In our system, each HMM has 3 hidden states and each state is modeled by a 3-component mixture of Gaussian. The following parameters of each HMM are learned by the **Baum-Welch** algorithm: (1) Prior probabilities of each state, (2) Transition probabilities between states and (3) Parameters of each state s (s=1,2,3): Mean vector $\mu_{s,m}$, covariance matrix $\Sigma_{s,m}$ and weight $w_{s,m}$ of each mixture component (Gaussian) (m=1,2,3).

The training and classification algorithm of weak classifiers are listed as follows:

Algorithm 1. Training of weak classifiers

1. Given Q training samples $\langle(x_1, y_1), ..., (x_Q, y_Q)\rangle$ where x_n is a sequence with action label y_n, $y_n \in \{1, ..., M\}$, n=1,...,Q, M is the number of action classes
2. Divide the Q samples into M groups such that each group contains samples with the same label.
3. for j=1 to N (N is the number of features)
      for i=1 to M
         3.1 Crop the training samples in group i, such that they contain only coordinates that belong to feature j
         3.2 Train $\text{HMM}_{i,j}$ using **Baum-Welch** algorithm

---

Algorithm 2. Classification algorithm based on weak classifier j

1. Given an observation sequence $O=O_1O_2...O_T$
2. for i=1 to M, Compute $P(O|\lambda_{i,j})$
3. Return $\underset{i:i=1,...,M}{\arg\max}(P(O|\lambda_{i,j}))$

Both **Forward** and **Baum-Welch** algorithm need to compute $P(O_t|s_t = s)$, the probability of observing O_t given that state s at time t. Unlike a discrete HMM, a continuous HMM uses a Probability Density Function (PDF) to estimate $P(O_t|s_t = s)$. This is because no point has a probability in a continuous distribution, only regions do. For the Gaussian mixture model used here, $P(O_t|s_t = s)$ is computed as follows:

$$\sum_{m=1}^{3}\left(w_{s,m}\frac{1}{(2\pi)^{\frac{d}{2}}|\Sigma_{s,m}|^{\frac{1}{2}}}e^{-\frac{1}{2}(O_t-\mu_{s,m})\Sigma_{s,m}^{-1}(O_t-\mu_{s,m})^T}\right) \qquad (2)$$

In practice, Log-likelihood $log(P(O_t|s_t = s))$ is used to avoid numerical underflow. Another consideration is that the probability of occurrence of the observation sequence $O_1O_2...O_T$ tends to decrease exponentially as T increases. But this causes no problem here because for feature j, the probability computed in each of $\text{HMM}_{i,j}$ $(i = 1, ..., M)$ decreases comparably.

The complexity of **Algorithm 2** is $O(MN_{st}^2T)$, where N_{st} is the number of states in HMM. Deciding automatically the appropriate value of N_{st} is difficult and therefore in practice, it is usually specified in advance. Our experiments show that an HMM of 3 states with a 3-component mixture Gaussian can capture rich dynamic information in the actions and can achieve desired high classification rate. So the complexity of **Algorithm 2** is approximately $O(MT)$.

The complexity of **Algorithm 1** is $O(NN_{it}N_{st}^2L_{all})$, where N_{it} is the number of iterations in **Baum-Welch** algorithm and L_{all} is the total length of training samples of all action classes. In our experiment, **Baum-Welch** algorithm usually converges in less than 5 iterations. So the complexity of **Algorithm 1** is approximately $O(NL_{all})$.

3.2   Boosting Classifiers Using AdaBoost.M2

Experiments show that individual learned HMM classifiers have reasonably good performance; for example, feature (all leg and torso related joints) alone can correctly classify 62.1% of 16 leg and torso related action classes. However, we expect much better performance from the final classifier. This can be done by combining HMM classifiers, considered to be weak classifiers. This is made possible due to the fact that each weak classifier has different discriminative power for different actions.

Inspired by success of boosting methods for many problems, particularly face detection of Viola and Jones [11], we use the AdaBoost [4] algorithm to combine results of weak classifiers and to discard less effective classifiers to reduce the computation cost. This algorithm works in an iterative way such that in each iterationthe newly selected classifiers focus more and more on the difficult training samples. In this paper, we use **AdaBoost.M2** [4], the multi-class version of AdaBoost. Some limitations of **AdaBoost.M2** for feature selection were stated in [13]; we believe that those limitations hold only when the weak classifiers have very limited discriminative power.

We rephrase the **AdaBoost.M2** algorithm here to accommodate our specific problem.

Algorithm 3. AdaBoost.M2 for action classification

1. Given Q training samples $\langle(x_1, y_1), ..., (x_Q, y_Q)\rangle$ where x_n is a sequence with action label y_n, $y_n \in \{1, ..., M\}$, $n=1,...,Q$
2. Train weak classifiers using **Algorithm 1** in section 3.1
3. Test these Q samples on each $\mathrm{HMM}_{i,j}$, record the value $P(x_n|\lambda_{i,j})$, $i=1,...,M$, $j=1,...,N$, $n=1,...,Q$
4. Let $B = \{(n, y) : n \in \{1, ..., Q\}, y \neq y_n\}$ be the set of all mislabels; Let $D^{(1)}(n, y) = 1/|B|$ for $(n, y) \in B$ be the initial distribution of mislabels
5. for k=1 to K (K is the number of iterations)

    5.1 Select a weak classifier h_k that has minimum
    pseudo-loss $\varepsilon_k = \frac{1}{2} \sum_{(n,y) \in B} D^{(k)}(n, y)(1 - P(x_n|\lambda_{y_n, h_k}) + P(x_n|\lambda_{y, h_k}))$

    5.2 Set $\beta_k = \varepsilon_k/(1 - \varepsilon_k)$

    5.3 Update $D^{(k)}$: $D^{(k+1)}(n, y) = \frac{D^{(k)}(n,y)}{Z_k}\beta_k^{\frac{1}{2}(1+P(x_n|\lambda_{y_n, h_k})-P(x_n|\lambda_{y, h_k}))}$

    where Z_k is normalization constant so that $D^{(k+1)}$ will be a distribution
6. Let $f = \sum_{k=1}^{K} (\log \frac{1}{\beta_k})P(x|\lambda_{y, h_k})$. Return the final classifier $h(x) = \underset{y \in \{1,...,M\}}{\arg\max} (f)$
    and likelihood $H(x) = \underset{y \in \{1,...,M\}}{\max} (f)$

The idea of this algorithm can be interpreted intuitively as follows:(1) $\log \frac{1}{\beta_k}$ is the weight of the selected classifier h_k. Intuitively, as $P(x_n|\lambda_{y_n, h_k})$ increases (which means h_k labels x_n more accurately), the pseudo-loss ε_k decreases and consequently $\log \frac{1}{\beta_k}$ increases. So in each iteration the new selected classifier has the strongest discriminative power given current $D^{(k)}$. (2)$D^{(k)}$, the distribution of mislabels, represents the importance of distinguishing incorrect label y on sample x_n. As $P(x_n|\lambda_{y,h_k})$ increases and $P(x_n|\lambda_{y_n,h_k})$ decreases (which means that h_k labels x_n less accurately), $D^{(k)}$ increases because $\varepsilon_k \leq \frac{1}{2}$ and thus $\beta_k \leq 1$. By maintaining this distribution, the algorithm can focus not only on the hard-to-classify samples but also on the hard-to-discriminate labels. This is the major improvement over **AdaBoost.M1**, the first version of multi-class AdaBoost [4].

Care needs to be taken when applying **AdaBoost.M2** on continuous HMMs because it is critical in **AdaBoost.M2** that the value of hypotheses generated by weak classifiers not exceed 1 so that the pseudo-loss ε_k is in the range of [0,0.5]. However, for a continuous HMM, the observation probability $P(x_n|\lambda_{i,j})$ computed by the **Forward** procedure is based on a Gaussian function, as shown in Eq.2. Keep in mind this is the probability *density* function. Therefore, $P(x_n|\lambda_{i,j})$ can be greater than 1 in practice. If this occurs, all $P(x_n|\lambda_{i,j})$ computed in step 3 of **Algorithm 3** will be normalized by a scale factor such that the maximum of all $P(x_n|\lambda_{i,j})$ does not exceed 1. (Theoretically, $P(x_n|\lambda_{i,j})$ can be an infinite number, which indicates the sample should be definitely labeled as action i, but this does not occur in our experiments.)

Results show that after combining 15 weak classifiers by the boosting procedure, the final classifier achieves a classification rate of 92.3% on the leg and torso related actions, showing the effectiveness of the algorithm.

4   The Segmentation Algorithm

Action classification method described in section 3 assumes that each input sequence belongs to one of the action classes. To achieve continuous action recognition, a (long) sequence needs to be segmented into contiguous (shorter) action segments. Such segmentation is as important as recognition itself.

Here is the definition of segmentation: Given an observation sequence $O = O_1 O_2 ... O_T$, a segmentation of O can be represented by a 3-tuple $S(1,T)= (N_S, s_p, a_p)$.

- N_S: the number of segments, $N_S \in \{1, ..., T\}$
- s_p: the set of start time of each segment, $s_p \in \{1, ..., T\}$, $p = 1, ..., N_S$, s_1 is always 1 and we add an additional point s_{N_S+1}=T+1 to avoid exceeding the array boundary
- a_p: the corresponding action labels of each segment, $a_p \in \{1, ..., M\}$

For a sub-sequence $O_{t1} O_{t1+1} ... O_{t2}$, we compute the following functions:

$$h(t1,t2) = \underset{y \in \{1,...,M\}}{\arg\max} \sum_{k=1}^{K} (\log \frac{1}{\beta_k}) P(O_{t1}...O_{t2}|\lambda_{y,h_k}) \qquad (3)$$

$$H(t1,t2) = \underset{y \in \{1,...,M\}}{\max} \sum_{k=1}^{K} (\log \frac{1}{\beta_k}) P(O_{t1}...O_{t2}|\lambda_{y,h_k}) \qquad (4)$$

$h(t1,t2)$ and $H(t1,t2)$ is the action label and likelihood computed by **Algorithm 3**.

Given a segmentation S of $O_1 O_2 ... O_T$, a likelihood function L is defined as:

$$L(1, T, S(1,T)) = \prod_{p=1}^{N_S} H(s_p, s_{p+1} - 1) \qquad (5)$$

A maximal likelihood function L^* is defined as:

$$L^*(1,T) = \max_{S(1,T)} L(1,T,S(1,T)) \qquad (6)$$

The goal of the segmentation problem is to find the maximal likelihood function $L^*(1,T)$ and the corresponding segmentation $S^*(1,T)$. Enumeration of all possible values of (N_S, s_p, a_p) is infeasible because of the combinatorial complexity. However, the problem can be solved in $O(T^3)$ time by a dynamic programming-based approach: Suppose a sub-sequence $O_{t1}...O_{t2}$ is initially labeled as $h(t1,t2)$ and t is the optimal segmentation point in between (if $O_{t1}...O_{t2}$ should be segmented). If $L^*(t1, t-1)L^*(t, t2)$ is larger than $H(t1, t2)$, then $O_{t1}...O_{t2}$ should be segmented at t. The idea is shown in Eq.7.

$$L^*(t1,t2) = \max_t(H(t1,t2), L^*(t1, t-1)L^*(t, t2)) \qquad (7)$$

This recursive definition of L^* is the basis of the following dynamic programming-based algorithm.

Algorithm 4. Segmentation algorithm
/*$L^*(t1,t2)$ abbr. as $L^*_{t1,t2}$, same for other variables*/

1. Given an observation sequence $O=O_1 O_2 ... O_T$. l_{min} is the limit of minimum length of a segment
2. Compute $h_{t1,t2}$ and $H_{t1,t2}$, $t1,t2 \in \{1,...,T\}$ and $t2 \geq t1 + l_{min} - 1$
3. /*too short to be segmented*/
   for $l=l_{min}$ to $2l_{min} - 1$
     for $t1=1$ to $T - l + 1$
       $L^*_{t1,t1+l-1}=H_{t1,t1+l-1}$
       Record the corresponding action labels
4. /*dynamic programming starts here*/
   for $l=2l_{min}$ to T
     for $t1=1$ to $T - l + 1$
       $L^*_{t1,t1+l-1}=\max(H_{t1,t1+l-1}, \max_t(L^*_{t1,t-1}L^*_{t,t1+l-1}))$
       where $t1 + l_{min} \leq t \leq t1 + l - l_{min}$
       Record the corresponding segmentation point and action labels
5. return $L^*_{1,T}$ and the corresponding $S^*_{1,T}$

We use l_{min} here to avoid over segmentation as well as impose a constraint on the stationary actions (or precisely, poses, e.g. stand) such that duration of a stationary action should be long enough.

The complexity of the above algorithm is $T^3/6$ in terms of computation of $L^*_{t1,t-1}L^*_{t,t1+l-1}$. The cost is still high if T is very large. Significant speedup can be achieved if there are pauses or stationary actions (which usually occur in a long sequence), which can be easily detected beforehand by sliding a temporal window and analyzing the mean and variance of motion within the sliding window. These pauses or stationary actions are then used to pre-segment the long sequence into several shorter sequences.

The above *step 2* requires computation of $P(O_{t1}...O_{t2}|\lambda)$, the probability of observing each valid sub-sequence $O_{t1}...O_{t2}$ by an HMM. To avoid repeated computation of such $P(O_{t1}...O_{t2}|\lambda)$ in the **Forward** procedure, we augment the **Forward** procedure so that instead of returning the probability of observing $O_{t1}...O_{t2}$ only, we return the probabilities of observing each sub-sequence of $O_{t1}...O_{t2}$ starting from O_{t1}.

5 Experimental Results

To validate the proposed action classification and segmentation algorithm, we tested it on a large MoCap database as well as several annotated and automatically tracked sequences to investigate the potential of its use with video data. The results on these two types of data are shown in section 5.1 and 5.2. In section 5.3, we show a comparison with our earlier template matching based approach algorithm [7] on the same dataset.

5.1 Results on MoCap Data

The 1979 MoCap sequences in our dataset contain 243,407 frames in total. We manually segmented these sequences such that each segment contains a whole course of one action. In total we have 3745 action segments. The distribution of these segments in each action class is not uniform. *Walk* has 311 segments while *lie2stand* has only 45 segments. The average number is 170. The length of these segments are also different, ranging from 43 to 95 frames. The average is 65 frames.

In **Experiment 1,** we randomly selected half of segments of each action class for training and the remainder for classification. In **Experiment 2**, we reduced the amount of training data to 1/3. We repeated these experiments five times and the average classification rate of each class is shown in Table 1.

The overall classification rate of each action group {*leg+torso, arm, head*} are $\{92.3\%, 94.7\%, 97.2\%\}_{Exp.1}$ and $\{88.1\%, 91.9\%, 94.9\%\}_{Exp.2}$, respectively.

As expected, the performance of Experiment 2 is lower, but not by much, indicating that the algorithm is robust in terms of the amount of available training data. Compared with Experiment 1, most of the first 3 best features (not shown here due to limited space) for each action did not change (although the order may be different). This shows consistency of **AdaBoost.M2** in selecting good classifiers.

Results show that individual learned HMM classifiers have reasonably good performance; for example, in Experiment 1, one feature (all leg and torso related joints) alone can correctly classify 62.1% of leg and torso related action

Table 1. Classification rate of each action class

action	walk	run	j upward	j forward	stand	sit	bow	lie
Exp.1	94.1%	95.5%	92.2%	91.2%	91.8%	92.4%	89.8%	88.7%
Exp.2	89.0%	91.3%	87.3%	86.6%	87.9%	90.5%	86.0%	84.8%
action	stand2sit	sit2stand	stand2bow	bow2stand	stand2lie	lie2stand	sit2lie	lie2sit
Exp.1	89.7%	89.8%	89.0%	88.3%	92.4%	88.2%	91.2%	91.8%
Exp.2	84.7%	86.6%	84.8%	86.5%	88.7%	84.5%	86.6%	86.1%
action	wave hand	point	lower arm	lift arm	nod	shake head		
Exp.1	95.8%	94.2%	92.7%	92.3%	97.9%	96.7%		
Exp.2	91.3%	92.8%	89.2%	89.4%	95.1%	94.8%		

classes. The effectiveness of **AdaBoost.M2** in combining good features can be clearly seen by a gain of about 30% (from 62.1% to 92.3%) in the classification rate.

In **Experiment 3**, we tested our segmentation/recognition algorithm on 122 unsegmented long sequences (from testing set) with average length of 949 frames (please see the supplementary material for some result videos). We use the classifier learned in Experiment 1 and we set l_{min}=20 frames to avoid over segmentation. The algorithm achieves a recognition rate of 89.7% (in terms of frames).

In terms of speed, on a P4 2.4GHz PC, Experiment 1 took 153 minutes for training and 42 minutes for classification ($\sim$47 fps). Experiment 2 took 76 minutes and 66 minutes ($\sim$41 fps). Experiment 3 took 68 minutes to segment 122 sequences ($\sim$28 fps). The results show that the classification as well as the segmentation/recognition algorithm works in real time.

5.2 Results on Annotated and Tracked Data

In **Experiment 4**, we used a 3-D annotation software and a 3-D tracking software developed in our group [6] to generate two annotated (994 frames in total) and one automatically tracked (159 frames) sequence.

Fig.3 shows some key frames of one annotated sequence. The rendered annotation results using a human character animation software called POSER (by Curious Labs) are displayed on the right. The ground truth action and the recognized action are shown at the top and the bottom, respectively.

Results show that most of actions have been correctly recognized although the segmentation is not perfect. Errors occur when the subject turns around because we don't model such actions in our action set. *Carry* was not recognized for the same reason. *Reach* and *crouch*, however, were recognized as *point* and *sit*, which are reasonable substitutions for *reach* and *crouch*.

The recognition rate on the annotated and tracked data is 88.5% and 84.3%, respectively. This is satisfactory considering a substantial amount of jittery noise contained in the data (root mean square position error rates of about 10 pixels ($\sim$10 cm) and joint angle errors of about 20°). The proposed algorithm, in

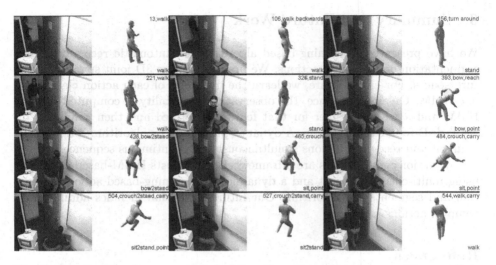

Fig. 3. Key frames of one annotated video. Ground truth and recognition result is shown in top-right and bottom-right, respectively.

general, is robust to these types of errors with short duration because of the longer-term dynamics captured by the HMMs.

5.3   Comparison with Template Matching Based Algorithm

We tested our earlier template matching based algorithm in [7] using exactly the same experimental setup. In [7], each action is represented by a template consisting of a set of channels with weights. Each channel corresponds to the evolution of one 3D joint coordinate and its weight is learned according to the Neyman-Pearson criterion. χ^2 function is used as the distance measurement between the template and the testing sequences. The results of [7] are listed as follows: **Exp.1**:{leg+torso:83.1%, arm:84.8%, head:88.4%}, **Exp.2**:{leg+torso:79.4%, arm: 80.5%, head: 82.3%}, **Exp.3**:80.1%, **Exp.4**:{annotated: 82.3%, tracked:80.6%}.

The new algorithm has significantly better results. We note that the detection results for the template matching based methods are inferior to those originally reported in [7] because the sequences in this test are much more demanding and include walking styles with large variations such as staggering, dribbling and catwalk. The method described in this paper outperforms template matching not only because Boosted HMMs provide a more powerful way to model such variations but also because it is less sensitive to temporal scale changes.

Also note that the recognition algorithm in [7] does not segment long sequences in Experiment 3. It simply searches for the best matched template within the preceding window. As action label at next frame may change, that leaves many small misclassified fragments. In contrast, the segmentation based method provide some global guidance for the process to make sure that the long sequence is not over segmented.

6 Summary and Future Work

We have presented a learning-based algorithm for automatic recognition and segmentation of 3d human actions. We first decompose 3D joint space into feature spaces. For each feature, we learn the dynamics of each action class using one HMM. Given a sequence, the observation probability is computed in each HMM and a weak classifier for that feature is formed and then combined by the **AdaBoost.M2** algorithm. A dynamic programming algorithm is applied to segment and recognize actions simultaneously in a continuous sequence.

Our major contributions are a framework that boosts HMM-based classifiers using multi-class AdaBoost and a dynamic programming-based action recognition and segmentation algorithm. Our future work plan includes adding more complex actions.

References

1. L. Campbell and A. Bobick. Recognition of human body motion using phase space constraints. In *Proc. of ICCV*, pp. 624-630, 1995.
2. J. Davis and A. Bobick. The Representation and Recognition of Action Using Temporal Templates. In *Proc. of CVPR*, pp. 928-934, 1997.
3. Alexei A. Efros, Alexander C. Berg, Greg Mori and Jitendra Malik. Recognizing Action at a Distance. In *Proc. of ICCV*, pp. 726-733, 2003.
4. Y. Freund and R.E. Schapire. A decision theoretic generalization of on-line learning and application to boosting. *Journal of Computer and System Science* 55(1), 1995, pp. 119-139.
5. S. Hongeng and R. Nevatia. Large-Scale Event Detection Using Semi-Hidden Markov Models In *Proc. of ICCV*, pp. 1455-1462, 2003.
6. M.W. Lee and R. Nevatia. Dynamic Human Pose Estimation using Markov chain Monte Carlo Approach. In *Proc. of the IEEE Workshop on Motion and Video Computing* (WACV/MOTION05), 2005.
7. F. Lv and R. Nevatia. 3D Human Action Recognition Using Spatio-Temporal Motion Templates. In *Proc. of the IEEE Workshop on Human-Computer Interaction* (HCI05), 2005.
8. L. R. Rabiner. A tutorial on Hidden Markov Models and selected applications in speech recognition. In *Proc. of the IEEE*, 77(2):257-286, 1989.
9. C. Rao, A. Yilmaz and M. Shah. View-Invariant Representation and Recognition of Actions. In *Int'l Journal of Computer Vision* 50(2), Nov. 2002, pp. 203-226.
10. E. Shechtman and M. Irani. Space-Time Behavior Based Correlation. In *Proc. of CVPR*, I pp. 405-412, 2005.
11. P. Viola and M. Jones. Rapid Object Detection Using a Boosted Cascade of Simple Features. In *Proc. of CVPR*, pp. 511-518, 2001.
12. A. Yilmaz and M.Shah. Actions Sketch: A Novel Action Representation. In *Proc. of CVPR*, I pp. 984-989, 2005.
13. P. Yin, I. Essa and J. M. Rehg. Asymmetrically Boosted HMM for Speech Reading In *Proc. of CVPR*, II pp. 755-761, 2004.

Segmenting Highly Articulated Video Objects with Weak-Prior Random Forests

Hwann-Tzong Chen[1], Tyng-Luh Liu[1], and Chiou-Shann Fuh[2]

[1] Institute of Information Science, Academia Sinica, Taipei 115, Taiwan
{pras, liutyng}@iis.sinica.edu.tw
[2] Department of CSIE, National Taiwan University, Taipei 106, Taiwan
fuh@csie.ntu.edu.tw

Abstract. We address the problem of segmenting highly articulated video objects in a wide variety of poses. The main idea of our approach is to model the prior information of object appearance via *random forests*. To automatically extract an object from a video sequence, we first build a random forest based on image patches sampled from the initial template. Owing to the nature of using a randomized technique and simple features, the modeled prior information is considered *weak*, but on the other hand appropriate for our application. Furthermore, the random forest can be dynamically updated to generate prior probabilities about the configurations of the object in subsequent image frames. The algorithm then combines the prior probabilities with low-level region information to produce a sequence of figure-ground segmentations. Overall, the proposed segmentation technique is useful and flexible in that one can easily integrate different cues and efficiently select discriminating features to model object appearance and handle various articulations.

1 Introduction

Object segmentation has been one of the fundamental and important problems in computer vision. A lot of efforts have been made to resolve the problem, but, partly due to the lack of a precise and objective definition itself, fully-automatic unconstrained segmentation is still an "unsolved" vision task. The predicament is further manifested by the success of those characterized with clear aims, e.g., edge or interest-point detection. Nevertheless, the bottom-up segmentation approaches based on analyzing low-level image properties have been shown to achieve stable and satisfactory performances [13], [20], [28], [36], even though the segmentation outcomes (e.g., see [17]) often contextually differ from those produced by humans [16], [21]. Humans have abundant experience on the contexts of images; with our prior knowledge we can infer an object's shape and depth, and thus produce *meaningful* segmentations that are unlikely to be derived by a general-purpose segmentation algorithm.

While fully automatic image segmentation seems to be an ill-posed problem, *figure-ground segmentation*, on the other hand, has more specific goals and is easier to evaluate the quality of segmenting results. Since the emphasis is on separating the target object(s) (of which some properties are known *a priori*)

A. Leonardis, H. Bischof, and A. Pinz (Eds.): ECCV 2006, Part IV, LNCS 3954, pp. 373–385, 2006.
© Springer-Verlag Berlin Heidelberg 2006

Fig. 1. Examples of unusual and highly articulated poses

from the background, it opens up many possibilities regarding how to impose prior knowledge and constraints on the segmentation algorithms. For instance, an algorithm may choose from some predefined object models, such as deformable templates [35] or pictorial structures [11], or learn from the training data [4] to construct the object representation. Once the representation is decided, the algorithm can yield segmentation hypotheses in a top-down fashion [4], and then examines the feasibility of hypothesized segmentations. Indeed top-down and bottom-up segmentation approaches are not mutually exclusive and, when properly integrated, they could result in a more efficient framework [30], [34].

In this paper we address figure-ground segmentation for objects in video. Particularly, we are interested in establishing a framework for extracting non-rigid, highly articulated objects, e.g., athletes doing gymnastics as shown in Fig. 1. The video sequences are assumed to be captured by moving cameras, and therefore background subtraction techniques are not suitable. Furthermore, since we are mostly dealing with unusual poses and large deformations, top-down approaches that incorporate class-specific object models such as active contours [2], exemplars [14], [29], pictorial structures [11], constellations of parts [12], deformable models [22], and deformable templates [35] are less useful here—the degree of freedom is simply too high, and it would require either a huge number of examples or many parameters to appropriately model all possible configurations of the specified object category. Hence, instead of considering *class-specific* segmentation [4], we characterize our approach as *object-specific* [34]: Given the segmented object and background in the initial image frame, the algorithm has to segment the same object in each frame of the whole image sequence, and the high-level prior knowledge about the object to be applied in the top-down segmentation process should be learned from the sole example.

1.1   Previous Work

In class-specific figure-ground segmentation, the top-down mechanism is usually realized by constructing an object representation for a specified object category and then running the segmentation algorithm under the guidance of the representation. Borenstein and Ullman [4] introduce the fragment-based representation that covers an object with class-related fragments to model the shape of the object. Their algorithm evaluates the quality of "covering with candidate fragments" to find an optimal cover as the segmenting result. Three criteria are used to determine the goodness of a cover: similarity between a fragment and an image region, consistency between overlapping fragments, and reliability (saliency) of fragments. Tu et al. [30] propose the image parsing framework that combine the bottom-up cues with the top-down generative models to simultaneously deal with segmentation, detection, and recognition. The experimental results in [30] illustrate the impressive performances of parsing images into background regions and rigid objects such as faces and text.

Despite the computational issues, Markov random fields (MRFs) have been widely used in image analysis through these years [15]. Recently several very efficient approximation schemes for solving MRFs [5], [33] and their successful use in producing excellent results for interactive figure-ground segmentation, e.g., [3], [6], [27], have made this group of approaches even more popular. Aiming for the class-specific segmentation, Kumar et al. [18] formulate the object category specific MRFs by incorporating top-down pictorial structures as the prior over the shape of the segmentation, and present the OBJ CUT algorithm to obtain segmentations under the proposed MRF model. Typically, graph-cut-based segmentation approaches use predefined parameters and image features in the energy functions [6]. Although the GMMRF model [3] allows adjustments to the color and contrast features through learning the corresponding parameters from image data, only low-level cues are considered. Ren et al. [26] propose to learn the integration of low-level cues (brightness and texture), middle-level cues (junctions and edge continuity), and high-level cues (shape and texture prior) in a probabilistic framework.

The segmentation task of our interest is related more closely to that of Yu and Shi [34], where they address the object-specific figure-ground segmentation. Given a sample of an object, their method can locate and segregate the same object under some view change in a test image. The algorithm takes account of both pixel-based and patch-based groupings through solving a constrained optimization regarding pixel-patch interactions. Still in Yu and Shi [34] the goal of segmentation is to identify rigid objects in images. We instead consider a figure-ground technique for video, and more importantly, for segmenting articulated objects with large deformations. We are also motivated by the work of Mori et al. [23] that considers detecting a human figure using segmentation. They use Normalized Cuts [28] to decompose an image into candidate segments. To generate the body configuration and the associated segmentation, their algorithm locates and then links those segments representing the limbs and torso of the target human. The experimental results reported in [23] show that the proposed technique can extract from images the baseball players in a wide variety of poses. Concerning the implementation details, their approach requires *logistic regression* to learn the weights of different cues from a set of hand-segmented image templates. In addition, several global constraints are enforced to reduce the complexity of searching a large number of candidate configurations. These constraints are indeed very strong prior knowledge defining what physically possible configurations of a human body can be, and consequently are not easy to be generalized to other object categories.

A different philosophy from those of the aforementioned approaches is using variational models [24] or level-set PDE-based methods [25] for image segmentation. Approaches of this kind are more flexible to handle deformations. However, integrating different cues or imposing top-down prior models in such frameworks is much more sophisticated, which involves adding intriguing terms accounting for the desired properties into the PDEs, and thus further complicates the numerical formulations, e.g., [8], [9]. It is also hard to include learning-based mechanisms such as parameter estimation and feature selection, to give suitable weights among low-level information and different aspects of prior knowledge.

1.2   Our Approach

Analogous to regularization for optimization problems, there is a trade-off between imposing strong prior knowledge and allowing flexibility of object configurations when we incorporate a top-down scheme into figure-ground segmentation. For the images shown in Fig. 1, class-specific shape (or structure) models, in general, are more restrictive for covering such a wide range of pose variations, otherwise the search space of possible configurations might be too large to be tractable.

We propose a new framework for object-specific segmentation that models the prior information by *random forests* [7], constructed from randomly sampled image patches. Owing to the nature of random forests, the modeled prior knowledge is *weak* but still sufficient for providing top-down probabilistic guidance on the bottom-up grouping. And this aspect of characteristic is crucial for our task. Moreover, the randomized technique also enables cue integration and feature selection to be easily achieved. We shall show that the proposed algorithm is useful and rather simple for video-based figure-ground segmentation, especially when the objects are non-rigid and highly articulated.

2   Learning Prior Models with Random Forests

In this section we first describe the image cues for constructing the prior models, and then explain the technique of embedding a prior model into a random forest. Given the template and the mask of an object, using Figs. 2a and 2b as an example, we seek to build a useful prior model with a random forest for subsequent video object segmentations. For the experiments presented in this paper, we use color, brightness, and gradient cues, though other cues such as texture and optical flow can be easily included in the same manner. Specifically, we first apply Gaussian blur to each color channel of the template as well as the gray-level intensity, and thus get the smoothed cues as illustrated in Figs. 2c and 2d. From the smoothed intensity we compute the gradient, and then further blur it to get the x and y derivatives as shown in Figs. 2e and 2f. Note that the values of all cues are normalized between 0 and 1. For convenience, these cues are combined to get a pseudo-image of six channels. We will treat the pseudo-image template as a pool of patches that constitute our prior knowledge about the object.

(a)	(b)	(c)	(d)	(e)	(f)

Fig. 2. Information used for constructing the prior models. (a) Template. (b) Mask. (c) RGB color cues. (d) Brightness cue. (e) x derivatives. (f) y derivatives.

2.1 Random Forests

Random forests by Breiman [7] are proposed for classification and regression, and are shown to be comparable with boosting and support vector machines (SVMs) through empirical studies and theoretical analysis. Despite their simplicity and the effectiveness in selecting features, random forest classifiers are far less popular than AdaBoost and SVMs in computer vision, though random forests are indeed closely related to and partly motivated by the shape-recognition approach of randomized trees [1]. Random forests have been used for multimedia retrieval by Wu and Zhang [32]. More recently, Lepetit et al. [19] consider randomized trees for keypoint recognition, and obtain very promising results.

To model the prior information of an object's appearance, we generate a forest of T random binary trees. Each tree is grown by randomly sampling N patches from the pseudo-image template; we run this process T times to obtain T trees. The typical window size of a patch we use in the experiments is 5×5. Since a pseudo-image contains six channels, we actually store each patch as a vector of $5 \times 5 \times 6$ elements (see the illustration at the right hand side of Fig. 3). Let $\mathbf{x}^k$ denote a patch, and $\{\mathbf{x}^k | \mathbf{x}^k \in \mathbb{R}^d\}_{k=1}^N$ be the sample set (hence $d = 150$). For each patch $\mathbf{x}^k$ we then obtain the label information y^k from the corresponding position (patch center) in the mask. Therefore, we have the labels $\{y^k | y^k \in \{\mathsf{F}, \mathsf{G}\}\}_{k=1}^N$ that record a patch belonging to figure (F) or ground (G). To grow a tree with $\{(\mathbf{x}^k, y^k)\}_{k=1}^N$ involves random feature selection and node impurity evaluation. The tree-growing procedure is described as follows.

1. At each tree-node, we randomly select M features. In this work we consider a feature as the difference between some ith and jth elements of a patch. That is, we repeat M times choosing at random a pair of element indices i and j. With a random pair of indices i and j defining a feature, each patch $\mathbf{x}^k$ would give a feature value $f = \mathbf{x}_i^k - \mathbf{x}_j^k$.

2. For each feature, we need to determine a threshold that best splits the patches reaching the current node by their feature values. The threshold of feature values for optimal splitting is obtained by maximizing the decrease in *variance impurity* of the distribution of the patches. The idea is to *purify* each child node such that the patches in a child node would almost carry the same label. (For brevity's sake, we skip the definition of impurity and the description of maximizing the impurity drop. The details can be found in [10], p. 400.)

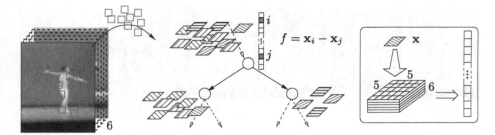

Fig. 3. Growing a random tree. The typical window size of a patch is 5 × 5. Since a pseudo-image contains six channels, we actually store a patch as a vector of 5 × 5 × 6 elements. A feature is defined as the difference between two randomly selected elements of a patch. We use the random feature (with an optimized threshold) to split the set of patches reaching the current node into two parts forming two child nodes, according to the feature values f of patches being greater or less than the threshold.

3. Among the M randomly selected features we pick the one that produces the maximum drop in impurity, and use this feature and its threshold to split the current patches into two child nodes according to the feature values of patches being greater or less than the threshold, as illustrated in Fig. 3.
4. We stop splitting a node (thus a leaf node) if the number of arriving patches is less than a chosen constant, or if the predefined limit of tree-height is met.
5. If there is no more node to be split, the growing process is done. Each internal node stores a feature and a splitting threshold, and each leaf node yields a probability $P(y = \mathsf{F}|\mathbf{x}$ reaches this leaf node), which is computed as the proportion of "the patches in this leaf node belonging to the figure F" to "all the patches that reach this leaf node."

The features used in the random trees cover a large number of combinations of differences between two channels with some spatial perturbations. For instance, they may represent the difference between the R and B channels of a patch, or represent two pixels being residing on or separated by an edge. Because the cues have been smoothed, the features are less sensitive to the exact positions they are selected. Moreover, these types of features can be efficiently computed; each computation costs only two memory accesses and one subtraction. Our experimental results show that they are also quite discriminating in most cases.

2.2 Prior Probabilities About the Object's Configuration

After constructing a forest of T trees by repeating the preceding procedure, we have a random forest that models the appearance prior of a target object. Then for each new image frame, we scan the whole image pixel by pixel to run every corresponding patch $\mathbf{x}$ through the random forest, and average the probabilities

new input   one tree   25 trees

Fig. 4. Prior probabilities

$\{P_t(y = \mathsf{F}|\mathbf{x})\}_{t=1}^{T}$ advised by the trees. The scheme thus provides top-down probabilistic guidance on the object's configuration. Fig. 4 illustrates the prior probabilities estimated by a single tree and by 25 random trees for a new input image. Suffice it to say, with a random forest of 25 trees, the object's appearance prior can be suitably modeled using the template and mask in Fig. 2. In the next section, we will show how to combine the top-down hints of prior probabilities with the bottom-up segmentations.

3   Applying Prior Models to Segmentation

In Figs. 5b and 5c we depict two segmenting results produced by Normalized Cuts [28]: one contains 4 segments and the other 70 segments. The results show that, even though directly using Normalized Cuts with a "few-segment" setting to obtain figure-ground segmentation might not be appropriate, the Normalized Cuts segmentation that produces many regions (over-segmentation) does provide useful low-level information about the segments of the object.

3.1   Solving Figure-Ground Segmentation

The key idea is to combine the low-level information of over-segmentation with the prior probabilities derived from the random-forest prior model to complete the figure-ground segmentation. Our algorithm can produce segmenting results like the one shown in Fig. 5d. In passing, based on the segmenting results, it is straightforward to highlight the object in the video or extract its contour, e.g., see Figs. 5e and 5f. We summarize our algorithm as follows.

Voting by prior probabilities. Inside each region of the over-segmentation derived from Normalized Cuts, compute the number of pixels whose prior probabilities are above, say, one standard deviation of the mean prior probabilities. That is, a pixel having a high enough prior probability casts one vote for the region to support it as a part of the figure.

Choosing candidates. A region will be considered as a candidate if it gets more than half of the total votes by its enclosing pixels.

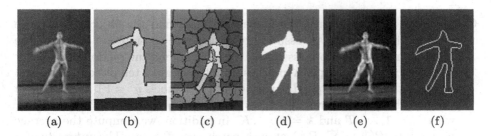

(a)   (b)   (c)   (d)   (e)   (f)

Fig. 5. (a) New input. (b) & (c) Two Normalized Cuts segmentations with 4 and 70 segments. (d) Figure-ground segmentation produced by our algorithm. Based on the segmentation result, it is straightforward to (e) highlight the object in the video, or (f) extract the contour for other uses such as action analysis.

Filling gaps. Apply, consecutively, morphological dilation and erosion (with a small radius) to all candidate regions. This will close some gaps caused by artifacts in low-level segmentation.

Merging the candidates. Compute the connected components of the outcome in the previous step to combine neighboring candidate regions. Set the largest component as the figure and the rest of the image as the background.

3.2 Locating the Video Object

So far we discuss merely the single-frame case, and assume that a loose bounding-box surrounding the object is given to point out the whereabouts of the object in each frame. Thus we take only the cropped image as input for the aforementioned algorithm. For video, we bring in a simple tracker to find the loose bounding-box of the object. This is also achieved by working on the prior probabilities. We just need to search nearby area of the object's previous location in the previous image frame to find a tight bounding-box that encloses mostly high prior probabilities. We then enlarge the tight bounding-box to get a loose one to include more backgrounds. The optimal tight bounding-box can be very efficiently located by applying the technique of *integral images*, as is used in [31]. Our need is to calculate the sum of prior probabilities inside each bounding-box and find the one yielding the largest sum. For that, we compute the integral image of the prior probabilities. Then calculating each sum would require only four accesses to the values at the bounding-box's corners in the integral image.

3.3 Updating the Random Forest

Since we are dealing with video, it is natural and convenient to update the random forest based on previous observations and segmenting results. The updated random forest would be consolidated with new discriminating features to distinguish the object from the changing backgrounds. We propose to update the random forest by cutting and growing trees. The following two issues are of concern to the updating: 1) which trees should be cut, and 2) which patches could be used to grow new trees.

Cutting old trees. Because the foreground mask and the object appearance given at the beginning are assumed to be accurate and representative, we use them to assess the goodness of the trees in the current random forest. For an assessment, we sample K patches from the original template to construct $\{\tilde{\mathbf{x}}^k\}_{k=1}^K$ that all correspond to the object (with labels $\tilde{y}^k = \mathsf{F}$). We run them through the random forest of T trees and get the probabilities $P_t(\tilde{y}^k = \mathsf{F}|\tilde{\mathbf{x}}^k)$, where $t = 1, \ldots, T$ and $k = 1, \ldots, K$. In addition, we compute the average probability $\bar{P}(\cdot) = \sum_t P_t(\cdot)$ of each patch over T trees. The *infirmity* of a tree is evaluated by

$$L_t = -\sum_k \bar{P}(\tilde{y}^k = \mathsf{F}|\tilde{\mathbf{x}}^k) \log P_t(\tilde{y}^k = \mathsf{F}|\tilde{\mathbf{x}}^k). \tag{1}$$

The negative logarithm of a probability measures the error made by a tree for a given patch. And the average probability $\bar{P}(\tilde{y}^k = \mathsf{F}|\tilde{\mathbf{x}}^k)$ gives a larger weight to the patch that is well predicted by most of the trees. Hence a tree will be penalized more by $\bar{P}(\tilde{y}^k = \mathsf{F}|\tilde{\mathbf{x}}^k)$ if it performs relatively poor than others on $\tilde{\mathbf{x}}^k$. We cut the top T' trees that give the largest values on L_t.

Growing new trees. We need to grow T' new trees to replace those being cut. The patches required for constructing new trees are sampled from three sources: 1) From the inside of the figure segmentation we sample the patches that are of very high prior probabilities and label them as the figure patches; 2) From the area outside the figure segmentation but inside the bounding-box, we sample the patches that are of very low prior probabilities and mark them as background patches; 3) From the area outside the loose bounding-box, we sample the patches that are of high prior probabilities, and also label them as background patches—these patches are prone to cause misclassifications.

After the updating, we have a mixture of old and new trees. The updated random forest still provides an effective prior model of the object, and becomes more robust against the varying background.

Note that our presentation in Section 3 is to first detail what needs to be done for each single frame, and then describe how to handle an image sequence. In practice, the algorithm of applying a prior model to segmenting a video object is carried out in the following order: 1) locating the bounding box, 2) solving figure-ground segmentation, and 3) updating the random forest.

4   Experiments

We test our approach with some dancing and gymnastics video clips downloaded from the Web[1]. Some of the image frames are shown in Fig. 6, as well as the prior probabilities and the figure-ground segmentations produced by our approach. The objects in these video sequences demonstrate a wide variety of poses. Many of the poses are unusual, though possible, and therefore provide ideal tests to emphasize the merits of our algorithm. Note that even though we only test on human figures, our approach is not restricted to a specific object category, and hence should be equally useful in segmenting other types of rigid or non-rigid objects.

The following are a summary of the implementation details and the parameters used. In our experiments the size of a random forest is $T = 25$. The height limit of a tree is set to 6. To grow each tree, we sample $N = 1800$ patches, each of size 5×5 as mentioned earlier, from the template image. (Specifically, the template image is enlarged and shrunk by 5% to add some scale variations. Therefore, we have three scales of the template for drawing samples; we sample 600 patches under each scale.) A typical template size is 150×100, which is also

---

[1] http://www.londondance.com, http://www.shanfan.com/videos/videos.html, http://www.rsgvideos.com

Fig. 6. The first two images shown in each of the five experiments are the template and the mask used for constructing the random forest. For each experiment we show three examples of the input frame, the prior probabilities, and the figure-ground segmentation produced by our approach.

the size of the loose bounding box used in the subsequent processes to locate the target object. Recall that, at each tree node, we need to randomly select M features as a trial, we have $M = 20$ for all the experiments. Regarding updating the random forest, for each updating we cut $T' = 10$ trees and grow new ones to keep the size of forest $(T = 25)$. Overall, we find the above setting of random forests can model the objects quite well.

Our current implementation of the proposed algorithm is in MATLAB and running on a Pentium 4, 3.4 GHz PC. About the running time, building the initial random forest of 25 trees takes 5 seconds. And it takes 25 seconds to produce the figure-ground segmentation for a 240×160 input image (including 15 seconds for Normalized Cuts, 5 seconds for computing the prior probabilities, and 3 seconds for updating the random forest).

5   Conclusion

We present a new randomized framework to solve figure-ground segmentation for highly articulated objects in video. Although previous works have shown that using top-down class-specific representations can improve figure-ground segmentations, such representations, which are usually built upon strong constraints and specific prior knowledge, might lack flexibility to model a wide variety of configurations of highly articulated objects. Our approach to the problem is based on modeling weak-prior object appearance with a random forest. Instead of constructing a representation for a specific object category, we analyze a video object by randomly drawing image patches from the given template and mask, and use the patches to construct the random forest as the prior model of the object. For an input image frame, we can derive the prior probabilities of the object's configuration from the random forest, and use the prior to guide the bottom-up grouping of over-segmented regions. Our experimental results on segmenting different video objects in various poses demonstrate the advantages of using random forests to model an object's appearance—a learning-based mechanism to select discriminating features and integrate different cues. For future work, we are interested in testing other filter-based cues to make our algorithm more versatile, as well as handling occlusion and multi-object segmentation.

Acknowledgements

This work was supported in part by grants NSC 94-2213-E-001-005, NSC 94-2213-E-001-020, and 94-EC-17-A-02-S1-032.

References

1. Y. Amit and D. Geman. Shape quantization and recognition with randomized trees. *Neural Computation*, 9:1545–1588, 1997.
2. A. Blake and M. Isard. *Active Contours: The Application of Techniques from Graphics, Vision, Control Theory and Statistics to Visual Tracking of Shapes in Motion.* Springer-Verlag, 1998.

3. A. Blake, C. Rother, M. Brown, P. Perez, and P.H.S. Torr. Interactive image segmentation using an adaptive GMMRF model. In *ECCV*, volume 1, pages 428–441, 2004.
4. E. Borenstein and S. Ullman. Class-specific, top-down segmentation. In *ECCV*, volume 2, pages 109–122, 2002.
5. Y. Boykov, O. Veksler, and R. Zabih. Markov random fields with efficient approximations. In *CVPR*, pages 648–655, 1998.
6. Y.Y. Boykov and M.P. Jolly. Interactive graph cuts for optimal boundary and region segmentation of objects in n-d images. In *ICCV*, volume 1, pages 105–112, 2001.
7. L. Breiman. Random forests. *Machine Learning*, 45(1):5–32, 2001.
8. T. Chan and W. Zhu. Level set based shape prior segmentation. In *CVPR*, volume 2, pages 1164–1170, 2005.
9. D. Cremers, F. Tischhauser, J. Weickert, and C. Schnorr. Diffusion snakes: Introducing statistical shape knowledge into the Mumford-Shah functional. *IJCV*, 50(3):295–313, December 2002.
10. R.O. Duda, P.E. Hart, and D.G. Stork. *Pattern Classification*. Wiley, 2001.
11. P.F. Felzenszwalb and D.P. Huttenlocher. Pictorial structures for object recognition. *IJCV*, 61(1):55–79, January 2005.
12. R. Fergus, P. Perona, and A. Zisserman. Object class recognition by unsupervised scale-invariant learning. In *CVPR*, volume 2, pages 264–271, 2003.
13. C.C. Fowlkes, D.R. Martin, and J. Malik. Learning affinity functions for image segmentation: Combining patch-based and gradient-based approaches. In *CVPR*, volume 2, pages 54–61, 2003.
14. D. Gavrila. Pedestrian detection from a moving vehicle. In *ECCV*, volume 2, pages 37–49, 2000.
15. S. Geman and D. Geman. Stochastic relaxation, Gibbs distributions, and the Bayesian restoration of images. *PAMI*, 6(6):721–741, November 1984.
16. http://www.cs.berkeley.edu/projects/vision/grouping/segbench/. *The Berkeley Segmentation Dataset and Benchmark*.
17. http://www.cs.berkeley.edu/~fowlkes/BSE/cvpr-segs/. *The Berkeley Segmentation Engine*.
18. M.P. Kumar, P.H.S. Torr, and A. Zisserman. OBJ CUT. In *CVPR*, volume 1, pages 18–25, 2005.
19. V. Lepetit, P. Lagger, and P. Fua. Randomized trees for real-time keypoint recognition. In *CVPR*, volume 2, pages 775–781, 2005.
20. J. Malik, S. Belongie, T. Leung, and J. Shi. Contour and texture analysis for image segmentation. *IJCV*, 43(1):7–27, June 2001.
21. D.R. Martin, C.C. Fowlkes, D. Tal, and J. Malik. A database of human segmented natural images and its application to evaluating segmentation algorithms and measuring ecological statistics. In *ICCV*, volume 2, pages 416–423, 2001.
22. T. McInerney and D. Terzopoulos. Deformable models in medical image analysis: A survey. *MIA*, 1(2):91–108, 1996.
23. G. Mori, X. Ren, A.A. Efros, and J. Malik. Recovering human body configurations: Combining segmentation and recognition. In *CVPR*, volume 2, pages 326–333, 2004.
24. D. Mumford and J. Shah. Boundary detection by minimizing functionals. In *CVPR*, pages 22–26, 1985.
25. N. Paragios and R. Deriche. Coupled geodesic active regions for image segmentation: A level set approach. In *ECCV*, volume 2, pages 224–240, 2000.

26. X. Ren, C. Fowlkes, and J. Malik. Cue integration for figure/ground labeling. In *NIPS 18*, 2005.
27. C. Rother, V. Kolmogorov, and A. Blake. GrabCut: interactive foreground extraction using iterated graph cuts. *ACM Trans. Graph.*, 23(3):309–314, 2004.
28. J. Shi and J. Malik. Normalized cuts and image segmentation. *PAMI*, 22(8): 888–905, August 2000.
29. K. Toyama and A. Blake. Probabilistic tracking in a metric space. In *ICCV*, volume 2, pages 50–57, 2001.
30. Z. Tu, X. Chen, A.L. Yuille, and S.C. Zhu. Image parsing: Unifying segmentation, detection, and recognition. In *ICCV*, pages 18–25, 2003.
31. P. Viola and M.J. Jones. Rapid object detection using a boosted cascade of simple features. In *CVPR*, volume 1, pages 511–518, 2001.
32. Y. Wu and A. Zhang. Adaptive pattern discovery for interactive multimedia retrieval. In *CVPR*, volume 2, pages 649–655, 2003.
33. J.S. Yedidia, W.T. Freeman, and Y. Weiss. Understanding belief propagation and its generalizations. *Exploring Artificial Intelligence in the New Millennium*, pages 239–269, 2003.
34. S.X. Yu and J. Shi. Object-specific figure-ground segregation. In *CVPR*, volume 2, pages 39–45, 2003.
35. A.L. Yuille, D.S. Cohen, and P.W. Hallinan. Feature extraction from faces using deformable templates. *IJCV*, 8(2):99–111, 1992.
36. S.C. Zhu and A. Yuille. Region competition: Unifying snakes, region growing, and Bayes/MDL for multiband image segmentation. *PAMI*, 18(9):884–900, September 1996.

SpatialBoost: Adding Spatial Reasoning to AdaBoost

Shai Avidan

Mitsubishi Electric Research Labs,
201 Broadway, Cambridge, MA, 02139
avidan@merl.com

Abstract. SpatialBoost extends AdaBoost to incorporate spatial reasoning. We demonstrate the effectiveness of SpatialBoost on the problem of interactive image segmentation. Our application takes as input a tri-map of the original image, trains SpatialBoost on the pixels of the object and the background and use the trained classifier to classify the unlabeled pixels. The spatial reasoning is introduced in the form of weak classifiers that attempt to infer pixel label from the pixel labels of surrounding pixels, after each boosting iteration. We call this variant of AdaBoost — SpatialBoost. We then extend the application to work with "GrabCut". In GrabCut the user casually marks a rectangle around the object, instead of tediously marking a tri-map, and we pose the segmentation as the problem of learning with outliers, where we know that only positive pixels (i.e. pixels that are assumed to belong to the object) might be outliers and in fact should belong to the background.

1 Introduction

Image segmentation is an ill-posed problem and automatic image segmentation is still an illusive target. This led to the development of interactive image segmentation algorithms that allow the user to intervene in the segmentation process with minimal effort.

Image segmentation can be categorized into "soft" and "hard" segmentation. In "soft" segmentation one is interested in recovering both the color and the transparency of the pixels, so that mixed pixels such as hair or fur could be handled, while in "hard" segmentation one is only interested in segmentation the pixels of the object from the background, without recovering their transparency. Here we focus on the latter and note that it can be used in its own right or as an initial guess for soft segmentation.

We treat image segmentation as a binary classification problem, where a classifier is trained on pixels of the object and pixels of the background and then used to classify the unlabeled pixels. We introduce *SpatialBoost* as our classifier. SpatialBoost extends the standard AdaBoost classifier to handle spatial reasoning. This is done by defining two types of weak classifiers. One type is the usual weak classifier that works on each pixel independently. The other type works on

A. Leonardis, H. Bischof, and A. Pinz (Eds.): ECCV 2006, Part IV, LNCS 3954, pp. 386–396, 2006.
© Springer-Verlag Berlin Heidelberg 2006

the predicted labels of a neighborhood of pixels, after each round of boosting. This allows SpatialBoost to learn spatial arrangements of pixels that can improve the overall quality of the classification. Both types of weak classifiers optimize the same target function and the implementation of SpatialBoost involves just a slight modification of the AdaBoost algorithm.

The three types of pixels (*object*, *background* and *unlabeled*) are defined in a tri-map that the user draw manually. This is often a laborious work and an easier user interface was recently suggested where the user casually marks a rectangle around the object and let the application take care of the rest. We show that our approach can be extended to handle this type of input as well by considering it as learning with outliers. That is, we assume that part of the pixels that are marked as positive (i.e. belong to the object) are actually outliers and should belong to the background.

2   Background

Our work brings together two lines of research. One focused on image segmentation and the other focused on extending AdaBoost to handle spatial information.

Interactive image segmentation has been studied extensively in the past. The Magic Wand [1] allows the user to pick pixels and then automatically cluster together pixels with similar color statistics. Other algorithms take as input a tri-map image. Their goal is to learn from the labeled object and background pixels enough information to correctly label the unlabeled pixels. Ruzon & Tomasi [12] and Chuang et al. [4] learn the local statistics of color distribution to predict the label of the unknown pixels. Because color does not carry spatial information they break the region of unlabeled pixels into many sub-regions, in ad-hoc fashion, and process each sub-region independently. In contrast, Boykov & Jolly [3] and later Blake et al. [2] use graph-cut algorithms that rely on color and contrast information, together with strong spatial prior to efficiently segment the image. This approach works on the entire image at once and there is no need to process multiple sub-regions separately. Finally, Rother et al. [11] eliminated the need for the creation of a tri-map by introducing GrabCut, where the user casually draw a rectangle around the object and the algorithm takes it from there. These methods are generative methods that seek to learn the likelihoods of the colors of the object and background and then, given the unlabeled pixels, determine to which color distribution they belong. We, on the other hand, take a discriminative approach where a classifier is trained on the labeled pixels and then applied to the unlabeled ones.

Efforts to extend AdaBoost to handle spatial reasoning were reported by Fink and Perona [8] who termed their method "Mutual Boost". They consider the problem of mutual detection of multiple objects in images and use the spatial relationship of AdaBoost classifiers during the detection iterations to improve overall performance. However, they use it for object detection and not for image segmentation. Torralba et al. [13] suggested "Boosted random fields" to combine AdaBoost and Belief propagation to handle interaction between neighboring pixels, for the purpose of using context to improve object detection.

3   SpatialBoost: AdaBoost with Spatial Reasoning

We pose image segmentation as a binary classification problem where a classifier is trained on the labeled pixels of the object and the background and then applied to the unlabeled pixels of the border region. In particular, the user constructs a tri-map image that defines pixels that are part of the *object*, part of the *background* or are *unlabeled*. We will term pixels that belong to the object as positive examples and pixels that belong to the background as negative examples. We can train a classifier on the labeled pixels and then apply the classifier to the unlabeled pixels. Recall that AdaBoost training, and testing, is done on each pixel independently, without any spatial interaction between neighboring pixels. Extending the feature vector of every pixel to capture some local image statistics can give a partial solution to the problem but can also pose several new problems. First, the dimensionality of the data grows, which in turn might require additional training data. Second, the interaction between neighboring pixels is limited to the particular image statistics selected. Finally, the information can not be *propagated* beyond the extent of the local image patch that was used to compute the local image statistics.

3.1   SpatialBoost

Within the context of AdaBoost, we give a simple extension that can incorporate spatial reasoning automatically. Given a collection of N data points and their labels, denoted $\{x_i, y_i\}_{i=1}^{N}$, AdaBoost minimizes the exponential loss function

$$J(H) = E(e^{-yH(x)}) \qquad (1)$$

as a way to minimize the zero-one loss function, where $H(x)$, termed the "strong" classifier, is a linear combination of T "weak" classifiers $h_i(x)$.

$$H(x) = \sum_{i=1}^{T} h_i(x) \qquad (2)$$

We will denote the weak classifiers $h_i(x)$ as *data* classifiers because they operate solely on the data point and do not model spatial interaction between the data points. However, the goal of AdaBoost is to minimize $J(H)$ and every weak classifier that helps the minimization can, and should, be used. In particular, we can use the current labels of the *neighbors* of the pixel to predict its label, in the next iteration of AdaBoost. That is, after each iteration of AdaBoost training we have, in addition to the feature vector of every pixel, the predicted labels of its neighbors. This is the additional information we want to capture and we do that by introducing a new "weak" classifier, that we term *spatial* classifier. In each iteration of AdaBoost training we now train two classifiers. A "data" classifier that was trained on each pixel independently and a "spatial" classifier that was trained on the predicted label of neighborhoods of pixels. AdaBoost now gets to choose the "weak" classifier that minimizes the classification error, be it

---

Algorithm 1. SpatialBoost - Training

Input: Training set $\{x_i, y_i\}_{i=1}^{N}$
            Number of iterations T
Output: A strong classifier $H(x)$

1. Initialize weights $\{w_i\}_{i=1}^{N}$ to $\frac{1}{N}$
2. Initialize estimated margins $\{\hat{y}_i\}_{i=1}^{N}$ to zero
3. For $t = 1...T$
   (a) Make $\{w_i\}_{i=1}^{N}$ a distribution
   (b) Set $x_i' = \{\hat{y}_j | x_j \in Nbr(x_i)\}$
   (c) Train weak *data* classifier h_t on the data $\{x_i, y_i\}_{i=1}^{N}$ and the weights $\{w_i\}_{i=1}^{N}$
   (d) Train weak *spatial* classifier h_t' on the data $\{x_i', y_i\}_{i=1}^{N}$ and the weights $\{w_i\}_{i=1}^{N}$
   (e) Set $\epsilon = \sum_{i=1}^{N} w_i |h_t(x_i) - y_i|$
   (f) Set $\epsilon' = \sum_{i=1}^{N} w_i |h_t'(x_i') - y_i|$
   (g) Set $\lambda_t = \begin{cases} 1 \text{ if } \epsilon < \epsilon' \\ 0 \text{ otherwise} \end{cases}$
   (h) Set $err = \lambda_t \epsilon + (1 - \lambda_t)\epsilon'$
   (i) Set weak classifier weight $\alpha_t = \frac{1}{2} log \frac{1-err}{err}$
   (j) Update examples weights

   $$w_i = w_i e^{(\alpha_t(\lambda_t |h_t(x_i) - y_i| + (1 - \lambda_t)|h_t'(x_i') - y_i|))}$$

   (k) Update margins $\hat{y}_i$ to be

   $$\hat{y}_i = \hat{y}_i + \alpha_t(\lambda_t h_t(x_i) + (1 - \lambda_t)h_t'(x_i'))$$

4. The strong classifier is given by $sign(H(x))$ where $H(x) = \sum_{t=1}^{T} \alpha_t(\lambda_t h_t(x) + (1 - \lambda_t)h_t'(x))$

---

the "data" classifier or the "spatial" classifier. As a result, the strong AdaBoost classifier might be a weighted sum of weak *data* and *spatial* classifiers where both types of classifiers work in concert to improve the same objective function. For the weak *spatial* classifiers we actually use the estimated margin of each data point, after each boosting round, instead of the label (which is the sign of the margin).

The SpatialBoost training algorithm is given in Algorithm 1. It takes as input a collection of labeled data points $\{x_i, y_i\}_{i=1}^{N}$ and a function $Nbr(x_i)$ that returns the list of neighbors of the point x_i. Once the strong classifier has been trained we can apply it to the unlabeled pixels of the image using Algorithm 2.

3.2 GrabCut – Learning with Outliers

Creating a tri-map image is time consuming and hence, Rother et al. [11] suggested GrabCut. In GrabCut the user merely draws a rectangle around the object and the system automatically takes care of the rest. Within the context of SpatialBoost this means nothing more than outlier rejection. Given the rectangle we know that all the pixels outside the rectangle are negative examples, while

---

Algorithm 2. SpatialBoost - Testing

Input: Unlabeled pixels $\{\mathbf{x_i}\}_{i=1}^{N}$
             The strong classifier $H(\mathbf{x})$
Output: Labels $\{y_i\}_{i=1}^{N}$

1. Initialize estimated margins $\{\hat{y}_i\}_{i=1}^{N}$ to zero
2. For $t = 1...T$
   (a) Set $\mathbf{x'_i} = \{\hat{y}_j | \mathbf{x_j} \in Nbr(\mathbf{x_i})\}$
   (b) Update margins $\hat{y}_i$ to be

$$\hat{y}_i = \hat{y}_i + \alpha_t(\lambda_t h_t(\mathbf{x_i}) + (1 - \lambda_t)h'_t(\mathbf{x'_i}))$$

3. Output $sign(\hat{y}_i)$

---

part of the positive pixels (i.e. pixels inside the rectangle) might be negative examples. Hence, we modify SpatialBoost to handle outliers. A simple approach to outlier rejection is to run SpatialBoost for several iterations and then mark the positive pixels with large weights (i.e. weights larger than a predefined threshold) as outliers, change their label to negative and repeat. In our case, we run SpatialBoost for several iterations (typically, 10 iterations), then take all the positive pixels that are still wrongly classified and have weight greater than $\frac{3}{N}$ (where N is the number of labeled pixels), flip their sign to be negative and restart SpatialBoost. We repeat this procedure for several times (typically, 5 times). Alternatively, one can adopt the BrownBoost algorithm [9].

3.3   The Feature Space

We are also interested in finding what is a good feature space to represent every pixel. Clearly, one can use the (R,G,B) color of every pixel as its feature vector but color carries no spatial information. This can be fixed in one of two ways. One way is to add spatial smoothness assumption, for instance by introducing a penalty term if two neighboring pixels disagree on their label. The second way is to consider more complicated feature spaces that capture both color and spatial information. In our experiments, we use feature vectors that capture the local HoG of every pixel, in addition to the color. This combined feature vector help disambiguate pixels. Working in a high-dimensional space makes it hard to model the distribution of the data points, as is done in generative methods. On the other hand, discriminative methods, such as AdaBoost or SpatialBoost, can give better results.

Also, since our feature space encodes both color and spatial information we do not have to break the image into multiple sub-regions and process each sub-region independently. Breaking the image into sub-region could improve our results, but we prefer to show the advantages of SpatialBoost without ad-hoc improvements.

4   Experiments

We show experiments on synthetic and real images.

4.1   Synthetic Images

To gain some intuition as to how SpatialBoost work we first present experiments
on synthetic images where we compare SpatialBoost and AdaBoost on a toy
problem of noise removal from binary images. Given a noisy binary image we
wish to infer the original "clean" image. To do so, we take a pair of clean/noisy
training images, that have the same local image statistics as our test image, and
train our classifier on them. We then apply the classifier to the noisy test image.
In our case we take the feature vector to be the 3×3 window around every
pixel, in the noisy image, and the label of each such data point is taken to be
the label of the center pixel of the window, in the corresponding clean image.
The neighborhood used by the function $Nbr()$ in the SpatialBoost algorithm is
taken to be a 5×5 window around every pixel. Figure 1 compare AdaBoost
and SpatialBoost. The size of the images is 100×100 pixels and the amount

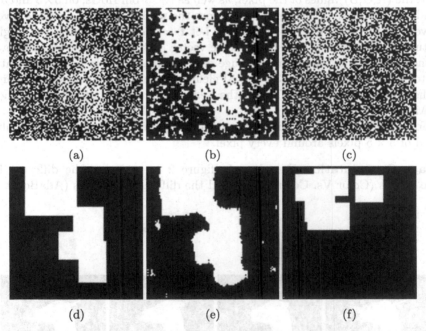

(a)   (b)   (c)

(d)   (e)   (f)

Fig. 1. Noise removal with 35% random noise. Given image (a) we want to infer image
(d). We show the results of two methods: AdaBoost (b) and SpatialBoost (e). For
training we used images (c) and (f). The "data" classifier takes every 3×3 window in
image (c) as a data point whose label is the value of its central pixel in image (f). The
"spatial" classifier takes every 5×5 window of the predicted labels in image (c) as a
data point.

of noise is 35%, that is we randomly flipped the sign of 35% of all the pixels in the image. One can see that SpatialBoost does a much better job in removing the noise then AdaBoost. This is because SpatialBoost allows information to *propagate* over time (i.e. iterations), whereas in AdaBoost the classification is much more localized.

4.2   Real Images

We now turn our attention to the problem of image segmentation and use the database published by [2].

Pre-processing. We compared two feature spaces. The first one is simply the (R,G,B) values of every pixel. The second feature space consists of color and local Histogram of Oriented Gradients (HoG). HoG is reminiscent of the SIFT detector [7] and has been used in several object detection and recognition applications [5, 6]. In particular, we compute it as follows.

We convert the color image into a gray scale image and compute its x and y derivatives, we then clip pixels whose x and y derivative are below a threshold (5 intensity values, in our case) and create an 8 bin Histogram of Oriented Gradients (HoG) in the neighborhood of each pixel. The feature vector contains both the (R,G,B) values of the pixel, as well as two 8-bin HoGs, on 3×3 and 5×5 windows, centered at the pixel. To improve the weak classifiers, we store several powers of the feature vector elements. Let $\mathbf{f} = [f_1, ..., f_n]$ denote the original feature vector, then we store the feature vector $[\mathbf{f}, \mathbf{f}^2, \mathbf{f}^3]$, that is, we raise every element to all the powers in the range one through three. In total, our feature vector consists of $57 = 3 * (3 + 8 + 8)$ elements. This is a cheap way of gaining kernel power, a-la kernel-SVM, for the weak classifier without implementing an SVM as our weak classifier.

For the *spatial* weak classifier we set the $Nbr()$ function to return a neighborhood of 5×5 pixels around every pixel.

Image Segmentation Results. In figure 2 we compare the different feature spaces (Color Vs. Color+HoG) and the different classifiers (AdaBoost Vs.

Fig. 2. Comparing feature space as well as AdaBoost Vs. SpatialBoost. First column: AdaBoost + RGB, Second column: SpatialBoost + RGB, Third column: AdaBoost + RGB + HoG, Fourth column: SpatialBoost + RGB + HoG.

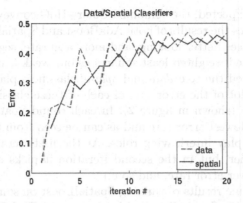

Fig. 3. Roles of *data* and *spatial* classifiers. The *x*-axis show the iteration number, the *y*-axis show the error rate of the *data* and *spatial* weak classifiers. In each iteration SpatialBoost chooses the weak classifier with the lowest error rate. As can be seen, In the first iteration the weak *data* classifier gives the lowest error rate, after that, the two types of weak classifier play interleaving roles.

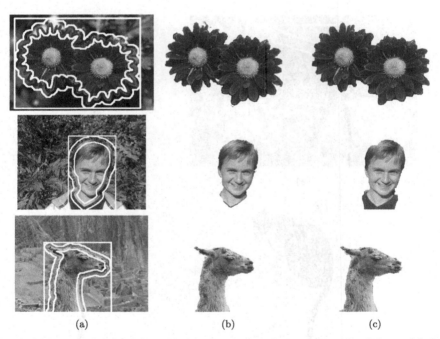

(a)   (b)   (c)

Fig. 4. Experiments on real data. Each row correspond to one example. Column (a) show the input image, column (b) show the results on the tri-map data and column (c) show the results on the GrabCut input. The tri-map and GrabCut inputs are overlaid on the original image. In the tri-map case, the inner most region is marked as positive, the outer most region is marked as negative and the region between the two is the test pixels to be classified. In the GrabCut method all the pixels outside the rectangle are marked as negative and all the pixels inside are marked as positive. The algorithm must determine which of the "positive" pixels is an outlier and should in fact belong to the background.

SpatialBoost). As expected, the combined Color+HoG conveys additional information that improves the results of both AdaBoost and SpatialBoost. Of the two, SpatialBoost produces better looking, and more accurate, segmentation results. In both cases we used weighted least squares as our weak learner.

Next, we measured the role *data* and *spatial* classifiers play in SpatialBoost. Figure 3 shows a plot of the error rate of each of these classifiers when trained on the llama image (shown in figure 2). In each round SpatialBoost picks the classifiers with the lowest error rate and as can be seen from the graph, the two types of classifiers play interleaving roles. At the first iteration, SpatialBoost picks a *data* classifier, but in the second iteration it picks a *spatial* classifiers because it has a lower error rate, and so on.

Figure 4 show some results of running SpatialBoost on some real images. We show results of running SpatialBoost with tri-map and GrabCut, as they appear in the database. No morphological post-processing operations are performed to enhance the results. We ran SpatialBoost on all 50 images in the database and found the average error rate to be 8.00% for the set of 30 training images and 8.23% for the set of 20 test images. The best results, for the tri-map input

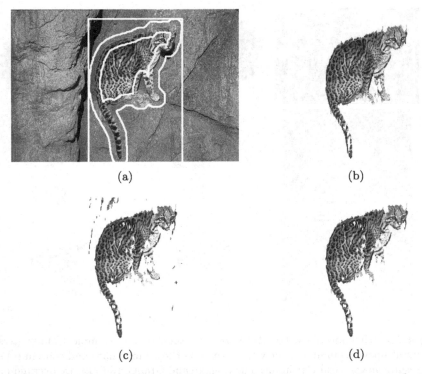

(a)   (b)

(c)   (d)

Fig. 5. Experiments on real data. Adding morphological post-processing can further improve results. Image (a) show the input image (with the tri-map and GrabCut boundaries overlaid), image (b) show the results with the tri-map input, image (c) show the results with the GrabCut input and image (d) show only the largest connected component of image (c).

reported by [2] are 7.9% on a test set of 20 out of the 50 images. They do not report results for the GrabCut input. We obtain an error rate of 8.84% for the 30 training images and 11.96% for the 20 test images, in the GrabCut case. In their follow-up work [11], where GrabCut was introduced, the authors show examples with multiple user inputs and so direct comparison is no longer possible.

A couple of comments are in order. First, we found that choosing small neighborhood windows gave better results, this is because larger neighborhood windows lead to blur that degrades segmentation performance. Second, we found that a large number of iterations actually help the segmentation as it allows the propagation phase to spread the information. Finally, the method takes a couple of seconds to run on a non-optimized MATLAB implementation.

In figure 5 we show results of combining SpatialBoost with basic morphological operations. In this case we cleaned the result of SpatialBoost in the case of GrabCut by detecting and keeping the largest connected component. The results on the tri-map input usually do not require the use of morphological post-processing operations.

SpatialBoost will automatically default to the standard AdaBoost algorithm in case there is no spatial information to be used for classification. Indeed, we tested spatialBoost on some of the UCI ML repostiroy [10] datasets (Ionosphere and Glass) and found that no "spatial" classifier was chosen. Specifically, the "spatial" classifier was trained on the predicted label of the 3 nearest examples, but apparently this information was not useful.

5   Conclusions

We give a simple extension to AdaBoost to handle spatial information. In addition to the usual weak *data* classifiers, we introduce weak *spatial* classifiers that work on the labels of the data points, after each iteration of the boosting algorithm. In each SpatialBoost iteration the algorithm chooses the best weak classifier (either *data* or *spatial* classifier) to be added. Results on synthetic and real images show the superiority of SpatialBoost over AdaBoost in cases that involve spatial reasoning.

References

1. Adobe System, 2002. Adobe Photoshop User Guide.
2. Blake, A. and Rother, C. and Brown, M. and Perez, P. and Torr, P. Interactive Image Segmentation using an adaptive GMMRF model. In *Proc. European Conf. Computer Vision*, 2004.
3. Boykov, Y. and Jolly, M.-P. Interactive graph cuts for optimal boundary and region segmentation of objects in N-D images. In *Proc. IEEE International Conference on Computer Vision*, 2001.
4. Chuang, y.-y., Curless, B., Salesin, D. and Szeliski, R. A Bayesian approach to digital matting. In *Proc IEEE Conf. on Computer Vision and Pattern Recognition*, 2001.

5. N. Dalal and B. Triggs. Histograms of Oriented Gradients for Human Detection. In *IEEE Conference on Computer Vision and Pattern Recognition* (CVPR), 2005.
6. W. T. Freeman and M. Roth. Orientation histograms for hand gesture recognition. In *Intl. Workshop on Automatic Face and Gesture Recognition*, 1995.
7. D. G. Lowe. Distinctive image features from scale-invariant keypoints. In *International Journal of Computer Vision* (IJCV, 60(2):91-110, 2004.
8. Fink, M. and Perona, P. Mutual Boosting for Contextual Inference. In *Adv. in Neural Information Processing Systems* (NIPS), 2003.
9. Freund, Y. An adaptive version of the boost by majority algorithm. In *Machine Learning*, 43(3):293-318, June 2001.
10. D.J. Newman, S. Hettich, C.L. Blake and C.J. Merz, UCI Repository of machine learning databases, url = "http://www.ics.uci.edu/~mlearn/MLRepository.html", University of California, Irvine, Dept. of Information and Computer Sciences, 1998.
11. Rother, C. and Kolmogorov, V. and Blake, A. GrabCut - Interactive Foreground Extraction using Iterated Graph Cuts, In *Proc. ACM Siggraph*, 2004.
12. Ruzon, M. and Tomasi, C. Alpha estimation in natural images. In *Proc IEEE Conf. on Computer Vision and Pattern Recognition*, 2000.
13. A. Torralba, K. P. Murphy and W. T. Freeman. contextual Models for Object Detection using Boosted Random Fields. In *Adv. in Neural Information Processing Systems* (NIPS), 2004.

Database-Guided Simultaneous Multi-slice 3D Segmentation for Volumetric Data

Wei Hong[2], Bogdan Georgescu[1], Xiang Sean Zhou[3],
Sriram Krishnan[3], Yi Ma[2], and Dorin Comaniciu[1]

[1] Integrated Data Systems Department, Siemens Corporate Research,
Princeton NJ 08540, USA
[2] Department of Electrical and Computer Engineering,
University of Illinois at Urbana-Champaign, Urbana IL 61801, USA
[3] Siemens Medical Solutions, Malvern PA 19355, USA

Abstract. Automatic delineation of anatomical structures in 3-D volumetric data is a challenging task due to the complexity of the object appearance as well as the quantity of information to be processed. This makes it increasingly difficult to encode prior knowledge about the object segmentation in a traditional formulation as a perceptual grouping task. We introduce a fast shape segmentation method for 3-D volumetric data by extending the 2-D database-guided segmentation paradigm which directly exploits expert annotations of the interest object in large medical databases. Rather than dealing with 3-D data directly, we take advantage of the observation that the information about position and appearance of a 3-D shape can be characterized by a set of 2-D slices. Cutting these multiple slices simultaneously from the 3-D shape allows us to represent and process 3-D data as efficiently as 2-D images while keeping most of the information about the 3-D shape. To cut slices consistently for all shapes, an iterative 3-D non-rigid shape alignment method is also proposed for building local coordinates for each shape. Features from all the slices are jointly used to learn to discriminate between the object appearance and background and to learn the association between appearance and shape. The resulting procedure is able to perform shape segmentation in only a few seconds. Extensive experiments on cardiac ultrasound images demonstrate the algorithm's accuracy and robustness in the presence of large amounts of noise.

1 Introduction

Three dimensional imaging technologies such as ultrasound, MRI and X-ray are developing rapidly. While 3-D volumetric data contain much richer information than 2-D images, 3-D volumetric data is still not widely used in clinical diagnosis mainly because quantitative analysis by human is much more time-consuming than analyzing 2-D images. Thus, automatic segmentation of anatomical structures in 3-D volumetric data is extremely important to have a fast quantitative analysis and to increase the use of volumetric data in clinical practice.

Segmentation of structures in 2-D images or 2-D video sequences has been extensive studied [1, 2, 3, 4]. However, automatically processing 3-D volumetric

A. Leonardis, H. Bischof, and A. Pinz (Eds.): ECCV 2006, Part IV, LNCS 3954, pp. 397–409, 2006.

data is much more challenging, due to the enormous amount of data and the resulting computational complexity. In the traditional formulation, segmentation is defined as a perceptual grouping task and solved through clustering or variational methods. However, as the difficulty of the desired segmentation increases, it becomes harder to incorporate prior knowledge into the grouping task. The 3-D active appearance model (3-D AMM) [5, 6] extends the 2-D AAM into 3-D. However, matching 3-D AAM to volumetric data is a non-linear optimization problem which requires heavy computation and good initialization to avoid local minima. Recently, segmentation methods based on prior knowledge learnt from large annotated databases through boosting [7, 8, 9] show promising performance on segmentation tasks with complex object appearance and noisy data. The advantage of boosting is that it can implicitly encode the large amount of prior knowledge relevant to the segmentation task and yield algorithms capable of running in real-time for 2-D images. However, there is no trivial way to implement it for 3-D volumetric data because the increase in dimension from two to three will dramatically increase the complexity of the algorithm.

Contributions. The main contribution of this paper is to propose a fast 3-D database-guided segmentation method that directly exploits expert annotation of the interest object in large databases. The key is to transform the 3-D learning problem into several 2-D learning problems solved simultaneously. By cutting multiple 2-D slices to represent a 3-D shape, the segmentation in 3-D is extremely accelerated. Haar-like rectangle features are used for appearance representation because they can be evaluated rapidly in 2-D by using the "integral images" [8]. It is difficult to directly use 3-D features and an "integral volume" due to the increased computational complexity. Also, the number of all possible 3-D features is much higher than the number of 2-D features, making the feature selection through boosting very difficult. Our method converts the 3-D problem into a 2-D problem while keeping most of the 3-D information. The computational complexity for evaluating features in our method is similar to the complexity for 2-D images. The 2-D features simultaneously obtained from all 2-D slices are used to solve two 3-D learning problems: 1. *Shape detection*, where a classifier is trained to distinguish between object appearance and non-object appearances (Section 3) and 2. *Shape inference*, where the association between an object appearance and its 3-D shape is solved by selecting the relevant features (Section 4).

The multiple slices of all 3-D shapes must be cut consistently according to their local coordinate systems. The local coordinates of each shape will be put in correspondence through shape alignment. Alignment of two 3-D shapes is in general a very hard problem because the meshes annotated by experts do not have *pairwise* correspondence. The task in our application is easier because some landmarks such as the principal axis and a representative plane (denoted by the A4C plane) are already known about the object of interest. The focus of this paper is segmentation of the left ventricle in 3-D ultrasound heart images however the method is general and can be applied to a wide range of anatomical object segmentation in volumetric data. In Section 2 we introduce an iterative algorithm to efficiently solve the alignment problem. Section 3 presents the method for shape detection followed by shape inference in Section 4 and experimental results in Section 5.

2 Non-rigid Linear 3-D Shape Alignment for Training Data

For all the shapes in the training database, the location, orientation, size, aspect ratio and non-linear deformation vary a lot (See Figure 1). The variation among these shapes must be eliminated to acquire their essential common characteristics and build their local coordinates.

Suppose that we have a mean shape which is the average of all the training shapes after alignment, all the training shapes must be aligned to this mean shape by transformations which will minimize the shapes variations. Ideally, a non-linear transformation can reduce the variation to zero. However, this transformation has to be searched at detection time. Thus, using an ideal non-linear transformation will considerably increase the search space. In our method, we only consider linear transformations, which provide a computationally feasible way to reduce the variation. The shape after the linear transformation will be very close to the mean shape and we denote it by the prototype of the original shape. The mean shape will be the average of all the prototypes.

Each training shape is represented by a 3-D triangle mesh annotated by experts. The mesh can be represented by a set of points (vertices), denoted as $P^0 \doteq \{\mathbf{X}_i = [X_i, Y_i, Z_i]^T \in \Re^3\}_{i=1}^N$ in world coordinates. N is the number of vertices of each mesh. For each point $\mathbf{X}$ on a shape, the corresponding point on the prototype shape is $\mathbf{x} \in \Re^3$ in its local coordinates. The prototype shape is denoted as $P \doteq \{\mathbf{x}_i = [x_i, y_i, z_i]^T \in \Re^3\}_{i=1}^N$. The mean shape is denoted as $\bar{P} \doteq \{\bar{\mathbf{x}}_i = [\bar{x}_i, \bar{y}_i, \bar{z}_i]^T \in \Re^3\}_{i=1}^N = \frac{1}{M} \sum P_j$. Among all the linear transformations, we assume that each shape is transformed to a prototype shape by rotating, translating, scaling and changing of aspect ratio. The linear transformation

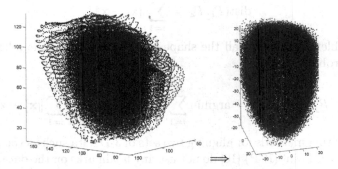

Fig. 1. Left: The location, orientation, size, aspect ratio and non-linear deformation of the shapes in the training set vary a lot. Right: The shapes aligned by proposed method.

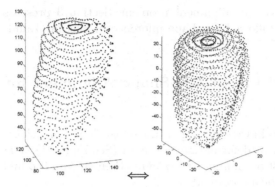

Fig. 2. Left: A shape used for training in world coordinates. Right: The prototype shape (black) and the mean shape (red) in their local coordinates.

between the original shape and its prototype (also between world coordinates and local coordinates) can be expressed as,

$$\mathbf{X} = RS\mathbf{x} + T, \tag{1}$$

$$\mathbf{x} = R^{-1}S^{-1}(\mathbf{X} - T), \tag{2}$$

where $R \in SO(3)$ is a rotation matrix, $S = \mathrm{diag}[w, d, h] \in \Re^{3 \times 3}$ is a scaling matrix and $T = [t_x, t_y, t_z]^T \in \Re^3$ is a translation vector. Figure 2 shows an example of a shape, its prototype shape and the mean shape. For each of the samples in the training set, the parameters of the transformation have to be estimated. A total of 9 parameters are needed to represent such a linear transformation, i.e., 3 parameters for R, 3 parameters for S and 3 parameters for T. In our data set of left ventricles, w and d are roughly equal. So we can simply set $w = d$ to reduce the total number of parameters to 8. h/w is defined to be the aspect ratio of the shape.

If the vertices of two shapes have pairwise correspondence, the distance of two shapes is defined as

$$\mathrm{dist}(P_1, P_2) \doteq \sum_{i=1}^{N} \|\mathbf{x}_i^1 - \mathbf{x}_i^2\| \tag{3}$$

The problem of aligning all the shapes can be written as the following optimization problem:

$$\{\bar{P}, R_j, S_j, T_j\}_{j=1}^{M} \doteq \mathrm{argmin} \sum_{j=1}^{M} \mathrm{dist}(P_j, \bar{P}) = \sum_{j=1}^{M} \sum_{i=1}^{N} \|\mathbf{x}_i^j - \bar{\mathbf{x}}_i\| \tag{4}$$

Most existing methods for aligning two sets of 3-D data such as the popular Iterative Closest Point (ICP) [10] do not use any landmarks on the data. They also usually only consider rigid motion and ignore the changing of aspect ratio. The non-linear optimization in those methods is prone to local minima. For our problem domain, we know the extrema of the principal axis which pass through the center of the left ventricle and a plane named apical-four-chamber plane (A4C plane) which passes through all 4 chambers of the heart. However, our 3-D data do not have pairwise correspondences. So the optimized mean shape and transformation parameters $\{\bar{P}, R_j, S_j, T_j\}_{j=1}^{M}$ still cannot have a closed-form solution. We introduce an iterative linear method to solve the optimization problem.

- Step 1: In the first step, the principal axis which links the two apexes of the shape is aligned to the z-axis. For each shape, the rotation matrix R_a needed for this transformation is,

$$R_a \doteq R_2 R_1^T, \quad R_1 = [\mathbf{v}, \mathbf{w}, \mathbf{v} \times \mathbf{w}], \quad R_2 = [\mathbf{u}, \mathbf{w}, \mathbf{u} \times \mathbf{w}], \quad \mathbf{w} = \mathbf{v} \times \mathbf{u}, \quad (5)$$

where $\mathbf{u}$ is the normalized principal axis vector and $\mathbf{v} = [0, 0, 1]^T$.
- Step 2: After the first step, all the shapes still have different angles of rotation along the z-axis. For each shape of a left ventricle, the A4C plane can determine the rotation along the z-axis. So in the second step, we rotate each mesh along its principal axis by certain degree so that the A4C plane of the left ventricle matches the x-z plane. The rotation is denoted as R_z,

$$R_z \doteq \begin{bmatrix} \cos\theta & \sin\theta & 0 \\ -\sin\theta & \cos\theta & 0 \\ 0 & 0 & 1 \end{bmatrix}, \quad (6)$$

where θ is the angle between the A4C plane and the x-z plane. The estimated rotation matrix of each shape should be $R = R_a * R_z$.
- Step 3: For all the meshes annotated by the experts, the vertices do not have one-to-one correspondence between two meshes except the two apexes. The points of the shape should correspond to the same physical points of the left ventricle. However it is impossible to determine automatically which points correspond the same physical points. So after we align the orientation of each mesh, we just move the centroid of each mesh to the origin of the coordinates and roughly evenly re-sample each mesh using polar coordinates. The re-sampled points will approximately have pairwise correspondences.
- Step 4: The mean shape $\bar{P}$ is calculated by $\bar{P} \doteq \frac{1}{M} \sum P_j$.
- Step 5: Finally, we need to align the position, scale and aspect ratio of all the shapes. For each shape, the parameters of S and T can be determined by solving the following equation,

$$\begin{bmatrix} \sum_{i=1}^{N}(x_i^2 + y_i^2) & 0 & \sum_{i=1}^{N}(x_i + y_i) & 0 & 0 \\ 0 & \sum_{i=1}^{N} z_i^2 & 0 & 0 & \sum_{i=1}^{N} z_i \\ \sum_{i=1}^{N} x_i & 0 & N & 0 & 0 \\ \sum_{i=1}^{N} y_i & 0 & 0 & N & 0 \\ 0 & \sum_{i=1}^{N} z_i & 0 & 0 & N \end{bmatrix} \begin{bmatrix} w \\ h \\ t_x \\ t_y \\ t_z \end{bmatrix} = \begin{bmatrix} \sum_{i=1}^{N}(x_i \bar{x}_i + y_i \bar{y}_i) \\ \sum_{i=1}^{N} z_i \bar{z}_i \\ \sum_{i=1}^{N} \bar{x}_i \\ \sum_{i=1}^{N} \bar{y}_i \\ \sum_{i=1}^{N} \bar{z}_i \end{bmatrix},$$

$$(7)$$

where $\mathbf{x} = [x, y, z]^T$, $\bar{\mathbf{x}} = [\bar{x}, \bar{y}, \bar{z}]^T$ and the estimated $S = \mathrm{diag}[w, w, h]$, $T = [t_x, t_y, t_z]$.

Steps 2 and 3 only need to be performed only once. Steps 1, 4 and 5 will be iterated until the change of the parameters is below a threshold determined by the working resolution.

After the convergence of the algorithm, the prototypes $\{\bar{P}\}_{j=1}^{M}$ of all shapes and their local coordinate transformations $\{R_j, S_j, T_j\}_{j=1}^{M}$ will be used to cut the multiple slices.

3   3-D Object Detection

The detection method we are using is based on boosted cascade of simple features, which has been widely used for real-time object detection[11, 8, 9]. However, most of such detection methods are only applied on 2-D images. Extending those methods to 3-D is not trivial and several problems must be addressed.

3.1   Multi-slice Representation of 3-D Data

One of the most popular sets of features for object detection is the Haar-like rectangular features, which can be computed very efficiently through the "integral images" [8]. However, in our problem domain, the enormous amount of 3-D data makes computing these features difficult. For example, for an 24×24-pixel 2-D image, there are already more than 180 thousand possible rectangle features. If we extend the rectangular features to cubical features, the number of possible features will be several million. Also, computing an "integral volume" is much slower than computing an integral image.

To avoid the difficulty in dealing with 3-D data directly, we first represent the 3-D data by 2-D slices simultaneously cut from the volume. These slices should be perpendicular to the surface of the shape in order to make the slices sensitive to the changing of the shape. So in the local coordinates we built in section 2 for each shape, we cut its prototype into vertical slices through the z-axis at different angles from the $x - z$ plane and cut horizontal slices at different z. For example, in Figure 3, there are two vertical slices at angle 0 and 90 degree from $x - z$ plane and one horizontal slice at $z = 0$. These three slices are already sufficient for detection purposes because any changes in the location, orientation or aspect ratio will cause large changes in at least one slice, since the slices coincide with the three coordinate axes. However, for the shape inference in Section 4, more slices are preferred to achieve better accuracy.

Rectangle features are computed simultaneously for each of the slice as shown in Figure 4. Features from all the 2-D slices consist the feature vector for the 3-D volume. The "integral image" is adopted to accelerate the computation of the features. The "integral mask" proposed in [9] is also needed to ensure correct computation for invalid image regions.

Training a detection classifier requires positive and negative samples. For the positive samples, the slices are obtained in local coordinates from the correct transformation we obtained in section 2. Several positive examples are shown in Figure 5 to demonstrate that the multiple slices capture the variations of the 3-D shapes. Some perturbation will be added to the correct transformation to

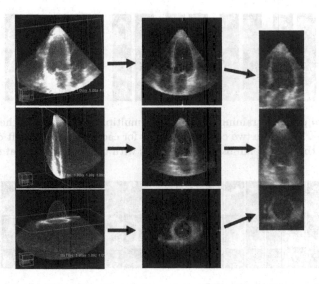

Fig. 3. An example of the slices that represent the 3-D volume. Two vertical slices are cut at 0 and 90 degree from the $x - z$ plane. One horizontal slice is cut at $z = 0$.

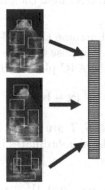

Fig. 4. Rectangle features are computed independently for each of the slice. Features from all the 2-D slices define the feature vector for the 3-D volume.

generate negative samples. Figure 6 shows positive samples and negative samples generated from one volume.

3.2   3-D Shape Detection

The detection of a 3-D shape is equivalent to finding the correct transformation between world coordinates and local coordinates of this object. From Equation 1, the transformation is determined by R, S and T, which contain 8 transformation parameters $[\omega_x, \omega_y, \omega_z, w, h, t_x, t_y, t_z]$, where ω_x, ω_y and ω_z are three Euler angles. Exhaustive searching in an 8 dimensional space would be very time-consuming. In the left ventricle detection problem, the A4C plane (i.e., the $x - z$ plane of local coordinates) is usually easy annotated by human or other

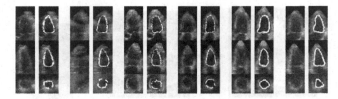

Fig. 5. Several positive training samples. The multiple slices capture the variations of the 3-D shapes. There are two columns of slices for each sample. The left columns show the slices and the right columns show the slices with the meshes annotated by experts.

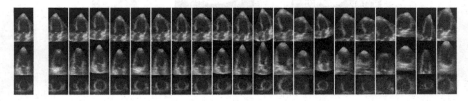

Fig. 6. Positive samples and negative samples generated from one volume. Only the leftmost one is a positive sample generated by correct local coordinates. All others are negative samples generated by incorrect local coordinates.

automatic detection. So we will assume the A4C is known so that we only need to search inside the A4C plane. Suppose that we know the normal vector $\mathbf{n}$ and a point $\mathbf{b}$ on the A4C plane. The A4C plane will be,

$$\mathbf{n}^T(\mathbf{x} - \mathbf{b}) = 0. \tag{8}$$

Suppose the initial transform R, S, T are R_0, S_0 and T_0. The initial rotation R_0 must satisfy that the y-axis of local coordinates is the normal of the A4C plane. It can be determined as,

$$R_0 = [\mathbf{u}_1, \mathbf{u}_2, \mathbf{u}_3], \quad \mathbf{u}_2 = \mathbf{n}, \ \mathbf{v} = [0, 0, 1]^T, \ \mathbf{u}_1 = \mathbf{u}_2 \times \mathbf{v}, \ \mathbf{u}_3 = \mathbf{u}_1 \times \mathbf{u}_2. \tag{9}$$

The initial scale matrix S_0 can be set to be the mean scale S_m for the training set. But the initial translation vector T_0 cannot be the mean translation vector T_m because it may not be on the A4C plane. So we will use the projection of T_m on the A4C plane as T_0, i.e.,

$$T_0 = T_m + \mathbf{n}\mathbf{n}^T(\mathbf{b} - T_m). \tag{10}$$

During the search, we will change the initial transformation R_0, S_0, T_0 by another relative transformation R_r, S_r, T_r. Since we need to fix our transformation inside the A4C plane, the only possible relative rotation is along y-axis.

$$R_r = \begin{bmatrix} \cos\omega_{ry} & 0 & \sin\omega_{ry} \\ 0 & 1 & 0 \\ -\sin\omega_{ry} & 0 & \cos\omega_{ry} \end{bmatrix}. \tag{11}$$

The relative translation $T_r = [t_{rx}, 0, t_{ry}]^T$ is a translation on the A4C plane.

The relative scale matrix is $S_r = \begin{bmatrix} w_r & 0 & 0 \\ 0 & w_r & 0 \\ 0 & 0 & h_r \end{bmatrix}$, where w_r is the changing of the width and h_r is the changing of the height.

So the overall transform from the prototype to the shape is,

$$\begin{aligned} \mathbf{x} &= RS\mathbf{x}_0 + T = R_0 R_r((S_0 + S_r)\mathbf{x}_0 + T_r) + T_0 \\ &= R_0 R_r(S_0 + S_r)\mathbf{x}_0 + R_0 R_r T_r + T_0. \end{aligned} \tag{12}$$

$$R = R_0 R_r, \quad S = S_0 + S_r, \quad T = R_0 R_r T_r + T_0 = RT_r + T_0. \tag{13}$$

The searching for $[w_{ry}, w_r, h_r, t_{rx}, t_{rz}]$ will be in a 5-dimensional space and will be performed on a coarse to fine fashion. In the coarse stage, the search range is determined by the statistics of the training data. After finding the maximum response of the detection classifier, a new iteration of searching will be performed. The initial point will be located at the maximum response found in the coarse stage and the search range will be reduced by half.

4   3-D Non-rigid Shape Inference

The problem is now to determine the shape associated with the detected object. This task is solved by finding the relevant features which best describe the non-rigid variations of the shapes around the mean. All the prototype shapes $\{P_j\}_{j=1}^M$ are clustered into K classes $\{C_i\}_{i=1}^K$ as shown in Figure 7 by the K-means algorithm. The rectangle feature vectors of each shape are acquired by the multi-slice presentation in Section 3.1. The best features vectors for each class $\{f_i\}_{i=1}^K$ that discriminate these classes of shapes are selected by the forward sequential feature selection [9]. For each input volume, we first find the linear non-rigid transformation of the shape by the detection method in Section 3.2. In local coordinates

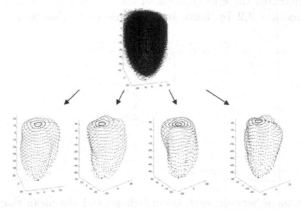

Fig. 7. All the prototype shapes $\{P_j\}_{j=1}^M$ are clustered into K classes $\{C_i\}_{i=1}^K$ by the K-means method

of the shape, the multiple slices are cut from its prototype to generate a query feature vector $\mathbf{f}_q$ for the shape in this volume. The distance of the query and a reference is,

$$d(\mathbf{f}_q, \mathbf{f}_r) = (\mathbf{f}_q - \mathbf{f}_r)^T \Sigma (\mathbf{f}_q - \mathbf{f}_r), \tag{14}$$

where $\mathbf{f}_q$ and $\mathbf{f}_r$ are the feature vectors of the query and the reference respectively. Σ is the Fisher linear discriminating matrix [12] learnt from the training samples.

The inferred shape $\hat{P}$ is computed by Nadaraya-Watson kernel-weighted average [13, 14] of the K prototype classes,

$$\hat{P} = \frac{\Sigma_{i=1}^{K} K_h(\mathbf{f}, \mathbf{f}_i) C_i}{\Sigma_{i=1}^{K} K_h(\mathbf{f}, \mathbf{f}_i)}, \tag{15}$$

where K_h is the Epanechnikov kernel [15] defined as,

$$K_h(\mathbf{f}, \mathbf{f}_i) = \begin{cases} \frac{3}{4}(1 - \frac{d(\mathbf{f}, \mathbf{f}_i)}{d(\mathbf{f}, \mathbf{f}_{[h]})}), & \text{for } \frac{d(\mathbf{f}, \mathbf{f}_i)}{d(\mathbf{f}, \mathbf{f}_{[h]})} \leq 1; \\ 0, & \text{otherwise,} \end{cases} \tag{16}$$

where $\mathbf{f}_{[h]}$ is the feature vector which has h^{th} smallest distance to $\mathbf{f}$.

5   Experiments

The proposed segmentation method was tested on two sets of 3-D ultrasound cardiac volumes of size $160 \times 144 \times 208 = 4,792,320$ voxels. The End-Diastolic(ED) set consists of 44 volumes and the End-Systolic(ES) set consists of 40 volumes. For each volume in the training sets, the A4C plane and a mesh of left ventricle with 1,139 vertices are annotated by experts.

We first demonstrate results of the 3-D shape alignment method introduced in Section 2. Figure 8 shows the distances between each aligned shape and the mean shape. The distance between two shapes is defined in Equation 3. The variation among the shapes is very small after the shape alignment.

Figure 9 illustrates the effectiveness of the 3-D multi-slice detection method described in Section 3.2 by leave one out method. The four curves indicate

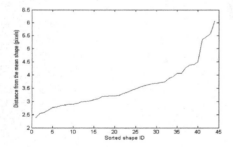
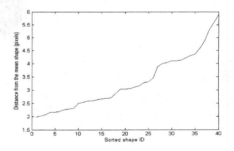

Fig. 8. The distances between each aligned shape and the mean shape. The shapes are sorted by their distances to the mean shape. Left: Results for ED volumes. Right Results for ES volumes.

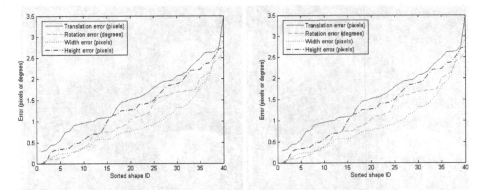

Fig. 9. The error of the translation, rotation, width and height for the left ventricle detection. Left: Results for ED volumes. Right Results for ES volumes.

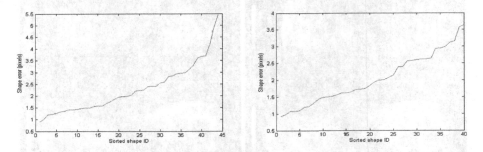

Fig. 10. The error of the entire segmentation procedure. Left: Results for ED volumes. Right Results for ES volumes.

errors of the translation $\|(\Delta t_x, \Delta t_z)\|$, rotation $|\Delta\omega_y|$, width $|\Delta w|$ and height $|\Delta h|$ respectively. The ground truth of these parameters are obtained by the shape alignment in Section 2.

The error of the entire segmentation procedure is shown in Figure 10. The automatic segmentation result of each volume is compared with the mesh annotated by experts. The error of the segmentation is the distance of the inferred shape and the ground truth in world coordinates. This error contains error both from the detection and shape inference.

The results in Figure 8 can be thought of as the error of another segmentation method which uses the ground truth of detection but does not use any shape inference. All the shapes are assumed to be the same as the mean shape. Comparing Figure 10 and Figure 8, we can conclude that the shape inference largely reduces the shape error even when the detection is not perfect.

Figure 11 shows additional segmentation results from volumes which do not have the meshes drawn by experts. The meshes found by our segmentation method visually fit the borders of the left ventricles very well.

The whole segmentation procedure takes about 3 seconds for each volume with 4, 792, 320 voxels on a Xeon 2.8GHz machine. Our algorithm is faster than

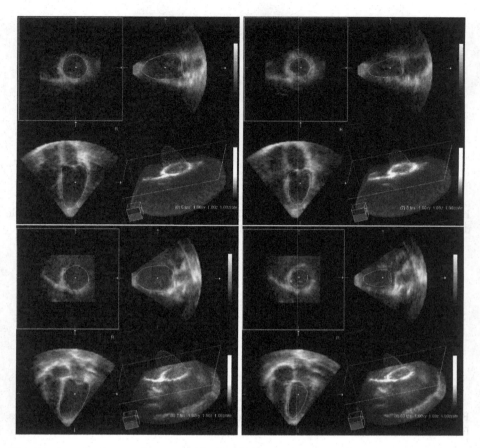

Fig. 11. Results from volumes which do not have the meshes drawn by experts. The meshes found by our segmentation method visually fit the boarders of the left ventricles very well.

3-D AAM models proposed in [5, 6]. Mitchell's work [5] requires 2-3 minutes for each frame on MRI data. Stegmann's 3-D AAM [6] takes 3.4 seconds on MRI data with 22,000 voxels.

6   Limitations and Future Work

We have proposed a fast method for segmenting anatomical objects from 3-D volumetric data. It overcomes the difficulty of working directly with 3-D data by simultaneously solving several 2-D problems. The method is learning-based and directly exploits expert annotations in medical databases.

Due to the difficulty of annotating 3-D shapes by hand, our training and testing sets are not very large or all-inclusive. In the future, more data will be collected and used to validate our method. In fact our method should only bene-fit from more training data. For the shape detection, it is also possible to utilize other local features or detection methods to generate a better initialization and reduce the searching range. For the non-rigid shape alignment, so far only linear transformations are considered. Integrating non-linear transformations might capture more complex variation of shapes.

References

1. Kass, M., Witkin, A., Terzopoulos, D.: Snakes: Active contour models. International Journal of Computer Vision **2** (1988) 321–331
2. T.F.Cootes, Edwards, G., C.J.Taylor: Active appearance models. In: Proc. 5th European Conference on Computer Vision. Volume 2. (1998) 484–498
3. Shi, J., Malik, J.: Normalized cuts and image segmentation. IEEE Transactions on Pattern Analysis and Machine Intelligence **22** (2000) 888–905
4. Comanicu, D., Meer, P.: Mean shift: A robust approach toward feature space analysis. IEEE Trans. Pattern Anal. Machine Intell. **24** (2002) 603–619
5. Mitchell, S., Bosch, J., Lelieveldt, B., van der Geest, R., Reiber, J., Sonka, M.: 3-d active appearance models: segmentation of cardiac mr and ultrasound images. IEEE Transactions on Medical Imaging **21** (2002) 1167–1178
6. Stegmann, M.B.: Generative Interpretation of Medical Images. PhD thesis, Technical University of Denmark (2004)
7. Freund, Y., Schapire, R.E.: A decision-theoretic generalization of on-line learning and an application to boosting. In: European Conference on Computational Learning Theory. (1995) 23–37
8. Viola, P., Jones, M.: Rapid object detection using a boosted cascade of simple features. In: Proceedings IEEE Conf. on Computer Vision and Pattern Recognition. (2001)
9. Georgescu, B., Zhou, X., Comaniciu, D., Gupta, A.: Database-guided segmentation of anatomical structures with complex appearance. In: Proceedings IEEE Conf. on Computer Vision and Pattern Recognition. (2005)
10. Besl, P.J., McKay, N.D.: A method for registration of 3-D shapes. IEEE Trans. Pattern Anal. Mach. Intell. **14** (1992) 239–256
11. Papageorgiou, C., Poggio, T.: A trainable system for object detection. Int. J. Comput. Vision **38** (2000) 15–33
12. Duda, R.O., Hart, P.E.: Pattern Classification and Scene Analysis. Wiley-Interscience (1973)
13. Nadaraya, E.A.: On estimating regression. Theory Prob. Appl. **10** (1964) 186–190
14. Watson, G.S.: Smooth regression analysis. Sankhy a, Series A **26** (1964) 359–372
15. Epanechnikov, V.: Nonparametric estimates of a multivariate probability density. Theory of Probability and its Applications **14** (1969) 153–158

Density Estimation Using Mixtures of Mixtures of Gaussians*

Wael Abd-Almageed and Larry S. Davis

Institute for Advanced Computer Studies, University of Maryland,
College Park, MD 20742
{wamageed, lsd}@umiacs.umd.edu

Abstract. In this paper we present a new density estimation algorithm using mixtures of mixtures of Gaussians. The new algorithm overcomes the limitations of the popular Expectation Maximization algorithm. The paper first introduces a new model selection criterion called the Penalty-less Information Criterion, which is based on the Jensen-Shannon divergence. Mean-shift is used to automatically initialize the means and covariances of the Expectation Maximization in order to obtain better structure inference. Finally, a locally linear search is performed using the Penalty-less Information Criterion in order to infer the underlying density of the data. The validity of the algorithm is verified using real color images.

1 Introduction

The Expectation Maximization algorithm (EM) [1] perhaps is the most frequently used parametric technique for estimating probability density functions (PDF) in both univariate and multivariate cases. It has been widely applied in computer vision [2], and pattern recognition [3] applications. In all of these areas, EM is used to model the PDF of a set of feature vectors using a given parametric model. Usually a mixture of Gaussians with a finite number of components is used to approximate the density function. The main advantage of EM is that it provides a closed-form analytical representation of the PDF. However, EM suffers a few limitations that will be discussed later.

This paper introduces a new nonparametric approach based on the mean-shift algorithm for overcoming the limitations of the EM algorithm. The paper is organized as follows. Section 2 briefly discusses the limitations of both the EM and the mean-shift algorithms. In Section 3 we introduce a new model selection criterion called the Penalty-less Information Criterion (PIC) that will be used in the subsequent sections. Section 4 presents a mean-shift- and PIC-based method for nonparametrizing the EM algorithm. The results of using the proposed algorithm are introduced in Section 5. Finally, Section 6 summarizes the paper and highlights directions for future research. Throughout the paper, we kindly encourage the reader to refer to the electronic copy for the clearer color version of the figures.

---

* This research has been funded, in part, by the Army Research Laboratory's Robotics Collaborative Technology Alliance program, contract number DAAD 19-012-0012 ARL-CTA-DJH.

A. Leonardis, H. Bischof, and A. Pinz (Eds.): ECCV 2006, Part IV, LNCS 3954, pp. 410–422, 2006.
© Springer-Verlag Berlin Heidelberg 2006

2   Expectation Maximization and Mean-Shift

2.1   Expectation Maximization

The Expectation Maximization is popular parametric approach for estimating the underlying density function of a set of data vectors in both the univariate and multivariate cases. Usually, the EM is used to approximate the underlying PDF using a mixture of Gaussian components. EM, however, sufferers from two major limitations. The first is that the number of components in the mixture must be *a priori* specified in order to obtain a reasonable estimate of the true PDF. This number must be accurately specified in order to balance the computational cost in both training and testing phases on one hand and the estimation accuracy on the other. The second limitation is that EM is highly sensitive to the initialization of the mean vectors and covariance matrices of the mixture.

Usually, the k-means algorithm (or similar algorithms) is used to initialize the mean vectors and covariance matrices of EM. Unfortunately, this approach sometimes drives EM towards the wrong mixture values. It sometimes also leads to numerical problems when estimating the covariance matrices.

Fig. 1.a shows the scatter plot of a bivariate data set drawn from a six-component Gaussian mixture. In Fig. 1.b the k-means algorithms correctly initialized the EM which helps convergence to the correct mixture parameters. In Fig. 1.c the k-means drives EM to converge to the wrong mixture parameters even though the data set has not changed. This example illustrates the significance of the initialization problem even when we know the true number of mixture components. The advantage of using EM here is its superior ability to infer the hidden structure of the data (assuming we can initialize it correctly).

Several attempts have been made to overcome the drawbacks of the EM algorithm. Figuerideo and Jain [4] broadly classify these methods into two categories: deterministic approaches and stochastic approaches. Deterministic methods, such as [5] and [6], are based on selecting the number of components according to some model selection criterion, which usually contains an increasing

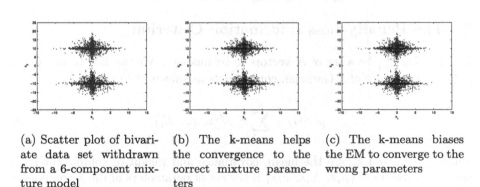

(a) Scatter plot of bivariate data set withdrawn from a 6-component mixture model

(b) The k-means helps the convergence to the correct mixture parameters

(c) The k-means biases the EM to converge to the wrong parameters

Fig. 1. Mixture parameter estimation using EM initialized by K-means

function that penalizes higher number of components. In [7] and [8] stochastic approaches based on Markov Chain Monte Carlo methods are used.

2.2 The Mean-Shift

The mode-finding algorithm introduced in [9] which is based on the mean-shift algorithm [10], compared to the k-means, consistently converges to the modes of the underlying density function. Therefore, for example, when applied to the data set in Fig. 1, the mean-shift successfully finds the two local maximum at $[0, -10]^T$ and $[0, 10]^T$ respectively.

The limitation of the mean-shift-based mode-finding algorithm is its inability to infer the hidden structure of the data. For example, Fig. 2.a shows a noisy image with a hidden structure (the reader is encouraged to refer to the electronic copy for a clearer image.) The 3D scatter plot of the RGB values of the image is shown in Fig. 2.b. When mean-shift is used to segment the image in Fig. 2, the result is a gray image with all pixels set to $[128, 128, 128]^T$ since mean-shift is technically "blind" to the structure of the data.

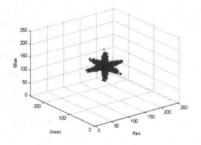

(a) A noisy image with a hidden structure

(b) The RGB scatter plot of the image in Fig. 2.a

Fig. 2. Noisy image with hidden structure

3   The Penalty-Less Information Criterion

Let $\mathbf{X} = \{\mathbf{x}_i\}_{i=1}^N$ be a set of N vectors to be modeled. We use EM to model the data by a mixture of k Gaussian components as shown in Equation 1,

$$p(\mathbf{x}|\Theta) = \sum_{i=1}^{k} \pi_i \, \mathcal{N}(\mathbf{x}, \, \mu_i, \, \Sigma_i) \qquad (1)$$

where μ_i, Σ_i and π_i are the mean, covariance and weight of component i, respectively and $\Theta = \{\mu_i s, \, \Sigma_i s, \, \pi_i s\}$ is the set of parameters of the k-component mixture model (such that $\sum_{i=1}^{k} \pi_i = 1$). The parameters set Θ can be estimated by applying the EM algorithm on $\mathbf{X}$. The set $\mathbf{X}$ can now be clusterized into k subsets (i.e. clusters) using the Mahalanobis distance based on Θ_k, such that

$$X = \bigcup_{i=1}^{k} X^i \tag{2}$$

where X^i is the subset of vectors that belong to cluster i.

For each cluster, i, we compute two estimates of the probability density function (PDF) underlying the data. First, we compute a parametric estimate of the PDF as shown in Equation 3

$$p_{EM}^i(x) = \pi_i \, \mathcal{N}(x, \, \mu_i, \Sigma_i) \tag{3}$$

where p_{EM}^i indicates the EM-based estimate of the PDF of subset X^i. The second PDF is a kernel density estimate (KDE) of the PDF of the cluster data given by

$$p_{KDE}^i(x) = \frac{1}{N^i} \sum_{j=1}^{N^i} \frac{1}{|H_j|} \mathcal{K} \left(\frac{x - x_j^i}{H_j} \right) \tag{4}$$

where N^i is the number of vectors in cluster i, H_j is the adaptive bandwidth matrix of vector j, x_j^i is vector number j of cluster i and $\mathcal{K}(.)$ is the kernel function. Since computing the kernel-based estimate of the PDF is computationally prohibitive in higher dimensions, we use the Improved Fast Guass Transform [11], which significantly reduces the complexity of the problem. The adaptive bandwidth is computed using the sample-point estimator of [12]. In this paper, we use the standard multivariate Gaussian as the kernel function.

We define the Penalty-less Information Criterion ($\mathcal{PIC}$) of a model with k components as the sum of weighted Jensen-Shannon divergence [13] between p_{EM}^i and p_{KDE}^i for all clusters as follows

$$\mathcal{PIC}_k = \sum_{i=1}^{k} \pi_i \, \mathcal{JSD}(p_{EM}^i, \, p_{KDE}^i) \tag{5}$$

where

$$\mathcal{JSD}(p_{EM}^i, \, p_{KDE}^i) = \frac{1}{2} \left(\mathcal{KLD}(p_{EM}^i, p_{Avg}^i) + \mathcal{KLD}(p_{KDE}^i, p_{Avg}^i) \right), \tag{6}$$

$$p_{Avg}^i = \frac{1}{2} \left(p_{EM}^i + p_{KDE}^i \right) \tag{7}$$

and

$$\mathcal{KLD}(p_1, \, p_2) = \int_{\forall x} p_1(x) \, \log \left(\frac{p_1(x)}{p_2(x)} \right) \, dx \tag{8}$$

Jensen-Shannon divergence is used here because it is a symmetric version of Kullback-Leibler $\mathcal{KLD}$ divergence. Symmetry is important to equally emphasize both estimates of the PDF; i.e. p_{KDE}^i and p_{EM}^i. To determine the model $\hat{k}$ that best represents the data set X, $\mathcal{PIC}$ is computed for a range of possible mixture components and the mixture with a minimum $\mathcal{PIC}$ is selected as shown in Equation 9.

$$\hat{k} = \arg_k \min \mathcal{PIC}_k \quad \text{and} \quad k = k_{min}, \, \ldots, \, k_{max} \tag{9}$$

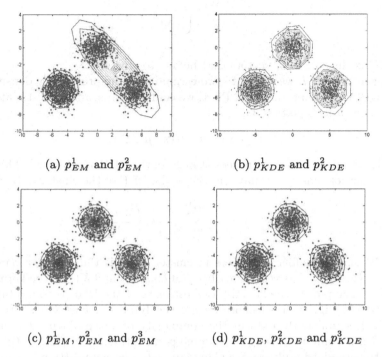

(a) p_{EM}^1 and p_{EM}^2 (b) p_{KDE}^1 and p_{KDE}^2

(c) p_{EM}^1, p_{EM}^2 and p_{EM}^3 (d) p_{KDE}^1, p_{KDE}^2 and p_{KDE}^3

Fig. 3. Data generated from three bivariate normal distributions. a and b:) fitting with a 2-component mixture, c and d:) fitting with 3-component mixture.

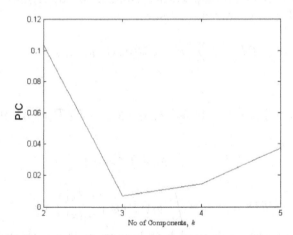

Fig. 4. The $\mathcal{PIC}$ for fitting the bivariate data of Fig. 3 using $k_{min} = 2$ and $k_{min} = 5$. The $\mathcal{PIC}$ is minimum at the correct number of components.

The search procedure is typical for many model selection criteria such as Bayesian Information Criterion (BIC). In that sense, $\mathcal{PIC}$ can be used alone as a model selection criterion. However, we will show in the next sections that within the proposed algorithm k_{min} and k_{max} are indeed constants.

Fig. 3 shows a simple example where bivariate data is generated using three normal distributions. The result of fitting the data using a two-component Gaussian mixture is shown in Fig. 3.a. The corresponding kernel density estimates of the two clusters is shown in Fig. 3.b. Because of the clear mis-modeling, the $\mathcal{PIC}$ value becomes relatively large. Fig. 3.c shows the result of fitting the data using a three-component mixture, which is similar to the kernel density estimates of the three clusters. As a result, the $\mathcal{PIC}$ value produced is relatively small. Repeating the same procedure for the range $k = \{2, 3, 4, 5\}$ results in the $\mathcal{PIC}$ values of Fig. 4, which has a clear minimum at the correct number of components.

4   Nonparametric EM Using Mixtures of Mixtures

Let $Y = \{x_i\}_{i=1}^{M}$ be a set of M vectors to be modeled. Here we use Y instead of X to denote the entire data set for reasons that will become clear later on. If we apply the mean-shift mode finding algorithm, proposed in [9], and only retain the modes with positive definite Hessian, we will obtain a set of m modes $Y_c = \{x_{c_j}\}_{j=1}^{m}$ which represent the local maxima points of the density function, where $m \ll M$. For details on computing the Hessian, the reader is referred to Han et al.'s method [14].

To infer the structure of the data, we start by partitioning Y into m partitions each of which corresponds to one of the detected modes. For all vectors of Y we compute a Mahalanobis-like distance δ defined by:

$$\delta(x_i|j) = (x_i - x_{c_j})^T P_j (x_i - x_{c_j})^T,$$
$$i = 1, 2, \ldots, M \quad \text{and} \tag{10}$$
$$j = 1, 2, \ldots, m$$

where P_j is the Hessian of mode j. The rationale here, as explained in [14] is to replace the covariance matrix, which may not be accurate at this point, by the Hessian which represents the local curvature around the mode x_{c_j}. Each vector is then assigned to a specific mode according to Equation 11.

$$C(i) = \arg_j \min \delta(x_i|j) \text{ and } j = 1, 2, \ldots, m \tag{11}$$

The data set can now be partitioned as

$$Y = \bigcup_{j=1}^{m} Y^j \tag{12}$$

where

$$Y^j = \{\forall x_i \in Y; \ C(i) \equiv j\} \tag{13}$$

It is important to note here that the partitioning of Equation 12 is different than that of Equation 2.

Each of the detected modes corresponds to either a single Gaussian, such as those of Fig. 3.a, or a mixture of more than one Gaussian such as that in Fig. 1.a.

To determine the complexity of density around a given mode x_{c_j}, we model the partition data Y_j using a mixture of Gaussians specific to partition j. In other words,

$$p(x|\Theta^j) = \sum_{i=1}^{k} \pi_i \, \mathcal{N}(x, \, \mu_i, \, \Sigma_i) \tag{14}$$

where Θ^j is the parameter set of the mixture associated with mode x_{c_j}. The initial values for the mean vectors are all set to x_{c_j}. The initial values for the covariance matrices are all set to P_j.

Since the structure of the data around x_{c_j} is unknown, we repeat the process for a search range of mixture complexities $[k_{min}, k_{max}]$ and compute $\mathcal{PIC}$ for each complexity. The mixture that minimizes the $\mathcal{PIC}$ is chosen to represent the given partition.

Applying the Penalty-less Information Criterion to all partitions results in m mixtures of Gaussians with different complexities. The underlying density of the entire data set Y is now modeled as a *mixture of mixtures of Gaussians* as follows

$$p(x|\Theta) = \sum_{j=1}^{m} \omega_j \, p(x|\Theta^j) \tag{15}$$

where $\Theta = \{\Theta^j, \, \omega_j; j = 1, 2, \ldots, , m\}$ is the set of all parameters. (Note that we extend the notation Θ here.) Finally, the weights of the mixtures ω_js are computed according to Equation 16.

$$\omega_j = \frac{\sum_{i=1}^{M} p(x_i|\Theta^j)}{\sum_{j=1}^{m} \sum_{i=1}^{M} p(x_i|\Theta^j)} \tag{16}$$

Algorithm 1 summarizes the proposed algorithm.

Algorithm 1. Nonparametric EM

Data: $Y = \{x_1, x_2, \ldots, x_i, \ldots, x_M\}$
Result: $\Theta^j s$ and $\omega^j s$
begin
    modes, $m \longleftarrow MeanShift(Y)$
    $Y^i s \longleftarrow PartitionFeatureSpace(Y, modes)$
    for $j \leftarrow 1$ **to** m **do**
        $X \longleftarrow Y^j$
        $N \longleftarrow M^j$
        for $k \longleftarrow k_{min}$ **to** k_{max} **do**
            $InitializeAllMeansAtTheModeLocation()$
            $InitializeAllCovariancesAtTheModeLocation()$
            PIC $_k$, $\Theta_k \longleftarrow ComputePIC(X, k)$
        $\hat{k}^j \longleftarrow \arg_k \min$ PIC $_k$
        $\Theta^j \longleftarrow \Theta_{\hat{k}^j}$
    $\omega_i s \longleftarrow EstimateMixtureWeights(Y)$
end

---

5 Experimental Results

5.1 Synthetic Data Example

Fig. 5 shows a set of bivariate vectors generated from a four-component Gaussian mixture. Three of the Gaussian components are co-centered at $[.5, .75]^T$ but with different covariance matrices. The fourth component is a simple component centered at $[.5, .2]^T$. The modes detected using mean-shift [9] are overlaid and marked by crosses. The result of the partitioning procedure of Equation 11 is also shown where the green points indicate Y^1 and the blue points indicate Y^2. The mode-based partitioning results in two partitions with different hidden structures. For each partition separately, the PIC is computed in the range $[k_{min} = 1, \ k_{max} = 4]$. In our experiments we use $k_{max} = 2^d$, where d is the dimensionality of the data. Fig. 6.a shows that the correct number of mixture components, $\hat{k}$ for the first partition Y^1 is $\hat{k} = 1$. On the other hand, the correct

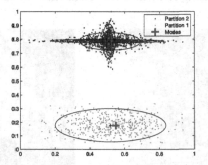

Fig. 5. Bivariate data generated from a 4-Gaussian mixture. The modes detected by the mean-shift are overlaied on the scatter plot.

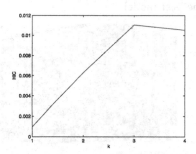

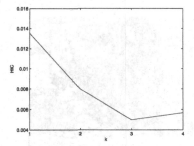

(a) The PIC values for differnet mixture complexities for the first partition, Y^1, of Fig. 5. The minimum PIC value corresponds to $k = 1$ mixture, which is the correct mixture

(b) The PIC values for differnet mixture complexities for the second partition, Y^2, of Fig. 5. The minimum PIC value corresponds to $k = 3$ mixture, which is the correct mixture

Fig. 6. The PIC values for different partitions Y^j

418   W. Abd-Almageed and L.S. Davis

number of components of the second partition Y^2 is $\hat{k} = 3$, due to the apparent complex structure of the data, as shown in Fig. 6.b.

5.2 Real Data Examples

To verify the performance of the proposed algorithm, it has been applied in an image segmentation setting. The results are compared to the those of standard model selection methods. The Luv color space was used throughout the following experiments.

Fig. 7.b shows the result of segmenting Fig. 7.a using the standard EM algorithm. The number of mixture components are selected using BIC as given by Equation 17.

$$\hat{k} = \arg_k \min -2 \log p(Y|\theta_k) + v_k \ \ln M \tag{17}$$

where θ_k and v_k are mixture model with k components and number of free parameters in θ_k, respectively. The initial values of the means and covariance matrices are selected using K-means. It is clear that the model over-segments the

(a) Original Image

(b) Segmented image using EM initialized using K-Means. BIC was used to select the best model

(c) Segmented Image using EM, with manually set number of mixture components

(d) Segmented Image using the proposed algorithm

Fig. 7. Image segmentations comparing the proposed algorithm against other traditional model selection methods

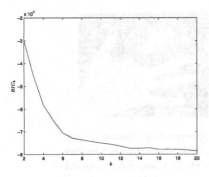
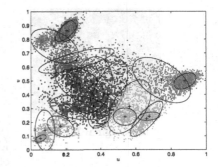

(a) BIC values for Fig. 7

(b) Hidden structures discovered by the proposed algorithm. Different colors correspond to different modes of the density function

Fig. 8. BIC values and hidden structure of Fig. 7

(a) Original Image

(b) Segmented image using EM initialized using K-Means. BIC was used to select the best model

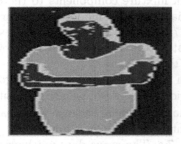

(c) Segmented Image using EM, with manually set number of mixture components

(d) Segmented Image using the proposed algorithm

Fig. 9. Image segmentations comparing the proposed algorithm against other traditional model selection methods

(a) Original Image

(b) Segmented Image using EM, with manually set number of mixture components. Good convergence of K-means

(c) Segmented Image using EM, with manually set number of mixture components. Bad convergence of K-means

(d) Segmented Image using the proposed algorithm

Fig. 10. Instability of the classical methods. Two different runs of the EM give different segmentation results.

image. The reason is that BIC only depends on the log likelihood of the feature vectors penalized by an increasing function of the number of free parameters.

The segmentation result in Fig. 7.c is obtained by visually inspecting the image and manually setting the number of mixture components to the correct value and using K-means to set the initial values of model parameters. The segmentation result are better than Fig. 7.c but not as accurate as desirable. Also, when the same experiment is repeated, the segmentation result will be different because of the random nature of the K-means.

Finally, Fig. 7.d shows the segmentation result using the proposed algorithm. The result is more accurate than the previous ones. Also, we are guaranteed to obtain the same result when repeating the experiment because the mean-shift must converge to the same stationary points every time it is applied.

Fig. 5.1.a shows the BIC values for Fig. 7.a. The curve does not have a local minima that suggests an appropriate model complexity. The ellipses in Fig. 5.1.b illustrate the hidden structures discovered by the proposed algorithm. Different modes of the density function require mixtures of variable complexities.

The same experiments was repeated for Fig. 9.a. Fig. 9.b shows the segmentation result of the EM with the BIC used to find the best model and the K-means used to initialize the model. The result of a manually selecting the number of mixture components is shown in Fig. 9.c. Finally, the result of the

Table 1. Number of data points and normalized run-time for model selection using both BIC search and proposed algorithm

	No. of points	BIC search run-time	Our run-time
Synthetic	2000	0.1583	0.0031
Woman	7598	0.0132	0.0041
House	12288	0.0525	0.0038
Hand	18544	0.2089	0.0040

proposed algorithm is shown in Fig. 9.d. The proposed algorithm yields better segmentation.

Fig. 10 illustrates the instability of using EM for density estimation and modeling. In both Fig. 10.b and Fig. 10.c the image is segmented using the EM with manually set number of mixture components and the K-means for initializing the mixture parameters. In Fig. 10.b the K-means helps the EM to converge to a good mixture, which yields a good segmentation. However, with the same number of components, K-means biases the EM to converge to a bad mixture, which results in a very poor segmentation result.

Table 1 compares the run-times of finding the best mixture model using BIC search ($k_{min} = 1$ and $k_{max} = 10$ and using our mixture of mixtures algorithm. The run-times are normalized by the number of data points. The large difference is due to two main reasons. The first is that BIC search is performed on the entire data set while our algorithm is based on partitioning the data set before applying the $\mathcal{PIC}$ search. The second reason is that the BIC search is applied on a wide range of potential complexities (because it uses the entire data set) while the $\mathcal{PIC}$ search is applied on a smaller range because of its local nature.

6   Conclusions and Future Research

This paper introduces a new method addressing the limitations of the popular Expectation Maximization algorithm; namely the *a priori* knowledge regarding the complexity of the mixture and difficulty of accurate initialization of mixture parameters.

The paper uses the mean-shift-based mode finding algorithm developed by Comaniciu and Meer in [9] to estimate the number of Gaussian mixtures that must be used to model the data. Then, a partitioning algorithm is performed to cluster the data into subsets. For each subset the regular EM is used to infer the hidden structure of the underlying density function. The mean vectors of the mixture is initialized at the mode location found by the mean-shift.

The paper also introduces a model selection criterion, $\mathcal{PIC}$, that is used to find the mixture that best fits the density of the mixture. The $\mathcal{PIC}$ compares the parametric representation of the density against a nonparametric estimate of PDF using the Jensen-Shannon divergence, without a penalty term.

Applying the proposed algorithm on 2D and 3D data sets shows the advantages of using the algorithm to obtaining a parametric representation of the underlying density without manually initializing the model. In the future, we plan to apply the proposed algorithm to other computer vision problems and compare its performance against other popular image segmentation algorithms.

References

1. Dempster, A., Laird, N., Rubin, D.: Maximum likelihood form incomplete data via the em algorithm. Journal of Royal Satistical Society, Series B **39** (1977)
2. Belongie, S., Carson, C., Greenspan, H., Malik, J.: Color- and texture-based image segmentation using em and its applications to content-based image retreval. In: Sixth International Conference on Computer Vision. (1998) 675–682
3. Abu-Naser, A., Galatsanos, N., Wernick, M., Schonfeld, D.: Object recognition based on impulse restoration with use of the expectation-maximization algorithm. Journal of the Optical Society of America A (Optics, Image Science and Vision) **15** (1998) 2327 – 40
4. Figueirdeo, M., Jain, A.: Unsupervised Learning of Finite Mixture Models. IEEE Trans. on Pattern Analysis and Machine Intelligence **24** (2002) 381–396
5. Dasgupta, A., Rafetry, A.: Detecting Features ni Spatial Point Patterns with Clutter Via Model-Based Clustering. J. of American Statistical Association (1998) 294–302
6. Campbell, J., Fraley, C., Murtagh, F., Raftery, A.: Linear Flaw Detection in Woven Textiles Using Model-Based clustering. Pattern Recognition Letters **18** (1997) 1539–1548
7. Neal, R.: Bayesian Mixture Modeling. In: Proc. of 11th Int'l Workshop on Maximum Entropy and Bayesian Methods of Statistical Analysis. (1992) 197–211
8. Bensmail, H., Celeus, G., Rafetry, A., Robert, C.: Inference in Model-Based Cluster Analysis. Statistics and Computing **7** (1997) 1–10
9. Comaniciu, D., Meer, P.: Mean Shift: A Robust Approach Toward Feature Space Analysis. IEEE Trans. Pattern Analysis and Machine Intelligence **24** (2002)
10. Fukunaga, K., Hostetler, L.D.: The estimation of a gradient of a density function, with applications in pattern recognition. IEEE Trans. on Information Theory **21** (1975) 32–40
11. Yang, C., Duraiswami, R., Gumerov, N., Davis, L.: Improved Fast Gauss Transform and Efficient Kernel Density Estimation. In: Proc. IEEE International Conference on Computer Vision. (2003)
12. Wand, M., Jones, M.: Kernel Smoothing. Chapman and Hall (1995)
13. Lin, J.: Divergence measuers based on the shannon entropy. IEEE Trans. Information Theory **37** (1991) 145–151
14. Han, H., and, D.C., Zhu, Y., Davis, L.: Incremental density approximation and kernel-based baesian filtering for object tracking. In: IEEE International Conference on Computer Vision and Pattern Recognition. (2004)

Example Based Non-rigid Shape Detection

Yefeng Zheng[1], Xiang Sean Zhou[2], Bogdan Georgescu[1],
Shaohua Kevin Zhou[1], and Dorin Comaniciu[1]

[1] Siemens Corporate Research, Princeton, NJ 08540, USA
[2] Siemens Medical Solutions, Malvern, PA 19355, USA
{yefeng.zheng, xiang.zhou, bogdan.georgescu, shaohua.zhou,
dorin.comaniciu}@siemens.com

Abstract. Since it is hard to handcraft the prior knowledge in a shape detection
framework, machine learning methods are preferred to exploit the expert annotation of the target shape in a database. In the previous approaches [1, 2], an optimal
similarity transformation is exhaustively searched for to maximize the response
of a trained classification model. At best, these approaches only give a rough
estimate of the position of a non-rigid shape. In this paper, we propose a novel
machine learning based approach to achieve a refined shape detection result. We
train a model that has the largest response on a reference shape and a smaller
response on other shapes. During shape detection, we search for an optimal non-
rigid deformation to maximize the response of the trained model on the deformed
image block. Since exhaustive searching is inapplicable for a non-rigid deformation space with a high dimension, currently, example based searching is used
instead. Experiments on two applications, left ventricle endocardial border detection and facial feature detection, demonstrate the robustness of our approach. It
outperforms the well-known ASM and AAM approaches on challenging samples.

1 Introduction

It is widely accepted that prior knowledge about the target shape is important and should
be used in shape detection. How to effectively use the prior knowledge is an active
research topic in non-rigid shape detection for a long time. Starting from the seminal paper by Kass et al. [3] on the active contour model (ACM), energy minimization
based approaches become a standard tool for non-rigid shape detection, where the prior
knowledge is encoded into an energy function. An active contour is driven by the external and internal forces. The external force is derived from input images, while the
internal force incorporates the prior knowledge of the target shape. In a standard setting
[3], active contour models use two parameters to adjust the elasticity and stiffness of
the shape. With such a limited flexibility, very little prior knowledge can be exploited
by ACMs and the contour often converges to an unrealistic shape. To mitigate this problem, the active shape model (ASM) [4] constraints the deformation of a shape. Given a
set of shapes, the principal component analysis (PCA) is applied to the shape space. The
deformation of the shape is constrained to a subspace spanned by a few eigenvectors
associated with the largest eigenvalues. The searching space can be further restricted
to a hyper-cube [4]. By adjusting the number of principal components preserved, ASM
can achieve a trade-off between the representation capability of the model and the constraints on the shape. If all principal components are used, ASM can represent any

A. Leonardis, H. Bischof, and A. Pinz (Eds.): ECCV 2006, Part IV, LNCS 3954, pp. 423–436, 2006.

shape, but no prior knowledge of the shape is used. On the other hand, if too few principal components are retained, an input shape cannot be well represented by the subspace. Therefore, there is an upper-bound of the detection accuracy given a specified choice of parameters. Both ACM and ASM only use the image contents around the shape boundaries, so they are more suitable for shapes with strong edges. The active appearance model (AAM) is a natural extension of ASM, where the variation of the appearance is constrained to a subspace too.

Along another research line, shape detection can be formulated as a classification problem: whether the given image block contains the target shape. Exhaustive searching in the similarity transformation space is often used to estimate the translation, rotation, and scale of the shape in an input image. Viola and Jones [1] proposed an efficient implementation of the AdaBoost algorithm [5, 6] for face detection. Given a large pool of simple features, AdaBoost can select a small feature set and the corresponding optimal weights for classification. The convolutional neural network (CNN) [2] is another classification based approach combing feature extraction, selection, and classifier training into the same framework. As a specially designed neural network, CNN is especially effective for two-dimensional images. One drawback of these classification based approaches is that only the similarity deformation of the shape can be estimated.

Since it is hard to handcraft the prior knowledge in a shape detection framework, we prefer a method directly exploiting the expert annotation of the target shape in a large database. Zhou et al. [7] proposed an approach to directly learn a regression function for the positions of control points. Though simple and elegant, the regression output is a multi-dimensional vector (often in the order of 100 for shape detection, depending on the application). Since regression for multi-dimensional output is hard, PCA is often exploited to restrict the shape deformation space. So, it suffers from the same limitations as ASM and AAM. Georgescu et al. [8] proposed the shape inference method to search for the most similar shape in the database. Particularly, the training set is clustered in the shape space into several clusters. A set of image features are selected to maximize the Fisher separation criterion. During shape detection, the input and training images are compared in the feature space to select a similar example shape for the input. As a heuristic metric, the Fisher separation criterion is optimal for very limited cases, such as the Gaussian distributions with the same covariance matrix. Both of the above approaches need a preprocessing step to estimate the rough position of a shape, which is often realized using a classification based approach [1, 8].

In this paper, we propose a novel learning based approach for non-rigid shape detection. Unlike the classification based approaches, we can output a refined detection result without the restriction to the similarity deformation. We train a model that has the largest response on the reference shape (in our case, we use the mean shape as the reference shape) and a smaller response on other shapes. The response of the model can be seen as a measure of the distance between a shape and the reference shape. During shape detection, we search for an optimal deformation (which corresponds to the optimal shape detection result) to maximize the response of the trained model. So, instead of distinguishing object and non-object as in the classification based approaches, our trained model distinguishes the reference shape from all the other shapes. One challenge, compared to the classification based approach, is that exhaustive searching is inapplicable for a non-rigid deformation space, which usually has a high dimension. Instead, example based searching is used. In this paper, we make the following contributions.

1. We propose a method to directly learn the relative distance in the shape space using image based features.
2. No assumption about the distribution of the shape or appearance is necessary in our approach.
3. The shape detection process can be seen as an optimization problem. Unlike the previous work, our objective function is learned, specified for a shape.

This paper is organized as follows. Our learning based non-rigid shape detection algorithm is described in detail in Section 2. In Section 3, we empirically compare our approach with several well-known algorithms, such as AAM and ASM. The paper concludes with a brief summary and a discussion of the limitations in Section 4.

2 Machine Learning Based Non-rigid Shape Detection

In this section we describe our problem formulation and learning method in detail. Our key problem is to train a model that has the largest response on the reference shape and a smaller response on other shapes. We can take the model response as a measure of the distance between a shape and the reference shape. Learning a regression function of the shape distance is a possible solution [7]. However, since the absolute magnitude of the distance measure is irrelevant, we formulate the learning as a ranking problem. Suppose we have a set of training images $I_1, I_2, \ldots, I_M$ and the corresponding annotated shapes $S_1, S_2, \ldots, S_M$. Suppose each shape S_i is represented with N control points P_i^n, $n = 1, 2, \ldots, N$. In our approach, the reference shape can be arbitrary. To reduce the distortion introduced in warping, the mean shape is used as the reference shape. Suppose the mean shape of the training set is $\bar{S}$, which can be calculated using the generalized Procrustes analysis [4]. For each shape S_i there is a warping template W_i which warps S_i toward the mean shape $\bar{S}$. Given a training image I_i, we can synthesize M warped images $I_i^1, I_i^2, \ldots, I_i^M$ using warping templates $W_1, W_2, \ldots, W_M$. Here, I_i^j is the warped image using image I_i and warping template W_j. These M synthesized images I_i^j, $j = 1, 2, \ldots, M$ can be sorted in the ascending order according to the shape distance $D_{i,j}$, which is defined as the average Euclidean distance between corresponding control points[1]

$$D_{i,j} = \frac{1}{N} \sum_{n=1}^{N} \| P_i^n - P_j^n \|. \tag{1}$$

The warped image using the *perfect* warping template, I_i^i, should be ranked on the top. By repeating the image synthesis for all training images, we obtain M ranked image

---

[1] Synthesized images can also be sorted in the deformed shape space. Suppose the shape of a warped image I_i^j is S_i^j. Images I_i^j for $j = 1, 2, \ldots, M$ can be sorted using the distance between S_i^j and the mean shape. Since the warping used in our approach is smooth, the difference between these two methods is small for warped images ranked on top.

lists, which have the following two characteristics. First, all synthesized images using the same image have the same appearance but a different shape. Second, all synthesized images that are ranked on the top in their own lists have the same shape (the mean shape $\bar{S}$) but different appearance. Refer to Fig. 1 for a graphical illustration. These characteristics help us to use a machine learning technique to learn a model whose ranking output is the most similar to the ground-truth.

2.1 Image Warping

Given a shape, we want to calculate the warping from it to the mean shape. Linear interpolation is used for image warping in AAM [9, 10]. The warping, however, is only piece-wise smooth. The thin plate spline (TPS) model [11] is often used for representing flexible coordinate transformations. The advantages of TPS are 1) the interpolation is smooth with derivatives of any order; 2) the model has no free parameters that need manual tuning; 3) it has closed-form solutions for both warping and parameter estimation; and 4) there is a physical explanation for its energy function. Two TPS models are used for a 2-D coordinate transformation. Suppose control point (x_i, y_i) corresponds to (u_i, v_i) for $i = 1, 2, \cdots, N$, let $z_i = f(x_i, y_i)$ be the target function value at location (x_i, y_i). We set z_i equal to u_i and v_i in turn to obtain one continuous transformation for each coordinate. The TPS interpolant $f(x, y)$ minimizes the following bending energy

$$I_f = \int \int_{\mathbb{R}^2} \left(\frac{\partial^2 f}{\partial x^2} \right)^2 + 2 \left(\frac{\partial^2 f}{\partial x \partial y} \right)^2 + \left(\frac{\partial^2 f}{\partial y^2} \right)^2 dx dy, \tag{2}$$

and has the solution of the form

$$f(x, y) = a_1 + a_x x + a_y y + \sum_{i=1}^{N} w_i U(\|(x_i, y_i) - (x, y)\|), \tag{3}$$

where $U(r)$ is the kernel function, taking the form of $U(r) = r^2 log r^2$. The parameters of the TPS models w and a are the solution of the following linear equation

$$\begin{bmatrix} K & P \\ P^T & 0 \end{bmatrix} \begin{bmatrix} w \\ a \end{bmatrix} = \begin{bmatrix} z \\ 0 \end{bmatrix}, \tag{4}$$

where $K_{ij} = U(\|(x_i, y_i) - (x_j, y_j)\|)$; the ith row of P is $(1, x_i, y_i)$; w and z are column vectors formed from w_i and z_i, respectively; and a is the column vector with elements a_1, a_x, and a_y.

To avoid holes in the warped image, we actually calculate the warping from the mean shape to the input shape. For each pixel in the warped image, we calculate its position in the input image. To reduce the computation, the simple closest pixel approximation is used to round the warped position to the integer grid. This warping information can be saved as a looking-up table. The expensive calculation of Equation (3) is only performed once and it is done off-line.

Fig. 1 (a) shows the mean shape of the left ventricle endocardial border in an ultrasound heart data set labeled using 17 control points. In the figure, we connect neighboring control points to visualize the border clearly. Fig. 1 (b) and (d) show two images,

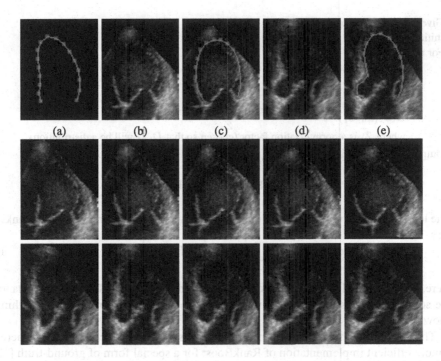

(a)   (b)   (c)   (d)   (e)

Fig. 1. Image warping for an ultrasound heart data set. (a) The mean shape of the left ventricle endocardial border, represented with 17 control points. In the figure, we connect neighboring control points to visualize the border clearly. (b) and (d) show two images with corresponding annotated shapes in (c) and (e), respectively. The second and third rows show synthesized images using (b) and (d), respectively. The ranks of these images from left to right are 1, 5, 10, 50, and 100.

and the corresponding shapes are shown in (c) and (e). Some synthesized images using (b) and (d) are shown in the second and third rows, respectively. They are sorted in the ascending order from left to right using the distance between the input shape and the warping shapes.

2.2   Learning the Shape Difference

In this section, we present the RankBoost [12] learning algorithm, which is used to learn the ranking of synthesized images. The goal of RankBoost learning is minimizing the (weighted) number of pairs of instances that are mis-ordered by the final ranking relative to the given ground-truth. Suppose the learner is provided with ground-truth about the relative ranking of an individual pair of instances x_0 and x_1. Suppose x_1 should be ranked above x_0, otherwise a penalty $D(x_0, x_1)$ is imposed (equal weighted penalty $D(x_0, x_1) = 1$ is used in our experiments). $D(x_0, x_1) = 0$ indicates no preference between x_0 and x_1. The penalty weights $D(x_0, x_1)$ can be normalized to a probability distribution

$$\sum_{x_0, x_1} D(x_0, x_1) = 1. \tag{5}$$

Given: Initial distribution D over $\mathcal{X} \times \mathcal{X}$.
Initialize: $D_1 = D$.
For $t = 1, 2, \ldots, T$
  - Train weak learner using distribution D_t to get weak ranking $h_t : \mathcal{X} \to \mathbb{R}$.
  - Choose $\alpha_t \in \mathbb{R}$.
  - Update:

$$D_{t+1}(x_0, x_1) = \frac{D_t(x_0, x_1) \exp[\alpha_t(h_t(x_0) - h_t(x_1))]}{Z_t}$$

  where Z_t is a normalization factor (chosen so that D_{t+1} will be a distribution).
Output the final ranking: $H(x) = \sum_{t=1}^{T} \alpha_t h_t(x)$.

Fig. 2. The RankBoost algorithm

The learning goal is searching for a final ranking function H that minimizes the ranking loss

$$rloss_D(H) = \sum_{x_0, x_1} D(x_0, x_1)[[H(x_1) \leq H(x_0)]]. \tag{6}$$

Here, $[[\pi]]$ is defined to be 1 if predicate π holds and 0 otherwise. Note that the instances are sorted in the descending order with respective to H. The RankBoost algorithm is shown in Fig. 2.

The above implementation is expensive in terms of space and computation. There is a more efficient implementation of RankBoost for a special form of ground-truth [12]. We say that the ranking ground-truth is *bipartite* if there exists disjoint subsets X_0 and X_1 of $\mathcal{X}$ such that the ground-truth ranks all instances in X_1 above all instances in X_0 and says nothing about any other pairs. In our approach, for a ranked image list, we want the top l images to be ranked above all the remaining images. We do not care about the relative ranking of synthesized images in different lists, so our ground-truth is not bipartite itself but a union of bipartite subsets. The efficient implementation of RankBoost is still applicable for this case, see [12] for details. Naturally, $l = 1$ should be used. Currently, example based searching is used for our shape detection method (discussed in Section 2.4). We select the top several closest prototypes in the database. Weighted average of the selected shapes are taken as the detection result. Therefore, the learning of ranking should not restrict to the top one in each list. A slightly larger l should be used ($l = 5$ in our following experiments).

There is an upper-bound for the ranking loss $rloss_D(H)$ on the training set [12].

Theorem 1: At time t, let

$$Z_t = \sum_{x_0, x_1} D_t(x_0, x_1) \exp\left[\alpha_t(h_t(x_0) - h_t(x_1))\right]. \tag{7}$$

The ranking loss of H on the training set is upper-bounded as

$$rloss_D(H) \leq \Pi_{t=1}^{T} Z_t. \tag{8}$$

For any given weak ranking function h_t, it can be shown that Z_t is a convex function of α_t and has a unique minimum [6]. The optimal α_t can be found numerically using the Newton-Raphson method. In our approach, each weaker learner uses only one feature.

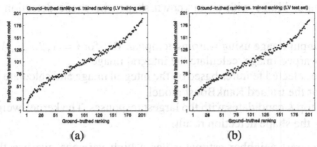

(a)   (b)

Fig. 3. Ground-truthed ranking vs. the average ranking by the trained RankBoost model for the left ventricle border detection. (a) On the training set. (b) On the test set.

For each feature, we search for an optimal α_t to minimize Z_t. The feature with the smallest Z_t value is selected as the weaker learner. So, the weaker learner training and optimal α_t searching are finished in one step.

Fig. 3 (a) and (b) show the ground-truthed ranking vs. the average ranking by the trained RankBoost model for the left ventricle endocardial border detection (presented in Section 3.1) on the training and test sets, respectively. As we can see, the ranking of the RankBoost model matches the ground-truth quite well.

2.3 Ranking vs. Classification

With bipartite ground-truth, the ranking problem is very similar to the classification problem. Formulated as a classification problem, instances in X_1 and X_0 form the positive and negative training samples, respectively. It is easy to verify that the objective function $rloss_D(H)$ of RankBoost, Equation (6), is equivalent to the error rate in AdaBoost [5], a corresponding learning algorithm for a classification problem. However, in our case, the ground-truth is not bipartite itself, but a union of bipartite subsets. We only care the relative ranking of synthesized images that are generated using the same image but different warping templates, e.g., I_i^m and I_i^n when $m \neq n$. We do not care the relative ranking of two synthesized images warped from different images, e.g., I_i^m and I_j^n if $i \neq j$. In our previous experiments, we tried to use AdaBoost to replace RankBoost in learning, but got worse results. Formulated as a ranking problem, the learning algorithm concentrates on learning the shape difference since the instances to be ranked have the same appearance but different shapes.

2.4 Shape Detection

We use the feature pool proposed in [1] for the learning task. A feature template is composed with several rectangular regions. The response of a feature is defined as the sum of intensities in some rectangles subtracted by the sum of intensities in the other rectangles. By moving and scaling the feature templates, a big feature pool (often in the magnitude of one million features) can be achieved. This feature pool is by no means optimal. For example, it cannot describe an edge with an orientation other than horizontal and vertical. The argument for using them is that there is an efficient implementation of feature extraction based on integral images. Please refer to [1] for details.

Given an input image with an unknown shape, the shape detection process is as follows.

1. Warp the input image using warping template W_i, for $i = 1, 2, \ldots, M$.
2. For each warped image, calculate the integral image.
3. Extract the selected features based on the integral image and calculate the combined response of the trained RankBoost model.
4. Select the top k candidates with the largest responses. The kernel-weighted average is taken as the shape detection result.

Since the nearest-neighbor estimator has a high variance, we use the Nadaraya-Watson kernel-weighted average [13] as the the final shape detection result

$$\hat{S} = \frac{\sum_{i=1}^{M} K_k(d_i) S_i}{\sum_{i=1}^{M} K_k(d_i)}, \tag{9}$$

where,

$$d_i = 1 - \frac{H_i - \min\{H_j\}}{\max\{H_j\} - \min\{H_j\}}. \tag{10}$$

Since the response H_i of the RankBoost model is not a distance measure, we normalize it to the range of $[0, 1]$ using the above equation. For the kernel K_k, we use the Epanechnikov quadratic kernel

$$K_k(d_i) = \begin{cases} 3/4 \left[1 - \left(\frac{d_i}{d_{[k]}}\right)^2\right] & \text{if } d_i \leq d_{[k]} \\ 0 & \text{otherwise} \end{cases}, \tag{11}$$

where k is the size of the neighborhood, and $d_{[k]}$ means the distance of the top k^{th} prototype. Using kernel-based smoothing, the detected shape is not restricted to those represented in the training set. In theory, any shape can be represented as a linear combination of a set of base shapes, which fully span the whole shape space.

The major computations of our approach include image warping, integral images calculation, and feature extraction. The speed of the whole procedure depends on the input image size and the number of warping templates. For left ventricle border detection presented in Section 3.1, the input image block size is 80×104 pixels. When 202 warping templates are used, we can process about 42 input image blocks per second (which means given an input image block, we finish all the above computations for all warping templates and output the detected shape) on a PC with dual 2.4 GHZ Xeon CPUs and 2 GB memory. The decomposed computation time for one input is 12.5 ms (52.8%) for image warping, 8.7 ms (36.8%) for integral image calculation, and 2.0 ms (8.4%) for feature extraction. Since the processing for each warping template is independent, our algorithm is well suited for parallel computing. On the same PC, if we using multi-thread techniques to make full use of the computation power, we can achieve the detection speed of about 77 inputs per second.

2.5 A More Efficient Implementation

In our feature pool, each feature is a linear combination of the intensities, and the RankBoost model is a linear combination of the selected features, as shown in Fig. 2. So,

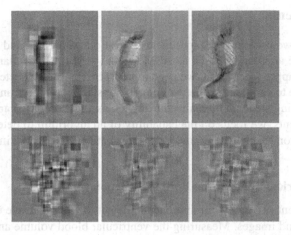

Fig. 4. Weight images. Top row: weight images for left ventricle endocardial border detection. Bottom row: weight images for facial feature detection. Left column: weight images aligned with the mean shapes. Middle and right columns: two back-warped weight images.

overall, the response of the trained RankBoost model is a linear combination of the intensities. We can organize the combination weights as an image. Fig. 4 shows the weight images learned by RankBoost for left ventricle endocardial border detection and facial feature detection (the weights are normalized to the range $[0, 255]$ for visualization purpose). Using weight images, shape detection is equivalent to searching for a warping template to maximize the dot-product of the warped image and the weight image.

$$\hat{W} = \arg\max_{W_i} I^i . I_w \tag{12}$$

Here, I^i is the warped image using warping template W_i, and I_w is the weight image. Image warping and dot-product calculation can be combined to achieve a more efficient implementation. Here, we back warp the weight image using each warping template, and store all back-warped weight images. This operation can be performed off-line. In shape detection, we calculate the dot-product of the input image and a back-warped weight image to calculate the response of the corresponding warping template. This implementation is more efficient than the integral image based approach. On the same PC, we achieve the speed of 54 inputs per second using one CPU, and 91 inputs per second using dual CPUs.

Beside increasing the speed, the weight-image based approach also provides more flexibility in feature design and warping interpolation. Any feature based on the linear combination of pixel intensities can be used, no need to be restricted to rectangular feature templates. In image warping, closest pixel approximation is not necessary any more, more accurate approximation such as bi-linear interpolation can be used as long as the interpolation is linear. Such extensions are the same efficient. At the current stage, we have not exploited such new possibilities to increase the shape detection accuracy. This is one direction of our future work.

3 Experiments

In this section, we present two experiments to test our approach, and compare it with other alternative approaches, such as ASM [4] and AAM [9]. Similar to the previous learning based approaches [7, 8], we need a preprocessing step to detect the rough position of a shape to compensate the variation in translation, rotation, and scale changes. This preprocessing step can be realized using a classification based approach [1, 2, 8]. In our experiments, we focus on the capability of an algorithm to detect the non-rigid shape deformation besides the similarity transformation, so the input images are rigidly aligned.

3.1 Left Ventricle Endocardial Border Detection

In this experiment, we apply our approach to detect the left ventricle endocardial borders in ultrasound images. Measuring the ventricular blood volume and the motion of ventricular border over various stages of the cardiac cycle are components with strong diagnostic power. The left ventricle is of particular interest because it pumps oxygenated blood out to distant tissues in the entire body. As shown in Fig. 7, ultrasound images are often affected by speckle noise, signal dropout, and imaging artifacts. In many cases, there is no clear border definition. A total of 404 ultrasound images of left ventricles are collected with the endocardial border manually annotated by experts using 17 points. The input image block is normalized to 80×104 pixels. The whole data set is split into two equal parts, one for training, the other for test.

The Matlab implementation of ASM by Dr. Ghassan Hamarneh at Simon Fraser University, Canada is used for comparison experiments. The source code is available at http://www.cs.sfu.ca/~hamarneh/software/asm/index.html. The AAM-API [10] developed by Dr. Mikkel B. Stegmann, available at http://www2.imm.dtu.dk/~aam/, is used for the AAM experiments. For both ASM and AAM, the mean shape is used for initialization. Multi-scale searching is often used in ASM and AAM and may achieve a better result under a relatively large initialization error [4, 9]. However, in our experiments, the samples have already been rigidly registered. Multi-scale searching doesn't improve the accuracy, therefore, it is not used. The

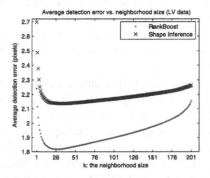

Fig. 5. Shape detection error vs. the neighborhood size, k, for kernel-weighted smoothing on the ultrasound heart test set. The proposed approach consistently outperforms the shape inference method at any k.

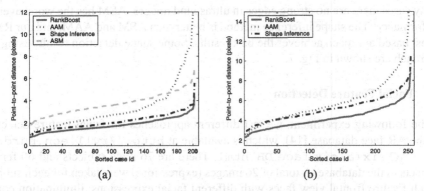

Fig. 6. Sorted detection errors using ASM, AAM, shape inference, and the proposed approach. (a) Left ventricle endocardial border detection. (b) Facial feature detection.

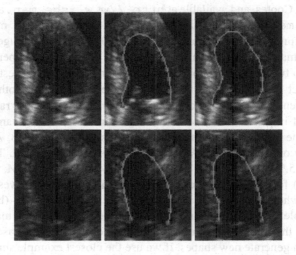

Fig. 7. Left ventricle endocardial border detection using our approach. Left column: input images. Middle column: detected shapes. Right column: expert drawn contours.

shape inference method [8] is also tested for comparison purpose. For all algorithms, the free parameters are tuned to achieve the best results on the test set.

The average point-to-point Euclidean distance, Equation (1), is used to evaluate the shape detection accuracy. The average detection error is 4.30 pixels for the mean shape, 3.70 pixels for ASM, and 3.33 pixels for AAM. Since the nearest-neighbor estimator has a high variance, kernel-weighted smoothing can significantly improve the performance of both shape inference and the proposed approach (as shown in Fig. 5). The detection error decreases from 2.70 pixels when $k = 1$ to the minimum of 2.14 pixels when $k = 34$ for shape inference. The proposed approach achieves the minimum detection error of 1.82 pixels when $k = 30$. Fig. 6 (a) shows the sorted errors (vertically these curves do not correspond to the same image). As shown in the figure, the performance variation of AAM is large compared to the other approaches. ASM is more stable, since the deformation of the shape is further restricted to a hyper-cube. Since in many cases there are no strong edges in ultrasound images, ASM has the worst average performance. The shape inference method is better than ASM and AAM, and our Rank-Boost based approach achieves the best results. Some shape detection results using our approach are shown in Fig. 7.

3.2   Facial Feature Detection

In the following experiment, we test different approaches for facial feature detection on the AR face database [14], which is available at http://rvl1.ecn.purdue.edu/~aleix/aleix_face_DB.html. There are 76 male subjects and 60 female subjects in the database. A total of 26 images (expressions) were taken for each subject, which feature frontal view faces with different facial expressions, illumination conditions, and occlusions (sun glasses and scarf). The original images are in color. In this experiment, they are converted to gray scale images. Manual markup using 22 points is provided by Dr. Cootes, and available at http://www.isbe.man.ac.uk/~bim/data/tarfd_markup/tarfd_markup.html. Currently, the markup is only available for expressions 01 (neutral expression), 02 (smile), 03 (anger), and 05 (left light on). One markup is shown in Fig. 8. Similar to the above experiment, we split the data set into two equal parts, one for training and the other for test. Samples from the same subject appear in either the training or test set, but not both. To avoid bias introduced by gender, the training and test sets have the same gender ratio.

The classical implementation of ASM only works for densely sampled points on curves. Since the 22 markup points are isolated, as shown in Fig. 8, ASM cannot be applied directly on this data set. All the other algorithms are tested. The average detection error is 5.93 pixels for the mean shape, 5.94 pixels for AAM, and 5.16 pixels (when $k = 37$) for shape inference. The proposed approach achieves the best result of 4.24 pixels when $k = 20$. The sorted errors are shown in Fig. 6 (b). One concern about an example based detection method is that the detected shape may be limited to those shapes in the training set. In our approach, however, kernel based smoothing is used, which can generate new shapes. If we use the closest example shape (i.e., $k = 1$) to represent the input shape, the lower-bound of the detection error is 4.31 pixels (the lower-bound is achieved when the closest shape searching is perfect). On this data set, we achieve a better result due to the use of kernel based smoothing.

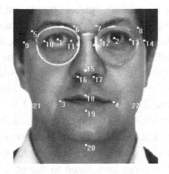

Fig. 8. Manual markup with 22 points for a face

Many samples in this data set are very challenging. For example, some male subjects have heavy beards, which reduces the detection accuracy of the chin (control points 20, 21, and 22). Expression 05 is captured with a strong left light turned on, so the left border of the face (control point 22) is often undistinguishable from the background. Another challenge is that about one third of the subjects wear glasses. AAM does not perform well on such a dual-mode distribution (wearing glasses or not). If we remove the subjects wearing glasses from both the training and test sets, the average detection error of AAM on the test set reduces from 5.94 pixels to 5.36 pixels.

4 Conclusions

In this paper, we proposed a novel non-rigid shape detection method by directly learning the relative distance in the shape space. No assumption about the distribution of the shape or appearance is necessary in our approach. Our shape detection process can be seen as an optimization problem. Unlike the previous work, our objective function is learned and specified for a shape. Experiments on left ventricle endocardial border detection and facial feature detection confirmed the robustness of our approach. It outperforms the well-known AAM and ASM approaches.

As a proof-of-concept, currently example based approach is used to for shape detection, whose speed is directly related to the size of the training set. When a large training set is available, the speed of example based approach may be too slow. In this case, the BoostMap method [15] can be exploited to speed up the searching. It has been shown that in some applications less than 10% candidates need to be evaluated with a slight performance deterioration.

References

1. Viola, P., Jones, M.: Rapid object detection using a boosted cascade of simple features. In: Proc. IEEE Conf. Computer Vision and Pattern Recognition. Volume 1. (2001) 511–518
2. Osadchy, R., Miller, M., LeCun, Y.: Synergistic face detection and pose estimation with energy-based model. In: Advances in Neural Information Processing Systems. MIT Press (2005) 1017–1024
3. Kass, M., Witkin, A., Terzopoulos, D.: Snakes: Active contour models. Int. J. Computer Vision 1(4) (1988) 321–331
4. Cootes, T.F., Taylor, C.J., Cooper, D.H., Graham, J.: Active shape models—their training and application. Computer Vision and Image Understanding 61(1) (1995) 38–59
5. Freund, Y., Schapire, R.E.: A decision-theoretic generalization of on-line learning and an application to boosting. J. Computer and System Sciences 55(1) (1997) 119–139
6. Schapire, R.E., Singer, Y.: Improved boosting algorithms using confidence-rated predictions. Machine Learning 37(3) (1999) 297–336
7. Zhou, S.K., Georgescu, B., Zhou, X.S., Comaniciu, D.: Image based regression using boosting method. In: Proc. Int'l Conf. Computer Vision. Volume 1. (2005) 541–548
8. Georgescu, B., Zhou, X.S., Comaniciu, D., Gupta, A.: Database-guided segmentation of anatomical structures with complex appearance. In: Proc. IEEE Conf. Computer Vision and Pattern Recognition. Volume 2. (2005) 429–436
9. Cootes, T.F., Edwards, G.J., Taylor, C.J.: Active appearance models. IEEE Trans. Pattern Anal. Machine Intell. 23(6) (2001) 681–685

10. Stegmann, M.B., Ersboll, B.K., Larsen, R.: FAME—a flexible appearance modeling environment. IEEE Trans. Medical Imaging **22**(10) (2003) 1319–1331
11. Bookstein, F.L.: Principal warps: Thin-plate splines and the decomposition of deformation. IEEE Trans. Pattern Anal. Machine Intell. **11**(6) (1989) 567–585
12. Freund, Y., Iyer, R., Schapire, R.E., Singer, Y.: An efficient boosting algorithm for combining preferences. J. Machine Learning Research **4**(6) (2004) 933–970
13. Hastie, T., Tibshirani, R., Friedman, J.: The Elements of Statistical Learning. Springer-Verlag (2001)
14. Martinez, A.M., Benavente, R.: The AR face database. Technical Report #24, CVC (1998)
15. Athitsos, V., Alon, J., Sclaroff, S., Kollios, G.: BoostMap: A method for efficient approximate similarity rankings. In: Proc. IEEE Conf. Computer Vision and Pattern Recognition. Volume 2. (2004) 268–275

Towards Safer, Faster Prenatal Genetic Tests: Novel Unsupervised, Automatic and Robust Methods of Segmentation of Nuclei and Probes

Christophe Restif

Department of Computing, Oxford Brookes University, Oxford OX33 1HX, UK
christophe.restif@centraliens.net

Abstract. In this paper we present two new methods of segmentation that we developed for nuclei and chromosomic probes – core objects for cytometry medical imaging. Our nucleic segmentation method is mathematically grounded on a novel parametric model of an image histogram, which accounts at the same time for the background noise, the nucleic textures and the nuclei's alterations to the background. We adapted an Expectation-Maximisation algorithm to adjust this model to the histograms of each image and subregion, in a coarse-to-fine approach. The probe segmentation uses a new dome-detection algorithm, insensitive to background and foreground noise, which detects probes of any intensity. We detail our two segmentation methods and our EM algorithm, and discuss the strengths of our techniques compared with state-of-the-art approaches. Both our segmentation methods are unsupervised, automatic, and require no training nor tuning: as a result, they are directly applicable to a wide range of medical images. We have used them as part of a large-scale project for the improvement of prenatal diagnostic of genetic diseases, and tested them on more than 2,100 images with nearly 14,000 nuclei. We report 99.3% accuracy for each of our segmentation methods, with a robustness to different laboratory conditions unreported before.

1 Introduction

Over the past twenty years, the age of pregnancy has been rising significantly, with increased risk of genetic disease for the children. Thanks to the progress made by research in genetics, many genetic diseases can now be treated at birth, sometimes even during pregnancy. However, current diagnostic methods require invasive procedures such as amniocentesis or cordocentesis, increasing the risk of miscarriage. It is known that a few fetal cells enter the maternal circulation: this opens the promise of a non-invasive diagnostic alternative. Isolating these cells non-destructively would give access to the whole genetic material of the foetus. Yet, such cells are rare: a sample of maternal blood will contain roughly 1 in 10^6 fetal cells, a ratio that can be reduced to about 1 in 10^4 with enrichment methods [1]. Computer vision can make their detection easier.

The cells used in this work are leucocytes. Their nuclei are treated with a blue fluorescent marker, and their telomeres with green fluorescent probes (see

A. Leonardis, H. Bischof, and A. Pinz (Eds.): ECCV 2006, Part IV, LNCS 3954, pp. 437–450, 2006.

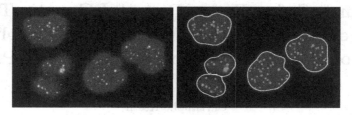

Fig. 1. Left: Image showing leucocyte nuclei (in blue), containing probes attached to the telomeres (in green). Right: nuclei and probes segmented with our method.

Fig. 1). Telomeres are the ending parts of chromosomes, and more abundant in fetal nuclei than in maternal ones. Measuring the green fluorescence in each nucleus is expected to be sufficient to single out the rare fetal nuclei within a sample of maternal blood, but it is still open to cytology research to assert it. The need for automatic image processing in this field of medical research is critical [2], and our work aims to meet this need.

Two significant issues impact the segmentation of such images. First, the nucleic fluorescence spreads into the background region immediately surrounding. Fig. 2 shows a typical nucleus, a profile of intensities across the image, and the histogram of the three segmented regions: it appears that the background is greatly affected near the nucleus. We use the term *illuminated background* to denote the background region where the intensity is increased by a nearby nucleus. Its extent is delimitated with a dotted line in Fig. 2. This region, hardly noticeable by eye, is critical to the correctness of the segmentation of the nuclei. The other issue is what we call *foreground noise*: unattached probes that cannot be perfectly washed out of the preparation sometimes accumulate as clumps and appear as bright spots, similar in intensity and shape to actual probes.

Previous work in this field is abundant, but is not usable in our context, where a large number of images taken in various laboratory conditions has to be analysed with minimal user interaction, and where, to reduce the time needed for diagnosis, the nuclei used are not cultured – as a result, they do not appear as convex and smooth as most image processing methods for nuclei segmentation require. In the following paragraphs we review the state-of-the-art methods. First, we review nucleic segmentation, then probe segmentation, and finally complete systems that are used in laboratories for similar purposes.

Nucleic segmentation methods can be classified in four categories: background subtraction, thresholding, watershed, and energy-based methods. For background subtraction, the background is generally either considered as uniformly noisy (with a histogram consisting of one Gaussian curve) [3], or is modeled with a reference image containing no objects, taken from an empty slide [2]. However, none of these models is satisfactory because of the background illumination near the nuclei. Threshold-based methods commonly used in cytometry, such as Otsu's [4] or Kittler and Illingworth's [5], assume that histograms are bimodal, or even consist of two Gaussians: this would be a crude and unrealistic estimate for our images (see histogram of a typical image in Fig. 2). Global thresholding

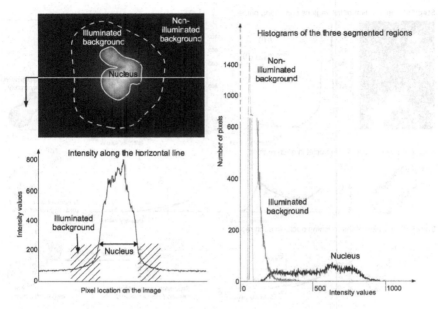

Fig. 2. Background illumination. Top left: image of a nucleus. Bottom left: intensity values along the horizontal line across the image. Right: Histograms of the three segmented regions (The vertical scale is bilinear, as reflected by the values on the side).

is bound to fail, because of cross-image intensity variations. Regarding local thresholding, the construction of a threshold surface introduces extra size and smoothness parameters, which have to be tuned, and are sensitive to the size and number of objects in an image. Watershed-based methods [6] are notorious for oversegmenting images; they require pre-processing with morphological operations to smooth the image, and post-processing to merge contiguous regions using shape, size and texture criteria. Most morphological operations use a filter, whose size and profile are to be tuned according to the image's properties and the smoothness required, and are thus little robust when automated. Region-merging is a long process, where the criteria for merging depend on the watershed results, and have to be tuned as well. Finally, energy-based methods, such as active contours [7], level sets, or graph cuts, require initialisation, internal energies modeling the final shape, external energies modeling the borders' characteristics, and parameters to balance them: these are difficult to tune even manually. Furthermore, in our context, the various nucleic textures and their impacts on the surrounding background are hard to model as local energy terms. Besides, the irregular shapes of uncultured nuclei elude typical internal energy terms. To summarise, these methods model the objects' characteristics independently, and require a complex parametrisation to link these models together.

Regarding probe segmentation, most methods are designed to segment only large bright probes, and usually less than four per nucleus. Existing probe-finding methods filter the image and threshold the intensities in order to keep a given percentage of bright pixels [8]. Two significant problems arise from the

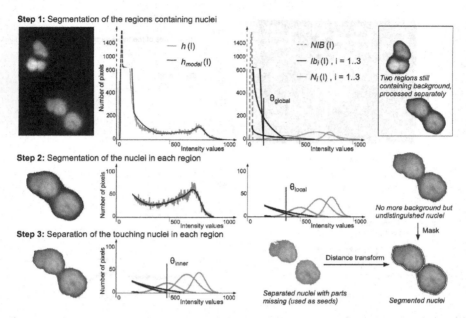

Fig. 3. The steps of nucleic segmentation. Top row, left to right: original image; its histogram with our adjusted model superimposed; the components of our model, used to find a global threshold removing most of the background; the segmented image, with two segmented regions containing nuclei but also some background. Middle row: one of these regions; its histogram and our adjusted model; the components of our model, used to find a local threshold, removing the remaining background; the segmented region, with no more background, but where the two nuclei are still undistinguised: it will be used as a mask for the final step of the segmentation. Bottow row: the segmented region; the components of our model, used to find an inner threshold, removing the darkest parts of the nuclei; the segmented nuclei, isolated but with parts missing: they are used as seeds, and grown with a fast distance transform within the mask defined above; the resulting segmentation of the region, with two separated nuclei and no background. See Section 3 for more details.

foreground noise. First, it flaws any histogram-based method by significantly increasing the number of high-intensity pixels. Second, as it is segmented as probes, existing methods need post-processing with a carefully designed classifier to distinguish it from the actual probes [9]. Also, existing systems measuring probes intensity require calibration, usually using a set of fluorescent beads [8], and are sensitive to changes in the fluorescence of the markers over time.

Finally, there are several integrated systems that are used in laboratory conditions for similar purposes; however, none of them is either automatic enough or general enough for clinical application. Many systems require expert human intervention at some point during the segmentation of each nucleus [10,11]. Automatic systems are not as general-purpose as ours: [12] require an extra specific marker on the nuclei's borders, while [13] only segments isolated convex elliptic nuclei; systems such as Castleman's [2] or Netten's [14], are only applicable to images with few nuclei and few probes.

Our approach to segmentation is designed to avoid from the beginning the problems mentioned above. For the nuclei, we use a unified model which encompasses seamlessly the background noise, the nucleic textures and the nuclei's alterations to the background. The parameters of our model are intuitive and are automatically adjusted to every image, using an adaptation of an Expectation-Maximisation algorithm. This way, our model adapts to images of varying intensities and qualities, with no prior assumptions, training or manual tuning. We use our model to find successive threshold values, first global then local, and to isolate touching nuclei – one of the most difficult tasks in cytometry. The three steps of our nuclei segmentation are illustrated in Fig. 3. For probe segmentation, we use a new dome-detection algorithm which is insensitive to background and foreground noise, and detects any number of probes of any intensity, with no calibration required. After segmentation, the locations and measures of the nuclei are stored in an XML database for later retrieval.

This article is organised as follows: in Section 2, we detail our novel model for histograms. In Section 3, we describe our Expectation-Maximisation algorithm adapted for histogram modeling. In Section 4, we present our new dome-detection method applied to probe segmentation. In Section 5, we compare our method with a typical watershed-based segmentation, discuss the results, and present the results obtained with our software to compare individuals' ages using telomeres intensities – a critical issue for non-invasive prenatal diagnosis as mentioned earlier. We conclude in Section 6 with an overview of our future work.

2   Model of the Histogram of an Image

As illustrated in Fig. 2, the histogram of a typical image consists of three overlapping parts: a sharp peak in the lowest values, a sharply decreasing curve in the medium values, and a plateau in the highest values. They correspond respectively to the non-illuminated background (NIB), illuminated background (IB), and nuclei (N). In this section we present the parametric functions we use to model each part, and emphasis our new model for the illuminated background.

Let $h(I)$ be an image histogram, consisting of parts NIB, IB and N, which we model with $h_{model}(I)$. We assume NIB contains A_b pixels, has a mean value I_b, and is affected by Gaussian noise of standard deviation σ_b. It is modeled with:

$$NIB(I) = \frac{A_b}{\sqrt{2\pi}\sigma_b} \exp\left(-\frac{(I-I_b)^2}{2\sigma_b^2}\right) . \qquad (1)$$

The part of the histogram corresponding to the highest intensities, N, reflects the nuclei's textures. They are very variable, within and across samples: in particular, variations affect the range of intensity values, the shape of the histogram and the number of peaks in it. Also, saturation can occur at high intensities, depending on the hardware used for imaging. To overcome these problems we model the nuclei's histograms with sums of Gaussians: this is both robust and flexible enough for our needs. As we do not know in advance how many nuclei an image contains, nor how many Gaussians are needed for each texture, we introduce a new parameter, n, the number of Gaussians modeling the nuclei. Each of these Gaussians i will model A_i pixels, with mean I_i and deviation σ_i:

$$N_i(I) = \frac{A_i}{\sqrt{2\pi}\sigma_i} \exp\left(-\frac{(I - I_i)^2}{2\sigma_i^2}\right), \ 1 \le i \le n. \tag{2}$$

Next we detail the model we use for the illuminated background. Let I_0 be the intensity at the nucleus' border, at distance R_0 from its center, and let I_b be the mean intensity of the non-illuminated background (see Eq.(1)). We model the intensity in the illuminated background, along a line normal to the nucleus' border, with a decreasing exponential (see Fig. 4):

$$I(r) = I_b + (I_0 - I_b) \cdot \exp\left(-\frac{r - R_0}{\rho}\right), \ \text{for } r \ge R_0, \tag{3}$$

where ρ is a constant controlling the slope of the intensity decay. This model cannot be fitted directly to an image for segmentation purposes, as it requires a prior segmentation of the nuclei. Nevertheless, it can be used to derive a model of the illuminated background's histogram. This latter model can be adjusted to the image histogram, as detailed in the next section. In the remaining of this section, we explain how we derive that model.

The expression of $I(r)$ in Eq. (3) can be inverted to define $r(I)$. This can be used to express the number of points $dn(r) = 2\pi r\, dr$ at distance r from the nucleus, as a function of the intensity, $dn(I)$. By integrating $dn(I)$ between I and $I + 1$, we obtain – by definition – the illuminated background's histogram. Introducing the new parameters $\alpha = \frac{\rho}{R_0}$ and $A = \pi R_0^2$, we obtain:

$$IB(I) = 2A\alpha \int_I^{I+1} \left(1 - \alpha \ln\frac{I - I_b}{I_0 - I_b}\right) \frac{dI}{I - I_b}. \tag{4}$$

Eq. (4) is independent of the nucleus' actual shape: it only depends on its area A and the dimensionless parameter α, controlling the extent of the illumination relative to the nucleus' size. It can be easily integrated with the change of variables $X = \frac{I - I_b}{I_0 - I_b}$. Also, this model is to be fitted to the histogram at values above the mean background value, with $I - I_b \gg 1$. Thus, a first-order expansion of $IB(I)$ with respect to $\frac{1}{I - I_b}$ is enough for our purpose. This leads to the definition of our new model for the histogram of the illuminated background:

$$IB(I) = \frac{2A\alpha^2}{I - I_b} \ln\left(\frac{I_0 - I_b}{I - I_b}\right). \tag{5}$$

The expression of $IB(I)$ in Eq. (5) is illustrated in Fig. 4, to the right. Its two parameters A and α correspond respectively to the area of the nucleus creating the illumination, and to the spatial decay of the illumination.

To link this model with that of the nuclei, we assume that each Gaussian modeling the nuclei's textures creates part of the background illumination. Let $IB_i(I)$ model the background illuminated by $N_i(I)$. Three of its four parameters are constrained by the rest of the model: namely, the area causing the

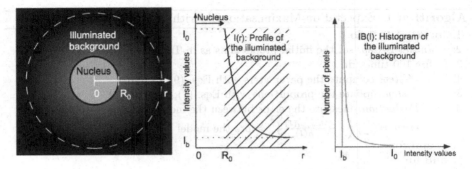

Fig. 4. Illustration of our model. Left: model of a circular nucleus. Center: model of the intensity values in the illuminated background, $I(r)$, defined in Eq. (3). Right: model of the histogram of the illuminated background, $IB(I)$, defined in Eq. (5).

illumination $A = A_i$ (see Eq. (2)), the mean intensity I_b of the non-illuminated background (see Eq. (1)), and the intensity I_0 at the nucleus' border. We set it to $I_0 = I_i - 2\sigma_i$. Using Eq. (2), it corresponds to the darker 5% of the nucleus' pixels, which we consider to be on the boundary. This way, the functions modeling the illuminated background are:

$$IB_i(I) = \frac{2\,A_i\,\alpha_i^2}{I - I_b}\,\ln\left(\frac{I_i - 2\sigma_i - I_b}{I - I_b}\right) \,,\, 1 \le i \le n \,. \tag{6}$$

Let Φ_n be the set of all the functions used, which are defined in Eqs. (1), (2) and (6). The model of the histogram is:

$$h_{model}(I) = \sum_{g \in \Phi_n} g(I) \,,\, \text{where } \Phi_n = \{NIB\} \cup \bigcup_{1 \le i \le n} \{IB_i, N_i\} \,. \tag{7}$$

It depends on the $4(n+1)$ parameters $n, A_b, I_b, \sigma_b, \{A_i, I_i, \sigma_i, \alpha_i\}_{1 \le i \le n}$. They are adjusted to an image histogram using an Expectation-Maximization algorithm, as detailed in the next section.

3   Expectation-Maximisation Algorithm for Histogram Modeling

Let $h(I)$ be an image histogram, consisting of parts NIB, IB and N, which we model with $h_{model}(I)$. Each intensity I in the histogram contains a proportion of pixels modeled by each function of our model. We define this proportion as:

$$p_f(I) = \frac{f(I)}{\sum_{g \in \Phi_n} g(I)} \,,\, \forall f \in \Phi_n = \{NIB\} \cup \bigcup_{1 \le i \le n} \{IB_i, N_i\} \,. \tag{8}$$

Knowing these proportions is enough to define the successive thresholds needed for our nucleic segmentation, as detailed at the end of this section. Given all

---

Algorithm 1. Expectation-Maximisation algorithm for histogram modeling

---
1: **for** $n = 1$ to 6 **do**
2:    *Initial E-step:* set the initial proportions as in Table 1
3:    **for** 100 times **do**
4:       *M-step:* compute the parameters with Eqs. (9) and (10).
5:       *E-step:* update the proportions with Eqs. (1), (2), (6), (8).
6:       *Evaluation:* measure the error between the model and the histogram as
       $error = \sum_I \left(1 - \frac{h_{model}(I)}{h(I)}\right)^2$. Store the model if the error is the lowest.
7:    **end for**
8: **end for**
9: **return** the model with the lowest error.

---

the parameters of the model, these proportions can be computed using Eqs. (1), (2), (6) and (8). Reciprocally, given all the proportions $p_f(I)$, $\forall I$, $\forall f \in \Phi_n$, the parameters of the model can be computed as described below. However, neither the parameters nor the proportions are available in the first place. This type of problem is commonly solved by Expectation Maximisation [15]. The EM algorithms commonly used in computer vision are adapted to mixture of Gaussian models. The algorithm we present as Algorithm 1 is adapted to histograms: the steps are the same, only the equations are different.

We now explain how to compute our model's parameters given a histogram $h(I)$ and all the proportions $p_f(I)$. The parameters of the Gaussians NIB and N_i are computed as the total, mean and deviation of a weighted histogram [16]:

$$A_i = \sum_I p_{N_i}(I) h(I) \, ; \, I_i = \sum_I p_{N_i}(I) h(I) I \, ; \, \sigma_i^2 = \sum_I p_{N_i}(I) h(I) (I - I_i)^2 . \quad (9)$$

The only unconstrained parameters of the functions IB_i are computed as:

$$\alpha_i = \frac{1}{|\ln \epsilon|} \sqrt{\frac{1}{A_i} \sum_{I=I_\epsilon}^{I_i - 2\sigma_i} p_{IB_i} h(I)}, \text{ where } \epsilon = 0.1 , I_\epsilon = I_b + \epsilon (I_0 - I_b) . \quad (10)$$

(See Appendix for details). The complete segmentation of the nuclei is performed in three steps, as illustrated on Fig. 3. First, we use the algorithm above to adjust our parametric model to the image histogram. Let:

$$\theta_{global} = \max\{I, \forall i, \min(p_{NIB}(I), p_{IB_i}(I)) \geq p_{N_i}(I)\} .$$

Below θ_{global}, all intensities contain more points from NIB or IB_i than from the corresponding N_i, and it is the highest such value. This is the global threshold we use to discard the non-illuminated and part of the illuminated background. Then, in each of the segmented regions, we apply the same algorithm to find a model of the histogram (without the NIB function this time). In the same way, we find the highest intensity containing more points from IB_i than from N_i, and use it as a local threshold θ_{local}. The newly segmented components

Table 1. Initial proportions' values for the EM algorithm. The histogram range $[0, I_{max}]$ is divided in $n+2$ parts. Intuitively, most dark pixels are modeled by NIB, most bright pixels by either one of the N_i, and most of the remaining pixels by the IB_i (see Fig. 2).

Intensity	$0 \ldots \frac{1}{n+2}I_{max}$	$\frac{1}{n+2}I_{max} \ldots \frac{2}{n+2}I_{max}$	$\frac{j}{n+2}I_{max} \ldots \frac{j+1}{n+2}I_{max}$ for $2 \leq j \leq n+1$
$p_{NIB}(I)$	0.9	0.1	0
$p_{IB_i}(I)$	0.1/n	0.9/n	0.1/n
$p_{N_i}(I)$	0	0	0.9/n if $i = j-1$, 0 else

do not contain background anymore; however, they might contain more than one nucleus. This problem is often solved by splitting components into convex parts [17], but cannot be applied here – uncultured nuclei may be concave. Instead, we consider the components' textures, which are already modeled by the N_i. We assume that there are several distinguishable nuclei in a component if it contains dark paths separating several bright parts. The threshold we use to define dark and bright for this test, called inner threshold θ_{inner}, is the lowest of the I_i. The connected components above θ_{inner} are considered as seeds: each one marks a unique nucleus. Then we extend the seeds into the regions above θ_{local} using a fast distance transform [18], and obtain the segmented nuclei. Fig. 3 shows the three steps of the segmentation, with the models adjusted to the histograms. Another example of a segmented image is shown in Fig. 1.

4   Dome-Finding Algorithm for Probe Segmentation

Once the nuclei are segmented, their telomere contents are to be evaluated, by segmenting the fluorescent probes in the green channel. Probes appear as small spots, each about a dozen pixels big. Background illumination is observed around the probes as well; however we cannot apply the same segmentation method as for the nuclei. This is for practical reasons: on a typical image, nuclei represent about 8% of the pixels in the image, and the illuminated background about 50%; but the probes only represent 0.3%, and the background around them, 2%. Adjusting our model using so few pixels would not be reliable enough.

Our novel method to segment probes is based on the following observations. Both background and foreground noise are characterized by high densities of local intensity maxima, distant by two or three pixels. Conversely, probes correspond to local maxima surrounded by pixels of decreasing intensity and few, if any, other local maxima within a distance of two or three pixels. Thus, we developed a peak-detection method sensitive to the density of local maxima. In addition, as it only measures pixels intensities relatively to their neighbours, our method can detect probes of high and low intensities, unlike traditional probe-finders restricted to few bright probes [2].

We segment probes as domes, starting from local maxima and gradually including neighbours if they form a dome around them. If a dome is large enough, we mark it as a probe; otherwise, we reject it. Around each local maximum, we consider three sets of neighbouring pixels, at increasing distances, as illustrated by different shades on gray in the left of Fig. 5. They form the level

Fig. 5. Left: the three level sets around a pixel, in three shades of gray, and all the downhill neighbours, indicated by the arrows. Middle: actual pixels values in the neighbourhood of a probe, and the segmented dome in gray. Right: actual pixels values in a zone of foreground noise; none of the local maxima is surrounded by a proper dome.

sets[1] of the dome, and approximate the shape of the probes. Formally, let p_M be a local maximum. The first level set consists of the 8 closest pixels: $LS_1 = \{p, d_\infty(p, p_M) = 1\}$. In the second level set are the twelve closest pixels that are not already in LS_1: $LS_2 = \{p, p \notin LS_1 \land d_1(p, LS_1) = 1\}$. Each pixel in these sets is assigned three neighbours, as indicated by the arrows in Fig. 5: we refer to them as *downhill neighbours*. If a pixel has a higher intensity than all its downhill neighbours, it is marked as being part of the dome.

By design, one complete dome corresponds to one probe. However, it happens that two probes are very close (two pixels apart), or that a probe is bigger than a dome (and contains two local maxima). In both cases, the dome construction above leads to two domes having one side in common that does not meet the downhill constraint, and which is therefore not included in any of the two domes. Since these cases are at the borderline but still valid, we accept domes with up to one of their four sides missing. Formally, a dome is marked as a segmented probe if it contains at least 75% of the pixels in LS_1 and 75% of LS_2. Domes with more pixels missing are rejected as noise (see middle and right of Fig. 5).

5   Results and Discussion

We start this section by presenting quantitative results obtained with our novel segmentation methods. Our data set contains 2,166 images, with nearly 14,000 nuclei and 317,000 probes overall. We compare our results with a typical watershed-based nucleic segmentation method. We also present an application of our methods, to compare the telomere intensities of two different individuals.

5.1   Accuracy of the Segmentation Methods

Nucleic Segmentation. We implemented our method on an iMac with a 1.8GHz PowerPC G5 and 1Gb of RAM, and processed our full dataset. For comparison,

---

[1] Here, the term *level set* refers to its original definition in topology, not to the segmentation method with the same name.

Table 2. Results of the nuclei segmentation

Method	Number of nuclei	Correctly segmented	Over segmented	Under segmented	Missed	Non existing
Watershed	2,779	2,232 - 80.3%	211 - 7.6%	212 - 7.6%	60 - 2.2%	64 - 2.3%
Ours	13,917	13,823 - 99.3%	31 - 0.22%	50 - 0.36%	8 - 0.06%	5 - 0.03%

we also implemented the watershed-based segmentation method for cytometry described in [19], as follows. The image is thresholded globally with the value found by the isodata algorithm; a distance transform is applied to the resulting image, followed by an h-dome extraction; the domes extracted are used as starting-points for the watershed algorithm, applied to the gradient transform of the original image. We implemented this method under the same conditions as ours, and tested it on a sample of 800 images, containing over 2,000 nuclei. The results of these two segmentation methods are listed in Table 2, and discussed below.

In terms of runtime, our method segments one nucleus in about one second (with no particular programming optimisation), which is about three times faster than the watershed-based one, and several times faster than manual segmentation. Our method has linear complexity, and no particular memory requirements (a histogram and the segmentation results). Once the histogram is built, our EM algorithm runs in constant time; the thresholding steps require one image scan. Conversely, the watershed-based method needs to store extra intermediate images, and the h-dome extraction requires an unknown number of image scans. Besides, this method takes several minutes to process images with no nuclei, and systematically segments objects in them. Our method processes empty images correctly and faster than images with nuclei.

The quantitative results, shown in Table 2, are significantly better with our method, which is due to its two main features. First, it finds the nucleic borders using a succession of threshold values that are adapted for each part of the image containing nuclei, while the other method uses a single global threshold. As a result, many more nuclei are missed, when darker that the global threshold, and many non-existing nuclei are segmented, which are in fact bright background regions. Secondly, our method uses a texture model to separate touching nuclei, and gets very low oversegmentation (when a nucleus is segmented in more than one object) and undersegmentation (when more than one nucleus are segmented as one object). Conversely, to find seeds, the watershed-based method replaces the nuclei's textures with a distance transform, which amounts to using only the nuclei's borders to separate them. This approach is bound to fail with uncultured nuclei, having concavities, as illustrated by the higher over- and undersegmentation rates. Similar quantitative results are reported in [20], for the same watershed-based method and for a contour-based method. Both methods correctly segment 80% of similar nuclei, and over- and under-segment a total of 15% of the dataset. Using successive watershed-based and contour-based methods, [13] reports a 99.4% segmentation accuracy, but their method requires the prior rejection of all the non-isolated, non-elliptic nuclei – corresponding to 30% of their data, but more than 50% of ours.

Our results can still be improved by basic post-processing. Missed objects cannot be recovered, but are very rare in the first place, while non-existing nuclei are hardly an issue. Oversegmentation happens when θ_{inner} is too high, and can be detected by the small size of the parts oversegmented. Undersegmentation is due to either θ_{global} or θ_{local} being too low, and results in bigger than average objects, which can be detected as such and processed with higher thresholds.

Probe Segmentation. The aim of segmenting probes is to measure the total fluorescence inside a nucleus, so oversegmentation is not an issue. Undersegmentation is prevented with our method, as a segmented probe has a minimum dome size. Overall, 99.3% of the probes were correctly found with our method. About 0.3% were missed, too wide to be detected as one dome. Most of them were dark, with little effect on the total fluorescence measured inside the nucleus; very rare wide and bright probes were ruled out as foreground noise (less than 0.1%). Finally, about 0.4% of the segmented objects were background, not probes; they were dark and did not affect the final measures.

5.2   Comparison of Individuals Ages Using Telomeres Intensities

As an application, we used our method to quantify the intensity of probes appearing in the nuclei for two individuals. This test was conducted to assess the differences in telomeric intensities between individuals of different ages. In particular the two populations of nuclei were not mixed. After using our segmentation, our program rejected the nuclei which were cropped at the edges of images. The results are shown in Fig. 6. The first histogram shows that the same number of probes per nucleus were segmented for the two individuals; the second histogram shows that the probes in the fetal nuclei are brighter. These result show that our method does not introduce bias in the number of probe segmented, and that there is a promising distinction between the individuals.

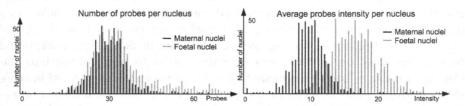

Fig. 6. Quantitative measures performed using our method on two populations of nuclei

Our software has proven reliable and robust enough to produce these results. Reducing the overlap between the two histograms is a subject for cytology research. Here again computer vision may help, as detailed in the next section.

6   Conclusions and Future Work

In this article we have detailed our new segmentation methods, presented a quantitative comparison of our nucleic segmentation with the widely used watershed method, and shown an application of our software for medical research. The nucleic segmentation method we developed is based on a new model of the image histogram, achieves a 99.3% accuracy and, to the best of our knowledge, is more robust and automatic than previously published work on this field. Also, we have presented some ideas to improve this rate further. As for the telomere probes, our method is robust against all sources of noise, and is also 99.3% accurate.

The segmentation techniques we developed can be used for various cytometric tasks. We have used it along with our telomeric segmentation method for a project of improved diagnostic methods. The quantitative results we have obtained show a promising distinction between the telomere intensities in individuals of different age. To improve the difference and reach the stage where a fetal nucleus can be detected within a population of maternal nuclei, we are participating in further work with cytologists. Not all uncultured nuclei will be usable in the final stage, where their genetic content is investigated. Some are damaged during the early processing of sample blood, and could be rejected before measuring the telomere intensities. These unusable nuclei can be detected by an expert cytometrist by their shapes. We are currently working with such experts on an automatic shape analysis of the segmented nuclei: our early work includes measuring the nuclei's concavities and using low-order Fourier reconstructions to define usability criteria. Rejecting these unusable nuclei before segmenting the telomeres would make our final comparison of populations more conclusive. At that stage, we will be in a stronger position to tell if this approach to non-invasive diagnostic alternative is reliable enough for a future clinical application.

The author thanks Prof. Clocksin, Dr Bray and Dr McCollum for their help and Prof. Hulten and Dr Ariosa for providing the images.

References

1. Hohmann, H., Michel, S., Reiber, W., Gunther, M., Claussen, U., von Eggeling, F.: How to enrich and analyse fetal cells from maternal blood. In: Fetal Cells and Fetal DNA in Maternal Blood, Karger (2001) 47–55
2. Merchant, F.A., Castleman, K.R.: Strategies for automated fetal cell screening. Human Reproduction Update 8 (2002) 509–521
3. Fang, B., Hsu, W., Lee, M.L.: On the accurate counting of tumor cells. IEEE Transactions on Nanobioscience 2 (2003) 94–103
4. Tanaka, T., Murase, Y., Oka, T.: Classification of skin tumors based on shape features of nuclei. In: Medicine and Biology Society. Volume 3. (2002) 1064–1066
5. Wu, K., Gauthier, D., Levine, M.D.: Live cell image segmentation. IEEE Transactions on Biomedical Engineering 42 (1995) 1–12
6. Lin, G., Adiga, U., Olson, K., Guzowski, J., Barnes, C., Roysam, B.: A hybrid 3D watershed algorithm incorporating gradient cues and object models for automatic segmentation of nuclei in confocal image stacks. Cytometry 56A (2003) 23–36
7. Lehmann, T., Bredno, J., Spitzer, K.: On the design of active contours for medical image segmentation. Methods of Information in Medicine 42 (2003) 89–98
8. Poon, S.S., Martens, U.M., Ward, R.K., Lansdorp, P.M.: Telomere length measurements using digital fluorescence microscopy. Cytometry 36 (1999) 267–278
9. Clocksin, W.F., Lerner, B.: Automatic analysis of fluorescence in-situ hybridisation images. In: British Machine Vision Conference. (2000) 666–674

10. Pelikan, D.M.V., Mesker, W.E., Scherjon, S.A., Kanhai, H.H.H., Tanke, H.J.: Improvement of the Kleihauer-Betke test by automated detection of fetal erythrocytes in maternal blood. Cytometry Part B (Clinical Cytometry) **54B** (2003) 1–9
11. de Solorzano, C.O., Garcia Rodriguez, E., Johnes, A., Pinkel, D., Gray, J., Sudar, D., Lockett, S.: Segmentation of confocal microscope images of cell nuclei in thick tissue sections. Journal of Microscopy **193** (1999) 212–226
12. de Solorzano, C.O., Malladi, R., Lelievre, S., Lockett, S.: Segmentation of nuclei and cells using membrane related protein markers. Microscopy **201** (2001) 404–415
13. Bamford, P., Lovell, B.: Method for accurate unsupervised cell nucleus segmentation. In: IEEE Engineering in Medicine and Biology. Volume 1. (2001) 133–135
14. Netten, H., Young, I., van Vliet, L., Tanke, H., Vroljik, H., Sloos, W.: Automation of fluorescent dot counting in interphase cell nuclei. Cytometry **28** (1997) 1–10
15. Theodoridis, S., Koutroumbas, K.: Pattern Recognition. 2nd edn. Elsevier (2003)
16. Smith, S.W. In: The scientist and engineer's guide to digital signal processing. California Technical Publishing (1997) 11–34
17. Kutalik, Z., Razaz, M., Baranyi, J.: Automated spatial and temporal image analysis of bacterial cell growth. In: BMVA Spatiotemporal Image Processing. (2004)
18. Felzenszwalb, P.F., Huttenlocher, D.P.: Distance transforms of sampled functions. Technical report, Cornell University (2004) TR2004-1963.
19. Malpica, N., de Solorzano, C.O., Vaquero, J.J., Santos, A., Vallcorba, I., Garcia-Sagrado, J.M., del Pozo, F.: Applying watershed algorithms to the segmentation of clustered nuclei. Cytometry **28** (1997) 289–297
20. Restif, C., Clocksin, W.: Comparison of segmentation methods for cytometric assay. In: Medical Image Understanding and Analysis. (2004) 153–156

Appendix

We use the notations of Section 2. The sum of histogram values of the illuminated background between any two values I_1 and I_2 is: $\sum_{I=I_1}^{I_2} IB(I) = \int_{I_1}^{I_2+1} dn(I)$. However, $dn(I)$ is only defined and positive between I_b and I_0, and is not summable near I_b. Let $I_\varepsilon = I_b + \varepsilon(I_0 - I_b)$, where $\varepsilon \in (0,1)$: $\sum_{I=I_\varepsilon}^{I_0-1} IB(I) = \int_{I_\varepsilon}^{I_0} dn(I)$. Developed to first order terms: $\sum_{I=I_\varepsilon}^{I_0-1} IB(I) = -2A\alpha^2 \int_{I_\varepsilon}^{I_0} \ln\left(\frac{I-I_b}{I_0-I_b}\right) \frac{dI}{I_0-I_b}$. Since $IB(I_0) = 0$, the sum can be extended to I_0, while the integral can be computed with a change of variable: $\sum_{I=I_\varepsilon}^{I_0} IB(I) = A\alpha^2 \ln^2 \varepsilon$. This gives the expression of α as a function of the histogram values: $\alpha = \frac{1}{|\ln \varepsilon|} \sqrt{\frac{1}{A} \sum_{I_\varepsilon}^{I_0} IB(I)}$.

Fast Memory-Efficient Generalized Belief Propagation*

M. Pawan Kumar and P.H.S. Torr

Department of Computing, Oxford Brookes University,
Oxford, UK, OX33 1HX
{pkmudigonda, philiptorr}@brookes.ac.uk
http://cms.brookes.ac.uk/computervision

Abstract. Generalized Belief Propagation (GBP) has proven to be a promising technique for performing inference on Markov random fields (MRFs). However, its heavy computational cost and large memory requirements have restricted its application to problems with small state spaces. We present methods for reducing both run time and storage needed by GBP for a large class of pairwise potentials of the MRF. Further, we show how the problem of subgraph matching can be formulated using this class of MRFs and thus, solved efficiently using our approach. Our results significantly outperform the state-of-the-art method. We also obtain excellent results for the related problem of matching pictorial structures for object recognition.

1 Introduction

Many tasks in Computer Vision, such as segmentation and object recognition, can be given a probabilistic formulation using Markov random fields (MRF). A popular method for performing inference on MRFs is Belief Propagation (BP) [1]. It is well known that on tree-structured MRFs, BP can be used to efficiently perform exact inference. For a general MRF, Yedidia *et al.* [2] proved that BP converges to stationary points of Bethe approximation of the free energy. They also proposed the Generalized Belief Propagation (GBP) algorithm which converges to stationary points of (the more accurate) Kikuchi approximation. Despite outperforming BP in terms of convergence and accuracy, there are few uses of GBP reported in the literature as it is computationally feasible only when the number of labels of the MRF is small.

Recent work has focused on tackling the problem of computational cost of message passing methods such as BP and GBP. Felzenszwalb and Huttenlocher [3, 4] put forward a method for speeding up message passing algorithms such as Viterbi, Forward-Backward and BP for a large class of pairwise potentials (e.g. Potts and linear model), when the labels are regularly discretized points in the parameter space. In our previous work [5], we extended these results to general

---

* This work was supported in part by the IST Programme of the European Community, under the PASCAL Network of Excellence, IST-2002-506778. This publication only reflects the authors' views.

A. Leonardis, H. Bischof, and A. Pinz (Eds.): ECCV 2006, Part IV, LNCS 3954, pp. 451–463, 2006.
© Springer-Verlag Berlin Heidelberg 2006

MRFs. However, little consideration thus far has been given to speeding up GBP, with the exception of Shental *et al.* [6] who describe an efficient GBP algorithm but only for the special case where the pairwise potentials form an Ising model.

The problem of reducing the large memory requirements has also met with little success. Felzenszwalb and Huttenlocher [4] observe that, when performing BP on a bipartite graph, the messages going to only a subset of sites are changed at each iteration. This allows them to reduce the memory requirements for grid graphs by half. Vogiatzis *et al.* [7] suggest a coarse-to-fine strategy for BP by grouping together similar labels. However this is restricted to labels lying on a grid. More importantly, it substantially changes the problem such that the messages and beliefs computed at any stage are not necessarily equivalent to those corresponding to the original MRF.

In this paper, show how to reduce the computational cost and memory requirements of GBP for a large class of pairwise potentials which we call the *robust truncated model*. This model divides all pairs of labels for the neighbouring sites into compatible and incompatible pairs and truncates the pairwise potentials of the incompatible pairs to a constant (see section 2 for details). Many vision applications such as object recognition [5], stereo and optical flow [4] use special cases of this model. Typically, the number of compatible labels n_C for a given label is much less than the total number of labels n_L, i.e. $n_C \ll n_L$.

We exploit the fact that, since the pairwise potentials of incompatible pairs of labels are constant, it results in many redundant computations in GBP which can be avoided. Let n_R be the number of regions formed by clustering the sites of the MRF and n_M be the size of the largest region. The main contributions of the paper are the following:

- We reduce the time complexity of GBP to $O(n_R n_M n_L^{n_M-1} n_C)$, (i.e. by a factor of n_L/n_C). Since $n_C \ll n_L$ for MRFs used in vision, this makes GBP computationally feasible (section 3).
- We observe that the approach described in [4] to reduce the memory requirements of BP by half for bipartite graphs can be extended to GBP (section 4).
- We show how the memory requirements of GBP can be reduced drastically (by a factor $(n_L/n_C)^{n_M-1}$) for a special case of the robust truncated model which can be used in various vision applications. Again, since $n_C \ll n_L$, GBP becomes memory efficient and thus, practically useful (section 4).
- We formulate the problem of subgraph matching using the special case of the robust truncated model and solve it accurately using the efficient GBP algorithm. Our results significantly outperform the state-of-the art methods (section 5).
- We obtain excellent results for the related problem of matching pictorial structures [8] for object recognition by using the efficient GBP algorithm (section 5).

It should be noted that our methods are applicable to other related message passing algorithms such as Viterbi, Forward-Backward, BP and tree-reweighted message passing [9]. For completeness, we first briefly describe the BP and GBP algorithms in the next section.

2 Belief Propagation and Its Generalization

This section briefly describes the standard belief propagation (BP) algorithm for performing inference on MRFs and formulates it using the *canonical* framework. This framework is then extended which results in the Generalized Belief Propagation (GBP) algorithm [2].

An MRF is defined by n_S sites along with a symmetric neighbourhood relationship $N(.)$ on them, i.e. $i \in N(j)$ if and only if $j \in N(i)$. Each site i can take a label $x_i \in \mathcal{X}_i$. We assume that the sets $\mathcal{X}_i$ are finite and discrete, i.e. $|\mathcal{X}_i| = n_L < \infty$. Associated with each configuration $\mathbf{x}$ of the MRF is its joint probability given by

$$\Pr(x_1, ..., x_{n_S}) = \frac{1}{Z} \prod_{ij} \phi_{ij}(x_i, x_j) \prod_i \phi_i(x_i). \tag{1}$$

Here, $\phi_i(x_i)$ is the unary potential of site i having label x_i, $\phi_{ij}(x_i, x_j)$ is the pairwise potential for two neighbouring sites i and j having labels x_i and x_j respectively and Z is the partition function. Note that the above equation assumes the MRF to be pairwise. However, this is not restrictive as any MRF can be converted into a pairwise MRF [2]. Performing inference on the MRF involves either determining the MAP configuration or obtaining the marginal posterior probabilities of each label. In this paper, we describe our approach in the context of max-product BP which provides the MAP configuration while noting that it is also equally applicable to sum-product BP which provides the marginal posteriors.

BP is a message passing algorithm proposed by Pearl [1]. It is an efficient approximate inference algorithm for MRFs with loops where each site i iteratively passes a message to its neighbouring site j. The message is a vector of dimension n_L whose elements are calculated as

$$m_{ij}^t(x_j) \leftarrow \alpha \max_{x_i} \phi_{ij}(x_i, x_j) \phi_i(x_i) \prod_{k \in N(i) \backslash j} m_{ki}^{t-1}(x_i), \tag{2}$$

where α is a normalization constant and $N(i) \backslash j$ is the set of all neighbouring sites of i excluding j. Note that x_j is used to index the message vector in the above equation such that $m_{ij}^t(x_j)$ corresponds to the x_j^{th} element of the vector m_{ij}^t. All messages are initialized to 1 and convergence is said to be achieved when the rate of change of all messages drops below a threshold. At convergence, the belief of a site i having a label x_i is given by

$$b_i(x_i) \leftarrow \alpha \phi_i(x_i) \prod_{j \in N(i)} m_{ji}(x_i), \tag{3}$$

and the MAP estimate is obtained by choosing the label x_i^* with the highest belief for every site i.

Yedidia *et al.* [2] proved that BP converges to the stationary points of the Bethe approximation of the free energy which clusters the sites of the MRF into *regions* of size at most 2. We denote the set of sites belonging to a region r by $\mathcal{S}(r)$. Region s is considered a sub-region of r if and only if $\mathcal{S}(s) \subset \mathcal{S}(r)$. Further, s is a *direct* sub-region of r if and only if the set $s \cup i$ is not a sub-region of r, for all regions i.

Every region r passes a message $m_{r \to s}$ to each of its direct sub-regions s. In order to compactly express what follows, we adopt the following notation. The message $m_{r \to s}(x_s)$ is simply written as $m_{r \to s}$ (i.e. the indexing is dropped). For example, $m_{ij \to j}$ stands for $m_{ij \to j}(x_j)$ in the following equations. We define $M(r)$ to be the set of messages going into a sub-region of r or going into r itself while starting outside r and its sub-regions. Let t be the set of all sites which belong to r but not to s, i.e. $t = r \backslash s$. The message update rule is given by

$$m_{r \to s} \leftarrow \alpha \max_{x_t} \phi_t(x_t) \prod_{m_{r' \to s'} \in M(r) \backslash M(s)} m_{r' \to s'}. \tag{4}$$

The potential $\phi_t(x_t)$ is defined as the product of the unary potentials of all sites in $r \backslash s$ and of all pairwise potentials between sites in r. It is easily verifiable that the above update equation is the same as equation (2). Upon convergence, the belief of r is given by

$$b_r \leftarrow \alpha \phi_r(x_r) \prod_{m_{r' \to s'} \in M(r)} m_{r' \to s'}. \tag{5}$$

The standard BP algorithm can be considered a special case of Generalized Belief Propagation (GBP). GBP converges to the stationary points of the Kikuchi approximation (which is more accurate than Bethe approximation) by allowing for regions of size more than 2. Fig. 1 shows an example of this for an MRF with 4 sites which results in 10 regions. It also shows the corresponding messages along with their directions. We define $M(r, s)$ to be the set of all messages starting from a sub-region of r and going to s or its sub-region. Then the GBP update equation is given by

$$m_{r \to s} \leftarrow \alpha \max_{x_t} \frac{\phi_t(x_t) \prod_{m_{r' \to s'} \in M(r) \backslash M(s)} m_{r' \to s'}}{\prod_{m_{r'' \to s''} \in M(r,s)} m_{r'' \to s''}}, \tag{6}$$

where $t = r \backslash s$. Note that, like BP, the message $m_{r \to s}$ in GBP is also indexed by x_s. For example, $m_{ijk \to ij}$ stands for $m_{ijk \to ij}(x_i, x_j)$ and thus, can be interpreted as an $n_L \times n_L$ matrix. Table 1 lists all the sets $M(r)$ and $M(r, s)$ for the example MRF in Fig. 1. Using equation (6), the messages $m_{ij \to i}$ and $m_{ijk \to ij}$ are given by

$$m_{ij \to i} \leftarrow \alpha \max_{x_j} \phi_j(x_j) \phi_{ij}(x_i, x_j) m_{ijk \to ij} m_{jk \to j}, \tag{7}$$

$$m_{ijk \to ij} \leftarrow \alpha \max_{x_t} \frac{\phi_k(x_k) \prod_{p,q \in \{i,j,k\}} \phi_{pq}(x_p, x_q) m_{jkl \to jk} m_{kl \to k}}{m_{ik \to i} m_{jk \to j}}. \tag{8}$$

Robust Truncated Model. In this paper, we consider the case where the pairwise potentials $\phi_{ij}(x_i, x_j)$ form a robust truncated model such that

$$\phi_{ij}(x_i, x_j) = f_{ij}(x_i, x_j), \quad \text{if } x_i \in \mathcal{C}_i(x_j),$$
$$= \tau_{ij}, \quad \text{otherwise}, \tag{9}$$

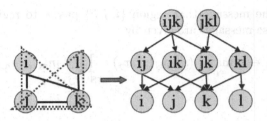

Fig. 1. *Left.* An example MRF with four sites. The solid lines show the interactions between the sites and describe a neighbourhood relationship on them. The dotted lines show the clustering of the sites into regions of size 3. *Right.* The sites are grouped to form ten regions for canonical GBP. The resulting messages and their directions are also shown using the arrows. For example, the top left arrow shows the message $m_{ijk \to ij}$ and the bottom left arrow shows the message $m_{ij \to i}$.

Table 1. Messages belonging to the sets $M(r)$ and $M(r,s)$ for each region r and its direct sub-region s shown in Fig. 1

r	$M(r)$	r	$M(r)$	r	s	$M(r,s)$
$\{ijk\}$	$m_{jkl \to jk}, m_{kl \to k}$	$\{kl\}$	$m_{jkl \to kl}, m_{ik \to k},$	$\{ijk\}$	$\{ij\}$	$m_{ik \to i},$
$\{jkl\}$	$m_{ijk \to jk}, m_{ij \to j}, m_{ik \to k}$		$m_{jk \to k}$			$m_{jk \to j}$
$\{ij\}$	$m_{ijk \to ij}, m_{ik \to i}, m_{jk \to j}$	$\{i\}$	$m_{ij \to i}, m_{ik \to i}$	$\{ijk\}$	$\{ik\}$	$m_{ij \to i},$
$\{ik\}$	$m_{ijk \to ik}, m_{ij \to i}, m_{jk \to k},$	$\{j\}$	$m_{ij \to j}, m_{jk \to j}$			$m_{jk \to k}$
	$m_{kl \to k}$	$\{k\}$	$m_{ik \to k}, m_{jk \to k},$	$\{ijk\}$	$\{jk\}$	$m_{ij \to j}, m_{ik \to k}$
$\{jk\}$	$m_{ijk \to jk}, m_{jkl \to jk}, m_{ij \to j},$		$m_{kl \to k}$	$\{jkl\}$	$\{jk\}$	$m_{kl \to k}$
	$m_{ik \to k}, m_{kl \to k}$	$\{l\}$	$m_{kl \to l}$	$\{jkl\}$	$\{kl\}$	$m_{jk \to k}$

where $\mathcal{C}_i(x_j)$ defines the subset of labels of i which are 'compatible' with x_j. In other words, the cost for an incompatible pair of labels is truncated to τ_{ij}. Included in this class are the commonly used Potts model i.e. $f_{ij}(x_i, x_j) = d_{ij}$, $\forall x_i \in \mathcal{C}_i(x_j)$, the truncated linear model i.e. $f_{ij}(x_i, x_j) = \exp(-|x_i - x_j|)$ and the truncated quadratic model i.e. $f_{ij}(x_i, x_j) = \exp(-(x_i - x_j)^2)$. In most problems, $f_{ij}(x_i, x_j) > \tau_{ij}$ and the number of labels n_C in $\mathcal{C}_i(x_j)$ are much smaller than n_L, i.e. $n_C \ll n_L$. Such MRFs have been successfully used for applications such as object recognition [5] and stereo [4]. Next, we describe our fast GBP algorithm.

3 Fast Generalized Belief Propagation

We now present a method for making GBP computationally efficient for MRFs whose pairwise potentials form a robust truncated model. This is a more general case than the Ising model addressed in [6]. Note that the choice of regions for GBP is not of concern in this paper since our method is independent of it. However, for clarity, we will only describe the method for MRFs that form complete graphs and where regions are formed by clustering all possible combinations of three sites. The extension to any other MRF is trivial. In this case, there are two types of messages: (i) $m_{ij \to j}$ is the message that region $\{i, j\}$ passes to site j and,

(ii) $m_{ijk \to jk}$ is the message that region $\{i, j, k\}$ passes to region $\{j, k\}$. Using equation (6), these messages are given by

$$m_{ij \to j} \leftarrow \alpha \max_{x_i} \phi_i(x_i) \phi_{ij}(x_i, x_j) \prod_{n \in \mathbf{S} \setminus \{i,j\}} m_{ni \to i} m_{nij \to ij}, \tag{10}$$

and

$$m_{ijk \to jk} \leftarrow \alpha \max_{x_i} \frac{\phi_i(x_i) \prod_{p,q \in \mathbf{R}} \phi_{pq}(x_p, x_q) \prod_{n \in \mathbf{S} \setminus \mathbf{R}} m_{ni \to i} m_{nij \to ij} m_{nik \to ik}}{m_{ij \to j} m_{ik \to k}}, \tag{11}$$

where $\mathbf{R} = \{i, j, k\}$ and $\mathbf{S}$ is the set of all n_S sites of the MRF. Obviously, most of the computational cost is contributed by messages $m_{ijk \to jk}$ which can be reduced significantly by making use of the special form of the pairwise potentials.

Since for any pair of sites i and j, most of the pairwise potential $\phi_{ij}(x_i, x_j)$ are constant (i.e. τ_{ij}), considerable speed-up is achieved by pre-computing all the terms which are common in the message update equations (10) and (11). In order to compute the messages $m_{ij \to j}$, we define

$$r_i(x_j) = \alpha \max_{x_i} \phi_i(x_i) \prod_{n \in \mathbf{S} \setminus \{i,j\}} m_{ni \to i} m_{nij \to ij}, \tag{12}$$

and

$$r_i'(x_j) = \alpha \max_{x_i \in \mathcal{C}_i(x_j)} \phi_i(x_i) f_{ij}(x_i, x_j) \prod_{n \in \mathbf{S} \setminus \{i,j\}} m_{ni \to i} m_{nij \to ij}. \tag{13}$$

The message $m_{ij \to j}$ is given by $\max\{r_i'(x_j), \tau_{ij} r_i(x_j)\}$. Note that no speed-up is obtained for the messages $m_{ij \to j}$ except in the special case of $\tau_{ij} = 0$ when each message can be computed as $\max\{r_i'(x_j)\}$ (i.e. independent of $r_i(x_j)$) in $O(n_C)$ time, where n_C is the number of labels in $\mathcal{C}_i(x_j)$. However, as noted above, the real concern is to reduce the complexity of the messages $m_{ijk \to jk}$.

We define

$$q_{ik}(x_j) = \sqrt{\alpha} \max_{x_i \notin \mathcal{C}_i(x_j)} \frac{\sqrt{\phi_i(x_i)} \prod_{n \in \mathbf{S} \setminus \{i,j,k\}} m_{nij \to ij} \sqrt{m_{ni \to i}}}{m_{ij \to j}}, \tag{14}$$

and

$$q_i'(x_j, x_k) = \alpha \max_{x_i \in \mathcal{C}_i(x_j, x_k)} \frac{\phi_i(x_i) \prod_{\{p,q\} \in \mathbf{R}} \phi_{pq} \prod_{n \in \mathbf{S} \setminus \mathbf{R}} m_{nij \to ij} m_{nik \to ik} m_{ni \to i}}{m_{ij \to j} m_{ik \to k}}, \tag{15}$$

where $\mathbf{R} = \{i, j, k\}$ and $\mathcal{C}_i(x_j, x_k) = \mathcal{C}_i(x_j) \cup \mathcal{C}_i(x_k)$. The time complexities of calculating $q_{ik}(x_j)$ and $q_i'(x_j, x_k)$ for a particular x_j and x_k are $O(n_L)$ and $O(n_C)$ respectively. Once these terms have been computed, the message $m_{ijk \to jk}$ can be obtained in $O(1)$ time as $\max\{q_i'(x_j, x_k), \phi_{jk} \tau_{ij} q_{ik}(x_j) \tau_{ik} q_{ij}(x_k)\}$.

The computational complexity of the overall algorithm is $O(n_S^3 n_L^2 n_C)$ (i.e. the number of messages). This is significantly better than the $O(n_S^3 n_L^3)$ time taken by ordinary GBP when n_L is very large. Again, for the special case of $\tau_{ij} = 0$, the messages can be computed even more efficiently as $q_i'(x_j, x_k)$, without computing the terms $q_{ik}(x_j)$. Note that the terms $q_{ik}(x_j)$ and $q_{ij}(x_k)$ would be computed using the same label $x_i \notin C_i(x_j, x_k)$ in equation (14) as the pairwise potentials $\phi_{ij}(x_i, x_j)$ and $\phi_{ik}(x_i, x_k)$ are constant for all such x_i (proof in appendix). Thus, the messages computed would be exactly equal to the messages in equation (11).

In general, this approach reduces the time complexity of GBP from $O(n_R n_M n_L^{n_M})$ to $O(n_R n_M n_L^{n_M-1} n_C)$, where n_R is the number of regions and n_M is size of the largest region. For example, in the case of BP over a complete graph, the only messages are of the form $m_{ij \to j}$ which can be computed efficiently using the above method in $O(n_S^2 n_L n_C)$ time instead of $O(n_S^2 n_L^2)$ time required by ordinary BP. Note that this is the same factor of speed-up obtained by the method described in [3] which cannot be extended to the GBP algorithm. Algorithm 1 shows the main steps involved in reducing the computational cost of GBP. Next, we describe our memory-efficient GBP algorithm.

Algorithm 1. Fast Generalized Belief Propagation

1. Using equations (12) and (13), calculate $r_i(x_j)$ and $r_i'(x_j)$, $\forall$ sites i, j and labels x_j.
2. Compute $m_{ij \to j} \leftarrow \max\{r_i'(x_j), \tau_{ij} r_i(x_j)\}$.
3. Using equations (14) and (15), calculate $q_{ik}(x_j)$ and $q_i'(x_j, x_k)$, $\forall$ i, j, k, x_j and x_k.
4. Compute $m_{ijk \to jk} \leftarrow \max\{q_i'(x_j, x_k), \phi_{jk} \tau_{ij} q_{ik}(x_j) \tau_{ik} q_{ij}(x_k)\}$.
5. Obtain the beliefs using equation (5).

---

4   Memory-Efficient Generalized Belief Propagation

We now present two approaches to reduce the memory requirements of GBP. The first approach extends the method of Felzenszwalb and Huttenlocher [4] for reducing the memory requirements of BP by half on bipartite graphs. The basic idea is that for a bipartite graph with the set of regions $A \cup B$, the message that a region in A passes to its sub-regions depends only on the messages coming from the regions in B and vice versa. In other words, if we know the messages coming from B, we can compute the messages within A. This suggests the strategy of alternating between computing messages for regions in A and B, thereby reducing the memory requirements by half.

We now describe the second approach which requires that $\tau_{ij} = 0$ for all pairs of site i and j. It is not surprising that further constraints need to be imposed on the robust truncated model. As mentioned above, the problem of reducing memory requirements has proven to be more difficult than that of reducing the time complexity and has met with limited success so far. However, we will demonstrate in section 5 that this restricted robust truncated model is still useful in a wide variety of vision applications.

The basic idea is to reduce the state space of the original MRF by dividing it into smaller MRFs whose labels are a subset of the labels of the original MRF.

However, these subsets are chosen such that the messages and beliefs computed on them are equivalent to those that would be obtained for the original problem. Specifically, we observe that when $\tau_{ij} = 0$, the messages $m_{ij \to j}$ and $m_{ijk \to jk}$ can be calculated using only $r_i'(x_j)$ and $q_i'(x_j, x_k)$ for all iterations of the GBP algorithm. Since $r_i'(x_j)$ and $q_i'(x_j, x_k)$ (and therefore the messages and the beliefs) are computed using $C_i(x_j)$ and $C_i(x_k)$, it would be sufficient to only include these in the smaller MRFs. Thus, each of smaller MRFs contains a subset of labels such that if x_j is included in an MRF, then $C_i(x_j)$ is also included in that MRF, for all sites i. These MRFs can then be solved one at a time using Algorithm 1 thereby greatly reducing the memory requirements since $n_C \ll n_L$. Moreover, this approach does not increase the computational cost of the fast GBP algorithm described in the previous section. Algorithm 2 illustrates the main steps of memory-efficient GBP.

Algorithm 2. Memory-Efficient Generalized Belief Propagation

1. Choose a subset of labels x_i for i. Choose all the labels $x_j \in C_j(x_i)$, $\forall$ sites j.
2. Solve the resultant small MRF using Algorithm 1. Note that $r_i(x_j)$ and $q_{ik}(x_j)$ need not be calculated.
3. Repeat step 2 with a different subset until all beliefs have been computed.

Note that our second approach achieves a considerable reduction in memory (of factor $(n_L/n_C)^{n_M-1}$) by restricting the form of the robust truncated model. Further, it is applicable to any general topology of the MRF, i.e. it is not restricted to only bipartite graphs. We now demonstrate our approach for subgraph matching and object recognition.

5 Experiments

In order to demonstrate the effectiveness of our approach, we generated several complete MRFs whose pairwise potentials form a robust truncated model with $\tau_{ij} = 0$. The regions are formed by clustering all possible combinations of three sites. Fig. 2 shows the average time and memory requirements for different values of the n_C/n_L (averaged over 100 MRFs). Note that when $n_C = n_L$ our approach reduces to the standard GBP algorithm. However, when $n_C \ll n_L$, it provides a significant reduction in time and memory requirements.

We now formulate two important problems, subgraph matching and object recognition, using the special case of the robust truncated model (i.e. $\tau_{ij} = 0$). It is observed that in both cases $n_C \ll n_L$ which allows us to solve these problems accurately using our fast, memory-efficient GBP algorithm.

5.1 Subgraph Matching

We use the fast, memory-efficient GBP algorithm to solve the problem of subgraph matching. Given two graphs $\mathcal{G}_1 = \{\mathcal{V}_1, \mathcal{E}_1\}$ and $\mathcal{G}_2 = \{\mathcal{V}_2, \mathcal{E}_2\}$, subgraph

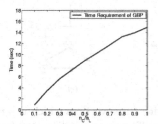 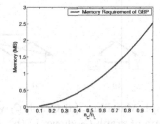

Fig. 2. Left: Average time taken by the efficient GBP algorithm for 100 random complete MRFs whose pairwise potentials satify the special case of the robust truncated model. The time complexity scales almost linearly with the factor n_C/n_L. Right: Average memory requirements which scales quadratically with n_C/n_L.

matching involves finding a mapping $f : \mathcal{V}_1 \to \mathcal{V}_2$ which minimizes the following energy function:

$$\sum_{v_i, v_j \in \mathcal{V}_1} \|l_{ij}^1 - l_{f(i)f(j)}^2\|, \tag{16}$$

where l_{ij}^k is the distance between vertices i and j of the kth graph. Many important computer vision problems, such as matching part-based models for object recognition can be thought of as special cases of this problem.

We define an MRF for determining the mapping $f(.)$ such that each site i represents a vertex v_i^1 in $\mathcal{V}_1$. Each label x_i represents a vertex v_i^2 in $\mathcal{V}_2$. For our example, we assume that all points $v_i^1 \in \mathcal{V}_1$ are equally likely to map to a point in $\mathcal{V}_2$, and hence the likelihood terms $\phi_i(x_i)$ are set to 0.5 (however this is not generally the case). The sites of the MRF form a complete graph as distances between all pairs of vertices should be preserved by the mapping. We define the pairwise potentials as

$$\phi_{ij}(\mathbf{x}_i, \mathbf{x}_j) = \begin{cases} d \text{ if } |l_{ij}^1 - l_{x_i x_j}^2| \le \epsilon \\ 0 \quad \text{otherwise}, \end{cases} \tag{17}$$

where ϵ is a constant which depends on the (expected) level of noise. In our experiments, we use $d = 1$. This favours the preservation of distance between corresponding pairs of vertices. Figure 3 shows an example of this formulation when $|\mathcal{V}_1| = 3$ and $|\mathcal{V}_2| = 4$.

Our problem thus reduces to obtaining the MAP estimate given the above MRF. For this purpose, we use the efficient GBP algorithm described in Algorithm 2. By restricting the region size to two, we obtain a time and memory efficient BP. Although less accurate, efficient BP is faster than efficient GBP. We compare the results with ordinary GBP and BP algorithms. For complete graphs, we found that GBP works well when the regions form a *star* pattern, i.e. the regions are of the form $\{1, i, j\}$ for all pairs $i > 1$ and $j > 1$. The common site '1' is chosen randomly. Note that this observation is consistent with that reported in [10].

We generated 1000 pairs of random graphs $\mathcal{G}_1$ and $\mathcal{G}_2$, with $|\mathcal{V}_1| = 0.25|\mathcal{V}_2|$ on an average. The number of vertices $|\mathcal{V}_2|$ were varied between 30 and 60.

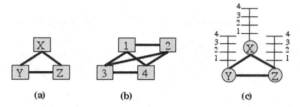

Fig. 3. Subgraph Matching. (a) Graph $\mathcal{G}_1$ with three vertices which is a rigidly transformed subgraph of graph $\mathcal{G}_2$ shown in (b). (c) The corresponding MRF formulation for subgraph matching. The MRF consists of three sites corresponding to the vertices X,Y and Z of $\mathcal{G}_1$. Each site has four possible labels corresponding to vertices 1,2,3 and 4 of $\mathcal{G}_2$. The interactions between the sites is shown using solid lines.

Table 2. Average time and space requirements of various methods for subgraph matching. Columns 4 and 5 show the requirements for smaller graphs with $|\mathcal{V}_2| = 20$.

Method	Time	Memory	Time (Small)	Memory (Small)	Accuracy (%)
BP	2 sec	4 MB	0.009 sec	0.08 MB	78.61
GBP	-	> 350 MB	6 sec	0.5 MB	95.79
Efficient BP	0.2 sec	0.4 MB	0.006 sec	0.008 MB	78.61
Efficient GBP	1.5 sec	3.5 MB	0.6 sec	0.07 MB	95.79
[11]	4.3 sec	0.1 MB	2.2 sec	0.02 MB	20.00

The vertices $|\mathcal{V}_1|$ were randomly selected subset of $|\mathcal{V}_2|$ with 7% noise added to them. The average number of correct matches for the vertices in $\mathcal{V}_1$ found using GBP were 95.79% (9421 out of 9835) compared to 78.61% (7732 out of 9835) found using BP. Thus, GBP provides much more accurate results than BP which should encourage its use in practice. We also significantly outperformed the state-of-the-art method by Chui and Rangarajan [11] (tested using their publically available code) on our challenging dataset. Table 2 summarizes the average time and space requirements for the various methods used. Note that due to large memory requirements of GBP, we ran another set of experiments on smaller graphs, i.e. $|\mathcal{V}_2| = 20$. The time and memory requirements for these smaller graphs are shown in the fourth and fifth column.

5.2 Object Recognition

We tested our approach for object recognition using a parts-based model called pictorial structures (PS) introduced by Fischler and Elschlager [8] and extended in [5]. PS are compositions of 2D patterns, i.e. parts, under a probablistic model for their shape, appearance and spatial layout (see [5] for details).

The connections between the parts of the PS form a complete graph. The pairwise potentials are defined as

$$\phi_{ij}(x_i, x_j) = \begin{cases} d & \text{if valid configuration,} \\ 0 & \text{otherwise.} \end{cases} \tag{18}$$

Method	Time	Memory
BP	59 sec	0.7 MB
GBP	240 sec	38 MB
Efficient BP	2 sec	0.09 MB
Efficient GBP	16 sec	0.5 MB

Fig. 4. Results of obtaining the MAP estimate of the parts of cows using the fast, memory-efficient GBP. The first row shows the input images. The detected parts are shown in the second row. The table on the right shows the average time and space requirements of various methods for object recognition.

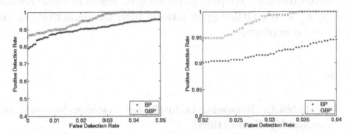

Fig. 5. Left: ROC curves for cow recognition. Right: Zoomed versions of a part of the ROC curve. Results indicate that better recognition performance is obtained using GBP compared to BP.

A configuration is valid if $x_{ij}^{min} \leq ||x_i - x_j|| \leq x_{ij}^{max}$. In all our experiments, we used $d = 1$. The parameters of the model are learnt in an unsupervised manner from videos as described in [5]. During recognition, the putative poses of the parts are found using a *tree cascade of classifiers* (see [5] for details). This allows us to efficiently prune the undesirable poses which result in a low potential $\phi_i(x_i)$. Again, for the above MRF, the regions form a *star* pattern with the *torso* part being the common site [10]. The MAP estimate of the pose for each part is obtained by performing inference using the fast, memory-efficient GBP algorithm.

Fig. 4 shows the results of our approach on some images containing cows. The cascade efficiently obtains approximately one hundred putative poses per part in 2 minutes. The MAP estimate of each of the parts obtained using GBP is shown in the second row. The table on the right summarizes the time and space requirements of the various methods for object recognition. Fig. 5 shows the ROC curves obtained using 450 positive and 2400 negative examples. Note that, as in the case of subgraph matching, GBP performs better than BP.

6   Summary and Conclusions

We have presented methods to overcome the problems of large computational complexity and space requirements in using GBP for the important case where the pairwise potentials form a robust truncated model. Specifically,

- We reduce the time complexity of GBP to $O(n_R n_M n_L^{n_M-1} n_C)$ for the case of robust truncated models.
- We reduce the memory requirements of GBP over bipartite MRFs by half.
- We further reduce the memory requirements of GBP for a general MRF by a factor of $(n_L/n_C)^{n_M-1}$ for a special case of the robust truncated model.

Further, we have demonstrated how the important problems of subgraph matching and object recognition can be formulated using the robust truncated model and solved efficiently using our approach. Our results significantly outperform the state-of-the-art method. We plan to investigate whether some restrictions can be relaxed (e.g. $\tau_{ij} = 0$). Other applications such as segmentation and optical flow also need to be explored.

References

1. Pearl, J.: Probabilistic Reasoning in Intelligent Systems: Networks of Plausible Inference. Morgan Kauffman (1998)
2. Yedidia, J., Freeman, W., Weiss, Y.: Bethe free energy, kikuchi approximations, and belief propagation algorithms. Technical Report TR2001-16, MERL (2001)
3. Felzenszwalb, P., Huttenlocher, D.: Fast algorithms for large state space HMMs with applications to web usage analysis. In: NIPS. (2003) 409–416
4. Felzenszwalb, P., Huttenlocher, D.: Efficient belief propagation for early vision. In: CVPR. (2004) I: 261–268
5. Kumar, M.P., Torr, P.H.S., Zisserman, A.: OBJ CUT. In: CVPR. (2005) I:18–25
6. Shental, N., Zomet, A., Hertz, T., Weiss, Y.: Learning and inferring image segmentation with the GBP typical cut algorithm. In: ICCV. (2003) 1243–1250
7. Vogiatzis, G., Torr, P.H.S., Seitz, S., Cipolla, R.: Reconstructing relief surfaces. In: BMVC. (2004) 117–126
8. Fischler, M., Elschlager, R.: The representation and matching of pictorial structures. TC **22** (1973) 67–92
9. Wainwright, M., Jaakkola, T., Willsky, A.: MAP estimation via agreement on (hyper)trees. Technical Report UCB/CSD-03-1226, UC Berkeley (2003)
10. Minka, T., Qi, Y.: Tree-structed approximations by expectation propagation. In: NIPS. (2003)
11. Chui, H., Rangarajan, A.: A new point matching algorithm for non-rigid registration. CVIU **89** (2003) 114–141

Appendix. The terms $q_{ik}(x_j)$ and $q_{ij}(x_k)$ described in equation (14) are obtained using the same label x_i.

Proof. The only terms which differ in $q_{ik}(x_j)$ and $q_{ij}(x_k)$ are $m_{nij \to ij}$ and $m_{nik \to ik}$ in the right-hand side of equation (14). Since all messages are initialized to 1 the proposition holds true for the first iteration. For subsequent iterations, consider the following equations:

$$m_{nij \to ij} \leftarrow \alpha \max_{x_n} \frac{\phi_n(x_n) \prod_{p,q \in \mathbf{R}_1} \phi_{pq}(x_p, x_q) \prod_{l \in \mathbf{S} \setminus \mathbf{R}_1} m_{ln \to n} m_{lni \to ni} m_{lnj \to nj}}{m_{ni \to i} m_{ni \to j}},$$

$$(19)$$

$$m_{nik \to ik} \leftarrow \alpha \max_{x_n} \frac{\phi_n(x_n) \prod_{p,q \in \mathbf{R}_2} \phi_{pq}(x_p, x_q) \prod_{l \in \mathbf{S} \setminus \mathbf{R}_2} m_{ln \to n} m_{lni \to ni} m_{lnj \to nk}}{m_{ni \to i} m_{nk \to k}},$$

$$(20)$$

where $\mathbf{R}_1 = \{n, i, j\}$ and $\mathbf{R}_2 = \{n, i, k\}$. The pairwise potentials $\phi_{ij}(x_i, x_j)$ and $\phi_{ik}(x_i, x_k)$ are constants for all $x_i \in \mathcal{C}_i(x_j)$ and $x_i \in \mathcal{C}_i(x_k)$ (over which the terms $q_{ik}(x_j)$ and $q_{ij}(x_k)$ are computed). The term $m_{lni \to ni}$ is common to both equations (19) and (20) and all other terms are constants for a particular pair of labels x_j and x_k. Thus, the above two messages are equivalent and it follows that $q_{ik}(x_j)$ and $q_{ij}(x_k)$ will be computed using the same label x_i.

Adapted Vocabularies for Generic Visual Categorization

Florent Perronnin, Christopher Dance, Gabriela Csurka, and Marco Bressan

Xerox Research Centre Europe, 6, chemin de Maupertuis, 38240 Meylan, France
{Firstname.Lastname}@xrce.xerox.com

Abstract. Several state-of-the-art Generic Visual Categorization (GVC) systems are built around a vocabulary of visual terms and characterize images with one histogram of visual word counts. We propose a novel and practical approach to GVC based on a universal vocabulary, which describes the content of all the considered classes of images, and class vocabularies obtained through the adaptation of the universal vocabulary using class-specific data. An image is characterized by a set of histograms - one per class - where each histogram describes whether the image content is best modeled by the universal vocabulary or the corresponding class vocabulary. It is shown experimentally on three very different databases that this novel representation outperforms those approaches which characterize an image with a single histogram.

1 Introduction

Generic Visual Categorization (GVC) is the pattern classification problem which consists in assigning one or multiple labels to an image based on its semantic content. We emphasize the use of the word "generic" as the goal is to classify a wide variety of objects and scenes. GVC is a very challenging task as one has to cope with variations in view, lighting and occlusion and with typical object and scene variations.

Several state-of-the-art GVC systems [14, 1, 4, 9, 16] were inspired by the *bag-of-words* (BOW) approach to text-categorization [13]. In the BOW representation, a text document is encoded as a histogram of the number of occurrences of each word. Similarly, one can characterize an image by a histogram of visual words count. The *visual vocabulary* provides a "mid-level" representation which helps to bridge the semantic gap between the low-level features extracted from an image and the high-level concepts to be categorized [1]. However, the main difference with text categorization is that there is no given visual vocabulary for the GVC problem and it has to be learned *automatically* from a training set.

To obtain the visual vocabulary, Sivic and Zisserman [14] and Csurka et al. [4] originally proposed to cluster the low-level features with the K-means algorithm, where each centroid corresponds to a visual word. To build a histogram, each feature vector is assigned to its closest centroid. Hsu and Chang [9] and Winn et al. [16] made use of the information bottleneck principle to obtain more discriminative vocabularies. Farquhar et al. also proposed a generative model, the Gaussian Mixture Model (GMM), to perform clustering [7]. In this case, a

A. Leonardis, H. Bischof, and A. Pinz (Eds.): ECCV 2006, Part IV, LNCS 3954, pp. 464–475, 2006.

low-level feature is not assigned to one visual word but to all words probabilistically, resulting in a continuous histogram representation. They also proposed to build the vocabulary by training class specific vocabularies and agglomerating them in a single vocabulary (see also the work of Leung and Malik [10] and Varma and Zisserman [15] for the related problem of texture classification). Although substantial improvements were obtained, we believe that this approach is unpractical for a large number of classes C. Indeed, if N is the size of the class-vocabularies, the size of the agglomerated vocabulary, and therefore of the histograms to be classified, will be $C \times N$ (c.f. the curse of dimensionality).

Our emphasis in this work is on developing a practical approach which scales with the number of classes. We define a *universal vocabulary*, which describes the visual content of all the considered classes, and *class vocabularies*, which are obtained through the *adaptation of the universal vocabulary* using class-specific data. While other approaches based on visual vocabularies characterize an image with a single histogram, in the proposed approach, an image is represented by a set of histograms of size $2 \times N$, one per class. Each histogram describes whether an image is more suitably modeled by the universal vocabulary or the corresponding adapted vocabulary.

The remainder of this paper is organized as follows. In section 2, we motivate the use of a universal vocabulary and of adapted class-vocabularies and describe the training of both types of vocabularies. In section 3, we show how to characterize an image by a set of histograms using these vocabularies. In section 4, we explain how to reduce significantly the computational cost of the proposed approach with a fast scoring procedure. In section 5, we show experimentally that the proposed representation outperforms those approaches which characterize an image with a single histogram. Finally, we draw conclusions.

2   Universal and Adapted Vocabularies

Let us first motivate the use of a universal vocabulary and of adapted class-vocabularies with a simple two-class problem where cats have to be distinguished from dogs.

A universal vocabulary is supposed to represent the content of all possible images and it is therefore trained with data from all classes under consideration. Since cats and dogs have many similarities, cats' and dogs' low-level feature vectors are likely to cluster into similar visual words such as "eye", "ear" or "tail". Hence, a histogram representation based on such a vocabulary is not powerful enough to help distinguish between cats and dogs. However, one can derive class vocabularies by adapting the universal vocabulary with class-specific data. Therefore, the universal "eye" word is likely to be specialized to "cat's eye" and "dog's eye" as depicted on Figure 1. Note that, although visual words are not guaranteed to be as meaningful as in the previous example, we believe that the combination of these universal and specific representations provides the necessary information to discriminate between classes.

As there exists a large body of work on the adaptation of GMMs, we represent a vocabulary of visual words by means of a GMM as done in [7]. Let us denote

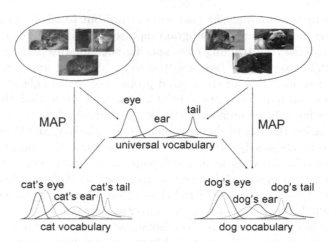

Fig. 1. The cats and dogs example: training a universal vocabulary with images from both classes and adapting this vocabulary to cat and dog vocabularies with class-specific data

by λ the set of parameters of a GMM. $\lambda = \{w_i, \mu_i, \Sigma_i, i = 1...N\}$ where w_i, μ_i and Σ_i denote respectively the weight, mean vector and covariance matrix of Gaussian i and where N denotes the number of Gaussians. Each Gaussian represents a word of the visual vocabulary: w_i encodes the relative frequency of word i, μ_i the mean of the word and Σ_i the variation around the mean. In the following, we assume that the covariance matrices are diagonal as (i) any distribution can be approximated with an arbitrary precision by a weighted sum of Gaussians with diagonal covariances and (ii) the computational cost of diagonal covariances is much lower than the cost involved by full covariances. We use the notation $\sigma_i^2 = \text{diag}(\Sigma_i)$.

If an observation x has been generated by the GMM, we have:

$$p(x|\lambda) = \sum_{i=1}^{N} w_i p_i(x). \tag{1}$$

The components p_i are given by:

$$p_i(x) = \frac{\exp\left\{-\frac{1}{2}(x - \mu_i)' \Sigma_i^{-1}(x - \mu_i)\right\}}{(2\pi)^{D/2}|\Sigma_i|^{1/2}} \tag{2}$$

where D is the dimensionality of the feature vectors and $|.|$ denotes the determinant operator.

We now explain how to train the universal and class vocabularies. The universal vocabulary is trained using maximum likelihood estimation (MLE) and the class vocabularies are adapted using the maximum a posteriori (MAP) criterion.

2.1   MLE Training of the Universal Vocabulary

Let $X = \{x_t, t = 1...T\}$ be the set of training samples. In the following, the superscript u denotes that a parameter or distribution relates to the universal vocabulary. The estimation of λ^u may be performed by maximizing the log-likelihood function $\log p(X|\lambda^u)$. This is referred to as MLE.

The standard procedure for MLE is the Expectation Maximization (EM) algorithm [5]. EM alternates two steps: (i) an expectation (E) step where the posterior probabilities of mixture occupancy (also referred to as occupancy probabilities) are computed based on the current estimates of the parameters, and (ii) a maximization (M) step, where the parameters are updated based on the expected complete data log-likelihood which depends on the occupancy probabilities computed in the E-step.

For the E-step, one simply applies Bayes formula to obtain:

$$\gamma_t(i) = p(i|x_t, \lambda^u) = \frac{w_i^u p_i^u(x_t)}{\sum_{j=1}^N w_j^u p_j^u(x_t)}. \tag{3}$$

The occupancy probability $\gamma_t(i)$ is the probability for observation x_t to have been generated by the i-th Gaussian.

The M-step re-estimation equations are [2]:

$$\hat{w}_i^u = \frac{1}{T} \sum_{t=1}^T \gamma_t(i) \tag{4}$$

$$\hat{\mu}_i^u = \frac{\sum_{t=1}^T \gamma_t(i) x_t}{\sum_{t=1}^T \gamma_t(i)} \tag{5}$$

$$(\hat{\sigma}_i^u)^2 = \frac{\sum_{t=1}^T \gamma_t(i) x_t^2}{\sum_{t=1}^T \gamma_t(i)} - (\hat{\mu}_i^u)^2 \tag{6}$$

where x^2 is a shorthand for $\text{diag}(xx')$.

Note that the initialization is an issue of paramount importance. Indeed EM is only guaranteed to converge to a local optimum and the quality of this optimum is largely dependent on the initial parameters. This initialization issue will be discussed in 5.

2.2 MAP Adaptation of Class Vocabularies

Let X be the set of adaptation samples. In the following, the superscript a denotes that a parameter or distribution relates to an adapted vocabulary.

The class vocabularies are estimated by adapting the universal vocabulary using the class training data and a form of Bayesian adaptation: MAP. The goal of MAP estimation is to maximize the posterior probability $p(\lambda^a|X)$ or equivalently $\log p(X|\lambda^a) + \log p(\lambda^a)$. Hence, the main difference with MLE lies in the assumption of an appropriate prior distribution of the parameters to be estimated. Therefore, it remains to (i) choose the prior distribution family and (ii) specify the parameters of the prior distribution.

The MAP adaptation of the GMM is a well-studied problem in the field of speech and speaker recognition [8, 12]. For both applications, one is interested in adapting a generic model, which reasonably describes the speech of any person, to more specific conditions using the data of a particular person. It was shown in [8] that the prior densities for GMM parameters could be adequately represented as a product of Dirichlet and normal-Wishart densities. When adapting a generic model with MAP to more specific conditions, it is natural to use the parameters of the generic model as a priori information on the location of the adapted parameters in the parameter space.

As shown in [8], one can also apply the EM procedure to MAP estimation. During the E-step, the occupancy probabilities γ are computed as was the case for MLE:

$$\gamma_t(i) = p(i|x_t, \lambda^a). \tag{7}$$

The M-step re-estimation equations are [8]:

$$\hat{w}_i^a = \frac{\sum_{t=1}^{T} \gamma_t(i) + \tau_i^w}{T + \sum_{i=1}^{N} \tau_i^w}, \tag{8}$$

$$\hat{\mu}_i^a = \frac{\sum_{t=1}^{T} \gamma_t(i) x_t + \tau_i^m \mu_i^u}{\sum_{t=1}^{T} \gamma_t(i) + \tau_i^m}, \tag{9}$$

$$(\hat{\sigma}_i^a)^2 = \frac{\sum_{t=1}^{T} \gamma_t(i) x_t^2 + \tau_i^s \left((\sigma_i^u)^2 + (\mu_i^u)^2\right)}{\sum_{t=1}^{T} \gamma_t(i) + \tau_i^s} - (\hat{\mu}_i^a)^2. \tag{10}$$

τ_i^w, τ_i^m and τ_i^s are relevance factors for the mixture weight, mean and variance parameters and keep a balance between the a priori information contained in the generic model and the new evidence brought by the class specific data. If a mixture component i was estimated with a small number of observations $\sum_{t=1}^{T} \gamma_t(i)$, then more emphasis is put on the a priori information. On the other hand, if it was estimated with a large number of observations, more emphasis will be put on the new evidence. Hence MAP provides a more robust estimate than MLE when little training data is available. The choice of parameter τ will be discussed in the section on experimental results.

3   Bipartite Histograms

Once the universal and adapted vocabularies have been properly estimated, we proceed as follows. For each class c, a novel vocabulary is obtained by merging the universal vocabulary and the adapted vocabulary of class c. This will be referred to as the *combined vocabulary* of class c. Note that the merging involves adjusting the weight parameters of the Gaussians to reflect the vocabulary size having doubled. In the case where the a priori probability $p(c)$ of class c is known, this can be done by multiplying the weights of the adapted vocabulary by $p(c)$ and the weights of the universal vocabulary by $(1 - p(c))$. The other parameters remain unchanged.

The rational behind this merging process is to make the Gaussians of the universal and adapted vocabularies "compete" to account for the feature vectors of an image. Indeed, if an image belongs to class c, it is more suitably described by the visual words of class c rather than by the words of the universal vocabulary.

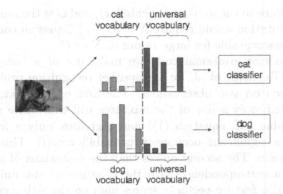

Fig. 2. Generating one bipartite histogram per category. Each histogram is subsequently fed to a different classifier.

On the other hand, if an image belongs to another class, then the visual words of the universal vocabulary will describe it more appropriately.

An image can therefore be characterized by a set of histograms - one per class - using these combined vocabularies. These histograms are said to be bipartite as half of the histogram reflects the contribution of the universal vocabulary in explaining the image while the other half reflects the contribution of the adapted vocabulary (c.f. Figure 2).

Interestingly, for a given image, summing the two halves of the bipartite histograms (i.e. summing the count of a word in the universal vocabulary part with the count of the corresponding word in the adapted vocabulary part) should lead to the same histogram approximately, whatever the class. Note that this histogram is the one we would obtain using only the universal vocabulary representation. Hence, the key of the success of the proposed approach is the ability to *separate for each class the relevant information from the irrelevant information*.

To classify these histograms, we use one Support Vector Machine (SVM) classifier per class. Each SVM is trained in a one-vs-all manner as done in [1, 4]. However, in [1, 4], as images are characterized by a single histogram, the same histograms are fed to the classifiers. In the proposed approach, each classifier is fed with different histograms, both at training and test time. Going back to our cats and dogs example, a "cat" classifier will be trained with histograms computed on the combined vocabulary of the class cat. In the same manner, at test time the histogram obtained with the combined vocabulary of the class cat will be fed to the cat classifier and the histogram obtained with the combined vocabulary of the class dog will be fed to the dog classifier.

4   Computational Cost

When estimating a histogram, the most intensive part is the Gaussian computation, i.e. the computation of the values $p_i(x)$ (c.f. equation (2)). If N is the number of Gaussians in the universal vocabulary, and C is the number of classes, a direct implementation would require $N \times (C+1)$ Gaussian computations per image. This is unacceptable for large values of N or C.

To reduce the computational cost, we make use of a fast scoring procedure devised by Reynolds et al. for the speaker recognition problem [12]. This technique is based on two observations. The first one is that, when a large GMM is evaluated, only a few of the mixtures will contribute significantly to the likelihood value (c.f. equation (1)) and therefore, only a few of the mixtures will have a significant occupancy probability $\gamma_t(i)$. This property was observed empirically. The second one is that the Gaussians of an adapted vocabulary retain a correspondence with the mixtures of the universal vocabulary. Therefore, if a feature vector x scores high on the i-th component of the universal vocabulary, it will score highly on the i-th Gaussians of all adapted vocabularies.

The fast scoring procedure operates as follows on each feature vector x_t:

1. Compute the likelihood $p_i^u(x_t)$ for all the mixture components i of the universal vocabulary (N Gaussian computations). Retain the K best components.
2. Compute the likelihood values $p_i^a(x_t)$ for the K corresponding components of the C adapted vocabularies ($K \times C$ Gaussian computations).
3. For the C combined vocabularies, compute the occupancy probabilities $\gamma_t(i)$ on the $2 \times K$ corresponding components. Assume that the occupancy probabilities are zero for the other components.

Hence, the number of Gaussian computations is reduced from $N \times (C+1)$ to $N + K \times C$. For large values of C this is reduction of the computational cost by a factor N/K. Typical values for N and K are $N = 1,024$ and $K = 5$. Note that we did not observe any significant decrease of the performance in our experiments with as little as $K = 2$ best components. Hence the value $K = 5$ is a rather conservative choice.

Returning to our cats and dogs example, this fast scoring procedure simply consists in first determining whether the input feature vector corresponds to an eye, a tail, etc. and then if it is a tail, whether it is more likely to be the tail of cat or the tail of a dog.

5   Experimental Validation

In this section, we carry out a comparative evaluation of the proposed approach on three very different databases: an in-house database of scenes, the LAVA7 database and the Wang database. The two approaches which will serve as a baseline are (i) the one which makes use only of the universal vocabulary (as in [14, 4]) and (ii) the one which agglomerates class-vocabularies into a single vocabulary (as in [7]). We consider a classification task, i.e. each image is to be assigned to one class and the measure of performance is the percentage of images assigned to their correct classes. In the following section, we describe the experimental setup. We then provide results.

5.1 Experimental Setup

The low-level local features are based on local histograms of orientations as described in [11]. These features were extracted on a regular grid at different scales. As all images were resized before the feature extraction step so that they contained (approximately) the same number of pixels, the same number of features was extracted from all images (approximately).

The dimensionality of feature vectors was subsequently reduced from 128 to 50 using Principal Component Analysis (PCA). This decorrelates the dimensions of the feature vectors and thus makes the diagonal covariance assumption more reasonable. Discarding the last components also removes noise and thus increases the performance. It also significantly reduces the cost of Gaussian computations.

To alleviate the difficult initialization problem when training the universal vocabulary with MLE, we used a strategy inspired by the vector quantization algorithm. We start with a vocabulary of one unique word and then increase the number of Gaussians iteratively. Each iteration consists of two steps: (i) all the Gaussians which were estimated at the previous step with more than a given number of observations are split into two by introducing a slight perturbation in the mean and (ii) EM is performed until convergence, i.e. until the log-likelihood difference between two iterations falls below a predefined threshold. These two steps can be repeated until the desired number of Gaussians is obtained. An advantage of increasing progressively the number of Gaussians is that it allows to monitor the recognition performance to select the optimum vocabulary size.

For MAP adaptation, to reduce the number of parameters to hand-tune, we enforced $\tau_i^w = \tau_i^m = \tau_i^s = \tau$. We tried different values for τ and found that values between 5 and 50 were reasonable. In our experiments, we set $\tau = 10$. We demonstrate below the influence of adapting either all parameters, i.e. the mixture weights, means and covariances, or a subset of the parameters.

As for classifying the histograms, we used linear SVMs for both the proposed approach and the approach based on a single vocabulary. The only parameter to set is the one which controls the trade-off between the margin and the number of misclassified points, commonly known as C. It was fixed to 300 in all the following experiments. Note that in the linear case the cost of classifying a histogram is independent of the number of support vectors and can be neglected compared to the cost of Gaussian computations.

5.2 Results

In-house database. The first set of experiments was carried out on an in-house database of 8 scenes relating to amusement parks, boats, New York city, tennis, sunrise/sunset, surfing, underwater and waterfalls. This is a challenging set as we collected the training data while the test material was collected independently by a third party. Approximately 12,000 images were available for training and 1,750 for testing.

We first determine which Gaussian parameters are the most crucial ones to adapt in the proposed approach. Results are presented on Figure 3(a) as the

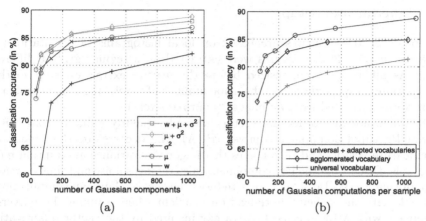

Fig. 3. Results on the in-house 8 scenes database. (a) Influence of the adaptation of the different Gaussian parameters (weight w, mean μ and covariance σ^2) on the classification accuracy. (b) Comparison of the proposed approach (universal + adapted vocabularies) with the two baseline systems (universal vocabulary and agglomerated vocabulary).

classification accuracy versus the number of Gaussian components, i.e. the vocabulary size. Clearly, adapting only the weights leads to a poor performance. Adapting either the means or the covariances has roughly the same impact and adapting both parameters leads to an additional small improvement. However, adapting the three parameters does not give further improvement. This experiment clearly shows that the relative frequency of a word (weight) in an adapted vocabulary has little influence; what matters is the location of the word (mean) and its variations (covariance). In the following, we adapt only the means and covariances.

We now compare the proposed approach with the two baseline approaches. Results are presented on Figure 3(b) as the classification accuracy versus the number of Gaussian computations per sample. For the two baselines, the number of Gaussian computations per sample is exactly the number of components. For the proposed approach, this is slightly higher (c.f. section 4). The proposed approach clearly outperforms the baselines. Indeed, it achieves an 88.8% accuracy while the approach based solely on a universal vocabulary achieves 81.4% accuracy and the approach based on an agglomerated vocabulary achieves an 84.9% accuracy for a vocabulary size of 1,024 visual words. This shows that the adapted vocabularies encode more discriminative information.

LAVA7 Database [4]. This database, also sometimes referred to as Xerox7 database [17], contains 1,776 images of seven objects: bikes, books, buildings, cars, faces, phones and trees. It served as a testbed for object recognition experiments during the course of the European LAVA project. The standard setup for running experiments on this database is a ten-fold cross-validation. Results are presented on Figure 4(a) as the classification accuracy versus the number of Gaussian computations per sample. We can see that the proposed approach outperforms the two baseline systems.

To the best of our knowledge, the best results reported on this database are those of Zhang et al. [17]. With their approach, which makes use of two feature extractors, two feature descriptors and an earth mover's distance (EMD) based kernel, they achieve a 94.3% accuracy but at a very high computational cost: the classification of an image takes on the order of 1 min on a modern PC. Running our non-optimized code on a 2.4 GHz AMD Opteron with 4GB RAM, our best system categorizes an image into one of the 7 categories with an accuracy of 95.8% in roughly 150 ms: approximately 125ms for the feature extraction and 25ms for the histogram building (the cost of the SVM classification can be neglected).

Wang Database [3]. This database contains 10 categories: Africa, beach, buildings, buses, dinosaurs, elephants, flowers, horses, mountains and food. Each category contains 100 images, which makes a total of 1,000 images. We used the same setup as in [3]: we randomly divided each category set into a training set and a test set, each with 50 images, and repeated the experiment 5 times. To prove that our good results are not restricted to SIFT-like features, we experimented with color features based on local mean and standard deviation in the RGB channels. Results are presented on Figure 4(b) as the classification accuracy versus the number of Gaussian computations per sample. We can observe that the proposed approach performs best, thus proving that our good results are not SIFT-specific. If we run separately two systems, one based on SIFT features and one based on color features, and if we do a late fusion (averaging the scores of the two systems), we get a 92.8% classification accuracy. To the best of our knowledge, the highest accuracy which had been previously reported on this database was 87.3% [6].

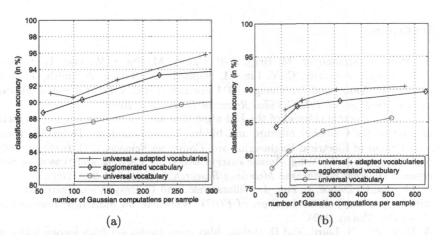

(a)   (b)

Fig. 4. Comparison of the proposed approach (universal + adapted vocabularies) with the two baseline systems (universal vocabulary and agglomerated vocabulary) on (a) the LAVA7 database and (b) the Wang database

6   Conclusion

We proposed a novel and practical approach to GVC based on a universal vocabulary, which describes the content of all the considered classes of images, and class vocabularies obtained from the universal vocabulary using class-specific data and MAP adaptation. An image is characterized by a set of histograms - one per class - where each histogram describes whether the image content is best modeled by the universal vocabulary or the corresponding class vocabulary. It was shown experimentally on three very different databases that this novel representation outperforms those approaches which characterize an image with a single histogram.

Note that, although less emphasis has been put on the reduction of the memory requirements, a simple approach could be used, if necessary, to reduce the number of Gaussians to store for each adapted vocabulary. As there exists a correspondence between the Gaussians in the universal and adapted vocabularies, one could save only those Gaussians which have significantly changed in the adapted vocabularies. This can be measured using various metrics such as the divergence, the Bhattacharya distance or the Gaussian overlap.

Also, although we have only considered a flat hierarchy of classes in this work, the proposed framework would be particularly suited to a hierarchical organization where the vocabularies of classes at a given level of the hierarchy would be adapted from their parent vocabularies.

Acknowledgments

This work was partially supported by the European project IST-2001-34405 LAVA (http://www.l-a-v-a.org) and the European project FP6-IST-511689 RevealThis (http://sifnos.ilsp.gr/RevealThis).

References

1. A. Amir, J. Argillander, M. Berg, S.-F. Chang, M. Franz, W. Hsu, G. Iyengar, J. Kender, L. Kennedy, C.-Y. Lin, M. Naphade, A. Natsev, J. Smith, J. Tesic, G. Wu, R. Yang, and D. Zhang. IBM research TRECVID-2004 video retrieval system. In *Proc. of TREC Video Retrieval Evaluation*, 2004.
2. J. Bilmes. A gentle tutorial of the EM algorithm and its application to parameter estimation for Gaussian mixture and hidden Markov models. Technical report, Department of Electrical Engineering and Computer Science, U.C. Berkeley, 1998.
3. Y. Chen, and J. Z. Wang. Image categorization by learning and reasoning with regions. *Journal of Machine Mearning Research*, 5(2004):913–939, 2004.
4. G. Csurka, C. Dance, L. Fan, J. Willamowski, and C. Bray. Visual categorization with bags of keypoints. In *Proc. of ECCV Workshop on Statistical Learning for Computer Vision*, 2004.
5. A. Dempster, N. Laird, and D. Rubin. Maximum likelihood from incomplete data via the EM algorithm. *Journal of the Royal Statistical Society*, 39(1):1–38, 1977.
6. T. Deselaers, D. Keysers, and H. Ney. Classification error rate for quantitative evaluation of content-based image retrieval systems. In *Proc. of ICPR*, 2004.

7. J. Farquhar, S. Szedmak, H. Meng, and J. Shawe-Taylor. Improving "bag-of-keypoints" image categorisation. Technical report, University of Southampton, 2005.
8. J.-L. Gauvain and C.-H. Lee. Maximum a posteriori estimation for multivariate Gaussian mixture observations of Markov chains. *IEEE Trans. on Speech and Audio Processing*, 2(2):291–298, Apr 1994.
9. W. H. Hsu and S.-F. Chang. Visual cue cluster construction via information bottleneck principle and kernel density estimation. In *Proc. of CIVR*, 2005.
10. T. Leung and J. Malik. Recognizing surfaces using three-dimensional textons. In *Proc. of ICCV*, 1999.
11. D. G. Lowe. Distinctive image features from scale-invariant keypoints. *Int. Journal of Computer Vision*, 60(2):91–110, 2004.
12. D. Reynolds, T. Quatieri, and R. Dunn. Speaker verification using adapted Gaussian mixture models. *Digital Signal Processing*, 10:19–41, 2000.
13. G. Salton and M. McGill. *Introduction to Modern Information Retrieval*. McGraw-Hill, 1983.
14. J. S. Sivic and A. Zisserman. Video google: A text retrieval approach to object matching in videos. In *Proc. of ICCV*, volume 2, pages 1470–1477, 2003.
15. M. Varma and A. Zisserman. A statistical approach to texture classification from single images. *Int. Journal of Computer Vision*, 62(1–2):61–81, 2005.
16. K. Winn, A. Criminisi, and T. Minka. Object categorization by learned visual dictionary. In *Proc. of ICCV*, 2005.
17. J. Zhang, M. Marszalek, S. Lazebnik, and C. Schmid. Local features and kernels for classification of texture and object categories: an in-depth study. INRIA, Research report 5737, 2005.

Identification of Highly Similar 3D Objects
Using Model Saliency

Bogdan C. Matei, Harpreet S. Sawhney, and Clay D. Spence

Sarnoff Corporation, 201 Washington Road, Princeton, NJ, USA

Abstract. We present a novel approach for identifying 3D objects from a database of models, highly similar in shape, using range data acquired in unconstrained settings from a limited number of viewing directions. We are addressing also the challenging case of identifying targets not present in the database. The method is based on learning offline *saliency* tests for each object in the database, by maximizing an objective measure of discriminability with respect to other similar models. Our notion of *model saliency* differs from traditionally used structural saliency that characterizes weakly the uniqueness of a region by the amount of 3D texture available, by directly linking discriminability with the Bhattacharyya distance between the distribution of errors between the target and its corresponding ground truth, respectively other similar models. Our approach was evaluated on thousands of queries obtained by different sensors and acquired in various operating conditions and using a database of hundreds of models. The results presented show a significant improvement in the recognition performance when using saliency compared to global point-to-point mismatch errors, traditionally used in matching and verification algorithms.

1 Introduction

In this paper we present a new approach for 3D object identification using 3D range data acquired by a laser scanner in unconstrained scenarios. We have assumed that the rough object category of the target is known using a feature-based classifier (indexer) which returns a list of possible candidate models, which are subsequently matched by minimizing the misalignment with the target. We illustrate our technique on *vehicle identification*, a very difficult task due to the high degree of similarity existing within classes of models such as sedans, vans or SUVs. In Figure 1 we have illustrated real 3D data overlapped onto its corresponding model (Toyota Tercel). Note the discrepancies between the data and the model and also the large degree of similarity between two models in the database which differ mostly only in the front and back regions.

The discriminability of global error measures, traditionally used in 3D object identification, is reduced by the high degree of similarity between models in the database, and operating conditions such as sensor noise, nearby clutter (for example, interior points and ground plane), incorrectly modeled or estimated articulations of moving parts, resulting in the decrease of the recognition rates. The method proposed in this paper addresses this problem and relies on learning *saliency tests*, by maximizing an objective measure of discriminability between a model and other models which are very similar in shape at a global scale, given a specific 3D range sensor and operating conditions.

A. Leonardis, H. Bischof, and A. Pinz (Eds.): ECCV 2006, Part IV, LNCS 3954, pp. 476–489, 2006.

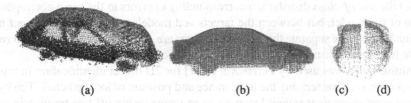

Fig. 1. (a) Overlap between the scene and its corresponding *Toyota Tercel* model. Note the significant difference in terms of nearby clutter (interiors ground plane, blooming effects (see the right front side of the vehicle), missing data in transparent regions corresponding to windows; (b) Overlap between the Toyota model (dark gray) and another close model (BMW, shown in light gray) after alignment; (c) Detail of the back; (d) Detail of the front.

During 3D object identification, the saliency tests associated with a model are verified and used in deciding whether to accept or reject that model.

The idea of using saliency to verify the identity of an object can be traced back to research done in cognitive psychology by Neisser [16] in modeling early vision in humans using *visual attention*. Neisser argued that recognition is done in *pre-attentive* and *attentive* stages. In the pre-attentive stage the visual system focuses the attention on salient features followed by a more detailed analysis in the attentive stage.

In general, the saliency of a feature is mostly understood as being related to its uniqueness [14]: the more frequent a feature is, the less salient it will be. For example, regions of an object having multiple local orientations are likely to be more distinctive in recognizing an object compared with planar regions, since all planar regions look alike. Lee et al. [15] recently proposed the *mesh saliency* as a measure derived from low-level human vision cues of regional importance for graphics meshes. Their saliency was defined with respect to structural properties of a surface by using Gaussian-weighted mean curvatures.

In feature-based object recognition we can employ the same concept to compute rotationally invariant surface descriptors such as spin-images [13] at those locations in an object in which the local 3D scatter is full rank. By reducing the impact of descriptors which are not distinctive and are likely shared amongst many models, the recognition performance can be improved. A main shortcoming of structural saliency is that it is not related directly to the discriminability of a particular object with respect to other objects. It only quantifies only our intuition that planar regions are not useful for recognizing generic objects.

In [5] the *relevance* of a feature is defined with respect to the distribution of features belonging to different classes within a region of the feature space. By using the relevance of feature in a k-nearest neighbor (NN) classifier, the authors in [5] showed improved classification performance. A similar concept was used in the *discriminant adaptive nearest neighbor* rule to adapt the metric in nearest neighbor classifiers [10].

We propose an alternative notion of *model saliency* which relates directly to maximizing the discriminability of a model with respect to other similar models based on computing the distance between two distributions: (i) the *in-class* distribution, corresponding to some specified *error measure* between targets of a given type and the corresponding ground truth model, computed within a certain support region of the model and (ii) the *out-of-class* distribution corresponding to errors in the same corresponding region of the model, but between the targets and models *other than the ground truth*. Obviously, the more separate the two distributions are, the more useful the salient region will be in separating an object from other possibly confusing candidates.

A similar idea was used by Ferencz et al. [7] for 2D object identification in training *hyper-features*, characterizing the appearance and position of local patches. The hyper-features were selected at salient locations in an image, using off-line training in which the mutual information between two distributions *self* and *others* was maximized. The self and other distributions were estimated using Gamma distributions using by-patches of positive and negative examples. However, unlike [7] in our 3D object identification application we are addressing different challenges: noisy 3D measurements affected by artifacts, large number of 3D models in the database very similar in shape, or nearby clutter.

In Section 2 we present a method for learning saliency tests for every model in the database. The saliency tests are verified using a battery of statistical relevance tests as discussed in Section 3. In Section 4 the proposed model saliency based 3D object identification method is evaluated on thousands of queries using a database of one hundred models. Conclusions are presented in Section 5.

2 Model Saliency

In this Section we describe the process of learning saliency tests by maximizing the discriminability of a model with respect to a number of similar models available from a database. We have employed only point cloud objects for the queries and the models in the database. The range sensors produce 3D point clouds and using surface reconstruction algorithms [11] to extract a mesh representation can be slow in practice and can result in additional artifacts due to noise and significant drop-outs in the data occurring in transparent and reflective regions. Models are also specified as point clouds rendered from faceted articulated models using a realistic range sensor simulator in order to ensure a good correspondence with the data acquired in real operating conditions in terms of resolution and relative pose between the sensor and the objects viewed.

2.1 Model Similarity Extraction

In computing saliency for a particular object, we are interested in determining what other models are similar in shape at a global scale and may be confused after the indexing and matching stages. The first step in extracting saliency for a model m_i, $i = 1, \ldots, M$, where M is the total number of models in the database, is to determine which models m_j, $j \neq i$ are similar to m_i.

Similarity measures between models were used by Huber et al. [12] for grouping objects into classes for 3D part-based classification. However, their measures were *relative*, which means that the similarity between two models is dependent on how many models are present in the database, and were computed using spin-images to eliminate small differences and extract only the commonalities between similar objects at a gross scale. In our object identification application we seek the opposite goal of finding distinctive elements between models in the database.

We define an *absolute* similarity measure $\xi(m_i, m_j) \in [0, 1]$ where $\xi(m_i, m_j) = 0$ means complete dissimilarity and $\xi(m_i, m_j) = 1$ denotes indistinguishable models. One of the most used surface dissimilarity measures is the average square error between the 3D point clouds, or the *point-to-point* distance [17].

Let $z_k^{m_i} \in \mathbb{R}^3$, $k = 1 \ldots, N_{m_i}$ denote the 3D data from model m_i and similarly, $z_l^{m_j} \in \mathbb{R}^3$, $l = 1 \ldots, N_{m_j}$ for model m_j. Thus the point-to-point (square) distance between model m_i and m_j is

$$D_0^2(m_i, m_j) = \frac{1}{N_{m_i}} \sum_{k=1}^{N_{m_i}} \| z_k^{m_i} - z_{l_k}^{m_j} \|^2 \tag{1}$$

where $z_{l_k}^{m_j}$ is the closest point from model m_j to $z_k^{m_i}$.

Models are aligned pairwise using the Iterated Closest Point algorithm (ICP) [2][9] by minimizing (1). The pose $\Pi_{m_i, m_j} \in \mathbb{R}^{4 \times 4}$ which aligns the model m_i with m_j can be obtained in close form using Arun's SVD algorithm [1]. The ICP algorithm requires an initial pose estimate Π_{m_i, m_j}^{ini} which is obtained using spin image matching [13].

An improved discriminant mismatch error measure, compared to the point-to-point distance, can be obtained by taking into account the local surface orientation. Chen and Medioni proposed the use of *point-to-plane* error measures to improve the convergence of the ICP algorithm [3]. We have employed the following *plane-to-plane* distance measure

$$D_1^2(m_i, m_j) = \frac{1}{N_{m_i}} \sum_{k=1}^{N_{m_i}} \min_{l=1,\ldots,N_{m_j}} \left(\frac{\| z_k^{m_i} - z_l^{m_j} \|^2}{\alpha_z^2} + \frac{1 - n_k^{m_i,\top} n_l^{m_j}}{\alpha_n^2} \right) \tag{2}$$

where $n_k^{m_i}$, $\| n_k^{m_i} \| = 1$ is the normal associated with the 3D point $z_k^{m_i}$ and α_z^2, α_n^2 are normalizing factors. The measure (2) is related to the Sobolev norms employing derivatives of a function up to some order K which are modern tools in the theory of differential equations and the study of chaos. Higher order terms such as curvature can be added to (2), by adding the distance between surface descriptors for the two surfaces such as the splash descriptor [3], or the spin-image which account for curvature by integration, and not differentiation which is very sensitive for noisy data. The resulting mismatch errors D_u, $u > 1$ can be used similarly to D_0, D_1 in our saliency computational framework.

Using the distances (1), (2) we can define a symmetric similarity measure

$$\xi_u(m_i, m_j) = \exp\left(-\frac{D_u^2(m_i, m_j) + D_u^2(m_j, m_i)}{\alpha_u^2} \right), \quad 0 \leq \xi_u(m_i, m_j) \leq 1 \tag{3}$$

where α_u^2 is a suitable normalizing factor and $u = 0, 1$. An example of the similarity scores ξ_0 is shown in Figure 2 for a Toyota Tercel model. Note the decrease in similarity scores which agrees also to our subjective notion of similarity. The normalizing factor α_u^2 is chosen depending on how much mismatches between models are penalized.

In computing $\xi(m_i, m_j)$ using (3) we need to align pairwise all the models from the database. The total number of required pairwise alignments is $M(M - 1)$, since $\Pi_{m_i, m_j} \neq \Pi_{m_j, m_i}^{-1}$.

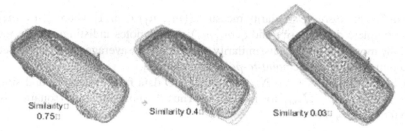

Fig. 2. Example of *absolute* similarity scores obtained using (3) for a Toyota Tercel against: BMW 318, Mazda 626, respectively, Nissan Frontier

2.2 Definition of Model Saliency

For each model m_i we determine the class of similar models $\Gamma_i = \{m_{j_1}, m_{j_2}, \ldots, \}$ such that $\xi_u(m_i, m_{j_k}) > \tau$. In our experiments we have employed $\tau = 0.7$ and $u = 0$ which provided a good balance between how many models are returned and the computational complexity involved. We have also limited the total number of models in Γ_i to $\nu_{max} = 20$ and guaranteed that at least $\nu_{min} = 2$ models are present, even if their similarity is smaller than τ.

Mathematically, we can express the learning of salient regions by defining a classification problem with two classes: self and others. The classifier is specified by: (i) a probability (likelihood) score derived from the surface dissimilarity measure D_u used; (ii) a support region x from the model, specified as a spherical region or oriented bounding box over which the likelihood is computed. According to Bayes rule a query q will be assigned to model m_i, iff $p(q \in m_i \mid Z, x, D_u) \geq p(q \notin m_i \mid Z, x, D_u)$, where Z is the available data from one single query q, x is a given region from model m_i and D_u is the surface dissimilarity measure used.

Assuming that the *a priori* probability of occurrence of a model $p(m_i)$ is uniform, the Bayes rule can be written in terms of the likelihood ratio

$$E[\Lambda(Z, x, D_u)] = E\left[\frac{p(Z \mid q \in m_i, x, D_u)}{p(Z \mid q \notin m_i, x, D_u)}\right] = \int \frac{p(Z \mid q \in m_i, x, D_u)}{p(Z \mid q \notin m_i, x, D_u)} p(Z) dZ \quad (4)$$

The larger the expected likelihood in (4), the better the region x and D_u will be in discriminating m_i from the set of models in Γ_i. We propose to define the saliency of a region using the Bhattacharyya coefficient, which has attractive metric properties, offers values between zero and one [4] and is defined for two probability distributions $p_1(y)$ and $p_2(y)$ as

$$BC(p_1(y), p_2(y)) = \int \sqrt{p_1(y) \, p_2(y)} dy \quad (5)$$

The Bhattacharyya coefficient is equal to one for two identical probabilities and is zero for disjoint probabilities. Thus, the saliency of a region x using surface dissimilarity measure D_u can be defined as

$$\beta(x, D_u) = 1 - \int \sqrt{p(Z \mid q \in m_i, x, D_u) p(Z \mid q \notin m_i, x, D_u)} dZ \quad (6)$$

Evaluating (6) requires the estimation of the *in-class* distribution $p(Z \mid q \in m_i, x, D_u)$ and the *out-of-class* distribution $p(Z \mid q \notin m_i, x, D_u)$. Standard density estimation based on sampling and kernel smoothing [8] can be employed to estimate a discretized version of (6)

$$\hat{\beta}(x, D_u) = 1 - \sum_{h=1}^{N_h} \sqrt{\hat{p}_h(Z \mid q \in m_i, x, D_u)\hat{p}_h(Z \mid q \notin m_i, x, D_u)} \qquad (7)$$

where N_h is the number of histogram bins used. Estimating $\hat{p}_h(Z \mid q \in m_i, x, D_u)$ and $\hat{p}_h(Z \mid q \in m_i, x, D_u)$ requires the availability of large amounts of training data Z for every model in the database. However, it is unrealistic that we can have sufficient examples belonging to each of the models from the database.

We propose to use *bootstrap* to generate new queries q^* by resampling from the available data. Bootstrap is a modern rigorous statistical tool which was developed by Efron [6] to numerically derive valid statistical measures about an estimate by resampling data solely from one input.

2.3   Learning Saliency Tests

Let Q denote the set of available training data for which we have available ground truth information. We align each query $q \in Q$ to its corresponding model m_i to find the pose Π_{q,m_i}, using the ICP algorithm which is initialized using matching of spin-images [13]. After the alignment, we compute the residuals $\epsilon_k^q = z_k^q - z_{l_k}^{m_i}$ between each query point z_k^q and its closest point $z_{l_k}^{m_i}$. The residuals $\zeta^q = \{\epsilon_k^q\}$ are stored together with the viewing direction V^q between the center of the model m_i and the 3D location of the range sensor under which the query q was acquired. In our 3D data, the information about the position of the sensor with respect to the target is known from GPS, while the distance from the sensor to the target is in general much larger compared to the target dimensions. Therefore, the viewing direction with respect to the model coordinate system of m_i can be found using the alignment Π_{q,m_i}.

The vehicle models are assumed to be aligned such that their back to front axis of symmetry is aligned to X axis and the vertical direction is parallel with the Z axis. The point cloud models are rendered from typically $N_v = 8$ views sampled at $45°$ azimuth angles and at an elevation angle which is constant and matches the expected operating conditions under which the 3D data is acquired. For each query q we store also the index $v^q = 1, \ldots N_v$ corresponding to the minimum angle between V_v and V^q. Let the residuals be $\Omega = \{(\zeta^q, v^q), q \in Q\}$. The residual set Ω is organized such that for every view index $v = 1, \ldots, N_v$ we have access to residuals ϵ_k^q, from queries q acquired from view closest to V_v, $\Omega = \{\Omega_v, v = 1, \ldots, N_v\}$.

The algorithm for computing the saliency is presented in the following:

1. Input is a model m_i for which we need to compute saliency together with the corresponding class of similar models $m_j \in \Gamma_i$, a 3D region x belonging to model m_i and an error measure D_u. We specify a region x as a cube centered at a point $c \in \mathbb{R}^3$ with side $2R$, though. We have used $R = 0.2$ m and $R = 0.5$ m to capture local and semi-local variation. Warp all the point clouds $m_j \in \Gamma_i$ towards m_i using

the pose determined off-line $\Pi(m_j, m_i)$. Let $m_{j(i)}$, be the warped model m_j in the coordinate system of m_i.

2. Select a random view $v^* = 1, \ldots, N_v$ and let $z^{m_i}_{k,v^*}$, $k = 1, \ldots, N_{m_i,v^*}$, where N_{m_i,v^*}, denote the 3D noise-free model points belonging to view v^*. We assume that the point cloud model m_i is obtained by concatenating all the views, hence $N_{m_i} = \sum_{v=1}^{N_v} N_{m_i,v}$

3. Sample with replacement from Ω_{v_b} residuals ϵ_k^* and generate bootstrapped measurements

$$z^{m_i*}_{k,v} = z^{m_i}_{k,v} + \epsilon_k^* \tag{8}$$

4. Create a new query q^* by using one, or by concatenating several bootstrapped views. Optionally, simulate other effects such as occlusions and artifacts in the data by randomly removing data. Align the query q^* to all the models $m_i, m_{j(i)} \in \Gamma_i$ to obtain the alignment parameters $\Pi_{q^*,m_i}, \Pi_{q^*,m_{j(i)}}$.

5. Compute the *in-class* error statistics $D_u(q^*, m_i, x)$ and the *out-of-class* error statistics $D_u(q^*, m_{j(i)}, x)$, where $D_u(q^*, m_k, x)$, as defined in (1), or (2) are restricted such that the summation is done only within region x from model m_i. Add the value $D_u(q^*, m_i, x)$ into the *in-class* histogram $\mathcal{H}_{in}(x)$ and the values $D_u(q^*, m_{j(i)})$ into the *out-of-class* histogram $\mathcal{H}_{out}(x)$. It is assumed that both the histograms have the same number of bins N_h and the same bin size.

6. Go to Step 2 until the number of samples required for computing $\mathcal{H}_{in}(x)$ and $\mathcal{H}_{out}(x)$ is sufficient.

7. Normalize and smooth each of the two histograms to eliminate the artifacts. Let $\hat{p}_{in,h}$, and $\hat{p}_{out,h}$ denote bin $h = 1, \ldots, N_h$ of the in-class and out-of-class histograms. The saliency of region x under the error statistic D_u (7) can be finally expressed as

$$\beta(x, D_u) = 1 - \sum_{h=1}^{N_h} \sqrt{\hat{p}_{in,h}\hat{p}_{out,h}} \tag{9}$$

We compute saliency measures (9) at dense locations c_k around the model m_i for the error measures D_u, $u = 0, 1$. Prior information about regions of a model which are prone to be affected by clutter (ex. cargo region) and artifacts in the data (dispersion of the data in highly reflective regions of a model such as headlights), are manually specified as oriented cuboids and used to eliminate candidate locations c_k at which saliency is calculated.

Most of the objects present in the database are symmetric with an axis of symmetry parallel with X direction and passing through the middle of the vehicles. The saliency values $\beta(x_k, D_u)$ are smoothed with a 3D smoothing kernel and symmetry is enforced by averaging smoothed saliency values at corresponding reflected locations c_k.

For computational efficiency we first sort the locations c_k were saliency was computed, in decreasing order of the saliency measure, separately for each distinct error measure employed. We retain only a certain fraction η of the most salient locations, while ensuring that enough regions of the model are represented, as illustrated in Figure 3. For each individual saliency test $T(m_i, x, D_u, \beta)$ we specify among others: model m_i for which the test was computed (including part information), 3D spherical region $x = (c, R)$, surface dissimilarity error measure D_u, saliency value β.

Saliency
Smoothed and
Symmetrized

Saliency
sampled

Fig. 3. Example of saliency computed for an *Acura Integra* model using point-to-point error measures D_0. The saliency is color coded from blue to red. Dark blue regions correspond to saliency close to zero, while red signifies highly salient regions with saliency close to one. The saliency was not computed in transparent regions (windows) as seen by the dark blue in the top row. Note that the saliency is symmetric and varies smoothly. In the bottom row we show the saliency after thresholding. Note that we retain only those locations from the front and back, which are most distinctive in identifying this specific model. These locations correspond to structural differences in the 3D shape which have the most power in separating the *Acura Integra* model from its own list of similar models in the database.

3   Verification of Saliency Tests

We employ next the saliency tests learned off-line for each of the models in the database to verify the identity of a target. We assume that an indexer and matcher modules are providing for each target a list of possible candidates containing with high probability the correct model together with articulation parameters such that the target is aligned to each model. The candidates are sorted according to global surface mismatch point-to-point surface mismatch errors minimized using a variant of the ICP algorithm which handles articulations.

The object identification module (verifier) analyzes sequentially each of the models returned by the matcher and *verifies* the corresponding saliency tests which were found to be most discriminating during learning. The first step in verifying each model is to preprocess the query and the model by:

1. Eliminating outliers in the scene. We mark as outliers all the query measurements which have a distance larger than $\rho = 2.5\sigma_z$, where σ_z is the standard deviation of the noise. For the range sensors employed $\sigma_z \approx 8$ cm, thus $\rho = 20$ cm.
2. Enforcing visibility constraints and performing *model culling* to eliminate 3D model points from regions which are self occluded and have no query points in vicinity.
3. Applying model annotations to mark query measurements as possible clutter or artifacts. Interior unmodeled clutter which are acquired due to transparency of windows can be eliminated by computing model interiors using ray-tracing. The model interior samples are used to mark the query measurements lying in the same corresponding voxels. For compact storage we extract only interior locations within 20 cm from the surface.

At the end of this preprocessing stage, query data is labeled as either: outliers, clutter/artifacts, interiors, or inliers. Model points are labeled as occluded or visible.

By verifying a saliency test $T(m_i, x, D_u, \beta)$, we make a decision to either: (i) discard the test as unreliable, occurring when there is not enough query data in the

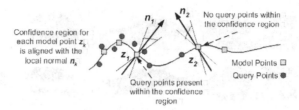

Fig. 4. The coverage of a saliency test is computed as the ratio between the number of models that are explained by data. For each model point He search for query measurements in regions aligned with the local surface normal.

corresponding 3D region x of the test; (ii) accept the test; (iii) reject the test. For (i) we determine whether a test can be evaluated by computing the coverage of the test, expressed as the ratio of the model points within x that can be explained by query measurements, with respect to the total number of model points in x, assuming relatively uniform sampling of the surfaces, as shown in Figure 4. We have employed a confidence threshold equal to 0.75 which was experimentally found to balance the fraction of saliency tests that are discarded, while ensuring an acceptance/rejection of a test to be taken with sufficient measurements present.

Assuming that a saliency test $T(m_i, x, D_u, \beta)$ can be reliably evaluated, we determine next whether to accept or reject it by applying several statistical relevance tests, such as likelihood ratio and χ^2 tests [18]. We apply the prescribed error measure D_u and compute the dissimilarity score $y_{m_i}^2 \triangleq D_u^2(q, m_i, x)$ between query q and model m_i within region x of m_i. The likelihood ratio of the test T is rejected when

$$\Lambda(T) = \frac{p_{in}(y_{m_i}|q \in m_i)}{p_{out}(y_{m_i}|q \notin m_i)} < \delta \tag{10}$$

where $p_{in}(y_{m_i}|q \in m_i)$ is the in-class probability (accept) and $p_{out}(y_{m_i}|q \notin m_i)$ is the out-of-class probability (reject) and δ is a threshold chosen depending on how stringent we are in rejecting an individual test. The in-class $p_{in}(y_{m_i}|q \in m_i)$ and out-of-class $p_{out}(y_{m_i}|q \notin m_i)$ probabilities were computed during off-line training. We have used $\delta = 1.1$ to allow a small tolerance to errors in data.

We employ the χ^2 test in addition to the likelihood test (10) under which the test T rejected iff

$$\frac{y_{m_i}^2}{\mu_{y_{m_i}}^2} \geq \frac{\chi_{p,1-\gamma}^2}{p}, \tag{11}$$

where p is the number of degrees of freedom of y^2, $\mu_{y_{m_i}}^2$ is the expected value of the residuals $y_{m_i}^2$, which is estimated from the distribution of residuals p_{in}, and $\chi_{p,1-\gamma}^2$ is the $1-\gamma$ quantile of a χ^2 distribution with p degrees of freedom. The number of degrees of freedom depends on the error measure used, for instance $p = 3$ for D_0, and $p = 5$ for D_1. Thus, an individual saliency test T_s is accepted when both (10) and (11) are obeyed, otherwise the test is rejected.

The saliency tests are grouped into semi-local regions B to be more robust to erroneous rejections of individual tests due to unaccounted outliers, wrong articulation estimates by the matcher. In combining the decision from several saliency tests we should note that: (i) rejecting a test is an indication that query does not belong to the corresponding model, no matter how salient a test is; (ii) accepting of a test should be weighted by how much *a priori* salient a test is.

We estimate the probability of rejecting a model given the tests in region B $p(q \notin m_i | B)$ as the ratio between the number of failed tests $N_{failed}(B)$ with respect to the number of tests which were measured $N_{measured}(B)$. We reject a region if $p(q \notin m_i | B) > 0.2$. Similarly to (10) we compute a saliency weighted log-likelihood ratio

$$\log(\Lambda(B)) = \frac{\sum_s \beta_s \log(\Lambda(T_s))}{\sum_s \beta_s} \tag{12}$$

where $0 \leq \beta_s \leq 1$ is the saliency of a test T_s. We reject the model hypothesis m_i if the $\Lambda(B) < \delta_1, \delta_1 < \delta$. The χ^2 (11) over a region B will reject a model iff

$$\frac{\sum_s \frac{y_{s,m_i}^2 \beta_s}{\mu_{y_s,m_i}^2}}{\sum_s \beta_s} > \frac{\chi_{p',1-\gamma}^2}{p'}, \quad p' = \sum_s p_s, \quad T_s \in B \text{ and } T_s \text{ accepted} \tag{13}$$

where p_s is the number of degrees of freedom of squared residuals y_{s,m_i}^2.

Note that in (12) and (13) we used only tests T_s which were accepted in order to eliminate the effect of tests failing badly locally due to unaccounted clutter or wrong pose estimation. Thus, we allow some of the saliency tests to pass with less stringent conditions, however at region level after weighting by the saliency we require more stringent conditions in order to accept it.

4   Experimental Results

We have evaluated the saliency based 3D object identification method proposed on a very challenging database of vehicle objects which are characterized by a high degree of similarity between their 3D shapes, such as sedans, vans or SUVs. In the experiments reported we have employed a database of 100 point-cloud models, rendered from faceted models of mostly civilian and military vehicles. Models have articulation information about moving parts (doors, trunks, hoods,etc.), information about transparent regions (ex. windows). For testing, we employed laser scanned data (LIDAR) acquired using a helicopter flying over an area of interest containing vehicles, clutter.

The registered data is segmented into volumes of interests (VOI) by a *target detection* module which also eliminates ground and vegetation clutter. The remaining 3D data (query) is passed onto the indexer and matcher modules which provide the 3D object identification with a list of putative candidates, together with articulation parameters such that the target and each point cloud model are coregistered. Examples of queries employed in our experiments are given in Figure 5. Note the fact that the target is viewed only from a limited set of viewpoints, covering typically three sides.

The 3D object identification module processes sequentially each candidate model returned by the indexer/matcher modules and *verifies* the salient tests learned offline and grouped within semi-local regions to increase the robustness to inaccuracies in

Fig. 5. Examples of queries employed for testing using *Collection I, II* data collections

alignment, outliers and unaccounted clutter. Each region is classified as accepted or rejected using a battery of statistical tests as discussed in Section 3. In general, we employ six to ten regions depending on the size of an object, each region containing tens of individual saliency tests. Failure of F regions will result in rejecting a candidate model. The parameter F is selected depending on the amount of false matches tolerated. In our experiments we have used $F = 2$. The experiments were run on a 2 GHz Pentium Mobile laptop. Each model can be verified in one to two seconds, including the overhead of loading and warping the models.

Our object recognition system was evaluated on thousands of queries using various range sensors and under different operating conditions (aerial, ground-based sensor). The queries were divided into training and testing data. The training data was employed for extracting saliency, as discussed in Section 2.3.

The testing data used for the evaluation results shown next comes from two data collections denoted as *Collection I* and *Collection II*. The distribution of queries among classes is shown in Table 2. Though we do not have precise calibrated information about the actual sensor noise, we have estimated that the standard deviation of the noise to be around 3" (or roughly 8 cm), largely along the viewing direction.

When the ground truth model corresponding to a query is present in the database, then the saliency based identification module should output only the correct model. We consider a recognition error the case in which the correct model is not returned, due to being either missed by the indexer and matcher modules, or because it is rejected after the verification of the prescribed saliency tests. If the ground truth model is not present in the database, then ideally no models should be returned.

Table 1. Distribution of queries used for testing

Collection I			Collection II		
Class	Number Queries	Number Queries with Model In Database	Class	Number Queries	Number Queries with Model in Database
Sedan	313	276	Sedan	260	232
Pick up	24	20	Pick up	20	20
Van	44	40	Van	28	20
SUV	40	20	SUV	32	12
Military	92	48	Military	76	32
Other	35	24	Other	32	20
Total	548	428	Total	448	336

The 3D object identification module will output generally more than one model, depending on the discriminability of a model, sensor noise, or whether distinctive features of a model were present in the query data. For example, military models tend to be quite distinct from each other, so wrong models are rarely accepted, while sedans tend to be similar to many other sedan models. The distribution of queries from the two data collections used is shown in Table 1.

A query is considered correctly recognized if: (i) the correct model, if any, is present in the list of identified objects; (ii) there are no models returned as recognized instances, which a human can judge as dissimilar with the target, or in other words it is hard for a human to distinguish between these models, given the quality of the data. Using the previous two criteria, the final recognition performance on the two data collections mentioned was found to be 96.5%.

In Table 2 we have displayed the average number of recognized models returned by the matcher and after saliency based verification. Note the significant reduction in the number of models returned after saliency is employed. The average lengths less than one in Table 2 can be easily understood since in the case of queries with no corresponding model in the database, ideally there shouldn't be any models returned, while for queries with models in the database, there may be recognition failures in recognizing the ground truth model.

The relatively large number of models returned, in the case of sedans for example, is due to the very challenging data available and to the high degree of similarity between models, as illustrated in Figure 6. For more discriminating models and better coverage, the list of identified models is much shorter, as shown in Figure 7. Assuming better data, with smaller noise, the discriminability of the saliency tests can be improved and thus smaller number of identified models.

Table 2. Average number of candidate models returned after indexer/matcher and after performing saliency based verification. (a) Using all queries. (b) Using queries that do not have a corresponding model in the database; (c) Using queries that have a corresponding model in database.

(a)

Collection Class	Collection I		Collection II	
	Matcher	Saliency Ident	Matcher	Saliency Ident
Sedan	24.6	12.5	19.2	10.2
Pick up	3.7	1.8	2.6	1.8
Van	8.7	4.1	5.5	3.4
SUV	4.6	1.8	3.3	2.6
Military	1.9	0.6	2.8	0.5
Other	0.9	0.7	0.8	0.5
Overall	15.6	7.8	12.4	6.5

(b)

Collection Class	Collection I		Collection II	
	Matcher	Saliency Ident	Matcher	Saliency Ident
Sedan	23.3	8.6	18.9	5.4
Pick up	5.8	1.8	-	-
Van	14	4.2	4.8	2.5
SUV	7.3	2.4	4.3	3.2
Military	3	0.2	4.1	0.3
Other	0.4	0.2	0.8	0.2
Overall	10.2	3.4	7.5	2.3

(c)

Collection Class	Collection I		Collection II	
	Matcher	Saliency Ident	Matcher	Saliency Ident
Sedan	24.8	13	19.2	10.8
Pick up	3.3	1.8	2.6	1.8
Van	8.1	4	5.8	3.7
SUV	1.9	1.2	1.7	1.4
Military	0.9	0.9	1	0.8
Other	1.2	0.9	0.8	0.8
Overall	17.2	9	14	8

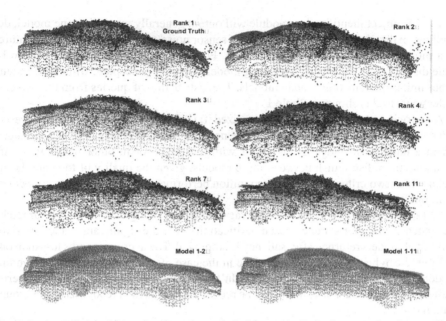

Fig. 6. Lack of distinguishing details, noise and significant similarity between the shapes of vehicles result in 11 identified models, from a total number of 26 models returned by the matcher. Query is a Pontiac GrandAm 1999. The models returned are: Dodge Avenger 1995 (rank 2), Ford Probe 1993 (rank 3), Chevy Malibu 1997 (rank 4), Buick Regal 1998 (rank 7) , Plymouth Neon 2000 (rank 11). Bottom row: comparison between the models: ground truth is plotted in dark gray and the corresponding model in light gray.

Fig. 7. Better coverage and less similarity between models result in only one identified model using saliency, compared to 15 models returned as possible candidates by the matcher. Query is Geo Metro 1990 plotted in red. Note the dissimilarity in the front between the Geo Metro 1990 (dark gray) and a Honda Civic 1990 (light gray) which is the rejected model ranked second using global scores (rightmost figure).

5   Conclusions

We have presented a novel 3D object identification approach based on learning salient features capable of discriminating between 3D objects highly similar in shape. The approach proposed shows a significant improvement in the ability of reducing the amount of identified objects, compared to using global error measures such as point-to-point distances, traditionally employed for object identification. The performance of the system was assessed using real LIDAR data on thousands of queries. We have addressed also the very challenging scenario of identifying objects which are not present in the database.

References

1. K. Arun, T. Huang, and S. Blostein, "Least-squares fitting of two 3D point sets," *PAMI*, vol. 9, pp. 698–700, 1987.
2. P. Besl and N. McKay, "A method for registration of 3d shapes," *PAMI*, vol. 18, pp. 540–547, 1992.
3. Y. Chen and G. Medioni, "Object modeling by registration of multiple range images," *IVC*, pp. 145–155, 1992.
4. D. Comaniciu, R. Visvanath, and P. Meer, "Kernel-based object tracking," *PAMI*, vol. 25, no. 5, pp. 564–577, 2003.
5. C. Domeniconi, J. Peng, and D. Gunopulos, "ocally adaptive metric nearest neighbor classification," *PAMI*, vol. 24, no. 9, pp. 1281–1285, 2002.
6. B. Efron and R. Tibshirani, *An Introduction to the Bootstrap*. Chapman & Hall, New York, 1993.
7. A. Ferencz, E. G. Learned-Miller, and J. Malik, "Learning hyper-features for visual identification," in *NIPS*, 2004.
8. K. Fukunaga, *Introduction to Statistical Pattern Recognition*. Academic Press, second edition edition, 1990.
9. N. Gelfand, L. Ikemoto, S. Rusinkiewicz, and M. Levoy, "Geometrically stable sampling for the ICP algorithm," in *3DIM 2003*, 2003.
10. T. Hastie, R. Tibshirani, and J. Friedman, *The elements of statistical learning. Data mining inference and prediction.* Springer, 2001.
11. H. Hoppe, T. DeRose, T. Duchamp, J. McDonald, and W. Stuetzle, "Surface reconstruction from unorganized points," in *ACM SIGGRAPH*, 1992, pp. 71–78.
12. D. Huber, A. Kapuria, R. Donamukkala, and M. Hebert, "Part-based 3D object classification," in *CVPR*, volume 2, (Washington,DC), June 2004, pp. 82–89.
13. A. Johnson and M. Hebert, "Surface matching for object recognition in complex three-dimensional scenes," *IVC*, vol. 16, pp. 635–651, 1998.
14. T. Kadir and A. Zisermann, "Scale, saliency and image description," *Commun. Assoc. Comp. Mach.*, vol. 24, pp. 381–395, 1981.
15. C. H. Lee, A. Varshney, and D. W. Jacobs, "Mesh saliency," in *ACM SIGGRAPH*, 2005, pp. 659 – 666.
16. U. Neisser, "Visual search," *Scientific American*, vol. 20, no. 12, pp. 94–102, 1964.
17. S. Rusinkiewicz and M. Levoy, "Efficient variants of the icp algorithm," in *Third International Conference on 3D Digital Imaging and Modeling (3DIM 2001)*, 2001.
18. L. Wasserman, *All of statistics. A concise course in statistical inferrence.* Springer, 2003.

Sampling Strategies for Bag-of-Features Image Classification

Eric Nowak[1,2], Frédéric Jurie[1], and Bill Triggs[1]

[1] GRAVIR-CNRS-INRIA,
655 avenue de l'Europe,
Montbonnot 38330, France
{Eric.Nowak, Bill.Triggs, Frederic.Jurie}@inrialpes.fr
http://lear.inrialpes.fr
[2] Bertin Technologie, Aix en Provence, France

Abstract. Bag-of-features representations have recently become popular for content based image classification owing to their simplicity and good performance. They evolved from texton methods in texture analysis. The basic idea is to treat images as loose collections of independent patches, sampling a representative set of patches from the image, evaluating a visual descriptor vector for each patch independently, and using the resulting distribution of samples in descriptor space as a characterization of the image. The four main implementation choices are thus how to sample patches, how to describe them, how to characterize the resulting distributions and how to classify images based on the result. We concentrate on the first issue, showing experimentally that for a representative selection of commonly used test databases and for moderate to large numbers of samples, random sampling gives equal or better classifiers than the sophisticated multiscale interest operators that are in common use. Although interest operators work well for small numbers of samples, the single most important factor governing performance is the number of patches sampled from the test image and ultimately interest operators can not provide enough patches to compete. We also study the influence of other factors including codebook size and creation method, histogram normalization method and minimum scale for feature extraction.

1   Introduction

This paper studies the problem of effective representations for automatic image categorization – classifying unlabeled images based on the presence or absence of instances of particular visual classes such as cars, people, bicycles, etc. The problem is challenging because the appearance of object instances varies substantially owing to changes in pose, imaging and lighting conditions, occlusions and within-class shape variations (see fig. 2). Ideally, the representation should be flexible enough to cover a wide range of visually different classes, each with large within-category variations, while still retaining good discriminative power between the classes. Large shape variations and occlusions are problematic for

A. Leonardis, H. Bischof, and A. Pinz (Eds.): ECCV 2006, Part IV, LNCS 3954, pp. 490–503, 2006.

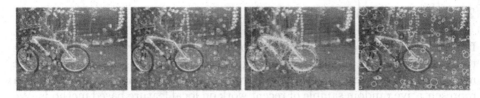

Fig. 1. Examples of multi-scale sampling methods. (1) Harris-Laplace (HL) with a large detection threshold. (2) HL with threshold zero – note that the sampling is still quite sparse. (3) Laplacian-of-Gaussian. (4) Random sampling.

rigid template based representations and their variants such as monolithic SVM detectors, but more local 'texton' or 'bag-of-features' representations based on coding local image patches independently using statistical appearance models have good resistance to occlusions and within-class shape variations. Despite their simplicity and lack of global geometry, they also turn out to be surprisingly discriminant, so they have proven to be effective tools for classifying many visual classes (e.g. [1, 2, 3], among others).

Our work is based on the bag-of-features approach. The basic idea of this is that a set of local image patches is sampled using some method (e.g. densely, randomly, using a keypoint detector) and a vector of visual descriptors is evaluated on each patch independently (e.g. SIFT descriptor, normalized pixel values). The resulting distribution of descriptors in descriptor space is then quantified in some way (e.g. by using vector quantization against a pre-specified codebook to convert it to a histogram of votes for (i.e. patches assigned to) codebook centres) and the resulting global descriptor vector is used as a characterization of the image (e.g. as feature vector on which to learn an image classification rule based on an SVM classifier). The four main implementation choices are thus how to sample patches, what visual patch descriptor to use, how to quantify the resulting descriptor space distribution, and how to classify images based on the resulting global image descriptor.

One of the main goals of this paper is to study the effects of different patch sampling strategies on image classification performance. The sampler is a critical component of any bag-of-features method. Ideally, it should focus attention on the image regions that are the most informative for classification. Recently, many authors have begun to use multiscale keypoint detectors (Laplacian of Gaussian, Förstner, Harris-affine, etc.) as samplers [4, 1, 2, 5, 6, 7, 8, 9, 10, 11], but although such detectors have proven their value in matching applications, they were not designed to find the most informative patches for image classification and there is some evidence that they do not do so [12, 13]. Perhaps surprisingly, we find that randomly sampled patches are often more discriminant than keypoint based ones, especially when many patches are sampled to get accurate classification results (see figure 1). We also analyze the effects of several other factors including codebook size and the clusterer used to build the codebook. The experiments are performed on a cross-section of commonly-used evaluation datasets to allow us to identify the most important factors for local appearance based statistical image categorization.

2 Related Work

Image classification and object recognition are well studied areas with approaches ranging from simple patch based voting to the alignment of detailed geometric models. Here, in keeping with our approach to recognition, we provide only a representative random sample of recent work on local feature based methods. We classify these into two groups, depending on whether or not they use geometric object models.

The geometric approaches represent objects as sets of parts whose positions are constrained by the model. Inter-part relationships can be modelled pairwise [4], in terms of flexible constellations or hierarchies [2, 14], by co-occurrence [15] or as rigid geometric models [8, 7]. Such global models are potentially very powerful but they tend to be computationally complex and sensitive to missed part detections. Recently, "geometry free" *bag-of-features* models based purely on characterizing the statistics of local patch appearances have received a lot of attention owing to their simplicity, robustness, and good practical performance. They evolved when texton based texture analysis models began to be applied to object recognition. The name is by analogy with the bag-of-words representations used in document analysis (e.g. [16]): image patches are the visual equivalents of individual "words" and the image is treated as an unstructured set ("bag") of these.

Leung *at al.* [3] sample the image densely, on each patch evaluating a bank of Gabor-like filters and coding the output using a vector quantization codebook. Local histograms of such 'texton' codes are used to recognize textures. Textons are also used in content based image retrieval, e.g. [17]. Lazebnik *et al.* [18] take a sparser bag-of-features approach, using SIFT descriptors over Harris-affine keypoints [9] and avoiding global quantization by comparing histograms using Earth Movers Distance [19]. Csurka *et al* [1] approach object classification using k-means-quantized SIFT descriptors over Harris-affine keypoints [9]. Winn *et al.* [13] optimize k-means codebooks by choosing bins that can be merged. Fergus *et al.* [5] show that geometry-free bag-of-features approaches still allow objects to be localized in images.

The above works use various patch selection, patch description, descriptor coding and recognition strategies. Patches are selected using keypoints [4, 1, 2, 5, 6, 7, 8, 9, 10, 11] or densely [3, 13, 15]. SIFT based [1, 6, 8, 10], filter based [3, 13] and raw patch based [4, 2, 5, 7, 11] representations are common. Both k-means [1, 3, 11, 13] and agglomerative [4, 7] clustering are used to produce codebooks, and many different histogram normalization techniques are in use. Our work aims to quantify the influence of some of these different choices on categorization performance.

3 Datasets

We have run experiments on six publicly available and commonly used datasets, three object categorization datasets and three texture datasets.

Fig. 2. Example of objects of Graz01 dataset: four images of the categories bike, car, person

Object datasets. *Graz01* contains 667, 640×480 pixel images containing three visual categories (bicycle, car, person) in approximately balanced proportions (see figure 2). *Xerox7*[1] contains 1776 images, each belonging to exactly one of the seven categories: bicycle, book, building, car, face, phone, tree. The set is unbalanced (from 125 to 792 images per class) and the images sizes vary (width from 51 to 2048 pixels). *Pascal-01*[2] includes four categories: cars, bicycles, motorbikes and people. A 684 image training set and a 689 image test set ('test set 1') are defined.

Texture datasets. *KTH-TIPS*[3] contains 810, 200×200 images, 81 from each of the following ten categories: aluminum foil, brown bread, corduroy, cotton, cracker, linen, orange peel, sandpaper, sponge and styrofoam. *UIUCTex*[4] contains 40 images per classes of 25 textures distorted by significant viewpoint changes and some non-rigid deformations. *Brodatz*[5] contains 112 texture images, one per class. There is no viewpoint change or distortion. The images were divided into thirds horizontally and vertically to give 9 images per class.

4 Experimental Settings

This section describes the default settings for our experimental studies. The multiscale Harris and LoG (Laplacian of Gaussian) interest points, and the randomly sampled patches are computed using our team's LAVA library[6]. The default parameter values are used for detection, except that detection threshold for interest points is set to 0 (to get as many points as possible) and – for comparability with other work – the minimum scale is set to 2 to suppress small regions (see §8).

---

[1] ftp://ftp.xrce.xerox.com/pub/ftp-ipc/
[2] http://www.pascal-network.org/challenges/VOC/
[3] http://www.nada.kth.se/cvap/databases/kth-tips/index.html
[4] http://www-cvr.ai.uiuc.edu/ponce_grp
[5] http://www.cipr.rpi.edu/resource/stills/brodatz.html
[6] http://lear.inrialpes.fr/software

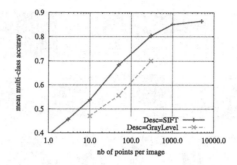

Fig. 3. Classifiers based on SIFT descriptors clearly out-perform ones based on normalized gray level pixel intensities, here for randomly sampled patches on the Graz dataset

We use SIFT [8] descriptors, again computed with the LAVA library with default parameters: 8 orientations and 4×4 blocks of cells (so the descriptor dimension is 128), with the cells being 3×3 pixels at the finest scale (scale 1). Euclidean distance is used to compare and cluster descriptors.

We also tested codings based on normalized raw pixel intensities, but as figure 3 shows, SIFT descriptor based codings clearly out-perform these. Possible reasons include the greater translation invariance of SIFT, and its robust 3-stage normalization process: it uses rectified (oriented) gradients, which are more local and hence more resistant to illumination gradients than complete patches, followed by blockwise normalization, followed by clipping and renormalization.

Codebooks are initialized at randomly chosen input samples and optimized by feeding randomly chosen images into online k-means (the memory required for true k-means would be prohibitive for codebooks and training sets of this size).

Descriptors are coded by hard assignment to the nearest codebook centre, yielding a histogram of codeword counts for each image. Three methods of converting histogram counts to classification features were tested: raw counts; simple binarization (the feature is 1 if the count is non-zero); and adaptive thresholding of the count with a threshold chosen to maximize the Mutual Information between the feature and the class label on the training set. MI based thresholding usually works best and is used as the default. Raw counts are not competitive so results for them are not presented below.

Soft *One-versus-one* SVM's are used for classification. In multi-class cases the class with the most votes wins. The SVM's are linear except in §9 where Gaussian kernels are used to make comparisons with previously published results based on nonlinear classifiers. The main performance metric is the unweighted mean over the classes of the recognition rate for each class. This is better adapted to unbalanced datasets than the classical "overall recognition rate", which is biased towards over-represented classes. By default we report average values over six complete runs, including the codebook creation and the category prediction. For most of the datasets the recognition rates are estimated using two-fold cross validation, but for Pascal-01 dataset we follow the PASCAL protocol and use the specified 'learning set'/'test set 1' split for evaluation.

5   Influence of the Sampling Method

The idea of representing images as collections of independent local patches has proved its worth for object recognition or image classification, but raises the question of which patches to choose. Objects may occur at any position and scale in the image so patches need to be extracted at all scales (e.g. [3, 13]). Dense sampling (processing every pixel at every scale, e.g. [12, 13]) captures the most information, but it is also memory and computation intensive, with much of the computation being spent on processing relatively featureless (and hence possibly uninformative) regions. Several authors argue that computation can be saved and classification performance can perhaps be improved by using some kind of salience metric to sample only the most informative regions. Example-based recognition proceeds essentially by matching new images to examples so it is natural to investigate the local feature methods developed for robust image

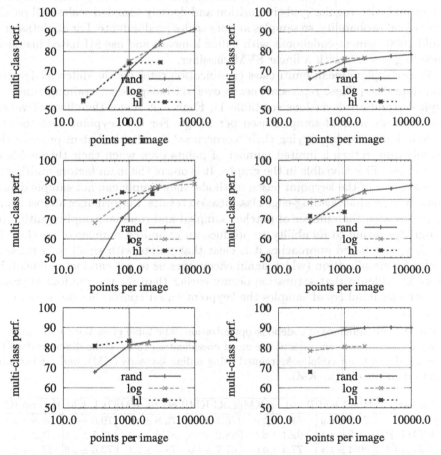

Fig. 4. Mean multi-class classification accuracy as a function of the number of sampled patches used for classification. Reading left to right and top to bottom, the datasets are: Brodatz, Graz01; KTH-TIPS, Pascal-01; UIUCTex and Xerox7.

matching in this context. In particular, many authors have studied recognition methods based on generic interest point detectors [4, 1, 2, 6, 7, 8, 9, 10, 11]. Such methods are attractive because they have good repeatability [8, 9] and transla- tion, scale, 2D rotation and perhaps even affine transformation invariance [20]. However the available interest or salience metrics are based on generic low level image properties bearing little direct relationship to discriminative power for visual recognition, and none of the above authors verify that the patches that they select are significantly more discriminative than random ones. Also, it is clear that one of the main parameters governing classification accuracy is simply the number of patches used, and almost none of the existing studies normalize for this effect.

We investigate these issues by comparing three patch sampling strategies. *Laplacian of Gaussian (LoG):* a multi-scale keypoint detector proposed by [21] and popularized by [8]. *Harris-Laplace (Harris):* the (non-affine) multi-scale key- point detector used in [18]. *Random (Rand):* patches are selected randomly from a pyramid with regular grids in position and densely sampled scales. All patches have equal probability, so samples at finer scales predominate. For all datasets we build 1000 element codebooks with online k-means and use MI-based histogram encoding (see §7) with a linear SVM classifier.

Figure 4 plots mean multi-class classification rates for the different detectors and datasets. (These represent means over six independent training runs – for typical standard deviations see table 1). Each plot shows the effect of varying the mean number of samples used per image. For the keypoint detectors this is done indirectly by varying their 'cornerness' thresholds, but in practice they usually only return a limited number of points even when their thresholds are set to zero. This is visible in the graphs. It is one of the main factors limiting the performance of the keypoint based methods: they simply can not sample densely enough to produce leading-edge classification results. Performance almost always increases with the number of patches sampled and random sampling ultimately dominates owing to its ability to produce an unlimited number of patches. For the keypoint based approaches it is clear that points with small cornerness are useful for classification (which again encourages us to use random patches), but there is evidence that saturation occurs earlier than for the random approach. For smaller numbers of samples the keypoint based approaches do predominate

Table 1. The influence of codebook optimization. The table gives the means and stan- dard deviations over six runs of the mean classification rates of the different detectors on each dataset, for codebooks refined using online k-means (KM), and for randomly sampled codebooks (no KM).

Dataset	Rand KM	Rand no KM	LoG KM	LoG no KM	H-L KM	H-L no KM
Graz01	74.2 ± 0.9	71.3 ± 0.9	76.1 ± 0.5	72.8 ± 0.9	70.0 ± 1.4	68.8 ± 2.0
KTHTIPS	91.3 ± 1.1	92.1 ± 0.4	88.2 ± 1.0	85.0 ± 1.8	83.1 ± 2.1	81.3 ± 1.1
Pascal-01	80.4 ± 1.4	77.4 ± 0.9	81.7 ± 1.0	78.7 ± 2.3	73.6 ± 2.3	67.8 ± 2.8
UIUCTex	81.3 ± 0.8	75.2 ± 1.4	81.0 ± 1.0	76.0 ± 0.8	83.5 ± 0.8	80.4 ± 0.8
Xerox7	88.9 ± 1.3	87.8 ± 0.5	80.5 ± 0.6	79.9 ± 0.9	66.6 ± 1.8	65.6 ± 1.5

in most cases, but there is no clear winner overall and in Xerox7 the random method is preferred even for small numbers of samples.

6   Influence of the Codebook

This section studies the influence of the vector quantization codebook size and construction method on the classification results.

Codebook size. The number of codebook centres is one of the major parameters of the system, as observed, e.g. by [1], who report that performance improves steadily as the codebook grows. We have run similar experiments, using online (rather than classical) k-means, testing larger codebooks, and studying the relationship with the number of patches sampled in the test image. Figure 5 shows the results. It reports means of multi-class error rates over 6 runs on the Xerox7 dataset for the three detectors. The other settings are as before. For each detector there are initially substantial gains in performance as the codebook size is increased, but overfitting becomes apparent for the large codebooks shown here. For the keypoint based methods there is also evidence of overfitting for

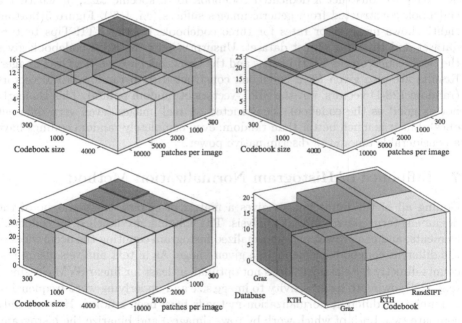

Fig. 5. All but bottom right: The influence of codebook size and number of points sampled per image for: random patches (top left); LoG detector (top right) and Harris detector (bottom left). Bottom right: the influence of the images used to construct the codebook, for KTH, Graz, and random SIFT vector codebooks on the KTH texture dataset and the Graz object dataset. The values are the means of the per-class classification error rates.

large numbers of samples, whereas the random sampler continues to get better as more samples are drawn. There does not appear to be a strong interaction between the influence of the number of test samples and that of the codebook size. The training set size is also likely to have a significant influence on the results but this was not studied.

Codebook construction algorithm. §4 presented two methods for constructing codebooks: randomly selecting centres from among the sampled training patches, and online k-means initialized using this. Table 1 compares these methods, again using 1000 element codebooks, MI-based normalization and a linear SVM classifier. 1000 patches per image are sampled (less if the detector can not return 1000). Except in one case (KTH-TIPS with random patches), the online k-means codebooks are better than the random ones. The average gain (2.7%) is statistically significant, but many of the individual differences are not. So we see that even randomly selected codebooks produce very respectable results. Optimizing the centres using online k-means provides small but worthwhile gains, however the gains are small compared to those available by simply increasing the number of test patches sampled or the size of the codebook.

Images used for codebook construction. One can also ask whether it is necessary to construct a dedicated codebook for a specific task, or whether a codebook constructed from generic images suffices (c.f. [13]). Figure 5(bottom right) shows mean error rates for three codebooks on the KTH-Tips texture dataset and the Graz object dataset. Unsurprisingly, the KTH codebook gives the best results on the KTH images and the Graz codebook on the Graz images. Results are also given for a codebook constructed from random SIFT vectors (random 128-D vectors, not the SIFT vectors of random points). This is clearly not as good as the codebooks constructed on real images (even very different ones), but it is much better than random: even completely random codings have a considerable amount of discriminative power.

7   Influence of Histogram Normalization Method

Coding all of the input images gives a matrix of counts, the analogue of the document-term matrix in text analysis. The columns are labelled by codebook elements, and each row is an unnormalized histogram counting the occurences of the different codebook elements in a given image. As in text analysis, using raw counts directly for classification is not optimal, at least for linear SVM classifiers (e.g. [22]), owing to its sensitivity to image size and underlying word frequencies. A number of different normalization methods have been studied. Here we only compare two, both of which work by rows (images) and binarize the histogram. The first sets an output element to 1 if its centre gets any votes in the image, the second adaptively selects a binarization threshold for each centre by maximizing the mutual information between the resulting binary feature and the class label over the training set [22]. As before we use 1000 element codebooks, online k-means, and a linear SVM. Results for two datasets are shown in figure 6 – other datasets give similar results.

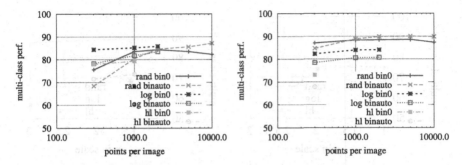

Fig. 6. The influence of histogram normalization on mean classification rate, for the Pascal-01 (left) and Xerox7 (right) datasets. Histogram entries are binarized either with a zero/nonzero rule (bin0) or using thresholds chosen to maximize mutual information with the class labels (binauto). Adaptive thresholding is preferable for dense sampling when there are many votes per bin on average.

Neither method predominates everywhere, but the MI method is clearly preferred when the mean number of samples per bin is large (here 10000 samples/image vs. 1000 centres). For example, on Xerox7, at 1000 samples/image the input histogram density is 27%, rising to 43% at 10000 samples/image. MI-based binarization reduces this to 13% in the later case, allowing the SVM to focus on the most relevant entries.

8 Influence of the Minimum Scale for Patch Sampling

Ideally the classifier should exploit the information available at all scales at which the object or scene is visible. Achieving this requires good scale invariance in the patch selection and descriptor computation stages and a classifier that exploits fine detail when it is available while remaining resistant to its absence when not. The latter is difficult to achieve but the first steps are choosing a codebook that is rich enough to code fine details separately from coarse ones and a binwise normalization method that is not swamped by fine detail in other bins. The performance of descriptor extraction at fine scales is critical for the former, as these contain most of the discriminative detail but also most of the aliasing and 'noise'. In practice, a minimum scale threshold is usually applied. This section evaluates the influence of this threshold on classification performance. As before we use a 1000 element codebook built with online k-means, MI-based normalization, and a linear SVM.

Figure 7 shows the evolution of mean accuracies over six runs on the Brodatz and Xerox7 datasets as the minimum scale varies from 1 to 3 pixels[7]. The performance of the LoG and Harris based methods decreases significantly as the minimum scale increases: the detectors return fewer patches than requested and useful information is lost. For the random sampler the number of patches is

---

[7] The other experiments in this paper set the minimum scale to 2. SIFT descriptors from the LAVA library use 4×4 blocks of cells with cells being at least 3×3 pixels, so SIFT windows are 12×12 pixels at scale 1.

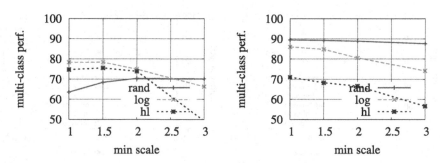

Fig. 7. The influence of the minimum patch selection scale for SIFT descriptors on the Brodatz (left) and Xerox7 (right) datasets

constant and there is no clear trend, but it is somewhat better to discard small scales on the Brodatz dataset, and somewhat worse on the Xerox7 dataset.

9   Results on the Pascal Challenge Dataset

The previous sections showed the usefulness of random sampling and quantified the influence of various parameters. We now show that simply by sampling

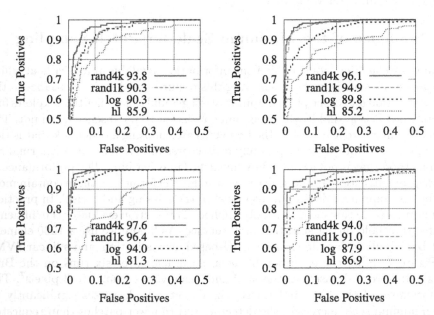

Fig. 8. ROC curves for the 4 categories of the PASCAL 2005 VOC challenge: top-left, bikes; top-right, cars; bottom-left, motorbikes; bottom-right, persons. The codebooks have 1000 elements, except that rand4k has 4000. Equal Error Rates are listed for each method.

Table 2. A comparison of our Rand4k method with the best results obtained (by different methods) during the PASCAL challenge and with the interest point based method of Zhang *et al.*

Method	motorbikes	bikes	persons	cars	average
Ours (rand4k)	97.6	93.8	94.0	96.1	95.4
Best Pascal [23]	97.7	93.0	91.7	96.1	94.6
Zhang *et al* [24]	96.2	90.3	91.6	93.0	92.8

large enough numbers of random patches, one can create a method that out-performs the best current approaches. We illustrate this on the Pascal-01 dataset from the 2005 PASCAL Visual Object Classification challenge because many teams competed on this and a summary of the results is readily available [23]. We use the following settings: 10 000 patches per image, online k-means, MI-based normalization, an RBF SVM with kernel width γ set to the median of the pairwise distances between the training descriptors, and either a 1000 element ('Rand1k') or 4000 element ('Rand4k') codebook. Figure 8 presents ROC curves for the methods tested in this paper on the 4 binary classification problems of the Pascal-01 Test Set 1. As expected the method Rand4k predominates. Table 2 compares Rand4k to the best of the results obtained during the PAS-CAL challenge [23] and in the study of Zhang *et al* [24]. In the challenge ('Best Pascal' row), a different method won each object category, whereas our results use a single method and fixed parameter values inherited from experiments on other datasets. The method of [24] uses a combination of sophisticated interest point detectors (Harris-Scale plus Laplacian-Scale) and a specially developed Earth Movers Distance kernel for the SVM, whereas our method uses (a lot of) random patches and a standard RBF kernel.

10   Conclusions and Future Work

The main goal of this article was to underline a number of empirical observations regarding the performance of various competing strategies for image representation in bag-of-features approaches to visual categorization, that call into question the comparability of certain results in the literature. To do this we ran head to head comparisons between different image sampling, codebook generation and histogram normalization methods on a cross-section of commonly used test databases for image classification.

Perhaps the most notable conclusion is that although interest point based samplers such as Harris-Laplace and Laplacian of Gaussian each work well in some databases for small numbers of sampled patches, they can not compete with simple-minded uniform random sampling for the larger numbers of patches that are needed to get the best classification results. In all cases, the number of patches sampled from the test image is the single most influential parameter governing performance. For small fixed numbers of samples, none of HL, LOG and random dominate on all databases, while for larger numbers of samples random sampling dominates because no matter how their thresholds are set, the interest operators saturate and fail to provide enough patches (or a broad enough variety of them) for competitive results. The salience cues that they optimize are useful for sparse feature based matching, but not necessarily optimal for image classification. Many of the conclusions about methods in the literature are questionable because they did not control for the different numbers of samples taken by different methods, and 'simple' dense random sampling provides better results than more sophisticated learning methods (§9).

Similarly, for multi-scale methods, the minimum image scale at which patches can be sampled (e.g. owing to the needs of descriptor calculation, affine normalization, etc.) has a considerable influence on results because the vast majority of patches or interest points typically occur at the finest few scales. Depending on the database, it can be essential to either use or suppress the small-scale patches. So the practical scale-invariance of current bag-of-feature methods is questionable and there is probably a good deal of unintentional scale-tuning in the published literature.

Finally, although codebooks generally need to be large to achieve the best results, we do see some evidence of saturation at attainable sizes. Although the codebook learning method does have an influence, even randomly sampled codebooks give quite respectable results which suggests that there is not much room for improvement here.

Future work. We are currently extending the experiments to characterize the influence of different clustering strategies and the interactions between sampling methods and classification more precisely. We are also working on random samplers that are biased towards finding more discriminant patches.

References

1. Csurka, G., Dance, C., Fan, L., Willamowski, J., Bray, C.: Visual categorization with bags of keypoints. In: ECCV'04 workshop on Statistical Learning in Computer Vision. (2004) 59–74
2. Fergus, R., Perona, P., Zisserman, A.: Object class recognition by unsupervised scale-invariant learning. In: CVPR03. (2003) II: 264–271
3. Leung, T., Malik, J.: Representing and recognizing the visual appearance of materials using three-dimensional textons. IJCV **43** (2001) 29–44
4. Agarwal, S., Awan, A., Roth, D.: Learning to detect objects in images via a sparse, part-based representation. PAMI **26** (2004) 1475–1490
5. Fergus, R., Fei-Fei, L., Perona, P., Zisserman, A.: Learning object categories from google's image search. In: ICCV. (2005) II: 1816–1823
6. Grauman, K., Darrell, T.: Efficient image matching with distributions of local invariant features. In: CVPR05. (2005) II: 627–634
7. Leibe, B., Schiele, B.: Interleaved object categorization and segmentation. In: BMVC. (2003)
8. Lowe, D.: Distinctive image features from scale-invariant keypoints. IJCV **60** (2004) 91–110
9. Mikolajczyk, K., Schmid, C.: An affine invariant interest point detector. In: ECCV. (2002) I: 128

10. Sivic, J., Zisserman, A.: Video google: A text retrieval approach to object matching in videos. In: ICCV03. (2003) 1470–1477
11. Weber, M., Welling, M., Perona, P.: Unsupervised learning of models for recognition. In: ECCV. (2000) I: 18–32
12. Jurie, F., Triggs, B.: Creating efficient codebooks for visual recognition. In: ICCV. (2005)
13. Winn, J., Criminisi, A., Minka, T.: Object categorization by learned universal visual dictionary. In: ICCV. (2005)
14. Bouchard, G., Triggs, B.: Hierarchical part-based visual object categorization. In: CVPR. Volume 1. (2005) 710–715
15. Agarwal, A., Triggs, B.: Hyperfeatures – multilevel local coding for visual recognition. In: ECCV. (2006)
16. Joachims, T.: Text categorization with support vector machines: learning with many relevant features. In: ECML-98, 10th European Conference on Machine Learning, Springer Verlag (1998) 137–142
17. Niblack, W., Barber, R., Equitz, W., Flickner, M., Glasman, D., Petkovic, D., Yanker, P.: The qbic project: Querying image by content using color, texture, and shape. SPIE 1908 (1993) 173–187
18. Lazebnik, S., Schmid, C., Ponce, J.: Affine-invariant local descriptors and neighborhood statistics for texture recognition. In: ICCV. (2003) 649–655
19. Rubner, Y., Tomasi, C., Guibas, L.: The earth mover's distance as a metric for image retrieval. IJCV 40 (2000) 99–121
20. Mikolajczyk, K., Tuytelaars, T., Schmid, C., Zisserman, A., Matas, J., Schaffalitzky, F., Kadir, T., Gool, L.V.: A comparison of affine region detectors. Int. J. Computer Vision 65 (2005) 43–72
21. Lindeberg, T.: Detecting salient blob-like image structures and their scales with a scale-space primal sketch: A method for focus-of-attention. IJCV 11 (1993) 283–318
22. Nowak, E., Jurie, F.: Vehicle categorization: Parts for speed and accuracy. In: VS-PETS workshop, in conjuction with ICCV 05. (2005)
23. et al., M.E.: The 2005 pascal visual object classes challenge. In Springer-Verlag, ed.: First PASCAL Challenges Workshop. (2006)
24. Zhang, J., Marszalek, M., Lazebnik, S., Schmid, C.: Local features and kernels for classifcation of texture and object categories: An in-depth study. Technical Report RR-5737, INRIA Rhône-Alpes, 665 avenue de l'Europe, 38330 Montbonnot, France (2005)

Maximally Stable Local Description for Scale Selection

Gyuri Dorkó and Cordelia Schmid

INRIA Rhône-Alpes, 655 Avenue de l'Europe, 38334 Montbonnot, France
{gyuri.dorko, cordelia.schmid}@inrialpes.fr

Abstract. Scale and affine-invariant local features have shown excellent performance in image matching, object and texture recognition. This paper optimizes keypoint detection to achieve stable local descriptors, and therefore, an improved image representation. The technique performs scale selection based on a region descriptor, here SIFT, and chooses regions for which this descriptor is maximally stable. Maximal stability is obtained, when the difference between descriptors extracted for consecutive scales reaches a minimum. This scale selection technique is applied to multi-scale Harris and Laplacian points. Affine invariance is achieved by an integrated affine adaptation process based on the second moment matrix. An experimental evaluation compares our detectors to Harris-Laplace and the Laplacian in the context of image matching as well as of category and texture classification. The comparison shows the improved performance of our detector.

1   Introduction

Local photometric descriptors computed at keypoints have demonstrated excellent results in many vision applications, including object recognition [1, 2], image matching [3], and sparse texture representation [4]. Recent work has concentrated on making these descriptors invariant to image transformations. This requires the construction of invariant image regions which are then used as support regions to compute invariant descriptors. In most cases a detected region is described by an independently chosen descriptor. It would, however, be advantageous to use a description adapted to the region. For example, for blob-like detectors which extract regions surrounded by edges, a natural choice would be a descriptor based on edges. However, adapted representations may not provide enough discriminative information, and consequently, a general descriptor, such as SIFT [5], could be a better choice. Many times this leads to better performance, yet less stable representations: small changes in scale or location can alter the descriptor significantly. We found that the most unstable component of keypoint-based scale-invariant detectors is the scale selection. We have, therefore, developed a detector which uses the descriptor to select the characteristic scales. Our feature detection approach consists of two steps. We first extract interest points at multiple scales to determine informative and repeatable locations. We then select the characteristic scale for each location by identifying maximally stable local descriptions. The chosen local description can be any measure computed on a

A. Leonardis, H. Bischof, and A. Pinz (Eds.): ECCV 2006, Part IV, LNCS 3954, pp. 504–516, 2006.

pixel neighborhood, such as color histograms, steerable filters, or wavelets. For our experiments we use the Scale Invariant Feature Transform (SIFT) [5], which has shown excellent performance for object representation and image matching [6]. The SIFT descriptor is computed on a 4x4 grid with an 8-bin orientation histogram for each cell, resulting in a 128-dimensional vector for a given local region.

Our method for scale-invariant keypoint detection and image representation has the following properties:

- Our scale selection method guarantees more stable descriptors than state-of-the-art techniques by explicitly using descriptors during keypoint detection. The stability criteria is developed to minimize the variation of the descriptor for small changes in scale.
- Repeatable locations are provided by interest point detectors (e.g. Harris), and therefore they have rich and salient neighborhoods. This consequently helps to choose repeatable and characteristic scales. We verify this experimentally, and show that our selection competes favorably with the best available detectors.
- The detector takes advantage of the properties of the local descriptor. This can include invariance to illumination or rotation as well as robustness to noise. Our experiments show that the local invariant image representation extracted by our algorithm leads to significant improvement for object and texture recognition.

Related Work. Many different scale- and affine-invariant detectors exist in the literature. Harris-Laplace [7] detects multi-scale keypoint locations with the Harris detector [8] and the characteristic scales are determined by the Laplacian operator. Locations based on Harris points are very accurate. However, scale estimation is often unstable on corner-like structures, because it depends on the exact corner location, i.e., shifts by one pixel may modify the selected scale significantly. The scale-invariant Laplacian detector [9] selects extremal values in location-scale space and finds blob-like structures. Blobs are well localized structures, but due to their homogeneity, the information content is often poor in the center of the region. The detector of Kadir et al. [10] extracts circular or elliptical regions in the image as maxima of the entropy scale-space of region intensity histograms. It extracts also blob-like structures, and has shown to be a more robust representation for some object categories [10]. Mikolajczyk et al. [11] show that it performs poorly for image matching, which might be due to the sparsity of the scale quantization. Edge and structure based scale-invariant detectors [12, 13, 14] also exist in the literature. Some of them have been evaluated in [11] and apart from MSER [14] have shown to be inferior to Harris-Laplace or Hessian-Laplace. The MSER (Maximally Stable Extremal Regions) detector [14] defines extremal regions as image segments where each inner-pixel intensity value is less (greater) than a certain threshold, and all intensities around the boundary are greater (less) than the same threshold. An extremal region is *maximally stable* when the area (or the boundary length) of the segment changes the least with respect to the threshold. This detector works particularly well on images with well defined edges, but it is less robust to noise and is not adapted to texture-like structures. It usually selects fewer regions than the other detectors.

Viewpoint invariance is sometimes required to achieve reliable image matching, object or texture recognition. Affine-invariant detectors [7, 9, 10, 12, 14] estimate the affine shape of the regions to allow normalization of the patch prior to descriptor computation. Lindeberg and Gårding [9] use an *affine adaptation* process based on the second moment matrix for the Laplacian detector. The affine extension of Harris-Laplace [7] is also based on this affine adaptation. The adaptation procedure is a post-processing step for the scale-invariant detections.

Overview. Our paper is organized as follows. In Section 2 we present our scale selection technique Maximally Stable Local SIFT Description (MSLSD) and introduce two detectors, Harris-MSLSD and Laplacian-MSLSD. We then compare their performance to Harris-Laplace and the Laplacian. In Section 3 we evaluate the detectors for image matching using a publicly available framework. Section 4 reports results for object category and texture classification. Finally, in Section 5 we conclude and outline future extensions.

2   Maximally Stable Local Description

In this section we present our method for selecting characteristic scales at keypoints and discuss the properties of our approach. We address two key features of interest point detectors: repeatability and description stability. *Repeatability* determines how well the detector selects the same region under various image transformations, and is important for image matching. In practice, due to noise and object variations, the corresponding regions are never exactly the same but their underlying descriptions are expected to be similar. This is what we call the *description stability*, and it is important for image matching and appearance based recognition.

The two properties, *repeatability* and *descriptor stability*, are in theory contradictory. A homogeneous region provides the most stable description, whereas its shape is in general not stable. On the other hand, if the region shape is stable, for example using edges as region boundaries, small errors in localization will often cause significant changes of the descriptor. Our solution is to apply the Maximally Stable Local Description algorithm to interest point locations only. These points have repeatable locations and informative neighborhoods. Our algorithm adjusts their scale parameters to stabilize the descriptions and rejects locations where the required stability cannot be achieved. The combination of repeatable location selection and descriptor stabilized scale selection provides a balanced solution.

Scale-invariant MSLSD detectors. To select characteristic locations with high repeatability we first detect interest points at multiple scales. We chose two widely used complementary methods, Harris [8] and the Laplacian [15, 16]. Harris detects corners, i.e., locations where the intensity varies significantly in several directions. The Laplacian detects blob-like structures. Its multi-scaled version detects extrema of the 2D Laplacian operator on multiple scales.

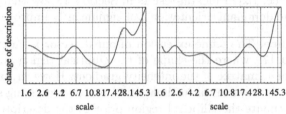

Fig. 1. Two examples for scale selection. The left and right graphs show the change in the local description as a function of scale for the left and right points respectively. The scales for which the functions have local minima are shown in the image. The bright thick circles correspond to the global minima.

The second step of our approach selects the characteristic scales for each keypoint location. We use *description stability* as criterion for scale selection: the scale for each location is chosen such that the corresponding representation (in our case SIFT [5]) *changes the least* with respect to scale. Fig. 1 illustrates our selection method for two Harris points. The two graphs show how the descriptors change as we increase the scale (the radius of the region) for the two keypoints. To measure the difference between SIFT descriptions we use the Euclidean distance as in [5]. The minima of the functions determine the scales where the descriptions are the most stable; their corresponding regions are depicted by circles in the image. Our algorithm selects the *absolute minimum* (shown as bright thick circles) for each point. Multi-scale points which correspond to the same image structure often have the same absolute minimum, i.e. result in the same region. In this case only one of them is kept in our implementation. To limit the number of selected regions an additional threshold can be used to reject unstable keypoints, i.e., if the minimum change of description is above a certain value the keypoint location is rejected. For each point we use a percentage of the maximum change over scales at the point location, set to 50% in our experiments.

Our algorithm is in the following referred to as *Maximally Stable Local SIFT Description* (MSLSD). Depending on the location detector we add the prefix H for Harris and L for Laplacian, i.e. H-MSLSD and L-MSLSD.

Illumination and rotation invariance. Our detectors are robust to illumination changes, as our scale selection is based on the SIFT descriptor. SIFT is normalized to unit length, and therefore offers invariance to scalar changes in image contrast. Since the descriptor is based on gradients, it is also invariant to an additive constant change in brightness, i.e., it is invariant to affine illumination changes.

The rotation invariance for SIFT can be achieved by extracting the dominant orientation and rotating the patch in this direction. If the keypoints have poorly defined orientations, the resulting descriptions are unstable and noisy. In our algorithm we orienting the patch in the dominant direction prior to the descriptor computation for each scale. Maximal description stability is then found for locations with well defined local gradients. In our experiments a -R suffix indicates rotation invariance. Experimental results in Section 4 show that our integrated estimation of the dominant orientation can significantly improve results.

Affine invariance. The affine extension of our detector is based on the affine adaptation in [9, 17], where the shape of the elliptical region is determined by the second moment matrix of the intensity gradient. However, unlike other detectors [4, 7], we do not use this estimation as a post-processing step after scale selection, but estimate the elliptical region prior to the descriptor computation for each scale. When the affine adaptation is unstable, i.e., sensitive to small changes of the initial scale, the descriptor changes significantly and the region is rejected. This improves the robustness of our affine-invariant representation. In our experiments an -*Aff* suffix indicates affine invariance. Full affine invariance requires rotation invariance, as the shape of each elliptical region is transformed into a circle reducing the affine ambiguity to a rotational one. Rotation normalization of the patch is, therefore, always included when affine invariance is used in our experiments.

3   Evaluation for Image Matching

This section evaluates the performance of our detectors for image matching based on the evaluation framework in [11], i.e., for the criteria repeatability rate and matching score. We compare our results to Harris-Laplace and LoG.

The repeatability rate measures how well the detector selects the same scene region under various image transformations. Each sequence has one reference image and five images with known homographies to the reference image. Regions are detected for the images and their accuracy is measured by the amount of overlap between the detected region and the corresponding region projected from the reference image with the known homography. Two regions are matched if their *overlap error* is sufficiently small:

$$1 - \frac{R_{\mu_a} \cap R_{(H^T \mu_b H)}}{R_{\mu_a} \cup R_{(H^T \mu_b H)}} < \epsilon_O$$

where R_μ is the elliptic or circular region extracted by the detector and H is the homography between the two images. The union $(R_{\mu_a} \cup R_{(H^T \mu_b H)})$ and the intersection $(R_{\mu_a} \cap R_{(H^T \mu_b H)})$ of the detected and projected regions are computed numerically. As in [11] the maximum possible overlap error ϵ_O is set to 40% in our experiments. The *repeatability score* is the ratio between the correct matches and the smaller number of detected regions in the pair of images.

The second criterion, the matching score, measures the discriminative power of the detected regions. Each descriptor is matched to its nearest neighbor in the second image. This match is marked as correct if it corresponds to a region match with maximum overlap error 40%. The matching score is the ratio between the correct matches and the smaller number of detected regions in the pair of images.

3.1   Viewpoint Changes

The performance of our detectors for viewpoint changes is evaluated on two different image sequences with viewpoint changes from 20 to 60 degrees. Fig. 2(a) shows sample images of the graffiti sequence. This sequence has well defined edges, whereas the wall sequence (Fig. 2(b)) is more texture-like.

Fig. 3 shows the repeatability rate and the matching score as well as the number of correct matches for different affine-invariant detectors. The ordering of the detectors is very similar for the criteria repeatability rate and matching score, as expected. On the graffiti sequence (Fig. 3, first row) the original Harris-Laplace (H-L-Aff) detector performs better than H-MSLSD-Aff. On the wall sequence results for H-MSLSD-Aff are slightly better than for H-L-Aff. This shows that the Laplacian scale selection provides good repeatability mainly in the presence of well defined edges. In case of the Laplacian our detector (L-MSLSD-Aff) out-performs the original one (LoG) for both sequences. This can be explained by the fact that LoG-Aff detects a large number of unstable (poorly repeatable)

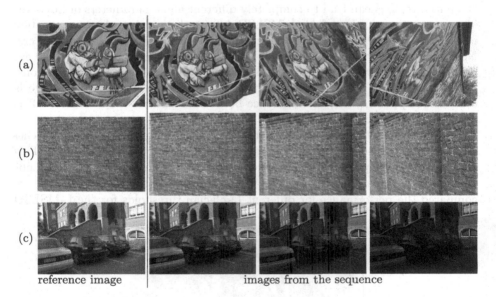

(a)

(b)

(c)

reference image | images from the sequence

Fig. 2. Image sequences used in the matching experiments. (a), (b) Viewpoint change. (c) Illumination change. The first column shows the reference image. These sequences may be downloaded from http://www.robots.ox.ac.uk/~vgg/research/affine/index.html.

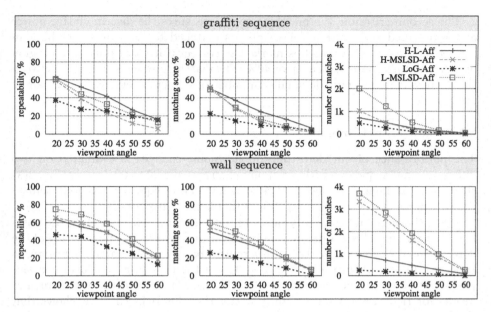

Fig. 3. Comparison of detectors for viewpoint changes. The repeatability rate, matching score and the number of correct matches are compared on the graffiti (first row) and on the wall (second row) sequence.

regions for nearly parallel edges, see Fig. 4. A small shift or scale change of the initial regions can lead to completely different affine parameters of LoG-Aff. These regions are rejected by L-MSLSD-Aff, as the varying affine parameters cause large changes in the local description over consecutive scale parameters. Note that in case of affine divergence both detectors reject the points. This example clearly shows that description stability leads to more repeatable regions. In case of natural scenes, as for example the wall sequence, this advantage is even more apparent, i.e., the difference between L-MSLSD-Aff over LoG-Aff is higher than for the graffiti sequence.

We can observe that we obtain a significantly higher number of correct matches with our detectors. This is due to a larger number of detected regions. This could increase the probability of accidental matches. To ensure that this did not bias our results—and to evaluate the effect of the detected region density—we compared the performance for different Laplacian thresholds for the L-MSLSD

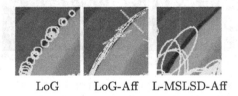

LoG   LoG-Aff   L-MSLSD-Aff

Fig. 4. Output of LoG detector on part of a graffiti image: the standard LoG detector (left), affine-invariant LoG (middle) and L-MSLSD-Aff (right)

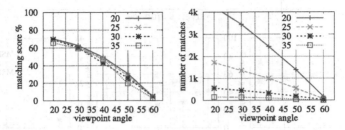

Fig. 5. Comparison of the matching score and the number of correct matches for several thresholds for the multi-scale Laplacian $(20, 25, 30, 35)$. Results are given for L-MSLSD on the wall sequence. A higher threshold results in less detections, and consequently a smaller number of absolute matches (second column).

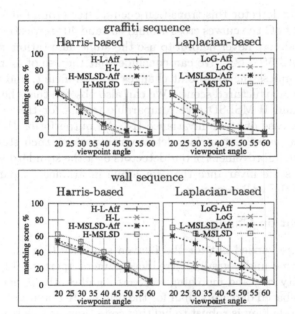

Fig. 6. Comparison of detectors with and without affine invariance on the graffiti (first row) and the wall (second row) sequence. The first column shows results for Harris- and the second for Laplacian-based detectors.

detector. Note that the Laplacian threshold determines the number of detections in location space, whereas the scale threshold rejects unstable locations and remains fixed throughout the paper. Fig. 5 shows that as the number of correct matches gradually decrease, the quality of the descriptors (matching score) stays the same. Consequently, we can conclude that the quality of the detections does not depend on the density of the extracted regions.

Fig. 6 shows that in case of small viewpoint changes the scale-invariant versions of the detectors perform better that the ones with affine invariance. It also allows to compare the scale-invariant detectors. On the graffiti images the original H-L performs better that its affine adapted version until 30° of viewpoint

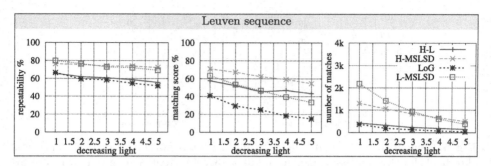

Fig. 7. Comparison of the detectors on the Leuven sequence (illumination changes)

change. For our detector this transition occurs later around 40°. In the case of
L-MSLSD and LoG the curves cross around 35° and 40° respectively. On the wall
sequence it is almost never helpful to use the affine adaptation, scale invariance
is sufficient until 55 − 60°. We can conclude that the use of affine invariance is
not necessary unless the viewpoint changes are significant, and that it is more
helpful in case of structured scenes. We can also observe that the scale-invariant
versions H-L and H-MSLSD give comparable results for the graffiti sequence,
whereas in the case of affine invariance H-L-Aff outperforms H-MSLSD-Aff. In
the other cases, our scale-invariant detectors outperform their standard versions.
In addition, the improvement of our detectors over the standard versions is more
significant for scale invariance than for affine invariance, in particular for the
Laplacian and the wall sequence.

3.2 Illumination Changes

Experiments are carried out for the Leuven sequence (Fig. 2 (c)), i.e., images
of the same scene under gradually reduced camera aperture. Fig. 7 shows that
the repeatability rate and matching score are significantly higher for our Harris-
and Laplacian-based detectors than for the original H-L and LoG. This confirms
that our scale selection is robust to lighting conditions as it is based on the SIFT
descriptor which is invariant to affine illumination changes.

3.3 Overall Performance

Mikolajczyk *et al.* [11] reported MSER (Maximally Stable Extremal Regions [14])
as the best affine-invariant detector on the three image sequences used here.
Fig. 8 compares the matching score of our detectors to the performance of MSER
on these sequences. Note that our results are directly comparable to the other
detectors reported in [11], as we use the same dataset and evaluation criteria. We
can observe that L-MSLSD outperforms MSER on the wall sequence and that
H-MSLSD performs better that MSER on the Leuven sequence. MSER gives
better results than other detectors on the graffiti images. Note that due to the
image structure of the graffiti scenes MSER selects significantly fewer keypoints
than the other detectors.

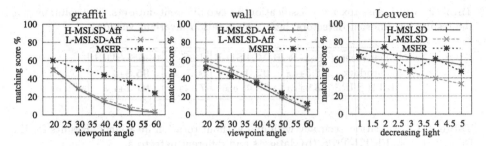

Fig. 8. Comparison of the matching scores obtained for our detectors, H-MSLSD-Aff and L-MSLSD-Aff, and MSER

4 Evaluation for Image Categorization

In this section we evaluate our new detectors for object and texture categorization. In both cases we perform image classification based on the bag-of-kepoints approach [18]. Images are represented as histograms of visual word occurrences, where the visual words are clusters of local descriptors. The histograms of the training images are used to train a linear SVM classifier. In the case of object categorization the output of the SVM determines the presence or absence of a category in a test image. For multi-class texture classification we use the 1-vs-1 strategy. Vocabularies are constructed by the K-Means algorithm. The number of clusters is fixed for each category, i.e., does not depend on the detector (400 for motorbikes and airplanes, 200 for bicycles, 100 for people, 1120 for Brodatz, and 1000 for KTH-TIPS). In all experiments we compare H-L to H-MSLSD and LoG to L-MSLSD and our representation is always SIFT.

Evaluation for category classification. The experiments are performed for four different datasets. Motorbikes and airplanes of the CalTech dataset [1] contain 800 images of objects and 900 images of background. Half of the sets are used for training and the other half for testing. The split of the positive sets is exactly the same as [1]. The TUGRAZ-1 dataset [2] contains people, bicycles, and a background class. We use the same training and test sets for two-class classification as [2].

Table 1. Comparison of object category classification results using our detectors (H-MSLSD and L-MSLSD) and their standard versions (H-L and LoG). Classification rates for four categories are reported at EER.

Category	H-L	H-MSLSD	LoG	L-MSLSD	Fergus *et al.* [1]	Opelt *et al.* [2]
\multicolumn{7}{c}{Caltech databases}						
Motorbikes	98.25	98.5	**98.75**	**98.75**	96.0	92.2
Airplanes	97.75	98.25	**99.0**	**99.0**	94.0	90.2
\multicolumn{7}{c}{TUGraz1 databases}						
Bicycles	92.0	**94.0**	90.0	92.0	*n.a.*	86.5
People	**86.0**	**86.0**	78.0	80.0	*n.a.*	80.8

Table 2. Multi-class texture classification for two different datasets. The columns give the results for different detectors, here their rotation invariant versions.

Database	H-L-R	H-MSLSD-R	LoG-R	L-MSLSD-R
Brodatz	88.3$_{\pm0.6}$	**92.0$_{\pm0.5}$**	90.5$_{\pm0.5}$	**95.8$_{\pm0.4}$**
KTH-TIPS	83.9$_{\pm1.1}$	**88.4$_{\pm0.9}$**	71.2$_{\pm1.5}$	**81.1$_{\pm1.2}$**

Table 3. Classification accuracy with and without rotation invariance. Results for the Brodatz (a) and KTH-TIPS (b) datasets and different detectors.

Brodatz		
Detector	no rot.inv.	rot.inv. (-R)
H-L	89.2$_{\pm0.6}$	← 88.3$_{\pm0.6}$
H-MSLSD	91.5$_{\pm0.6}$	→ 92.0$_{\pm0.5}$
LoG	90.1$_{\pm0.5}$	→ 90.5$_{\pm0.5}$
L-MSLSD	94.2$_{\pm0.5}$	→ 95.8$_{\pm0.4}$

(a)

KTH-TIPS		
Detector	no rot.inv.	rot.inv. (-R)
H-L	85.8$_{\pm1.1}$	← 83.9$_{\pm1.1}$
H-MSLSD	88.1$_{\pm1.2}$	→ 88.4$_{\pm0.9}$
LoG	73.1$_{\pm1.5}$	← 71.2$_{\pm1.5}$
L-MSLSD	80.9$_{\pm1.3}$	→ 81.1$_{\pm1.2}$

(b)

Table 1 reports the classification rate at the EER[1] for four databases and four different detectors. The last two columns give results from the literature. We can observe that in most cases our detectors give better results when compared to their standard versions. In the remaining cases the results are exactly the same. This demonstrates that the local description based on our detectors is more stable and representative of the data.

Evaluation for texture classification. Experiments are carried out on two different texture databases: Brodatz [19] and KTH-TIPS [20]. The Brodatz dataset consists of 112 different texture images, each of which is divided into 9 non-overlapping sub-images. The KTH-TIPS texture dataset contains 10 texture classes with 81 images per class. Images are captured at 9 scales, viewed under three different illumination directions and three different poses. Our training set contains 3 sub-images per class for Brodatz and 40 images per class for KTH-TIPS. Each experiment is repeated 400 times using different random splits and results are reported as the average accuracy on the folds with their standard deviation over the 400 runs. Table 2 compares the results of our detectors H-MSLSD-R and L-MSLSD-R to H-L-R and LoG-R. Note that we use the rotation invariant version here, as rotation invariance allows to group similar texture structures. We can observe that our scale selection technique, MSLSD, improves the results significantly in all cases.

Table 3 analyzes the influence of rotation invariance on the representation. Results for Harris-Laplace and LoG are in general better *without*, whereas results for our detectors are always better *with* rotation invariance. The poor performance of the existing detectors is due to an unstable estimation of the orientation leading to significant errors/noise in the descriptions. Note that the orientation of the patch is estimated after the region detection. In our MSLSD method rotation

---

[1] Point on the ROC curves for which $p(TruePositives) = 1 - p(FalsePositives)$.

estimation is integrated into the scale selection criterion which implies that only regions with stable dominant gradients are selected, and it therefore improves the quality of the image representation.

5   Conclusion and Future Work

This paper introduced a new approach for selecting characteristic scales based on the stability of the local description. We experimentally evaluated this technique for the SIFT descriptor, i.e. Maximally Stable Local SIFT Description (MSLSD). We also demonstrated how a stable estimate of affine regions and orientation can be integrated in our method. Results for MSLSD versions of Harris and Laplacian points outperformed in many cases their corresponding state-of-the-art versions with respect to repeatability and matching. For object category classification MSLSD achieved better or similar results for four datasets. In the context of texture classification our approach always outperformed the standard versions of the detectors.

Future work includes the evaluation of our maximally stable local description approach with other keypoint detectors as well as other descriptors. Our scale selection could also be applied to a dense image representation, which would require an additional criterion for selecting discriminative regions.

Acknowledgments

This research was supported by the European project LAVA.

References

1. Fergus, R., Perona, P., Zisserman, A.: Object class recognition by unsupervised scale-invariant learning. In: CVPR, Madison, Wisconsin, USA. Volume II. (2003) 264–271
2. Opelt, A., Fussenegger, M., Pinz, A., Auer, P.: Weak hypotheses and boosting for generic object detection and recognition. In: ECCV, Prague, Czech Republic. Volume II. (2004) 71–84
3. Schaffalitzky, F., Zisserman, A.: Multi-view matching for unordered image sets. In: ECCV, Copenhagen, Denmark. Volume I. (2002) 414–431
4. Lazebnik, S., Schmid, C., Ponce, J.: Sparse texture representation using affine-invariant neighborhoods. In: CVPR, Madison, Wisconsin, USA. Volume 2. (2003) 319–324
5. Lowe, D.G.: Distinctive image features from scale-invariant keypoints. IJCV 60(2) (2004) 91–110
6. Mikolajczyk, K., Schmid, C.: A performance evaluation of local descriptors. In: CVPR, Madison, Wisconsin, USA. Volume 2. (2003) 257–263
7. Mikolajczyk, K., Schmid, C.: Scale and affine invariant interest point detectors. IJCV 60(1) (2004) 63–86
8. Harris, C., Stephens, M.: A combined corner and edge detector. In: Alvey Vision Conference. (1988) 147–151

9. Lindeberg, T., Garding, J.: Shape-adapted smoothing in estimation of 3D depth cues from affine distortions of local 2D brightness structure. In: ECCV, Stockholm, Sweden. (1994) 389–400

10. Kadir, T., Zisserman, A., Brady, M.: An affine invariant salient region detector. In: ECCV, Prague, Czech Republic. Volume I. (2004) 228–241

11. Mikolajczyk, K., Tuytelaars, T., Schmid, C., Zisserman, A., Matas, J., Schaffalitzky, F., Kadir, T., Gool, L.V.: A comparison of affine region detectors. IJCV 65(1/2) (2005) 43–72

12. Tuytelaars, T., Van Gool, L.: Matching widely separated views based on affine invariant regions. IJCV 59(1) (2004) 61–85

13. Jurie, F., Schmid, C.: Scale-invariant shape features for recognition of object categories. In: CVPR, Washington, DC, USA. Volume II. (2004) 90–96

14. Matas, J., Chum, O., Urban, M., Pajdla, T.: Robust wide baseline stereo from maximally stable extremal regions. In: BMVC, Cardiff, England. (2002) 384–393

15. Blostein, D., Ahuja, N.: A multi-scale region detector. Computer Vision, Graphics and Image Processing 45(1) (1989) 22–41

16. Lindeberg, T.: Feature detection with automatic scale selection. International Journal of Computer Vision 30(2) (1998) 79–116

17. Baumberg, A.: Reliable feature matching across widely separated views. In: CVPR, Hilton Head Island, South Carolina, USA. Volume I. (2000) 774–781

18. Csurka, G., Bray, C., Dance, C., Fan, L.: Visual categorization with bags of keypoints. In: Workshop on Statistical Learning in Computer Vision, ECCV. (2004) 1–22

19. Brodatz, P.: Textures: A Photographic Album for Artists and Designers. Dover Publications, New York (1966)

20. Hayman, E., Caputo, B., Fritz, M., Eklundh, J.O.: On the significance of real-world conditions for material classification. In: ECCV, Prague, Czech Republic. Volume IV. (2004) 253–266

Scene Classification Via pLSA

Anna Bosch[1], Andrew Zisserman[2], and Xavier Muñoz[1]

[1] Computer Vision and Robotics Group, University of Girona, 17071 Girona
{aboschr, xmunoz}@eia.udg.es
[2] Robotics Research Group, University of Oxford, Oxford OX1 3PJ
az@robots.ox.ac.uk

Abstract. Given a set of images of scenes containing multiple object categories (e.g. grass, roads, buildings) our objective is to discover these objects in each image in an unsupervised manner, and to use this object distribution to perform scene classification. We achieve this discovery using probabilistic Latent Semantic Analysis (pLSA), a generative model from the statistical text literature, here applied to a bag of visual words representation for each image. The scene classification on the object distribution is carried out by a k-nearest neighbour classifier.

We investigate the classification performance under changes in the visual vocabulary and number of latent topics learnt, and develop a novel vocabulary using colour SIFT descriptors. Classification performance is compared to the supervised approaches of Vogel & Schiele [19] and Oliva & Torralba [11], and the semi-supervised approach of Fei Fei & Perona [3] using their own datasets and testing protocols. In all cases the combination of (unsupervised) pLSA followed by (supervised) nearest neighbour classification achieves superior results. We show applications of this method to image retrieval with relevance feedback and to scene classification in videos.

1 Introduction

Classifying scenes (such as mountains, forests, offices) is not an easy task owing to their variability, ambiguity, and the wide range of illumination and scale conditions that may apply. Two basic strategies can be found in the literature. The first uses low-level features such as colour, texture, power spectrum, etc. This approaches consider the scene as an individual object [16, 17] and is normally used to classify only a small number of scene categories (indoor versus outdoor, city versus landscape etc...). The second strategy uses an intermediate representations before classifying scenes [3, 11, 19], and has been applied to cases where there are a larger number of scene categories (up to 13).

In this paper we introduce a new classification algorithm based on a combination of unsupervised probabilistic Latent Semantic Analysis (pLSA) [6] followed by a nearest neighbour classifier. The pLSA model was originally developed for topic discovery in a text corpus, where each document is represented by its word frequency. Here it is applied to images represented by the frequency of "visual words". The formation and performance of this "visual vocabulary" is investigated in depth. In particular we compare sparse and dense feature descriptors

A. Leonardis, H. Bischof, and A. Pinz (Eds.): ECCV 2006, Part IV, LNCS 3954, pp. 517–530, 2006.

over a number of modalities (colour, texture, orientation). The approach is inspired in particular by three previous papers: (i) the use of pLSA on sparse features for recognizing compact object categories (such as Caltech cars and faces) in Sivic *et al.* [15]; (ii) the dense SIFT [9] features developed in Dalal and Triggs [2] for pedestrian detection; and (iii) the semi-supervised application of Latent Dirichlet Analysis (LDA) for scene classification in Fei Fei and Perona [3]. We have made extensions over all three of these papers both in developing new features and in the classification algorithm. Our work is most closely related to that of Quelhas *et al.* [12] who also use a combination of pLSA and supervised classification. However, their approach differs in using sparse features and is applied to classify images into only three scene types.

We compare our classification performance to that of three previous methods [3, 11, 19] using the authors' own databases. The previous works used varying levels of supervision in training (compared to the unsupervised object discovery developed in this paper): Fei Fei and Perona [3] requires the category of each scene to be specified during learning (in order to discover the *themes* of each category); Oliva and Torralba [11] require a manual ranking of the training images into 6 different properties; and Vogel and Schiele [19] require manual classification of 59582 local patches from the training images into one of 9 *semantic concepts*. As will be seen, we achieve superior performance in all cases.

We briefly give an overview of the pLSA model in Section 2. Then in Section 3 we describe the classification algorithm based on applying pLSA to images. Section 4 describes the features used to form the visual vocabulary and the principal parameters that are investigated. A description of datasets and a detailed description of the experimental evaluation is given in Sections 5 and 6.

2   pLSA Model

Probabilistic Latent Semantic Analysis (pLSA) is a generative model from the statistical text literature [6]. In text analysis this is used to discover topics in a document using the bag-of-words document representation. Here we have *images* as *documents* and we discover *topics as object categories* (e.g. grass, houses), so that an image containing instances of several objects is modelled as a mixture of topics. The models are applied to images by using a *visual* analogue of a *word*, formed by vector quantizing colour, texture and SIFT feature like region descriptors (as described in Section 4). pLSA is appropriate here because it provides the correct statistical model for clustering in the case of multiple object categories per image. We will explain the model in terms of images, visual words and topics.

Suppose we have a collection of images $D = d_1,...,d_N$ with words from a visual vocabulary $W = w_1,...,w_V$. One may summarize the data in a V × N co-occurrence table of counts $N_{ij} = n(w_i, d_j)$, where $n(w_i, d_j,)$ denotes how often the word w_i occurred in an image d_j. In pLSA there is also a latent variable model for co-occurrence data which associates an unobserved class variable $z \in Z = z_1,...,z_Z$ with each observation. A joint probability model $P(w, d)$ over V × N is defined by the mixture:

$$P(w|d) = \sum_{z \in Z} P(w|z)P(z|d) \qquad (1)$$

$P(w|z)$ are the topic specific distributions and, each image is modelled as a mixture of topics, $P(z|d)$. For a fuller explanation of the model refer to [5, 6, 15].

3   Classification

In training the topic specific distributions $P(w|z)$ are learnt from the set of training images. Each training image is then represented by a Z-vector $P(z|d_{train})$, where Z is the number of topics learnt. Determining both $P(w|z)$ and $P(z|d_{train})$ simply involves fitting the pLSA model to the entire set of training images. In particular it is not necessary to supply the identity of the images (i.e. which category they are in) or any region segmentation.

Classification of an unseen test image proceeds in two stages. First the document specific mixing coefficients $P(z|d_{test})$ are computed, and then these are used to classify the test images using a K nearest neighbour scheme. In more detail document specific mixing coefficients $P(z|d_{test})$ are computed using the fold-in heuristic described in [5]. The unseen image is projected onto the simplex spanned by the $P(w|z)$ learnt during training, i.e. the mixing coefficients $P(z_k|d_{test})$ are sought such that the Kullback-Leibler divergence between the measured empirical distribution and $P(w|d_{test}) = \sum_{z \in Z} P(w|z)P(z|d_{test})$ is minimized. This is achieved by running EM in a similar manner to that used in learning, but now only the coefficients $P(z_k|d_{test})$ are updated in each M-step with the learnt $P(w|z)$ kept fixed. The result is that the test image is represented by a Z-vector. The test image is then classified using a K Nearest Neighbours

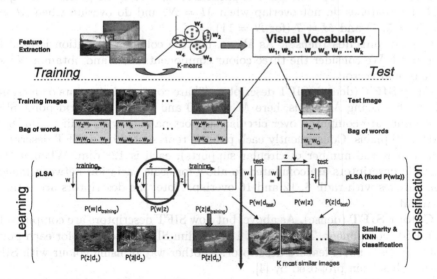

Fig. 1. Overview of visual vocabulary formation, learning and classification stages

classifier (KNN) on the Z-vectors of the training images. An Euclidean distance function is used. In more detail, the KNN selects the K nearest neighbours of the new image within the training database. Then it assigns to the new picture the label of the category which is most represented within the K nearest neighbours. Figure 1 shows graphically the learning and classification process.

4   Visual Words and Visual Vocabulary

In the formulation of pLSA, we compute a co-occurrence table, where each image is represented as a collection of visual words, provided from a visual vocabulary. This visual vocabulary is obtained by vector quantizing descriptors computed from the training images using k-means, see the illustration in the first part of Figure 1. Previously both sparse [1, 7, 14] and dense descriptors, e.g. [2, 8, 18], have been used. Here we carry out a thorough comparison over dense descriptors for a number of visual measures (see below) and compare to a sparse descriptor. We vary the normalization, sizes of the patches, and degree of overlap. The words produced are evaluated by assessing their classification performance over three different databases in Section 5.

We investigate four dense descriptors, and compare their performance to a previously used sparse descriptor. In the dense case the important parameters are the size of the patches (N) and their spacing (M) which controls the degree of overlap:

Grey patches (dense). As in [18], and using only the grey level information, the descriptor is a N × N square neighbourhood around a pixel. The pixels are row reordered to form a vector in an N^2 dimensional feature space. The patch size tested are $N = 5, 7$ and 11. The patches are spaced by M pixels on a regular grid. The patches do not overlap when $M = N$, and do overlap when $M = 3$ (for $N = 5, 7$) and $M = 7$ (for $N = 11$).

Colour patches (dense). As above, but the colour information is used for each pixel. We consider the three colour components HSV and obtain a $N^2 \times 3$ dimensional vector.

Grey SIFT (dense). SIFT descriptors [9] are computed at points on a regular grid with spacing M pixels, here $M = 5, 10$ and 15. At each grid point SIFT descriptors are computed over circular support patches with radii $r = 4, 8, 12$ and/or 16 pixels. Consequently each point is represented by n SIFT descriptors (where n is the number of circular supports), each is 128-dim. When $n > 1$, multiple descriptors are computed to allow for scale variation between images. The patches with radii 8, 12 and 16 overlap. Note, the descriptors are rotation invariant.

Colour SIFT (dense). As above, but now SIFT descriptors are computed for each HSV component. This gives a 128 × 3 dim-SIFT descriptor for each point. Note, this is a novel feature descriptor. Another way of using colour with SIFT features has been proposed by [4].

Grey SIFT (sparse). Affine co-variant regions are computed for each grey scale image, constructed by elliptical shape adaptation about an interest point

[10]. These regions are represented by ellipses. Each ellipse is mapped to a circle by appropriate scaling along its principal axis and a 128-dim SIFT descriptor computed. This is the method used by [1, 7, 14, 15].

5   Datasets and Methodology

5.1   Datasets

We evaluated our classification algorithm on three different datasets: (i) Oliva and Torralba [11], (ii) Vogel and Schiele [19], and (iii) Fei Fei and Perona [3]. We will refer to these datasets as OT, VS and FP respectively. Figure 2 shows example images from each dataset, and the contents are summarized here:

OT: includes 2688 images classified as 8 categories: 360 coasts, 328 forest, 374 mountain, 410 open country, 260 highway, 308 inside of cities, 356 tall buildings, 292 streets. The average size of each image is 250 × 250 pixels.

VS: includes 702 natural scenes consisting of 6 categories: 144 coasts, 103 forests, 179 mountains, 131 open country, 111 river and 34 sky/clouds. The size of the images is 720 × 480 (landscape format) or 480 × 720 (portrait format). Every scene category is characterized by a high degree of diversity and potential ambiguities since it depends strongly on the subjective perception of the viewer.

FP: contains 13 categories and is only available in greyscale. This dataset consists of the 2688 images (8 categories) of the OT dataset plus: 241 suburb residence, 174 bedroom, 151 kitchen, 289 living room and 216 office. The average size of each image is approximately 250 × 300 pixels.

Fig. 2. Example images from the three different datasets used. (a) from dataset OT [11], (b) from dataset VS [19], and (c) from the dataset FP [3]. The remaining images of this dataset are the same as in OT but in greyscale.

5.2   Methodology

The classification task is to assign each test image to one of a number of categories. The performance is measured using a confusion table, and overall performance rates are measured by the average value of the diagonal entries of the confusion table.

Datasets are split randomly into two separate sets of images, half for training and half for testing. We take 100 random images from the training set to find the optimal parameters, and the rest of the training images are used to compute the vocabulary and pLSA topics. A vocabulary of visual words is learnt from about 30 random training images of each category.

The new classification scheme is compared to two baseline methods. These are included in order to gauge the difficulty of the various classification tasks. The baseline algorithms are:

Global colour model. The algorithm computes global HSV histograms for each training image. The colour values are represented by a histogram with 36 bins for H, 32 bins for S, and 16 bins for V, giving a 84-dimensional vector for each image. A test image is classified using KNN (with $K = 10$).

Global texture model. The algorithm computes the orientation of the gradient at each pixel for each training image (greyscale). These orientations are collected into a 72 bin histogram for each image. The classification of a test image is again carried out using KNN.

Moreover the KNN classifier is also applied directly to the bag-of-words (BOW) representation (i.e. to $P(w|d)$) in order to assess the gain in using pLSA (where the KNN classifier is applied to the topic distribution $P(z|d)$).

6   Classification Results

We investigate the variation of classification performance with change in visual vocabulary, number of topics etc for the case of the OT dataset. The results for the datasets FP and VS use the optimum parameters selected for OT and are given in Section 6.2 below. For the OT dataset three classification situations are considered: classification into 8 categories, and also classification within the two subsets of natural (4 categories), and man-made (4 categories) images. The latter two are the situations considered in [11]. We carry out experiments with normalized images (zero mean and unit standard deviation) and unnormalized images.

Excluding the preprocessing time of feature detection and visual vocabulary formation, it takes about 15 mins to fit the pLSA model to 1600 images (Matlab implementation on a 1.7GHz Computer).

6.1   Classification of the OT Dataset

We first investigate how classification performance (on the validation set – see Section 5.2) is affected by the various parameters: the number of visual words

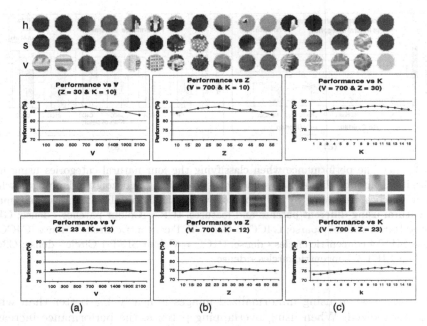

Fig. 3. Performance under variation in various parameters for the 8 category OT classification. Top: example visual words and performance for dense colour SIFT $M = 10$, $r = 4, 8, 12$ and 16 (each column shows the HSV components of the same word). Lower example visual words and performance for grey patches with $N = 5$ and $M = 3$. (a) Varying number of visual words, V, (b) Varying number of topics, Z, (c) Varying number k (KNN).

(V in the k-means vector quantization), the number of topics (Z in pLSA), and the number of neighbours (K in kNN). Figure 3 shows this performance variation for two types of descriptor – dense colour SIFT with $M = 10$ and four circular supports, and grey patches with $N = 5$ and $M = 3$. Note the mode in the graphs of V, Z and K in both cases. This is quite typical across all types of visual words, though the position of the modes vary slightly. For example, using colour SIFT the mode is at $V = 1500$ and $Z = 25$, while for grey patches the mode is at $V = 700$ and $Z = 23$. For K the performance increases progressively until K is between 10 and 12, and then drops off slightly. In the following results the optimum choice of parameters is used for each descriptor type.

To investigate the statistical variation we repeat the dense colour SIFT experiment ($r = 4, 8, 12, 16$ and $M = 10$) 15 times with varying random selection of the training and test sets, and building the visual vocabulary afresh each time. All parameters are fixed with the number of visual words $V = 1500$, the number of topics $Z = 25$ and the number of neighbours $K = 10$. We obtained performance values between 79% and 86% with a mean of 84.78% and standard deviation of 1.93%.

We next investigate the patch descriptors in more detail. Figure 4a shows the results when classifying the images of natural scenes with colour-patches. The

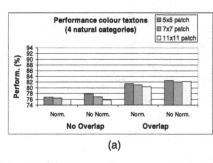 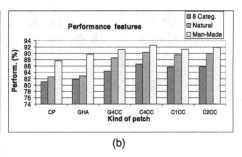

(a)   (b)

Fig. 4. (a) The performance when classifying the four natural categories using normalized and unnormalized images and with overlapping and non-overlapping patches. Colour patches are used. (b) Performance when classifying all categories, man-made and natural using different patches and features. (CP = Colour patches - dense; GHA = Grey Harris Affine - sparse; G4CC = Grey SIFT concentric circles - dense; C4CC = Colour SIFT 4 concentric circles - dense; C1CC = Colour SIFT 1 Circle - dense; C2CC = Colour SIFT 2 concentric circles - dense.

performance when using unnormalized images is nearly 1% better than when using normalized. When using overlapping patches, the performance increases by almost 6% compared to no overlap. Similar results occur for the man-made and all scene category sets. Comparing results when classifying the images using only grey level information or using colour, it can be seen that colour brings an increment of around 6-8%. This is probably because colour is such an important factor in outdoor images, and helps to disambiguate and classify the different objects in the scene. For colour patches the best performance is obtained when using the 5×5 patch over unnormalized images, with $M = 3$, $V = 900$, $Z = 23$ and $K = 10$.

The performance of SIFT features is shown in Figure 4b. The best results are obtained with dense and not sparse descriptors. This is almost certainly because we have more information on the images: in the sparse case the only information is where a Harris detector fires and, especially for natural images, this is a very impoverished representation. Again colour is a benefit with better results obtained using colour than grey SIFT. The performance using grey SIFT when classifying natural images is 88.56% and increase 2% when using colour SIFT, both with four concentric support regions. The difference when using these vocabularies with man-made images is not as significant. This reiterates that colour in natural images is very important for classification. Turning to the performance variation with the number of support regions for dense SIFT. It can be seen that best results are obtained using four concentric circles. With only one support region to represent each patch, results are around 1% worse. This is probably because of lack of invariance to scale changes (compared to using four support regions to represent each point).

All the results above are for $P(z|d)$ with the KNN algorithm. Now we investigate classifying the BOW representation directly. We use $V = 1500$, $Z = 25$, $K = 10$, $M = 10$ and four concentric circles. When classifying the 4 natural

Table 1. Rates obtained different features when using database OT: GP (Grey Patches), CP (Colour Patches), G4CC (Grey SIFT four Concentric Circles), C4CC (Colour SIFT four Concentric Circles), PS (Colour Patches and Colour SIFT), BOW (Bag-of-Words), GlC (Global colour), GlT (Global Texture).

Visual Vocabulary	GP	CP	G4CC	C4CC	PS	BOW	GlC	GlT
All categ.	71.51	77.05	84.39	86.65	82.6	82.53	55.12	62.21
Natural categ.	75.43	82.47	88.56	90.28	84.05	88.74	59.53	69.61
Man-made categ.	77.44	83.56	91.17	92.52	89.34	89.67	66.11	73.14

images in the OT dataset, the results using the topic distribution is 90.28 and with the bag-of-words directly the classification performance decreases by only around $1, 5\%$, to 88.74%. However for 8 categories, the performance decreases by nearly 4%, from 86.65 to 82.53%. Using the 13 categories from the FP dataset, the performance falls 8.4%, from 73.4% to 64.8%. Thus there is a clear gain in using pLSA (over the BOW) when classifying a large number of categories.

Table 1 summarizes the results for the three OT image sets (all 8 categories, 4 natural and 4 man-made) covering the different vocabularies: grey and colour patches, grey and colour SIFT, BOW classification and the two baseline algorithms. From these results it can be seen that: (i) The baseline texture algorithm works better than the baseline colour in all three cases. Despite its simplicity the performance of the baseline texture algorithm on man-made images (73.14%) is very high, showing that these images may be easily classified from their edge directions. (ii) For the various descriptors there are clear performance conclusions: man-made is always better classified than natural (as expected from the baseline results); SIFT type descriptors are always superior to patches; colour is always superior to grey level. The best performance (86.65% for all 8 categories) is obtained using colour SIFT with $M = 10$ and four concentric circles. (iii) Somewhat surprizingly, better results are obtained using the SIFT vocabulary alone, rather than when merging both vocabularies (patches and SIFT). This may be because the parameters (V, Z and K) have been optimized for a single vocabulary, not under the conditions of using multiple vocabularies. This issue will be investigated further.

The best classified scenes are *highway* and *forest* with 95.61% and 94.86% of correct classified images respectively. The most difficult scenes to classify are *open country*. There is confusion between the *open country* and *coast* scenes. These are also the most confused categories in [11].

Figure 5 shows examples of segmentation of four topics using the colour SIFT vocabulary. Circular patches are painted according to the maximum posterior $P(z|w, d)$:

$$P(z|w, d) = \frac{P(w|z)P(z|d)}{\sum_{z_l \in Z} P(w|z_l)P(z_l|d)} \qquad (2)$$

For each visual word in the image we choose the topic with maximum posterior $P(z|w, d)$ and paint the patch with its associated colour, so each colour represents a different topic (the topic colour is chosen randomly). To simplify the figures

Fig. 5. Topics segmentation. Four topics (clouds – top left, sky – top right, vegetation – lower left, and snow/rocks in mountains – lower right) are shown. Only circular regions with a topic posterior $P(z|w, d)$ greater than 0.8 are shown.

we only paint one topic each time. Note that topics represent consistent regions across images (enabling a coarse segmentation) and there is a straightforward correspondence between topic and object.

Decreasing the number of training images. We evaluate now the classification performance when less training data is available. The OT dataset is split into 2000 training images and 688 test images. A varying number of nt labelled images from the training set are used to learn the pLSA topics and for the KNN. The classification performance is compared using $P(z|d)$ and BOW vectors. The vocabulary has $V = 1500$ words, and $Z = 25$ and $K = 10$. Four support regions are used for each point spaced at $M = 10$. Table 2 shows the results. The gap between pLSA and BOW increases as the number of labelled training images decreases, as was demonstrated in [12].

Table 2. Comparison of $P(z|d)$ and BOW performance as the number of training images used in KNN is decreased. The classification task is into 8 categories from the OT dataset.

# img. (nt)	2000	1600	1024	512	256	128	32
Perf. $P(z|d)$	86.9	86.7	84.6	79.5	75.3	68.2	58.7
Perf. BOW	83.1	82.6	80.4	72.8	60.2	52.0	47.3

Summary. The best results are obtained using dense descriptors – colour SIFT with four circular support. Overlap increases the performance. When using the SIFT vocabulary the values for the parameters giving the best results are $M = 10$ pixels with radius for the concentric circles support regions of $r = 4, 8, 12$ and 16 pixels and $V = 1500$, $Z = 25$ and $K = 10$. For patches the best results are for $N = 5$, $M = 3$, $V = 900$, $Z = 23$ and $K = 10$. In both, colour information is used. The result that dense SIFT gives the best performance was also found by [2] in the case of pedestrian detection. It it interesting that the same feature applies both to more distributed categories (like grass, mountains) as well as the compact objects (pedestrians) of their work where essentially only the boundaries are salient.

6.2   Comparison to Previous Results

We compare the performance of our classification algorithm to the supervised approaches of Vogel and Schiele [19] and Oliva and Torralba [11], and the semi-supervised approach of Fei Fei and Perona [3], using the same datasets that they tested their approaches on. For each dataset we use the same parameters and type of visual words ($V = 1500$, $Z = 25$ and $K = 10$ with SIFT and four circular supports spaced at $M = 10$). We used colour for OT and VS and grey for FP. The visual vocabulary is computed independently for each dataset, as described in section 5.2. We return to the issue of sharing vocabularies across datasets in section 6.3. The results are given in Table 3.

Table 3. Comparison of our algorithm with other methods using their own databases

Dataset	# of categ.	our perf.	authors' perf.
OT	8	86.65	–
OT	4 Natural	90.2	89.0 [11]
OT	4 Man-Made	92.5	89.0 [11]
VS	6	85.7	74.1 [19]
FP	13	73.4	65.2 [3]

Note that much better results are obtained with the four natural scenes of OT, than with the six of VS. This is because the images in VS are much more ambiguous than those of OT and consequently more difficult to classify. Our method outperforms all of the previous methods, despite the fact that our training is unsupervised in the sense that the scene identity of each image is unknown at the pLSA stage and is not required until the KNN classification step. This is in contrast to [3], where each image is labelled with the identity of the scene to which it belongs during the training stage. In [19], the training requires manual annotation of 9 semantic concepts for 60000 patches, while in [11] training requires manual annotation of 6 properties for thousands of scenes. We are not using the same split into training and testing images as the original authors: for OT we use approximately 200 images per category which means *less* training images (and more testing images) than [11], who used between 250 and 300 training images per category. For VS we used 350 images for training and 350 also for testing which also means *less* training images than [19] who used approximately 600 training images. When working with FP we used 1344 images for training, which is slightly *more* than [3], who used 1300 (100 per category) training images.

Discussion. The superior performance (compared to [3, 19]) could be due to the use of better features and how they are used. In the case of Vogel and Schiele, they learn 9 topics (called *semantic concepts*) that correspond to those that humans can observe in the images: *water, trees, sky* etc. for 6 categories. Fei Fei and Perona learn 40 topics (called *themes*) for 13 categories. They do not say if these topics correspond to natural objects. In our case, we discover between

22 and 30 topics for 8 categories. These topics can vary depending if we are working with colour features (where topics can distinguish objects with different colours like *light sky, blue sky, orange sky, orange foliage, green foliage* etc...) or only grey SIFT features (objects like *trees* and *foliage, sea, buildings* etc...). In contrast to [19] we discover objects that sometimes would not be distinguished in a manual annotation, for example *water with waves* and *water without waves*. Our superior performance compared to [11] could be due to their method of scene interpretation. They use the spatial envelope modeled in a holistic way in order to obtain the structure (shape) of the scene using coarsely localized information. On the other hand, in our approach specific information about objects is used for scene categorization.

6.3   Other Applications

We applied the pLSA based classifier in three other situations. The first one is also a classification task, but combining the images of two different datasets, the second is a relevance feedback application, and the third is scene retrieval for the film *Pretty Woman* [Marshall, 1990]. In all the following the descriptor is dense colour SIFT with circular support and $V = 700$, $Z = 22$ and $K = 10$ (these are the optimal parameter values when working with the four natural scenes).

Vocabulary generalization. In this classification test, we train the system with the four natural scenes of the OT dataset (*coast, forest, mountains* and *open country*) and test using the same four scene categories from the VS dataset. This tests whether the vocabulary and categories learnt from one dataset generalizes to another. We obtain a performance of 88.27% of correctly classified images. Note, this performance is worse than that obtained when classifying the same categories using only the OT database. This is because (i) images within the same database are more similar, and (ii) the images in VS are more ambiguous and not all represented in OT. To address (i) we will investigate using vocabularies composed from both databases.

Relevance Feedback (RF). [20] proposed a method for improving the retrieval performance, given a probablistic model. It is based on moving the query point in the visual word space toward good example points (relevant images) and

Fig. 6. Example frames from the film Pretty Woman with their classification. The classifier is trained on the OT dataset.

away from bad example points (irrelevant images). The vector moving strategy uses the Rocchio's formula [13]. To test RF we simulate the user's feedback using 25 random images of each category. For each query image, we carry out n iterations. At each iteration the system examines the top 20, 40 or 60 images that are most similar to the query excluding the positive examples labelled in previous iterations. Images from the same category as the initial query will be used as positive examples, and other images as negative examples. We used 200 query images, 25 of each category, in OT dataset. Best results are obtained when considering the top 60 images, The first 100 images can be retrieved with an average precision of 0.75. The most difficult category to retrieve is *open country* while the better retrieved are *forest* and *highway* followed by *tall buildings*. This is in accordance with the classification results.

Classifying film frames into scenes. In this test the images in OT are again used as training images (8 categories), and key frames from the movie *Pretty Woman* are used as test images. We used one of every 100 frames from the movie to form the testing set. In this movie there are only a few images that could be classified as the same categories used in OT, and there are many images containing only people. So it is a difficult task for the system to correctly classify the key frames. However, the results obtained (see Figure 6) are very encouraging and show again the success of using pLSA in order to classify scenes according to their topic distribution.

7   Conclusions

We have proposed a scene classifier that learns categories and their distributions in unlabelled training images using pLSA, and then uses their distribution in test images as a feature vector in a supervised nearest neighbour scheme. In contrast to previous approaches [3, 11, 19], our topic learning stage is completely unsupervised and we obtain significantly superior performance. We studied the influence of various descriptor parameters and have shown that using dense SIFT descriptors with overlapping patches gives the best results for man-made as well as for natural scene classification. Furthermore, discovered topics correspond fairly well with different objects in the images, and topic distributions are consistent between images of the same category. It is probably this freedom in choosing appropriate topics for a dataset, together with the optimized features and vocabularies, that is responsible for the superior performance of the scene classifier over previous work (with manual annotation). Moreover, the use of pLSA is never detrimental to performance, and it gives a significant improvement over the original BOW model when a large number of scene categories are used.

Acknowledgements

Thanks to A.Torralba, J.Vogel and F.F.Li for providing their datasets and to Josef Sivic for discussions. This work was partially funded by the research grant BR03/01 from the University of Girona and by the EC NOE Pascal.

References

1. Csurka, G., Bray, C., Dance, C., Fan, L.: Visual categorization with bags of keypoints. SLCV Workshop, ECCV, (2004) 1–22
2. Dalal, N., Triggs, B.: Histograms of oriented gradients for human detection. CVPR, San Diego, California (2005)
3. Fei-Fei, L., Perona, P.: A bayesian hierarchical model for learning natural scene categories. CVPR, Washington, DC, USA, (2005) 524–531
4. Geodeme, T., Tuytelaars, T., Vanacker, G., Nuttin, M., Van Gool, L. Omnidirectional Sparse Visual Path Following with Occlusion-Robust Feature Tracking. OMNIVIS Workshop, ICCV (2005)
5. Hofmann, T.: Probabilistic latent semantic indexing. ACM SIGIR, (1998)
6. Hofmann, T.: Unsupervised learning by probabilistic latent semantic analysis. Machine Learning 41 (2001) 177–196
7. Lazebnik, S., Schmid, C., Ponce, J.: A sparse texture representation using affine-invariant regions. CVPR, volume 2, (2003) 319–324
8. Leung, T., Malik, J.: Representing and recognizing the visual appearance of materials using three-dimensional textons. IJCV 43 (2001) 29–44
9. Lowe, D.: Distinctive image features from scale invariant keypoints. IJCV 60 (2004) 91–110
10. Mikolajczyk, K., Schmid, C.: Scale and affine invariant interest point detectors. IJCV 60 (2004) 63–86
11. Oliva, A., Torralba, A.: Modeling the shape of the scene: a holistic representation of the spatial envelope. IJCV (42) 145–175
12. Quelhas, P., Monay, F., Odobez, J., Gatica-Perez, D., Tuytelaars, T., Van Gool, L.: Modeling scenes with local descriptors and latent aspects. ICCV, Beijing, China, (2005)
13. Rocchio, J.: Relevance feedback in information retrieval. In the SMART Retrieval System - Experiments in Automatic Document Processing, Prentice Hall, Englewood Cliffs, NJ (1971)
14. Sivic, J., Zisserman, A.: Video Google: A text retrieval approach to object matching in videos. ICCV, (2003)
15. Sivic, J., Russell, B., Efros, A., Zisserman, A., Freeman, W.T.: Discovering objets and their locations in images. In: ICCV, Beijing, China (2005)
16. Szummer, M., Picard, R.W.: Indoor-outdoor image classification. ICCV, Bombay, India (1998) 42–50
17. Vailaya, A., Figueiredo, A., Jain, A., Zhang, H.: Image classification for content-based indexing. T-IP 10 (2001)
18. Varma, M., Zisserman, A.: Texture classification: Are filter banks necessary? CVPR, volume 2, Madison, Wisconsin (2003) 691–698
19. Vogel, J., Schiele, B.: Natural scene retrieval based on a semantic modeling step. CIVR, Dublin, Ireland (2004)
20. Zhang, R., Zhang, Z.: Hidden semantic concept discovery in region based image retrieval. CVPR, Washington, DC, USA (2004)

Probabilistic Linear Discriminant Analysis

Sergey Ioffe*

Fujifilm Software, 1740 Technology Dr., Ste. 490, San Jose, CA 95110
sioffe@gmail.com

Abstract. Linear dimensionality reduction methods, such as LDA, are often
used in object recognition for feature extraction, but do not address the problem of
how to use these features for recognition. In this paper, we propose Probabilistic
LDA, a generative probability model with which we can both extract the features
and combine them for recognition. The latent variables of PLDA represent both
the class of the object and the view of the object within a class. By making examples of the same class share the class variable, we show how to train PLDA
and use it for recognition on previously unseen classes. The usual LDA features
are derived as a result of training PLDA, but in addition have a probability model
attached to them, which automatically gives more weight to the more discriminative features. With PLDA, we can build a model of a previously unseen class
from a single example, and can combine multiple examples for a better representation of the class. We show applications to classification, hypothesis testing,
class inference, and clustering, on classes not observed during training.

1 Introduction

There is a long tradition of using linear dimensionality reduction methods for object
recognition [1, 2]. Most notably, these include Principal Component Analysis (PCA)
and Linear Discriminant Analysis (LDA). While PCA identifies the linear subspace in
which most of the data's energy is concentrated, LDA identifies the subspace in which
the data between different classes is most spread out, relative to the spread within each
class. This makes LDA suitable for recognition problems such as classification. One
of the questions that dimensionality reduction methods do not answer is: what do we
do with the lower-dimension representation of the data? A common technique is to
project the data onto a PCA subspace, thus eliminating singularities, and then find an
LDA subspace. However, after the projection, how do we combine the components
of the resulting multivariate representation? Clearly some dimensions (for example,
the dominant projection directions identified by LDA) have to be more important than
others, but how do we incorporate this difference in importance into recognition? How
do we perform tasks such as classification and hypothesis testing on examples of classes
we haven't seen before, and how do we take advantage of multiple examples of a new
class?

In this paper, we reformulate the problem of dimensionality reduction for recognition
in the probabilistic context. It has long been known that LDA maximizes the likelihood
of a Gaussian mixture model and is mathematically equivalent to linear regression of

---

* The author is currently at Google.

A. Leonardis, H. Bischof, and A. Pinz (Eds.): ECCV 2006, Part IV, LNCS 3954, pp. 531–542, 2006.
© Springer-Verlag Berlin Heidelberg 2006

the class assignment labels [3, 4]. Such regression, however, is useful only when LDA is used to classify examples of the classes represented in the training data. One of the many problems in which this assumption is false is face recognition. For example, having trained a system, we need to be able to determine whether two face views belong to the same person, even though we have not seen this person before. In these cases, we are not able to build an accurate probability model for the new person (since we have only one example), nor is a discrete class label defined for an example of a previously unseen class.

In a Gaussian mixture model with common class-conditional covariances, each class is described by its center, and the support of the prior distribution of the class centers is a finite set of points. This is not sufficient for handling new classes, and in this work we solve this problem by making the prior of the class centers continuous. We can learn this prior (which models the differences between classes) as well as the common variance of the class-conditional distributions (which models the differences between examples of the same class). We will show that by maximizing the model likelihood we arrive at the features obtained by Linear Discriminant Analysis. However, in Probabilistic LDA, we also obtain a principled method of combining different features so that the more discriminative features have more impact on recognition.

Probabilistic LDA is a general method that can accomplish a wide variety of recognition tasks. In "one-shot learning" [5], a single example of a previously unseen class can be used to build the model of the class. Multiple examples can be combined to obtain a better representation of the class. In hypothesis testing, we can compare two examples, or two groups of examples, to determine whether they belong to the same (previously unseen) class. This can further be used to cluster examples of classes not observed before, and automatically determine the number of clusters.

The method proposed in this paper is to LDA what Probabilistic PCA [6] is to PCA. Namely, we will derive the commonly used feature extraction method using a probabilistic approach, and obtain the method not just to compute the features, but also to combine them. While PPCA is used to model a probability density of data, PLDA can be used to make probabilistic inferences about the class of data.

2   Linear Discriminant Analysis

Linear Discriminant Analysis (LDA) is commonly used to identify the linear features that maximize the between-class separation of data, while minimizing the within-class scatter [7]. Consider a training data set containing N examples $\{\mathbf{x}^1 \ldots \mathbf{x}^N\}$, where each example $\mathbf{x}^i$ is a column vector of length d. Each training example belongs to one of the K classes. Let $\mathcal{C}_k$ be the set of all examples of class k, and let $n_k = |\mathcal{C}_k|$ be the number of examples in class $k = 1 \ldots K$. In LDA, the within-class and between-class scatter matrices are computed:

$$S_w = \frac{\sum_k \sum_{i \in \mathcal{C}_k} (\mathbf{x}^i - \mathbf{m}_k)(\mathbf{x}^i - \mathbf{m}_k)^T}{N}, \ S_b = \frac{\sum_k n_k (\mathbf{m}_k - \mathbf{m})(\mathbf{m}_k - \mathbf{m})^T}{N} \quad (1)$$

where $\mathbf{m}_k = \frac{1}{n_k} \sum_{i \in \mathcal{C}_k} \mathbf{x}^i$ is the mean of kth class, and $\mathbf{m} = \frac{1}{N} \sum_i \mathbf{x}^i$ is the mean of the data set. We seek the linear transformation $\mathbf{x} \rightarrow W^T \mathbf{x}$ that maximizes the between-class variance relative to the within-class variance, where W is a $d \times d'$ matrix, with d' being the desired number of dimensions. It can be shown that the columns of the optimal W are the generalized eigenvectors such that $S_b \mathbf{w} = \lambda S_w \mathbf{w}$, corresponding to the d' largest eigenvalues. One consequence of this result is that W simultaneously diagonalizes the scatter matrices $W^T S_b W$ and $W^T S_w W$. In other words, LDA decorrelates the data both between and within classes.

The LDA projections can be derived by fitting a Gaussian Mixture Model to the training data [3]. The mixture model that results can be used to classify examples of the classes represented in the training data, but not the novel classes. A different probability model is required for that purpose, and is provided by Probabilistic LDA.

3 Probabilistic LDA

A Gaussian mixture model can be thought of as a latent variable model where the observed node x represents the example, and the latent variable y is the center of a mixture component and represents the class (Fig. 1a). Members of the same class share the class variable y. The class-conditional distributions

$$P(\mathbf{x} \,|\, \mathbf{y}) = \mathcal{N}(\mathbf{x} \,|\, \mathbf{y}, \Phi_w)$$

have a common covariance matrix Φ_w, and the prior on the class variable assigns a probability mass to each of the finite number of points: $P(\mathbf{y}) = \sum_{k=1}^{K} \pi_k \delta(\mathbf{y} - \mu_k)$. When the centers μ_k are constrained to lie in a low-dimensional (but unknown) subspace, likelihood maximization with respect to μ_k, π_k and Φ_w recovers the standard LDA projections [3]. We want to extend the probabilistic framework to be able to handle classes not represented in the training data. To this end, we propose to modify the latent variable prior and make it continuous. In particular, to enable efficient inference and closed-form training, we shall impose a Gaussian prior:

$$P(\mathbf{y}) = \mathcal{N}(\mathbf{y} \,|\, \mathbf{m}, \Phi_b)$$

We will require Φ_w to be positive definite, and Φ_b to be positive semi-definite. It is a well-known result from linear algebra that Φ_w and Φ_b can be simultaneously diagonalized: $V^T \Phi_b V = \Psi$ and $V^T \Phi_w V = I$, where the diagonal matrix Ψ and non-singular matrix V are found by solving a generalized eigenproblem. By defining $A = V^{-T}$, we have $\Phi_w = AA^T$ and $\Phi_b = A\Psi A^T$. Our model is then:

$$\begin{array}{ll} \mathbf{x} = \mathbf{m} + A\mathbf{u} & \text{where} \\ \mathbf{u} \sim \mathcal{N}(\cdot \,|\, \mathbf{v}, \mathbf{I}) & \text{and} \\ \mathbf{v} \sim \mathcal{N}(\cdot \,|\, 0, \Psi) & \end{array} \qquad (2)$$

Here v represents the class, and u represents an example of that class in the projected space — just as $\mathbf{y} = \mathbf{m} + A\mathbf{v}$ and $\mathbf{x} = \mathbf{m} + A\mathbf{u}$ do in the data space. Here, Ψ is diagonal, $\Psi \geq 0$. The corresponding graphical model is shown in Fig. 1b.

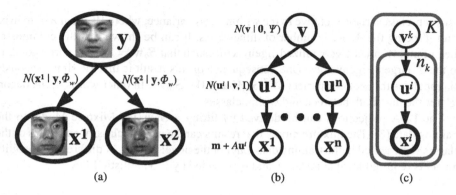

Fig. 1. (a) Modeling class and view. The latent variable $\mathbf{y}$ represents the class center, and the examples of the class are drawn from a Gaussian distribution centered at $\mathbf{y}$. If the prior on $\mathbf{y}$ is discrete, this is a mixture model. For the model to generalize to previously unseen classes, we instead impose a Gaussian prior $\mathcal{N}(\mathbf{y} \mid \mathbf{m}, \Phi_b)$ on the class center, which leads to Probabilistic LDA. (b) By diagonalizing the covariances Φ_b and Φ_w, PLDA models the class center $\mathbf{v}$ and examples $\mathbf{u}$ in the latent space where the variables are independent. The example $\mathbf{x}$ in the original space is related to its latent representation $\mathbf{u}$ via an invertible transformation A. All the recognition activities take place in the latent space. (c) A set of examples $\mathbf{x}$ grouped into K clusters, where examples within the kth cluster share the class variable $\mathbf{v}^k$. The latent variables $\mathbf{v}$ and $\mathbf{u}$ are hidden and can be integrated out. In the training data, the grouping of examples into clusters is given, and we learn the model parameters by maximizing the likelihood. If, instead, the model parameters are fixed, likelihood maximization with respect to the class assignment labels solves a clustering problem.

3.1   Inference in the Latent Space

The main advantage of PLDA is that it allows us to make inference about the classes not present during training. One example of such a situation is face recognition. The model parameters are learned from training data, but the trained system must deal with examples of novel individuals. This is different from many other object recognition tasks where the training data contains examples of all the classes.

In the problem of classification, we are given a gallery $(\mathbf{x}^1 \dots \mathbf{x}^M)$ containing one example from each of M classes, as well as a probe example $\mathbf{x}^p$. We know that the probe belongs to one of the M classes in the gallery, and need to determine which one. We will answer this question by maximizing the likelihood. This is more easily accomplished in the latent space, where we apply the transform $\mathbf{u} = A^{-1}(\mathbf{x} - \mathbf{m})$ to all of the data, which decorrelates the data as shown in Eqn. (2). Consider an example $\mathbf{u}^g$ from the gallery. Let us compute $P(\mathbf{u}^p \mid \mathbf{u}^g)$, the probability of the probe example coming from the same class as the gallery example. By performing the inference on the class variable, we have

$$P(\mathbf{v} \mid \mathbf{u}) = \mathcal{N}(\mathbf{v} \mid \tfrac{\Psi}{\Psi + \mathbf{I}}\mathbf{u}, \tfrac{\Psi}{\Psi + \mathbf{I}}) \tag{3}$$

Since $\mathbf{u}^p$ and $\mathbf{u}^g$ are conditionally independent given $\mathbf{v}$ (see Fig. 1), we have

$$P(\mathbf{u}^p \mid \mathbf{u}^g) = \mathcal{N}(\mathbf{u}^p \mid \tfrac{\Psi}{\Psi + \mathbf{I}}\mathbf{u}^g, \mathbf{I} + \tfrac{\Psi}{\Psi + \mathbf{I}}) \tag{4}$$

To classify a probe example, we compute $P(\mathbf{u}^p \mid \mathbf{u}^g)$ for $g = 1 \ldots M$, and pick the maximum. With PLDA, we were able to combine the knowledge about the general structure of the data, obtained during training, and the examples of new classes, yielding a principled way to perform classification[1].

We can also combine multiple examples of a class into a single model, improving the recognition performance. If n independent examples $\mathbf{u}_{1 \ldots n}^g$ of a class are in the gallery to be used for classification, then we can show that

$$P(\mathbf{u}^p \mid \mathbf{u}_{1 \ldots n}^g) = \mathcal{N}(\mathbf{u}^p \mid \tfrac{n\Psi}{n\Psi + \mathbf{I}} \bar{\mathbf{u}}^g, \mathbf{I} + \tfrac{\Psi}{n\Psi + \mathbf{I}})$$

where $\bar{\mathbf{u}}^g = \frac{1}{n}(\mathbf{u}_1^g + \cdots + \mathbf{u}_n^g)$.

Another common recognition problem is that of hypothesis testing. Given two examples of previously unseen classes, we need to determine whether they belong to the same class. Methods such as LDA do not solve this problem, but with PLDA it is easily accomplished. For two examples $\mathbf{u}^p$ and $\mathbf{u}^g$, we compute the likelihoods $P(\mathbf{u}^p)P(\mathbf{u}^g)$ and $\mathcal{P}(\mathbf{u}^p, \mathbf{u}^g) = \int P(\mathbf{u}^p \mid \mathbf{v}) P(\mathbf{u}^g \mid \mathbf{v}) P(\mathbf{v}) d\mathbf{v}$ corresponding to the two examples belonging to different classes and the same class, respectively, and use the ratio of the two to classify. More generally, if the probe contains multiple examples of an object and the gallery contains multiple examples of another object, we compute the likelihood ratio

$$R(\{\mathbf{u}_{1 \ldots m}^p\}, \{\mathbf{u}_{1 \ldots n}^g\}) = \frac{\text{likelihood(same)}}{\text{likelihood(diff)}} = \frac{\mathcal{P}(\mathbf{u}_{1 \ldots m}^p, \mathbf{u}_{1 \ldots n}^g)}{\mathcal{P}(\mathbf{u}_{1 \ldots m}^p)\mathcal{P}(\mathbf{u}_{1 \ldots n}^g)} \tag{5}$$

where

$$\mathcal{P}(\mathbf{u}^{1 \ldots n}) = \int P(\mathbf{u}^1 \mid \mathbf{v}) \cdots P(\mathbf{u}^n \mid \mathbf{v}) P(\mathbf{v}) d\mathbf{v}$$

$$= \prod_{t=1}^d \frac{1}{(2\pi)^{n/2}(\psi_t + \frac{1}{n})^{1/2}} \exp\left(-\frac{(\bar{u}_t)^2}{2(\psi_t + \frac{1}{n})} - \frac{\sum_{i=1}^n (u_t^i - \bar{u}_t)^2}{2}\right) \tag{6}$$

is the distribution of a set of examples, given that they belong to the same class. Here, for the tth feature, $\bar{u}_t = \frac{1}{n}\sum_{i=1}^n u_t^i$. Since Ψ is diagonal, the contributions of different features to $\mathcal{P}$ are decoupled. For priors π_{same} and π_{diff}, the probability that all the examples are of the same class is $(1 + \frac{\pi_{\text{diff}}/\pi_{\text{same}}}{R})^{-1}$. If $R > \frac{\pi_{\text{diff}}}{\pi_{\text{same}}}$, the two groups of examples belong to the same class; otherwise, they do not. Being able to compare two groups of examples makes it also possible to use PLDA for clustering.

The between-class feature variances ψ_t indicate how discriminative the features are. In PLDA, the better features automatically contribute more to recognition. As a special case, consider a completely non-discriminative feature, for which $\psi = 0$. It can be seen that this feature does not contribute to R (Eqn. (5)), or to the other equations above, at all. Therefore, we can perform dimensionality reduction by keeping only the rows of A^{-1} corresponding to non-zero ψ. If we want to use at most d' dimensions, we impose the constraint that no more than d' entries of Ψ be non-zero. We will show how to do this in the next section.

---

[1] The problem of outliers, not belonging to any of the gallery classes, is also solved by PLDA, where we define $P(\mathbf{u}^p \mid \emptyset) = \mathcal{N}(\mathbf{u}^p \mid 0, \Psi + \mathbf{I})$.

3.2   Learning the Model Parameters

The unknown parameters of PLDA are the mean $\mathbf{m}$, the covariance matrix Ψ, and the loading matrix A (or, equivalently, the variances Φ_b and Φ_w). These parameters can be learned in the maximum likelihood framework. Given N training patterns separated into K classes (Fig. 1c), we can compute the likelihood of the data. We will make the assumption that all examples are independently drawn from their respective classes. The log-likelihood is

$$\ell(\mathbf{x}^{1...N}) = \sum_{k=1}^{K} \ln \mathcal{P}(\mathbf{x}^i : i \in \mathcal{C}_k) \tag{7}$$

where

$$\mathcal{P}(\mathbf{x}^1 \ldots \mathbf{x}^n) = \int \mathcal{N}(\mathbf{y} \mid 0, \Phi_b) \mathcal{N}(\mathbf{x}^1 \mid \mathbf{y}, \Phi_w) \cdots \mathcal{N}(\mathbf{x}^n \mid \mathbf{y}, \Phi_w) d\mathbf{y}$$

is the joint probability distribution of a set of n patterns, provided they belong to the same class. Computing the integral, we get: $\ln \mathcal{P}(\mathbf{x}^{1...n}) = C - \frac{1}{2}(\ln |\Phi_b + \frac{\Phi_w}{n}| + \mathrm{tr}((\Phi_b + \frac{\Phi_w}{n})^{-1}(\bar{\mathbf{x}} - \mathbf{m})(\bar{\mathbf{x}} - \mathbf{m})^T) + (n-1) \ln |\Phi_w| + \mathrm{tr}(\Phi_w^{-1}(\sum_{i=1}^{n}(\mathbf{x}^i - \bar{\mathbf{x}})(\mathbf{x}^i - \bar{\mathbf{x}})^T)))$ where $\bar{\mathbf{x}} = \frac{1}{n}\sum_{i=1}^{n} \mathbf{x}^i$ and C is a constant term that we can ignore.

Let us consider the case where each of the classes in the training data is represented by the same number n of examples. Maximizing Eqn. (7) with respect to $\mathbf{m}$, we find $\mathbf{m} = \frac{1}{N} \sum_i \mathbf{x}^i$. Substituting it back, we finally obtain

$$\ell(\mathbf{x}^{1...N}) = -\frac{c}{2}\left(\ln |\Phi_b + \frac{1}{n}\Phi_w| + \mathrm{tr}((\Phi_b + \frac{1}{n}\Phi_w)^{-1} S_b) \right.$$
$$\left. + (n-1) \ln |\Phi_w| + n\mathrm{tr}(\Phi_w^{-1} S_w) \right) \tag{8}$$

where S_b and S_w are defined in Eqn. (1). We need to maximize the value of ℓ with respect to Φ_b and Φ_w, subject to Φ_w being positive definite, Φ_b being positive semi-definite, and, in the case of dimensionality reduction, $\mathrm{rank}(\Phi_b) \leq d'$. Without these constraints, simple matrix calculus would yield

$$\Phi_w = \frac{n}{n-1} S_w, \quad \Phi_b = S_b - \frac{1}{n-1} S_w$$

Therefore, if the scatter matrices S_w and S_b are diagonal then so are the covariances Φ_w and Φ_b. In fact, this diagonalization property holds even if the above constraints are imposed. According to Eqn. (2), $\Phi_b = A\Psi A^T$, where A is invertible. For fixed Ψ, unconstrained optimization of Eqn. (8) with respect to A^{-1} makes both $A^{-1}S_b A^{-T}$ and $A^{-1}S_w A^{-T}$ diagonal. Therefore, the columns of A^{-T} contain the generalized vectors of S_b and S_w, and the projection of data into the latent space (where the recognition takes place) is the LDA projection discussed in §2. Finally optimizing (8) with respect to Ψ, subject to $\Psi \geq 0$ and $\mathrm{rank}(\Psi) \leq d'$, we obtain the method for learning the parameters of our model (2). This method is shown in Fig. 2.

Our method was derived for the case where each class in the training data is represented by the same number n of examples. This may not be true in practice, in which case we can resample the data to make the number of examples the same, use EM (as shown in §5), or use approximations. We took the latter approach, using the closed-form solution in Fig. 2 where n was taken to be the average number of examples per class.

Given: Training examples $\mathbf{x}^{1\cdots N}$ from K classes, with $n = N/K$ examples per class
Find: Parameters $\mathbf{m}, A, \Psi$ maximizing the likelihood of the PLDA model (Eqn. (2), Fig. 1).

1. Compute the scatter matrices S_b and S_w (Eqn. (1)). Find the matrix W of generalized eigenvectors with columns such that $S_b\mathbf{w} = \lambda S_w\mathbf{w}$. Then, $\mathbf{x} \rightarrow W^T\mathbf{x}$ is the LDA projection, and $\Lambda_b = W^T S_b W$ and $\Lambda_w = W^T S_w W$ are both diagonal.
2. Set

$$\mathbf{m} = \tfrac{1}{N} \sum_{i=1}^{N} \mathbf{x}^i$$

$$A = W^{-T} \left(\tfrac{n}{n-1}\Lambda_w\right)^{1/2}$$

$$\Psi = \max\left(0, \tfrac{n-1}{n}(\Lambda_b/\Lambda_w) - \tfrac{1}{n}\right)$$

3. To reduce the dimensionality to d', keep the d' largest elements of Ψ and set the rest to zero. In the latent space $\mathbf{u} = A^{-1}(\mathbf{x} - \mathbf{m})$, only the features corresponding to non-zero entries of Ψ are needed for recognition.

Fig. 2. Fitting the parameters of the PLDA model

4 Results

With Probabilistic LDA, we model the variations in the appearance of any object, as well as the differences in the appearance of different objects. This makes PLDA a general model, useful for a variety of recognition tasks on examples of previously unseen classes. We will show its applications to class inference, classification, hypothesis testing, and clustering.

4.1 Class Inference

By modeling both within-class and between-class variations, PLDA allows us to isolate the class component of an example. This emphasizes the features that make different objects distinct, discarding the information not useful for recognition.

From Eqn. (3), we can show that the MAP estimate (and also the expectation) of the class center $\mathbf{y}$ corresponding to example $\mathbf{x}$ is $\hat{\mathbf{y}} = \mathbf{m} + A\hat{\mathbf{v}} = \mathbf{m} + A(\Psi + I)^{-1}\Psi A^{-1}(\mathbf{x} - \mathbf{m})$. In Fig. 3, we demonstrate the class inference on faces from the PIE database [8]. Each row of Fig. 3a contains one person, but the view variations within each row are large. In Fig. 3b we show the estimate of the class center. Most of the variation within rows has been eliminated, while different rows look distinct.

4.2 Classification

One natural task for PLDA is classification, and we apply it to face recognition. We trained the system on a set faces extracted from videos, each of which was automatically cropped and contrast-normalized. We reduce the dimensionality using PCA and capturing around 96% of the energy. In the resulting subspace, we train the PLDA model as described in §3.

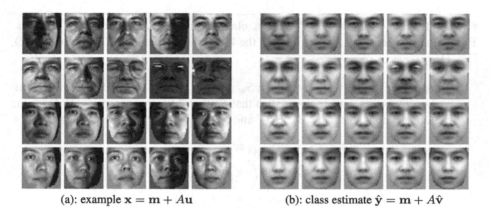

(a): example $\mathbf{x} = \mathbf{m} + A\mathbf{u}$ (b): class estimate $\hat{\mathbf{y}} = \mathbf{m} + A\hat{\mathbf{v}}$

Fig. 3. Class inference with PLDA. (a) Faces from the PIE dataset. Rows correspond to different people. (b) We estimate the class variable $\mathbf{y}$ from each example $\mathbf{x}$. This emphasizes the information relevant to recognition, and largely takes out the view variations. This makes the images within the same class look similar, and those of different classes different. The inference was done on each image independently. The system has never seen images from these classes before.

Each test case consists of a gallery containing one example of each of M people from the FERET database [9] (the training data was collected by us and did not include any FERET images). The probe $\mathbf{x}^p$ contains a different image of one of those M people, and is classified by maximizing the likelihood $P(\mathbf{x}^p \mid \mathbf{x}^g)$ (Eqn. (4)). In Fig. 4a we compare the performance of PLDA to that of LDA. In LDA-based classification, we project the data onto a d'-dimensional space, normalize it so that each feature has the same within-class variance, and classify the probe by finding the nearest neighbor from the gallery (equivalent to a maximum-likelihood decision rule). Although the features extracted by PLDA are the same as LDA, the probability model in PLDA makes it consistently outperform LDA of any dimensionality d', for any gallery size. Note that with PLDA we do not need to choose the best value for d', since the probability model automatically gives less importance to the less discriminative features. On the other hand, d' affects the performance of LDA (here, $d' = 80$ seems to be the best choice).

4.3   Hypothesis Testing

While PLDA lets us perform classification better than LDA, there are many tasks that LDA does not address at all. In hypothesis testing, we need to determine whether two examples belong to the same class or not. More generally, given two groups of examples, where each group belongs to one class, we need to determine whether the two classes are the same. This is accomplished by PLDA by comparing the likelihood ratio R (Eqn. (5)) with the prior ratio. We use the COIL database [10], containing 72 images of each of 100 objects. We randomly select 68 objects to use for training, and test on the 32 remaining objects. An error results when two examples of the same object selected from the test set are classified as different (false negative), or when two examples of different objects are classified as the same (false positive). The images were sampled to 32×32 pixels, and PCA (computed on the training set) was used to extract 200 features.

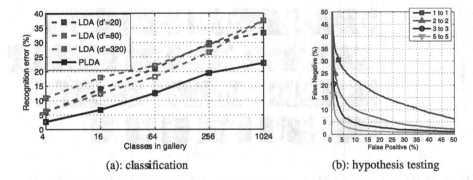

(a): classification   (b): hypothesis testing

Fig. 4. (a) Evaluating the classification performance of LDA (with varying dimensions d') and PLDA on the FERET face data set. A test gallery contains M classes, with one example per class. The probe is a different example of one of the M classes, and needs to be labeled. We plot the misclassification rate as a function of M. PLDA significantly outperforms LDA. The training and test data came from different sources and have no people in common. **(b)** Hypothesis testing using PLDA. We determine whether two examples belong to the same class or not by comparing the likelihood ratio R with the prior ratio. The top curve shows the false positive and false negative rates computed for the COIL database, with the marker corresponding to equal priors. We can also compare two *groups* of examples, where each contains several examples of one class. Combining multiple examples yields better models of the new classes, reducing the error rates. Different classes were used for training and testing.

In Fig. 4b, we show the error rates, where the ratio of priors $\frac{\pi_{\text{diff}}}{\pi_{\text{same}}}$ moves us along the curve (the marker corresponds to equal priors). With PLDA we can compare groups of examples too, and we show that by comparing several examples of one class with several examples of the other we get much better accuracy than with single examples. We expect that a non-linear dimensionality reduction such as LLE [11] would make the data better suited for the Gaussian model in PLDA, further reducing the error rates.

4.4 Clustering

While in classification we have the gallery of labeled objects, a different, unsupervised approach is needed when no class labels are available. In that case, we need to cluster the examples, so that each cluster roughly corresponds to one class. Methods such as K-means can be used, but suffer from the arbitrary choice of metric and the need to specify the number of clusters in advance. With PLDA, we can automatically determine the optimal number of classes.

We approach clustering as the likelihood maximization problem. Each split of examples into clusters corresponds to a graphical model (Fig. 1c) in which all examples within one cluster share the class variable, and the likelihood of the clustering is computed by integrating out the class variables, which can be done in closed form (Eqn. (6)). Because the set of examples can be split into clusters in an exponential number of ways, we cannot compute the likelihood of each clustering. Instead, we use agglomerative clustering as an approximate search mechanism. We start with each example in its own cluster, and at each iteration merge two clusters. When two clusters are merged, the log-likelihood ℓ increases by $\ln R$, where R is the likelihood ratio defined in Eqn. (5).

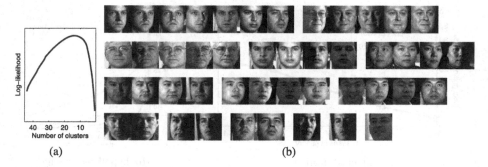

Log-likelihood

40 30 20 10
Number of clusters

(a)   (b)

Fig. 5. PLDA makes it possible to cluster examples and automatically determine the optimal number of clusters. We approach clustering as likelihood maximization, and use agglomerative clustering. At each step we merge the clusters with the largest likelihood ratio R; this increases the log-likelihood by $\ln R$. **(a)** The log-likelihood ℓ as a function of the number of clusters. The maximum is reached at 14 clusters. **(b)** The clusters maximizing the likelihood. If we give each person a label A through H, the clusters are: *(BBBBBDC), (AAAAA), (FFFFF), (DDDD), (IIII), (HHHH), (GGGG), (EEEE), (EG), (HC), (CC), (I), (C), (C).*

Therefore, at each iteration, we merge the two clusters with the maximum R, and update the log-likelihood as $\ell \leftarrow \ell + \ln R$. The point in this process at which ℓ reaches its maximum tells us the (approximately) optimal way to cluster the data, including the number of clusters.

We tested the clustering algorithm on the PIE dataset, by randomly selecting 5 images of each of the 9 dataset collectors (the training data didn't include any PIE images). In Fig. 5a we plot the log-likelihood ℓ against the number of clusters. The graph has a maximum, which tells us how many clusters are needed (14 in this case). Fig. 5b shows the corresponding clusters. While the clustering is not perfect, it largely corresponds to the true classes of the examples.

5   Combining Probabilistic PCA and Probabilistic LDA

Usually, a dimensionality reduction such as PCA must be used before applying LDA to eliminate singularities in the problem. Using PCA before PLDA works very well for recognition, but it may be desirable to use PLDA to model the probability distribution in the original space, and not the PCA-projected subspace. This suggests combining PLDA with Probabilistic PCA [6] instead.

Probabilistic PCA fits the data with a model $\mathbf{x} \sim \mathcal{N}(\cdot \mid \mathbf{m} + A\mathbf{u}, \Sigma)$ where the latent variable $\mathbf{u} \sim \mathcal{N}(\cdot \mid 0, \mathbf{I})$, and $\Sigma = \sigma^2 \mathbf{I}$. We will combine PPCA with PLDA (Eqn. (2)), to obtain the following model:

$$\mathbf{x} \sim \mathcal{N}(\cdot \mid \mathbf{m} + A\mathbf{u}, \Sigma), \quad \text{where} \quad \mathbf{u} \sim \mathcal{N}(\cdot \mid \mathbf{v}, \mathbf{I}) \quad \text{and} \quad \mathbf{v} \sim \mathcal{N}(\cdot \mid 0, \Psi) \qquad (9)$$

If D is the dimensionality of the data and d is the desired dimensionality of the latent space, we constrain A to be of size $D \times d$. We find the parameters of the model by using Expectation Maximization (e.g. [7]). Note that by letting $d = D$ and setting $\sigma \rightarrow 0$ we obtain an EM method for fitting the PLDA model which doesn't require that each class be represented by the same number of training examples.

We can further extend PPCA+PLDA to model wider, non-linear view variations, by defining a mixture model in which each mixture component j has its own linear transformation (m_j, A_j). We can think of A_j as coarsely representing the view, and $u - v$ as capturing finer view variations. The class variable v is shared by all examples of the same class, even those from different mixture components. The recognition tasks and EM-based training can be performed approximately, using an additional step assigning each example to one of the mixture components. This allows us to project each example into the latent space, and perform the recognition activities there. Note that if an example comes from a class represented by v, and belongs to the jth mixture component, then its expected value is $m_j + A_j v$, which is the representation used in asymmetric bilinear models [12]. However, unlike the bilinear models, ours is a probability model, and training it does not require the ground-truth view labels, which may be hard to obtain. Experiments with the PPCA+PLDA mixture model will be a part of our future research.

6 Discussion

We presented a novel generative model that decomposes a pattern into the class and the view. Probabilistic Linear Discriminant Analysis (PLDA) is related to LDA and Probabilistic PCA, and can be thought of as LDA with a probability distributions attached to the features. The probability distribution models the data through the latent variables corresponding to the class and the view. This allows us to perform inference and recognition. The model automatically gives more importance to the more discriminative features, which helps us avoid a search for the optimal number of features. On the other hand, we can perform dimensionality reduction with PLDA, by imposing an upper limit on the rank of the between-class variance. As an extension, we also proposed a PPCA+PLDA model that doesn't require PCA pre-processing, and a PPCA+PLDA Mixture for modeling wider view variations.

One of the most important advantages of PLDA, compared to LDA and its previously proposed probabilistic motivations, is that the probability distributions are learned not only for the examples within a class but for the class center as well. This makes PLDA perfectly suited for a wide variety of recognition problems on classes we have not seen before. A model of a class can be built from a single example (one-shot learning), and is further improved by combining multiple examples of a class. We can perform classification ("what is the class of the example?"), hypothesis testing ("do the two examples belong to the same class?"), and clustering.

Just like any linear model, PLDA performs best when the data obey the linear assumptions. However, it can be applied to non-linear distributions if the features are extracted first that linearize the data. One option is to embed the data in a linear manifold (e.g. [11]), and use PLDA there. Alternatively, we can use the kernel trick inside PLDA, by extracting non-linear features from the data using Kernel LDA [13], and then computing the probability distribution of each feature independently.

Acknowledgments. Many thanks to David Forsyth, Thomas Leung and Troy Chinen for discussions and suggestions, and to the paper's area chair and reviewers for very helpful comments and literature pointers.

References

1. Belhumeur, P.N., Hespanha, J., Kriegman, D.J.: Eigenfaces vs. fisherfaces: Recognition using class specific linear projection. IEEE Trans. PAMI **19**(7) (1997) 711–720
2. Pentland, A., Moghaddam, B., Starner, T.: View-based and modular eigenspaces for face recognition. In: Proc. of IEEE CVPR, Seattle, WA (1994)
3. Hastie, T., Tibshirani, R.: Discriminant analysis by Gaussian mixtures. Journal of the Royal Statistical Society series B **58** (1996) 158–176
4. Bach, F., Jordan, M.: A probabilistic interpretation of canonical correlation analysis. Technical Report 688, Department of Statistics, UC Berkeley (2005)
5. Fei-Fei, L., Fergus, R., Perona, P.: A bayesian approach to unsupervised one-shot learning of object categories. In: ICCV. (2003)
6. Tipping, M., Bishop, C.: Probabilistic principal component analysis. Technical Report NCRG/97/010, Neural Computing Research Group, Aston University. (1997)
7. Bishop, C.: Neural networks for pattern recognition. Oxford University Press (1995)
8. Sim, T., Baker, S., Bsat, M.: The cmu pose, illumination, and expression (pie) database. Proc. IEEE International Conference on Automatic Face and Gesture Recognition (2002)
9. Phillips, P., Wechsler, H., Huang, J., Rauss, P.: The feret database and evaluation procedure for face recognition algorithms. IVC **16**(5) (1998) 295–306
10. Nene, S., Nayar, S., Murase, H.: Columbia object image library: Coil. Technical Report CUCS-006-96, Department of CS, Columbia University (1996)
11. Roweis, S.T., Saul, L.K.: Nonlinear dimensionality reduction by locally linear embedding. Science **290** (2000) 2323–2326
12. Tenenbaum, J.B., Freeman, W.T.: Separating style and content with bilinear models. Neural Computation **12**(6) (2000) 1247–1283
13. Mika, S., Ratsch, G., Weston, J., Scholkopf, B., Muller, K.: Fisher discriminant analysis with kernels. Proceedings of IEEE Neural Networks for Signal Processing Workshop (1999)

A New 3-D Model Retrieval System Based on *Aspect-Transition Descriptor*

Soochahn Lee[1], Sehyuk Yoon[2], Il Dong Yun[3], Duck Hoon Kim[4],
Kyoung Mu Lee[1], and Sang Uk Lee[1]

[1] School of Electrical Engineering and Computer Science,
Seoul National University, Seoul, 151-742, Republic of Korea
redhouse@diehard.snu.ac.kr, kyoungmu@snu.ac.kr,
sanguk@ipl.snu.ac.kr
[2] Service Planning Department, KT corporation,
Seognam, Kyonggi-do, 463-711, Republic of Korea
uniqness@kt.co.kr
[3] School of Electronics and Information Engineering,
Hankuk University of Foreign Studies,
Yongin, 449-791, Republic of Korea
yun@hufs.ac.kr
[4] Institute for Robotics and Intelligent Systems,
University of Southern California,
Los Angeles, CA 90089, USA
duckkim@usc.edu

Abstract. In this paper, we propose a new 3-D model retrieval system using the *Aspect-Transition Descriptor* which is based on the aspect graph representation [1, 2] approach. The proposed method differs from the conventional aspect graph representation in that we utilize transitions as well as aspects. The process of generating the *Aspect-Transition Descriptor* is as follows: First, uniformly sampled views of a 3-D model are separated into a stable and an unstable view sets according to the local variation of their 2-D shape. Next, adjacent stable views and unstable views are grouped into clusters and we select the characteristic aspects and transitions by finding the representative view from each cluster. The 2-D descriptors of the selected characteristic aspects and transitions are concatenated to form the 3-D descriptor. Matching the *Aspect-Transition Descriptors* is done using a modified Hausdorff distance. To evaluate the proposed 3-D descriptor, we have evaluated the retrieval performance on the Princeton benchmark database [3] and found that our method outperforms other retrieval techniques.

1   Introduction

For years, 3-D model retrieval has been of interest for applications mostly in specialized areas such as mechanical CAD, molecular biology, and computer graphics. With the recent increase in the number and variety of 3-D models, however, new types of applications intended for the general public, such as personalized 3-D cyber-rooms and avatars, and tools for creating amateur 3-D animated

A. Leonardis, H. Bischof, and A. Pinz (Eds.): ECCV 2006, Part IV, LNCS 3954, pp. 543–554, 2006.
© Springer-Verlag Berlin Heidelberg 2006

motion pictures have been gaining interest. In order to make this a reality, tools for easy authoring of new 3-D models, the construction of large databases of 3-D models, and the efficient and accurate retrieval of 3-D models from the database are problems that must be solved. Especially, for these kinds of applications that are not related to only a few classes of models, it is necessary to develop a 3-D model retrieval system that is not task-dependent and can accurately retrieve free-form objects.

The problem of retrieving the relevant 3-D models from the database is closely linked to how the model is described, *i.e.*, which characteristic the 3-D descriptor is based on. Whether it is based on the 3-D geometry or, as shown in Fig. 1, the projected 2-D views of the model divides 3-D descriptors into geometry-based [4, 5, 6, 7, 8] and view-based [9, 10] ones. Geometry-based descriptors utilize different geometrical attributes such as shape histograms [4] of vertices and the distribution of distances of two random points on the model [5]. Descriptors based on more complex geometrical attributes include extended Gaussian images [6], spherical extent functions [7], and spherical harmonic descriptors [8]. On the other hand, view-based descriptors are all based on 2-D views, but differ in how the viewpoints are organized or selected.

As 3-D models become free-form, it becomes almost impossible to extract high-order geometrical attributes. Since geometry-based descriptors are based on primitive geometrical attributes, they rely on extensive statistical information to characterize 3-D models. But it can be difficult to determine the amount of statistical information needed for accurate description of models. View-based descriptors, however, do not suffer from this problem since they intuitively encapsule the information needed to discriminate between inter-class differences and intra-class similarities for any class of 3-D models. Also, view-based descriptors have the advantage that 3-D model retrieval systems based on it is able to provide a more user friendly interface by enabling the user to utilize a 2-D image or sketch as a query input. It is worthy to note that the Light Field Descriptor [9], which belongs to view-based descriptors, is producing superior results compared to other geometry-based descriptors [3].

Unlike the Light Field Descriptor [9] which samples the 3-D model at vertices of a regular dodecahedron, the aspect graph representation [1, 2] focuses on generating aspects and connecting them into a graph. Specifically, aspects that have small change in the projected shape of the model with change of viewpoint are connected by transitions in which the change in projected shape is dramatic. Note that, in this paper, aspects and transitions correspond to stable views and unstable views, respectively. Aspect graph representations have been defined for special classes of models such as polyhedra [11], solids of revolution [12, 13], piece-wise smooth objects [14], and algebraic surfaces [15]. However, one main issue arises, *i.e.*, how to reduce the number of aspects for complex shapes or free-form models. Ikeuchi and Kanade [16] proposed a method to group views using similar features extracted from the model, and Weinshall and Werman [17] formally analyzed the notion of view stability and view likelihood which can be used to determine characteristic views. Recently, Cyr and Kimia [10] proposed a

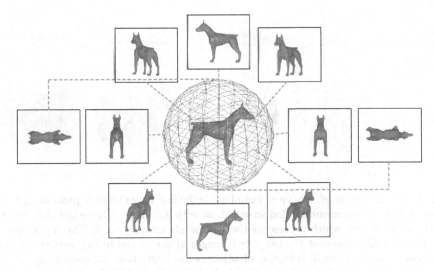

Fig. 1. Describing a 3-D model using its projected images at various viewpoints

new aspect graph representation which first groups views using a region-growing approach based on the similarity between adjacent views and then defines the aspect as the characteristic view for each group. Their approach has advantages that it is applicable to free-form objects and it reduces the number of aspects needed to describe a 3-D model.

The proposed method is similar to that of Cyr and Kimia [10] in that we also focus in grouping views and defining aspects using characteristic views. The main difference is that we utilize not only stable views but also unstable views, *i.e.*, transitions as well as aspects. This is based on the observation that transitions may contain more additional information compared to similar aspects. Specifically, we first classify views on the view sphere into stable views and unstable views using *local variation* which is a notion that will be made clearer in Section 2. Next, we separately group the stable views and unstable views into clusters based on similarity and define the aspect for stable view clusters and the transition for unstable view clusters by finding the characteristic views of each cluster. We call the 3-D descriptor constructed using the aspects and transitions the *Aspect-Transition Descriptor*. Consequently, the *Aspect-Transition Descriptor* utilizes only the most representative aspects, and as a result utilizes a small number of views. Note that, we avoid the need to align the 3-D models in the process of constructing descriptors.

The paper is organized as follows: In Section 2, the proposed view classification method and the process of generating the *Aspect-Transition Descriptor* are explained in detail. Then Section 3 illustrates the matching technique based on the Hausdorff distance for the proposed retrieval system. Section 4 presents and analyzes the performance of the proposed retrieval system from experiments conducted using the Princeton benchmark database [3]. Finally, Section 5 concludes this paper.

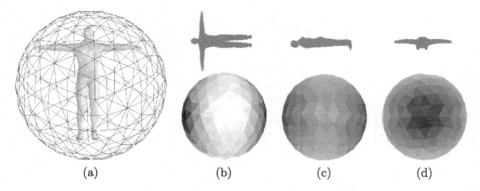

Fig. 2. Visualization of the view sampling and view classification process. (a) The wireframe is the twice subdivided icosahedron with 320 faces. The bright dots are the centers of each face which represents the viewpoints actually used. The top shapes in (b), (c), and (d) represent the projected images of the model in (a), and the bottom polyhedra represent the distribution of adjacent local variations for each image. Bright faces indicate low local variation, while dark faces indicate high local variation.

2   Generation of the *Aspect-Transition Descriptor*

2.1   View Sampling and Classification

The generation of the *Aspect-Transition Descriptor* begins with view sampling. View sampling is the process of sampling the view of the 3-D model from various viewpoints on the view sphere which is a sphere normalized relative to the size of the model. Here, the viewpoints in the sampling process must be uniformly distributed on the view sphere, so the geometry of regular polyhedra is used. Also, the number of viewpoints must be large enough to sufficiently sample the shape of the model. Therefore, we somewhat over-sample the model using the center point of the faces in a twice subdivided icosahedron as viewpoints [18]. Specifically, we create 320 sampled views of the 3-D model.

Next, we classify the sampled views into stable views and unstable views based on *local variation* which is the approximation of local shape variation extensively explored in [17]. Unfortunately, the notion of differentiation of local shape variation is practically inapplicable, so we approximate that notion with computing the dissimilarity of each view V_i with its neighboring views V_j on the assumption that the sampled views are sufficiently dense. This approximation denoted as $L(V_i)$ is called *local variation* and is defined by

$$L(V_i) = \sum_j \frac{d(V_i, V_j)}{g(V_i, V_j)},\qquad(1)$$

where $d(V_i, V_j)$ is the dissimilarity between V_i and V_j, and $g(V_i, V_j)$ is the geometric distance between the viewpoints of the two views. Here, the dissimilarity is computed using 2-D descriptors as image metrics for each view. We will discuss 2-D descriptors in Section 2.3.

Now, using local variation as the criteria, the stable view set **SV** and the unstable view set **UV** is defined as follows:

$$\mathbf{SV} = \left\{ V_{sv} \,\Big|\, L(V_{sv}) < \frac{1}{n}\sum_i L(V_i) - \theta_{sv} \right\}, \tag{2}$$

$$\mathbf{UV} = \left\{ V_{uv} \,\Big|\, L(V_{uv}) > \frac{1}{n}\sum_i L(V_i) - \theta_{uv} \right\}, \tag{3}$$

where n is the total number of sampled views, and θ_{sv} and θ_{uv} are thresholds based on the standard deviation of the *local variation* values that control the number of stable and unstable views. Fig. 3 shows an example of a stable view and an unstable view with its neighboring views.

2.2 Selecting Characteristic Views

After dividing stable views and unstable views, we separately select characteristic views from each set. Here, characteristic aspects and transitions are selected in a similar manner. Specifically, as characteristic aspects and transitions are selected by first grouping adjacent stable views and then finding the most representative view in each group.

Characteristic aspects are selected by the following steps: First, we assign each stable view to be in its own group. Next, we calculate the distance between every group and merge the two groups with the shortest distance where distance is the dissimilarity of the two views. After merging two groups, we assign a new

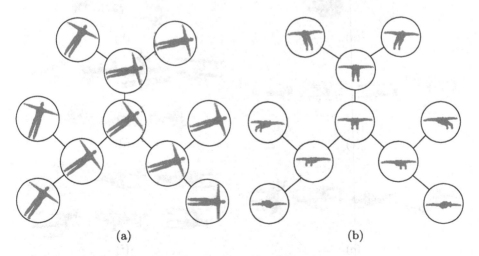

(a)   (b)

Fig. 3. Illustration of neighboring views for (a) a stable view and (b) an unstable view where the center image is the corresponding view. The connected neighboring views are from viewpoints connected on the twice subdivided icosahedron of Fig. 2(a).

representative view such that the sum of dissimilarity between other views and that cluster is the smallest. The above process is iterated until the sum of the maximum dissimilarity between the representative view and other views for each group grows larger than a certain threshold. Finally, the representative views for the remaining groups of stable views are defined as the characteristic aspects. We select characteristic transitions by the same process using the set of unstable views instead of stable views.

The characteristic aspects and transitions for several models are presented in Fig. 4. We can see that viewpoints of the characteristic aspects and transitions based on the proposed method are unevenly spaced which enables the appropriate information corresponding to aspects and transitions to be extracted.

2.3   Extracting the *Aspect-Transition Descriptor*

Now that the characteristic aspects and transitions have been selected, the remaining process is to construct the *Aspect-Transition Descriptor*. Since the *Aspect-Transition Descriptor* is constructed by concatenating 2-D descriptors of the selected characteristic aspects and views, we focus mainly on which 2-D descriptor to be utilized.

The method for describing 2-D images can be classified into two main classes, which are contour-based descriptor and region-based descriptor. Specifically, the contour-based descriptor utilizes only the information of the boundary of the shape, while the region-based descriptor utilizes all the pixels that constitute the shape region. Both the descriptors can be viewed as only partial information

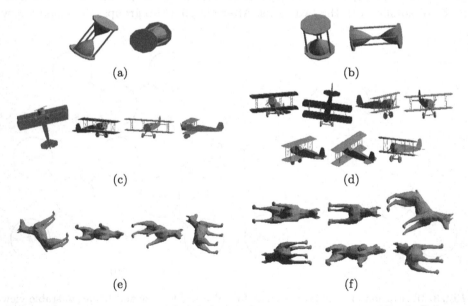

(a)

(b)

(c)

(d)

(e)

(f)

Fig. 4. Characteristic aspects (a, c, e) and characteristic transitions (b, d, f) for an hourglass (a, b) a biplane (c, d), and a dog (e, f)

of the image since the contour-based descriptor loses the interior information of the shape and cannot describe unconnected regions, and the region-based descriptor loses the detailed boundary information. Therefore, we utilize the Angular Radial Transform (ART) [19] and the Curvature Scale Space (CSS) [20] descriptors as the region based and contour based descriptors, respectively. Here, the actual extraction of the 2-D descriptors is performed at the time of view sampling for every view in order to use the descriptors as the basis of both dissimilarity and local variation in the view classification process described in Section 2.1.

Figs. 5 and 6 show the characteristic aspects and transitions of a cocktail glass selected using the CSS [20] descriptor and those of an hourglass using the ART [19] descriptor, respectively. Fig. 5(a) shows that the aspects represent a circular shape since the circular shape will have the smallest variation to change of viewpoint, and the median of the frontal and top view since at this point the shape variation exerts a local minima. On the other hand, Fig. 5(b) shows that transitions are selected from viewpoints where a viewpoint change brings a change in the topology of the contour shape, *i.e.*, from two overlapped circles to two connected circles. For the case of the hourglass, it can be seen in Fig. 6(a) that viewpoints for the aspects are located straight in front and at the top of the model, while the left transition in Fig. 6(b) is located at a region diagonal to the front or top of the model. Here, the right part of Fig 6(b) is selected as a transition since one of the pillars in occluding the two cones which could be in non-occlusion by changing the viewpoint a little bit.

Finally, the *Aspect-Transition Descriptor* is constructed by concatenating the 2-D descriptors for the characteristic aspects and transitions.

(a)   (b)

Fig. 5. (a) Characteristic aspects and (b) characteristic transitions for a cocktail glass model using the CSS [20] descriptor as the dissimilarity measure

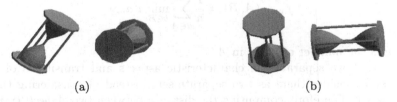

(a)   (b)

Fig. 6. (a) Characteristic aspects and (b) characteristic transitions for an hourglass model using the ART [19] descriptor as the dissimilarity measure

3   Computing the Distance Between Two *Aspect-Transition Descriptors*

Now, the remaining problem is how to compute the distance between *Aspect-Transition Descriptors*. Generally, the number of both the characteristic aspects and transitions varies according to the complexity of a given 3-D model. Therefore, a specific distance measure is required for computing the distance between *Aspect-Transition Descriptors*. Here, we convert with this problem into the problem of matching two point sets of which the numbers of elements are different.

The Hausdorff distance is widely used as a metric defining the distance between two point sets. Formally, given two point sets A and B, the Hausdorff distance is defined as follows:

$$f(A, B) = \max \left\{ \overrightarrow{f}(A, B), \overrightarrow{f}(B, A) \right\}, \tag{4}$$

where $\overrightarrow{f}(A, B)$ and $\overrightarrow{f}(B, A)$ imply the directed Hausdorff distance. Here, the directed Hausdorff distance $\overrightarrow{f}(A, B)$ is represented in the following equation:

$$\overrightarrow{f}(A, B) = \max_{a \in A} \min_{b \in B} d(a, b). \tag{5}$$

Here, a and b imply a point in A and B, respectively, and $d(a, b)$ is the distance between a and b. In general, $\overrightarrow{f}(A, B)$ is not equal to $\overrightarrow{f}(B, A)$ since the directed Hausdorff distance is not commutative.

Although the Hausdorff distance is suitable for computing the distance between two point sets of which the numbers of elements are different, some modifications must be done in order to be utilized in our retrieval system. Considering that the Hausdorff distance ultimately measures only the maximum of minimum distances between two point sets and discards all other minimum distances, we need to modify this to take the similarities between all of the characteristic aspects and transitions into account. Specifically, the modified Hausdorff distance uses the average instead of the maximum as follows:

$$f_{\text{mod}}(A, B) = \max \left\{ \overrightarrow{f_{\text{mod}}}(A, B), \overrightarrow{f_{\text{mod}}}(B, A) \right\}, \tag{6}$$

where

$$\overrightarrow{f_{\text{mod}}}(A, B) = \frac{1}{n} \sum_{a \in A} \min_{b \in B} d(a, b). \tag{7}$$

Here, n is the number of views in A.

Note that we separate the characteristic aspects and transitions of a 3-D model and consider them as two separate sets instead of considering them as one view set. Therefore, computing the distance between two *Aspect-Transition Descriptors* can be considered as combining the computed similarities of the aspects and transitions for the two models.

4   Experimental Results

We evaluated the performance of our retrieval system on the Princeton benchmark database [3]. The database contains 1814 models divided into two sets of 907 models for training and testing. Since training is not needed here, we used only the testing set which is classified into 92 classes. Generally, the performance of a retrieval system heavily depends on the database and categorization of 3-D models. The Princeton benchmark [3] is well organized and is recently being established as the standard benchmark for comparing the performance of 3-D model retrieval algorithms.

To compare the performance of several descriptors, we use three well-known measures: The first-tier, second-tier, and precision-recall plot [3]. The first-tier and second-tier are the percentage of models in the query's class that is retrieved in the top $|C| - 1$ matches and in the top $2 \times (|C| - 1)$ matches, respectively, where $|C|$ implies the number of models in a class C. The precision-recall plot describes the relationship between the precision and the recall of the retrieval system. Specifically, for a query model in a class C with $|C|$ models, the precision is the ratio of the retrieved members of class C in the top K matches to K, and the recall is the ratio of the retrieved members of class C in the top K matches to $|C|$. Note that the recall and precision are inversely proportional since increasing K raises the recall but brings a decrease in precision.

As described in Section 2.2, the classification of stable and unstable views and the number of selected characteristic views in the view selection process are determined by threshold values. In our implementation, the view classification thresholds θ_{sv} and θ_{uv} are both set to 0.5. Fig. 7 shows the the precision-recall plots for the following three cases: the first is when the threshold for the ART descriptor is 0.3 for selecting characteristic aspects and 0.2 for selecting characteristic transitions. Next, the second is the precision-recall plots for the cases using both aspects and transitions with both thresholds 0.8 for the ART descriptor and both 0.3 for the CSS descriptor. Here, the computed distances of aspects and transitions are combined by simple averaging. Finally, the third, which yielded the best performance, is when using the ART and CSS descriptors combined with thresholds 0.8 and 0.3 for ART and CSS, respectively. The distances computed using ART and CSS were combined by weighted averaging as $d_{combined} = 0.3 \times d_{ART} + 0.7 \times d_{CSS}$. Also, we note that the retrieval performance in the case of combined aspects and transitions with threshold 0.8 (18.7 views per model) is substantially better than the case using only aspects with a lower threshold 0.3 which has more views (19.5 views per model).

Next, the results of the first-tier and second-tier for our descriptor and several others evaluated on the Princeton benchmark database [3] are given in Table 1. Specifically, the results of D2 Shape Distribution(D2), Extended Gaussian Image (EGI), Complex EGI (CEGI), Shape Histograms (SHELLS, SECTORS, SECSHEL), Spherical Extent Function (EXT), Radialized EXT (REXT), Gaussian Euclidian Distance Transform (GEDT), Spherical Harmonic Descriptor (SHD),

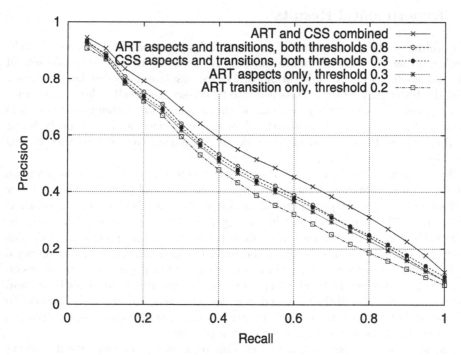

Fig. 7. The precision-recall plots using various parameters tested on the Princeton benchmark database [3]

and Light Field Descriptor (LFD) are compared to our method. It can be seen that the results of the *Aspect-Transition Descriptor* gives the best results. Specifically, the *Aspect-Transition Descriptor* outperforms the Light Field Descriptor [9] by 1.6% for the first tier and 1.4% for the second tier.

Finally, the precision-recall plots of the proposed descriptor and other descriptors discussed above are given in Fig. 8. It can be seen that the proposed method provide the best retrieval performance. Also, the proposed descriptor has the advantage that a smaller number of sampled views can be utilized to construct the proposed descriptor compared to the Light Field Descriptor.

5   Conclusion

We proposed a new 3-D descriptor called the *Aspect-Transition Descriptor* and described a novel retrieval system based on this descriptor. The *Aspect-Transition Descriptor* is a view-based descriptor based on the aspect graph representation, which particularly utilizes transitions as well as aspects to describe a 3-D model. This is based on the intuitive observation that transitions encapsule as much information of the model as aspects. From this, the proposed descriptor is able to achieve the information that was overlooked by traditional aspect graph representations. We also adopted a method to compare the

Table 1. First and second tier results using various 3-D descriptors on the Princeton benchmark database [3]

Shape Descriptor	First Tier	Second Tier
Proposed(ATD)	39.6%	50.1%
LFD	38.0%	48.7%
REXT	32.7%	43.2%
SHD	30.9%	41.1%
GEDT	31.3%	40.7%
EXT	28.6%	37.9%
SECSHEL	26.7%	35.3%
VOXEL	26.7%	35.0%
SECTORS	24.9%	33.4%
CEGI	21.1%	28.7%
EGI	19.7%	27.7%
D2	15.8%	23.5%
SHELLS	11.1%	17.3%

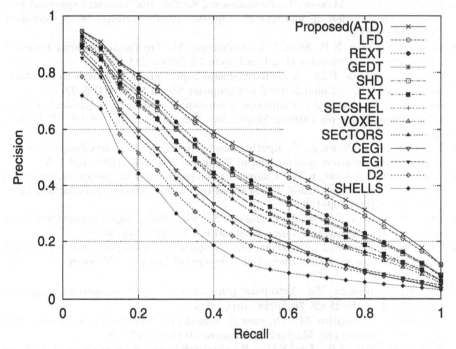

Fig. 8. The precision-recall plot of our retrieval system tested on the Princeton benchmark database [3] compared with other 3-D descriptors tested on the same database

distance of *Aspect-Transition Descriptor*s based on the Hausdorff distance. We have evaluated our retrieval system on the Princeton benchmark [3] and found that our system gives the best overall results.

References

1. Koenderink, J.J., van Doorn, A.J.: The singularities of the visual mapping. Biological Cybernetics **24** (1976) 51–59
2. Koenderink, J.J., van Doorn, A.J.: The internal representation of solid shape with respect to vision. Biological Cybernetics **32** (1979) 211–216
3. Shilane, P., Min, P., Kazhdan, M.M., Funkhouser, T.A.: The princeton shape benchmark. In: Proceedings of Shape Modeling International. (2004) 167–178
4. Ankerst, M., Kastenmüller, G., Kreigel, H.P., Seidl, T.: Nearest neighbor classification in 3d protein databases. In: Proceedings of the Seventh International Conference on Intelligent Systems for Molecular Biology. (1999) 34–43
5. Osada, R., Funkhouser, T., Chazelle, B., Dobkin, D.: Matching 3D models with shape distributions. In: Proceedings of Shape Modeling International. (2001) 154–166
6. Horn, B.K.P.: Extended gaussian images. Proceedings of the IEEE **72** (1984) 1656–1678
7. Vranic, D., Saupe, D.: 3D model retrieval with spherical harmonics and moments. In: Proceedings of the DAGM:The German Association for Pattern Recognition. (2001) 392–397
8. Kazhdan, M., Funkhouser, T., Rusinkiewicz, S.: Rotation invariant spherical harmonic representation of 3d shape descriptors. In: Proceedings of on Geometry Processing. (2003)
9. Chen, D.Y., Tian, X.P., Shen, Y.T., Ouhyoung, M.: On visual similarity based 3d model retrieval. Computer Graphics Forum **22** (2003) 223–232
10. Cyr, C.M., Kimia, B.B.: A similarity-based aspect-graph approach to 3d object recognition. International Journal of Computer Vision **57** (2004) 5–22
11. Shimshoni, I., Ponce, J.: Finite-resolution aspect graphs of polyhedral objects. IEEE Transcations on Pattern Analsis and Machine Intelligence **19** (1997) 315–327
12. Kriegman, D.J., Ponce, J.: Computing exact aspect graphs of curved objects: Solids of revolution. International Journal of Computer Vision **5** (1990) 119–135
13. Eggert, D.W., Bowyer, K.W.: Computing the perspective projection aspect graph of solids of revolution. IEEE Transcations on Pattern Analsis and Machine Intelligence **15** (1993) 109–128
14. Shokoufandeh, A., Marsic, I., Dickinson, S.: View-based object recognition using saliency maps. Image and Vision Computing **17** (1999) 445–460
15. Petitjean, S., Ponce, J., Kriegman, D.: Computing exact aspect graphs of curved objects:algebraic surfaces. International Journal of Computer Vision **9** (1992) 231–255
16. Ikeuchi, K., Kanade, T.: Automatic generation of object recognition programs. Proceedings of the IEEE **76** (1988) 1016–1035
17. Weinshall, D., Werman, M.: On view likelihood and stability. IEEE Transcations on Pattern Analsis and Machine Intelligence **19** (1997) 97–108
18. Kim, D.H., Yun, I.D., Lee, S.U.: Regular polyhedral descriptor for 3-d object retrieval system. In: Proceedings of International Conference on Image Processing (3). (2003) 592–532
19. Manjunath, B., Salembier, P., Sikora, T.: Introduction to MPEG-7. Wiley (2002)
20. Mokhtarian, F., Mackworth, A.K.: A theory of multiscale, curvature-based shape representation for planar curves. IEEE Transcations on Pattern Analsis and Machine Intelligence **14** (1992) 789–805

Unsupervised Patch-Based Image Regularization and Representation

Charles Kervrann[1,2] and Jérôme Boulanger[1,2]

[1] IRISA/INRIA Rennes, Projet Vista, Campus Universitaire de Beaulieu,
35 042 Rennes Cedex, France
[2] INRA - MIA, Domaine de Vilvert, 78 352 Jouy-en-Josas, France

Abstract. A novel adaptive and patch-based approach is proposed for image regularization and representation. The method is unsupervised and based on a pointwise selection of small image patches of fixed size in the variable *neighborhood* of each pixel. The main idea is to associate with each pixel the weighted sum of data points within an adaptive neighborhood and to use image patches to take into account complex spatial interactions in images. In this paper, we consider the problem of the adaptive neighborhood selection in a manner that it balances the accuracy of the estimator and the stochastic error, at each spatial position. Moreover, we propose a practical algorithm with no hidden parameter for image regularization that uses no library of image patches and no training algorithm. The method is applied to both artificially corrupted and real images and the performance is very close, and in some cases even surpasses, to that of the best published denoising methods.

1 Introduction

Most of the more efficient regularization methods are based on energy functionals minimization since they are designed to explicitly account for the image geometry, involving the adjustment of global weights that balance the contribution of prior smoothness terms and a fidelity term [23, 28]. Thus, related partial differential equations (PDE) and variational methods have shown impressive results to tackle the problem of edge-preserving smoothing [24, 28, 32] and more recently the problem of image decomposition [1]. Moreover, other smoothing algorithms aggregate information over a neighborhood of fixed size, based on two basic criteria: a spatial criterion to select points in the vicinity of the current point and a brightness criterion in order to choose only points which are similar in some sense. In view of this generic approach, a typical filter is the sigma filter [19] and a continuous version of this filter gives the well-known nonlinear Gaussian filter [14]. Finally, if we substitute a Gaussian window to the hard disk-shaped window around the current position, we get variants of the *bilateral filtering* [31], controlled by setting the standard deviations in both spatial and brightness domains. Nevertheless, as effective as bilateral filtering and variants, they lacked a theoretical basis and some connections to better understood methods have been

A. Leonardis, H. Bischof, and A. Pinz (Eds.): ECCV 2006, Part IV, LNCS 3954, pp. 555–567, 2006.

investigated. In particular, the relationships between bilateral filtering and iterative *mean-shift* algorithm, local mode filtering, clustering, local M-estimators, non-linear diffusion, regularization approaches combining nonlocal data and nonlocal smoothness terms, and Beltrami flow, can be found in [33, 11, 3, 22, 29].

Nevertheless, we note that all cited methods have a relatively small number of regularity parameters that control the global amount of smoothing being performed. They are usually chosen to give a good and global visual impression and are sometimes heuristically chosen [31]. Furthermore, when local characteristics of the data differ significantly across the image domain, selecting local smoothing parameters seems more satisfying and, for instance, has been addressed in [4, 13, 5, 8]. But, what makes image regularization very hard, is that natural images often contain many irrelevant objects. To develop better image enhancement algorithms that can deal with such a structured noise, we need explicit models for the many regularities and geometries seen in local patterns. This corresponds to another line of work which consists in modeling non-local pairwise interactions from training data [35] or a library of natural image patches [12, 27]. The idea is to improve the traditional Markov random field (MRF) models by learning potential functions from examples and extended neighborhoods for computer vision applications [35, 12, 27]. In our framework, we will also assume that small image patches in the semi-local neighborhood of a point contains the essential process required for local smoothing. Thus, the proposed patch-based regularization approach is conceptually very simple being based on the key idea of iteratively increasing a window at each pixel and adaptively weighting input data. The data points with a similar patch to the central patch will have larger weights in the average. We use 7×7 or 9×9 image patches to compute these weights since they are able to capture most of local geometric patterns and texels seen in images. Note also that, it has been experimentally confirmed that intuitive exemplar-based approaches are fearsome for 2D texture synthesis [10] and image inpainting [34, 9]. Nevertheless, we propose here a theoretical framework for choosing a semi-local neighborhood adapted to each pixel. This neighborhood which could be large, is chosen to balance the accuracy of the pointwise estimator and the stochastic error, at each spatial position [20]. This adaptation method is a kind of change-point detection procedure, initiated by Lepskii [20]. By introducing spatial adaptivity, we extend the work earlier described in [7] which can be considered as an extension of bilateral filtering [31] to image patches. The related works to our approach are the unsupervised recent *non-local means* algorithm [7], nonlinear Gaussian filters [31, 33, 22] and statistical smoothing schemes [25, 16, 17], but are enhanced via incorporating either a variable window scheme or patch-based weights. Finally, to our knowledge, the more related competitive methods for image denoising, are recent wavelet-based methods [30, 26]. In our experiments, we have then reported the results when these methods are applied to a commonly-used image dataset [26]. We show that the performance of our method surpasses most of the already published and very competitive denoising methods [30, 26, 27, 7].

2   Patch-Based Approach

Consider the following basic image model: $Y_i = u(\mathbf{x}_i) + \varepsilon_i, i = 1, \ldots, |G|$ where $\mathbf{x}_i \in G \subset \mathbb{R}^d$, $d \geq 2$, represents the spatial coordinates of the discrete image domain of $|G|$ pixels, and $Y_i \in \mathbb{R}_+$ is the observed intensity at location $\mathbf{x}_i$. We suppose the errors ε_i to be independent, distributed Gaussian zero-mean random variables with unknown variances σ^2. In order to recover $u : \mathbb{R}^d \to \mathbb{R}$ from noisy observations, we suppose there exists repetitive patterns in the semi-local neighborhood of a point $\mathbf{x}_i$. In particular, we assume that the unknown image $u(\mathbf{x}_i)$ can be calculated as the weighted average of input data over a variable neighborhood Δ_i around that pixel $\mathbf{x}_i$. Henceforth, the points $\mathbf{x}_j \in \Delta_i$ with a similar regularized patch $\mathbf{u}_j$ to the reference regularized image patch $\mathbf{u}_i$ will have larger weights in the average. Now, we just point out that our ambition is not to learn generic image priors from a database of image patches as already described in [35, 12, 27], but we just consider image patches as non-local image features, and adapt kernel regression techniques for image regularization.

For simplicity, an image patch $\mathbf{u}_i$ is modeled as a fixed size square window of $p \times p$ pixels centered at $\mathbf{x}_i$. In what follows, $\mathbf{u}_i$ will denote indifferently a patch or a vector of p^2 elements where the pixels are concatenated along a fixed lexicographic ordering. As with all exemplar-based techniques, the size of image patches must be specified in advance [10, 34, 9, 7]. We shall see that a 7×7 or 9×9 patch is able to take care of the local geometries and texture in the image while removing undesirable distortions. In addition, the proposed approach requires no training step and may be then considered as *unsupervised*. This makes the method somewhat more attractive for many applications.

Another important question under such an estimation approach is how to determine the size and shape of the variable neighborhood (or window) Δ_i at each pixel, from image data. The selected window must be different at each pixel to take into account the inhomogeneous smoothness of the image. For the sake of parsimony, the set $\mathcal{N}_\Delta$ of admissible neighborhoods will be arbitrarily chosen as a geometric grid of nested square windows $\mathcal{N}_\Delta = \{\Delta_{i,n} : |\Delta_{i,n}| = (2^n+1) \times (2^n+1), n = 1, \ldots, N_\Delta\}$, where $|\Delta_{i,n}| = \#\{\mathbf{x}_j \in \Delta_{i,n}\}$ is the cardinality of $\Delta_{i,n}$ and N_Δ is the number of elements of $\mathcal{N}_\Delta$. For technical reasons, we will require the following conditions: $\Delta_{i,n}$ is centered at $\mathbf{x}_i$ and $\Delta_{i,n} \subset \Delta_{i,n+1}$. Finally, we focus on the *local L_2 risk* as an objective criterion to guide the optimal selection of the smoothing window for constructing the "best" possible estimator. This optimization will be mainly accomplished by starting, at each pixel, with a small window $\Delta_{i,0}$ as a *pilot* estimate, and increasing $\Delta_{i,n}$ with n. The use of variable and overlapping windows combined with adaptive weights contributes to the regularization performance with no block effect.

Adaptive estimation procedure. The proposed procedure is iterative [25, 17] and works as follows. At the initialization, we choose a local window $\Delta_{i,0}$ containing only the point of estimation $\mathbf{x}_i$ ($|\Delta_{i,0}| = 1$). A first estimate $\widehat{u}_{i,0}$ (and its variance $\widehat{v}_{i,0}^2 = \mathrm{Var}(\widehat{u}_{i,0})$) is then given by: $\widehat{u}_{i,0} = Y_i$ and $\widehat{v}_{i,0}^2 = \widehat{\sigma}^2$ where an estimated variance $\widehat{\sigma}^2$ has been plugged in place of σ^2 since the variance of errors are supposed to be unknown. At the next iteration, a larger window $\Delta_{i,1}$ with $\Delta_{i,0} \subset \Delta_{i,1}$ centered at $\mathbf{x}_i$ is considered. Every point $\mathbf{x}_j$ from $\Delta_{i,1}$ gets a weight $\pi_{i \sim j,1}$ defined by comparing pairs of $p \times p$ regularized patches $\widehat{\mathbf{u}}_{i,0} = \left(\widehat{u}_{i,0}^{(1)}, \cdots, \widehat{u}_{i,0}^{(p^2)} \right)^T$ and $\widehat{\mathbf{u}}_{j,0} = \left(\widehat{u}_{j,0}^{(1)}, \cdots, \widehat{u}_{j,0}^{(p^2)} \right)^T$ obtained at the first iteration. Note that p is fixed for all the pixels in the image. As usual, the points $\mathbf{x}_j$ with a similar patch to $\widehat{\mathbf{u}}_{i,0}$ will have weights close to 1 and 0 otherwise. Then we recalculate an new estimate $\widehat{u}_{i,1}$ defined as the *weighted average* of data points lying in the neighborhood $\Delta_{i,1}$. We continue this way, increasing with n the considered window $\Delta_{i,n}$ while $n \leq N_\Delta$ where N_Δ denotes the maximal number of iterations of the algorithm. For each $n \geq 1$, the studied maximum likelihood (ML) estimator $\widehat{u}_{i,n}$ and its variance $\widehat{v}_{i,n}^2$ can be then represented as

$$\widehat{u}_{i,n} = \sum_{\mathbf{x}_j \in \Delta_{i,n}} \pi_{i \sim j,n} Y_j, \quad \widehat{v}_{i,n}^2 = \widehat{\sigma}^2 \sum_{\mathbf{x}_j \in \Delta_{i,n}} \left[\pi_{i \sim j,n} \right]^2 \qquad (1)$$

where the weights $\pi_{i \sim j,n}$ are continuous variables and satisfy the usual conditions $0 \leq \pi_{i \sim j,n} \leq 1$ and $\sum_{\mathbf{x}_j \in \Delta_{i,n}} \pi_{i \sim j,n} = 1$. In our modeling, these weights are computed from pairs of regularized $p \times p$ patches $\widehat{\mathbf{u}}_{i,n-1}$ and $\widehat{\mathbf{u}}_{j,n-1}$ obtained at iteration $n-1$ and p is fixed for all the pixels in the image. In what follows, n will coincide with the iteration and we will use $\widehat{n}(\mathbf{x}_i)$ to designate the index of the "best" window $\widehat{\Delta}(\mathbf{x}_i) \overset{def}{=} \Delta_{i,\widehat{n}(\mathbf{x}_i)}$ and the "best" estimate $\widehat{u}(\mathbf{x}_i) \overset{def}{=} \widehat{u}_{i,\widehat{n}(\mathbf{x}_i)}$. Among all non-rejected window $\Delta_{i,n}$ from N_Δ, the optimal window is chosen as

$$\widehat{\Delta}(\mathbf{x}_i) = \arg \max_{\Delta_{i,n} \in N_\Delta} \left\{ |\Delta_{i,n}| : |\widehat{u}_{i,n} - \widehat{u}_{i,n'}| \leq \varrho \widehat{v}_{i,n'}, \text{ for all } 1 \leq n' < n \right\}$$

where ϱ is a positive constant. Throughout this paper, we shall see the rational behind this pointwise statistical rule and the proposed strategy that updates the pointwise estimator when the neighborhood increases at each iteration [25].

Adaptive weights. In order to compute the similarity of between patches $\widehat{\mathbf{u}}_{i,n}$ and $\widehat{\mathbf{u}}_{j,n}$, a distance must be first considered. In [10, 34, 9, 7], several authors showed that the L_2 distance $\|\widehat{\mathbf{u}}_{i,n} - \widehat{\mathbf{u}}_{j,n}\|^2$ is a reliable measure to compare image patches. To make a decision, we have rather used a normalized distance

$$\mathrm{dist}(\widehat{\mathbf{u}}_{i,n-1}, \widehat{\mathbf{u}}_{j,n-1}) = \frac{1}{2} \left[(\widehat{\mathbf{u}}_{i,n-1} - \widehat{\mathbf{u}}_{j,n-1})^T \widehat{\mathbf{V}}_{i,n-1}^{-1} (\widehat{\mathbf{u}}_{i,n-1} - \widehat{\mathbf{u}}_{j,n-1}) \right. \qquad (2)$$
$$\left. + (\widehat{\mathbf{u}}_{j,n-1} - \widehat{\mathbf{u}}_{i,n-1})^T \widehat{\mathbf{V}}_{j,n-1}^{-1} (\widehat{\mathbf{u}}_{j,n-1} - \widehat{\mathbf{u}}_{i,n-1}) \right]$$

where $\widehat{\mathbf{V}}_{\cdot,n-1}$ is $p^2 \times p^2$ diagonal matrix of the form (the symbol "$\cdot$" is used to denote a spatial position)

$$\widehat{\mathbf{V}}_{\cdot,n-1} = \begin{pmatrix} \left(\widehat{v}_{\cdot,n-1}^{(1)} \right)^2 & 0 & \cdots & 0 \\ \vdots & \vdots & \vdots & \vdots \\ 0 & \cdots & 0 & \left(\widehat{v}_{\cdot,n-1}^{(p^2)} \right)^2 \end{pmatrix}$$

and $\widehat{v}_{\cdot,n-1}^{(\ell)}, \ell = 1, \cdots, p^2$, is the local standard deviation of the estimator $\widehat{u}_{\cdot,n-1}^{(\ell)}$, and the index ℓ is used to denote a spatial position in an image patch $\widehat{\mathbf{u}}_{\cdot,n-1} = \left(\widehat{u}_{\cdot,n-1}^{(1)}, \cdots, \widehat{u}_{\cdot,n-1}^{(\ell)}, \cdots, \widehat{u}_{\cdot,n-1}^{(p^2)}\right)^T$. Moreover, we used a symmetrized distance to test both the hypotheses that $\mathbf{x}_j$ belongs to the region $\Delta_{i,n}$ and $\mathbf{x}_i$ belongs to the region $\Delta_{j,n}$, at the same time. Accordingly, the hypothesis $\widehat{\mathbf{u}}_{i,n-1}$ and $\widehat{\mathbf{u}}_{j,n-1}$ are similar, is accepted if the distance is small, i.e. $\mathrm{dist}(\widehat{\mathbf{u}}_{i,n-1}, \widehat{\mathbf{u}}_{j,n-1}) \leq \lambda_\alpha$. In our modeling, the parameter $\lambda_\alpha \in \mathbb{R}_+$ is chosen as a quantile of a $\chi^2_{p^2,1-\alpha}$ distribution with p^2 degrees of freedom, and controls the probability of type I error for the hypothesis of two points to belong to the same region: $\mathbb{P}\{\mathrm{dist}(\widehat{\mathbf{u}}_{i,n-1}, \widehat{\mathbf{u}}_{j,n-1}) \leq \lambda_\alpha\} = 1 - \alpha$. All these tests ($|\Delta_{i,n}|$ tests) have to be performed at a very high significance level, our experience suggesting to use a $1 - \alpha = 0.99$-quantile. Henceforth, we introduce the following commonly-used weight function

$$\pi_{i \sim j,n} = \frac{K\left(\lambda_\alpha^{-1}\,\mathrm{dist}(\widehat{\mathbf{u}}_{i,n-1}, \widehat{\mathbf{u}}_{j,n-1})\right)}{\displaystyle\sum_{\mathbf{x}_j \in \Delta_{i,n}} K\left(\lambda_\alpha^{-1}\,\mathrm{dist}(\widehat{\mathbf{u}}_{i,n-1}, \widehat{\mathbf{u}}_{j,n-1})\right)} \qquad (3)$$

with $K(\cdot)$ denoting a monotone decreasing function, e.g. a kernel $K(x) = \exp(-x/2)$. Due to the fast decay of the exponential kernel, large distances between estimated patches lead to nearly zero weights. Note that the use of weights enables to relax the structural assumption the neighborhood is a variable square window.

An "ideal" smoothing window. In this section, we address the problem of the automatic selection of the window $\Delta_{i,\cdot}$ adapted for each pixel $\mathbf{x}_i$. It is well understood that the local smoothness varies significantly for point to point in the image and *global risk* measures cannot wholly reflect the performance of estimators at a point. Then, a classical way to measure the performance of the estimator $\widehat{u}_{i,n}$ to its target value $u(\mathbf{x}_i)$ is to choose the *local L_2 risk*, which is explicitly decomposed into the sum of the squared bias $\widehat{b}_{i,n}^2$ and variance $\widehat{v}_{i,n}^2$:

$$\left[\mathbb{E}|\widehat{u}_{i,n} - u(\mathbf{x}_i)|^2\right]^{1/2} = |\widehat{b}_{i,n}^2 + \widehat{v}_{i,n}^2|^{1/2}. \qquad (4)$$

Our goal is then to minimize this *local L_2 risk* with respect to the size of the window $\Delta_{i,n}$, at each pixel in the image. Actually, the optimal solution explicitly depends on the smoothness of the "true" function $u(\mathbf{x}_i)$ which is unknown, and so, of less practical interest [16]. A natural way to bring some further understanding of the situation is then to individually analyze the behavior of the bias and variance terms when $\Delta_{i,n}$ increases or decreases with n as follows:

– The bias term $\widehat{b}_{i,n} = \mathbb{E}\left[\widehat{u}_{i,n} - u(\mathbf{x}_i)\right]$ is nonrandom and characterizes the accuracy of approximation of the function u at the point $\mathbf{x}_i$. As it explicitly depends on the unknown function $u(\mathbf{x}_i)$, its behavior is doubtful. Nevertheless, if we use the geometric inequality $|\mathbf{x}_j - \mathbf{x}_i| \leq \frac{\sqrt{2}}{2}|\Delta_{i,n}|^{1/2}$ and assume that there exists a real constant $0 < C_1 < \infty$ such that

$|u(\mathbf{x}_j) - u(\mathbf{x}_i)| \leq C_1|\mathbf{x}_j - \mathbf{x}_i|$, then $|\widehat{b}_{i,n}| \leq \frac{C_1}{\sqrt{2}}|\Delta_{i,n}|^{1/2}$. Accordingly, $|\widehat{b}_{i,n}|^2$ is of the order $O(|\Delta_{i,n}|)$ and typically increases when $\Delta_{i,n}$ increases (see also [16]).

- The behavior of the variance term is just opposite. The errors are independent and the stochastic term $\widehat{v}_{i,n}^2$ can be exactly computed on the basis of observations. Since $0 \leq \pi_{i \sim j,n} \leq 1$ and $\sum_{\mathbf{x}_j \in \Delta_{i,n}} \pi_{i \sim j,n} = 1$, it follows that $\widehat{\sigma}^2|\Delta_{i,n}|^{-1} \leq \widehat{v}_{i,n}^2 \leq \widehat{\sigma}^2$. In addition, we can reasonably assume that there exits a constant $0 \leq \gamma^2 \leq 1$ such that $\widehat{v}_{i,n}^2 \approx \widehat{\sigma}^2|\Delta_{i,n}|^{-\gamma^2}$. Accordingly, as $\Delta_{i,n}$ increases, more data is used to construct the estimate $\widehat{u}_{i,n}$, and so $\widehat{v}_{i,n}^2$ decreases.

Therefore, the bias and standard deviation terms are monotonous functions with opposite behaviors. In order to approximately minimize the local L_2 risk with respect to $|\Delta_{i,n}|$, a natural idea would be to minimize an upper bound of the form

$$\mathbb{E}|\widehat{u}_{i,n} - u(\mathbf{x}_i)|^2 \leq \frac{C_1^2}{2}|\Delta_{i,n}| + \widehat{\sigma}^2|\Delta_{i,n}|^{-\gamma^2}.$$

Unfortunately, the size of the optimal window defined as $|\Delta^\star(\mathbf{x}_i)| = \left[\frac{2\gamma^2\widehat{\sigma}^2}{C_1^2}\right]^{\frac{1}{\gamma^2+1}}$ cannot be used in practice since C_1 and γ are unknown. However, for this optimal solution $|\Delta^\star(\mathbf{x}_i)|$, it can be easily shown that the ratio between the optimal bias $b^\star(\mathbf{x}_i)$ and the optimal standard deviation $v^\star(\mathbf{x}_i)$ is not image dependent, i.e. $|b^\star(\mathbf{x}_i)| \leq \gamma v^\star(\mathbf{x}_i)$. Accordingly, the ideal window will be chosen as the largest window $\Delta_{i,n}$ such that $\widehat{b}_{i,n}$ is still not larger than $\gamma\widehat{v}_{i,n}$, for some real value $0 \leq \gamma^2 \leq 1$: $\Delta^\star(\mathbf{x}_i) = \sup_{\Delta_{i,n} \in \mathcal{N}_\Delta}\{|\Delta_{i,n}| : \widehat{b}_{i,n} \leq \gamma\widehat{v}_{i,n}\}$.

Now, we just point out that the estimator $\widehat{u}_{i,n}$ is usually decomposed as $\widehat{u}_{i,n} = u(\mathbf{x}_i) + \widehat{b}_{i,n} + \nu_i$ where $\nu_i \sim \mathcal{N}(0, \mathbb{E}[\nu_i^2])$. Hence, $\mathbb{E}[\widehat{u}_{i,n}] = u(\mathbf{x}_i) + \widehat{b}_{i,n}$, $\mathbb{E}[\nu_i^2] = \mathbb{E}[|\widehat{u}_{i,n} - u(\mathbf{x}_i) - \widehat{b}_{i,n}|^2] \overset{def}{=} \widehat{v}_{i,n}^2$ and the following inequality $|\widehat{u}_{i,n} - u(\mathbf{x}_i)| \leq \widehat{b}_{i,n} + \varkappa\widehat{v}_{i,n}$ holds with a high probability for $0 < \varkappa < \infty$. Accordingly, we can modify the previous definition of the *ideal* window as follows

$$\Delta^\star(\mathbf{x}_i) = \sup_{\Delta_{i,n} \in \mathcal{N}_\Delta}\{|\Delta_{i,n}| : |\widehat{u}_{i,n} - u(\mathbf{x}_i)| \leq (\gamma + \varkappa)\,\widehat{v}_{i,n}\}, \tag{5}$$

which depends no longer on $\widehat{b}_{i,n}$. In the next section, we shall see that a practical *data-driven* window selector based on this definition of $\Delta^\star(\mathbf{x}_i)$ which is yet related to the ideal and unobserved function $u(\mathbf{x}_i)$, can actually be derived.

A data-driven local window selector. In our approach, the collection of estimators $\{\widehat{u}_{i,1}, \ldots, \widehat{u}(\mathbf{x}_i)\}$ is naturally ordered in the direction of increasing $|\Delta_{i,n}|$ where $\widehat{u}(\mathbf{x}_i)$ can be thought as the best possible estimator with the smallest variance. A selection procedure can be then described based on pairwise comparisons of an essentially one-dimensional family of competing estimators $\widehat{u}_{i,n}$. In this modeling, the differences $\widehat{u}_{i,n} - \widehat{u}_{i,n'}$ are Gaussian random variables with known variances $\text{Var}(\widehat{u}_{i,n} - \widehat{u}_{i,n'}) \leq \widehat{v}_{i,n'}^2$ with $1 \leq n' < n$, and expectations equal to the bias differences $\widehat{b}_{i,n} - \widehat{b}_{i,n'}$. From the definition of $\Delta^\star(\mathbf{x}_i)$ (see (5)), we derive $|\widehat{u}_{i,n'} - \widehat{u}_{i,n}| \leq (2\gamma + \varkappa)\widehat{v}_{i,n'}$, $1 \leq n' < n$, and, among all good candidates $\{\widehat{u}_{i,n}\}$ satisfying this inequality, one choose the one with the smallest variance $\widehat{v}_{i,n}^2$. Following the above discussion, a window selector will be then based on the following pointwise rule [20, 21]:

$$\widehat{\Delta}(\mathbf{x}_i) = \arg \max_{\Delta_{i,n} \in \mathcal{N}_\Delta} \{|\Delta_{i,n}| : |\widehat{u}_{i,n} - \widehat{u}_{i,n'}| \leq \varrho\widehat{v}_{i,n'}, \text{ for all } 1 \leq n' < n\} \quad (6)$$

where $\varrho = (2\gamma + \varkappa)$. This rule actually ensures the balance between the stochastic term and the bias term, and means that we take the largest window such that the estimators $\widehat{u}_{i,n}$ and $\widehat{u}_{i,n'}$ are not too different, in some sense, for all $1 \leq n' < n$ (see [18]). Hence, if an estimated point $\widehat{u}_{i,n'}$ appears far from the previous ones, this means that the bias is already too large and the window $\Delta_{i,n}$ is not a good one. This idea underlying our construction definitely belongs to Lepskii [20, 21].

Implementation. At the initialization, we naturally choose $|\Delta_{i,0}| = 1$, the fixed size of $p \times p$ patches and choose the number of iterations N_Δ. In addition, the noise variance $\widehat{\sigma}^2$ is robustly estimated from input data (see [17]). To complete

---

Algorithm.   Let $\{p, \alpha, \varrho, N_\Delta\}$ be the parameters

---

Initialization: compute $\widehat{\sigma}^2$ and set $\widehat{u}_{i,0} = Y_i$ and $\widehat{v}_{i,0}^2 = \widehat{\sigma}^2$ for each $\mathbf{x}_i \in G$.

Repeat

– for each $\mathbf{x}_i \in G$
  • compute

$$\pi_{i \sim j, n} = \frac{K\left(\lambda_\alpha^{-1} \operatorname{dist}(\widehat{\mathbf{u}}_{i,n-1}, \widehat{\mathbf{u}}_{j,n-1})\right)}{\displaystyle\sum_{\mathbf{x}_j \in \Delta_{i,n}} K\left(\lambda_\alpha^{-1} \operatorname{dist}(\widehat{\mathbf{u}}_{i,n-1}, \widehat{\mathbf{u}}_{j,n-1})\right)}$$

$$\widehat{u}_{i,n} = \sum_{\mathbf{x}_j \in \Delta_{i,n}} \pi_{i \sim j, n} Y_j, \qquad \widehat{v}_{i,n}^2 = \widehat{\sigma}^2 \sum_{\mathbf{x}_j \in \Delta_{i,n}} [\pi_{i \sim j, n}]^2$$

  • choose the window as

$$\widehat{\Delta}(\mathbf{x}_i) = \arg \max_{\Delta_{i,n} \in \mathcal{N}_\Delta} \{|\Delta_{i,n}| : |\widehat{u}_{i,n} - \widehat{u}_{i,n'}| \leq \varrho\widehat{v}_{i,n'}, \text{ for all } 1 \leq n' < n\}.$$

  If this rule is violated at iteration n, we do not accept $\widehat{u}_{i,n}$ and keep the estimate $\widehat{u}_{i,n-1}$ as the final estimate at $\mathbf{x}_i$, i.e. $\widehat{u}(\mathbf{x}_i) = \widehat{u}_{i,n-1}$ and $\widehat{n}(\mathbf{x}_i) = n - 1$. This estimate is unchanged at the next iterations and $\mathbf{x}_i$ is "frozen".
– increment n

while $n \leq N_\Delta$.

Fig. 1. Patch-based image regularization algorithm

the procedure, we choose $\varrho \in [2,4]$ in order to get a good accuracy for the pointwise estimator (see [18] for the proof) and λ_α as a $1 - \alpha = 0.99$-quantile of a $\chi^2_{p^2,1-\alpha}$ distribution. Finally, the complexity of the algorithm given in Fig. 1, is of the order $p \times p \times |G| \times (|\Delta_{.,1}| + \ldots + |\Delta_{.,N_\Delta}|)$.

3   Experimental Results

Our results were measured by the peak signal-to-noise ratio (PSNR) in decibels (db) as $\text{PSNR} = 10\log_{10}(255^2/\text{MSE})$ with $\text{MSE} = |G|^{-1}\sum_{\mathbf{x}_i \in G}(u_o(\mathbf{x}_i) - \widehat{u}(\mathbf{x}_i))^2$ where u_0 is the noise-free original image. We have done simulations on a commonly-used set of images available at http://decsai.ugr.es/~javier/denoise/test_images/ and described in [26]. In all our experiments, we have chosen image patches of 9×9 pixels and set the algorithm parameters as follows: $\lambda_{0.01} = \chi^2_{81,0.01} = 113.5, \varrho = 3$ and $N_\Delta = 4$ (see [18]). The processing of a 256×256 image required typically about 1 minute ($p = 9$) on a PC (2.0 Ghz, Pentium IV) using a C++ implementation. The potential of the estimation method is mainly illustrated with the 512×512 *lena* image (Fig. 2a) corrupted by an additive white-Gaussian noise (WGN) (Fig. 2b, PSNR $= 22.13$ db, $\sigma = 20$). In Fig. 2c, the noise is reduced in a natural manner and significant geometric features, fine textures, and original contrasts are visually well recovered with no undesirable

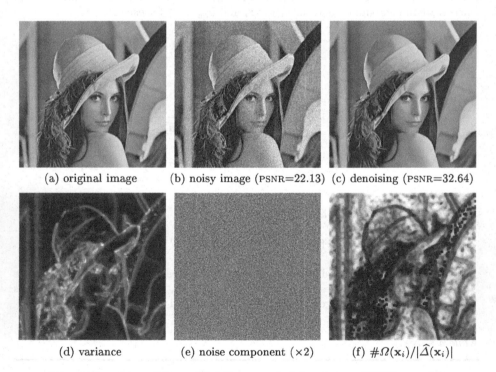

(a) original image   (b) noisy image (PSNR=22.13)   (c) denoising (PSNR=32.64)

(d) variance   (e) noise component (×2)   (f) $\#\Omega(\mathbf{x}_i)/|\widehat{\Delta}(\mathbf{x}_i)|$

Fig. 2. Denoising of the artificially corrupted *lena* image (WGN, $\sigma = 20$)

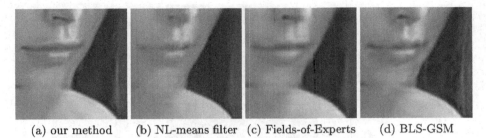

(a) our method   (b) NL-means filter   (c) Fields-of-Experts   (d) BLS-GSM

Fig. 3. Denoising results on the noisy *lena* image (WGN, $\sigma = 20$). a) Our method (PSNR = 32.64), b) NL-means filter [7] (PSNR=31.09), c) Fields-of-Experts [27] (PSNR=31.92), d) wavelet-based denoising method (BLS-GSM) [26] (PSNR=32.66).

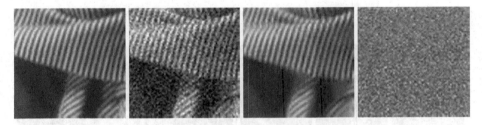

Fig. 4. Detail of the *barbara* image. From left to right: original image, artificially corrupted image (WGN, $\sigma = 30$), result of our patch-based method, difference between the noisy image and the regularized image (noise component).

artifacts (PSNR = 32.64 db). The noise component is shown in Fig. 2e (magnification factor of 2) and has been estimated by calculating the difference between the noisy image (Fig. 2b) and the recovered image (Fig. 2c). The estimated noise component contains few geometric structures and is similar to a simulated white Gaussian noise. To better appreciate the accuracy of the denoising process, the variance $\widehat{v}^2(\mathbf{x}_i)$ of the pointwise estimator $\widehat{u}(\mathbf{x}_i)$ is shown in Fig. 2d where dark values correspond to high-confidence estimates. As expected, pixels with a low level of confidence are located in the neighborhood of image discontinuities. Figure 2f shows the probability of a patch $\widehat{u}(\mathbf{x}_i)$ occurring in $\widehat{\Delta}(\mathbf{x}_i)$:
$$\mathbb{P}\{\widehat{u}(\mathbf{x}_i) \text{ occurring in } \widehat{\Delta}(\mathbf{x}_i)\} \overset{def}{=} \#\Omega(\mathbf{x}_i)/|\widehat{\Delta}(\mathbf{x}_i)|$$ where $\Omega(\mathbf{x}_i)$ is used to denote the set $\{\mathbf{x}_j \in \widehat{\Delta}(\mathbf{x}_i) : \text{dist}(\widehat{u}(\mathbf{x}_i), \widehat{u}(\mathbf{x}_j)) \leq \lambda_\alpha\}$. In Fig. 2f, dark values correspond low probabilities of occurrence and, it is confirmed that repetitive patterns in the neighborhood of image discontinuities are mainly located along image edges. Our approach is also compared to the *non-local means* algorithm [7] using 7×7 image patches and a fixed search window of 21×21 pixels as recommended by the authors: the visual impression and the numerical results are improved using our algorithm (see Fig. 3b). Finally, we have compared the performance of our method to the Wiener filtering (WF) (Matlab function `wiener2`) and other competitive methods [28, 31, 24], including recent patch-based approaches [7, 27] and pointwise adaptive estimation approaches [25, 17]. We point out that, visually

Fig. 5. Real noisy photographs (top) and restoration results (bottom)

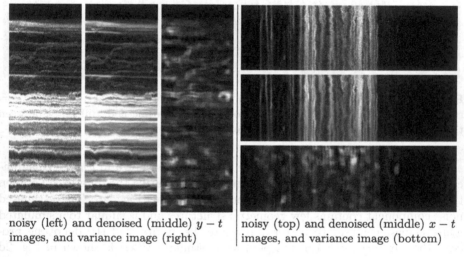

noisy (left) and denoised (middle) $y - t$ images, and variance image (right)

noisy (top) and denoised (middle) $x - t$ images, and variance image (bottom)

Fig. 6. Results on a 2D image depicting trajectories of vesicles of transport in the spatio-temporal planes $y - t$ (left) and $x - t$ (right) (analysis of Rab proteins involved in the regulation of transport from the Golgi apparatus to the endoplasmic reticulum).

and quantitatively, our very simple and unsupervised algorithm favorably compares to any of these denoising algorithms, including the more sophisticated and best known wavelet-based denoising methods [30, 26] (see Fig. 3d) and learned filters-based denoising methods [27] (see Fig. 3c). In Table 1 (a), we reported the best available published PSNR results for the same image dataset [26] ; we note that our method nearly outperforms any of the tested methods in terms of PSNR. Also, if the PSNR gains are marginal for some images, the visual difference can be significant as shown in Fig. 3 where less artifacts are visible using our method (see also Fig. 4). Nevertheless, other competitive unsupervised patch-based methods exist (e.g. see [15, 2]), but we did not report the results on this

Table 1. Performances of our method when applied to test noisy (WGN) images

Image σ/PSNR	Lena 20/22.13	Barbara 20/22.18	Boats 20/22.17	House 20/22.11	Peppers 20/22.19
Our method	**32.64**	**30.37**	**30.12**	**32.90**	**30.59**
Buades et al. [7]	31.09	29.38	28.60	31.54	29.05
Kervrann [17]	30.54	26.50	28.01	30.70	28.23
Polzehl et al. [25]	29.74	26.05	27.74	30.31	28.40
Portilla et al. [26]	32.66	30.32	30.38	32.39	30.31
Roth et al. [27]	31.92	28.32	29.85	32.17	30.58
Rudin et al. [28]	30.48	27.07	29.02	31.03	28.51
Starck et al. [30]	31.95	-	-	-	-
Tomasi et al. [31]	30.26	27.02	28.41	30.01	28.88
Wiener filering	28.51	26.99	27.97	28.74	28.10

(a) Performances of denoising algorithms when applied to test noisy (WGN) images.

σ/PSNR	Lena 512^2	Barbara 512^2	Boats 512^2	House 256^2	Peppers 256^2
5 / 34.15	37.91	37.12	36.14	37.62	37.34
10 / 28.13	35.18	33.79	33.09	35.26	34.07
15 / 24.61	33.70	31.80	31.44	34.08	32.13
20 / 22.11	32.64	30.37	30.12	32.90	30.59
25 / 2017	31.73	29.24	29.20	32.22	29.73
50 / 14.15	28.38	24.09	25.93	28.67	25.29
75 / 10.63	25.51	22.10	23.69	25.49	22.31
100 / 8.13	23.32	20.64	21.78	23.08	20.51

patch size	Lena 512^2	Barbara 512^2	Boats 512^2	House 256^2	Peppers 256^2
3 × 3	32.13	28.97	29.86	32.69	30.86
5 × 5	32.52	29.97	30.15	33.05	30.98
7 × 7	32.63	30.27	30.17	33.03	30.80
9 × 9	32.64	30.37	30.12	32.90	30.59

(b) Performances of our method ($p=9, N_\Delta=4, \alpha=0.01$) for different signal-to-noise ratios (WGN).

(c) Performances of our method ($N_\Delta = 4, \alpha = 0.01$) for different patch sizes (WGN, $\sigma = 20$)

image dataset since they are not available. These methods must be considered for future comparisons. To complete the experiments, Table 1 (b) shows the PSNR values using our patch-based regularization method when applied to this set of test images for a wide range of noise variance. Moreover, we have also examined some complementary aspects of our approach. Table 1 (c) shows the PSNR values obtained by varying the patch size. Note the PSNR values are close for every patch size and the optimal patch size depends on the image contents. Nevertheless, a patch 9 × 9 seems appropriate in most cases and a smaller patch can be considered for processing piecewise smooth images.

In the second part of experiments, the effects of the patch-based regularization is approach are illustrated on real old photographs. The set of parameters is unchanged for processing all these test images: $p = 9, N_\Delta = 4, \alpha = 0.01$. In most cases, a good compromise between the amount of smoothing and preservation of edges and textures is automatically reached. In that case, the noise variance $\widehat{\sigma}^2$ is automatically estimated from image data. The reconstruction of images is respectively shown in Fig. 5. Note that geometric structures are well preserved and the noise component corresponding to homogeneous artifacts is removed.

Finally, we have applied the patch-based restoration method to noisy 2D images extracted from a temporal 2D+time ($xy - t$) sequence of 120 microscopy images in intracellular biology, showing a large number of small fluorescently labeled moving vesicles in regions close to the Golgi apparatus (courtesy of Curie Institute). The reading of observed trajectories is easier if the patch-based estimation method is applied to both noisy $x-t$ or $y-t$ projection images shown in Fig. 6 (see also [6]).

4   Conclusion

We have described a novel adaptive regularization algorithm where patch-based weights and variable window sizes are jointly used. The use of variable and overlapping windows contributes to the regularization performance with no block effect, enhances the flexibility of the resulting local regularizers and make them possible to cope well with spatial inhomogeneities in natural images. An advantage of the method is that internal parameters can be easily chosen and are relatively stable. The algorithm is able to regularize both piecewise-smooth and textured natural images since they contain enough redundancy. Actually, the performance of our simple algorithm is very close to that of the best already published denoising methods. In the future, we plan to study the automatic patch size selection to better adapt to image contents.

References

1. Aujol, J.F., Aubert, G., Blanc-Fraud, L., Chambolle, A.: Image decomposition into a bounded variation component and an oscillating component. J. Math. Imag. Vis. **22** (2005) 71-88
2. Awate, S.P., Whitaker, R.T.: Higher-order image statistics for unsupervised, information-theoretic, adaptive, image filtering. In: Proc. CVPR'05, San Diego (2005)
3. Barash, D., Comaniciu, D.: A Common framework for nonlinear diffusion, adaptive smoothing, bilateral filtering and mean shift. Image Vis. Comp. **22** (2004) 73-81
4. Black, M.J., Sapiro, G.: Edges as outliers: anisotropic smoothing using local image statistics. In: Proc. Scale-Space'99, Kerkyra (1999)
5. Brox, T., Weickert, J.: A TV flow based local scale measure for texture discrimination. In: Proc. ECCV'04, Prague (2004)
6. Boulanger, J., Kervrann, C., Bouthemy, P.: Adaptive spatio-temporal restoration for 4D fluoresence microscopic imaging. In: Proc. MICCAI'05, Palm Springs (2005)
7. Buades, A., Coll, B., Morel, J.M.: Image denoising by non-local averaging. In: Proc. CVPR'05, San Diego (2005)
8. Comaniciu, D., Ramesh, V., Meer, P.: The variable bandwidth mean-shift and data-driven scale selection. In: Proc. ICCV'01, Vancouver (2001)
9. Criminisi, A., Pérez, P., Toyama, K.: Region filling and object removal by exemplar-based inpainting. IEEE T. Image Process. **13** (2004) 1200-1212
10. Efros, A., Leung, T.: Texture synthesis by non-parametric sampling. In: Proc. ICCV'99, Kerkyra (1999)
11. Elad, M.: On the bilateral filter and ways to improve it. IEEE T. Image Process. **11** (2002) 1141-1151
12. Freeman, W.T., Pasztor, E.C., Carmichael, O.T.: Learning low-level vision. Int. J. Comp. Vis. **40** (2000) 25-47
13. Gilboa, G., Sochen, N., Zeevi, Y.Y.: Texture preserving variational denoising using an adaptive fidelity term. In: Proc. VLSM'03, Nice (2003)

14. Godtliebsen, F., Spjotvoll, E., Marron, J.S.: A nonlinear Gaussian filter applied to images with discontinuities. J. Nonparametric Stat. **8** (1997) 21-43

15. Jojic, N., Frey, B., Kannan, A.: Epitomic analysis of appearance and shape. In: Proc. ICCV'03, Nice (2003)

16. Katkovnik, V., Egiazarian, K., Astola, J.: Adaptive window size image denoising based on intersection of confidence intervals (ICI) rule. J. Math. Imag. Vis. **16** (2002) 223-235

17. Kervrann, C.: An adaptive window approach for image smoothing and structures preserving. In: Proc. ECCV'04, Prague (2004)

18. Kervrann, C., Boulanger, J.: Local adaptivity to variable smoothness for exemplar-based image denoising and representation. INRIA RR-5624 (2005)

19. Lee, J.S.: Digital image smoothing and the sigma filter. Comp. Vis. Graph. Image Process. **24** (1983) 255-269

20. Lepskii, O.: On a problem of adaptive estimation on white Gaussian noise. Th. Prob. Appl. **35** (1980) 454-466

21. Lepskii, O.V., Mammen, E., Spokoiny, V.G.: Optimal spatial adaptation to inhomogeneous smoothness: an approach based on kernel estimates with variable bandwidth selectors. Ann. Stat. **25** (1997) 929-947

22. Mrazek, P., Weickert, J., Bruhn, A.: On robust estimation and smoothing with spatial and tonal kernels. Preprint 51, U. Bremen (2004)

23. Mumford, D., Shah, J.: Optimal approximations by piecewise smooth functions and variational problems. Comm. Pure and Appl. Math. **42** (1989) 577-685

24. Perona. P., Malik, J.: Scale space and edge detection using anisotropic diffusion. IEEE T. Patt. Anal. Mach. Intell. **12** (1990) 629-239

25. Polzehl, J., Spokoiny, V.: Adaptive weights smoothing with application to image restoration. J. Roy. Stat. Soc. B **62** (2000) 335-354

26. Portilla, J., Strela, V., Wainwright, M., Simoncelli, E.: Image denoising using scale mixtures of Gaussians in the wavelet domain. IEEE T. Image Process. **12** (2003) 1338-1351

27. Roth, S., Black, M.J.: Fields of experts: a framework for learning image priors with applications. In: Proc. CVPR'05, San Diego (2005)

28. Rudin, L., Osher, S., Fatemi, E.: Nonlinear Total Variation based noise removal algorithms. Physica D (2992) **60** (1992) 259-268

29. Sochen, N., Kimmel, R., Bruckstein, A.M.: Diffusions and confusions in signal and image processing. J. Math. Imag. Vis. **14** (2001) 237-244

30. Starck, J.L., Candes, E., Donoho, D.L.: The Curvelet transform for image denoising. IEEE T. Image Process. **11** (2002) 670-684

31. Tomasi, C., Manduchi, R.: Bilateral filtering for gray and color images. In: Proc. ICCV'98, Bombay (1998)

32. Tschumperlé, D.: Curvature-preserving regularization of multi-valued images using PDE's. In: Proc. ECCV'06, Graz (2006)

33. van de Weijer, J., van den Boomgaard, R.: Local mode filtering. In: Proc. CVPR'01, Kauai (2001)

34. Zhang, D., Wang, Z.: Image information restoration based on long-range correlation. IEEE T. Circ. Syst. Video Technol. **12** (2002) 331-341

35. Zhu, S.C., Wu, Y., Mumford, D.: Filters, random fields and maximum entropy (FRAME): Towards a unified theory for texture modeling. Int. J. Comp. Vis. **27** (1998) 107-126

A Fast Approximation of the Bilateral Filter Using a Signal Processing Approach

Sylvain Paris and Frédo Durand

Massachusetts Institute of Technology,
Computer Science and Artificial Intelligence Laboratory

Abstract. The bilateral filter is a nonlinear filter that smoothes a signal while preserving strong edges. It has demonstrated great effectiveness for a variety of problems in computer vision and computer graphics, and a fast version has been proposed. Unfortunately, little is known about the accuracy of such acceleration. In this paper, we propose a new signal-processing analysis of the bilateral filter, which complements the recent studies that analyzed it as a PDE or as a robust statistics estimator. Importantly, this signal-processing perspective allows us to develop a novel bilateral filtering acceleration using a downsampling in space and intensity. This affords a principled expression of the accuracy in terms of bandwidth and sampling. The key to our analysis is to express the filter in a higher-dimensional space where the signal intensity is added to the original domain dimensions. The bilateral filter can then be expressed as simple linear convolutions in this augmented space followed by two simple nonlinearities. This allows us to derive simple criteria for down-sampling the key operations and to achieve important acceleration of the bilateral filter. We show that, for the same running time, our method is significantly more accurate than previous acceleration techniques.

1 Introduction

The bilateral filter is a nonlinear filter proposed by Tomasi and Manduchi to smooth images [1]. It has been adopted for several applications such as texture removal [2], dynamic range compression [3], and photograph enhancement [4, 5]. It has also be adapted to other domains such as mesh fairing [6, 7], volumetric denoising [8] and exposure correction of videos [9]. This large success stems from several origins. First, its formulation and implementation are simple: a pixel is simply replaced by a weighted mean of its neighbors. And it is easy to adapt to a given context as long as a distance can be computed between two pixel values (*e.g.* distance between hair orientations in [10]). The bilateral filter is also non-iterative, *i.e.* it achieves satisfying results with only a single pass. This makes the filter's parameters relatively intuitive since their action does not depend on the cumulated effects of several iterations.

On the other hand, the bilateral filter is nonlinear and its evaluation is computationally expensive since traditional acceleration, such as performing convolution after an FFT, are not applicable. Elad [11] proposes an acceleration method using Gauss-Seidel iterations, but it only applies when multiple iterations of the

A. Leonardis, H. Bischof, and A. Pinz (Eds.): ECCV 2006, Part IV, LNCS 3954, pp. 568–580, 2006.

filter are required. Durand and Dorsey [3] describe a linearized version of the filter that achieves dramatic speed-ups by downsampling the data, achieving running times under one second. Unfortunately, this technique is not grounded on firm theoretical foundations, and it is difficult to evaluate the accuracy that is sacrificed. In this paper, we build on this work but we interpret the bilateral filter in terms of signal processing in a higher-dimensional space. This allows us to derive an improved acceleration scheme that yields equivalent running times but dramatically improves numerical accuracy.

Contributions. This paper introduces the following contributions:

- An interpretation of the bilateral filter in a signal processing framework. Using a higher dimensional space, we formulate the bilateral filter as a convolution followed by simple nonlinearities.
- Using this higher dimensional space, we demonstrate that the convolution computation can be downsampled without significantly impacting the result accuracy. This approximation technique enables a speed-up of several orders of magnitude while controlling the error induced.

2   Related Work

The bilateral filter was first introduced by Smith and Brady under the name "SUSAN" [12]. It was rediscovered later by Tomasi and Manduchi [1] who called it the "bilateral filter" which is now the most commonly used name. The filter replaces each pixel by a weighted average of its neighbors. The weight assigned to each neighbor decreases with both the distance in the image plane (the *spatial domain S*) and the distance on the intensity axis (the *range domain R*). Using a Gaussian G_σ as a decreasing function, and considering a grey-level image I, the result I^{bf} of the bilateral filter is defined by:

$$I_{\mathbf{p}}^{\text{bf}} = \frac{1}{W_{\mathbf{p}}^{\text{bf}}} \sum_{\mathbf{q} \in S} G_{\sigma_{\text{s}}}(\|\mathbf{p} - \mathbf{q}\|) \, G_{\sigma_{\text{r}}}(|I_{\mathbf{p}} - I_{\mathbf{q}}|) \, I_{\mathbf{q}} \qquad (1\text{a})$$

$$\text{with} \quad W_{\mathbf{p}}^{\text{bf}} = \sum_{\mathbf{q} \in S} G_{\sigma_{\text{s}}}(\|\mathbf{p} - \mathbf{q}\|) \, G_{\sigma_{\text{r}}}(|I_{\mathbf{p}} - I_{\mathbf{q}}|) \qquad (1\text{b})$$

The parameter σ_{s} defines the size of the spatial neighborhood used to filter a pixel, and σ_{r} controls how much an adjacent pixel is downweighted because of the intensity difference. W^{bf} normalizes the sum of the weights.

Barash [13] shows that the two weight functions are actually equivalent to a single weight function based on a distance defined on $S \times R$. Using this approach, he relates the bilateral filter to adaptive smoothing. Our work follows a similar idea and also uses $S \times R$ to describe bilateral filtering. Our formulation is nonetheless significantly different because we not only use the higher-dimensional space for the definition of a distance, but we also use convolution in this space. Elad [11] demonstrates that the bilateral filter is similar to the Jacobi algorithm, with the specificity that it accounts for a larger neighborhood instead of the closest adjacent pixels usually considered. Buades *et al.* [14] expose an asymptotic analysis of the Yaroslavsky filter [15] which is a special case of the bilateral filter with a step function as spatial weight. They prove that asymptotically, the Yaroslavsky filter behaves as the Perona-Malik filter, *i.e.* it alternates between smoothing and shock formation depending on the gradient intensity. Durand and Dorsey [3] cast their study into the robust statistics framework [16, 17]. They show that the bilateral filter is a *w*-estimator [17] (p.116). This explains the role of the range weight in terms of sensitivity to outliers. They also point out that the bilateral filter can be seen as an extension of the Perona-Malik filter using a larger neighborhood. Mrázek *et al.* [18] relate bilateral filtering to a large family of nonlinear filters. From a single equation, they express filters such as anisotropic diffusion and statistical estimators by varying the neighborhood size and the involved functions. The main difference between our study and existing work is that the previous approaches link bilateral filtering to another nonlinear filter based on PDEs or statistics whereas we cast our study into a signal processing framework. We demonstrate that the bilateral filter can be mainly computed with linear operations, the nonlinearities being grouped in a final step.

Several articles [11, 19, 14] improve the bilateral filter. They share the same idea: By exploiting the local "slope" of the image intensity, it is possible to better represent the local shape of the signal. Thus, they define a modified filter that better preserve the image characteristics *e.g.* they avoid the formation of shocks. We have not explored this direction since the formulation becomes significantly more complex. It is however an interesting avenue for future work.

The work most related to ours are the speed-up techniques proposed by Elad [11] and Durand and Dorsey [3]. Elad [11] uses Gauss-Seidel iterations to accelerate the convergence of iterative filtering. Unfortunately, no results are shown – and this technique is only useful when the filter is iterated to reach the stable point, which is not its standard use of the bilateral filter (one iteration or only a few). Durand and Dorsey [3] linearize the bilateral filter and propose a downsampling scheme to accelerate the computation down to few seconds or less. However, no theoretical study is proposed, and the accuracy of the approximation is unclear. In comparison, we base our technique on signal processing grounds which help us to define a new and meaningful numerical scheme. Our algorithm performs low-pass filtering in a higher-dimensional space than Durand and Dorsey's [3]. The cost of a higher-dimensional convolution is offset by the accuracy gain, which yields better performance for the same accuracy.

3   Signal Processing Approach

We decompose the bilateral filter into a convolution followed by two nonlinearities. To cast the filter as a convolution, we define a homogeneous intensity that will allow us to obtain the normalization term $W_{\mathrm{p}}^{\mathrm{bf}}$ as an homogeneous component after convolution. We also need to perform this convolution in the product space of the domain and the range of the input signal. Observing Equations (1), the nonlinearity comes from the division by W^{bf} and from the dependency on the pixel intensities through $G_{\sigma_r}(|I_\mathbf{p} - I_\mathbf{q}|)$. We study each point separately and isolate them in the computation flow.

3.1   Homogeneous Intensity

A direct solution to handle the division is to multiply both sides of Equation (1a) by $W_\mathbf{p}^{\mathrm{bf}}$. The two equations are then almost similar. We underline this point by rewriting Equations (1) using two-dimensional vectors:

$$\begin{pmatrix} W_\mathbf{p}^{\mathrm{bf}} I_\mathbf{p}^{\mathrm{bf}} \\ W_\mathbf{p}^{\mathrm{bf}} \end{pmatrix} = \sum_{\mathbf{q} \in \mathcal{S}} G_{\sigma_\mathbf{s}}(\|\mathbf{p} - \mathbf{q}\|) \, G_{\sigma_r}(|I_\mathbf{p} - I_\mathbf{q}|) \begin{pmatrix} I_\mathbf{q} \\ 1 \end{pmatrix} \tag{2}$$

To maintain the property that the bilateral filter is a weighted mean, we introduce a function W whose value is 1 everywhere:

$$\begin{pmatrix} W_\mathbf{p}^{\mathrm{bf}} I_\mathbf{p}^{\mathrm{bf}} \\ W_\mathbf{p}^{\mathrm{bf}} \end{pmatrix} = \sum_{\mathbf{q} \in \mathcal{S}} G_{\sigma_\mathbf{s}}(\|\mathbf{p} - \mathbf{q}\|) \, G_{\sigma_r}(|I_\mathbf{p} - I_\mathbf{q}|) \begin{pmatrix} W_\mathbf{q} I_\mathbf{q} \\ W_\mathbf{q} \end{pmatrix} \tag{3}$$

By assigning a couple $(W_q I_q, W_q)$ to each pixel q, we express the filtered pixels as linear combinations of their adjacent pixels. Of course, we have not "removed" the division since to access the actual value of the intensity, the first coordinate (WI) has still to be divided by the second one (W). This can be compared with homogeneous coordinates used in projective geometry. Adding an extra coordinate to our data makes most of the computation pipeline computable with linear operations; a division is made only at the final stage. Inspired by this parallel, we call the couple (WI, W) the *homogeneous intensity*.

Although Equation (3) is a linear combination, this does not define a linear filter yet since the weights depend on the actual values of the pixels. The next section addresses this issue.

3.2   The Bilateral Filter as a Convolution

If we ignore the term $G_{\sigma_r}(|I_\mathbf{p} - I_\mathbf{q}|)$, Equation (3) is a classical convolution by a Gaussian kernel: $(W^{\mathrm{bf}} I^{\mathrm{bf}}, W^{\mathrm{bf}}) = G_{\sigma_\mathbf{s}} \otimes (WI, W)$. But the range weight depends on $I_\mathbf{p} - I_\mathbf{q}$ and there is no summation on I. To overcome this point, we introduce an additional dimension ζ and sum over it. With the Kronecker symbol $\delta(\zeta)$ (1 if $\zeta = 0$, 0 otherwise) and $\mathcal{R}$ the interval on which the intensity is defined, we rewrite Equation (3) using $\left[\delta(\zeta - I_\mathbf{q}) = 1 \right] \Leftrightarrow \left[\zeta = I_\mathbf{q} \right]$:

$$\begin{pmatrix} W_\mathbf{p}^{\mathrm{bf}} I_\mathbf{p}^{\mathrm{bf}} \\ W_\mathbf{p}^{\mathrm{bf}} \end{pmatrix} = \sum_{\mathbf{q} \in \mathcal{S}} \sum_{\zeta \in \mathcal{R}} G_{\sigma_\mathbf{s}}(\|\mathbf{p} - \mathbf{q}\|) \, G_{\sigma_r}(|I_\mathbf{p} - \zeta|) \, \delta(\zeta - I_\mathbf{q}) \begin{pmatrix} W_\mathbf{q} I_\mathbf{q} \\ W_\mathbf{q} \end{pmatrix} \tag{4}$$

Equation (4) is a sum over the product space $\mathcal{S} \times \mathcal{R}$. We now focus on this space. We use lowercase names for the functions defined on $\mathcal{S} \times \mathcal{R}$. The product $G_{\sigma_\mathbf{s}} G_{\sigma_r}$ defines a Gaussian kernel $g_{\sigma_\mathbf{s}, \sigma_r}$ on $\mathcal{S} \times \mathcal{R}$:

$$g_{\sigma_\mathbf{s}, \sigma_r} : \quad (\mathbf{x} \in \mathcal{S}, \zeta \in \mathcal{R}) \quad \mapsto \quad G_{\sigma_\mathbf{s}}(\|\mathbf{x}\|) \, G_{\sigma_r}(|\zeta|) \tag{5}$$

From the remaining part of Equation (4), we build two functions i and w:

$$i: \quad (\mathbf{x} \in \mathcal{S}, \zeta \in \mathcal{R}) \quad \mapsto \quad I_{\mathbf{x}} \tag{6a}$$

$$w: \quad (\mathbf{x} \in \mathcal{S}, \zeta \in \mathcal{R}) \quad \mapsto \quad \delta(\zeta - I_{\mathbf{x}}) \, W_{\mathbf{x}} \tag{6b}$$

The following relations stem directly from the two previous definitions:

$$I_{\mathbf{x}} = i(\mathbf{x}, I_{\mathbf{x}}) \quad \text{and} \quad W_{\mathbf{x}} = w(\mathbf{x}, I_{\mathbf{x}}) \quad \text{and} \quad \forall \zeta \neq I_{\mathbf{x}}, \, w(\mathbf{x}, \zeta) = 0 \tag{7}$$

Then Equation (4) is rewritten as:

$$\begin{pmatrix} W_{\mathbf{p}}^{\mathrm{bf}} \, I_{\mathbf{p}}^{\mathrm{bf}} \\ W_{\mathbf{p}}^{\mathrm{bf}} \end{pmatrix} = \sum_{(\mathbf{q}, \zeta) \in \mathcal{S} \times \mathcal{R}} g_{\sigma_s, \sigma_r}(\mathbf{p} - \mathbf{q}, I_p - \zeta) \begin{pmatrix} w(\mathbf{q}, \zeta) \, i(\mathbf{q}, \zeta) \\ w(\mathbf{q}, \zeta) \end{pmatrix} \tag{8}$$

The above formula corresponds to the value at point $(\mathbf{p}, I_{\mathbf{p}})$ of a convolution between g_{σ_s, σ_r} and the two-dimensional function (wi, w):

$$\begin{pmatrix} W_{\mathbf{p}}^{\mathrm{bf}} \, I_{\mathbf{p}}^{\mathrm{bf}} \\ W_{\mathbf{p}}^{\mathrm{bf}} \end{pmatrix} = \left[g_{\sigma_s, \sigma_r} \otimes \begin{pmatrix} wi \\ w \end{pmatrix} \right] (\mathbf{p}, I_{\mathbf{p}}) \tag{9}$$

According to the above equation, we introduce the functions i^{bf} and w^{bf}:

$$(w^{\mathrm{bf}} \, i^{\mathrm{bf}}, w^{\mathrm{bf}}) = g_{\sigma_s, \sigma_r} \otimes (wi, w) \tag{10}$$

Thus, we have reached our goal. The bilateral filter is expressed as a convolution followed by nonlinear operations:

$$\begin{aligned}
\textbf{linear:} \quad & (w^{\mathrm{bf}} \, i^{\mathrm{bf}}, w^{\mathrm{bf}}) = g_{\sigma_s, \sigma_r} \otimes (wi, w) & (11\mathrm{a}) \\[2mm]
\textbf{nonlinear:} \quad & I_{\mathbf{p}}^{\mathrm{bf}} = \dfrac{w^{\mathrm{bf}}(\mathbf{p}, I_{\mathbf{p}}) \, i^{\mathrm{bf}}(\mathbf{p}, I_{\mathbf{p}})}{w^{\mathrm{bf}}(\mathbf{p}, I_{\mathbf{p}})} & (11\mathrm{b})
\end{aligned}$$

The nonlinear section is actually composed of two operations. The functions $w^{\mathrm{bf}} \, i^{\mathrm{bf}}$ and w^{bf} are evaluated at point $(\mathbf{p}, I_{\mathbf{p}})$. We name this operation *slicing*. The second nonlinear operation is the division. In our case, slicing and division commute *i.e.* the result is independent of their order because g_{σ_s, σ_r} is positive and w values are 0 and 1, which ensures that w^{bf} is positive.

3.3   Intuition

To gain more intuition about our formulation of the bilateral filter, we propose an informal description of the process before discussing further its consequences.

The spatial domain $\mathcal{S}$ is a classical xy image plane and the range domain $\mathcal{R}$ is a simple axis labelled ζ. The w function can be interpreted as the "plot in the $xy\zeta$ space of $\zeta = I(x, y)$" *i.e.* w is null everywhere except on the points

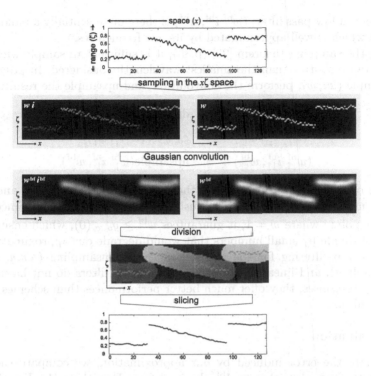

Fig. 1. Our computation pipeline applied to a 1D signal. The original data (top row) are represented by a two-dimensional function (wi, w) (second row). This function is convolved with a Gaussian kernel to form $(w^{\mathrm{bf}} i^{\mathrm{bf}}, w^{\mathrm{bf}})$ (third row). The first component is then divided by the second (fourth row, blue area is undefined because of numerical limitation, $w^{\mathrm{bf}} \approx 0$). Then the final result (last row) is extracted by sampling the former result at the location of the original data (shown in red on the fourth row).

$(x, y, I(x, y))$ where it is equal to 1. The wi product is similar to w. Instead of using binary values 0 or 1 to "plot I", we use 0 or $I(x, y)$ $i.e.$ it is a plot with a pen whose brightness equals the plotted value.

Then using these two functions wi and w, the bilateral filter is computed as follows. First, we "blur" wi and w $i.e.$ we convolve wi and w with a Gaussian defined on $xy\zeta$. This results in the functions $w^{\mathrm{bf}} i^{\mathrm{bf}}$ and w^{bf}. For each point of the $xy\zeta$ space, we compute $i^{\mathrm{bf}}(x, y, \zeta)$ by dividing $w^{\mathrm{bf}}(x, y, \zeta) \, i^{\mathrm{bf}}(x, y, \zeta)$ by $w^{\mathrm{bf}}(x, y, \zeta)$. The final step is to get the value of the pixel (x, y) of the filtered image I^{bf}. This directly corresponds to the value of i^{bf} at $(x, y, I(x, y))$ which is the point where the input image I was "plotted". Figure 1 illustrates this process on a simple 1D image.

4   Fast Approximation

We have shown that the bilateral filter can be interpreted as a Gaussian filter in a product space. Our acceleration scheme directly follows from the fact that this operation is a low-pass filter. $(w^{\mathrm{bf}} i^{\mathrm{bf}}, w^{\mathrm{bf}})$ is therefore essentially a band-limited function which is well approximated by its low frequencies.

Using the sampling theorem [20] (p.35), it is sufficient to sample with a rate at least twice shorter than the smallest wavelength considered. In practice, we downsample (wi, w), perform the convolution, and upsample the result:

$$(w_{\downarrow} i_{\downarrow}, w_{\downarrow}) = \text{downsample}(wi, w) \tag{12a}$$

$$(w_{\downarrow}^{\mathrm{bf}} i_{\downarrow}^{\mathrm{bf}}, w_{\downarrow}^{\mathrm{bf}}) = g_{\sigma_{\mathrm{s}}, \sigma_{\mathrm{r}}} \otimes (w_{\downarrow} i_{\downarrow}, w_{\downarrow}) \tag{12b}$$

$$(w_{\downarrow\uparrow}^{\mathrm{bf}} i_{\downarrow\uparrow}^{\mathrm{bf}}, w_{\downarrow\uparrow}^{\mathrm{bf}}) = \text{upsample}(w_{\downarrow}^{\mathrm{bf}} i_{\downarrow}^{\mathrm{bf}}, w_{\downarrow}^{\mathrm{bf}}) \tag{12c}$$

The rest of the computation remains the same except that we slice and divide $(w_{\downarrow\uparrow}^{\mathrm{bf}} i_{\downarrow\uparrow}^{\mathrm{bf}}, w_{\downarrow\uparrow}^{\mathrm{bf}})$ instead of $(w^{\mathrm{bf}} i^{\mathrm{bf}}, w^{\mathrm{bf}})$, using the same $(\mathbf{p}, I_{\mathbf{p}})$ points. Since slicing occurs at points where $w = 1$, it guarantees $w^{\mathrm{bf}} \geq g_{\sigma_{\mathrm{s}}, \sigma_{\mathrm{r}}}(0)$, which ensures that we do not divide by small numbers that would degrade our approximation.

We use box-filtering for the prefilter of the downsampling (a.k.a. average downsampling), and linear upsampling. While these filters do not have perfect frequency responses, they offer much better performances than schemes such as tri-cubic filters.

4.1   Evaluation

To evaluate the error induced by our approximation, we compare the result $I_{\downarrow\uparrow}^{\mathrm{bf}}$ from the fast algorithm to I^{bf} obtained from Equations (1). For this purpose, we compute the peak signal-to-noise ratio (PSNR) considering $\mathcal{R} = [0; 1]$:

$$\text{PSNR}(I_{\downarrow\uparrow}^{\mathrm{bf}}) = -10 \, \log_{10} \left(\tfrac{1}{|\mathcal{S}|} \sum_{\mathbf{p} \in \mathcal{S}} \left| I_{\downarrow\uparrow}^{\mathrm{bf}}(\mathbf{p}) - I^{\mathrm{bf}}(\mathbf{p}) \right|^2 \right).$$

We have chosen three images as different as possible to cover a broad spectrum of content. We use (see Figure 4):

- An artificial image with various edges and frequencies, and white noise.
- An architectural picture structured along two main directions.
- And a photograph of a natural scene with a more stochastic structure.

The box downsampling and linear upsampling schemes yield very satisfying results while being computationally efficient. We experimented several sampling rates $(s_{\mathrm{s}}, s_{\mathrm{r}})$ for $\mathcal{S} \times \mathcal{R}$. The meaningful quantities to consider are the ratios $\left(\frac{s_{\mathrm{s}}}{\sigma_{\mathrm{s}}}, \frac{s_{\mathrm{r}}}{\sigma_{\mathrm{r}}} \right)$ that indicate how many high frequencies we ignore compared to the bandwidth of the filter we apply. Small ratios correspond to limited approximations and high ratios to more aggressive downsamplings. A consistent approximation is a sampling rate proportional to the Gaussian bandwidth (i.e. $\frac{s_{\mathrm{s}}}{\sigma_{\mathrm{s}}} \approx \frac{s_{\mathrm{r}}}{\sigma_{\mathrm{r}}}$) to achieve similar accuracy on the whole $\mathcal{S} \times \mathcal{R}$ domain. The results plotted in Figure 2 show that this remark is globally valid in practice. A closer look at the plots reveals that $\mathcal{S}$ can be slightly more aggressively downsampled than $\mathcal{R}$. This is probably due to the nonlinearities and the anisotropy of the signal.

Figure 3-left shows the running times for the architectural picture with the same settings. In theory, the gain from space downsampling should be twice the

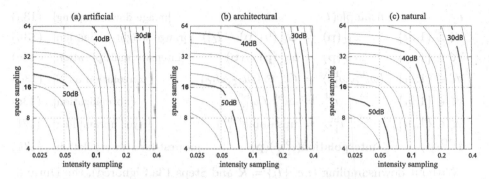

Fig. 2. Accuracy evaluation. All the images are filtered with ($\sigma_s = 16, \sigma_r = 0.1$). The PSNR in dB is evaluated at various sampling of $\mathcal{S}$ and $\mathcal{R}$ (greater is better). Our approximation scheme is more robust to space downsampling than range downsampling. It is also slightly more accurate on structured scenes (a,b) than stochastic ones (c).

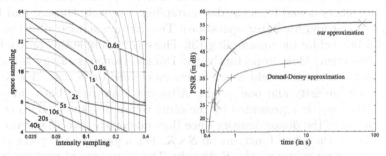

Fig. 3. Left: Running times on the architectural picture with ($\sigma_s = 16, \sigma_r = 0.1$). The PSNR isolines are plotted in gray. Exact computation takes about 1h. • Right: Accuracy-versus-time comparison. Both methods are tested on the architectural picture (1600×1200) with the same sampling rates of $\mathcal{S}\times\mathcal{R}$ (from left to right): (4;0.025) (8;0.05) (16;0.1) (32;0.2) (64;0.4).

one from range downsampling since $\mathcal{S}$ is two-dimensional and $\mathcal{R}$ one-dimensional. In practice, the nonlinearities and caching issues induce minor deviations. Combining this plot with the PSNR plot (in gray under the running times) allows for selecting the best sampling parameters for a given error tolerance or a given time budget. As a simple guideline, using sampling steps equal to σ_s and σ_r produce results without visual difference with the exact computation (see Fig. 4). Our scheme achieves a speed-up of two orders of magnitude: Direct computation of Equations (1) lasts about one hour whereas our approximation requires one second. This dramatic improvement opens avenues for interactive applications.

4.2   Comparison with the Durand-Dorsey Speed-Up

Durand and Dorsey also describe a linear approximation of the bilateral filter [3]. Using evenly spaced intensity values $I_1..I_n$ that cover $\mathcal{R}$, their scheme can be summarized as (for convenience, we also name G_{σ_s} the 2D Gaussian kernel):

$$\iota_\downarrow = \text{downsample}(I) \qquad\qquad\qquad \text{[image downsampling]} \quad (13a)$$

$$\forall \zeta \in \{1..n\} \qquad \omega_{\downarrow\zeta}(\mathbf{p}) = G_{\sigma_r}(|\iota_\downarrow(\mathbf{p}) - I_\zeta|) \quad \text{[range weight evaluation]} \quad (13b)$$

$$\forall \zeta \in \{1..n\} \qquad \omega\iota_{\downarrow\zeta}(\mathbf{p}) = \omega_{\downarrow\zeta}(\mathbf{p})\,\iota_\downarrow(\mathbf{p}) \quad \text{[intensity multiplication]} \quad (13c)$$

$$\forall \zeta \in \{1..n\} \qquad (\omega\iota_{\downarrow\zeta}^{bf}, \omega_{\downarrow\zeta}^{bf}) = G_{\sigma_s} \otimes (\omega\iota_{\downarrow\zeta}, \omega_{\downarrow\zeta}) \quad \text{[convolution on } \mathcal{S}\text{]} \quad (13d)$$

$$\forall \zeta \in \{1..n\} \qquad \iota_{\downarrow\zeta}^{bf} = \omega\iota_{\downarrow\zeta}^{bf} / \omega_{\downarrow\zeta}^{bf} \quad \text{[normalization]} \quad (13e)$$

$$\forall \zeta \in \{1..n\} \qquad \iota_{\downarrow\uparrow\zeta}^{bf} = \text{upsample}(\iota_{\downarrow\zeta}^{bf}) \quad \text{[layer upsampling]} \quad (13f)$$

$$I^{DD}(\mathbf{p}) = \text{interpolation}(\iota_{\downarrow\uparrow\zeta}^{bf})(\mathbf{p}) \quad \text{[nearest layer interpolation]} \quad (13g)$$

Without downsampling (*i.e.* $\{I_i\} = \mathcal{R}$ and Steps 13a,f ignored), the Durand-Dorsey scheme is equivalent to ours because Steps 13b,c,d correspond to a convolution on $\mathcal{S} \times \mathcal{R}$. Indeed, Step (13b) computes the values of a Gaussian kernel on $\mathcal{R}$. Step (13c) actually evaluates the convolution on $\mathcal{R}$, considering that $\iota_\downarrow(\mathbf{p})$ is the only nonzero value on the ζ axis. With Step (13d), the convolution on $\mathcal{S}$, these three steps perform a 3D convolution using a separation between $\mathcal{R}$ and $\mathcal{S}$.

The differences comes from the downsampling approach. Durand and Dorsey interleave linear and nonlinear operations: The division is done after the convolution 13d but before the upsampling 13f. There is no simple theoretical base to estimate the error. More importantly, the Durand-Dorsey strategy is such that the intensity ι and the weight ω are functions defined on $\mathcal{S}$ only. A given pixel has only one intensity and one weight. After downsampling, both sides of the discontinuity may be represented by the same values of ι and ω. This is a poor representation of the discontinuities since they inherently involve several values. In comparison, we define functions on $\mathcal{S} \times \mathcal{R}$. For a given image point in $\mathcal{S}$, we can handle several values on the $\mathcal{R}$ domain. The advantage of working in $\mathcal{S} \times \mathcal{R}$ is that this characteristic is not altered by downsampling. It is the major reason why our scheme is more accurate than the Durand-Dorsey technique, especially on discontinuities.

Figure 3-right shows the precision achieved by both approaches relatively to their running time, and Figure 4 illustrates their visual differences. There is no gain in extreme downsampling since nonlinearities are no more negligible. Both approaches also have a plateau in their accuracy *i.e.* beyond a certain point, precision gains increase slowly with sampling refinement but ours reaches a higher accuracy ($\approx$ 55dB compared to $\approx$ 40dB). In addition, for the same running time, our approach is always more accurate (except for extreme downsampling).

4.3   Implementation

All the experiments have been done an Intel Xeon 2.8GHz using the same code base in C++. We have implemented the Durand-Dorsey technique with the same libraries as our technique. 2D and 3D convolutions are made using FFT. The domains are padded with zeros over 2σ to avoid cross-boundary artefacts. There are no other significant optimizations to avoid bias in the comparisons. A production implementation could therefore be improved with techniques such as separable convolution. Our code is publicly available on our webpage. The software is open-source, under the MIT license.

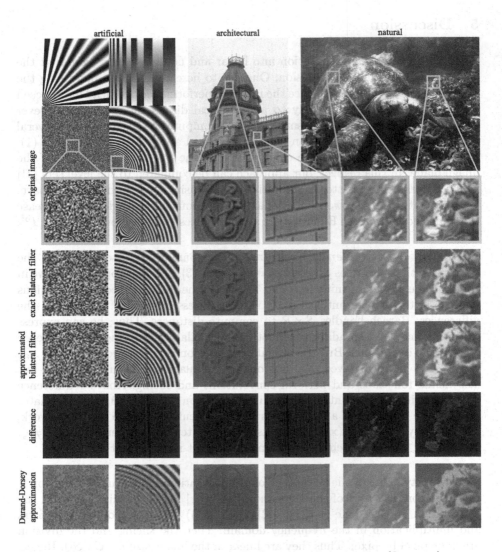

Fig. 4. We have tested our approximated scheme on three images (first row): an artificial image (512 × 512) with different types of edges and a white noise region, an architectural picture (1600 × 1200) with strong and oriented features, and a natural photograph (800 × 600) with more stochastic textures. For clarity, we present representative close-ups (second row). Full resolution images are available on our website. Our approximation produces results (fourth row) visually similar to the exact computation (third row). A color coded subtraction (fifth row) reveals subtle differences at the edges (red: negative, black: 0, and blue: positive). In comparison, the Durand-Dorsey approximation introduces large visual discrepancies: the details are washed out (bottom row). All the filters are computed with $\sigma_s = 16$ and $\sigma_r = 0.1$. Our filter uses a sampling rate of (16,0.1). The sampling rate of the Durand-Dorsey filter is chosen in order to achieve the same (or slightly superior) running time. Thus, the comparison is done fairly, using the same time budget.

5   Discussion

Dimensionality. Our separation into linear and nonlinear parts comes at the cost of the additional ζ dimension. One has to be careful before increasing the dimensionality of a problem since the incurred performance overhead may exceed the gains, restricting our study to a theoretical discussion. We have however demonstrated that this formalism allows for a computation scheme that is several orders of magnitude faster than a straightforward application of Equation (1). This advocates performing the computation in the $\mathcal{S} \times \mathcal{R}$ space instead of the image plane. In this respect, our approach can be compared to the level sets [21] which also describe a better computation scheme using a higher dimension space.

Note that using the two-dimensional homogeneous intensity does not increase the dimensionality since Equation (1) also computes two functions: W^{bf} and I^{bf}.

Comparison with *Generalized Intensity*. Barash also uses points in the $\mathcal{S} \times \mathcal{R}$ space that he names *generalized intensities* [13]. Our two approaches have in common the global meaning of $\mathcal{S}$ and $\mathcal{R}$: The former is related to pixel positions and the latter to pixel intensities. It is nevertheless important to highlight the differences. Barash handles $\mathcal{S} \times \mathcal{R}$ to compute distances. Thus, he can express the difference between adaptive smoothing and bilateral filtering as a difference of distance definitions. But the actual computation remains the same. Our use of $\mathcal{S} \times \mathcal{R}$ is more involved. We not only manipulate points in this space but also define functions and perform convolutions and slicing. Another difference is our definition of the intensity through a function (i or i^{bf}). Barash associates directly the intensity of a point to its $\mathcal{R}$ component whereas in our framework, the intensity of a point $(\mathbf{x}, \zeta)$ is *not* its ζ coordinate *e.g.* in general $i^{\mathrm{bf}}(\mathbf{x}, \zeta) \neq \zeta$. In addition, our approach leads to a more efficient implementation.

Complexity. One of the advantage of our separation is that the convolution is the most complex part of the algorithm. Using $| \cdot |$ for the cardinal of a set, the convolution can be done in $\mathcal{O}\left(|\mathcal{S}|\,|\mathcal{R}|\log(|\mathcal{S}|\,|\mathcal{R}|)\right)$ with fast Fourier transform and multiplication in the frequency domain. Then the slicing and the division are done pixel by pixel. Thus they are linear in the image size *i.e.* $\mathcal{O}\left(|\mathcal{S}|\right)$. Hence, the algorithm complexity is dominated by the convolution. This result is verified in practice as shown by Table 1. The convolution time rapidly increases as the sampling becomes finer. This validates our choice of focussing on the convolution.

Table 1. Time used by each step at different sampling rates of the architectural image. Upsampling is included in the nonlinearity time because our implementation computes $i_{\downarrow\uparrow}^{\mathrm{bf}}$ only at the $(\mathbf{x}, I_{\mathbf{x}})$ points rather than upsampling the whole $\mathcal{S} \times \mathcal{R}$ space.

sampling $(\sigma_{\mathrm{s}}, \sigma_r)$	(4,0.025)	(8,0.05)	(16,0.1)	(32,0.2)	(64,0.4)
downsampling	1.3s	0.23s	0.09s	0.07s	0.06s
convolution	63s	2.8s	0.38s	0.02s	0.01s
nonlinearity	0.48s	0.47s	0.46s	0.47s	0.46s

6   Conclusions

We have presented a fast approximation technique of the bilateral filter based on a signal processing interpretation. From a theoretical point of view, we have introduced the notion of homogeneous intensity and demonstrated a new approach of the space-intensity domain. We believe that these concepts can be applied beyond bilateral filtering, and we hope that these contributions will inspire new studies. From a practical point of view, our approximation technique yields results visually similar to the exact computation with interactive running times. This technique paves the way for interactive applications relying on quality image smoothing.

Future Work. Our study translates almost directly to higher dimensional data (*e.g.* color images or videos). Analyzing the performance in these cases will provide valuable statistics. Exploring deeper the frequency structure of the $\mathcal{S} \times \mathcal{R}$ domain seems an exciting research direction.

Acknowledgement. We thank Soonmin Bae, Samuel Hornus, Thouis Jones, and Sara Su for their help with the paper. This work was supported by a National Science Foundation CAREER award 0447561 "Transient Signal Processing for Realistic Imagery," an NSF Grant No. 0429739 "Parametric Analysis and Transfer of Pictorial Style," a grant from Royal Dutch/Shell Group and the Oxygen consortium. Frédo Durand acknowledges a Microsoft Research New Faculty Fellowship, and Sylvain Paris was partially supported by a Lavoisier Fellowship from the French "Ministère des Affaires Étrangères."

References

1. Tomasi, C., Manduchi, R.: Bilateral filtering for gray and color images. In: Proc. of International Conference on Computer Vision, IEEE (1998) 839–846
2. Oh, B.M., Chen, M., Dorsey, J., Durand, F.: Image-based modeling and photo editing. In: Proc. of SIGGRAPH conference, ACM (2001)
3. Durand, F., Dorsey, J.: Fast bilateral filtering for the display of high-dynamic-range images. ACM Trans. on Graphics **21** (2002) Proc. of SIGGRAPH conference.
4. Eisemann, E., Durand, F.: Flash photography enhancement via intrinsic relighting. ACM Trans. on Graphics **23** (2004) Proc. of SIGGRAPH conference.
5. Petschnigg, G., Agrawala, M., Hoppe, H., Szeliski, R., Cohen, M., Toyama, K.: Digital photography with flash and no-flash image pairs. ACM Trans. on Graphics **23** (2004) Proc. of SIGGRAPH conference.
6. Jones, T.R., Durand, F., Desbrun, M.: Non-iterative, feature-preserving mesh smoothing. ACM Trans. on Graphics **22** (2003) Proc. of SIGGRAPH conference.
7. Fleishman, S., Drori, I., Cohen-Or, D.: Bilateral mesh denoising. ACM Trans. on Graphics **22** (2003) Proc. of SIGGRAPH conference.
8. Wong, W.C.K., Chung, A.C.S., Yu, S.C.H.: Trilateral filtering for biomedical images. In: Proc. of International Symposium on Biomedical Imaging, IEEE (2004)
9. Bennett, E.P., McMillan, L.: Video enhancement using per-pixel virtual exposures. ACM Trans. on Graphics **24** (2005) 845 – 852 Proc. of SIGGRAPH conference.

10. Paris, S., Briceño, H., Sillion, F.: Capture of hair geometry from multiple images. ACM Trans. on Graphics **23** (2004) Proc. of SIGGRAPH conference.
11. Elad, M.: On the bilateral filter and ways to improve it. IEEE Trans. On Image Processing **11** (2002) 1141–1151
12. Smith, S.M., Brady, J.M.: SUSAN – a new approach to low level image processing. International Journal of Computer Vision **23** (1997) 45–78
13. Barash, D.: A fundamental relationship between bilateral filtering, adaptive smoothing and the nonlinear diffusion equation. IEEE Trans. on Pattern Analysis and Machine Intelligence **24** (2002) 844
14. Buades, A., Coll, B., Morel, J.M.: Neighborhood filters and PDE's. Technical Report 2005-04, CMLA (2005)
15. Yaroslavsky, L.P.: Digital Picture Processing. Springer Verlag (1985)
16. Huber, P.J.: Robust Statistics. Wiley-Interscience (1981)
17. Hampel, F.R., Ronchetti, E.M., Rousseeuw, P.M., Stahel, W.A.: Robust Statistics – The Approach Based on Influence Functions. Wiley Interscience (1986)
18. Mrázek, P., Weickert, J., Bruhn, A.: On Robust Estimation and Smoothing with Spatial and Tonal Kernels. In: Geometric Properties from Incomplete Data. Springer (to appear)
19. Choudhury, P., Tumblin, J.E.: The trilateral filter for high contrast images and meshes. In: Proc. of Eurographics Symposium on Rendering. (2003)
20. Smith, S.: Digital Signal Processing. Newnes (2002)
21. Osher, S., Sethian, J.A.: Fronts propagating with curvature-dependent speed: Algorithms based on Hamilton-Jacobi formulations. J. of Comp. Physics. (1988)

Learning to Combine Bottom-Up and Top-Down Segmentation

Anat Levin and Yair Weiss*

School of Computer Science and Engineering,
The Hebrew University of Jerusalem
www.cs.huji.ac.il/~{alevin, yweiss}

Abstract. Bottom-up segmentation based only on low-level cues is a notoriously difficult problem. This difficulty has lead to recent top-down segmentation algorithms that are based on class-specific image information. Despite the success of top-down algorithms, they often give coarse segmentations that can be significantly refined using low-level cues. This raises the question of how to combine both top-down and bottom-up cues in a principled manner.

In this paper we approach this problem using supervised learning. Given a training set of ground truth segmentations we train a fragment-based segmentation algorithm *which takes into account both bottom-up and top-down cues simultaneously*, in contrast to most existing algorithms which train top-down and bottom-up modules separately. We formulate the problem in the framework of Conditional Random Fields (CRF) and derive a novel feature induction algorithm for CRF, which allows us to efficiently search over thousands of candidate fragments. Whereas pure top-down algorithms often require hundreds of fragments, our simultaneous learning procedure yields algorithms with a handful of fragments that are combined with low-level cues to efficiently compute high quality segmentations.

1 Introduction

Figure 1 (replotted from [2]) illustrates the importance of combining top-down and bottom-up segmentation. The leftmost image shows an image of a horse and the middle column show three possible segmentations based only on low-level cues. Even a sophisticated bottom-up segmentation algorithm (e.g. [10, 11]) has difficulties correctly segmenting this image.

The difficulty in pure low-level segmentation has led to the development of top-down, class-specific segmentation algorithms [3, 9, 16]. These algorithms fit a deformable model of a known object (e.g. a horse) to the image - the shape of the deformed model gives an estimate of the desired segmentation. The right-hand column of figure 1 shows a top-down segmentation of the horse figure obtained by the algorithm of [3]. In this algorithm, image fragments from horses in a training database are correlated with the novel image. By combining together the segmentations of the fragments, the novel image is segmented. As can be seen, the top-down segmentation is better than any of the bottom-up segmentations but still misses important details.

* Research supported by the EU under the DIRAC Project. EC Contract No.027787.

A. Leonardis, H. Bischof, and A. Pinz (Eds.): ECCV 2006, Part IV, LNCS 3954, pp. 581–594, 2006.

Input   Bottom-up   Top-down

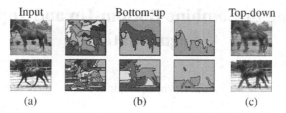

(a)   (b)   (c)

Fig. 1. The relative merits of the bottom-up and the top-down approaches, replotted from [2]. (a) Input image. (b) The bottom-up hierarchical segmentation at three different scales. (c) The top-down approach provides a meaningful approximation for the figureground segmentation of the image, but may not follow exactly image discontinuities.

In recent years, several authors have therefore suggested combining top-down and bottom-up segmentation [2, 15, 12, 5]. Borenstein et al. [2] choose among a discrete set of possible low-level segmentations by minimizing a cost function that includes a bias towards the top-down segmentation. In the *image parsing* framework of Tu et al. [12] object-specific detectors serve as a proposal distribution for a data-driven Monte-Carlo sampling over possible segmentations. In the *OBJ-CUT* algorithm [5] a layered pictorial structure is used to define a bias term for a graph-cuts energy minimization algorithm (the energy favors segmentation boundaries occurring at image discontinuities).

These recent approaches indeed improve the quality of the achieved segmentations by combining top-down and bottom-up cues at run-time. However, the training of the bottom-up and top-down modules is performed *independently*. In the work of Borenstein and colleagues, training the top-down module consists of choosing a set of fragments from a huge set of possible image fragments. This training is performed *without taking into account low-level cues*. In the image parsing framework [12], the top-down module are object detectors trained using AdaBoost to maximize detection performance. Again, this training is performed without taking into account low-level cues. In the *OBJ-CUT* algorithm, the training of the pictorial structures is performed using a combination of AdaBoost (for the local detectors) and Gaussian modeling (for the relative location of parts). Once again, this training does not take into account low-level cues.

Figure 2(a) shows a potential disadvantage of training the top-down model while ignoring low-level cues. Suppose we wish to train a segmentation algorithm for octopi. Since octopi have 8 tentacles and each tentacle has multiple degrees of freedom,

(a)   (b)

Fig. 2. (a) Octopi: Combining low-level information can significantly reduce the required complexity of a deformable model. (b) Examples from horses training data. Each training image is provided with its segmentation mask.

any top-down algorithm would require a very complex deformable template to achieve reasonable performance. Consider for example the top-down algorithm of Borenstein and Ullman [3] which tries to cover the segmentations in the dataset with a subset of image fragments. It would obviously require a huge number of fragments to achieve reasonable performance. Similarly, the layered pictorial structure algorithm of Kumar et al. [5] would require a large number of parts and a complicated model for modeling the allowed spatial configurations.

While Octopi can appear in a large number of poses, their low-level segmentation can be easy since their color is relatively uniform and (depending on the scene) may be distinct from the background. Thus an algorithm that trains the top-down module while taking into account the low-level cues can choose to devote far less resources to the deformable templates. The challenge is to provide a principled framework for simultaneous training of the top-down and bottom-up segmentation algorithms.

In this paper we provide such a framework. The algorithm we propose is similar *at run-time* to the OBJ-CUT and Borenstein et al. algorithms. As illustrated in figure 3, at run-time a novel image is scanned with an object detector which tries all possible subimages until it finds a subimage that is likely to contain the object (for most of the databases in this paper the approximate location was known so no scanning was performed). Within that subimage we search for object parts by performing normalized correlation with a set of fragments (each fragment scans only a portion of the subimage where it is likely to occur thus modeling the spatial interaction between fragment locations). The location of a fragment gives rise to a local bias term for an energy function. In addition to the local bias, the energy function rewards segmentation boundaries occurring at image discontinuities. The final segmentation is obtained by finding the global minimum of the energy function.

While our algorithm is similar at run-time to existing segmentation algorithms, the *training* method is unique in that it *simultaneously takes into account low-level and high-level cues*. We show that this problem can be formulated in the context of Conditional Random Fields [7, 6] which leads to a convex cost function for simultaneous training of both the low-level and the high-level segmenter. We derive a novel feature-induction for CRFs which allows us to efficiently learn models with a small number of fragments. Whereas pure top-down algorithms often require hundreds of fragments, our simultaneous learning procedure yields algorithms with a handful of fragments that are combined with low-level cues to efficiently compute high quality segmentations.

2   Segmentation Using Conditional Random Fields

Given an image I, we define the energy of a binary segmentation map x as:

$$E(x; I) = \nu \sum_{i,j} w_{ij} |x(i) - x(j)| + \sum_k \lambda_k |x - x_{F_k, I}| \tag{1}$$

This energy is a combination of a pairwise low-level term and a local class-dependent term.

(a)	(b)	(c)	(d)

Fig. 3. System overview: (a) Detection algorithm applied to an input image (b) Fragments search range, dots indicate location of maximal normalized correlation (c) Fragments local evidence, overlaid with ground truth contour (d) Resulting segmentation contour

The low level term is defined via a set of affinity weights $w(i, j)$. $w(i, j)$ are high when the pixels (i, j) are similar and decrease to zero when they are different. Similarity can be defined using various cues including intensity, color, texture and motion as used for bottom up image segmentation [10]. Thus minimizing $\sum_{i,j} w_{ij}|x(i) - x(j)|$ means that labeling discontinuities are cheaper when they are aligned with the image discontinuities. In this paper we used 8-neighbors connectivity, and we set:

$$w_{ij} = \frac{1}{1 + \sigma d_{ij}^2}$$

where d_{ij} is the RGB difference between pixels i and j and $\sigma = 5 \cdot 10^4$.

The second part of eq 1 encodes the local bias, defined as a sum of local energy terms each weighted by a weight λ_k. Following the terminology of Conditional Random Fields, we call each such local energy term a feature. In this work, these local energy terms are derived from image fragments with thresholds. To calculate the energy of a segmentation, we shift the fragment over a small window (10 pixels in each direction) around its location in its original image. We select the location in which the normalized correlation between the fragment and the new image is maximal (see Fig 3(b)). The feature is added to the energy, if this normalized correlation is large than a threshold. Each fragment is associated with a mask fragment x_F extracted from the training set (Fig 8 shows some fragments examples). We denote by $x_{F,I}$ the fragment mask x_F placed over the image I, according to the maximal normalized correlation location. For each fragment we add a term to the energy function which penalizes for the number of pixels for which x is different from the fragment mask $x_{F,I}$, $|x - x_{F,I}| = \sum_{i \in F} |x(i) - x_{F,I}(i)|$. Where $i \in F$ means the pixel i is covered by the fragment F after the fragment was moved to the maximal normalized correlation location (see Fig 3(c)).

Our goal in this paper is to learn a set of fragments $\{F_k\}$, thresholds and weights $\{\lambda_k\}$, ν that will favor the true segmentation. In the training stage the algorithm is provided a set of images $\{I_t\}_{t=1:T}$ and their binary segmentation masks $\{x_t\}_{t=1:T}$, as in figure 2(b). The algorithm needs to select features and weights such that minimizing the energy with the learned parameters will provide the desired segmentation.

2.1   Conditional Random Fields

Using the energy (eq. 1) we define the likelihood of the labels x conditioned on the image I as

$$P(x|I) = \frac{1}{Z(I)} e^{-E(x;I)} \quad \text{where:} \quad Z(I) = \int_x e^{-E(x;I)}$$

That is, x forms a Conditional Random Field (CRF) [7]. The goal of the learning process is to select a set of fragments $\{F_k\}$, thresholds and weights $\{\lambda_k\}$, ν that will maximize the sum of the log-likelihood over training examples: $\ell(\vec{\lambda}, \nu; \vec{F}) = \sum_t \ell^t(\vec{\lambda}, \nu; \vec{F})$

$$\ell^t(\vec{\lambda}, \nu; \vec{F}) = \log P(x_t|I_t; \vec{\lambda}, \nu, \vec{F}) = -E(x_t; I_t, \vec{\lambda}, \nu, \vec{F}) - \log Z(I_t; \vec{\lambda}, \nu, \vec{F}) \quad (2)$$

The idea of the CRF log likelihood is to select parameters that will maximize the likelihood of the ground truth segmentation for training examples. Such parameters should minimize the energy of the true segmentations x_t, while maximizing the energy of all other configurations.

Below we list several useful properties of the CRF log likelihood:

1. For a given features set $\vec{F} = [F_1, ..., F_K]$, if there exists a parameter set $\vec{\lambda}^* = [\lambda_1^*, .., \lambda_K^*]$, ν^* for which the minimum of the energy function is exactly the true segmentation: $x_t = \arg\min_x E(x; I_t, \vec{\lambda}^*, \nu^*, \vec{F})$. Then selecting $\alpha\vec{\lambda}^*, \alpha\nu^*$ with $\alpha \to \infty$ will maximize the CRF likelihood, since: $P(x_t|I_t; \alpha\vec{\lambda}^*, \alpha\nu^*, \vec{F}) = 1$ (see [8]).

2. The CRF log likelihood is *convex* with respect to the weighting parameters λ_k, ν as discussed in [7].

3. The derivative of the log-likelihood with respect to the coefficient of a given feature is known to be the difference between the expected feature response, and the observed one. This can be expressed in a simple closed form way as:

$$\frac{\partial \ell^t(\vec{\lambda}, \nu; \vec{F})}{\partial \lambda_k} = \frac{\partial \log P(x_t|I_t; \vec{\lambda}, \nu, \vec{F})}{\partial \lambda_k}$$

$$= \sum_{i \in F_k} \sum_r p_i(r)|r - x_{F_k, I_t}(i)| - \sum_{i \in F_k} |x_t(i) - x_{F_k, I_t}(i)|$$

$$= <|x_t - x_{F_k, I_t}|>_{P(x_t|I_t; \vec{\lambda}, \nu, \vec{F})} - <|x_t - x_{F_k, I_t}|>_{Obs} \quad (3)$$

$$\frac{\partial \ell^t(\vec{\lambda}, \nu; \vec{F})}{\partial \nu} = \frac{\partial \log P(x_t|I_t; \vec{\lambda}, \nu, \vec{F})}{\partial \nu}$$

$$= \sum_{ij} \sum_{rs} p_{ij}(r, s) w_{ij} |r - s| - \sum_{ij} w_{ij} |x_t(i) - x_t(j)|$$

$$= <|x_t(i) - x_t(j)|>_{P(x_t|I_t; \vec{\lambda}, \nu, \vec{F})} - <|x_t(i) - x_t(j)|>_{Obs} \quad (4)$$

Where $p_i(r), p_{ij}(r, s)$ are the marginal probabilities $P(x_i = r|I_t; \vec{\lambda}, \nu, \vec{F})$, $P(x_i = r, x_j = s|I_t; \vec{\lambda}, \nu, \vec{F})$.

Suppose we are given a set of features $\vec{F} = [F_1, ...F_K]$ and the algorithm task is to select weights $\vec{\lambda} = [\lambda_1, .., \lambda_K]$, ν that will maximize the CRF log likelihood. Given that the cost is convex with respect to $\vec{\lambda}$, ν it is possible to randomly initialize the weights vector and run gradient decent, when the gradients are computed using equations 3,4. Note that gradient decent can be used for selecting the optimal weights, without computing the explicit CRF log likelihood (eq 2).

Exact computation of the derivatives is intractable, due to the difficulty in computing the marginal probabilities $p_i(r), p_{ij}(r, s)$. However, any approximate method for estimating marginal probabilities can be used. One approach for approximating the marginal probabilities is using Monte Carlo sampling, like in [4, 1]. An alternative approach is to approximate the marginal probabilities using the beliefs output of sum product belief propagation or generalized belief propagation. Similarly, an exact computation of the CRF log likelihood (eq 2) is challenging due to the need to compute the log-partition function $Z(I) = \int_x e^{-E(x;I)}$. Exact computation of $Z(I)$ is in general intractable (except for tree structured graphs). However, approximate inference methods can be used here as well, such as the Bethe free energy or the Kikuchi approximations [14]. Monte-Carlo methods can also be used. In this work we have approximated the marginal probabilities and the partition function using sum product tree-reweighted belief propagation [13], which provides a rigorous bound on the partition function, and has better convergence properties than standard belief propagation. Tree reweighted belief propagation is described in the Appendix.

2.2 Features Selection

The learning algorithm starts with a large pool of candidate local features. In this work we created a 2, 000 features pool, by extracting image fragments from training images. Fragments are extracted at random sizes and random locations. The learning goal is to select from the features pool a small subset of features that will construct the energy function E, in a way that will maximize the conditional log likelihood $\sum_t \log P(x_t|I_t)$. Since the goal is to select a small subset of features out of a big pool, the required learning algorithm for this application is more than a simple gradient decent.

Let E_k denote the energy function at the k'th iteration. The algorithm initializes E_0 with the pairwise term and adds local features in an iterative greedy way, such that in each iteration a single feature is added: $E_k(x; I) = E_{k-1}(x; I) + \lambda_k|x - x_{F_k,I}|$. In each iteration we would like to add the feature F_k that will maximize the conditional log likelihood. We denote by $L_k(F, \lambda)$ the possible likelihood if the feature F, weighted by λ, is added at the k'th iteration:

$$L_k(F, \lambda) = \ell(\vec{\lambda}_{k-1}, \lambda, \nu; \vec{F}_{k-1}, F) = \sum_t \log P\left(x_t|I_t; \ E_{k-1}(x_t; I_t) + \lambda|x - x_{F,I}|\right)$$

Straightforward computation of the likelihood improvement is not practical since in each iteration, it will require inference for each candidate feature and for every possible weight λ we may assign to this feature. For example, suppose we have 50 training images, we want to scan 2, 000 features, 2 possible λ values, and we want to perform 10 features selection iterations. This results in 2, 000, 000 inference operations. Given that each inference operation itself is not a cheap process, the resulting computation can not be performed in a reasonable time. However, we suggest a novel efficient way to approximate the possible contribution from each of the candidate features.

Observation: *A first order approximation to the conditional log likelihood can be computed efficiently, without a specific inference process per feature.*

Proof:

$$L_k(F, \lambda) \approx \ell_{k-1}(\vec{\lambda}_{k-1}, \nu) + \lambda \left. \frac{\partial L_k(F, \lambda)}{\partial \lambda} \right|_{\lambda=0} \tag{5}$$

where

$$\left. \frac{\partial L_k(F, \lambda)}{\partial \lambda} \right|_{\lambda=0} = <|x_t - x_{F,I_t}| >_{P(x_t|I_t; \vec{\lambda}_{k-1}, \nu, \vec{F}_{k-1})} - <|x_t - x_{F,I_t}| >_{Obs} \tag{6}$$

and $\ell_{k-1}(\vec{\lambda}_{k-1}, \nu) = \sum_t \log P(x_t|I_t; E_{k-1})$. We note that computing the above first order approximation requires a single inference process on the previous iteration energy E_{k-1}, from which the local beliefs (approximated marginal probabilities) $\{b_{t,i}^{k-1}\}$ are computed. Since the gradient is evaluated at the point $\lambda = 0$, it can be computed using the $k - 1$ iteration beliefs and there is no need for a specific inference process per feature.   □

Computing the first order approximation for each of the training images is linear in the filter size. This enables scanning thousands of candidate features within several minutes. As evident from the gradient formula (eq 6) and demonstrated in the experiments section, the algorithm tends to select fragments that: (1) have low error in the training set (since it attempts to minimize $<|x_t - x_{F,I_t}| >_{Obs}$) and (2) are not already accounted for by the existing model (since it attempts to maximize $<|x_t - x_{F,I_t}| >_{P(x_t|I_t; \vec{\lambda}_{k-1}, \nu, \vec{F}_{k-1})}$). First order approximation to the log-likelihood function were also used by [17] to select features for exponential models fitting.

Once the first order approximations have been calculated we can select a small set of the features $F_{k_1} ... F_{k_N}$ with the largest approximated likelihood gains. For each of

---

Algorithm 1. Features Selection

Initialization: $E_0(x_t; I_t) = \nu \sum_{ij} w_{ij} |x_t(i) - x_t(j)|$.
for k=1 to maxItr

1. Run tree-reweighted belief propagation using the $k-1$ iteration energy $E_{k-1}(x_t; I_t)$. Compute local beliefs $\{b_{t,i}^{k-1}\}$.
2. For each feature F compute the approximated likelihood using eq 5.
   Select the N features $F_{k_1} ... F_{k_N}$ with largest approximated likelihood gains.
3. For each of the features $F_{k_1} ... F_{k_N}$, and for each scale $\lambda \in \{\lambda^1, ..., \lambda^M\}$, run tree-reweighted belief propagation and compute the likelihood $L_k(F_{k_n}, \lambda^m)$
4. Select the feature and scale with maximal likelihood gain:

$$(F_{k_n}, \lambda^m) = \arg \max_{n=1:N, \, m=1:M} L_k(F_{k_n}, \lambda^m)$$

Set $\lambda_k = \lambda^m$, $F_k = F_{k_n}$, $E_k(x; I) = E_{k-1}(x; I) + \lambda_k |x - x_{F_k, I}|$.

---

the selected features, and for each of a small discrete set of possible λ values $\lambda \in \{\lambda^1, ..., \lambda^M\}$, we run an inference process and evaluate the explicit conditional log likelihood. The optimal feature (and scale) is selected and added to the energy function E. The features selection steps are summarized in Algorithm 1.

Once a number of features have been selected, we can also optimize the choice of weights $\{\lambda_k\}, \nu$ using several gradient decent steps. Since the cost is convex with respect to the weights a local optimum is not an issue.

3   Experiments

In our first experiment we tried to segment a synthetic octopus dataset. Few sample images are shown in Fig 4. It's clear that our synthetic octopi are highly non rigid objects. Any effort to fully cover all the octopi tentacles with fragments (like [2, 9, 5]), will require a huge number of different fragments. On the other hand, there is a lot of edges information in the images that can guide the segmentation. The first feature selected by our algorithm is located on the octopi head, which is a rigid part common to all examples. This single feature, combined with pairwise constraints was enough to propagate the true segmentation to the entire image. The MAP segmentation given the selected feature is shown in Fig 4.

We then tested our algorithm on two real datasets, of horses [3, 2] and cows [9]. We measured the percentage of mislabeled pixels in the segmented images on training and testing images, as more fragments are learned. Those are shown for horses in Fig 5(a), and for cows in Fig 5(b). Note that after selecting 3 fragments our algorithm performs at over 95% correct on test data for the horse dataset. The algorithm of Borenstein et al. [2] performed at 95% for pixels in which its confidence was over 0.1 and at 66% for the rest of the pixels. Thus our overall performance seems comparable (if not better) even though we used far less fragments. The OBJ-CUT algorithm also performs at around 96% for a subset of this dataset using a LPS model of 10 parts whose likelihood function takes into consideration chamfer distance and texture and is therefore significantly more complex than normalized correlation.

Fig. 4. Results on synthetic octopus data. Top: Input images. Middle: response of the local feature, with the ground truth segmentation contour overlaid in red. Bottom: MAP segmentation contour overlaid on input image.

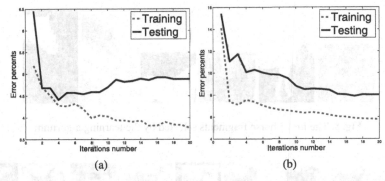

(a)   (b)

Fig. 5. Percents of miss-classified pixels: (a) Horses data (b) Cows data Note that after 4 fragments our algorithm performs at over 95% correct on test data for the horse dataset. These results are comparable if not better than [2, 5] while using a simpler model.

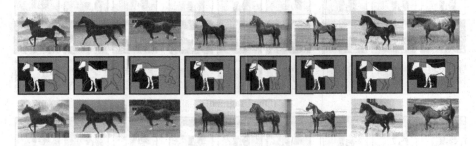

Fig. 6. Testing results on horses data. Top row: Input images. Second row: Response of the local features and the boundary feature, with the ground truth segmentation contour overlaid in red. Bottom row: MAP segmentation contour overlaid on input image.

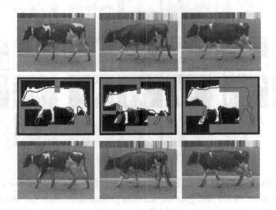

Fig. 7. Testing results on cows' data with 4 features. Top row: Input images. Second row: Response of the local features and the boundary feature, with the ground truth segmentation contour overlaid in red. Bottom row: MAP segmentation contour overlaid on input image.

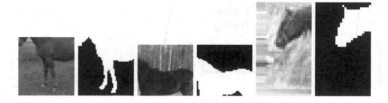

Fig. 8. The first 3 horse fragments selected by the learning algorithm

(Input Images)

(One Fragment)

(Two Fragments)

(Three Fragments)

Fig. 9. Training results on horses data. For each group: Top row - response of the local features and the boundary feature, with the ground truth segmentation contour overlaid in red. Middle row - MAP segmentation. Bottom row - MAP segmentation contour overlaid on input image.

In the horses and cows experiments we rely on the fact that we are searching for a shape in the center of the window, and used an additional local feature predicting that the pixels lying on the boundary of the subimage should be labeled as background.

In Fig 6 we present several testing images of horses, the ground truth segmentation, the local features responses and the inferred segmentation. While low level information adds a lot of power to the segmentation process, it can also be misleading. For example, the example on the right of Fig 9 demonstrates the weakness of the low level information.

In Fig 7 we present segmentation results on cows test images, for an energy function consisting of 4 features. The segmentation in this case is not as good as in the horses' case, especially in the legs. We note that in most of these examples the legs are in a different color than the cow body, hence the low-level information can not easily propagate labeling from the cow body to its legs. The low level cue we use in the work is quite simple- based only on the RGB difference between neighboring pixels. It's possible that using more sophisticated edges detectors [10] will enable a better propagation.

The first 3 horse fragments that were selected by the algorithm are shown in Fig 8. In Fig 9 we illustrate the first 3 training iterations on several training images. Quite a good segmentation can be obtained even when the response of the selected features does not cover the entire image. For example the first fragment was located around the horse's front legs. As can be seen in the first 3 columns of Fig 9, some images can be segmented quite well based on this single local feature. We can also see that the algorithm tends to select new features in image areas that were mislabeled in the previous iterations. For example, in several horses (mainly the 3 middle columns) there is still a problem in the upper part, and the algorithm therefore selects a second feature in the upper part of the horse. Once the second fragment was added there are still several mislabeled head areas (see the 3 right columns), and as a result the 3rd fragment is located on the horse head.

4   Discussion

Evidence from human vision suggests that humans utilize significant top-down information when performing segmentation. Recent works in computer vision also suggest that segmentation performance in difficult scenes is best approached by combining top-down and bottom-up cues. In this paper we presented an algorithm that learns how to combine these two disparate sources of information into a single energy function. We showed how to formulate the problem as that of estimation in Conditional Random Fields which will provably find the correct parameter settings if they exist. We introduced a novel feature induction algorithm for CRFs that allowed us to efficiently search over thousands of image fragments for a small number of fragments that will improve the segmentation performance. Our learned algorithm achieves state-of-the-art performance with a small number of fragments combined with very rudimentary low-level cues.

Both the top-down module and the bottom-up module that we used can be significantly improved. Our top-down module translates an image fragment and searches for the best normalized correlation, while other algorithms also allow rescaling and rotation of the parts and use more sophisticated image similarity metrics. Our bottom-up module uses only local intensity as an affinity function between pixels, whereas other algorithms have successfully used texture and contour as well. In fact, one advantage of the CRFs framework is that we can learn the relative weights of different affinity functions. We believe that by improving both the low-level and high-level cues we will obtain even better performance on the challenging task of image segmentation.

5 Appendix: Tree-Reweighted Belief Propagation and Tree-Reweighted Upper Bound

In this section we summarize the basic formulas from [13] for applying tree-rewighted belief propagation and for computing the tree-rewighted upper bound.

For a given graph G, we let $\boldsymbol{\mu_e} = \{\mu_e | e \in E(G)\}$ represent a vector of edge appearance probabilities. That is, μ_e is the probability that the edge e appears in a spanning tree of the graph G, chosen under a particular distribution on spanning trees. For 2D-grid graphs with 4-neighbors connectivity a reasonable choice of edges distributions is $\boldsymbol{\mu_e} = \{\mu_e = \frac{1}{2} | e \in E(G)\}$ and for 8-neighbors connectivity, $\boldsymbol{\mu_e} = \{\mu_e = \frac{1}{4} | e \in E(G)\}$.

The edge appearance probabilities are used for defining a tree-rewighted massages passing scheme. Denote the graph potentials as: $\Psi_i(x_i) = e^{-E_i(x_i)}$, $\Psi_{ij}(x_i, x_j) = e^{-E_{ij}(x_i, x_j)}$, and assume $P(x)$ can be factorized as: $P(x) \propto \prod_i \Psi_i(x_i) \prod_{i,j} \Psi_{ij}(x_i, x_j)$. The tree-rewighted massages passing scheme is defined as follows:

1. Initialize the messages $m^0 = m^0_{ij}$ with arbitrary positive real numbers.
2. For iterations n=1,2,3,... update the messages as follows:

$$m_{ji}^{n+1}(x_i) = \kappa \sum_{x'_j} exp(-\frac{1}{\mu_{ij}} E_{ij}(x_i, x'_j) - E_j(x'_j)) \left\{ \frac{\prod_{k \in \Gamma(j) \backslash i} \left[m_{kj}^n(x'_j) \right]^{\mu_{kj}}}{\left[m_{ij}^n(x'_j) \right]^{(1-\mu_{ji})}} \right\}$$

where κ is a normalization factor such that $\sum_{x_i} m_{ji}^n(x_i) = 1$.

The process converges when $m_{ji}^{n+1} = m_{ji}^n$ for every ij.

Once the process has converged, the messages can be used for computing the local and pairwise beliefs:

$$b_i(x_i) = \kappa \ exp(-E_i(x_i)) \prod_{k \in \Gamma(i)} [m_{ki}(x_i)]^{\mu_{ki}} \qquad (7)$$

$$b_{ij}(x_i, x_j) = \kappa \ exp(-\frac{1}{\mu_{ij}} E_{ij}(x_i, x_j) - E_i(x_i) - E_j(x_j))$$

$$\frac{\prod_{k \in \Gamma(i) \backslash j} [m_{ki}(x_i)]^{\mu_{ki}} \prod_{k \in \Gamma(j) \backslash i} [m_{kj}(x_j)]^{\mu_{kj}}}{[m_{ji}(x_i)]^{(1-\mu_{ij})} [m_{ij}(x_j)]^{(1-\mu_{ji})}} \qquad (8)$$

We define a pseudo-marginals vector $\vec{q} = \{q_i, q_{ij}\}$ as a vector satisfying: $\sum_{x_i} q_i(x_i) = 1$ and $\sum_{x_j} q_{ij}(x_i, x_j) = q_i(x_i)$. In particular, the beliefs vectors in equations 7,8 are a peseudo-marginals vector. We use the peseudo-marginals vectors for computing the tree-rewighted upper bound.

Denote by θ the energy vector $\theta = \{E_i, E_{ij}\}$. We define an "average energy" term as: $\vec{q} \cdot \theta = \sum_i \sum_{x_i} -q_i(x_i)E_i(x_i) + \sum_{ij} \sum_{x_i, x_j} -q_{ij}(x_i, x_j)E_{ij}(x_i, x_j)$. We define the single node entropy: $H_i(q_i) = -\sum_{x_i} q_i(x_i) \log q_i(x_i)$. Similarly, we define the mutual information between i and j, measured under q_{ij} as: $I_{ij}(q_{ij}) = \sum_{x_i,x_j} q_{ij}(x_i,x_j) \log \frac{q_{ij}(x_i,x_j)}{\left(\sum_{x'_j} q_{ij}(x_i,x'_j)\right)\left(\sum_{x'_i} q_{ij}(x'_i,x_j)\right)}$. This is used to define a free energy: $\mathcal{F}(\vec{q};\mu_e;\theta) \triangleq -\sum_i H_i(q_i) + \sum_{ij} \mu_{ij} I_{ij}(q_{ij}) - \vec{q} \cdot \theta$.

In [13] Wainwright et al prove that $\mathcal{F}(\vec{q};\mu_e;\theta)$ provides an upper bound for the log partition function:

$$\log Z = \int_x exp(-\sum_i E_i(x_i) - \sum_{ij} E_{ij}(x_i,x_j)) \leq \mathcal{F}(\vec{q};\mu_e;\theta)$$

They also show that the free energy $\mathcal{F}(\vec{q};\mu_e;\theta)$ is minimized using the peseudo-marginals vector $\vec{b}$ defined using the tree-reweighted messages passing output. Therefore the tighter upper bound on $\log Z$ is provided by $\vec{b}$.

This result follows the line of approximations to the log partition function using free energy functions. As stated in [14], when standard belief propagation converges, the output beliefs vector is a stationary point of the bethe free energy function, and when generalized belief propagation converges, the output beliefs vector is a stationary point of the Kikuchi free energy function. However, unlike the bethe free energy and Kikuchi approximations, the tree-reweighted free energy is *convex* with respect to the peseudo-marginals vector, and hence tree-reweighted belief propagation can not end in a local minima.

A second useful property of using the tree-reweighted upper bound as an approximation for the log partition function, is that computing the likelihood derivatives (equations 3-4) using the beliefs output of tree-reweighted massages passing, will result in *exact* derivatives for the upper bound approximation.

In this paper we used $\mathcal{F}(\vec{b};\mu_e;\theta)$ as an approximation for the log partition function, where $\vec{b}$ is the output of tree-reweighted belief propagation. We also used the tree-reweighted beliefs $\vec{b}$ in the derivatives computation (equations 3-4), as our approximation for the marginal probabilities.

References

1. A. Barbu and S.C. Zhu. Graph partition by swendsen-wang cut. In *Proceedings of the IEEE International Conference on Computer Vision*, 2003.
2. E. Borenstein, E. Sharon, and S. Ullman. Combining top-down and bottom-up segmentation. In *Proceedings of the IEEE Conference on Computer Vision and Pattern Recognition Workshop on Perceptual Organization in Computer Vision*, June 2004.
3. E. Borenstein and S. Ullman. Class-specific, top-down segmentation. In *Proc. of the European Conf. on Comput. Vision*, May 2002.
4. X. He, R. Zemel, and M. Carreira-Perpi. Multiscale conditional random fields for image labeling. In *Proceedings of the IEEE Conference on Computer Vision and Pattern Recognition*, 2004.
5. M. Pawan Kumar, P.H.S. Torr, and A. Zisserman. Objcut. In *Proceedings of the IEEE Conference on Computer Vision and Pattern Recognition*, 2004.
6. S. Kumar and M. HebertMultiscale. Discriminative random fields: A discriminative framework for contextual interaction in classification. In *Proceedings of the IEEE International Conference on Computer Vision*, 2003.

7. John Lafferty, Andrew McCallum, and Fernando Pereira. Conditional random fields: Probabilistic models for segmenting and labeling sequence data. In *Proc. 18th International Conf. on Machine Learning*, pages 282–289. Morgan Kaufmann, San Francisco, CA, 2001.
8. Yann LeCun and Fu Jie Huang. Loss functions for discriminative training of energy-based models. In *Proc. of the 10-th International Workshop on Artificial Intelligence and Statistics (AIStats'05)*, 2005.
9. B. Leibe, A. Leonardis, and B. Schiele. Combined object categorization and segmentation with an implicit shape model. In *Proceedings of the Workshop on Statistical Learning in Computer Vision*, Prague, Czech Republic, May 2004.
10. J. Malik, S. Belongie, T. Leung, and J. Shi. Contour and texture analysis for image segmentation. In K.L. Boyer and S. Sarkar, editors, *Perceptual Organization for artificial vision systems*. Kluwer Academic, 2000.
11. E. Sharon, A. Brandt, and R. Basri. Segmentation and boundary detection using multiscale intensity measurements. In *Proceedings of the IEEE Conference on Computer Vision and Pattern Recognition*, 2001.
12. Z.W. Tu, X.R. Chen, A.L Yuille, and S.C. Zhu. Image parsing: segmentation, detection, and recognition. In *Proceedings of the IEEE International Conference on Computer Vision*, 2003.
13. M. J. Wainwright, T. Jaakkola, and A. S. Willsky. Tree-reweighted belief propagation and approximate ml estimation by pseudo-moment matching. In *9th Workshop on Artificial Intelligence and Statistics*, 2003.
14. J. S. Yedidia, W.T. Freeman, and Y. Weiss. Constructing free-energy approximations and generalized belief propagation algorithms. *IEEE Transactions on Information Theory*, 51:2282–2312, 2005.
15. S.X. Yu and J. Shi. Object-specific figure-ground segregation. In *Proceedings of the IEEE Conference on Computer Vision and Pattern Recognition*, 2003.
16. A. Yuille and P. Hallinan. Deformable templates. In *Active Vision, A. Blake and A. Yuille, Eds. MIT press*, 2002.
17. Song Chun Zhu, Zing Nian Wu, and David Mumford. Minimax entropy principle and its application to texture modeling. *Neural Computation*, 9(8):1627–1660, 1997.

Multi-way Clustering Using Super-Symmetric Non-negative Tensor Factorization

Amnon Shashua, Ron Zass, and Tamir Hazan

School of Engineering and Computer Science, The Hebrew University, Jerusalem
{shashua, zass, tamirr}@cs.huji.ac.il

Abstract. We consider the problem of clustering data into $k \geq 2$ clusters given complex relations — going beyond pairwise — between the data points. The complex n-wise relations are modeled by an n-way array where each entry corresponds to an affinity measure over an n-tuple of data points. We show that a probabilistic assignment of data points to clusters is equivalent, under mild conditional independence assumptions, to a super-symmetric non-negative factorization of the closest hyper-stochastic version of the input n-way affinity array. We derive an algorithm for finding a local minimum solution to the factorization problem whose computational complexity is proportional to the number of n-tuple samples drawn from the data. We apply the algorithm to a number of visual interpretation problems including 3D multi-body segmentation and illumination-based clustering of human faces.

1 Introduction

We address the fundamental problem of grouping feature vectors (points) on the basis of multi-wise similarity or coherency relationships among n-tuples of points. The case of pairwise ($n = 2$) relationships has drawn much attention in statistical, graph theoretical and computer vision literature. For example, a clustering task of a collection of points $\mathbf{x}_1, ..., \mathbf{x}_m$ in Euclidean space R^n may be induced by a symmetric "affinity" matrix $K_{ij} = e^{-\|\mathbf{x}_i - \mathbf{x}_j\|^2/\sigma^2}$ which would serve as the input to a process aimed at assigning the m points into $k \geq 2$ classes. The greatly popular "spectral" clustering technique, for example, looks for the k leading eigenvectors of a normalized version of K as a new coordinate system which in ideal settings would map the original coordinates of the points to k points in R^k, one per each cluster [10, 11]. Graph theoretical methods perform normalization on the affinity matrix (producing the Laplacian of K) whereby the second smallest eigenvector splits the points into two clusters [15, 8], and more recently it was shown that conditionally independent statements on the unknown labels given the data points lead to the finding that $K = GG^\top$, $G \geq 0$, where G contains the probabilistic assignments of points to clusters [20].

It has been recently pointed out by a number of authors [1, 5, 21] that for many computer vision and machine learning applications a pairwise affinity relationship among points does not capture the complexity of the problem. For example, if a parametric model requires d points for a definition, then $n \geq d+1$

A. Leonardis, H. Bischof, and A. Pinz (Eds.): ECCV 2006, Part IV, LNCS 3954, pp. 595–608, 2006.

points can be used to provide an affinity value by taking the square residual error Δ^2 of the least-squares fit of the n points to the model and translating it into a probability value $\kappa(\mathbf{x}_{i_1}, ..., \mathbf{x}_{i_n}) = e^{-\Delta^2/\sigma^2}$, where $1 \leq i_1, ..., i_n \leq m$. The affinities form an n-way (tensor) super-symmetric array $K_{i_1,...,i_n} = \kappa(\mathbf{x}_{i_1}, ..., \mathbf{x}_{i_n})$ which like as above is the input for a clustering of the m points into $k \geq 2$ clusters. Computer vision applications for parametric models include (i) 3D-from-2D multi-body segmentation where under an affine model one would need $n \geq 5$ points to determine an affinity value [17] and under a perspective model $n \geq 9$ points are required [9]; (ii) segmenting 3D objects taken from the same pose but under varying illumination conditions — for matte surfaces ignoring self-shadowing one would need $n \geq 4$ pictures for determining an affinity, i.e., the likelihood that the four pictures are of the same 3D surface [13], and (iii) multi-model selection in general.

We address in this paper the problem of clustering m points into $k \geq 2$ clusters given an n-way super-symmetric affinity array $K \in [m] \times .. \times [m] = [m]^{\times n}$. We will first describe the state of the art in this domain and then proceed to describe our contribution.

1.1   Previous Work on n-Way Clustering and Our Approach

Clustering from an n-way affinity array is new to computer vision and machine learning but has been a topic of extensive research in VLSI and PCB clustering placement since the early 70s. A convenient representation of the problem is given by a *hypergraph*, with m vertices and $\binom{m}{n}$ different hyper-edges, where the vertices correspond to the points (circuit elements in VLSI) to be clustered into $k \geq 2$ parts and the hyper-edges (nets connecting circuit elements) correspond to subsets of vertices where the degree n of an edge is the number of vertices spanned by it.

The techniques employed by the VLSI/PCB community for hypergraph partitioning into clusters are largely heuristic in nature — for a review see [2]. The recent work coming out from the vision and machine learning communities [1, 5, 21] seek an approximate graph that best resembles the original hypergraph. For example, [1] define a pairwise affinity as a weighted average over all n-tuple affinities containing the two points in question — this can be viewed as a projection of the original tensor K onto a two-dimensional matrix by a weighted sum of its the slices. Similarly, [5] defines a pairwise affinity between points $\mathbf{x}_r, \mathbf{x}_s$ as a sum of products $K_{r,i_2,...,i_n} K_{s,i_2,...,i_n}$ over all $i_2, ..., i_n$. Finally, [21] performs a multiplicative normalization with the vertices degrees (the sum of weights incident to a vertex) as part of creating a Laplacian of the hypergraph. Both [1, 21] are consistent with graph theoretical research which define hypergraph Laplacians by summing up all the weights incident to pairs of vertices [12], while the work of [5] is inspired by "high order SVD" literature (referenced therein).

The idea of projecting the hypergraph onto a graph is not without merit. However, the projection from a high-order affinity array to a pairwise affinity would have a high SNR for *simple* problems. Problems with a small number of clusters having a high number of points per cluster relative to the affinity degree would benefit from the projection approach. Generally, however, a projection induces information-loss and the pairwise affinities will get increasingly obscured with increasing affinity degree — and since we have here a "curse of dimensionality" effect, a rapid decline of pairwise affinity SNR is expected with increasing problem complexity.

Rather than performing a projection we work with the full affinity tensor. Our approach enables us to define any affinity degree we desire — including one obtained by projection of the original tensor to a lower degree one, and in particular to a pairwise affinity. Starting from a super-symmetric tensor K of any degree, we show that a general probabilistic argument on conditional independence introduces a simple connection between K and the desired $m \times k$ probabilistic partition matrix $G \geq 0$. The connection is two fold (i) the "balancing" requirement on the cluster sizes requires K to be hyper-stochastic, and (ii) G is obtained by a super-symmetric non-negative factorization (SNTF) of K. The algorithm we derive for performing the SNTF is based on a positive-preserving gradient descent scheme. The scheme also supports partial sampling of the affinity tensor which is necessary since it is practically impossible to fill in, or even store, a full high-degree affinity array. The complexity of the update step is $O(mkp)$ where $p \leq \binom{m}{n}$ is the number of samples.

The work presented here is an outgrowth of our algebraic treatment of pairwise affinity clustering showing that K is completely positive [20] and of a general treatment of tensor ranks and conditional independence with latent variables [14].

2   Probabilistic Clustering from n-Way Affinity Arrays

Let $\mathcal{D} = \{\mathbf{x}_1, ..., \mathbf{x}_m\}$ be points in R^d which we wish to assign to k clusters $C_1, .., C_k$ and let $y_i \in \{1, ..., k\}$ be the associated (unknown) labels. We assume that we have a way to measure the probability, which for now is simply an affinity measure in the range $(0, 1]$, that any n-tuple of points $\mathbf{x}_{i_1}, ..., \mathbf{x}_{i_n}$, $1 \leq i_j \leq m$, belong to the same cluster. For example, if we know that the clusters are defined as $n-1$ dimensional subspaces, then $k(\mathbf{x}_{i_1}, ..., \mathbf{x}_{i_n}) = e^{-\Delta}$, where Δ is the volume defined by the n-tuple, would be a reasonable measure of n-tuple affinity.

Given the affinities $k(\mathbf{x}_{i_1}, ..., \mathbf{x}_{i_n})$, which form an n-way array K indexed by $K_{i_1, ..., i_n}$, we wish to assign a probability $g_{r,s} = P(y_s = r \mid \mathcal{D})$ of point $\mathbf{x}_s$ belonging to cluster C_r. The desired membership probabilities form a non-negative $m \times k$ matrix $G = [\mathbf{g}_1, ..., \mathbf{g}_k]$, thus our goal is to find G given K. We will derive below an algebraic constraint on the n-way array K and relate it, by means of factorization and linear constraints, to the desired matrix G.

Consider the labels y_i as *latent* variables and assume that $y_1 \perp ... \perp y_m \mid \mathcal{D}$, i.e., that the labels are independent of each other given the entire set of data points. Then, the probability $P(y_{i_1} = r, ..., y_{i_n} = r \mid \mathcal{D})$ that $\mathbf{x}_{i_1}, ..., \mathbf{x}_{i_n}$ belong to cluster C_r, is factorizable:

$$P(y_{i_1} = r, ..., y_{i_n} = r \mid \mathcal{D}) = P(y_{i_1} = r \mid \mathcal{D}) \cdots P(y_{i_n} = r \mid \mathcal{D}).$$

The probability that the n-tuple are clustered together is given by marginalization:

$$K_{i_1,\ldots,i_n} = \sum_{r=1}^{k} P(y_{i_1} = r \mid \mathcal{D}) \cdots P(y_{i_n} = r \mid \mathcal{D}) = \sum_{r=1}^{k} g_{r,i_1} \cdots g_{r,i_n},$$

which translate to the fact that K should be a rank=k super-symmetric tensor:

$$K = \sum_{r=1}^{k} \mathbf{g}_r^{\otimes n}, \quad \mathbf{g}_r \geq 0,$$

where $\mathbf{g}^{\otimes n}$ denotes the rank-1 tensor $\mathbf{g} \otimes \mathbf{g} \otimes \ldots \otimes \mathbf{g}$. In other words, the cluster assignment probabilities are related to a non-negative super-symmetric factorization of the input n-way array K. To complete the algebraic relation between K and G we need to consider the constraints on K such that the n-way affinity array will indeed represent a distribution:

Proposition 1. *Given uniform priors on the distribution of labels, i.e., $P(y_i = j) = 1/k$ for all $i = 1, \ldots, m$, the n-way array K must be hyper-stochastic:*

$$\sum_{i_1,\ldots,i_{j-1},i_{j+1},\ldots,i_n} K_{i_1,\ldots,i_n} = \left(\frac{m}{k}\right)^{n-1} \mathbf{1}, \quad j = 1,\ldots,n$$

where $\mathbf{1}$ is the m-dimensional vector $(1,\ldots,1)$.

Proof: From the definition of G we have that the rows sum to 1: $\sum_r P(y_s = r \mid \mathcal{D}) = \sum_r g_{rs} = 1$. Therefore, the uniform priors means that each column sums to m/k: $\sum_s g_{rs} = m/k$. The rows and columns sums propagate to a (scaled) hyper-stochastic constraint on K:

$$\sum_{i_1,\ldots,i_{j-1},i_{j+1},\ldots,i_n} K_{i_1,\ldots,i_n} = \sum_{r=1}^{k} g_{r,i_j} \sum_{i_1,\ldots,i_{j-1},i_{j+1},\ldots,i_n} g_{r,i_1} \cdots g_{r,i_{j-1}} g_{r,i_{j+1}} \cdots g_{r,i_n}$$

$$= \sum_{r=1}^{k} g_{r,i_j} \left(\sum_{i_1} g_{r,i_1}\right) \cdots \left(\sum_{i_{j-1}} g_{r,i_{j-1}}\right) \left(\sum_{i_{j+1}} g_{r,i_{j+1}}\right) \cdots \left(\sum_{i_n} g_{r,i_n}\right)$$

$$= \left(\frac{m}{k}\right)^{n-1} \sum_{r=1}^{k} g_{r,i_j} = \left(\frac{m}{k}\right)^{n-1}$$

$\square$

Note that the hyper-stochasticity constraint is "balanced partitions" in disguise. The uniform prior assumption in fact constraints the dataset to form k "balanced" clusters. Since we do not wish to *enforce* strictly a balanced partition we will seek only a "soft" version of the hyper-stochastic constraint by adopting the following scheme: (i) find a hyper-stochastic approximation F to the input affinity array K, and (ii) given F, perform a super-symmetric non-negative tensor factorization (SNTF), i.e., find $\mathbf{g}_1, \ldots, \mathbf{g}_k \geq 0$ that minimize the Frobenius norm $\|F - \sum_r \mathbf{g}_r^{\otimes n}\|^2$.

Finding a hyper-stochastic approximation to K can be done by repeating a normalization step which is an extension of the symmetrized Sinkhorn [16, 20] rows and columns normalization procedure for matrices. The following proposition forms a normalization algorithm which converges to a super-symmetric hyper-stochastic array:

Proposition 2. *For any non-negative super-symmetric n-way array $K^{(0)}$, iterating the process:*

$$K_{i_1,\dots,i_n}^{(t+1)} = \frac{K_{i_1,\dots,i_n}^{(t)}}{(a_{i_1} \cdots a_{i_n})^{1/n}},$$

where

$$a_i = \sum_{i_2,\dots,i_n} K_{i,i_2,\dots,i_n}, \qquad i = 1,\dots,m$$

converges to a hyper-stochastic array.

The proof is in Appendix B. In the pairwise affinity ($n = 2$) case, the results above state that $K = GG^{\top}$ and that prior to factorizing K we should normalize it by replacing it with $F = D^{-1/2}KD^{-1/2}$ where D is a diagonal matrix holding the row sums of K. If we iterate this normalization procedure we will obtain a doubly-stochastic approximation to K. This is consistent with [20] which argues that the conditional independence statements $y_i \perp y_j \mid \mathcal{D}$ lead to the finding that $K = GG^{\top}$ which also underlies the k-means, spectral clustering and normalized cuts approaches. In other words, the conditional independence assumptions we made at the start are already built-in into the conventional pairwise affinity treatment — we have simply acknowledged them and extended them beyond pairwise affinities.

3   The SNTF Algorithm

We are given a n-way affinity array $K \in [d_1] \times \dots \times [d_n]$ with $d_i = m$ being the number of data points to be clustered. An entry $K_{i_1,\dots,i_n}$ with $1 \le i_j \le m$ denotes the (un-normalized) probability of the n-point tuple $\mathbf{x}_{i_1}, \dots, \mathbf{x}_{i_n}$ to be clustered together. The tensor K is super-symmetric because the probability $K_{i_1,\dots,i_n}$ does not depend on the order of the n points. Furthermore, we can ignore entries with repeating indices and focus only on the case $i_1 \ne \dots \ne i_n$ (this is crucial for the success of the algorithm). For practical reasons, we would like to store only a single representative of each n-tuple (instead of $n!$ entries), thus we focus only on the entries $i_1 < i_2 < \dots < i_n$. Accordingly, we define the order-restricted Frobenius (semi) norm:

$$\|K\|_o^2 = <K, K>_o = \sum_{1 \le i_1 < i_2 < \dots < i_n \le m} K_{i_1,\dots,i_n}^2,$$

where $<A, B>_o$ is the inner-product (restricted to strictly ascending order) operation. Note that when K is super-symmetric then

$$\|K\|_o^2 = \frac{1}{n!} \sum_{i_1 \ne \dots \ne i_n} K_{i_1,\dots,i_n}^2$$

which is the restriction of the Frobenius norm to non-repeating indices. As mentioned in the previous section, we pass K through a normalization process and obtain a normalized version denoted by F. Our goal is to find a non-negative matrix $G_{m \times k}$ whose columns are denoted by $\mathbf{g}_1, ..., \mathbf{g}_k$ such as to minimize the following function:

$$f(G) = \frac{1}{2}\|F - \sum_{j=1}^{k} \mathbf{g}_j^{\otimes n}\|_o^2,$$

We derive below a positive-preserving update rule: $g_{r,s} \leftarrow g_{r,s} - \delta_{rs}\partial f/\partial g_{r,s}$. We start with the derivation of the partial derivative $\partial f/\partial g_{r,s}$. The differential df is derived below:

$$df = d\frac{1}{2} < F - \sum_{j=1}^{k} \mathbf{g}_j^{\otimes n}, F - \sum_{j=1}^{k} \mathbf{g}_j^{\otimes n} >_o = <\sum_{j=1}^{k} \mathbf{g}_j^{\otimes n} - F, d(\sum_{j=1}^{k} \mathbf{g}_j^{\otimes n}) >_o$$

$$= < \sum_{j=1}^{k} \mathbf{g}_j^{\otimes n} - F, \sum_{j}(d\mathbf{g}_j) \otimes \mathbf{g}_j^{\otimes(n-1)} + \mathbf{g}_j \otimes (d\mathbf{g}_j) \otimes \mathbf{g}_j^{\otimes(n-2)} + ... + \mathbf{g}_j^{\otimes(n-1)} \otimes d\mathbf{g}_j >_o$$

The partial derivative with respect to $g_{r,s}$ (the s'th entry of $\mathbf{g}_r$) is:

$$\frac{\partial f}{\partial g_{rs}} = <\sum_{j=1}^{k} \mathbf{g}_j^{\otimes n} - F, \mathbf{e}_s \otimes \mathbf{g}_r^{\otimes(n-1)} + ... + \mathbf{g}_r^{\otimes(n-1)} \otimes \mathbf{e}_s >_o$$

where $\mathbf{e}_s$ is the standard vector $(0, 0, .., 1, 0, ..0)$ with 1 in the s'th coordinate. It will be helpful to introduce the following notation: let $1 \leq i_2 < ... < i_n \leq m$ and let $1 \leq s \leq m$ be different from $i_2, ..., i_n$, then $s \rightarrow i_2, .., i_n$ is an ascending n-tuple index (i.e., s is inserted into $i_2, ..., i_n$ in the appropriate position). Thus, for example:

$$< F, \mathbf{a} \otimes \mathbf{b} \otimes \mathbf{b} + \mathbf{b} \otimes \mathbf{a} \otimes \mathbf{b} + \mathbf{b} \otimes \mathbf{b} \otimes \mathbf{a} >_o = \sum_{i_1 \neq i_2 < i_3} F_{i_1 \rightarrow i_2, i_3} a_{i_1} b_{i_2} b_{i_3}$$

Using the above short-hand notation, the partial derivative becomes:

$$\frac{\partial f}{\partial g_{r,s}} = \sum_{j=1}^{k} g_{j,s} \sum_{s \neq i_2 < ... < i_n} \prod_{q=2}^{n} g_{j,i_q} g_{r,i_q} - \sum_{s \neq i_2 < ... < i_n} F_{s \rightarrow i_2, .., i_n} \prod_{q=2}^{n} g_{r,i_q} \qquad (1)$$

We will be using a "positive preserving" gradient descent scheme $g_{rs} \leftarrow g_{rs} - \delta_{rs}\partial f/\partial g_{rs}$. Following [7] we set the gradient step size δ_{rs} as follows:

$$\delta_{rs} = \frac{g_{rs}}{\sum_{j=1}^{k} g_{j,s} \sum_{s \neq i_2 < ... < i_n} \prod_{q=2}^{n} g_{j,i_q} g_{r,i_q}} \qquad (2)$$

After substitution of eqn. 2 into the gradient descent equation we obtain a multiplicative update rule:

$$g_{rs} \leftarrow \frac{g_{rs} \sum_{s \neq i_2 < ... < i_n} F_{s \rightarrow i_2, .., i_n} \prod_{q=2}^{n} g_{r,i_q}}{\sum_{j=1}^{k} g_{j,s} \sum_{s \neq i_2 < ... < i_n} \prod_{q=2}^{n} g_{j,i_q} g_{r,i_q}} \qquad (3)$$

The update rule preserves positivity, i.e., if the initial guess for G is non-negative and F is super-symmetric and non-negative, then all future updates will maintain non-negativity. The proof that the update rule reduces $f(G)$ and converges to a local minima is presented in Appendix A.

There are a couple of noteworthy points to make. First, removing from consideration entries in F that correspond to repeated indices makes the energy function $f(g_{r,s})$ be quadratic (when all other entries of G are fixed) which in turn is the key for the update rule above to reduce the energy at each step. Second, each sample of n-tuple corresponds to $n!$ entries of the affinity tensor K. As the dimension grows, any algorithm for processing K becomes unpractical as simply recording the measurements is unwieldy. The scheme we presented above records only the $\binom{m}{n}$ entries $1 \leq i_1 < ... < i_n \leq m$ instead of m^n in return for keeping a lexicographic order during measurement recording and during the update process of $g_{r,s}$ (access to $F_{s \to i_2,...,i_n}$).

Next, for large arrays, the need to sample all the possible (ordered) n-tuples out of m points introduces an excessive computational burden. In fact, it is sufficient to sample only a relatively small fraction of all n-tuples for most clustering problems. The sampling introduces vanishing entries in K that do not correspond to low affinity of the corresponding n-tuple but to the fact that the particular tuple was not sampled — those should be weighted-out in the criteria function $f(G)$. A "weighted" version of the scheme above requires merely a straightforward modification of the update rule:

$$g_{rs} \leftarrow \frac{g_{rs} \sum_{s \neq i_2 < ... < i_n} W_{s \to i_2,...,i_n} F_{s \to i_2,...,i_n} \prod_{q=2}^{n} g_{r,i_q}}{\sum_{j=1}^{k} g_{j,s} \sum_{s \neq i_2 < ... < i_n} W_{s \to i_2,...,i_n} \prod_{q=2}^{n} g_{j,i_q} g_{r,i_q}} \qquad (4)$$

where $W_{i_1,...,i_n} \geq 0$, $i_1 < ... < i_n$, is a weight associated with the entry $K_{i_1,...,i_n}$. In particular we are interested in the binary weighting scenario where the weight is zero if the n-tuple $\mathbf{x}_{i_1}, ..., \mathbf{x}_{i_n}$ was not sampled and '1' otherwise. To summarize, the n-way clustering algorithm is presented below:

1. Construct K: sample n-tuples $\mathbf{x}_{i_1}, ..., \mathbf{x}_{i_n}$, $i_1 < ... < i_n$, and set $K_{i_1,...,i_n} = k(\mathbf{x}_{i_1}, ..., \mathbf{x}_{i_n})$. Set $W_{i_1,...,i_n} = 1$.
2. Normalize K: apply the iterative normalization scheme which generates F (Prop. 2).
3. Factor F: starting with an initial guess for $G \geq 0$, iteratively update the entries $g_{r,s}$ one at a time using eqn. 4 until convergence is reached.

Note that only sampled entries participate in the algorithm, therefore the complexity of each update step (eqn. 4) is a constant factor of the number of samples. The complexity of the algorithm is $O(mkp)$ where $p \leq \binom{m}{n}$ is the number of samples (number of non-vanishing entries of W).

4   Experiments

We begin by studying the performance of the SNTF algorithm on synthetic data compared to the graph projection methods [1, 5, 21]. A comparative study

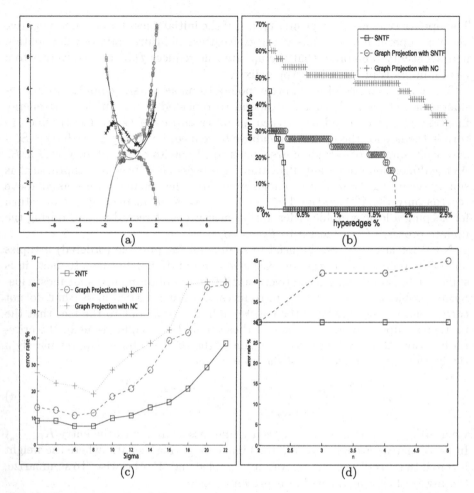

Fig. 1. Synthetic study of clustering $m = 200$ points arranged in $k = 5$ 3rd-order curves (i.e., affinity degree is $n = 5$). See text for details on each display.

of graph projection against outlier rejection algorithms (like RANSAC) and the multi-level hypergraph partitioning algorithms used in the VLSI community was presented in [1] showing a significant advantage to graph projection. Therefore we will focus our comparative study on the performance relationship between SNTF and graph projection.

The graph projection approximates the original hypergraph with a graph followed by spectral clustering. In practice, when the affinity degree n is large one needs to use sampling, i.e., during the projection not all hyper-edges are used since their number grows exponentially with the affinity degree ([5] addressed the sampling issue). We expect the graph projection to work well when the problem is "simple", i.e., when a projection from $\binom{m}{n}$ hyper-edges to $\binom{m}{2}$ edges can be done with minimal information loss – in those cases it is worthwhile to reduce the problem size from a hypergraph to a graph rather than working directly with

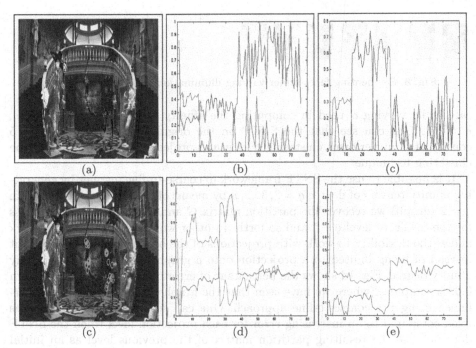

Fig. 2. 3D-from-2D motion segmentation. (a) shows a picture with 76 points over four separate bodies, (b,c) show the resulting four columns of the partition matrix G using SNTF with a 9-way affinity array. The bottom row shows the results after projecting the affinity array onto a matrix. The projection resulted in significant information-loss which caused performance degradation.

the full affinity tensor. On the other hand, when the number of points is large or when the affinity degree is high, one would expect a significant information-loss during projection with a resulting degraded performance.

In our first experiment we generated $m = 200$ points in the 2D plane laying on $k = 5$ 3rd-order polynomials with added Gaussian noise. The number of hyper-edges (entries of the affinity tensor K) is $\binom{200}{5}$ and since a 3rd-order 1D polynomial is determined by four coefficients we have $n = 5$. We ran SNTF, graph projection using Normalized-Cuts (NC) and graph projection using SNTF (i.e., the same algorithm described in this paper but for $n = 2$). We varied the runs according to the sampling percentage ranging from $0.02\% - 2.5\%$ of sampled hyper-edges. Fig. 1a shows the input data and Fig. 1b shows the clustering error percentage of the three runs per sampling. The error of the SNTF is indeed higher than the graph projection when the sampling is very low (0.02%), i.e., when the affinity tensor is very sparse and thus the projection onto a graph (matrix) does not suffer from information-loss. As the sampling rate increases the performance of the SNTF on $n = 5$ original affinity tensor significantly outperforms both graph projection runs and reaches perfect clustering much earlier (0.2% compared to 1.5% sampling). Fig. 1c compares the error rate of SNTF and graph projections (NC and SNTF with $n = 2$) using 0.15% sampling

Fig. 3. Segmenting faces under varying illumination conditions. See text.

rate while varying σ used in computing the affinity from the residual Δ, i.e., $e^{-\Delta^2/\sigma^2}$. One can see that the SNTF on the original affinity degree $n = 5$ consistently outperforms clustering over graph projections — regardless of the clustering technique.

It is possible to use the SNTF framework in coarse-to-fine manner by generating affinity tensors of degree $q = 2, 3, ..., n$ by means of projection. Starting from $q = 2$ (graph) we recover the partition matrix G and use it as the initial guess for the SNTF of level $q + 1$ and so forth. In other words, the SNTF framework allows the flexibility to work with projections of the original affinity tensor, but instead of being limited to a projection onto a graph we could work with any affinity degree. Fig. 1d shows the percentage of error on the same data but with 0.02% sampling (where we have seen that the graph projection has the upper-hand) using the coarse-to-fine approach. One can see that the error remains fixed compared to an increasing error for each projection level when the SNTF does not use the resulting partition matrix of the previous level as an initial guess. This also confirms that there is a tradeoff between the complexity of the energy landscape introduced in high-degree affinities and the information loss introduced by aggressive projections. Ideally, one should work with a projection to the smallest affinity degree with minimal information loss. The advantage of the SNTF framework is that we are free to choose the affinity degree, whereas with graph projection the affinity degree is set to $n = 2$.

We move next to a 3D motion segmentation experiment. Fig. 2a shows a frame from "Matrix Reloaded" where we track 76 points arranged on four different moving bodies: the background (moving due to camera motion) and three separate people moving independently from the background motion. The points were tracked across two successive frames and our task is to perform a segmentation (clustering) of the points and assign each point to the proper moving body. It is well known that under perspective projection each pair of matching points p_i, p_i' in the image plane represented in homogenous coordinates satisfy a bilinear constraint: $p_i'^\top F p_i = 0$ where F is a 3×3 matrix iff the corresponding 3D points are part of a single moving object [9]. Therefore, we need $n = 9$ points in order to obtain an affinity measurement, i.e., the likelihood that the 9-tuple arise form the same moving object. The affinity tensor has $\binom{76}{9}$ entries and we sample roughly one million entries from it with a proximity bias, i.e., once a point is sampled the next point is biased towards close points according to a Normal distribution. We ran SNTF with $k = 4$ clusters on the 9-degree (sampled) affinity tensor. Fig. 2b,c shows the four columns of the partition matrix G. Recall that the entries of each column represent the assignment probability of the corresponding point to the cluster associated with the column. The values of G induce a clear-cut segmentation of the points to four separate bodies and the assignments are shown in Fig. 2a as varying color and shape. This particular segmentation problem is sufficiently challenging both for the graph projection approach and to the geometric-specific methods of [19, 18]. With regard to graph projection, the projection from a 9-degree affinity to a pairwise affinity is very aggressive with significant information-loss. Fig. 2e,f shows the four columns of G recovered from SNTF with $n = 2$ (followed by a projection) — one can see that one of the moving bodies got lost.

Finally we ran an experiment on segmenting faces under varying illumination conditions. It is well known that under certain surface property assumptions (Lambertian) the space of pictures of a 3D object ignoring cast-shadows lie in a 3D subspace [13]. We therefore need a 4th-degree affinity measured over quadruples of pictures. Fig. 3 shows a sequence of pictures of a person under varying illumination conditions adopted from the AR dataset. We had 21 pictures spanning three different persons and we ran SNTF using 4-degree affinity tensor with $k = 3$ clusters. The three columns of the partition matrix G are shown in the right display. The pictures are unambiguously assigned to the correct person. Similar results of comparable quality were also obtained by graph projection.

Acknowledgments

We thank Alex Samorodnitsky for assistance in proving Proposition 2 and acknowledge the financial support from ISF grant 189/03 and GIF grant 773/2004.

References

1. S. Agrawal, J. Lim, L. Zelnik-Manor, P. Perona, D. Kriegman, and S. Belongie. Beyond pairwise clustering. In *Proceedings of the IEEE Conference on Computer Vision and Pattern Recognition*, 2005.
2. C.J. Alpert and A.B. Kahng. Recent directions in netlist partitioning. *The VLSI Journal*, 19(1-2):1–81, 1995.
3. C.M. Fiduccia and R.M. Mattheyses. A linear time heuristic for improving network partitions. In *Proc. of the 19th IEEE Design Automation Conference*, pages 175–181, 1982.
4. I.M. Gelfand, M.M. Karpanov, and A.V. Zelevinsky. *Discriminants, Resultants and multidimensional determinants*. Birkhauser Boston, 1994.
5. V.M. Govindu. A tensor decomposition for geometric grouping and segmentation. In *Proceedings of the IEEE Conference on Computer Vision and Pattern Recognition*, 2005.
6. B.W. Kernighan and S. Lin. An efficient heuristic procedure for partitioning graphs. *The Bell System Technical Journal*, 49(2), 1970.
7. D. Lee and H. Seung. Learning the parts of objects by non-negative matrix factorization. *Nature*, 401:788–791, 1999.
8. T. Leighton and S. Rao. An approximate max-flow min-cut theorem for uniform multicommodity flow problems with applications to approximate algorithms. In *Proceedings Symposium on Foundations of Comp. Sci.*, 1988.
9. H.C. Longuet-Higgins. A computer algorithm for reconstructing a scene from two projections. *Nature*, 293:133–135, 1981.

10. A.Y. Ng, M.I. Jordan, and Y. Weiss. On spectral clustering: Analysis and an algorithm. In *Proceedings of the conference on Neural Information Processing Systems (NIPS)*, 2001.
11. P. Perona and W. Freeman. A factorization approach to grouping. In *Proceedings of the European Conference on Computer Vision*, 1998.
12. J.A. Rodriguez. On the Laplacian eigenvalues and metric parameters of hypergraphs. *Linear and Multilinear Algebra*, 50(1):1–14, 2002.
13. A. Shashua. Illumination and view position in 3D visual recognition. In *Proceedings of the conference on Neural Information Processing Systems (NIPS)*, Denver, CO, December 1991.
14. A. Shashua and T. Hazan. Non-negative tensor factorization with applications to statistics and computer vision. In *Proceedings of the International Conference on Machine Learning (ICML)*, 2005.
15. J. Shi and J. Malik. Normalized cuts and image segmentation. *IEEE Transactions on Pattern Analysis and Machine Intelligence*, 22(8), 2000.
16. R. Sinkhorn. A relationship between arbitrary positive matrices and doubly stochastic matrices. *Ann. Math. Statist.*, 35:876–879, 1964.
17. S. Ullman and R. Basri. Recognition by linear combination of models. *IEEE Transactions on Pattern Analysis and Machine Intelligence*, 13:992–1006, 1991.
18. R. Vidal, Y. Ma, S. Soatto, and S. Sastry. Two-view multibody structure from motion. *International Journal of Computer Vision*, 2004.
19. L. Wolf and A. Shashua. Two-body segmentation from two perspective views. In *Proceedings of the IEEE Conference on Computer Vision and Pattern Recognition*, Hawaii, Dec. 2001.
20. R. Zass and A. Shashua. A unifying approach to hard and probabilistic clustering. In *Proceedings of the International Conference on Computer Vision*, Beijing, China, Oct. 2005.
21. D. Zhou, J. Huang, and B. Scholkopf. Beyond pairwise classification and clustering using hypergraphs. Technical report, Max Planck Institute for Biol. Cybernetics, TR-143, August 2005.

A Proof of Convergence: The Update Rule

Let $f(g_{rs})$ be the energy as a function of g_{rs} (all other entries of G remain constant) and let g'_{rs} be the updated value according to eqn. 3. We wish to show that if we make a gradient descent with a step size δ_{rs} given by eqn. 2 (which as we saw leads to a positive-preserving update), then $f(g'_{rs}) \leq f(g_{rs})$. They key is that δ_{rs} is smaller than the inverse second derivative:

Proposition 3. *The update scheme $g'_{rs} = g_{rs} - \delta_{rs}\partial f/\partial g_{rs}$, with δ_{rs} given by eqn. 2 and the partial first derivative is given by eqn. 1, reduces the optimization function, i.e., $f(g'_{rs}) \leq f(g_{rs})$.*

Proof: The second derivative is:

$$\frac{\partial^2 f}{\partial g_{rs}\partial g_{rs}} = \sum_{s \neq i_2 < ... < i_n} \prod_{q=2}^{n} g^2_{r,i_q},$$

and the step size δ_{rs} satisfies:

$$\delta_{rs} = \frac{g_{rs}}{\sum_{j=1}^{k} g_{j,s} \sum_{s \neq i_2 < \ldots < i_n} \prod_{q=2}^{n} g_{j,i_q} g_{r,i_q}} \leq \frac{g_{rs}}{g_{r,s} \sum_{s \neq i_2 < \ldots < i_n} \prod_{q=2}^{n} g_{r,i_q}^2}$$

$$= \frac{1}{\partial^2 f / \partial g_{rs} \partial g_{rs}}$$

The Taylor expansion of $f(g_{rs} + h)$ with $h = -\delta_{rs} \partial f / \partial g_{rs}$ is:

$$f(g_{rs}') = f(g_{rs}) - \delta_{rs} (\frac{\partial f}{\partial g_{rs}})^2 + \frac{1}{2} \delta_{rs}^2 (\frac{\partial f}{\partial g_{rs}})^2 \frac{\partial^2 f}{\partial g_{rs} \partial g_{rs}},$$

from which follows:

$$f(g_{rs}) - f(g_{rs}') = \delta_{rs} (\frac{\partial f}{\partial g_{rs}})^2 (1 - \frac{1}{2} \delta_{rs} \frac{\partial^2 f}{\partial g_{rs} \partial g_{rs}}) \geq 0,$$

since $\delta_{rs} \partial^2 f / \partial g_{rs} \partial g_{rs} \leq 1$. $\qquad\qquad\qquad\qquad\qquad\qquad$ ☐

We apply the update rule in a Gauss-Seidel fashion according to a row-major raster scan of the entries of G (a row-major raster scan has the advantage of enabling efficient caching). Since the energy is lower-bounded, twice differentiable, and is monotonically decreasing via the update rule, yet cannot decrease beyond the lower bound (i.e., positive preserving), then the process will converge onto a local minimum of the optimization function $\frac{1}{2}\|F - \sum_{j=1}^{k} g_j^{\otimes n}\|^2$ with entries with repeated indices ignored.

B   Proof of Convergence: Normalization Scheme

We prove the following proposition:

For any non-negative super-symmetric n-way array $K^{(0)}$, without vanishing slices, iterating the process:

$$K_{i_1,\ldots,i_n}^{(t+1)} = \frac{K_{i_1,\ldots,i_n}^{(t)}}{(a_{i_1} \cdots a_{i_n})^{1/n}}, \tag{5}$$

where

$$a_i = \sum_{i_2,\ldots,i_n} K_{i,i_2,\ldots,i_n}, \qquad i = 1, \ldots, m$$

converges to a hyper-stochastic array.

Proof: we define the *hyper-permanent* (following the definition of hyperdeterminant [4]):

$$hperm(K) = \sum_{\sigma_2 \in S_m} \cdots \sum_{\sigma_n \in S_m} \prod_{i=1}^{m} K_{i,\sigma_2(i),\ldots,\sigma_n(i)},$$

where S_m is the permutation group of m letters. Let K' be the n-way array following one step of the normalization step described in eqn. 5. We have:

$$\prod_{i=1}^{m}(a_i a_{\sigma_2(i)} \cdots a_{\sigma_n(i)})^{1/n} = \prod_{i=1}^{m}(a_i^n)^{1/n} = \prod_{i=1}^{m}a_i,$$

from which we can conclude that:

$$hperm(K') = \frac{1}{\prod_{i=1}^{m}a_i}hperm(K).$$

To show that the normalization scheme monotonously increases the hyper-permanent of the n-way array we need to show that $\prod_{i=1}^{m}a_i \leq 1$. From the arithmetic-geometric means inequality it is sufficient to show that $\sum_{i=1}^{m}a_i \leq m$. From the definition of a_i we have:

$$\sum_{i=1}^{m}a_i = \sum_{i,i_2,...,i_n}K_{i,i_2,...,i_n}\frac{1}{(a_i a_{i_2}\cdots a_{i_n})^{1/n}}. \tag{6}$$

From the arithmetic-geometric means inequality $(\prod_{i=1}^{m}x_i)^{1/m} \leq (1/m)\sum_i x_i$, replace x_i with $1/a_i$ (recall that $a_i > 0$) and obtain:

$$\frac{1}{(a_1 a_2 \cdots a_m)^{1/m}} \leq \frac{1}{m}\sum_{i=1}^{m}\frac{1}{a_i},$$

and in general for any n-tuple $1 \leq i_1 < ... < i_n \leq m$:

$$\frac{1}{(a_{i_1}\cdots a_{i_n})^{1/n}} \leq \frac{1}{n}(\frac{1}{a_{i_1}} + ... + \frac{1}{a_{i_n}}). \tag{7}$$

By substituting the inequality eqn. 7 into eqn. 6 while noting that:

$$\sum_{i,i_2,..,i_n}K_{i,i_2,...,i_n}\frac{1}{a_{i_j}} = \sum_{i_j=1}^{m}\frac{1}{a_{i_j}}\sum_{i,i_2,...,i_{j-1}i_{j+1},...,i_n}K_{i,i_2,...,i_{j-1}i_{j+1},...,i_n} = m,$$

we obtain that $\sum_i a_i \leq m$ as required. Therefore, we conclude so far that each step of the normalization scheme increases the hyper-determinant of the previous step. The hyper-permanent is bounded from above since:

$$hperm(K) \leq \prod_{i=1}^{m}a_i \leq 1,$$

therefore the process must converge. The process converges when $hperm(K') = hperm(K)$ which can happen only of $a_1 = ... = a_m = 1$. □

Author Index

Lecture Notes in Computer Science

For information about Vols. 1–3850

please contact your bookseller or Springer

Vol. 3901: P.M. Hill (Ed.), Logic Based Program Synthesis and Transformation. X, 179 pages. 2006.

Vol. 3899: S. Frintrop, VOCUS: A Visual Attention System for Object Detection and Goal-Directed Search. XIV, 216 pages. 2006. (Sublibrary LNAI).

Vol. 3898: K. Tuyls, P.J. 't Hoen, K. Verbeeck, S. Sen (Eds.), Learning and Adaption in Multi-Agent Systems. X, 217 pages. 2006. (Sublibrary LNAI).

Vol. 3897: B. Preneel, S. Tavares (Eds.), Selected Areas in Cryptography. XI, 371 pages. 2006.

Vol. 3896: Y. Ioannidis, M.H. Scholl, J.W. Schmidt, F. Matthes, M. Hatzopoulos, K. Boehm, A. Kemper, T. Grust, C. Boehm (Eds.), Advances in Database Technology - EDBT 2006. XIV, 1208 pages. 2006.

Vol. 3895: O. Goldreich, A.L. Rosenberg, A.L. Selman (Eds.), Theoretical Computer Science. XII, 399 pages. 2006.

Vol. 3894: W. Grass, B. Sick, K. Waldschmidt (Eds.), Architecture of Computing Systems - ARCS 2006. XII, 496 pages. 2006.

Vol. 3893: L. Atzori, D.D. Giusto, R. Leonardi, F. Pereira (Eds.), Visual Content Processing and Representation. IX, 224 pages. 2006.

Vol. 3891: J.S. Sichman, L. Antunes (Eds.), Multi-Agent-Based Simulation VI. X, 191 pages. 2006. (Sublibrary LNAI).

Vol. 3890: S.G. Thompson, R. Ghanea-Hercock (Eds.), Defence Applications of Multi-Agent Systems. XII, 141 pages. 2006. (Sublibrary LNAI).

Vol. 3889: J. Rosca, D. Erdogmus, J.C. Príncipe, S. Haykin (Eds.), Independent Component Analysis and Blind Signal Separation. XXI, 980 pages. 2006.

Vol. 3888: D. Draheim, G. Weber (Eds.), Trends in Enterprise Application Architecture. IX, 145 pages. 2006.

Vol. 3887: J.R. Correa, A. Hevia, M. Kiwi (Eds.), LATIN 2006: Theoretical Informatics. XVI, 814 pages. 2006.

Vol. 3886: E.G. Bremer, J. Hakenberg, E.-H.(S.) Han, D. Berrar, W. Dubitzky (Eds.), Knowledge Discovery in Life Science Literature. XIV, 147 pages. 2006. (Sublibrary LNBI).

Vol. 3885: V. Torra, Y. Narukawa, A. Valls, J. Domingo-Ferrer (Eds.), Modeling Decisions for Artificial Intelligence. XII, 374 pages. 2006. (Sublibrary LNAI).

Vol. 3884: B. Durand, W. Thomas (Eds.), STACS 2006. XIV, 714 pages. 2006.

Vol. 3882: M.L. Lee, K.-L. Tan, V. Wuwongse (Eds.), Database Systems for Advanced Applications. XIX, 923 pages. 2006.

Vol. 3881: S. Gibet, N. Courty, J.-F. Kamp (Eds.), Gesture in Human-Computer Interaction and Simulation. XIII, 344 pages. 2006. (Sublibrary LNAI).

Vol. 3880: A. Rashid, M. Aksit (Eds.), Transactions on Aspect-Oriented Software Development I. IX, 335 pages. 2006.

Vol. 3879: T. Erlebach, G. Persinao (Eds.), Approximation and Online Algorithms. X, 349 pages. 2006.

Vol. 3878: A. Gelbukh (Ed.), Computational Linguistics and Intelligent Text Processing. XVII, 589 pages. 2006.

Vol. 3877: M. Detyniecki, J.M. Jose, A. Nürnberger, C. J. '. van Rijsbergen (Eds.), Adaptive Multimedia Retrieval: User, Context, and Feedback. XI, 279 pages. 2006.

Vol. 3876: S. Halevi, T. Rabin (Eds.), Theory of Cryptography. XI, 617 pages. 2006.

Vol. 3875: S. Ur, E. Bin, Y. Wolfsthal (Eds.), Hardware and Software, Verification and Testing. X, 265 pages. 2006.

Vol. 3874: R. Missaoui, J. Schmidt (Eds.), Formal Concept Analysis. X, 309 pages. 2006. (Sublibrary LNAI).

Vol. 3873: L. Maicher, J. Park (Eds.), Charting the Topic Maps Research and Applications Landscape. VIII, 281 pages. 2006. (Sublibrary LNAI).

Vol. 3872: H. Bunke, A. L. Spitz (Eds.), Document Analysis Systems VII. XIII, 630 pages. 2006.

Vol. 3871: E.-G. Talbi, P. Liardet, P. Collet, E. Lutton, M. Schoenauer (Eds.), Artificial Evolution. XI, 310 pages. 2006.

Vol. 3870: S. Spaccapietra, P. Atzeni, W.W. Chu, T. Catarci, K.P. Sycara (Eds.), Journal on Data Semantics V. XIII, 237 pages. 2006.

Vol. 3869: S. Renals, S. Bengio (Eds.), Machine Learning for Multimodal Interaction. XIII, 490 pages. 2006.

Vol. 3868: K. Römer, H. Karl, F. Mattern (Eds.), Wireless Sensor Networks. XI, 342 pages. 2006.

Vol. 3866: T. Dimitrakos, F. Martinelli, P.Y.A. Ryan, S. Schneider (Eds.), Formal Aspects in Security and Trust. X, 259 pages. 2006.

Vol. 3865: W. Shen, K.-M. Chao, Z. Lin, J.-P.A. Barthès, A. James (Eds.), Computer Supported Cooperative Work in Design II. XII, 659 pages. 2006.

Vol. 3863: M. Kohlhase (Ed.), Mathematical Knowledge Management. XI, 405 pages. 2006. (Sublibrary LNAI).

Vol. 3862: R.H. Bordini, M. Dastani, J. Dix, A.E.F. Seghrouchni (Eds.), Programming Multi-Agent Systems. XIV, 267 pages. 2006. (Sublibrary LNAI).

Vol. 3861: J. Dix, S.J. Hegner (Eds.), Foundations of Information and Knowledge Systems. X, 331 pages. 2006.

Vol. 3860: D. Pointcheval (Ed.), Topics in Cryptology – CT-RSA 2006. XI, 365 pages. 2006.

Vol. 3858: A. Valdes, D. Zamboni (Eds.), Recent Advances in Intrusion Detection. X, 351 pages. 2006.

Vol. 3857: M.P.C. Fossorier, H. Imai, S. Lin, A. Poli (Eds.), Applied Algebra, Algebraic Algorithms and Error-Correcting Codes. XI, 350 pages. 2006.

Vol. 3855: E. A. Emerson, K.S. Namjoshi (Eds.), Verification, Model Checking, and Abstract Interpretation. XI, 443 pages. 2005.

Vol. 3854: I. Stavrakakis, M. Smirnov (Eds.), Autonomic Communication. XIII, 303 pages. 2006.

Vol. 3853: A.J. Ijspeert, T. Masuzawa, S. Kusumoto (Eds.), Biologically Inspired Approaches to Advanced Information Technology. XIV, 388 pages. 2006.

Vol. 3852: P.J. Narayanan, S.K. Nayar, H.-Y. Shum (Eds.), Computer Vision – ACCV 2006, Part II. XXXI, 977 pages. 2006.

Vol. 3851: P.J. Narayanan, S.K. Nayar, H.-Y. Shum (Eds.), Computer Vision – ACCV 2006, Part I. XXXI, 973 pages. 2006.